CHILTON'S
REPAIR MANUAL

ISUZU 1981-91

Covers all U.S. and Canadian models of Amigo • Impulse • I-Mark • Pickups • Rodeo • Stylus • Trooper and Trooper II

Senior Vice President	Ronald A. Hoxter
Publisher and Editor-In-Chief	Kerry A. Freeman, S.A.E.
Executive Editors	Dean F. Morgantini, S.A.E., W. Calvin Settle, Jr., S.A.E.
Managing Editor	Nick D'Andrea
Special Products Manager	Ken Grabowski, A.S.E., S.A.E.
Senior Editors	Jacques Gordon, Michael L. Grady, Debra McCall, Kevin M. G. Maher, Richard J. Rivele, S.A.E., Richard T. Smith, Jim Taylor, Ron Webb
Project Managers	Martin J. Gunther, Will Kessler, A.S.E., Richard Schwartz
Production Manager	Andrea Steiger
Product Systems Manager	Robert Maxey
Director of Manufacturing	Mike D'Imperio
Editor	Jim Steele

CHILTON BOOK COMPANY

CONTENTS

1 GENERAL INFORMATION and MAINTENANCE

2 ENGINE PERFORMANCE and TUNE-UP

3 ENGINE and ENGINE OVERHAUL

4 EMISSION CONTROLS

5 FUEL SYSTEM

6 CHASSIS ELECTRICAL

7  DRIVE TRAIN

8  SUSPENSION and STEERING

9  BRAKES

10  BODY

11 MECHANIC'S DATA

SAFETY NOTICE

Proper service and repair procedures are vital to the safe, reliable operation of all motor vehicles, as well as the personal safety of those performing repairs. This book outlines procedures for servicing and repairing vehicles using safe, effective methods. The procedures contain many NOTES, CAUTIONS and WARNINGS which should be followed along with standard safety procedures to eliminate the possibility of personal injury or improper service which could damage the vehicle or compromise its safety.

It is important to note that repair procedures and techniques, tools and parts for servicing motor vehicles, as well as the skill and experience of the individual performing the work vary widely. It is not possible to anticipate all of the conceivable ways or conditions under which vehicles may be serviced, or to provide cautions as to all of the possible hazards that may result. Standard and accepted safety precautions and equipment should be used during cutting, grinding, chiseling, prying, or any other process that can cause material removal or projectiles.

Some procedures require the use of tools specially designed for a specific purpose. Before substituting another tool or procedure, you must be completely satisfied that neither your personal safety, nor the performance of the vehicle will be endangered.

Although the information in this guide is based on industry sources and is as complete as possible at the time of publication, the possibility exists that the manufacturer made later changes which could not be included here. While striving for total accuracy, Chilton Book Company cannot assume responsibility for any errors, changes, or omissions that may occur in the compilation of this data.

PART NUMBERS

Part numbers listed in this reference are not recommendations by Chilton for any product by brand name. They are references that can be used with interchange manuals and aftermarket supplier catalogs to locate each brand supplier's discrete part number.

SPECIAL TOOLS

Special tools are recommended by the vehicle manufacturer to perform their specific job. Use has been kept to a minimum, but where absolutely necessary, they are referred to in the text by the part number of the tool manufacturer. These tools can be purchased under the appropriate part number, from Isuzu or regional distributor, or, an equivalent tool can be purchased locally from a tool supplier or parts outlet. Before substituting any tool for the one recommended, read the SAFETY NOTICE at the top of this page.

ACKNOWLEDGMENTS

The Chilton Book Company expresses its appreciation to Isuzu Motor Corp. for their generous assistance.

Copyright © 1991 by Chilton Book Company
All Rights Reserved
Published in Radnor, Pennsylvania 19089 by Chilton Book Company
ONE OF THE ABC PUBLISHING COMPANIES, A PART OF CAPITAL CITIES/ABC, INC.

Manufactured in the United States of America
890   0987

Chilton's Repair Manual: Isuzu 1981–91
ISBN 0-8019-8219-7 pbk.
Library of Congress Catalog Card No. 91-055218

General Information and Maintenance

HOW TO USE THIS BOOK

Chilton's Repair Manual for 1981–91 Isuzu cars and trucks is intended to help you learn more about the inner workings of your vehicle and save you money on its upkeep and operation.

The first two Chapters will be the most used, since they contain maintenance and tune-up information and procedures. Studies have shown that a properly tuned and maintained car or truck can get at least 10% better gas mileage (which translates into lower operating costs) and periodic maintenance will catch minor problems before they turn into major repair bills. The other Chapters deal with the more complex systems of your car or truck. Operating systems from engine through brakes are covered to the extent that the average do-it-yourselfer becomes mechanically involved. This book will not explain such things as rebuilding the differential for the simple reason that the expertise required and the investment in special tools make this task impractical and uneconomical. It will give you the detailed instructions to help you change your own brake pads and shoes, tune-up the engine, replace spark plugs and filters, and do many more jobs that will save you money, give you personal satisfaction and help you avoid expensive problems.

A secondary purpose of this book is a reference guide for owners who want to understand their car or truck and/or their mechanics better. In this case, no tools at all are required. Knowing just what a particular repair job requires in parts and labor time will allow you to evaluate whether or not you're getting a fair price quote and help decipher itemized bills from a repair shop.

Before attempting any repairs or service on your car or truck, read through the entire procedure outlined in the appropriate chapter. This will give you the overall view of what tools and supplies will be required. There is nothing more frustrating than having to walk to the bus stop on Monday morning because you were short one gasket on Sunday afternoon. So read ahead and plan ahead. Each operation should be approached logically and all procedures thoroughly understood before attempting any work. Some special tools that may be required can often be rented from local automotive jobbers or places specializing in renting tools and equipment. Check the yellow pages of your phone book.

All Chapters contain adjustments, maintenance, removal and installation procedures, and overhaul procedures. When overhaul is not considered practical, we tell you how to remove the failed part and then how to install the new or rebuilt replacement. In this way, you at least save the labor costs. Backyard overhaul of some components (such as the alternator or water pump) is just not practical, but the removal and installation procedure is often simple and well within the capabilities of the average car or truck owner.

Two basic mechanic's rules should be mentioned here. First, whenever the LEFT side of the car or truck or engine is referred to, it is meant to specify the DRIVER'S side of the car or truck. Conversely, the RIGHT side of the car or truck means the PASSENGER'S side. Second, all screws and bolts are removed by turning counterclockwise, and tightened by turning clockwise, unless otherwise noted.

Safety is always the most important rule. Constantly be aware of the dangers involved in working on or around an automobile and take proper precautions to avoid the risk of personal injury or damage to the vehicle. See the section in this Chapter, Servicing Your Vehicle Safely, and the SAFETY NOTICE on the acknowledgment page before attempting any service procedures and pay attention to the instructions provided. There are 3 common mistakes in mechanical work:

1. Incorrect order of assembly, disassembly or adjustment. When taking something apart or putting it together, doing things in the wrong order usually just costs you extra time; however it CAN break something. Read the entire procedure before beginning disassembly. Do everything in the order in which the instructions say you should do it, even if you can't immediately see a reason for it. When you're taking apart something that is very intricate (for example, a carburetor), you might want to draw a picture of how it looks when assembled at one point in order to make sure you get everything back in its proper position. We will supply exploded views whenever possible, but sometimes the job requires more attention to detail than an illustration provides. When making adjustments (especially tune-up adjustments), do them in order. One adjustment often affects another and you cannot expect satisfactory results unless each adjustment is made only when it cannot be changed by any other.

2. Overtorquing (or undertorquing) nuts and bolts. While it is more common for overtorquing to cause damage, undertorquing can cause a fastener to vibrate loose and cause serious damage, especially when dealing with aluminum parts. Pay attention to torque specifications and utilize a torque wrench in assembly. If a torque figure is not available remember that, if you are using the right tool to do the job, you will probably not have to strain yourself to get a fastener tight enough. The pitch of most threads is so slight that the tension you put on the wrench will be multiplied many times in actual force on what you are tightening. A good example of how critical torque is can be seen in the case of spark plug installation, especially where you are putting the plug into an aluminum cylinder head. Too little torque can fail to crush the gasket, causing leakage of combustion gases and consequent overheating of the plug and engine parts. Too much torque can damage the threads or distort the plug, which changes the spark gap at the electrode. Since more and more manufacturers are using aluminum in their engine and chassis parts to save weight, a torque wrench should be in any serious do-it-yourselfer's tool box.

There are many commercial chemical products available for ensuring that fasteners won't come loose, even if they are not torqued just right (a very common brand is Loctite®). If you're worried about getting something together tight enough to hold, but loose enough to avoid mechanical damage during assembly, one of these products might offer substantial insurance. Read the label on the package and make sure the product is compatible with the materials, fluids, etc. involved before choosing one.

3. Crossthreading. This occurs when a part such as a bolt is screwed into a nut or casting at the wrong angle and forced, causing the threads to become damaged. Crossthreading is more likely to occur if access is difficult. It helps to clean and lubricate fasteners, and to start threading with the part to be installed going straight in, using your fingers. If you encounter resistance, unscrew the part and start over again at a different angle until it can be inserted and turned several times without much effort. Keep in mind that many parts, especially spark plugs, use tapered threads so that gentle turning will automatically bring the part you're threading to the proper angle if you don't force it or resist a change in angle. Don't put a wrench on the part until it's been turned in a couple of times by hand. If you suddenly encounter resistance and the part has not seated fully, don't force it. Pull it back out and make sure it's clean and threading properly.

Always take your time and be patient; once you have some experience, working on your car or truck will become an enjoyable hobby.

TOOLS AND EQUIPMENT

Naturally, without the proper tools and equipment it is impossible to properly service your vehicle. It would be impossible to catalog each tool that you would need to perform each or every operation in this book. It would also be unwise for the amateur to rush out and buy an expensive set of tools an the theory that he may need one or more of them at sometime.

The best approach is to proceed slowly, gathering together a good quality set of those tools that are used most frequently. Don't be misled by the low cost of bargain tools. It is far better to spend a little more for better quality. Forged wrenches, 6- or 12-point sockets and fine tooth ratchets are by far preferable to their less expensive counterparts. As any good mechanic can tell you, there are few worse experiences than trying to work on a car or truck with bad tools. Your monetary savings will be far outweighed by frustration and mangled knuckles.

Certain tools, plus a basic ability to handle tools, are required to get started. A basic mechanics tool set, a torque wrench, and, a Torx® bits set. Torx® bits are hexlobular drivers which fit both inside and outside on special Torx® head fasteners used in various places.

Begin accumulating those tools that are used most frequently; those associated with routine maintenance and tune-up.

In addition to the normal assortment of screwdrivers and pliers you should have the following tools for routine maintenance jobs (your car or truck uses metric fasteners):

1. Metric wrenches, sockets and combination open end/box end wrenches in sizes from 3mm to 19mm, and a spark plug socket ($^{13}/_{16}$ in.) If possible, buy various length socket drive extensions. One break in this department is that the metric sockets available in the U.S. will all fit the ratchet handles and extensions you may already have (¼ in., ⅜ in., and ½ in. drive).

2. One set of metric combination (one end open and one end box) wrenches.

3. Wire-type spark plug feeler gauge.

4. Blade-type feeler gauges.

5. Slot and Phillips head screwdrivers in various sizes.

6. Oil filter strap wrench, necessary for removing oil filters (never used, though, for installing the filters).

7. Funnel, for pouring fresh oil or automatic transmission fluid from quart oil bottles.

8. Pair of slip-lock pliers.

9. Pair of vise-type pliers.

10. Adjustable wrench.

11. A hydraulic floor jack of at least 1½ ton capacity. If you are serious about maintaining your own car or truck, then a floor jack is as necessary as a spark plug socket. The greatly

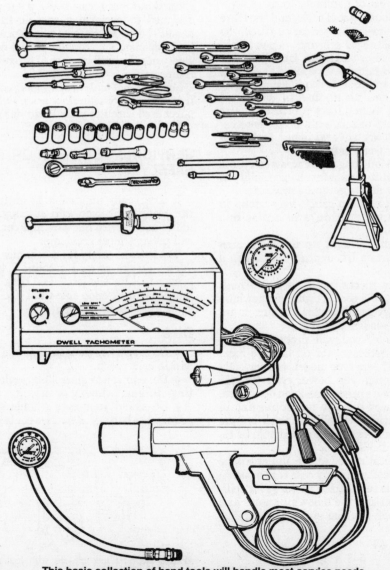

This basic collection of hand tools will handle most service needs

increased utility, strength, and safety of a hydraulic floor jack makes it pay for itself many times over through the years.

12. At least 4 sturdy jackstands for working underneath the car or truck. Any other type of support (bricks, wood and especially cinderblocks) is just plain dangerous.

13. An inductive timing light.

In addition to the above items there are several others that are not absolutely necessary, but handy to have around. These include oil-dry (cat box litter works just as well and may be cheaper), a transmission funnel and the usual supply of lubricants, antifreeze and fluids, although these can be purchased as needed. This is a basic list for routine maintenance, but only your personal needs and desires can accurately determine your list of necessary tools.

This is an adequate set of tools, and the more work you do yourself on your car or truck, the larger you'll find the set growing—a pair of pliers here, a wrench or two there. It makes more sense to have a comprehensive set of basic tools as listed above, and then to acquire more along the line as you need them, than to go out and plunk down big money for a professional size set you may never use. In addition to these basic tools, there are several other tools and gauges you may find useful.

1. A compression gauge. The screw-in type is slower to use but it eliminates the possibility of a faulty reading due to escaping pressure.

2. A manifold vacuum gauge, very useful in troubleshooting ignition and emissions problems.

3. A drop light, to light up the work area (make sure yours is UL approved, and has a shielded bulb).

4. A volt/ohm meter (multi-tester). These are handy for use if a wire is broken somewhere and are especially necessary for working on today's electronics-laden vehicles.

As a final note, you will probably find a torque wrench necessary for all but the most basic work. The beam type models are perfectly adequate, although the newer click (break-away) type are more precise, and you don't have to crane your neck to see a torque reading in awkward situations. The breakaway torque wrenches are more expensive and should be recalibrated periodically.

Torque specification for each fastener will be given in the procedure in any case that a specific torque value is required. If no torque specifications are given, use the following values as a guide, based upon fastener size:

Bolts marked 6T
6mm bolt/nut — 5–7 ft. lbs.
8mm bolt/nut — 12–17 ft. lbs.
10mm bolt/nut — 23–34 ft. lbs.
12mm bolt/nut — 41–59 ft. lbs.
14mm bolt/nut — 56–76 ft. lbs.

Bolts marked 8T
6mm bolt/nut — 6–9 ft. lbs.
8mm bolt/nut — 13–20 ft. lbs.
10mm bolt/nut — 27–40 ft. lbs.
12mm bolt/nut — 46–69 ft. lbs.
14mm bolt/nut — 75–101 ft. lbs.

Special Tools

Normally, the use of special factory tools is avoided for repair procedures, since these are not readily available for the do-it-yourself mechanic. When it is possible to perform the job with more commonly available tools, it will be pointed out, but occasionally, a special tool was designed to perform a specific function and should be used. Before substituting another tool, you should be convinced that neither your safety nor the performance of the vehicle will be compromised.

Some special tools are available commercially from major tool manufacturers. Others can be purchased through your Isuzu dealer.

SERVICING YOUR CAR OR TRUCK SAFELY

It is virtually impossible to anticipate all of the hazards involved with automotive maintenance and service but care and common sense will prevent most accidents.

The rules of safety for mechanics range from "don't smoke around gasoline," to "use the proper tool for the job." The trick to avoiding injuries is to develop safe work habits and take every possible precaution.

Do's

● Do keep a fire extinguisher and first aid kit within easy reach.

● Do wear safety glasses or goggles when cutting, drilling, grinding or prying.

● Do shield your eyes whenever you work around the battery. Batteries contain sulphuric

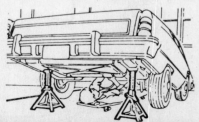

Always support the vehicle with jackstands when working underneath it

acid. In case of contact with the eyes or skin, flush the area with water or a mixture of water and baking soda and get medical attention immediately.

• Do use safety stands for any undercar service. Jacks are for raising vehicles; safety stands are for making sure the vehicle stays raised until you want it to come down. Whenever the vehicle is raised, block the wheels remaining on the ground and set the parking brake.

• Do disconnect the negative battery cable when working on the electrical system. The primary ignition system can contain up to 40,000 volts.

• Do properly maintain your tools. Loose hammerheads, mushroomed punches and chisels, frayed or poorly grounded electrical cords, excessively worn screwdrivers, spread wrenches (open end), cracked sockets, slipping ratchets, or faulty droplight sockets can cause accidents and injuries.

• Do use the proper size and type of tool for the job being done.

• Do, when possible, pull on a wrench handle rather than push on it, and adjust your stance to prevent a fall.

• Do be sure that adjustable wrenches are tightly adjusted on the nut or bolt and pulled so that the face is on the side of the fixed jaw.

• Do select a wrench or socket that fits the nut or bolt. The wrench or socket should sit straight, not cocked.

• Do strike squarely with a hammer — avoid glancing blows.

• Do set the parking brake and block the drive wheels if the work requires that the engine be running.

Don'ts

• Don't run an engine in a garage or anywhere else without proper ventilation — EVER! Carbon monoxide is poisonous. It takes a long time to leave the human body and you can build up a deadly supply of it in your system by simply breathing in a little every day. Always use power vents, windows, fans or open the garage doors.

• Don't work around moving parts while wearing a necktie or other loose clothing. Short sleeves are much safer than long, loose sleeves and hard toed shoes with neoprene soles protect your toes and give a better grip on slippery surfaces. Jewelry is not safe when working around a car. Long hair should be hidden under a hat or cap.

• Don't use pockets for toolboxes. A fall or bump can drive a screwdriver deep into your body. Even a wiping cloth hanging from the back pocket can wrap around a spinning shaft or fan.

• Don't smoke when working around gasoline, cleaning solvent or other flammable material.

• Don't smoke when working around the battery. When the battery is being charged, it gives off explosive hydrogen gas.

• Don't use gasoline to wash your hands. There are excellent soaps available. Gasoline may contain lead, and lead can enter the body through a cut, accumulating in the body until you are very ill. Gasoline also removes all the natural oils from the skin so that bone dry hands will absorb oil and grease.

• Don't service the air conditioning system unless you are equipped with the necessary tools and training. The refrigerant, R-12, is extremely cold and when exposed to the air, will instantly freeze any surface it comes in contact with, including your eyes. Although the refrigerant is normally non-toxic, R-12 becomes a deadly poisonous gas in the presence of an open flame. One good whiff of the vapors from burning refrigerant can be fatal.

SERIAL NUMBER IDENTIFICATION

Vehicle Identification Plate

The vehicle identification number is embossed on a plate, that is attached to the top left corner of the instrument panel. The number is visible through the windshield from the outside of the vehicle. The eighth digit of the number, indicates the engine model and the tenth digit represents the model year (example is K for 1989).

Engine Number

The gasoline engine serial number is stamped on the top right front corner of the engine. The diesel serial number is stamped on the left rear corner of the engine block.

The Impulse equipped with the 4ZC1-T and 4ZD1 engine, has the number stamped on the left rear corner of the engine block, near the en-

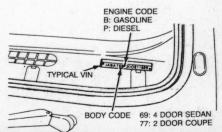

Vehicle identification number—early model (VIN)

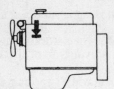

G180Z engine serial number location

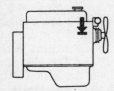

G200Z engine serial number location

4XCI-U engine serial number location

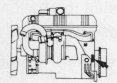

4ZCI-T engine serial number location

Diesel engine serial number location

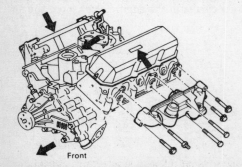

Front

V6 engine serial number location

gine to transaxle mounting. On the I-Mark equipped with the G180Z engine, the number is stamped on the top right corner of the engine block. The I-Mark equipped with the 4FB1 diesel engine, has the number stamped on the left rear corner of the engine block. The I-Mark (FWD) equipped with the 4XC1-U, 4XC1-T and the 4XE1 engines, have the number stamped on the flange near the transaxle mounting, toward the front of the vehicle. The 1989-91 Troopers and Rodeos are available with V6 engines. The engine serial number is located on top of the rocker arm covers.

Transmission Number

Both manual transmissions have their serial numbers on the side of the main case. The automatic location is similar.

ROUTINE MAINTENANCE

Air Cleaner

Carbureted and throttle body injected engines have air cleaner assemblies mounted directly above the fuel system on the engine. Multi-port fuel injected engines have air cleaner assemblies mounted away from the intake runners out the way. The MPI assembly is a rectangular shape. Depending on the model, remove the retaining screws or snaps to access the air cleaner element.

Replace the air cleaner element every 30,000 miles with driven in normal conditions and 15,000 when driven in dusty conditions.

Gasoline Fuel Filter

The early model carbureted I-mark and Impulse have the fuel filter located either at the fuel tank inside the trunk or near the carburetor in the engine compartment.

The P'UP, Amigo and Rodeo are equipped with the fuel filter located directly in front of the fuel tank.

On the Trooper/Trooper II, the fuel filter is located along the inner side of the right frame rail, near the rear of the vehicle.

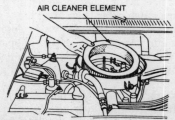

AIR CLEANER ELEMENT

Air cleaner element

ENGINE IDENTIFICATION

Year	Model	Engine Displacement cu. in. (cc)	Engine Series Identification	No. of Cylinders	Engine Type
1981	I-Mark	110.8 (1816)	G180Z	4	OHC
	I-Mark	111 (1815)	4FBI-Diesel	4	OHC
	Pick-up	110.8 (1816)	G180Z	4	OHC
	Pick-up	136.6 (2238)	C223	4	Diesel/OHV
1982	I-Mark	110.8 (1816)	G180Z	4	OHC
	I-Mark	111 (1815)	4FBI-Diesel	4	OHC
	Pick-up	110.8 (1816)	G180Z	4	OHC
	Pick-up	136.6 (2238)	C223	4	Diesel/OHV
1983	I-Mark	110.8 (1816)	G180Z	4	OHC
	I-Mark	111 (1815)	4FBI-Diesel	4	OHC
	Impulse	118.9 (1949)	G200Z	4	SOHC
	Pick-up	116 (1950)	G180Z	4	OHC
	Pick-up	136.6 (2238)	C223	4	Diesel/OHV
1984	I-Mark	110.8 (1816)	G180Z	4	OHC
	I-Mark	111 (1815)	4FBI-Diesel	4	OHC
	Impulse	118.9 (1949)	G200Z	4	SOHC
	Pick-up	119 (1950)	G200Z	4	OHC
	Pick-up	136.6 (2238)	C223	4	Diesel/OHV
1985	I-Mark (RWD)	110.8 (1816)	G180Z	4	OHC
	I-Mark (RWD)	111 (1815)	4FBI-Diesel	4	OHC
	I-Mark (FWD)	90 (1471)	4XCI-U	4	OHC
	Impulse	118.9 (1949)	G200Z	4	SOHC
	Impulse Turbo	121 (1983)	4ZCI-T	4	Turbo SOHC
	Pick-up	119 (1950)	G200Z	4	OHC
	Pick-up	136.6 (2238)	C223	4	Diesel/OHV
1986	I-Mark	90 (1471)	4XCI-U	4	OHC
	Impulse	118.9 (1949)	G200Z	4	SOHC
	Impulse Turbo	121 (1983)	4ZCI-T	4	Turbo SOHC
	Pick-up	119 (1950)	G200Z	4	OHC
	Pick-up	138 (2250)	4ZDI	4	OHC
	Pick-up	136.6 (2238)	C223	4	OHV Diesel
	Trooper II	138 (2250)	4ZDI	4	OHC
	Trooper II	136 (2238)	C223-T	4	OHV Diesel
1987	I-Mark	90 (1471)	4XCI-U	4	OHC
	Impulse	118.9 (1949)	G200Z	4	SOHC
	Impulse Turbo	121 (1983)	4ZCI-T	4	Turbo OHC
	Pick-up	119 (1949)	G200Z	4	OHC
	Pick-up	138 (2250)	4ZDI	4	OHC
	Pick-up	136.6 (2238)	C223	4	Diesel OHV
	Pick-up	136.6 (2238)	C223T	4	Turbo OHV
	Trooper II	156 (2559)	4ZE1	4	OHC

ENGINE IDENTIFICATION (cont.)

Year	Model	Engine Displacement cu. in. (cc)	Engine Series Identification	No. of Cylinders	Engine Type
1988	I-Mark	90 (1471)	4XCI-U	4	OHC
	I-Mark (Turbo)	90 (1471)	4XC1-T	4	Turbo OHC
	Impulse Turbo	121.7 (1994)	4ZCI-T	4	Turbo OHC
	Impulse	138 (2254)	4ZD1	4	OHC
	Pick-up	119 (1949)	G200Z	4	OHC
	Pick-up	138 (2250)	4ZDI	4	OHC
	Pick-up	136.6 (2238)	C223	4	Diesel OHV
	Pick-up	136.6 (2238)	C223T	4	Turbo OHV
	Trooper II	156 (2559)	4ZE1	4	OHC
1989	I-Mark	90 (1471)	4XCI-U	4	OHC
	I-Mark (Turbo)	90 (1471)	4XC1-T	4	Turbo OHC
	Impulse (DOHC)	92 (1588)	4XE1	4	DOHC
	Impulse (Turbo)	121.7 (1994)	4ZC1-T	4	Turbo OHC
	Impulse	138 (2254)	4ZD1	4	OHC
	Pick-up	138 (2250)	4ZDI	4	OHC
	Pick-up	156 (2559)	4ZE1	4	OHC
	Trooper II	156 (2559)	4ZE1	4	OHC
	Trooper II	171 (2800)	V6 2.8L	6	OHV
	Amigo	138 (2250)	4ZD1	4	OHC
	Amigo	156 (2559)	4ZE1	4	OHC
1990	Impulse DOHC	92 (1588)	4XE1	4	DOHC
	Pick-up	138 (2250)	4ZDI	4	OHC
	Pick-up	156 (2559)	4ZE1	4	OHC
	Trooper II	156 (2559)	4ZE1	4	OHC
	Trooper II	171 (2800)	V6 2.8L	6	OHV
	Amigo	138 (2250)	4ZD1	4	OHC
	Amigo	156 (2559)	4ZE1	4	OHC
1991	Stylus	92 (1588)	4XE1	4	SOHC
	Stylus	92 (1588)	4XE1	4	DOHC
	Impulse	92 (1588)	4XE1	4	DOHC
	Impulse	92 (1588)	4XE1	4	Turbo DOHC
	Pick-up	138 (2250)	4ZD1	4	OHC
	Pick-up	156 (2559)	4ZE1	4	OHC
	Trooper II	156 (2559)	4ZE1	4	OHC
	Trooper II	171 (2800)	V6 2.8L	6	OHV
	Amigo	138 (2250)	4ZD1	4	OHC
	Amigo	156 (2559)	4ZE1	4	OHC
	Rodeo	156 (2559)	4ZE1	4	OHC
	Rodeo	191 (3100)	CPC	6	OHV

REMOVAL AND INSTALLATION

1. Properly relieve the fuel system pressure.
2. Raise and safely support the vehicle.
3. Using 2 pairs of vise grips, pinch off the fuel line on each side of the fuel filter. Filters that use hex fittings, use a backup and flarenut wrench to loosen the inlet and outlet fittings.
4. Remove the fuel hose clamps and the fuel hoses from each side of the filter.
5. Remove the mounting bolt and the filter.

To install:

6. Using a new filter, install it to the vehicle; be sure its directional arrow faces forward.
7. Install the fuel hoses and fuel hose clamps to the filter.
8. Remove the vise grips.
9. Start the engine and check for leaks at the filter.

Diesel Fuel Filter

The fuel filter is located near the battery.

REMOVAL AND INSTALLATION

1. Properly relieve the fuel system pressure. Disconnect the negative battery cable.
2. Disconnect the water separator sensor wire from the connector.
3. Using a filter wrench, remove the fuel filter.
NOTE: *When removing the fuel filter, be careful not to spill the fuel from the cartridge.*
4. Drain the fuel cartridge and remove the sensor from the cartridge.

To install:

5. Lubricate the new sensor O-ring with diesel fuel and install the sensor onto the cartridge.
6. Lubricate the cartridge O-ring with diesel fuel. Install the cartridge until the O-ring contacts the sealing surface face, then, tighten the cartridge ⅔ of a turn with a filter wrench.
7. Connect the electrical connector to the sensor.
8. Depress the priming pump, located on top of the cartridge, 30–40 times to fill the cartridge.
NOTE: *The pumping force will increase as the filter becomes filled.*
9. Start the engine and check for leakage around the sealing portions.

DRAINING WATER FROM THE SYSTEM

1. Using a 0.2L (about 1 pint) container, place it at the end of the vinyl hose, located under the drain plug of the separator.
2. Loosen the drain plug 5 turns.
3. Depress the priming pump about 10 times until the water is drained from the filter.
4. Tighten the drain plug.

5. Depress the priming pump several times.
6. Start the engine and check for leakage around the drain plug.
7. Make sure the **FILTER** light remains out.

Positive Crankcase Ventilation (PCV)

The carbureted gasoline 4 cyl. engines do not use a PCV valve. In place of the valve is a regulating orifice in the intake manifold. Blow-by gases are drawn through the regulating orifice into the intake manifold for reburning. During wide open throttle, the engine vacuum is not sufficient to draw enough vapor through the manifold, allowing part to be drawn into the air cleaner via the rear end of the rocker arm cover.

The fuel injected gasoline 4 cyl. and V6 engines use a PCV valve. The PCV valve meters the flow at a rate depending upon the manifold vacuum. If the manifold vacuum is high, the PCV restricts the flow to the intake manifold. If abnormal, operating conditions occur, excessive amounts of internal exhaust gases back flow through the crankcase vent tube into the air filter to be burned by normal combustion.

The crankcase ventilation system (PCV) must be operating correctly to provide complete scavenging of the crankcase vapors. Fresh air is supplied to the crankcase from the air filter, mixed with the internal exhaust gases, passed through the PCV valve or orifice and into the intake manifold.

If the engine is idling roughly, a quick check of the PCV valve can be made. While the engine is idling, pull the PCV valve from the valve cover, place your thumb over the end of the PCV valve and check for vacuum. If no vacuum exists, check for a plugged PCV valve, manifold port, hoses or deteriorated hoses. Turn the engine "OFF", remove the PCV valve and shake it. Listen for the rattle of the check needle inside the valve. If it does not rattle, replace the valve.

The PCV system should be checked at every oil change and serviced every 30,000 miles.
NOTE: *Never operate an engine without a PCV valve or a ventilation system, for it can become damaged.*

Diesel Engine

Check the diaphragm valve for damage and adhesion to the seating surface. Check the oil separator element for wear if any abnormal conditions are found, replace the PCV valve assembly.

Evaporative Canister

To limit gasoline vapor discharge into the air this system is designed to trap fuel vapors,

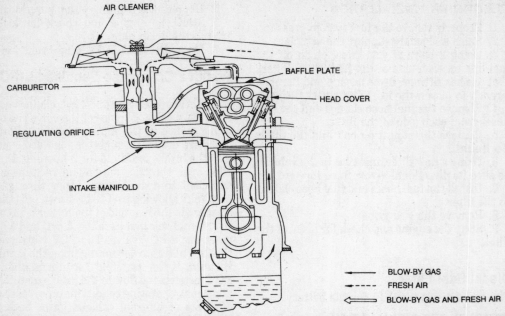

AIR CLEANER

CARBURETOR

REGULATING ORIFICE

INTAKE MANIFOLD

BAFFLE PLATE

HEAD COVER

→ BLOW-BY GAS
------ FRESH AIR
⇐ BLOW-BY GAS AND FRESH AIR

PVC system—carbureted 4-cylinder gas engines do not use a valve. They use a regulating orifice located in the intake manifold

which normally escape from the fuel tank and carburetor. Vapor arrest is accomplished through the use of the charcoal canister. This canister absorbs fuel vapors and stores them until they can be removed to be burned in the engine. Removal of the vapors from the canister to the engine is accomplished by a carburetor, throttle body assembly or solenoid operated bowl vent. In addition to the carburetor modifications and the canister, the fuel tank requires a non-vented gas cap. The domed fuel tank posi-

tions a vent high enough above the fuel to keep the vent pipe in the vapor at all times. The single vent pipe is routed directly to the canister. From the canister, the vapors are routed to the PCV system, where they will be burned during normal combustion.

SERVICING

Make sure the hoses are connected properly and not damaged.

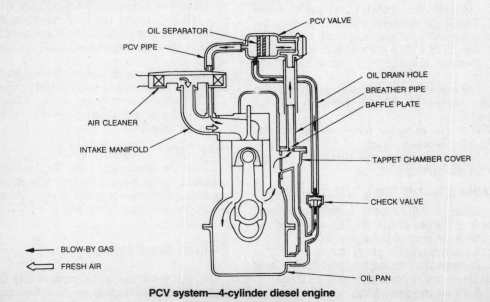

OIL SEPARATOR

PCV PIPE

PCV VALVE

AIR CLEANER

INTAKE MANIFOLD

OIL DRAIN HOLE

BREATHER PIPE

BAFFLE PLATE

TAPPET CHAMBER COVER

CHECK VALVE

← BLOW-BY GAS
⇐ FRESH AIR

OIL PAN

PCV system—4-cylinder diesel engine

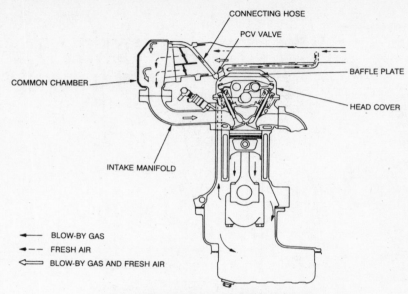

CONNECTING HOSE

PCV VALVE

BAFFLE PLATE

HEAD COVER

COMMON CHAMBER

INTAKE MANIFOLD

← BLOW-BY GAS

←-- FRESH AIR

⇐ BLOW-BY GAS AND FRESH AIR

PCV system—4-cylinder gas EFI 4ZEI engine

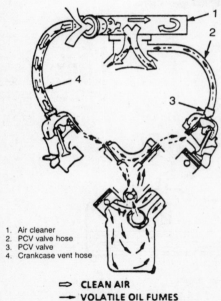

1. Air cleaner
2. PCV valve hose
3. PCV valve
4. Crankcase vent hose

⇨ CLEAN AIR

➡ VOLATILE OIL FUMES

--➡ MIXTURE OF AIR AND FUMES

PCV system—6-cylinder engine

FUNCTIONAL TEST — V6 ONLY

Canister Purge Valve

1. Apply a short length of hose to the lower tube of the purge valve and attempt to blow through the hose. Little or no air should pass through into the canister.

2. With a hand vacuum pump, apply 15 Hg (51 kPa) of vacuum through the control valve tube (upper tube). The diaphragm should hold vacuum for at least 20 seconds, if not the canister has to be replaced.

Fuel Tank Pressure Control Valve

1. Apply 15 Hg (51 kPa) of vacuum to the control vacuum tube. The diaphragm should hold vacuum for at least 20 seconds. If it does not, the diaphragm is leaking and the valve must be replaced.

2. With the vacuum applied to the control vacuum tube, apply a short hose to the valve's tank tube side and blow into the tube. The air should pass through the valve. If no air passes through the valve, the valve should be replaced.

Battery

All Isuzu vehicles have a "maintenance free" battery as standard equipment, eliminating the need for fluid level checks and the possibility of specific gravity tests. Nevertheless, the battery does require some attention.

Once a year, the battery terminals and the cable clamps should be cleaned. Remove the side terminal bolts and the cables, negative cable first. Clean the cable clamps and the battery terminals with a wire brush until all corrosion, grease, etc. is removed and the metal is shiny. It is especially important to clean the inside of the clamp thoroughly, since a small deposit of foreign material or oxidation there will prevent a sound electrical connection and inhibit either starting or charging. Special tools are available for cleaning the side terminal clamps and terminals.

Before installing the cables, loosen the battery hold-down clamp, remove the battery, and check the battery tray. Clear it of any debris and check it for soundness. Rust should be

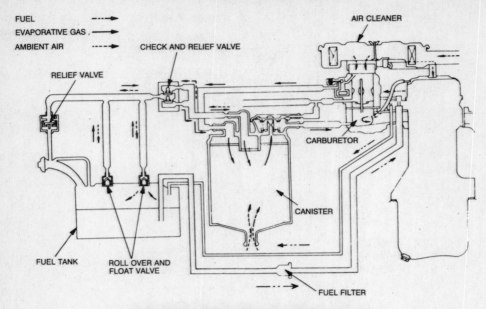

FUEL ----->
EVAPORATIVE GAS , ---->
AMBIENT AIR ---->

AIR CLEANER

CHECK AND RELIEF VALVE

RELIEF VALVE

CARBURETOR

CANISTER

FUEL TANK

ROLL OVER AND
FLOAT VALVE

FUEL FILTER

Evaporative control system—4-cylinder gas engine

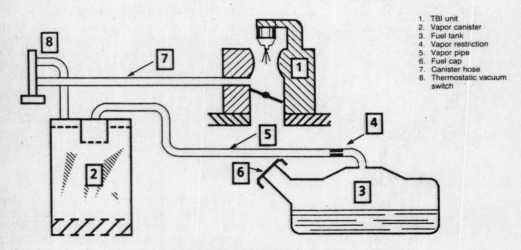

1. TBI unit
2. Vapor canister
3. Fuel tank
4. Vapor restriction
5. Vapor pipe
6. Fuel cap
7. Canister hose
8. Thermostatic vacuum
   switch

Evaporative control system—V6 engine

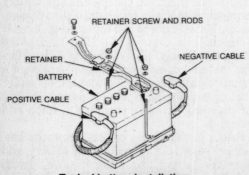

RETAINER SCREW AND RODS

RETAINER

NEGATIVE CABLE

BATTERY

POSITIVE CABLE

Typical battery installation

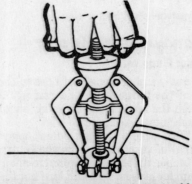

Use a puller to remove the battery cable

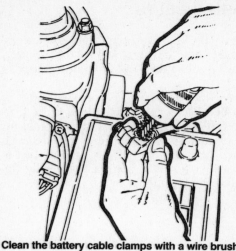

Clean the battery cable clamps with a wire brush

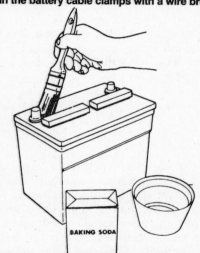

BAKING SODA

Cleaning the battery with baking soda and water

wire-brushed away, and the metal given a coat of anti-rust paint. Replace the battery and tighten the hold-down clamp securely, but be careful not to overtighten, which will crack the battery case.

After the clamps and terminals are clean, re-install the cables, negative cable last. Give the clamps and terminals a thin external coat of grease after installation, to retard corrosion.

Check the cables at the same time that the terminals are cleaned. If the cable insulation is cracked or broken, or if the ends are frayed, the cable should be replaced with a new cable of the same length and gauge.

NOTE: *Keep flames or sparks away from the battery; it gives off explosive hydrogen gas. Battery electrolyte contains sulphuric acid. If you should get any on your skin or in your eyes, flush the affected areas with plenty of clear water; if it lands in your eyes, get medical help immediately.*

Testing the Maintenance Free Battery

Maintenance free batteries do not require normal attention as far as fluid level checks are concerned. However, the terminals require periodic cleaning, which should be performed at least once a year.

The sealed top battery cannot be checked for charge in the normal manner, since there is no provision for access to the electrolyte. To check the condition of the battery:

1. If the indicator eye on top of the battery is dark, the battery has enough fluid. If the eye is light, the electrolyte fluid is too low and the battery must be replaced.

2. If a green dot appears in the middle of the eye, the battery is sufficiently charged. Proceed to Step 4. If no green dot is visible, charge the battery as in Step 3.

3. Charge the battery at this rate:
CAUTION: *Do not charge the battery for more than 50 amp/hours. If the green dot appears, or if electrolyte squirts out of the vent hole, stop the charge and proceed to Step 4.*
It may be necessary to tip the battery from side to side to get the green dot to appear after charging.

4. Connect a battery load tester and a voltmeter across the battery terminals (the battery cables should be disconnected from the battery). Apply a 300 amp load to the battery for 15 seconds to remove the surface charge. Remove the load.

5. Wait 15 seconds to allow the battery to recover. Apply the appropriate test load, as specified in the load test chart in this Chapter.

Battery Load Test

1. Apply the load for 15 seconds while reading the voltage. Disconnect the load.

2. Check the results against the following chart. If the battery voltage is at or above the specified voltage for the temperature listed, the battery is good. If the voltage falls below what's listed, the battery should be replaced.

Belts

TENSION CHECKING AND ADJUSTMENT
V-Belts

Check the drive belts every 15,000 miles or twelve months for evidence of wear such as cracking, fraying, and incorrect tension. Determine belt tension at a point halfway between the pulleys by pressing on the belt with moderate thumb pressure. If the distance between the pulleys (measured at the center of the pulley) is 330–400mm (13–16 in.), the belt should deflect 13mm (½ in.) at the halfway point of its longest straight run; 6mm (¼ in.) if the distance is

HOW TO SPOT WORN V-BELTS

V-Belts are vital to efficient engine operation—they drive the fan, water pump and other accessories. They require little maintenance (occasional tightening) but they will not last forever. Slipping or failure of the V-belt will lead to overheating. If your V-belt looks like any of these, it should be replaced.

This belt has deep cracks, which cause it to flex. Too much flexing leads to heat build-up and premature failure. These cracks can be caused by using the belt on a pulley that is too small. Notched belts are available for small diameter pulleys.

Cracking or weathering

Oil and grease on a belt can cause the belt's rubber compounds to soften and separate from the reinforcing cords that hold the belt together. The belt will first slip, then finally fail altogether.

Softening (grease and oil)

Glazing is caused by a belt that is slipping. A slipping belt can cause a run-down battery, erratic power steering, overheating or poor accessory performance. The more the belt slips, the more glazing will be built up on the surface of the belt. The more the belt is glazed, the more it will slip. If the glazing is light, tighten the belt.

Glazing

The cover of this belt is worn off and is peeling away. The reinforcing cords will begin to wear and the belt will shortly break. When the belt cover wears in spots or has a rough jagged appearance, check the pulley grooves for roughness.

Worn cover

This belt is on the verge of breaking and leaving you stranded. The layers of the belt are separating and the reinforcing cords are exposed. It's just a matter of time before it breaks completely.

Separation

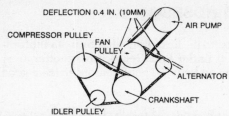

V-belt routing—1981–85 gasoline engine I-Mark

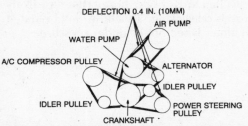

V-belt routing—P'UP with G180Z and G200Z engines

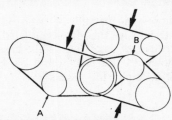

V-belt routing—early model Impulse

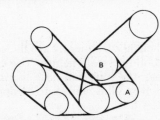

V-belt routing—early model Trooper II

Serpentine belt routing—2.8L V6 Trooper II

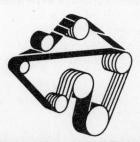

Serpentine belt routing—3.1L V6 Rodeo

178–300mm (7–12 in.). If the defection is found to be too much or too little, loosen the mounting bolts and make the adjustments.

Before you attempt to adjust any of your engine's belts, you should take an old rag soaked in solvent and clean the mounting bolts of any road grime which has accumulated there. On some of the harder-to-reach bolts, an application of penetrating oil will make them easier to loosen. When you're adjusting belts, especially on 4 cylinder engines with air conditioning and power steering, it would be especially helpful to have a variety of socket extensions and universals to get to those hard-to-reach bolts.

NOTE: *When adjusting the air pump belt, if you are using a pry bar, make sure that you pry against the cast iron end cover and not against the aluminum housing. Excessive force on the housing itself will damage it.*

Serpentine Belts

After 1989, the V6 engines are equipped with a serpentine belt and automatic belt tensioner. The tension is maintained by a spring loaded pulley/tensioner. The indicator mark on the moveable portion of the tensioner must be within the limits of the slotted area on the stationary portion of the tensioner. Any reading outside the limits indicates either a defective belt or tensioner.

To remove the belt, install a ½ in. racthet handle into the square slot in the tensioner and move far enough to slide the belt off the pulleys. Mark the belt routing for installation.

Hoses

HOSE REPLACEMENT

Upper and lower radiator hoses and all heater hoses should be checked for deterioration, leaks and loose hose clamps every 15,000 miles. To remove the hoses:

6-rib "V" belt
Serpentine belt

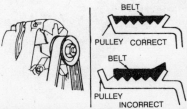

Proper serpentine belt alignment

HOW TO SPOT BAD HOSES

Both the upper and lower radiator hoses are called upon to perform difficult jobs in an inhospitable environment. They are subject to nearly 18 psi at under hood temperatures often over 280°F., and must circulate nearly 7500 gallons of coolant an hour—3 good reasons to have good hoses.

A good test for any hose is to feel it for soft or spongy spots. Frequently these will appear as swollen areas of the hose. The most likely cause is oil soaking. This hose could burst at any time, when hot or under pressure.

Swollen hose

Cracked hoses can usually be seen but feel the hoses to be sure they have not hardened; a prime cause of cracking. This hose has cracked down to the reinforcing cords and could split at any of the cracks.

Cracked hose

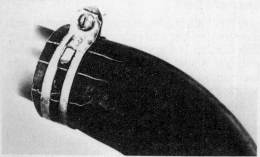

Weakened clamps frequently are the cause of hose and cooling system failure. The connection between the pipe and hose has deteriorated enough to allow coolant to escape when the engine is hot.

Frayed hose end (due to weak clamp)

Debris, rust and scale in the cooling system can cause the inside of a hose to weaken. This can usually be felt on the outside of the hose as soft or thinner areas.

Debris in cooling system

1. Drain the radiator.
2. Loosen the hose clamps at each end of the hose to be removed.
3. Working the hose back and forth, slide it off its connection and then install a new hose if necessary.
4. Position the hose clamps at least 6mm (¼ in.) from the end of the hose and tighten them.

NOTE: *Always make sure that the hose clamps are beyond the bead and placed in the center of the clamping surface before tightening them.*

Cooling System

Once a month, the engine coolant level should be checked. This is quickly accomplished by observing the level of coolant in the recovery tank, which is the translucent tank mounted to the right of the radiator, and connected to the radiator filler neck by a length of hose. As long as coolant is visible in the tank between the "Full Cold" and "Full Hot" marks the coolant level is O.K.

If coolant is needed, a 50/50 mix of ethylene glycol based antifreeze and clear water should always be used for additions, both winter and summer. Add coolant to the recovery tank through the capped opening. If adding coolant to the radiator, make sure the engine is cool before removing the radiator cap.

The radiator hoses, clamps, and radiator cap should be checked at the same time as the coolant level. Hoses which are brittle, cracked, or swollen should be replaced. Clamps should be checked for tightness (screwdriver-tight only — do not allow the clamp to cut into the hose or crush the fitting). The radiator cap gasket should be checked for any obvious tears, cracks or swelling, or any signs of incorrect seating in the radiator neck.

CAUTION: *To avoid injury when working with a hot engine, cover the radiator cap with a thick cloth. Wear a heavy glove to protect your hand. Turn the radiator cap slowly to the first stop, and allow all the pressure to vent (indicated when the hissing noise stops). When the pressure has been released, press down and remove the cap the rest of the way.*

The cooling system should be drained, flushed and refilled every 2 years or 30,000 miles, according to the manufacturer's recommendations. However, many mechanics prefer to change the coolant every year; it is cheap insurance against corrosion, overheating or freezing.

1. Remove the radiator cap when the engine is cool. See the preceding "CAUTION" about removing the cap.
2. With the radiator cap removed, run the engine until heat can be felt in the upper hose, indicating that the thermostat is open. The heater should be turned on to its maximum heat position, so that the core is flushed out.
3. Shut off the engine and open the drain cock in the bottom of the radiator. Drain the radiator.
4. Close the drain cock and fill the system with clear water. A cooling system flushing additive can be added, if desire.
5. Run the engine until it is hot again.
6. Drain the system, then flush with water until it runs clear.
7. Clean out the coolant recovery tank: remove the cap leaving the hoses in place. Remove the tank and drain it of any coolant. Clean it out with soap and water, empty it, and install it.
8. Close the drain cock and fill the radiator with a 50/50 mix of ethylene glycol based antifreeze and water to the base of the radiator filler neck. Fill the coolant recovery tank with the same mixture to the "Full Hot" mark. Install the recovery tank cap.
9. Run the engine until the upper radiator hose is hot again (radiator cap still off). With the engine idling, add the 50/50 mix of antifreeze and water to the radiator until the level reaches the bottom of the filler neck. Shut off the engine and install the radiator cap, aligning the arrows with the overflow tube. Turn off the heater.

Air Conditioning System

Regular maintenance of the air conditioning system includes periodic checks of the drive belt tension. In addition, the system should be operated for at least 5 minutes every month. This ensures an adequate supply of lubricant to the bearings and also helps to prevent the seals and hoses from drying out. To do this comfortably in the winter months, turn the air conditioning "ON", place the temperature control lever on "WARM" or "HI" position and turn the blower fan to its highest setting. This will engage the compressor, circulating the lubricating oils within the system, but prevents the discharge of cold air. The system should be checked for proper refrigerant charge using the procedure given below.

GENERAL SERVICING PROCEDURES

The most important aspect of air conditioning service is the maintenance of pure and adequate charge of refrigerant in the system. A refrigeration system cannot function properly if a significant percentage of the charge is lost. Leaks are common because the severe vibration encountered in an automobile can easily cause a sufficient cracking or loosening of the air condi-

AIR CONDITIONING SERVICE CHART

Year	Model	Compressor	R-12 capacity (ounces)	Oil capacity (ounces) ③	Gauge Pressure Low	Gauge Pressure High	Gauge Setting Location Low	Gauge Setting Location High
1981–85	I-Mark (RWD)	Diesel-Kiki (A-6)	30.0	5.00	15–20 ① 21–26 ②	120–140 ① 185–210 ②	Compressor	Receiver/drier
1985–90	I-Mark (FWD)	Diesel-Kiki (A-6)	28.0	5.70	28–43 ②	213–256 ②	Suction line	Receiver/drier
1981–91	Pick-up, Amigo	Diesel-Kiki (A-6)	32.0–35.0	5.00	14 ① 16 ②	130–135 ① 195–190 ②	Compressor	Receiver/drier
1983–89	Impulse	Diesel-Kiki (A-6)	30.0	5.00	28–43 ②	213–256 ②	Compressor	Receiver/drier
1990–91	Impulse	DKV-14D	27.0	6.70	28–43 ②	213–256 ②	Suction line	Next to Receiver/drier
1986–91	Trooper	Diesel-Kiki (A-6)	33.5	5.00	28–43 ②	213–256 ②	Compressor	Receiver/drier
		Radial-4	33.5	6.00	28–43 ②	213–256 ②	Compressor	Receiver/drier
1991	Rodeo	Diesel-Kiki (A-6)	35.0	5.00	28–43 ②	213–256 ②	Evap. low side	Discharge line
		Radial-4	35.0	6.00	28–43 ②	213–256 ②	Suction line	Discharge line
1991	Stylus	DKV-14D	26.5	6.76	28–43 ②	213–256 ②	Suction line	Discharge line

① at 70° degrees
② at 90° degrees
③ Total system capacity
④ U.S. Quart

tioning fittings. As a result, the extreme operating pressures of the system force refrigerant out.

The problem can be understood by considering what happens to the system as it is operated with a continuous leak. Because the expansion valve regulates the flow of refrigerant to the evaporator, the level of refrigerant there is fairly constant. The accumulator stores any excess of refrigerant, and so a loss will first appear there as a reduction in the level of liquid. As this level nears the bottom of the vessel, some refrigerant vapor bubbles will begin to appear in the stream of liquid supplied to the expansion valve. This vapor decreases the capacity of the expansion valve very little. As the quantity of liquid in the condenser decreases, the operating pressure will drop there and throughout the high side of the system. As the R-12 continues to be expelled, the pressure available to force the liquid through the expansion valve will continue to decrease, and, eventually, the expansion valve will prove to be too much of a restriction for adequate flow.

At this point, low side pressure will start to drop, and severe reduction in cooling capacity, marked by freeze-up of the evaporator coil, will result. Eventually, the operating pressure of the evaporator will be lower than the pressure of the atmosphere surrounding it, and air will be drawn into the system wherever there are leaks in the low side.

Because all atmospheric air contains at least some moisture, water will enter the system and mix with the R-12 and the oil. Trace amounts of moisture will cause sludging of the oil, and corrosion of the system. Saturation and clogging of the receiver/drier filter, and freezing of the expansion valve will eventually result. As air fills the system to a greater and greater extend, it will interfere more and more with the normal flows of refrigerant and heat.

A list of general precautions that should be observed while doing this follows:

1. Keep all tools as clean and dry as possible.
2. Thoroughly purge the service gauges and hoses of air and moisture before connecting them to the system. Keep them capped when not in use.
3. Thoroughly clean any refrigerant fitting before disconnecting it, in order to minimize the entrance of dirt into the system.
4. Plan any operation that requires opening the system beforehand in order to minimize the length of time it will be exposed to open air. Cap or seal the open ends to minimize the entrance of foreign material.
5. When adding oil, pour it through an extremely clean and dry tube or funnel. Keep the oil capped whenever possible. Do not use oil that has not been kept tightly sealed.
6. Use only refrigerant 12. Purchase refrigerant intended for use in only automotive air conditioning system. Avoid the use of refriger-

ant 12 that may be packaged for another use, such as cleaning, or powering a horn, as it is impure.

7. Completely evacuate any system that has been opened to replace a component, other than when isolating the compressor, or that has leaked sufficiently to draw in moisture and air. This requires evacuating air and moisture with a good vacuum pump for at least one hour.

If a system has been open for a considerable length of time it may be advisable to evacuate the system for up to 12 hours (overnight).

8. Use a wrench on both halves of a fitting that is to be disconnected, so as to avoid placing torque on any of the refrigerant lines.

ADDITIONAL PREVENTIVE MAINTENANCE CHECKS

Antifreeze

In order to prevent heater core freeze-up during air conditioner operation, it is necessary to maintain permanent type antifreeze protection of $+15°F$ $(-9°C)$ or lower. A reading of $-15°F$ $(-26°C)$ is ideal since this protection also supplies sufficient corrosion inhibitors for the protection of the engine cooling system.

WARNING: *Do not use antifreeze longer than specified by the manufacturer.*

Radiator Cap
To install:

For efficient operation of an air conditioned car's cooling system, the radiator cap should

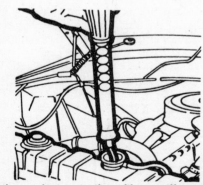

Testing coolant protection with an antifreeze tester

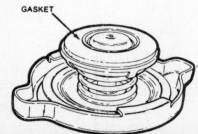

GASKET

Check the radiator cap gasket for cuts or cracks

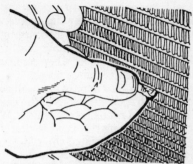

Clean the radiator and condenser fins of debris

have a holding pressure which meets manufacturer's specifications. A cap which fails to hold these pressure should be replaced.

Condenser

Any obstruction of or damage to the condenser configuration will restrict the air flow which is essential to its efficient operation. It is therefore, a good rule to keep this unit clean and in proper physical shape.

NOTE: *Bug screens are regarded as obstructions.*

Condensation Drain Tube

This single molded drain tube expels the condensation, which accumulates on the bottom of the evaporator housing, into the engine compartment.

If this tube is obstructed, the air conditioning performance can be restricted and condensation buildup can spill over onto the vehicle's floor.

SAFETY PRECAUTIONS

Because of the importance of the necessary safety precautions that must be exercised when working with air conditioning systems and R-12 refrigerant, a recap of the safety precautions are outlined.

1. Avoid contact with a charged refrigeration system, even when working on another part of the air conditioning system or vehicle. If a heavy tool comes into contact with a section of copper tubing or a heat exchanger, it can easily cause the relatively soft material to rupture.

2. When it is necessary to apply force to a fitting which contains refrigerant, as when checking that all system couplings are securely tightened, use a wrench on both parts of the fitting involved, if possible. This will avoid putting torque on the refrigerant tubing. (It is advisable, when possible, to use tube or line wrenches when tightening these flare nut fittings.)

3. Do not attempt to discharge the system by merely loosening a fitting, or removing the service valve caps and cracking these valves. Pre-

cise control is possibly only when using the service gauges. Place a rag under the open end of the center charging hose while discharging the system to catch any drops of liquid that might escape. Wear protective gloves when connecting or disconnecting service gauge hoses.

4. Discharge the system only in a well ventilated area, as high concentrations of the gas can exclude oxygen and act as an anesthetic. When leak testing or soldering this is particularly important, as toxic gas is formed when R-12 contacts any flame.

5. Never start a system without first verifying that both service valves are backseated, if equipped, and that all fittings throughout the system are snugly connected.

6. Avoid applying heat to any refrigerant line or storage vessel. Charging may be aided by using water heated to less than 125°F (52°C) to warm the refrigerant container. Never allow a refrigerant storage container to sit out in the sun, or near any other source of heat, such as a radiator.

7. Always wear goggles when working on a system to protect the eyes. If refrigerant contacts the eye, it is advisable in all cases to see a physician as soon as possible.

8. Frostbite from liquid refrigerant should be treated by first gradually warming the area with cool water, and then gently applying petroleum jelly. A physician should be consulted.

9. Always keep refrigerant can fittings capped when not in use. Avoid sudden shock to the can which might occur from dropping it, or from banging a heavy tool against it. Never carry a refrigerant can in the passenger compartment of a car.

10. Always completely discharge the system before painting the vehicle (if the paint is to be baked on), or before welding anywhere near the refrigerant lines.

TEST GAUGES

Most of the service work performed in air conditioning requires the use of a set of two gauges, one for the high (head) pressure side of the system, the other for the low (suction) side.

The low side gauge records both pressure and vacuum. Vacuum readings are calibrated from 0 to 30 in. Hg and the pressure graduations read from 0 to no less than 60 psi.

The high side gauge measures pressure from 0 to at last 600 psi.

Both gauges are threaded into a manifold

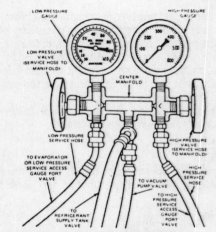

Air conditioning manifold gauge set

| | Amount of refrigerant | Almost no refrigerant | Insufficient | Suitable | Too much refrigerant |
Check item					
Temperature of high pressure and low pressure lines		Almost no difference between high pressure and low pressure side temperature	High pressure side is warm and low pressure side is fairly cold	High pressure side is hot and low pressure side is cold	High pressure side is abnormally hot
State in sight glass		Bubbles flow continuously. Bubbles will disappear and something like mist will flow when refrigerant is nearly gone.	The bubbles are seen at intervals of 1-2 seconds.	Almost transparent. Bubbles may appear when engine speed is raised and lowered. No clear difference exists between these two conditions.	No bubbles can be seen
Pressure of system		High pressure side is abnormally low.	Both pressure on high and low pressure sides are slightly low.	Both pressures on high and low pressure sides are normal.	Both pressures on high and low pressure sides are abnormally high.
Repair		Stop compressor immediately and conduct an overall check.	Check for gas leakage, repair as required, replenish and charge system.		Discharge refrigerant from service valve of low pressure side.

Using a sight glass to determine the relative refrigerant charge

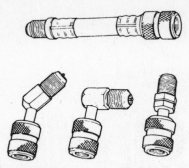

High pressure gauge port valve adapters

that contains two hand shut-off valves. Proper manipulation of these valves and the use of the attached test hoses allow the user to perform the following services:

1. Test high and low side pressures.
2. Remove air, moisture, and contaminated refrigerant.
3. Purge the system (of refrigerant).
4. Charge the system (with refrigerant).

The manifold valves are designed so that they have no direct effect on gauge readings, but serve only to provide for, or cut off, flow of refrigerant through the manifold. During all testing and hook-up operations, the valves are kept in a close position to avoid disturbing the refrigeration system. The valves are opened only to purge the system or refrigerant or to charge it.

INSPECTION

CAUTION: *The compressed refrigerant used in the air conditioning system expands into the atmosphere at a temperature of −21.7°F (−30°C) or lower. This will freeze any surface, including your eyes, that it contacts. In addition, the refrigerant decomposes into a poisonous gas in the presence of a flame. Do not open or disconnect any part of the air conditioning system.*

Sight Glass Check

NOTE: *All models are equipped with a sight glass on top of the receiver/drier. Another way to find out if the system has enough refrigerant is to install a set of test gauges.*

You can safely make a few simple checks to determine if your air conditioning system needs service. The tests work best if the temperature is warm (about 70°F [21°C]).

NOTE: *If your vehicle is equipped with an aftermarket air conditioner, the following system check may not apply. You should contact the manufacturer of the unit for instructions on systems checks.*

1. Operation of the air conditioning blower at all four speeds with the mode button in any position except OFF and engagement of the compressor clutch would indicate that the electrical circuit are functioning properly. (The blower will not operate in any speed with the mode button in the OFF position.)

2. The same hand felt temperature of the evaporator inlet pipe and the accumulator surface of an operating system would indicate a properly charged system.

3. Operation of the air conditioning control selector (mode) button to distribute air from designed outlets would indicate proper functioning.

NOTE: *If it is determined that the system has a leak, it should be corrected as soon as possible. Leaks may allow moisture to enter and cause a very expensive rust problem. Exercise the air conditioner for a few minutes, every two weeks or so, during the cold months. This avoids the possibility of the compressor seals drying out from lack of lubrication.*

TESTING THE SYSTEM

1. Connect a gauge set. Refer to the illustrations for proper gauge hook-up.
2. Close (clockwise) both gauge set valves.
3. Mid-position both service valves, if equipped with an aftermarket installation.
4. Park the vehicle in the shade. Start the engine, set the parking brake, place the transmission in **N** and establish an idle of 1,500 rpm.
5. Run the air conditioning system for full cooling, but NOT in the **MAX** or **COLD** mode.
6. Insert a thermometer into the center air outlet.
7. Use the accompanying performance chart for a specifications reference. If pressures are abnormal, refer to the air conditioner service chart in this Chapter.

WARNING: *These pressures are the norm for an ambient temperature of 70°F or 90°F (21 or 32°C). Higher air temperatures along with high humidity will cause higher system pressures. At idle speed and an ambient temperature of 110°F (43°C), the high pressure reading can exceed 300 psi.*

Under these extreme conditions, you can keep the pressures down by directing a large electric floor fan through the condenser.

DISCHARGING THE SYSTEM

CAUTION: *Due to the environmental impact the refrigerant has on atmosphere, discharge the refrigerant into a recycling station instead of purging into the atmosphere.*

1. Remove the caps from the high and low pressure charging valves in the high and low pressure lines.
2. Turn both manifold gauge set hand valves to the fully closed (clockwise) position.

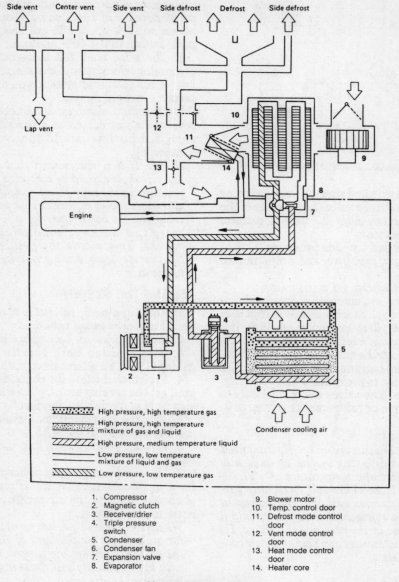

Side vent   Center vent   Side vent   Side defrost   Defrost   Side defrost

Lap vent

Engine

High pressure, high temperature gas

High pressure, high temperature mixture of gas and liquid

High pressure, medium temperature liquid

Low pressure, low temperature mixture of liquid and gas

Low pressure, low temperature gas

Condenser cooling air

1. Compressor
2. Magnetic clutch
3. Receiver/drier
4. Triple pressure switch
5. Condenser
6. Condenser fan
7. Expansion valve
8. Evaporator
9. Blower motor
10. Temp. control door
11. Defrost mode control door
12. Vent mode control door
13. Heat mode control door
14. Heater core

Air conditioning system

3. Connect the manifold gauge set.

4. If the gauge set hoses do not have the gauge port actuating pins, install fitting adapters on the manifold gauge set hoses. If the vehicle does not have a service access gauge port valve, connect the gauge set low pressure hose to the evaporator service access gauge port valve. A special adapter may be required to attach the manifold gauge set to the high pressure service access gauge port valve.

5. Connect the center hose to the refrigerant recycling station.

6. Open the low pressure gauge valve slightly and allow the system pressure to bleed into the recycling station.

7. When the system is just about empty, open the high pressure valve very slowly to avoid losing an excessive amount of refrigerant oil. Allow any remaining refrigerant to escape.

EVACUATING THE SYSTEM

NOTE: *This procedure requires the use of a vacuum pump.*

1. Connect the manifold gauge set.

2. Discharge the system into the refrigerant recycling station.

3. On 1981 and later models, make sure that the low pressure gauge set hose is connected to the low pressure service gauge port on the top

of the compressor or in the suction line and the high pressure hose connected to the high pressure service gauge port on the receiver/drier or discharge line. Refer to the gauge connection illustrations in this Chapter.

4. Connect the center service hose to the inlet fitting of the vacuum pump.

5. Turn both gauge set valves to the wide open position.

6. Start the pump and note the low side gauge reading.

7. Operate the pump until the low pressure gauge reads 25–30 in. Hg. Continue running the vacuum pump for 10 minutes more. If you have replaced some component in the system, run the pump for an additional 30 minutes.

8. To Leak test the system. Close both gauge set valves. Turn off the pump. The needle should remain stationary at the point at which the pump was turned off. If the needle drops to zero rapidly, there is a leak in the system which must be repaired.

TROUBLE	POSSIBLE CAUSE	CORRECTION
No cooling or insufficient cooling	1. Magnetic clutch does not run	• Refer to diagnosis chart "A/C CONTROL SYSTEM" in this section
	2. Compressor is not rotating properly	
	• Drive belt loosened or broken	• Adjust the drive belt to the specified tension or replace the drive belt
	• Magnetic clutch face is not clean and slips.	• Clean the magnetic clutch face or replace
	• Incorrect clearance between magnetic plate drive plate and pulley.	• Adjust the clearance
	• Compressor oil leaks from shaft seal or shell	• Replace the compressor
	• Compressor seized	• Replace the compressor
	3. Insufficient or excessive charge of refrigerant	• Check charge of refrigerant
	4. Leaks in the refrigerant system	• Check refrigerant system for leaks and refrigerant line connection or repair as necessary
	5. Condenser clogged	• Clean the condenser
	6. Temperature control link unit of the heater unit defective	• Repair the link unit
	7. Unsteady operation due to foreign substance in expansion valve	• Replace the expansion valve
Insufficient velocity of cooling air	1. Evaporator clogged or frosted	• Check evaporator core and replace or clean the core
	2. Air leaking from cooling unit or air duct	• Check evaporator and duct connection, then repair as necessary
	3. Blower motor does not rotate properly	

A/C diagnosis chart

RESULT	SYMPTOM	TROUBLE CAUSE	CORRECTION
Discharge (High) pressure gauge abnormally high	Reduced or no air flow through the condenser	• Condenser clogged or dirty • Condenser or radiator motor does not operate properly	• Clean • Check voltage and motor • Refer to diagnosis chart of condenser fan
	No bubbles in sight glass when condenser is cooled by water	• Excessive refrigerant in system	• Discharge refrigerant as required
	Refrigerant line to the condenser is excessive hot	• Restricted flow of refrigerant in system	• Check expansion valve
	After stopping air conditioner, pressure drops approx. 196 kPa (28 psi.) quickly	• Air in system	• Evacuate and charge refrigerant system

A/C diagnosis chart

LEAK TESTING

Some leak tests can be performed with a soapy water solution. There must be at least a 8 oz. charge in the system for a leak to be detected. The most extensive leak tests are performed with either a Halide flame type leak tester or the more preferable electronic leak tester.

In either case, the equipment is expensive, and, the use of a Halide detector can be **extremely** hazardous!

CHARGING THE SYSTEM

CAUTION: *NEVER OPEN THE HIGH PRESSURE SIDE WITH A CAN OF REFRIGERANT CONNECTED TO THE SYSTEM! OPENING THE HIGH PRESSURE SIDE WILL OVERPRESSURIZE THE CAN, CAUSING IT TO EXPLODE!*

1. Start and run the engine until it reaches operating temperature. Then set the air conditioning mode control button on **OFF**.

RESULT	SYMPTOM	TROUBLE CAUSE	CORRECTION
Discharge (High) pressure gauge abnormal low	Insufficient cooling and excessive bubbles in the sight glass	• Insufficient refrigerant in system	• Check for leaks and charge refrigerant as required
	Frost or dew seen on refrigerant line before and after receiver/dehydrator or expansion valve and low-pressure gauge indicates vacuum	• Unsatisfactory valve operation because of clogged expansion or defective temperature sensor of expansion valve • Refrigerant restricted by moisture or dirt in refrigerant freezing	• Evacuate and charge the refrigerant • Clean or replace the expansion valve • Replace the receiver/dehydrator
	When stopping air conditioner, high and low pressure gauge balanced quickly	• Compressor seal defective • Poor compression due to defective gasket of compressor	• Replace compressor
Suction (Low) pressure gauge abnormal high	Low pressure gauge is lowered after condenser is cooled by water	• Excessive refrigerant in system	• Discharge refrigerant as necessary
	Low pressure hose of around the compressor refrigerant line connector is lower than around evaporator	• Unsatisfactory operation of valve due to defective temperature sensor of expansion valve • Expansion valve opens too long • Compressor suction strainer defective	• Clean or replace expansion valve • Replace compressor
	When stopping air conditioner, high and low pressure gauge is balanced soon	• Compressor gasket is defective	• Replace compressor
	Air conditioner turns off before the room temperature is sufficiently cool	• Electro thermo sensor defective	• Check the electro thermo sensor and replace as necessary
Suction (Low) pressure abnormal low	Condenser is not hot and excessive bubble in sight glass	• Insufficient refrigerant	• Charge refrigerant as required
	Frost on the expansion valve inlet line	• Expansion valve clogged	• Clean or replace the expansion valve
	A distinct difference in temperature develops between the inlet and outlet refrigerant lines of the receiver/dehydrator is frosted.	• Receiver/dehydrator clogged	• Replace the receiver/dehydrator

A/C diagnosis chart

RESULT	SYMPTOM	TROUBLE CAUSE	CORRECTION
Suction (Low) pressure abnormal low	Expansion valve outlet refrigerant line is not cold and low-pressure gauge indicates vacuum	• The temperature sensor of the expansion valve is defective, and the valve cannot regulate the correct flow of the refrigerant	• Replace the expansion valve
Suction (Low) and Discharge (High) pressure abnormal high	No bubbles in sight glass after condenser is cooled by water	• Excessive refrigerant in system	• Discharge refrigerant as required
	Reduce air flow through condenser	• Condenser clogged • Condenser or radiator motor does not rotate properly	• Clean • Check voltage and motor
	Suction (Low) pressure hose is not cold	• Air in system	• Evacuate and charge refrigerant
Suction (Low) and Discharge (High) pressure abnormal low	Excessive bubbles in the sight glass	• Insufficient refrigerant in system	• Check for leaks and repair • Charge refrigerant as required

A/C diagnosis chart

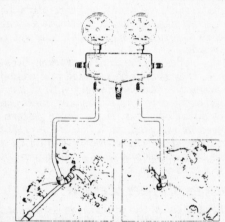

Suction line/discharge line gauge hook-up

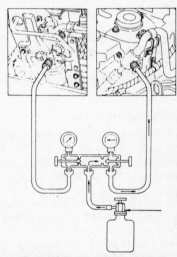

Suction line/receiver-drier gauge hook-up

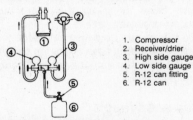

1. Compressor
2. Receiver/drier
3. High side gauge
4. Low side gauge
5. R-12 can fitting
6. R-12 can

Compressor/receiver-drier gauge hook-up

2. With the R-12 cans inverted, open the R-12 source valve(s) and allow one 14 oz. can of liquid R-12 to flow into the system through the low side service fitting.

3. As soon as one can of R-12 has been added to the system, immediately engage the compressor by setting the air conditioning control button to **NORM** and the blower speed on **HI**, to draw in the remainder of the R-12 charge. Do not let the low side gauge exceed 50 psi, if it

does close the gauge valve until the pressure drops.

NOTE: *The charging operation can be speeded up by using a large volume fan to pass air over the condenser. If the condenser temperature is maintained below the charging cylinder temperature, R-12 will enter the system more rapidly.*

4. Turn off the R-12 source valve and run engine for 30 seconds to clear the lines and gauges.

CAUTION: *Do NOT disconnect the gauge hoses while the engine is running. The extreme pressure may cause personal injury.*

5. With the engine NOT running, remove the charging low side hose adapter from the compressor or suction line service fitting. Un-

screw rapidly to avoid excess R-12 escape from the system.

CAUTION: *Never remove a gauge line from its adapter when the line is connected to the air conditioning system. Always remove the line adapter from the service fitting to disconnect a line. Do not remove charging hose at the gauge set while attached to the accumulator. This will result in complete discharge of the system due to the depressed Schrader valve in service low side fitting, and may cause personal injury due to escaping R-12.*

6. Replace protective cap on compressor or suction line fitting.

7. Turn engine off, if not done so.

8. Leak check system with electronic leak detector J-29547 or equivalent.

9. Start engine.

10. With the system fully charged and leak checked, continue to operate the system performance.

CAUTION: *NEVER ALLOW THE HIGH PRESSURE SIDE READING TO EXCEED 240 psi!*

Refer to the "Air Conditioning Service Chart" in this chapter for the recommended refrigerant charges.

NOTE: *Remember that most disposible cans are only 14 oz., not 16 oz.*

ADDING REFRIGERANT OIL

Refrigerant oil can be purchased in raw or pressurized cans. The raw oil can be added when the system is discharged and has no pressure or forced in under pressure using a oil injection pump. The can is pressurized with R-12 and has 4 oz. of refrigerant oil per can. The oil is added in the same manner as the refrigerant.

Refrigerant oil must be added after the system has been discharged, if not using a pressurized can. The air conditioner system requires a specific amount of 525 viscosity refrigerant oil ONLY. New oil quantities must be added during component replacement. Refer to the "Air Conditioning Service Chart" in this chapter.

With no signs of excessive leakage, add as follows:

1. If the Diesel-Kiki or R-4 compressor are removed, the oil in the compressor should be drained, measured and recorded. Added the same amount plus 1 oz. (30ml) to the new compressor.

NOTE: *When installing a new compressor, drain the new compressor and add the amount of oil in step 1. Do not add the amount in step 1 without draining the compressor first because the system will be overfilled.*

2. If the evaporator is removed, add 1.7 oz. (50mL) of oil.

3. If the condensor is removed, add 1 oz. (30mL) of oil.

4. If the receiver/drier is removed, the oil in it must be drained, measured and recorded. The same amount of new oil must be replaced. If installing a new receiver, add 1 oz. (30mL).

With signs of excessive leakage, add oil as follows:

1. If less than 3 oz. (89mL) is drained out of the receiver/drier, 3 oz. (89mL) of oil should be installed.

2. If more than 3 oz. (89mL) of oil was drained, add that amount.

Windshield Wipers

For maximum effectiveness and longest element life, the windshield and wiper blades should be kept clean. Dirt, tree sap, road tar and so on will cause streaking, smearing and blade deterioration if left on the glass. It is advisable to wash the windshield carefully with a commercial glass cleaner at least once a month. Wipe off the rubber blades with the wet rag afterwards.

If the blades are found to be cracked, broken or torn, they should be replaced immediately. Replacement intervals will vary with usage, although ozone deterioration usually limits blade life to about one year. If the wiper pattern is smeared or streaked, or if the blade chatters across the glass, the elements should be replaced. It is easiest and most sensible to replace the elements in pairs.

WIPER REFILL REPLACEMENT

The element of the wiper blade uses a spring type retainer on the end of the element. To remove the element, insert and rotate a screwdriver. Slide the element upward out of the housing retaining tabs.

To install the new element, slide it into the housing retaining tabs, lining up the slot in the element with the housing tab and snap the element into place.

Tires and Wheels

TIRE ROTATION

Tire rotation is recommended every 6000 miles or so, to obtain maximum tire wear. The pattern you use depends on whether or not your car has a usable spare. Radial tires should not be cross-switched (from one side of the car to the other); they last longer if their direction of rotation is not changed. Snow tires sometimes have directional arrows molded into the side of the carcass; the arrow shows the direction of rotation. They will wear very rapidly if the rotation is reversed.

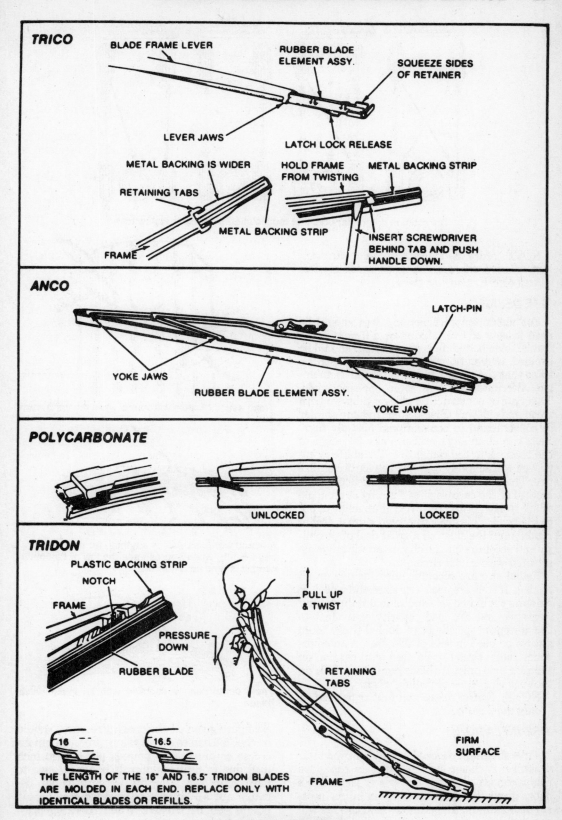

TRICO

BLADE FRAME LEVER

RUBBER BLADE ELEMENT ASSY.

SQUEEZE SIDES OF RETAINER

LEVER JAWS

LATCH LOCK RELEASE

METAL BACKING IS WIDER

HOLD FRAME FROM TWISTING

METAL BACKING STRIP

RETAINING TABS

METAL BACKING STRIP

FRAME

INSERT SCREWDRIVER BEHIND TAB AND PUSH HANDLE DOWN.

ANCO

LATCH-PIN

YOKE JAWS

RUBBER BLADE ELEMENT ASSY.

YOKE JAWS

POLYCARBONATE

UNLOCKED

LOCKED

TRIDON

PLASTIC BACKING STRIP

NOTCH

FRAME

PULL UP & TWIST

PRESSURE DOWN

RUBBER BLADE

RETAINING TABS

16

16.5

FIRM SURFACE

THE LENGTH OF THE 16" AND 16.5" TRIDON BLADES ARE MOLDED IN EACH END. REPLACE ONLY WITH IDENTICAL BLADES OR REFILLS.

FRAME

Wiper insert replacement

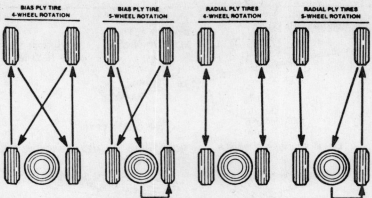

Tire rotation diagrams; note that radials should not be cross-switched

NOTE: *Mark the wheel position or direction of rotation on radial tires or studded snow tires before removing them.*

TIRE DESIGN

For maximum satisfaction, tires should be used in sets of five. Mixing or different types (radial, bias-belted, fiberglass belted) should be avoided. Conventional bias tires are constructed so that the cords run bead-to-bead at an angle. Alternate plies run at an opposite angle. This type of construction gives rigidity to both tread and sidewall. Bias-belted tires are similar in construction to conventional bias ply tires. Belts run at an angle and also at a 90° angle to the bead, as in the radial tire. Tread life is improved considerably over the conventional bias tire. The radial tire differs in construction, but instead of the carcass plies running at an angle of 90° to each other, they run at an angle of 90° to the bead. This gives the tread a great deal of rigidity and the sidewall a great deal of flexibility and accounts for the characteristic bulge associated with radial tires.

Radial tire are recommended for use on all models. If they are used, tire sizes and wheel diameters should be selected to maintain ground clearance and tire load capacity equivalent to the minimum specified tire. Radial tires should always be used in sets of five, but in an emergency radial tires can be used with caution on the rear axle only. If this is done, both tires on the rear should be of radial design.

NOTE: *Radial tires should never be used on only the front axle.*

TIRE INFLATION

Tires should be checked weekly for proper air pressure. A chart, located either in the glove compartment or on the driver's or passenger's door, gives the recommended inflation pressures. Maximum fuel economy and tire life will result if the pressure is maintained at the high-

Tread wear indicators will appear when the tire is worn out

A penny works as well as anything for checking tire tread depth; when you can see the top of Lincoln's head, it is time for a new tire

Tread depth can be checked with an inexpensive gauge

est figure given on the chart. Pressures should be checked before driving since pressure can increase as much as 6 pounds per square inch (psi) due to heat buildup. It is a good idea to have your own accurate pressure gauge, because not all gauges on service station air pumps can be trusted. When checking pressures, do not neglect the spare tire. Note that some spare tires require pressures considerably higher than those used in the other tires.

While you are about the task of checking air pressure, inspect the tire treads for cuts, bruises and other damage. Check the air valves to be sure that they are tight. Replace any missing valve caps.

Check the tires for uneven wear that might indicate the need for front end alignment or tire rotation. Tires should be replaced when a tread wear indicator appears as a solid band across the tread.

When buying new tires, give some thought to the following points, especially if you are considering a switch to larger tires or a different profile series:

1. All 4 tires must be of the same construction type. This rule cannot be violated. Radial, bias, and bias-belted tires must not be mixed.

2. The wheels should be the correct width for

Troubleshooting Basic Wheel Problems

Problem	Cause	Solution
The car's front end vibrates at high speed	• The wheels are out of balance • Wheels are out of alignment	• Have wheels balanced • Have wheel alignment checked/adjusted
Car pulls to either side	• Wheels are out of alignment • Unequal tire pressure • Different size tires or wheels	• Have wheel alignment checked/adjusted • Check/adjust tire pressure • Change tires or wheels to same size
The car's wheel(s) wobbles	• Loose wheel lug nuts • Wheels out of balance • Damaged wheel • Wheels are out of alignment • Worn or damaged ball joint • Excessive play in the steering linkage (usually due to worn parts) • Defective shock absorber	• Tighten wheel lug nuts • Have tires balanced • Raise car and spin the wheel. If the wheel is bent, it should be replaced • Have wheel alignment checked/adjusted • Check ball joints • Check steering linkage • Check shock absorbers
Tires wear unevenly or prematurely	• Incorrect wheel size • Wheels are out of balance • Wheels are out of alignment	• Check if wheel and tire size are compatible • Have wheels balanced • Have wheel alignment checked/adjusted

Troubleshooting Basic Tire Problems

Problem	Cause	Solution
The car's front end vibrates at high speeds and the steering wheel shakes	• Wheels out of balance • Front end needs aligning	• Have wheels balanced • Have front end alignment checked
The car pulls to one side while cruising	• Unequal tire pressure (car will usually pull to the low side) • Mismatched tires • Front end needs aligning	• Check/adjust tire pressure • Be sure tires are of the same type and size • Have front end alignment checked
Abnormal, excessive or uneven tire wear See "How to Read Tire Wear"	• Infrequent tire rotation • Improper tire pressure • Sudden stops/starts or high speed on curves	• Rotate tires more frequently to equalize wear • Check/adjust pressure • Correct driving habits
Tire squeals	• Improper tire pressure • Front end needs aligning	• Check/adjust tire pressure • Have front end alignment checked

the tire. Tire dealers have charts of tire and rim compatibility. A mismatch will cause sloppy handling and rapid tire wear. The tread width should match the rim width (inside bead to inside bead) within 25mm (1 in.). For radial tires, the rim width should be 80% or less of the tire (not tread) width.

3. The height (mounted diameter) of the new tires can change speedometer accuracy, engine speed at a given road speed, fuel mileage, acceleration, and ground clearance. Tire manufacturers furnish full measurement specifications.

4. The spare tire should be usable, at least for short distance and low speed operation, with the new tires.

5. There should not be any body interference when loaded, on bumps, or in turns.

NOTE: *The tires will perform well at all normal loads when inflated as recommended on the Tire Placard (located on the driver's door of your car).*

STORAGE

Store the tires at the proper inflation pressure if they are mounted on wheels. Keep them in a cool dry place, laid on their sides. If the tires are stored in the garage or basement, do not let them stand on a concrete floor; set them on strips of wood.

CARE OF SPECIAL WHEELS

An aluminum wheel may become porous and leak air. Locate the leak by inflating the assembly to 40 psi and dipping the assembly into water. Mark the leak areas. Remove the tire from the wheel and scuff the inside rim surface with

Tire Size Comparison Chart

"60 Series"	"70 Series"	"78 Series"	1965–77	"60 Series"	"70 Series"	"80 Series"
"Letter" sizes			Inch Sizes	Metric-inch Sizes		
		Y78-12	5.50-12, 5.60-12 6.00-12	165/60-12	165/70-12	155-12
		W78-13	5.20-13	165/60-13	145/70-13	135-13
		Y78-13	5.60-13	175/60-13	155/70-13	145-13
			6.15-13	185/60-13	165/70-13	155-13, P155/80-13
A60-13	A70-13	A78-13	6.40-13	195/60-13	175/70-13	165-13
B60-13	B70-13	B78-13	6.70-13 6.90-13	205/60-13	185/70-13	175-13
C60-13	C70-13	C78-13	7.00-13	215/60-13	195/70-13	185-13
D60-13	D70-13	D78-13	7.25-13			
E60-13	E70-13	E78-13	7.75-13			195-13
			5.20-14	165/60-14	145/70-14	135-14
			5.60-14	175/60-14	155/70-14	145-14
			5.90-14			
A60-14	A70-14	A78-14	6.15-14	185/60-14	165/70-14	155-14
	B70-14	B78-14	6.45-14	195/60-14	175/70-14	165-14
	C70-14	C78-14	6.95-14	205/60-14	185/70-14	175-14
D60-14	D70-14	D78-14				
E60-14	E70-14	E78-14	7.35-14	215/60-14	195/70-14	185-14
F60-14	F70-14	F78-14, F83-14	7.75-14	225/60-14	200/70-14	195-14
G60-14	G70-14	G77-14, G78-14	8.25-14	235/60-14	205/70-14	205-14
H60-14	H70-14	H78-14	8.55-14	245/60-14	215/70-14	215-14
J60-14	J70-14	J78-14	8.85-14	255/60-14	225/70-14	225-14
L60-14	L70-14		9.15-14	265/60-14	235/70-14	
	A70-15	A78-15	5.60-15	185/60-15	165/70-15	155-15
B60-15	B70-15	B78-15	6.35-15	195/60-15	175/70-15	165-15
C60-15	C70-15	C78-15	6.85-15	205/60-15	185/70-15	175-15
	D70-15	D78-15				
E60-15	E70-15	E78-15	7.35-15	215/60-15	195/70-15	185-15
F60-15	F70-15	F78-15	7.75-15	225/60-15	205/70-15	195-15
G60-15	G70-15	G78-15	8.15-15/8.25-15	235/60-15	215/70-15	205-15
H60-15	H70-15	H78-15	8.45-15/8.55-15	245/60-15	225/70-15	215-15
J60-15	J70-15	J78-15	8.85-15/8.90-15	255/60-15	235/70-15	225-15
	K70-15		9.00-15	265/60-15	245/70-15	230-15
L60-15	L70-15	L78-15, L84-15	9.15-15			235-15
	M70-15	M78-15				255-15
		N78-15				

Note: Every size tire is not listed and many size comparisons are approximate, based on load ratings. Wider tires than those supplied new with the vehicle, should always be checked for clearance.

80 grit sandpaper. Apply a thick layer of adhesive/sealant part number 1052366 or equivalent to the leak area and allow six hours to dry.

Clean special wheels with a special mag wheel cleaner or mild soap and water. Do not use harsh detergents or solvents because the protective coating may be damaged.

FLUIDS AND LUBRICANTS

Fuel Recommendations

Gasoline Engines

The engine is designed to operate on unleaded gasoline ONLY and is essential for the proper operation of the emission control system. The use of unleaded fuel will reduce spark plug fouling, exhaust system corrosion and engine oil deterioration.

In most parts of the United States, fuel with an octane rating of 87 should be used; in high altitude areas, fuel with an octane rating as low as 85 may be used. However, the high performance engines are recommended to use a fuel with an octane rating of 93 or greater. Using fuels with a lower octane may decrease engine performance, increase emissions and engine wear.

In some areas, fuel consisting of a blend of alcohol may be used; this blend of gasoline and alcohol is known as gasohol. When using gasohol, never use blends exceeding 10% ethanol or 5% methanol.

NOTE: *The use of fuel with excessive amounts of alcohol may jeopardize the new car warranties.*

Diesel Engines

Fuel manufacturers produce two grades of diesel fuel, No. 1 and No. 2, for use in automotive diesel engines. Generally speaking, No. 2 fuel is recommended over No. 1 for driving in temperatures above 20°F (−7°C). In fact, in many areas, No. 2 diesel is the only fuel available. By comparison, No. 2 diesel fuel is less volatile than No. 1 fuel, and gives better fuel economy. No. 2 fuel is also a better injection pump lubricant.

Two important characteristics of diesel fuel are its cetane number and its viscosity.

The cetane number of a diesel fuel refers to the ease with which a diesel fuel ignites. High cetane numbers mean that the fuel will ignite with relative ease so that it ignites well in an engine being cranked at low temperatures. Naturally, the lower the cetane number, the higher the temperature must be to ignite the fuel. Most commercial fuels have cetane numbers that range from 35 to 65. No. 1 diesel fuel generally has a higher cetane rating than No. 2 fuel.

Viscosity is the ability of a liquid, in this case diesel fuel, to flow. Using straight No. 2 diesel fuel below 20°F (−7°C) can cause problems, because this fuel tends to become cloudy, meaning wax crystals begin forming in the fuel. 20°F (−7°C) is often called the cloud point for No. 2 fuel. In extreme cold weather, No. 2 fuel can stop flowing altogether. In either case, fuel flow is restricted, which can result in a no start condition or poor engine performance. Fuel manufacturers often winterize No. 2 diesel fuel by using various fuel additives and blends (No. 1 diesel fuel, kerosene, etc.) to lower its winter time viscosity. Generally speaking, though, No. 1 diesel fuel is more satisfactory in extremely cold weather.

NOTE: *No. 1 and No. 2 diesel fuels will mix and burn with no ill effects, although the engine manufacturer will undoubtedly recommend one or the other. Consult the owner's manual for information.*

Depending on local climate, most fuel manufacturers make winterized No. 2 fuel available seasonally.

Many automobile manufacturers (Oldsmobile, for example) publish pamphlets giving the locations of diesel fuel stations nationwide. Contact the local dealer for information.

Do not substitute home heating oil for automotive diesel fuel. While basic characteristics of these oils are similar, the heating oil is not capable of meeting diesel cetane ratings. This means that using it might offer not only hard starting but engine knock; even under warm operating conditions. This could result in unnecessary engine wear or damage.

Further, furnace oil is not blended for operation at colder temperatures as most heating oil filters are located indoors. It could easily clog fuel filters with wax.

The equipment used in burning furnace oil does not contain the extremely fine machined surfaces or extremely tiny nozzle openings used in a diesel engine fuel system. Very small amounts of dirt and abrasives that will pass right through a heating oil fuel system could play havoc with your diesel's injection system. Finally, minimum standards regarding sulphur and ash that help keep deposits out of your diesel engine and minimize corrosion may not be met by furnace oil.

One more word on diesel fuels. Don't thin diesel fuel with gasoline. The result is the most highly explosive mixture possible in your fuel tank and unwarranted danger. Fuel thinned with gasoline may not adequately lubricate the injection system, leading to premature pump and nozzle failure and need for an expensive

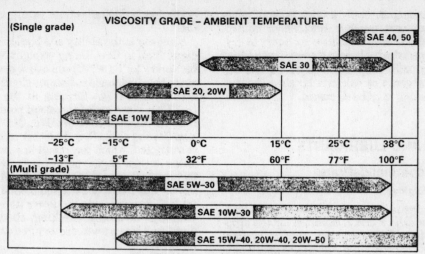

Gasoline engine oil viscosity chart

overhaul. Cetane rating will also be effected in an undesirable way.

It's best to buy No. 1 or blended No. 2 fuel for wintertime use. If you must use some means to keep No. 2 fuel from waxing, blend it with No. 1 or use a quality anti-waxing agent.

Oil Recommendations

When adding oil to the crankcase or changing the oil or filter, it is important that oil of an equal quality to original equipment be used in your vehicle. The use of inferior oils may void the warranty, damage your engine, or both.

The SAE (Society of Automotive Engineers) grade number of oil indicates the viscosity of the oil (its ability to lubricate at a given temperature). The lower the SAE number, the lighter the oil; the lower the viscosity, the easier it is to crank the engine in cold weather but the less the oil will lubricate and protect the engine at high temperatures. This number is marked on every oil container.

Oil viscosities should be chosen from those oils recommended for the lowest anticipated temperatures during the oil change interval. Multigrade oils have been developed because of the need for an oil that embodies both good lubrication at high temperatures and easy cranking in cold weather. All oils are thick at low temperatures and thin out as the temperature rises. Basically, a multigrade oil is thinner at lower temperatures and thicker at high temperatures relative to straight weight oils. For example, a 10W–40 oil (the W stands for winter) exhibits the characteristics of a 10 weight (SAE 10) oil when the vehicle is first started and the oil is cold. Its lighter weight allows it to travel to the lubricating surfaces quicker and offer less resistance to starter motor cranking than, say,

a straight 30 weight (SAE 30) oil. But after the engine reaches operating temperature, the 10W–40 oil begins acting like straight 40 weight (SAE 40) oil, its heavier weight providing greater lubrication with less chance of foaming than a straight 30 weight oil would *at that temperature* .

NOTE: *Single grade (straight weight) oils such as SAE 30 are more satisfactory than multi-viscosity oils for highway driving in diesel engines.*

GASOLINE ENGINE OIL

The API (American Petroleum Institute) designation, also found on the oil container, indicates the classification of engine oil used under certain given operating conditions. Only oils designated for use Service **SE**, or **SF** heavy duty detergent should be used in your vehicle. For 1984 and later models, only **SF** or **SG** oils are approved by Isuzu. Oils of the SE, SF and SG type perform many functions inside the engine besides their basic function of lubrication. Through a balanced system of metallic detergents and polymeric dispersants, the oil prevents high and low temperature deposits and also keeps sludge and dirt particles in suspension. Acids, particularly sulphuric acid, as well as other by-products of engine combustion are neutralized by the oil. If these acids are allowed to concentrate, they can cause corrosion and rapid wear of the internal engine parts.

CAUTION: *Non-detergent or straight mineral oils should not be used in your GM engine.*

DIESEL ENGINE OIL

Diesel engines require different engine oil from those used in gasoline engines. Besides do-

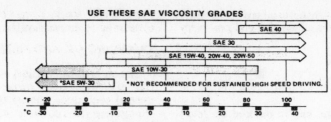

USE THESE SAE VISCOSITY GRADES

SAE 40

SAE 30

SAE 15W-40, 20W-40, 20W-50

SAE 10W-30

*SAE 5W-30   * NOT RECOMMENDED FOR SUSTAINED HIGH SPEED DRIVING.

| °F | -20 | 0 | 20 | 40 | 60 | 80 | 100 |
| °C | -30 | -20 | -10 | 0 | 10 | 20 | 30 | 40 |

Diesel engine oil viscosity chart

ing the things gasoline engine oil does, diesel oil must also deal with increased engine heat and the diesel blow-by gases, which create sulphuric acid, a highly corrosive compound.

Under the American Petroleum Institute (API) classifications, gasoline engine oil codes begin with an **S**, and diesel engine oil codes begin with a **C**. This first letter designation is followed by a second letter code which explains what type of service (heavy, moderate, light) the oil is meant for. For example, the top of a typical oil can will include: **API SERVICES SC, SD, SE, CA, CB, CC**. This means the oil in the can is a good, moderate duty engine oil when used in a diesel engine.

It should be noted here that the further down the alphabet the second letter of the API classification is, the greater the oil's protective qualities are (CD is the severest duty diesel engine oil, CA is the lightest duty oil, etc.) The same is true for gasoline engine oil classifications (SG is the severest duty gasoline engine oil, SA is the lightest duty oil, etc.).

Many diesel manufacturers recommend an oil with both gasoline and diesel engine API classifications. Consult the owner's manual for specifications.

The top of the oil can will also contain an SAE (Society of Automotive Engineers) designation, which gives the oil's viscosity. A typical designation will be: SAE 10W–30, which means the oil is a winter viscosity oil, meaning it will flow and give protection at low temperatures.

On the diesel engine, oil viscosity is critical, because the diesel is much harder to start (due to its higher compression) than a gasoline engine. Obviously, if you fill the crankcase with a very heavy oil during the winter (SAE 20W–50, for example) the starter is going to require a lot of current from the battery to turn the engine. And, since batteries don't function well in cold weather in the first place, you may find yourself stranded some morning. Consult the owner's manual for recommended oil specifications for the climate you live in.

SYNTHETIC OIL

There are excellent synthetic and fuel efficient oils available that, under the right circum-

stances, can help provide better fuel mileage and better engine protection. However, these advantages come at a price, which can be three or four times the price per quart of conventional motor oils.

Before pouring any synthetic oils into your vehicle's engine, you should consider the condition of the engine and the type of driving you do. Also, check the vehicle's warranty conditions regarding the use of synthetics.

Generally, it is best to avoid the use of synthetic oil in both brand new and older, high mileage engines. New engines require a proper break-in, and the synthetics are so slippery that they can prevent this; most manufacturers recommend that you wait at least 5,000 miles before switching to a synthetic oil. Conversely, older engines are looser and tend to use more oil; synthetics will slip past worn parts more readily than regular oil, and will be used up faster. If your vehicle already leaks and/or uses oil (due to worn parts and bad seals or gaskets), it will leak and use more with a slippery synthetic inside.

Consider your type of driving. If most of your accumulated mileage is on the highway at higher, steadier speeds, a synthetic oil will reduce friction and probably help delivery better fuel mileage. Under such ideal highway conditions, the oil change interval can be extended, as long as the oil filter will operate effectively for the extended life of the oil. If the filter can't do its job for this extended period, dirt and sludge will build up in your engine's crankcase, sump, oil pump and lines, no matter what type of oil is used. If using synthetic oil in this manner, you should continue to change the oil filter at the recommended intervals.

Vehicles used under harder, stop-and-go, short hop circumstances should always be serviced more frequently and for these vehicles synthetic oil may not be a wise investment. Because of the necessary shorter change interval needed for this type of driving, you cannot take advantage of the long recommended change interval of most synthetic oils.

Finally, most synthetic oils are not compatible with conventional oils and cannot be added to them. This means you should always carry a couple of quarts of synthetic oil with you while on a long trip, as not all service stations carry this oil.

OIL LEVEL CHECK

Every time you stop for fuel, check the engine oil as follows:

1. Make sure the car is parked on level ground.

2. When checking the oil level it is best for the engine to be at normal operating temperature, although checking the oil immediately after stopping will lead to a false reading. Wait a few minutes after turning off the engine to allow the oil to drain back into the crankcase.

3. Open the hood and locate the dipstick which will be on either the right or left side depending upon your particular engine. Pull the dipstick from its tube, wipe it clean and then reinsert it.

4. Pull the dipstick out again and, holding it horizontally, read the oil level. The oil should be between the "FULL" and "ADD" marks, dots or in the checkered area on the dipstick. If the oil is below the bottom mark, add oil of the proper viscosity through the capped opening in the top of the cylinder head cover.

5. Replace the dipstick and check the oil level again after adding any oil. Be careful not to overfill the crankcase. Approximately 1 quart of oil will raise the level from the upper mark to the "FULL" mark. Excess oil will generally be consumed at an accelerated rate.

CHANGING OIL AND FILTER

The oil is to be changed every 3,000 miles or the interval in your owner's manual. Under normal conditions, change the filter at first oil change and then at every other oil change, unless 6 months pass between changes. We recommend that the oil filter be changed every time the oil is changed. About a quart of dirty oil remains in the old filter. For a few dollars, it is a small expense for extended engine life.

REMOVAL AND INSTALLATION

1. Allow the engine to reach normal operating temperature. Turn the engine OFF and allow to sit for about five minutes. Raise the car and support on jackstands. Remove the oil pan plug and drain oil into a catch pan.

2. Using an oil filter wrench, remove the oil filter and place it in the oil catch pan. Using a clean rag, wipe oil filter mounting surface.

To install:

3. When installing the oil filter, place a small amount of oil on the sealing gasket and tighten the filter only hand tight. Install the oil pan plug and torque to 20 ft. lbs. (27 Nm).

4. Make sure the plug is tight in the pan. Using a funnel, add oil through the valve cover

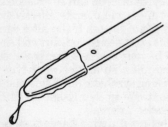

Oil level dipstick—early model engines

Oil level dipstick—late model engines

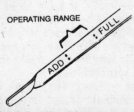

Oil level dipstick—V6 engines

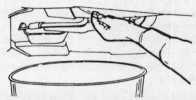

By keeping inward pressure on the plug as you unscrew it, oil will not escape past the threads

Remove the oil filter with a strap wrench

Coat the new oil filter gasket with clean engine oil

Install the new oil filter by hand

Add oil through the capped opening in the cylinder head cover

cap. Lower car, start the engine and inspect for oil leaks.

WARNING: *Run the engine at idle speed only until the oil pressure starts to rise. Engine damage may occur if the engine is raced with no oil pressure.*

Transmission and Transaxle

FLUID RECOMMENDATION

Manual

Use engine oil for all the manual transmissions and transaxles, except for the Borg Warner T5R. The BW T5R uses Dexron®II automatic transmission fluid. The BW transmission is used in the 1991 Rodeo (4×2) with the V6 engine.

Automatic

Use only Dexron®II Automatic Transmission Fluid.

FLUID LEVEL CHECK

Manual

The oil in the manual transmission should be checked every 12 months or 15,000 miles.

1. Allow the engine to reach normal operating temperature, raise the vehicle and support with jackstands and remove the filler plug from the side of the transmission/transaxle housing. Remove the speedometer driven gear assembly to check the fluid on the front wheel drive I-Mark.

2. If lubricant begins to trickle out of the hole, there is enough and you need not go any further. Otherwise, carefully insert your finger (watch out for sharp threads) and check to see if the oil is up to the edge of the hole.

3. If not, add oil through the hole until the level is at the edge of the hole. Most engine oils come in a plastic bottle with a nozzle; making

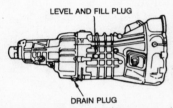

Manual transmission drain and fill plugs

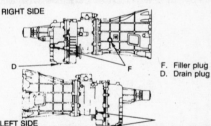

Manual transmission/transfer case drain and fill plugs—they are separate units and have to be drained independently

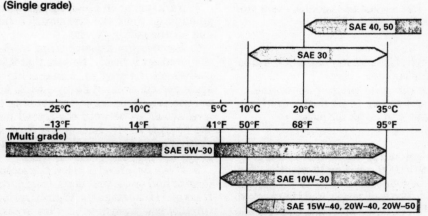

Manual transmission and transaxle oil viscosity chart

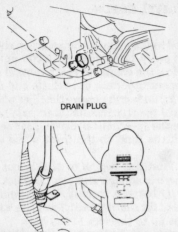

DRAIN PLUG

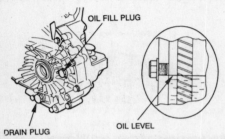

I-Mark (FWD) manual transaxle drain and fill—refill through the speedometer gear assembly

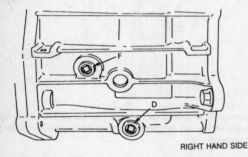

OIL FILL PLUG

DRAIN PLUG   OIL LEVEL

Impulse/Stylus (FWD) manual transaxle drain and fill plugs

Automatic transaxle level check

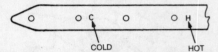

COLD   HOT

Automatic transmission/transaxle dipstick—others similar

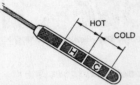

HOT
COLD

Late model automatic transmission dipstick—maintain a leave between the COLD line at 68–86°F (20–30°C) and a level between the HOT line at 158–176°F (70–80°C)

Add automatic transmission fluid through the dipstick tube

F

D

RIGHT HAND SIDE

Borg Warner T5R manual transmission—1991 Rodeo (4 × 2), use Dexron®II fluid ONLY

additions simple. Use a turkey baster if the area does not permit access.

4. Replace the filler plug or speedometer driven gear and torque to 20 ft. lbs. (27 Nm). Run the engine and check for leaks.

Automatic

Check the automatic transmission fluid level at least every 15,000 miles or 12 months. The dipstick can be found in the rear of the engine compartment. The fluid level should be checked only when the transmission is hot (normal operating temperature). The transmission is considered hot after about 20 miles of highway driving.

NOTE: *If you have driven for a prolonged period of time or in city traffic in hot weather, wait until the fluid cools down, about 30 minutes before checking the fluid level.*

1. Park the car on a level surface with the engine idling. Shift the transmission into Park and set the parking brake.

2. Remove the dipstick, wipe it clean and then reinsert it firmly. Be sure that it has been pushed all the way in. Remove the dipstick again and check the fluid level while holding it horizontally. With the engine running, the fluid level should be between the second notch and the "FULL HOT" line. If the fluid must be checked when it is cool, the level should be between the first and second notches.

3. If the fluid level is below the second notch (engine hot) or the first notch (engine cold), add Dexron®II automatic transmission fluid through the dipstick tube. This is easily done with the aid of a funnel. Check the level often as

you are filling the transmission. Be extremely careful not to overfill it. Overfilling will cause slippage, seal damage and overheating. **Approximately 1 pint of ATF will raise the fluid level from one notch/line to the other.**

NOTE: *Use only Dexron®II ATF. The use of any other fluid will cause severe damage to the transmission.*

The fluid on the dipstick should always be a bright red color. If it is discolored (brown or black), or smells burnt, serious transmission troubles, probably due to overheating, should be suspected. The transmission should be inspected by a qualified technician to locate the cause of the burnt fluid.

DRAIN AND REFILL
Manual

NOTE: *Before removing the oil from the transmission, drive the car to ensure that the oil has been warmed and the sediment has been stirred.*

Replace the transmission/transaxle fluid at the first 15,000 miles and then every 30,000 miles.

1. Raise the car and support on jack stands. Place an oil catch pan under the transmission.
2. Remove the plugs from the bottom and the side of the transmission. Allow the oil to drain into the pan. Remove the speedometer driven gear for the FWD I-Mark.
3. Refer to the "Oil Viscosity" chart for oil application. Replace the bottom plug and torque to 20 ft. lbs. (27 Nm). Install the new oil through the hole in the side of the transmission. Fill until the oil is level with the fill hole or to the level on the speedometer gear assembly. Replace the plug and lower the car.

Automatic

1. Drive the vehicle until it has reached normal operation temperature. Raise and support the car on jack stands. Place an oil catch pan under the transmission.

NOTE: *Some models have transmission oil pan drain plugs, if so remove the plug and allow the fluid to drain into the catch pan. If not, the oil pan has to be removed to drain the fluid.*

2. Remove all of the oil pan bolts, except for two corner bolts, which must be loosened 3 complete turns.
3. Using a rubber mallet, strike the opposite corner of the pan with one hand and hold up the oil pan with the other. Allow the fluid to drain and remove the pan. Remove the filter/screen.
4. Clean the oil pan and screen. Clean the mating surface of the transmission/transaxle with a scraper. Wash the mating surfaces with solvent to remove the oil film.
5. Install a new filter.
6. Install a new pan gasket, making sure it is in the proper position. Use the pan bolts to hold the gasket in place.
7. Raise the oil pan into position and tighten the bolts. Torque the bolts to 120 inch lbs. (10 Nm).
8. Add new transmission fluid through the dipstick tube. Start the engine and shift the transmission through the gear while the drive wheels are off the ground. Fill the transmission to the COLD level and check for leaks. Drive the vehicle and adjust the level to the HOT line. DO NOT overfill.

Transfer Case
FLUID RECOMMENDATIONS AND LEVEL CHECK
Manual

The manual transmission/transfer case is a complete unit and the fluid from the transmission lubricates the transfer case. Use engine oil to refill the manual transmission/transfer case. Refer to the "Oil Viscosity" chart in the manual transmission section.

Automatic

The automatic transmission and transfer case are separate units. The level has to be check individually. Use Dexron®II automatic transmission fluid in both units.

Remove the oil filler plug, if no fluid comes out of the hole, fill the transfer case with Dexron®II until the fluid spills out of the hole. Install the plug and torque to 20 ft. lbs. (27 Nm).

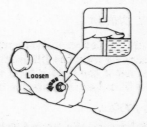

Transfer case fill plug—automatic transmission only

1990 Impulse 4 × 4

The manual transaxle and transfer case are separate units. The transfer case fluid is SAE 80W-90 GL-5 gear lubricant. Do NOT use engine oil in this assembly.

To check the lubricant level, remove the filler plug, if no lube comes out of the hole, fill the transfer case with gear lubricant until the lube

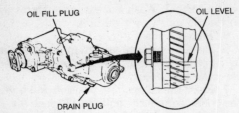

OIL FILL PLUG

OIL LEVEL

DRAIN PLUG

4 × 4 transfer case oil drain and fill plug—4 × 4 Impulse, use SAE 80W-90 GL-5 gear lube; use engine oil in the transmission

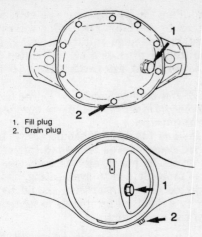

1. Fill plug
2. Drain plug

Rear differential drain and fill plugs

spills out of the hole. Install the plug and torque to 20 ft. lbs. (27 Nm).

DRAIN AND REFILL

1. Raise the vehicle and support with jackstands. Place a catch pan under the transfer case.

2. Remove the drain plug at the bottom of the transfer case. Allow the fluid to drain into the pan.

3. Install the drain plug and torque to 20 ft. lbs. (27 Nm).

4. Remove the filler plug and refill the transfer case with engine oil for the transfer case with a manual transmission, Dexron®II for the transfer case with a automatic transmission and SAE 80W-90 GL-5 gear lube for the *Impulse transfer case.* Install the fill plug and torque to 20 ft. lbs. (26 Nm).

Differential (Drive Axle)

FLUID RECOMMENDATION

Use only standard GL-5 hypoid type gear oil, SAE 80W or SAE 80W/90 for temperatures under 50°F (10°C) and SAE 140W for temperatures over 50°F (10°C).

FLUID LEVEL CHECK

With the car parked on a level surface, remove the filler plug from the differential housing. Check to see if the fluid is level with the bottom of the filler hole. Replace the plug.

DRAIN AND REFILL

1. Raise and support the car on 4 jack stands. Place a container under the differential to catch the fluid.

2. If a bottom plug exists, remove it, if not, remove the bolts retaining the cover to the housing. Pry the cover from the differential housing and allow the fluid to drain into the catch pan. Use a suction pump to remove the fluid if available.

3. Clean and inspect the differential. With the cover and housing washed free of oil, apply sealer to the mating surfaces.

4. Using a new gasket, install the cover and torque the bolts. Fill the differential with fluid (if a bottom plug was removed, replace it), installing it through the filler plug hole.

5. When the fluid level has reached the bottom of the filler hole, replace the filler plug. Lower the car and inspect for leaks.

Coolant

FLUID RECOMMENDATION

When adding or changing the fluid in the system, create a 50/50 mixture of high quality ethylene glycol antifreeze and water.

LEVEL CHECK

The fluid level may be checked by observing the fluid level marks of the recovery tank, if so equipped. The level should be below the "MIN" mark when the system is cold. At normal operating temperatures, the level should be between the "MIN" and the "MAX" marks. Only add coolant to bring the level to the "MAX" mark.

If the system is not equipped with a recovery tank, allow the engine to cool down before opening the radiator cap. Open the cap and add coolant to bring the level to about 13mm (½ in.) below the filler neck.

CAUTION: *Should it be necessary to remove the radiator cap, make sure that the system has had time to cool, reducing the internal pressure.*

DRAIN, FLUSH AND REFILL

The cooling system should be drained, thoroughly flushed and refilled at least every 30,000 miles or 24 months. These operations should be done with the engine cold.

1. Remove the radiator and recovery tank caps. Run the engine until the upper radiator

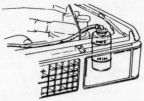

Coolant recovery tank—fill to the MAX mark when hot

Brake master cylinder—remote

Radiator drain plug

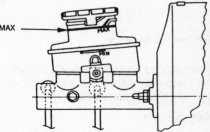

Brake master cylinder—integral

hose gets hot. This means that the thermostat is open and the coolant is flowing through the system.

2. Turn the engine "OFF" and place a large container under the radiator. Open the drain valve at the bottom of the radiator. Open the block drain plugs to speed up the draining process, if so equipped.

3. Close the drain valves and add water until the system is full. Repeat the draining and filling process several times, until the liquid is nearly colorless.

4. After the last draining, fill the system with a 50/50 mixture of ethylene glycol and water. Run the engine until the system is hot and add coolant, if necessary. Replace the caps and check for any leaks.

Brake Master Cylinder
FLUID RECOMMENDATION

When adding or replacing the brake fluid, always use a top quality fluid, such as Delco Supreme II or DOT-3. DO NOT allow the brake fluid container or master cylinder reservoir to remain open for long periods of time; brake fluid absorbs moisture from the air, reducing its effectiveness and causing corrosion in the lines. Isuzu recommends that silicone brake should not be used in the brake system. Damage to the rubber parts may result.

FLUID LEVEL

The master cylinder — located in the left rear section of the engine compartment — consists of an aluminum body and a translucent nylon reservoir with minimum and maximum fill indicators. The fluid level of the reservoirs should be kept near the top of the MAX marks.

NOTE: *Be careful not to spill any brake fluid on painted surfaces, for it eats the paint.*

Any sudden decrease in the fluid level indicates a possible leak in the system and should be checked out immediately.

Clutch Master Cylinder
FLUID RECOMMENDATIONS

When adding or replacing the clutch fluid, always use a top quality fluid, such as Delco Supreme II or DOT-3. DO NOT allow the clutch fluid container or cylinder reservoir to remain open for long periods of time; brake fluid absorbs moisture from the air, reducing its effectiveness and causing corrosion in the lines. Isuzu recommends that silicone brake should not be used in the clutch system. Damage to the rubber parts may result.

FLUID LEVEL

The clutch master cylinder — located in the left rear section of the engine compartment, near the brake master cylinder — consists of an aluminum body and a translucent nylon reservoir with minimum and maximum fill indicators. The fluid level of the reservoirs should be kept near the top of the MAX marks.

NOTE: *Be careful not to spill any brake fluid on painted surfaces, for it eats the paint.*

Any sudden decrease in the fluid level indicates a possible leak in the system and should be checked out immediately.

Power Steering Pump
FLUID RECOMMENDATION

When filling or replacing the fluid of the power steering pump reservoir, **use Dexron®II**

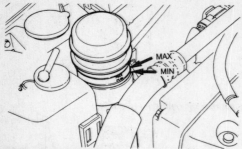

Power steering reservoir

automatic transmission fluid only. Any other fluid may cause damage to the internal power steering components.

LEVEL CHECK

Power steering fluid level should be checked at least once every 12 months or 7,500 miles. To prevent possible overfilling, check the fluid level only when the fluid has warmed to operating temperatures and the wheels are turned straight ahead. If the level is low, fill the pump reservoir until the fluid level measures "Full" or "Max" in the reservoir. Low fluid level usually produces a moaning sound as the wheels are turned (especially when standing still or parking) and increases steering wheel effort.

NOTE: *Isuzu recommends that you use Dexron® II automatic transmission fluid. Any other fluid is not an acceptable substitute.*

Manual Steering Gear

Use chassis grease to lubricate the manual rack and pinion assembly during overhaul.

Use SAE 80W-90 GL-5 gear lubricant in the P'UP manual steering box. Remove the fill plug on the side cover to refill the steering box with lubricant

Chassis Greasing

All original suspension components have no provision for grease fittings. Some replacement components do have grease fittings. If equipped with fittings, use a pressurized grease gun to inject a small amount of chassis grease about every 15,000 miles. Do not overfill the components, grease seal damage may occur. Use spray lithium grease to lubricate the stabilizer and strut rod bushings.

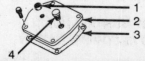

1. Lock nut
2. Side cover
3. Gasket
4. Fill plug

Manual steering gear fill plug—use SAE 80W-90 GL-5 gear lubricant

Body Lubrication
HOOD LATCH AND HINGES

Clean the latch surfaces and apply clean engine oil or all purpose lithium grease to the latch pilot bolts, spring anchor and hood hinges as well. Use a chassis grease to lubricate all the pivot points in the latch release mechanism.

DOOR HINGES

The gas tank filler door, car door, and rear hatch or trunk lid hinges should be wiped clean and lubricated with clean engine oil. Silicone spray also works well on these parts, but must be applied more often. Use engine oil to lubricate the trunk of hatch lock mechanism and the lock bolt and striker. The door lock cylinders can be lubricated easily with a shot silicone spray or one of the many dry penetrating lubricants commercially available.

PARKING BRAKE LINKAGE

Use chassis grease on the parking brake cable where it contacts the guides, links, levers, and pulleys. The grease should be a water resistant one for durability under the car.

ACCELERATOR LINKAGE

Lubricate the carburetor stud, carburetor lever, throttle body and the accelerator pedal lever at the support inside the car with clean engine oil or silicone spray.

TRANSMISSION SHIFT LINKAGE

Lubricate the shift linkage with water resistant chassis grease.

Front Wheel Bearings
Rear Wheel Drive

REMOVAL AND INSTALLATION

CAUTION: *Some brake pads contain asbestos, which has been determined to be a cancer causing agent. Never clean the brake surfaces with compressed air! Avoid inhaling any dust from any brake surface! When cleaning brake surfaces, use a commercially available brake cleaning fluid.*

1. Raise and safely support the vehicle. Remove the wheel assembly. Remove the dust cap.
2. Remove the cotter pin, nut and outer roller bearing assembly from the hub. Remove the brake rotor/hub from the spindle.
3. Pry out the inner bearing lip seal and remove the inner bearing assembly.
4. Wash all parts in a cleaning solvent and dry with compressed air. Do NOT allow the bearing to turn while dry with compressed air.
5. Check the bearings for pitting or scoring.

Also check for smooth rotation and lack of noise.

To install:

6. Thoroughly lubricate the bearings with new "High Tempurature" wheel bearing lubricant.

7. Apply a light coat of lubricant to the spindle and inside surface of the hub.

8. Place the inner bearing in the race of the hub and install a new grease seal. Do not allow the seal to twist in the bore.

9. Install the hub assembly on the spindle.

10. Install the outer wheel bearing, washer and adjust nut.

11. To adjust the wheel bearings, torque the nut to 22 ft. lbs. (30 Nm) while turning the hub, back off the nut completely and then tighten finger tight. If the slot in the nut is not aligned with the spindle, tighten only enough to align.

12. Install a new cotter pin and bend over. Install the dust cap on the hub.

13. Install the brake caliper and support assembly.

14. Install the wheel assembly.

ADJUSTMENT

1. With the wheel raised, remove the hub cap and dust cap and then remove the cotter pin and nut retainer from the end of the spindle.

2. While rotating the wheel, tighten the spindle nut to 22 ft. lbs.

3. Turn the hub 2–3 turns and loosen the nut just enough so it can be turned by hand.

4. Turn the nut all the way hand tight and check to be sure the hub has no freeplay.

5. Measure the starting torque by pulling a wheel hub stud with a pull scale. Tighten the spindle nut so the pull scale reads 1.1–2.6 lbs. (0.5–1.2 lbs.). When the hub begins to rotate.

NOTE: *Make sure the brake pads are not in contact with the drum when measuring rotating torque.*

6. Install the nut retainer, new cotter pin, dust cap and hub cap.

TRAILER TOWING

Towing a trailer will affect handling, durability and economy. Your safety and satisfaction depend upon proper use of correct equipment. Also, you should avoid overloads and other abusive use.

Factory trailer towing packages are available on most vehicles. However, if you are installing a trailer hitch and wiring on your vehicle, there are a few thing that you ought to know.

Information on trailer towing, special equipment and optional equipment is available at your local dealership. You can write to American Isuzu Motors Inc. 2300 Pellissier Place, Whittier, CA 90601-9979

Trailer Weight

Trailer weight is the first, and most important, factor in determining whether or not your vehicle is suitable for towing the trailer you have in mind. The horsepower-to-weight ratio should be calculated. The basic standard is a ratio of 35:1. That is, 35 pounds of GVW (gross vehicle weight) for every horsepower.

To calculate this ratio, multiply you engine's rated horsepower by 35, then subtract the weight of the vehicle, including passengers and luggage. The resulting figure is the ideal maximum trailer weight that you can tow. One point to consider: a numerically higher axle ratio can offset what appears to be a low trailer weight. If the weight of the trailer that you have in mind is somewhat higher than the weight you just calculated, you might consider changing your rear axle ratio to compensate.

Hitch Weight

There are three kinds of hitches: bumper mounted, frame mounted, and load equalizing.

Bumper mounted hitches are those which attach solely to the vehicle's bumper. Many states prohibit towing with this type of hitch, when it attaches to the vehicle's stock bumper, since it subjects the bumper to stresses for which it was not designed. Aftermarket rear step bumpers, designed for trailer towing, are acceptable for use with bumper mounted hitches.

CAUTION: *Do NOT attach any hitch to the bumper bar on the vehicle. A hitch attachment may be made through the bumper mounting locations, but only if an additional attachment is also made.*

Frame mounted hitches can be of the type which bolts to two or more points on the frame, plus the bumper, or just to several points on the frame. Frame mounted hitches can also be of the tongue type, for Class I towing, or, of the receiver type, for classes II and III.

Load equalizing hitches are usually used for large trailers. Most equalizing hitches are welded in place and use equalizing bars and chains to level the vehicle after the trailer is hooked up.

The bolt-on hitches are the most common, since they are relatively easy to install.

Check the gross weight rating of your trailer. Tongue weight is usually figured as 10% of gross trailer weight. Therefore, a trailer with a maximum gross weight of 2,000 lbs. (907 kg) will have a maximum tongue weight of 200 lbs. (91 kg) Class I trailers fall into this category. Class II trailers are those with a gross weight rating of 2,000–3,500 lbs. (907–1,588 kg), while Class III trailers fall into the 3,500–6,000 lbs. (1,588–2,722 kg) category. Class IV trailers are those over 6,000 lbs. (2,722 kg) and are for use with fifth wheel trucks, only.

When you have determined the hitch that you'll need, follow the manufacturer's installation instructions, exactly, especially when it comes to fastener torques. The hitch will subjected to a lot of stress and good hitches come with hardened bolts. Never substitute an inferior bolt for a hardened bolt.

More frequent service is required when using your vehicle to pull a trailer. The automatic transmission fluid, engine oil/filter and rear axle lubricant change requirements for change. Change the engine oil/filter every 3,000 miles (5,000 km), transmission and rear axle fluid every 15,000 miles (25,000 km).

Wiring

Wiring the vehicle for towing is fairly easy. There are a number of good wiring kits available and these should be used, rather than trying to design your own. All trailers will need brake lights and turn signals as well as tail lights and side marker lights. Most states require extra marker lights for overly wide trailers. Also, most states have recently required back-up lights for trailers, and most trailer manufacturers have been building trailers with back-up lights for several years.

Additionally, some Class I, most Class II and just about all Class III trailers will have electric brakes.

Add to this number an accessories wire, to operate trailer internal equipment or to charge the trailer's battery, and you can have as many as seven wires in the harness.

Determine the equipment on your trailer and buy the wiring kit necessary. The kit will contain all the wires needed, plus a plug adapter set which included the female plug, mounted on the bumper or hitch, and the male plug, wired into, or plugged into the trailer harness.

When installing the kit, follow the manufacturer's instructions. The color coding of the wires is standard throughout the industry.

One point to note, some domestic vehicles, and most imported vehicles, have separate turn signals. On most domestic vehicles, the brake lights and rear turn signals operate with the same bulb. For those vehicles with separate turn signals, you can purchase an isolation unit so that the brake lights won't blink whenever the turn signals are operated, or, you can go to your local electronics supply house and buy four diodes to wire in series with the brake and turn signal bulbs. Diodes will isolate the brake and turn signals. The choice is yours. The isola-

tion units are simple and quick to install, but far more expensive than the diodes. The diodes, however, require more work to install properly, since they require the cutting of each bulb's wire and soldering in place of the diode.

One final point, the best kits are those with a spring loaded cover on the vehicle mounted socket. This cover prevents dirt and moisture from corroding the terminals. Never let the vehicle socket hang loosely. Always mount it securely to the bumper or hitch.

PUSHING AND TOWING

All Isuzu models covered in this guide, equipped with automatic transmissions can not be push started. The vehicle can be towed, however, with the transmission in Neutral as long as the speed does not exceed 35 mph and the distance does not exceed 15 miles. If the above speeds and distances must be exceeded, the vehicle's driveshaft must be disconnected first, or the drive wheels raised. The tow truck operator typically has a special dolly for this purpose. Towing with the rear wheels raised also requires the steering wheels to be locked in the straight ahead position (do not rely on the steering column lock for this purpose).

JUMP STARTING A DUAL BATTERY DIESEL

The batteries are connected in parallel circuit (positive terminal to positive terminal, negative terminal to negative terminal). Hooking the batteries up in parallel circuit increases battery cranking power without increasing total battery voltage output (12 volts). On the other hand, hooking two 12 volt batteries up in a series circuit (positive terminal to negative terminal, positive terminal to negative terminal) increases total battery output to 24 volts (12 volts + 12 volts).

CAUTION: *NEVER hook the batteries up in a series circuit or the entire electrical system will be severely damaged. This may even start a fire!*

In the event that a dual battery diesel must be jump started, use the following procedure.

1. Open the hood and locate the batteries. On GM diesels, the manufacturer usually suggests using the battery on the driver's side of the vehicle to make the connection.

2. Position the donor vehicle so that the jumper cables will reach from its battery (must be 12 volt, negative ground) to the appropriate battery in the diesel. Do not allow the vehicles to touch.

JUMP STARTING A DEAD BATTERY

The chemical reaction in a battery produces explosive hydrogen gas. This is the safe way to jump start a dead battery, reducing the chances of an accidental spark that could cause an explosion.

Jump Starting Precautions

1. Be sure both batteries are of the same voltage.
2. Be sure both batteries are of the same polarity (have the same grounded terminal).
3. Be sure the vehicles are not touching.
4. Be sure the vent cap holes are not obstructed.
5. Do not smoke or allow sparks around the battery.
6. In cold weather, check for frozen electrolyte in the battery. Do not jump start a frozen battery.
7. Do not allow electrolyte on your skin or clothing.
8. Be sure the electrolyte is not frozen.
CAUTION: *Make certain that the ignition key, in the vehicle with the dead battery, is in the OFF position. Connecting cables to vehicles with on-board computers will result in computer destruction if the key is not in the OFF position.*

Jump Starting Procedure

1. Determine voltages of the two batteries; they must be the same.
2. Bring the starting vehicle close (they must not touch) so that the batteries can be reached easily.
3. Turn off all accessories and both engines. Put both cars in Neutral or Park and set the handbrake.
4. Cover the cell caps with a rag—do not cover terminals.
5. If the terminals on the run-down battery are heavily corroded, clean them.
6. Identify the positive and negative posts on both batteries and connect the cables in the order shown.
7. Start the engine of the starting vehicle and run it at fast idle. Try to start the car with the dead battery. Crank it for no more than 10 seconds at a time and let it cool off for 20 seconds in between tries.
8. If it doesn't start in 3 tries, there is something else wrong.
9. Disconnect the cables in the reverse order.
10. Replace the cell covers and dispose of the rags.

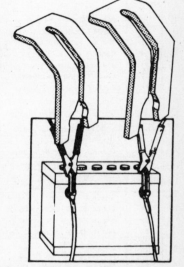

Side terminal batteries occasionally pose a problem when connecting jumper cables. There frequently isn't enough room to clamp the cables without touching sheet metal. Side terminal adaptors are available to alleviate this problem and should be re-

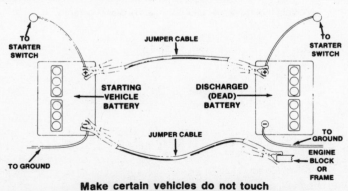

Make certain vehicles do not touch

This hook-up for negative ground cars only

Item No.	MILEAGE ONLY ITEMS	IN THOUSANDS OF MILES (USE ODOMETER READING)														
		3.75	7.5	15	22.5	30	37.5	45	52.5	60	67.5	75	82.5	90	97.5	105
1	ROTATE TIRES AND ADJUST TIRE PRESSURE		X	X	X	X	X	X	X	X	X	X	X	X	X	X
2	CHANGE FRONT & REAR AXLE LUBRICANT					X				X				X		
3	CHANGE MANUAL TRANSMISSION & TRANSFER CASE LUBRICANT					X				X				X		
5	REPLACE AIR CLEANER ELEMENT					X				X				X		
6	REPACK FRONT WHEEL BEARINGS					X				X				X		
7	CHANGE AUTOMATIC TRANSMISSION FLUID					X				X				X		
8	REPLACE FUEL LINE FILTER					X				X				X		
9	CHECK & ADJUST VALVE CLEARANCE				X			X			X			X		
11	REPLACE POWER STEERING RUBBER HOSES									X						
12	CHANGE POWER STEERING FLUID						X						X			
14	ADJUST ENGINE IDLE SPEED	X				X				X				X		

Item No.	MILEAGE/MONTHS whichever comes first	EVERY MONTHS OR	IN THOUSANDS OF MILES (USE ODOMETER READING)														
			3.75	7.5	15	22.5	30	37.5	45	52.5	60	67.5	75	82.5	90	97.5	105
15	* OWNER SAFETY CHECKS	12		X	X	X	X	X	X	X	X	X	X	X	X	X	X
16	LUBRICATE BODY & CHASSIS			X	X	X	X	X	X	X	X	X	X	X	X	X	X
17	CHECK FLUID & LUBRICANT LEVELS			X	X	X	X	X	X	X	X	X	X	X	X	X	X
18	CHECK FRONT & REAR PROPELLER SHAFT			X	X	X	X	X	X	X	X	X	X	X	X	X	X
19	CHECK SUSPENSION & STEERING			X	X	X	X	X	X	X	X	X	X	X	X	X	X
20	CHECK TIRES, WHEELS & DISC BRAKES			X	X	X	X	X	X	X	X	X	X	X	X	X	X
21	CHECK BRAKE LINES & HOSES			X	X	X	X	X	X	X	X	X	X	X	X	X	X
22	CHECK EXHAUST SYSTEM			X	X	X	X	X	X	X	X	X	X	X	X	X	X
23	DRAIN WATER FROM FUEL FILTER			X	X	X	X	X	X	X	X	X	X	X	X	X	X
24	CHANGE ENGINE OIL			X	X	X	X	X	X	X	X	X	X	X	X	X	X
25	CHANGE ENGINE OIL FILTER			X	X	X	X	X	X	X	X	X	X	X	X	X	X
26	CHECK & LUBE BRAKE & CLUTCH PEDALS				X	X	X	X	X	X	X	X	X	X	X	X	X
27	CHECK DRUM BRAKES & PARKING BRAKES				X	X	X	X	X	X	X	X	X	X	X	X	X
28	CHECK & CLEAN COOLING SYSTEM				X	X	X	X	X	X	X	X	X	X	X	X	X
29	INSPECT FUEL CAP, LINES & TANK				X	X	X	X	X	X	X	X	X	X	X	X	X
30	CHECK THROTTLE LINKAGE				X	X	X	X	X	X	X	X	X	X	X	X	X
31	CHECK BUMPERS				X	X	X	X	X	X	X	X	X	X	X	X	X
32	LUBE FRONT & REAR PROPELLER SHAFTS (4WD only)				X	X	X	X	X	X	X	X	X	X	X	X	X
33	CHECK STEERING GEAR				X	X	X	X	X	X	X	X	X	X	X	X	X
35	CHECK DRIVE BELTS (Except California)	12					X				X				X		
	CHECK DRIVE BELTS (California only)	24					X				X				X		
38	AIR CONDITIONING SHOULD BE CHECKED EVERY 12 MONTHS																

* OWNER SAFETY CHECKS ARE EXPLAINED ON FOLLOWING PAGES.

Vehicle maintenance schedule—early diesel engines

Item No.	MILEAGE ONLY ITEMS	IN THOUSANDS OF MILES (USE ODOMETER READING)										
		5.0	7.5	15	22.5	30	37.5	45	52.5	60	67.5	75
1	ROTATE TIRES AND ADJUST TIRE PRESSURE		●	●	●	●	●	●	●	●	●	●
2	CHANGE FRONT & REAR AXLE LUBRICANT		●			●				●		
3	CHANGE MANUAL TRANSMISSION & TRANSFER CASE LUBRICANT		●			●				●		
4	REPLACE SPARK PLUGS					●				●		
5	REPLACE AIR CLEANER ELEMENT					●				●		
6	REPACK FRONT WHEEL BEARINGS					●				●		
7	CHANGE AUTOMATIC TRANSMISSION FLUID					●				●		
8	REPLACE FUEL LINE FILTER (Except California)					●				●		
9	CHECK & ADJUST VALVE CLEARANCE				●			●			●	
10	CHECK SPARK PLUG & COIL WIRES (Except California)					●				●		
11	REPLACE POWER STEERING RUBBER HOSES							●				
12	CHANGE POWER STEERING FLUID						●				●	
13	CHECK THERMOSTATICALLY CONTROLLED AIR CLEANER (Except California)									●		
14	ADJUST ENGINE IDLE SPEED (Except California)	●		●		●		●		●		●
	ADJUST ENGINE IDLE SPEED (California Only)	●										

Item No.	MILEAGE/MONTHS Whichever comes first	EVERY MONTHS OR	IN THOUSANDS OF MILES (USE ODOMETER READING)									
			7.5	15	22.5	30	37.5	45	52.5	60	67.5	75
15	●OWNER SAFETY CHECKS	12	●	●	●	●	●	●	●	●	●	●
16	LUBRICATE BODY & CHASSIS		●	●	●	●	●	●	●	●	●	●
17	CHECK FLUID & LUBRICANT LEVELS		●	●	●	●	●	●	●	●	●	●
18	CHECK FRONT & REAR PROPELLER SHAFT		●	●	●	●	●	●	●	●	●	●
19	CHECK SUSPENSION & STEERING		●	●	●	●	●	●	●	●	●	●
20	CHECK TIRES, WHEELS, & DISC BRAKES		●	●	●	●	●	●	●	●	●	●
21	CHECK BRAKE LINES & HOSES		●	●	●	●	●	●	●	●	●	●
22	CHECK EXHAUST SYSTEM		●	●	●	●	●	●	●	●	●	●
24	CHANGE ENGINE OIL		●	●	●	●	●	●	●	●	●	●
25	CHANGE ENGINE OIL FILTER		●	●	●	●	●	●	●	●	●	●
26	CHECK & LUBE BRAKE & CLUTCH PEDALS		●	●	●	●	●	●	●	●	●	●
27	CHECK DRUM BRAKES & PARKING BRAKES		●	●	●	●	●	●	●	●	●	●
28	CHECK & CLEAN COOLING SYSTEM		●	●	●	●	●	●	●	●	●	●
29	INSPECT FUEL CAP, LINES, & TANK		●	●	●	●	●	●	●	●	●	●
30	CHECK THROTTLE LINKAGE		●	●	●	●	●	●	●	●	●	●
31	CHECK BUMPERS		●	●	●	●	●	●	●	●	●	●
32	LUBE FRONT & REAR PROPELLER SHAFTS (4WD only)		●	●	●	●	●	●	●	●	●	●
33	CHECK STEERING GEAR	12										
34	CHECK CARBURETOR CHOKE & HOSES	24				●				●		
35	CHECK DRIVE BELTS	24				●				●		
36	CHECK DISTRIBUROR AND DISTRIBUTOR ADVANCE MECHANISM (Except California)	24				●				●		
37	CHECK AIR INJECTION REACTOR SYSTEM (Except California)	24				●				●		
38	AIR CONDITIONING SHOULD BE CHECKED EVERY 12 MONTHS.											

● OWNER SAFETY CHECKS ARE EXPLAINED ON FOLLOWING PAGES.

Vehicle maintenance schedule—early gas engines

MILEAGE ONLY ITEMS		IN THOUSANDS OF MILES (USE ODOMETER READING)												
		7.5	15	22.5	30	37.5	45	52.5	60	67.5	75	82.5	90	97.5
1	CHANGE FRONT & REAR AXLE OIL		x		x				x				x	
2	CHANGE MANUAL TRANSMISSION AND TRANSFER CASE OIL		x		x				x				x	
3	ADJUST ENGINE IDLE SPEED	x							x		x		x	
4	ADJUST VALVE CLEARANCE		x			x		x	x		x		x	
5	REPLACE AIR CLEANER ELEMENT					x			x				x	
6	REPLACE SPARK PLUGS					x			x				x	
7	CHANGE ENGINE COOLANT					x							x	
8	REPLACE TIMING BELT								x					
9	REPLACE O₂ SENSOR												x	
10	ROTATE TIRES	x	x	x	x	x	x	x	x	x	x	x	x	x
11	CHANGE POWER STEERING FLUID					x			x				x	
12	REPACK FRONT WHEEL BEARINGS					x			x				x	
13	CLEAN RADIATOR CORE AND A/C CONDENSER								x					
14	INSPECT SPARK PLUG WIRE								x					

MILEAGE/MONTHS whichever comes first		MONTHS OR EVERY	IN THOUSANDS OF MILES (USE ODOMETER READING)												
			7.5	15	22.5	30	37.5	45	52.5	60	67.5	75	82.5	90	97.5
1	CHECK BATTERY FLUID LEVEL	12	x	x	x	x	x	x	x	x	x	x	x	x	x
2	CHECK ENGINE COOLANT LEVEL	12	x	x	x	x	x	x	x	x	x	x	x	x	x
3	CHECK BRAKE AND CLUTCH FLUID LEVEL	12	x	x	x	x	x	x	x	x	x	x	x	x	x
4	CHECK FLUID LEAKS	12	x	x	x	x	x	x	x	x	x	x	x	x	x
5	CHANGE ENGINE OIL	12	x	x	x	x	x	x	x	x	x	x	x	x	x
6	REPLACE ENGINE OIL FILTER	12	x		x		x		x	x		x			x
7	CHECK COOLING AND HEATER HOSES	12		x			x			x		x		x	
8	CHECK EXHAUST SYSTEM	12	x	x	x	x	x	x	x	x	x	x	x	x	x
9	CHECK FUEL LINE AND FUEL TANK/CAP	12								x					
10	CHECK ENGINE DRIVE BELTS	24				x				x				x	
11	CHECK TIRES AND WHEELS	12	x	x	x	x	x	x	x	x	x	x	x	x	x
12	ADJUST STEERING GEAR PLAY	24				x				x				x	
13	CHECK BRAKE LINES AND HOSE	12	x	x	x	x	x	x	x	x	x	x	x	x	x
14	CHECK DISC BRAKES	12		x			x			x		x		x	
15	CHECK PARKING BRAKE	12		x			x			x		x		x	
16	ADJUST BRAKE PEDAL PLAY	12		x			x			x		x		x	
17	CHECK ACCELERATOR PEDAL AND CABLE	6	x	x	x	x	x	x	x	x	x	x	x	x	x
18	LUBE SUSPENSION	6	x	x	x	x	x	x	x	x	x	x	x	x	x
19	LUBE BODY AND CHASSIS	6	x	x	x	x	x	x	x	x	x	x	x	x	x
20	LUBE FRONT AND REAR PROPELLER SHAFT	6	x		x		x		x		x		x		x
21	CHECK CLUTCH LINES AND HOSE	12					x			x				x	
22	* CHECK AUTOMATIC TRANSMISSION AND TRANSFER CHAIN CASE FLUID	12					x			x				x	
23	CHECK AUTO CRUISE CONTROL LINKAGE AND HOSES	12		x	x		x			x		x		x	
24	LUBE CLUTCH PEDAL SPRING, BUSHING AND CLEVIS PIN	6		x			x			x		x		x	
25	CHECK CLUTCH PEDAL FREE PLAY	12		x			x			x		x		x	
26	CHECK PROPELLER SHAFT FLANGE TORQUE	12	x		x		x		x		x		x		x
27	CHECK STARTER SAFETY SWITCH	12	x	x	x	x	x	x	x	x	x	x	x	x	x
28	CHECK THROTTLE LINKAGE	12		x			x			x		x		x	

* : CHANGE IS NEEDED ONLY UNDER SEVERE DRIVING CONDITIONS

Vehicle maintenance schedule—late model 4-cylinder engines

MILEAGE ONLY ITEMS	IN THOUSANDS OF MILES (USE ODOMETER READING)												
	7.5	15	22.5	30	37.5	45	52.5	60	67.5	75	82.5	90	97.5
1 CHANGE FRONT & REAR AXLE OIL		x		x				x				x	
2 CHANGE MANUAL TRANSMISSION AND TRANSFER CASE OIL		x		x				x				x	
3 ADJUST IGNITION TIMING								x					
4 CHECK THERMOSTATICALLY CONTROLLED AIR CLEANER				x				x				x	
5 REPLACE AIR CLEANER ELEMENT				x				x				x	
6 REPLACE SPARK PLUGS				x				x				x	
7 CHANGE ENGINE COOLANT				x								x	
8 CHECK THROTTLE BODY MOUNTING BOLT TORQUE	x	x	x	x	x	x	x	x	x	x	x	x	x
9 CHECK PCV SYSTEM								x					
10 INSPECT SPARK PLUG WIRE								x					
11 ROTATE TIRES	x	x	x	x	x	x	x	x	x	x	x	x	x
12 CHANGE POWER STEERING FLUID				x				x				x	
13 REPACK FRONT WHEEL BEARINGS				x				x				x	
14 CLEAN RADIATOR CORE AND A/C CONDENSER								x					
15 CHANGE TRANSFER CASE OIL (AUTOMATIC TRANSMISSION)		x		x				x				x	

MILEAGE/MONTHS whichever comes first	MONTHS OR EVERY	IN THOUSANDS OF MILES (USE ODOMETER READING)												
		7.5	15	22.5	30	37.5	45	52.5	60	67.5	75	82.5	90	97.5
1 CHECK BATTERY FLUID LEVEL	12	x	x	x	x	x	x	x	x	x	x	x	x	x
2 CHECK ENGINE COOLANT LEVEL	12	x	x	x	x	x	x	x	x	x	x	x	x	x
3 CHECK BRAKE AND CLUTCH FLUID LEVEL	12	x	x	x	x	x	x	x	x	x	x	x	x	x
4 CHECK FLUID LEAKS	12	x	x	x	x	x	x	x	x	x	x	x	x	x
5 CHANGE ENGINE OIL	12	x	x	x	x	x	x	x	x	x	x	x	x	x
6 REPLACE ENGINE OIL FILTER	12	x		x		x		x		x		x		x
7 CHECK COOLING AND HEATER HOSES	12		x		x		x		x		x		x	
8 CHECK EXHAUST SYSTEM	12	x	x	x	x	x	x	x	x	x	x	x	x	x
9 CHECK FUEL LINE AND FUEL TANK/CAP	12								x					
10 CHECK ENGINE DRIVE BELTS	24				x				x				x	
11 CHECK TIRES AND WHEELS	12	x	x	x	x	x	x	x	x	x	x	x	x	x
12 ADJUST STEERING GEAR PLAY	24				x				x				x	
13 CHECK BRAKE LINES AND HOSE	12	x	x	x	x	x	x	x	x	x	x	x	x	x
14 CHECK DISC BRAKES	12		x		x		x		x		x		x	
15 CHECK PARKING BRAKE	12		x		x		x		x		x		x	
16 ADJUST BRAKE PEDAL PLAY	12		x		x		x		x		x		x	
17 CHECK ACCELERATOR PEDAL AND CABLE	6	x	x	x	x	x	x	x	x	x	x	x	x	x
18 LUBE SUSPENSION	6	x	x	x	x	x	x	x	x	x	x	x	x	x
19 LUBE BODY AND CHASSIS	6	x	x	x	x	x	x	x	x	x	x	x	x	x
20 LUBE FRONT AND REAR PROPELLER SHAFT	6	x		x		x		x		x		x		x
21 CHECK CLUTCH LINES AND HOSE	12				x				x				x	
22 CHECK AUTO CRUISE CONTROL LINKAGE AND HOSES	12		x		x		x		x		x		x	
23 LUBE CLUTCH PEDAL SPRING, BUSHING AND CLEVIS PIN	6		x		x		x		x		x		x	
24 CHECK CLUTCH PEDAL FREE PLAY	12		x		x		x		x		x		x	
25 CHECK PROPELLER SHAFT FLANGE TORQUE	12	x		x		x		x		x		x		x
26 CHECK STARTER SAFETY SWITCH	12	x	x	x	x	x	x	x	x	x	x	x	x	x
27 CHECK THROTTLE LINKAGE	12		x		x		x		x		x		x	
28 *CHECK AUTOMATIC TRANSMISSION FLUID	12				x				x				x	

* CHANGE IS NEEDED ONLY UNDER SEVERE DRIVING CONDITIONS

Vehicle maintenance schedule—late model 6-cylinder engines

CAPACITIES

Year	Model	Engine Displacement code (cc)	Engine Crankcase		Transmission (pts.)			Drive Axle (pts.)	Fuel Tank (gal.)	Cooling System (qts.)
			with Filter	without Filter	4-Spd	5-Spd	Auto.			
1981	I-Mark	G180Z (1800)	4.0	3.5	2.7	3.8	13.4	2.1	13.7	6.9
	I-Mark	4FBI (1817)	5.5	5.0	2.7	3.8	13.4	2.1	13.7	7.4
	Pick-up	G180Z (1800)	5.2	4.1	2.7	3.3	13.4	2.7	13.2 ①	8.5
	Pick-up	C223 (2238)	6.3	5.8	2.7	3.3	13.4	2.7	13.2 ①	9.5 ②
1982	I-Mark	G180Z (1800)	4.0	3.5	2.7	3.8	13.4	2.1	13.7	6.9
	I-Mark	4FBI (1817)	5.5	5.0	2.7	3.8	13.4	2.1	13.7	7.4
	Pick-up	G180Z (1800)	5.2	4.1	2.7	3.3	13.4	2.7	13.2 ①	8.5
	Pick-up	C223 (2238)	6.3	5.8	2.7	3.3	13.4	2.7	13.2 ①	9.5 ②
1983	I-Mark	G180Z (1800)	4.0	3.5	2.7	3.8	13.4	2.1	13.7	6.9
	I-Mark	4FBI (1817)	5.5	5.0	2.7	3.8	13.4	2.1	13.7	7.4
	Impulse	G200Z (1950)	3.8	3.4	—	3.3	13.4	2.5	15.1	9.4
	Pick-up	G180Z (1800)	5.2	4.1	2.7	3.3	13.4	2.7	13.2 ①	8.5
	Pick-up	C223 (2238)	6.3	5.8	2.7	3.3	13.4	2.7	13.2 ①	9.5 ②
1984	I-Mark	G180Z (1800)	4.0	3.5	2.7	3.8	13.4	2.1	13.7	6.9
	I-Mark	4FBI (1817)	5.5	5.0	2.7	3.8	13.4	2.1	13.7	7.4
	Impulse	G200Z (1950)	3.8	3.4	—	3.3	13.4	2.5	15.1	9.4
	Pick-up	G200Z (1950)	3.7	3.3	2.6	3.3	12.6	2.7	13.2 ①	8.5
	Pick-up	C223 (2238)	6.0	5.6	2.6	3.3	12.6	2.7	13.2 ①	9.5 ②
1985	I-Mark (RWD)	G180Z (1800)	4.0	3.5	2.7	3.8	13.4	2.1	13.7	6.9
	I-Mark (RWD)	4FBI (1817)	5.5	5.0	2.7	3.8	13.4	2.1	13.7	7.4
	I-Mark (FWD)	4XC1-U (1471)	3.4	3.0	—	2.8	12.6	—	11.1	6.8
	Impulse	G200Z (1950)	3.8	3.4	—	3.3	13.4	2.5	15.1	9.4
	Impulse Turbo	4ZC1-T (1983)	3.8	3.4	—	3.3	13.4	3.1	15.1	9.6
	Pick-up	G200Z (1950)	3.7	3.3	2.6	3.3	12.6	2.7	13.2 ①	8.5
	Pick-up	C223 (2238)	6.0	5.6	2.6	3.3	12.6	2.7	13.2 ①	9.5 ②
1986	I-Mark (FWD)	4XC1-U (1471)	3.4	3.0	—	2.8	12.6	—	11.1	6.8
	Impulse	G200Z (1950)	3.8	3.4	—	3.3	13.4	2.5	15.1	9.4
	Impulse Turbo	4ZC1-T (1983)	3.8	3.4	—	3.3	13.4	3.1	15.1	9.6
	Pick-up	G200Z (1950)	4.4	4.0	2.6	3.2	12.6	2.7	13.2 ①	8.5
	Pick-up	4ZD1 (2250)	4.4	4.0	2.6	3.2	12.6	2.7	13.2 ①	8.5
	Pick-up	C223 (2238)	6.0	5.3	2.6	3.2	12.6	2.7	13.2 ①	9.6 ②
	Pick-up	C223T (2238)	6.0	5.3	2.6	3.2	12.6	2.7	13.2 ①	11.2
	Trooper II	4ZD1 (2250)	4.4	4.0	—	9.7	—	3.2	21.9	8.5
	Trooper II	C223T (2238)	6.0	5.3	—	9.7	—	3.2	21.9	10.0
1987	I-Mark (FWD)	4XC1-U (1471)	3.4	3.0	—	2.8	12.6	—	11.1	6.8
	I-Mark (FWD)	4XC1-UT (1471)	3.4	3.0	—	2.3	13.6	—	11.1	6.8
	Impulse	G200Z (1950)	3.8	3.4	—	3.3	13.3	2.5	15.1	9.4
	Impulse Turbo	4ZC1-T (1983)	3.8	3.4	—	3.3	13.3	3.1	15.1	9.6
	Pick-up	G200Z (1950)	4.4	4.0	2.6	3.2	12.6	2.7	13.2 ①	8.5
	Pick-up	4ZD1 (2250)	4.4	4.0	2.6	3.2	12.6	2.7	13.2 ①	8.5
	Pick-up	C223, C223-T	6.0	5.3	2.6	3.2	12.6	2.7	13.2 ①	9.6
	Trooper II	4ZE1 (2559)	4.4	4.0	—	6.2	12.0	1.9	21.9	8.5
1988	I-Mark	4XC1-U (1471)	3.4	3.0	—	2.8	12.6	—	11.1	6.8
	I-Mark	4XC1-UT (1471)	3.4	3.0	—	2.3	13.6	—	11.1	6.8
	Impulse	4ZD1 (2254)	3.8	3.4	—	3.3	13.7	3.1	15.1	9.3
	Impulse Turbo	4ZC1-T (1994)	3.8	3.4	—	3.3	13.7	3.1	15.1	9.5
	Pick-up	G200Z (1950)	4.4	4.0	2.6	3.2	12.6	2.7	13.2 ①	8.5

CAPACITIES (cont.)

Year	Model	Engine Displacement code (cc)	Engine Crankcase with Filter	without Filter	Transmission (pts.) 4-Spd	5-Spd	Auto.	Drive Axle (pts.)	Fuel Tank (gal.)	Cooling System (qts.)
1988	Pick-up	4ZD1 (2250)	4.4	4.0	2.6	3.2	12.6	2.7	13.2 ①	8.5
	Pick-up	C223, C223 Turbo	6.0	5.3	2.6	3.2	12.6	2.7	13.2 ①	9.6
	Trooper II	4ZE1 (2559)	4.4	4.0	—	6.2	12.0	1.9	21.9	8.5
1989	I-Mark	4XC1-U (1471)	3.4	3.0	—	2.0	13.8	—	11.1	6.8
	I-Mark	4XC1-T (1471)	3.4	3.0	—	2.0	13.8	—	11.1	7.5
	I-Mark	4XE1 (1588)	3.4	3.0	—	2.0	13.8	—	11.1	6.8
	Impulse	4ZD1 (2254)	3.8	3.4	—	3.3	13.7	3.2	15.1	9.3
	Impulse	4ZC1-T (1994)	3.8	3.4	—	3.3	13.7	3.2	15.1	9.5
	Pick-up	4ZD1 (2250)	4.2	3.8	—	3.2	—	3.1	14.0 ③	9.5
	Pick-up	4ZE1 (2559)	5.2	4.8	—	3.2	14.6	3.8	14.0 ③	9.5
	Trooper II	4ZE1 (2559)	5.2	4.8	—	6.2	12.0	3.8	22.0	8.5
	Trooper II	2.8L V6 (2800)	4.5	4.0	—	6.2	9.3	3.8	22.0	10.6
	Amigo	4ZD1 (2250)	4.2	3.8	—	3.3	—	3.2	22.0	9.5
	Amigo	4ZE1 (2559)	5.2	4.8	—	6.2	14.6	3.8	22.0	9.5
1990–91	Impulse	4XE1 (1588)	4.6	4.0	—	4.0	14.0	1.4	12.4	7.3 ④
	Impulse	4XE1-T (1588)	4.6	4.0	—	4.0	14.0	1.4	12.4	7.9
	Stylus	4XE1 (1588)	3.4	3.0	—	4.0	13.8	—	12.4	7.2 ④
	Stylus	4XE1-W (1588)	4.4	3.8	—	4.0	13.8	—	12.4	7.3
	Pick-up	4ZD1 (2250)	4.2	3.8	—	3.2	—	3.1	14.0 ③	9.5
	Pick-up	4ZE1 (2559)	5.2	4.8	—	3.2	14.6	3.8	14.0 ③	9.5
	Trooper II	4ZE1 (2559)	5.2	4.8	—	6.2	12.0	3.8	22.0	8.5
	Trooper II	2.8L V6 (2800)	4.5	4.0	—	6.2	9.3	3.8	22.0	10.6
	Amigo	4ZD1 (2250)	4.2	3.8	—	3.3	—	3.2	22.0	9.5
	Amigo	4ZE1 (2259)	5.2	4.8	—	6.2	14.6	3.8	22.0	9.5
	Rodeo	4ZE1 (2559)	5.8	5.4	—	6.2	19.0	4.0	22.0	9.5
	Rodeo	3.1L V6 (3100)	4.3	3.8	—	4.8	19.0	4.0	22.0	11.4

① 19.1 gals.; heavy duty
② 11 qts. with auto. trans.
③ 20 gals.; heavy duty
④ 7.8 qts. with auto. trans.

3. Shut off all electrical equipment on both vehicles. Turn off the engine of the donor vehicle, set the parking brakes on both vehicles and block the wheels. Also, make sure both vehicles are in **NEUTRAL** (manual transmission models) or **PARK** (automatic transmission models).

4. Using the jumper cables, connect the positive (+) terminal of the donor vehicle battery to the positive terminal of one (not both) of the diesel batteries.

5. Using the second jumper cable, connect the negative (−) terminal of the donor battery to a solid, stationary, metallic point on the diesel (alternator bracket, engine block, etc.). Be very careful to keep the jumper cables away from moving parts (cooling fan, alternator belt, etc.) on both vehicles.

6. Start the engine of the donor vehicle and run it at moderate speed.

7. Start the engine of the diesel.

8. When the diesel starts, disconnect the battery cables in the reverse order of attachment.

JACKING

All models covered in this guide are equipped from the factory with a scissor or a screw-type jack. This jack was only designed to aid tire changing in emergency situations; it was NOT designed as a maintenance tool. Never get under the vehicle when it is supported by only a jack.

NOTE: *A sturdy set of jackstands (at least two) and a hydraulic floor jack of at least 1½ ton capacity are two of the best investments you can make if you are serious about maintaining your own vehicle. The added safety and utility of a hydraulic floor jack makes this tool pay for itself many times over through the years.*

Drive-on ramps are also commercially available; they raise the front end of the vehicle up about 10–12 in. (254–305mm). Make sure yours are of all-welded construction and made from strong, square tubing. You must make sure the rear wheels are blocked when using ramps.

CAUTION: *NEVER Use concrete cinder blocks for supporting any type of vehicle. Their use can be extremely dangerous, as they easily break if the load is not perfectly distributed.*

Regardless of the method of jacking or hoisting the vehicle, there are only certain areas of the undercarriage and suspension you can safely use to support the vehicle. See the accompanying illustration, and make sure that only the shaded areas are used. Also, be especially careful not to damage the catalytic converter when jacking or supporting the vehicle.

Engine Performance and Tune-Up

2

TUNE-UP PROCEDURES

In order to extract the full measure of performance and economy from your engine it is essential that it be properly tuned at regular intervals. A regular tune-up will keep your vehicle's engine running smoothly and will prevent the annoying minor breakdowns and poor performance associated with an untuned engine.

A complete tune-up should be performed every 30,000 miles or twenty four months, which-

ever comes first. This interval should be halved if the vehicle is operated under severe conditions, such as trailer towing, prolonged idling, continual stop and start driving, or if starting or running problems are noticed. It is assumed that the routine maintenance described in Chapter 1 has been kept up, as this will have a decided effect on the results of a tune-up. All of the applicable steps of a tune-up should be followed in order, as the result is a cumulative one.

GASOLINE ENGINE TUNE-UP SPECIFICATIONS

Year	Model	Engine Displacement cc (cu. in.)	Spark Plugs Type	Spark Plugs Gap (in.)	Ignition Timing (deg./rpm)	Intake Valve Opens (deg.)	Compression Pressure (psi)	Idle Speed (rpm)	Valve Clearance (in.) cold In.	Valve Clearance (in.) cold Ex.
1983–87	Impulse	G200Z (119)	BPR-6ES11 NGK	0.039– 0.043	12°/900	21°	178	850– 950	0.006	0.010
1984–88	Pick-up	G200Z (119)	BPR-6ES11 NGK	0.040	6°/900 ①	21°	170	800– 950	0.006	0.010
1985–89	I-Mark	4XC1-U (90)	BPR-6ES11 NGK	0.040	3°/600 ②	17°	178	1000 AT 750 MT	0.006	0.010
1985–89	Impulse	4ZC1-T (121)	BPR-6ES11 NGK	0.040	12°/900	21°	178	850– 950	0.006	0.010
1988–89	I-Mark	4XC1-T (90)	BPR-6ES11 NGK	0.043	15°/950	17°	170	950	0.006	0.010
1986–91	Pick-up, Trooper II, Amigo	4ZD1 (138)	BPR-6ES11 NGK	0.040	6°/900 ①	21°	170	900 AT 800 MT	0.006	0.010
1987–91	Pick-up, Trooper II, Amigo, Rodeo	4ZE1 (156)	BPR-6ES11 NGK	0.040	12°/900	13°	170	850– 950	0.008	0.008
1989–91	Trooper II	2.8L V6 (171)	R43TSK	0.450	10°/800	—	150	800	Hyd.	Hyd.
1991	Rodeo	3.1L V6 (191)	R43TSK	0.450	10°/800	—	150	800	Hyd.	Hyd.

MT: manual transmission
AT: automatic transmission
Hyd.: hydraulic lifter
① 6°/800 with manual trans.
② 3°/850 with automatic trans.

DIESEL TUNE-UP SPECIFICATIONS

Year	Model	Valve Clearance (cold) Intake (in.)	Exhaust (in.)	Intake Valve Opens (deg.)	Injection Pump Setting (deg.)	Injection Pressure (psi) New	Used	Idle Speed (rpm)	Cranking Compression Pressure (psi)
1981–88	C223	0.016	0.016	16°	15° ①	1493	1493	750 ②	441
1981–85	4FBI	0.010	0.014	32°	12°	1706–1848	1706–1848	575–675 ③	441
1986–88	C223-T	0.016	0.016	16°	10°	1920	1920	750 ②	441

① 13°; California model
② 850; automatic trans.
③ 675–775; automatic trans.

If the specifications on the tune-up sticker in the engine compartment disagree with the Tune-Up Specifications chart in this Chapter, the figures on the sticker must be used. The sticker often reflects changes made during the production run.

Spark Plugs

A typical spark plug consists of a metal shell surrounding a ceramic insulator. A metal electrode extends downward through the center of the insulator and protrudes a small distance. Located at the end of the plug and attached to the side of the outer metal shell is the side electrode. The side electrode bends in at a 90° angle so that its tip is even with, and parallel to, the tip of the center electrode. The distance between these two electrodes (measured in thousandths of an inch) is called the spark plug gap. The spark plug in no way produces a spark but merely provides a gap across which the current can arc. The coil produces anywhere from 20,000 to 40,000 volts or more, which travels to the distributor where it is distributed through the spark plug wires to the spark plugs. The current passes along the center electrode and jumps the gap to the side electrode, and, in so doing, ignites the air/fuel mixture in the combustion chamber.

SPARK PLUG HEAT RANGE

Spark plug heat range is the ability of the plug to dissipate heat. The longer the insulator (or the farther it extends into the engine), the hotter the plug will operate; the shorter the insulator the cooler it will operate. A plug that ab-

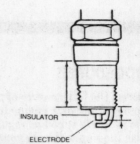

INSULATOR

ELECTRODE

Spark plug heat range

Adjust the electrode gap by bending the side electrode

FLEX SOCKET WRENCH

Using a flex wrench—2.8L V6 engine

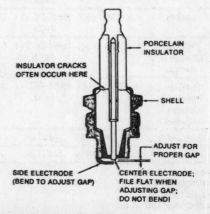

PORCELAIN INSULATOR

INSULATOR CRACKS OFTEN OCCUR HERE

SHELL

ADJUST FOR PROPER GAP

SIDE ELECTRODE (BEND TO ADJUST GAP)

CENTER ELECTRODE; FILE FLAT WHEN ADJUSTING GAP; DO NOT BEND!

Cross section of a spark plug

Check the spark plug gap using a filler gauge

sorbs little heat and remains too cool will quickly accumulate deposits of oil and carbon since it is not hot enough to burn them off. This leads to plug fouling and consequently to misfiring. A plug that absorbs too much heat will have to deposits, but, due to the excessive heat, the electrodes will burn away quickly and in some instances, pre-ignition may result. Pre-ignition takes place when plug tips get so hot that they glow sufficiently to ignite the fuel/air mixture before the actual spark occurs. This early ignition will usually cause a pinging during low speeds and heavy loads.

The general rule of thumb for choosing the correct heat range when picking a spark plug is: if most of your driving is long distance, high speed travel, use a colder plug; if most of your driving is stop and go, use a hotter plug. Original equipment plugs are compromise plugs, but most people never have occasion to change their plugs from the factory recommended heat range.

REPLACING SPARK PLUGS

A set of spark plugs usually requires replacement after 20,000–30,000 miles (32,000–48,000 km) on cars or trucks with electronic ignition, depending on your style of driving. In normal operation, plug gap increases about 0.001 in. (0.0254mm) for every 1,000–2,500 miles. As the gap increases, the plug's voltage requirement also increases. It requires a greater voltage to jump the wider gap and about two to three times as much voltage to fire a plug at high speeds than at idle.

When you're removing spark plugs, you should work on one at a time. Don't start by removing the plug wires all at once, because unless you number them, they may become mixed up. Take a minute before you begin and number the wires with tape. The best location for numbering is near where the wires come out of the cap.

Twist and pull on the rubber boot to remove the spark plug wires; never pull on the wire itself

1. Twist the spark plug boot and remove the boot and wire from the plug. Do not pull on the wire itself as this will ruin the wire.

2. If possible, use a brush or rag to clean the area around the spark plug. Make sure that all the dirt is removed so that none will enter the cylinder after the plug is removed.

3. Remove the spark plug using the proper size socket. Either a 5/8 in. or $^{13}/_{16}$ in. size socket depending on the engine. Turn the socket counterclockwise to remove the plug. Be sure to hold the socket straight on the plug to avoid breaking the plug, or rounding off the hex on the plug.

4. Once the plug is out, check it against the plugs shown in the Color section in this book to determine engine condition. This is crucial since plug readings are vital signs of engine condition.

5. Use a round wire feeler gauge to check the plug gap. The correct size gauge should pass through the electrode gap with a slight drag. If you're in doubt, try one size smaller and one larger. The smaller gauge should go through easily while the larger one should not go through at all. If the gap is incorrect, use the electrode bending tool on the end of the gauge to adjust the gap. When adjusting the gap, always bend the side electrode. The center electrode is non-adjustable.

6. Squirt a drop of penetrating oil on the threads of the new plug and install it. Don't oil the threads too heavily. Turn the plug in clockwise by hand until it is snug.

7. When the plug is finger tight, tighten it with a wrench. Take care not to overtighten. Torque to 15 ft. lbs. (20 Nm).

8. Install the plug boot firmly over the plug. Proceed to the next plug.

CHECKING AND REPLACING SPARK PLUG CABLES

Visually inspect the spark plug cables for burns, cuts, or breaks in the insulation. Check the spark plug boots and the nipples on the distributor cap and coil. Replace any damaged wiring. If no physical damage is obvious, the wires can be checked with an ohmmeter for excessive resistance.

When installing a new set of spark plug cables, replace the cables one at a time so there will be no mixup. Start by replacing the longest cable first. Install the boot firmly over the spark plug. Route the wire exactly the same as the original. Insert the nipple firmly into the tower on the distributor cap. Repeat the process for each cable.

Measure the resistance of the spark plug cable with an ohmmeter. Replace the cable if the resistance is not within 9.6–22.4kΩ.

WARNING: *Never kink or pull on the cable. The synthetic conductor may become damaged. Never stick a needle or the pointed end of a probe into the cable during a timing check.*

FIRING ORDERS

NOTE: *To avoid confusion, remove and tag the wires one at a time, for replacement.*

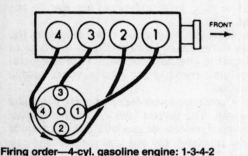

Firing order—4-cyl. gasoline engine: 1-3-4-2

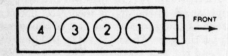

Firing order—diesel engine: 1-3-4-2

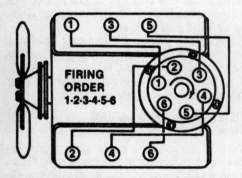

Firing order—6-cyl. gasoline engine: 1-2-3-4-5-6

IGNITION TIMING

ADJUSTMENT

Gasoline Engines

EXCEPT 4XE1 AND V6 ENGINE

NOTE: *On the 2.0L and 2.3L engines, be sure to set the air gap in the distributor before timing the engine.*

The timing marks are located near the front crankshaft pulley and consist of a pointer with graduations attached to the engine block and a mark on the crankshaft pulley.

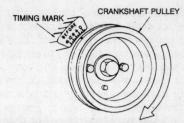

Timing indicator—gasoline 4-cyl. engines

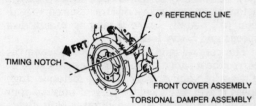

Timing indicator—gasoline 6-cyl. engines

Timing indicator—I-Mark (FWD) gasoline engine

1. Check and correct the air gap in the distributor.

2. Locate and clean the timing marks on the crankshaft pulley and the front of the engine.

3. Using an inductive pick-up timing light, connect it to the No. 1 spark plug wire. Attach a tachometer to the ignition coil.

4. If the distributor is equipped with a vacuum advance, disconnect and plug the vacuum line.

5. Make sure all wires from the timing light and tachometer are clear of the fan and belts. Start the engine.

6. Adjust the idle to the correct rpm.

7. Aim the timing light at the timing marks. Adjust the distributor until the timing marks are aligned.

8. Tighten the distributor mounting bolt and check the timing again.

9. Turn the engine **OFF** and remove the timing light and tachometer. Connect the distributor vacuum line.

V6 ENGINE

1. Set the parking brake and block the drive wheels.

2. Operate the engine to normal operating temperatures and turn the air conditioning **OFF**, if equipped.

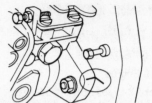

Diesel injection pump timing mark—all diesel engines

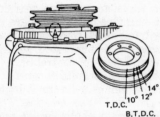

Diesel crankshaft timing indicator—4FB1 engine

3. Verify that the Check Engine light is not turned **ON**.

4. Place the Electronic Spark Timing (EST) into the bypass mode by disconnect the timing connector.

NOTE: *The EST is a single wire connector, located under the center console in the passenger compartment. Do not disconnect the 4-wire connector from the distributor.*

5. Using an inductive pick-up timing light, connect it to the No. 1 spark plug wire.

6. Check and/or adjust the engine speed to 800 rpm.

7. Loosen the distributor hold-down bolt and turn the distributor until the timing mark, on the crankshaft pulley, is aligned with the 10° BTDC timing mark on the timing cover.

8. Tighten the distributor hold-down bolt.

9. Reconnect the timing connector and clear the ECM trouble code(s).

1.6L 4XE1 IMPULSE AND STYLUS

NOTE: *The 4XE1 DOHC Turbo engine with the Direct Ignition System is adjusted in the same manner as the non-turbo and Stylus. Adjust the camshaft angle sensor instead of the distributor.*

1. Apply the parking brake, start the engine and place the transmission shifter in Neutral.

2. Check that the CHECK ENGINE light is not turned ON.

3. Connect the terminals 1 and 3 of the ALDL (assembly line diagnostic link) with a jumper wire.

4. Connect a timing light to the No. 1 spark plug wire.

5. Loosen the distributor hold down bolt and adjust the timing to specifications found in the "Tune-up" specifications chart in this Chapter.

NOTE: *If the adjustment is impossible because of large fluctuations, open the throttle valve a little to increase the engine speed to 1500–2000 rpm. The fluctuation will be reduced for easy confirmation.*

6. Torque the distributor hold down to 17 ft. lbs. (24 Nm).

7. Remove the jumper wire and make sure the CHECK ENGINE light turns OFF.

8. Idle speed in NOT necessary because it is controlled by the ECM.

INJECTION TIMING

ADJUSTMENT

Diesel Engine

1. Check to see if the notched line on the injection pump and mounting plate are aligned.

2. Bring the No. 1 piston to top dead center on the compression stroke by turning the crankshaft. The correct notch must be used for alignment as the damper pulley is provided with a total of seven notches.

3. Remove the front upper timing belt cover, check the timing belt for proper tension and alignment of the timing marks.

4. Remove the cam cover and rear plug, then check that the fixing plate fits smoothly into the slit at the rear end of the camshaft, then remove the fixing plate J-29761.

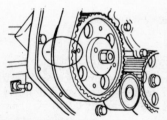

Timing marks—4FB1 engine

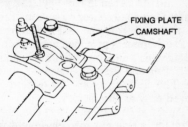

Camshaft fixing plate—4FB1 engine

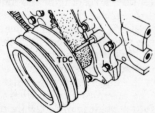

Timing indicator—C223 diesel engine

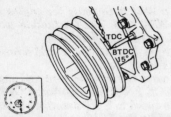

Timing to specifications—refer to specification chart, C223 engine

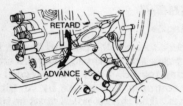

Injection pump timing—all diesel engines

Valve adjustment procedure

5. Disconnect the injection pipe from the injection pump and remove the distributor head screw and gasket, then install a static timing gauge. Set the lift about 0.040 in. (1mm) from the plunger.

6. Bring the piston in No. 1 cyl. to a point 45–60° before top dead center by turning the crankshaft, then calibrate the dial indicator to zero.

7. The damper is provided with notched lines as illustrated. The four lines at one side are for static timing and should be used for service purposes. The three lines are for dynamic timing and used only at the factory.

8. Turn the crankshaft until the line 12° on the damper is brought into alignment with the pointer, then take a reading of the dial indicator. *Standard reading 0.020 in. (0.5mm).*

9. If the reading on the dial indicator deviates from the specified range, hold the crankshaft to the "Injection Pump Setting" in the diesel tune-up specifications chart. Loosen the two nuts on the injection pump flange.

10. Move the pump to a point where the dial indicator gives a reading of 0.020 in. (0.5mm). Tighten the flange nuts.

ELECTRONIC IGNITION

General Information

SYSTEM OPERATION

Except 2.8L Engine

There are 2 types of ignition systems used on Isuzu engines: one uses a conventional centrifugal advance type distributor and the other uses a fully transistorized type distributor.

Conventional type distributors are made up of the distributor shaft, rotor shaft, rotor head, breaker assembly, reluctor, governor flyweight, pinion gear and vacuum control unit.

Transistorized distributors consist of dust bushing, rotor, pinion and a crank angle sensor built into the distributor housing. The crank angle sensor uses a photo-electric pick-up to measure piston position and engine speed.

2.8L V6 Engine

The computer controlled Electronic Spark Timing (EST) ignition system used on the V6 engines consists of the battery, distributor, engine control switch, spark plugs, primary and secondary wiring.

The computer, or Electronic Control Module (ECM), monitors the information from the engine sensor network. The ECM uses this information to calculate the proper spark timing and tell the distributor when to make timing modifications.

The distributor does not have centrifugal advance weights, springs or a vacuum advance unit.

The V6 engines is equipped with Electronic Spark Control (ESC). At the heart of the ESC system is the knock sensor which is mounted to the engine block. The knock sensor is connected to the electronic spark control module which is located on the right fender panel in the engine compartment or on a bracket mounted to the block. In response to engine knock, the sensor transmits a signal to the electronic spark module ("half function box"). The spark control module sends the signal to the ECM which in turn tells the distributor to retard the spark timing up to 20° to reduce spark knock in the engine.

NOTE: *For further information pertaining to the electronic ignition system, refer to Chapters 3 and 4.*

AIR GAP SETTING

On the G200Z and 4ZD1 engines, the air gap setting in the distributor should be checked and adjusted before the ignition timing is adjusted.

1. Remove the distributor cap, O-ring and rotor.

2. Use a feeler gauge to measure the air gap

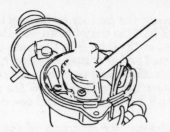

Air gap setting—G200Z and 4ZD1 engines

at the pick up coil projection. The gap should be 0.008–0.016 in. (0.20–0.40mm) for the G200Z engine, or 0.012–0.020 in. (0.30–0.50mm) for the 4ZD1 engine; adjust it, if necessary.

3. Loosen the screws and move the signal generator until the gap is correct. Tighten the screws and recheck the gap.

NOTE: *The electrical parts in this system are not repairable. If found to be defective, they must be replaced.*

VALVE LASH

ADJUSTMENT

All Engines Except 4XE1 (1.6L DOHC) and V6

NOTE: *The valves are adjusted with the engine COLD. It is best to allow an engine to sit overnight before beginning a valve adjustment. While all valve adjustments must be made as accurately as possible, it is better to have the valve adjustment slightly loose rather than slightly tight. A burned valve may result from overly tight valve adjustments.*

1. Remove the rocker arm cover and discard the gasket.

2. Make sure both the cylinder head and camshaft retaining bolts are tightened to the proper torque.

Cylinder / Valve	1	2	3	4
Intake	○	○	●	●
Exhaust	○	●	○	●

Note: ○ When piston in No. 1 cylinder is at TDC on compression stroke.
● When piston in No. 4 cylinder is at TDC on compression stroke.

Valve adjusting sequence—all 4-cyl. gasoline engines

CYLINDER NO.	1		2		3		4	
VALVES	I	E	I	E	I	E	I	E
STEP. 1	○	○	○			○		
STEP. 2				○	○		○	○

I: INTAKE VALVE
E: EXHAUST VALVE

Valve adjusting sequence—4FB1 diesel engines

Cylinder No.	1		2		3		4	
Valves	E	I	I	E	E	I	I	E
Step 1	○	○	○		○			
Step 2				◎		◎	◎	◎

I: INTAKE VALVE
E: EXHAUST VALVE

Valve adjusting sequence—C223 and C233-T diesel engine

3. Rotate the crankshaft pulley until the No. 1 piston is at TDC of the compression stroke.

NOTE: *To make sure the piston is on the correct stroke, remove the spark plug and place a finger over the hole. Feel for air being forced out of the spark plug hole. Both valves on No. 1 cylinder will be closed. Stop turning the crankshaft when the TDC timing mark on the crankshaft pulley is directly aligned with the timing mark pointer.*

4. With the No. 1 piston at TDC of the compression stroke, adjust the clearances according to the "Valve Adjusting Sequence" illustrations in this Chapter.

5. Adjust the clearance by loosening the locknut and turning the adjusting screw. Retightening the locknut when the proper thickness feeler gauge passes between the camshaft or valve stem and has a slight drag when the clearance is corrected.

6. Rotate the crankshaft 1 complete revolution (360°) to position the No. 4 piston at TDC of its compression stroke and adjust the clearances as shown in the illustration.

7. After adjustment, use a new gasket, sealant and install the rocker arm cover.

4XE1-WT (DOHC) Engine

NOTE: *Inspect and adjust the valve clearance when the engine is COLD. Retorque the camshaft bearing cap bolts to 7 ft. lbs. (10 Nm) before inspecting and adjusting valve clearances.*

1. Remove the cylinder head cover as outlined in Chapter 3.

2. Remove all spark plugs.

3. Set the No. 1 cylinder to top dead center on the compression stroke by turning the crankshaft pulley and align the notched line with the 0 mark on the timing cover. Check that the tappets on the No. 1 have play and tappets on the No. 4 have no play. If not, turn the crankshaft one revolution and align the marks as above.

4. **The allowable valve clearance is 0.004–0.008 in. (0.10–0.20mm) for intake and 0.008–0.012 in. (0.20–0.30mm).**

5. Measure the clearance between the cam lobe and adjuster (shim) of the valves with. Refer to the "Valve Adjuster Sequence" illustration in this Chapter.

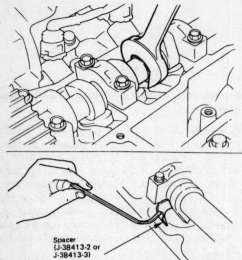

Spacer
(J-38413-2 or
J-38413-3)

Press down the tappet by the cam lift, turning camshaft and place the spacer on the upper circumference of the tappet from outside of the cylinder head

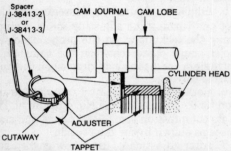

Spacer
J-38413-2
or
J-38413-3/

CAM JOURNAL   CAM LOBE

CYLINDER HEAD

ADJUSTER

CUTAWAY

TAPPET

Release cam lift by turning the camshaft and hold the tappet down with the spacer. Remove the adjuster shim from the spark plug side with a small prybar and magnetic finger

	Cylinder	1	2	3	4
Valve					
Intake		O	O	●	●
Exhaust		O	●	O	●

Note: O When piston in No. 1 cylinder is at TDC on compression stroke.
● When piston in No. 4 cylinder is at TDC on compression stroke.

Valve adjusting sequence—4XE1-WT (DOHC) engine

6. Record the measurement which are out of the allowable clearance.

7. Turn the crankshaft one revolution and measure the remaining valves, refer to the "Valve Adjuster Sequence" illustration.

8. The valve are adjusted by replacing the shims.

9. Press down the tappet by the cam lift, turning the camshaft. Place the spacer tool J–38413–2 on the upper circumference of the tappet from the outside of the cylinder head.

10. Release the cam lift by turning the camshaft and hold the tappet down with the spacer tool. Remove the shim from the spark plug side with a small prybar or magnetic finger. Use the cutaway in the tappet to remove the shim.

11. Determine the thickness of the shim by using the following formula and accompanying chart:

a. Measure the thickness of the original shim with a micrometer.

b. Calculate the thickness of an available shim so that the valve clearance comes within the allowable value.

- Ta = thickness of the available shim
- M = measured valve clearance
- To = thickness of original shim
- M + To = Ta

c. Select the available shim with a thickness as close as possible to the calculated values.

12. Install the shim by placing it into the tappet. Press down the tappet by turning the camshaft and remove the spacer tool.

13. Install the cylinder head cover.

V6 Engines

1. Remove the rocker arm cover as outlined in Chapter 3.

2. Rotate the crankshaft until the No. 1 cylinder is on the TDC of its compression stroke.
NOTE: *When the notch on the damper pulley is aligned with the 0 timing mark and the rocker arms of the No. 1 cylinder do not move, the engine is at the TDC of the compression stroke of the No. 1 cylinder.*

3. With the engine at TDC of the No. 1 cylinder, adjust the following valves:
Exhaust: 1, 2 and 3
Intake: 1, 5 and 6

4. Back out the adjusting nut until lash is felt.

5. Tighten the adjusting nut until the lash is removed, then, turn the nut 1½ additional turns to center the lifter plunger.

6. Rotate the engine 1 complete revolution

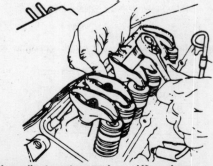

Valve adjustment procedure—V6 engines

and reposition the notch on the damper pulley with the **0** mark on the timing tab; this is the No. 4 cylinder firing position.

7. With the engine at TDC of the No. 4 cylinder, adjust the following valves:

Exhaust: 4, 5 and 6

Intake: 2, 3 and 4

8. Back out the adjusting nut until lash is felt.

9. Tighten the adjusting nut until the lash is removed, plus, turn the nut 1½ additional turns to center the lifter plunger.

10. Using a new gasket and sealant, install the rocker arm covers.

CARBURETED ENGINE FUEL SYSTEM

IDLE SPEED ADJUSTMENT

All Engines

NOTE: *The idle speed adjusting screws is located on the passenger side of the carburetor*

Measured clearance		Original Adjuster (Shim) Thickness (mm)
mm	inch	(columns: 2.52 through 3.48 in 0.02 mm increments)
0.000–0.025	0.000–0.001	… 1 1 2 2 3 3 4 4 5 5 6 6 7 7 8 8 9 9 10 10 10 11 11 12 12 13 13 14 14 15 15 16 16 17
0.026–0.050	0.001–0.002	… 1 1 1 2 2 3 3 3 4 4 5 5 5 6 6 7 7 7 8 8 9 9 9 10 10 11 11 12 12 13 13 13 14 15 15 16 16 17 17 17
0.051–0.075	0.002–0.003	… 1 1 1 2 2 3 3 3 4 4 5 5 5 6 6 7 7 7 8 8 9 9 9 10 10 11 11 11 12 12 13 13 14 14 15 15 16 16 17 17 17 18
0.076–0.100	0.003–0.004	… 1 1 2 2 2 3 3 4 4 4 5 5 6 6 6 7 7 8 8 8 9 9 10 10 10 11 11 12 12 13 13 14 14 15 15 16 16 17 17 18 18 18
0.101–0.200	0.004–0.008	Replacement not to be required
0.201–0.225	0.008–0.009	2 2 2 3 3 4 4 4 5 5 6 6 6 7 7 8 8 9 9 9 10 10 11 11 11 12 12 13 13 13 14 14 15 15 16 16 17 17 18 18 18 19 19
0.226–0.250	0.009–0.010	2 3 3 3 4 4 5 5 5 6 6 7 7 7 8 8 9 9 10 10 11 11 11 12 12 13 13 13 14 15 15 16 16 17 17 18 18 19 19 19
0.251–0.275	0.010–0.011	3 3 3 4 4 5 5 6 6 7 7 7 8 8 9 9 10 10 11 11 11 12 12 13 13 14 14 15 15 16 16 17 17 17 18 18 19 19 19
0.276–0.300	0.011–0.012	3 4 4 4 5 5 6 6 6 7 7 8 8 9 9 10 10 10 11 11 12 12 13 13 14 14 15 15 16 16 16 17 17 18 18 19 19
0.301–0.325	0.012–0.013	4 4 4 5 5 6 6 6 7 7 8 8 9 9 10 10 11 11 12 12 13 13 14 14 15 15 16 16 16 17 17 18 18 19 19
0.326–0.350	0.013–0.014	4 5 5 5 6 6 7 7 8 8 9 9 10 10 11 11 11 12 12 13 13 14 15 15 16 16 17 17 18 18 19 19
0.351–0.375	0.014–0.015	5 5 5 6 6 7 7 8 8 9 9 10 10 11 11 11 12 13 13 14 14 15 15 16 16 17 17 18 18 19 19 19
0.376–0.400	0.015–0.016	5 6 6 6 7 7 8 8 9 9 10 10 11 11 12 12 12 13 14 14 15 15 16 16 17 17 18 18 19 19
0.401–0.425	0.016–0.017	6 6 6 7 7 8 8 9 9 10 10 11 11 12 12 13 13 14 14 15 15 16 16 17 17 18 18 18 19
0.426–0.450	0.017–0.018	6 7 7 7 8 8 9 9 10 10 11 11 11 12 13 13 14 14 15 15 16 16 17 17 18 18 19 19 19
0.451–0.475	0.018–0.019	7 7 7 8 8 9 9 10 10 11 11 12 12 13 13 14 14 15 15 16 16 17 17 18 18 19 19 19
0.476–0.500	0.019–0.020	7 8 8 8 9 9 10 10 11 11 12 12 13 13 14 14 15 15 16 16 17 17 18 18 19 19
0.501–0.525	0.020–0.021	8 8 8 9 9 10 10 11 11 12 12 13 13 14 14 15 15 16 16 17 17 18 18 19 19
0.526–0.550	0.021–0.022	8 9 9 9 10 10 11 11 12 12 13 13 14 14 15 15 16 16 17 17 18 18 19 19
0.551–0.575	0.022–0.023	9 9 9 10 10 11 11 12 12 13 13 14 14 15 15 16 16 17 17 18 18 19 19
0.576–0.600	0.023–0.024	9 10 10 10 11 11 12 12 13 13 14 14 15 15 16 16 17 17 18 18 18 19 19
0.601–0.625	0.024–0.025	10 10 10 11 11 12 12 13 13 14 14 15 15 16 16 17 17 18 18 19 19
0.626–0.650	0.025–0.026	10 11 11 11 12 12 13 13 14 14 15 15 16 16 17 17 18 18 19 19
0.651–0.675	0.026–0.027	11 11 11 12 12 13 13 14 14 15 15 16 16 17 17 18 18 19 19 19
0.676–0.700	0.027–0.028	11 12 12 12 13 13 14 14 15 15 16 16 17 17 18 18 19 19
0.701–0.725	0.028–0.029	12 12 12 13 13 14 14 15 15 16 16 17 17 18 18 19 19
0.726–0.750	0.029–0.030	12 13 13 13 14 14 15 15 16 16 17 17 18 18 19 19
0.751–0.775	0.030–0.031	13 13 13 14 14 15 15 16 16 17 17 18 18 19 19
0.776–0.800	0.031–0.032	13 14 14 14 15 15 16 16 17 17 18 18 19 19
0.801–0.825	0.032–0.033	14 14 14 15 15 16 16 17 17 18 18 19 19 19
0.826–0.850	0.033–0.034	14 15 15 15 16 16 17 17 18 18 19 19 19
0.851–0.875	0.034–0.035	15 15 15 16 16 17 17 18 18 19 19
0.876–0.900	0.035–0.036	15 16 16 16 17 17 18 18 19 19
0.901–0.925	0.036–0.037	16 16 16 17 17 18 18 18 19 19
0.926–0.950	0.0365–0.0374	16 17 17 17 18 18 19 19 19
0.951–0.975	0.037–0.038	17 17 17 18 18 19 19 19
0.976–1.000	0.038–0.039	17 18 18 18 19 19
1.001–1.025	0.039–0.040	18 18 18 19 19
1.026–1.050	0.040–0.041	18 18 18 19 19
1.051–1.075	0.041–0.042	19 19 19
1.076–1.100	0.042–0.043	19

Thickness of available adjuster (Shim)

NO in Chart	Thickness (mm)	NO in Chart	Thickness (mm)
1	2.55	11	3.05
2	2.60	12	3.10
3	2.65	13	3.15
4	2.70	14	3.20
5	2.75	15	3.25
6	2.80	16	3.30
7	2.85	17	3.35
8	2.90	18	3.40
9	2.95	19	3.45
10	3.00		

How to use the chart

[Example]
Measured clearance; 0.550mm
Original adjuster thickness; 2.96mm
(Thickness mark (2.96) is printed
on the adjuster surface)

1. Draw straight lines as shown in the chart.
2. Select No.17 available adjuster to be replaced by finding cross point of straight lines.
3. Replace the 2.96mm adjuster with No.17 (3.35mm) adjuster.

Measured clearance		Original Adjuster (Shim) Thickness (mm)
mm	inch	2.96
0.526–0.550		→ 17

Adjuster shim selection chart (intake)

at the throttle cable side on G180Z and G200Z engines.

1. Firmly set the parking brake and block the drive wheels.

2. Place the transmission in **N**.

3. Operate the engine until it reaches normal operating temperatures. Be sure the choke is fully open and the air cleaner is installed. If equipped, turn the air conditioning **OFF**.

4. Disconnect and plug the distributor vacuum, the canister purge and EGR vacuum lines.

Shut off the vacuum to the idle compensator by bending the rubber hose.

5. Turn the throttle adjusting screw to the required idle speed.

6. If equipped with air conditioning, turn air conditioning control to **MAX COLD** and the blower on **HIGH**.

7. Open throttle to approximately ⅓ opening and allow it to close.

NOTE: *The speed-up solenoid should reach full travel.*

Thickness of available adjuster (Shim)

NO in Chart	Thickness (mm)	NO in Chart	Thickness (mm)
1	2.55	11	3.05
2	2.60	12	3.10
3	2.65	13	3.15
4	2.70	14	3.20
5	2.75	15	3.25
6	2.80	16	3.30
7	2.85	17	3.35
8	2.90	18	3.40
9	2.95	19	3.45
10	3.00		

Note; Thickness mark is printed on the surface to be contacted with tappet.

How to use the chart

[Example]
Measured clearance; 0.550mm
Original adjuster thickness; 2.96mm
(Thickness mark (2.96) is printed on the adjuster surface)

1. Draw straight lines as shown in the chart.
2. Select No.15 available adjuster to be replaced by finding cross point of straight lines.
3. Replace the 2.96mm adjuster with No.15 (3.25mm) adjuster.

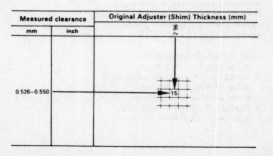

Adjuster shim selection chart (exhaust)

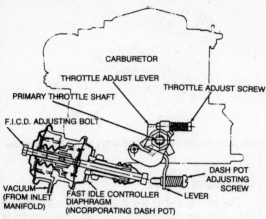

CARBURETOR

THROTTLE ADJUST LEVER

THROTTLE ADJUST SCREW

PRIMARY THROTTLE SHAFT

F.I.C.D. ADJUSTING BOLT

DASH POT
ADJUSTING
SCREW

VACUUM
(FROM INLET
MANIFOLD)

FAST IDLE CONTROLLER
DIAPHRAGM
(INCORPORATING DASH POT)

LEVER

Adjusting screws on the 4XC1-U carburetor

8. Adjust the speed-up solenoid screw to 850–950 rpm.

IDLE MIXTURE ADJUSTMENT

Except California Engines

1. Firmly set the parking brake and block the drive wheels.
2. Place the transmission in **N**.
3. Remove the carburetor assembly.
4. Using a drill, drill a hole through the sealing plug covering the idle mixture screw and pry the plug from the carburetor.
5. Reinstall the carburetor.

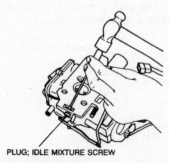

PLUG; IDLE MIXTURE SCREW

Removing the mixture screw plug—carbureted engines except 4XC1-U

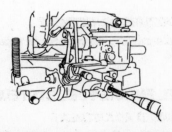

Idle mixture screw concealment plug removal—4XC1-U engine

6. Operate the engine until it reaches normal operating temperatures. Be sure the choke is fully open and the air cleaner is installed. If equipped, turn the air conditioning **OFF**.
7. Disconnect and plug the distributor vacuum, the canister purge and EGR vacuum lines. Shut off the vacuum to the idle compensator by bending the rubber hose.
8. Turn the throttle adjusting screw until the engine speed reaches the specification in the "Tune-up" chart in this Chapter.
9. Turn the idle mixture screw all the way in and back out 3 turns.
10. Turn the throttle adjusting screw until the engine speed is 800 rpm (manual transmission) or 900 rpm (automatic transmission).
11. Adjust the idle mixture screw to achieve the maximum speed.
12. Reset the throttle adjusting screw until the engine speed reaches the specification in the "Tune-up" chart.
13. Turn the idle mixture screw counterclockwise (lean) until the engine speed is 750–850 rpm (manual transmission) or 850–950 rpm (automatic transmission).
14. Reinstall a mixture adjustment plug.

California Engines

1. Firmly set the parking brake and block the drive wheels.
2. Place the transmission in **N**.
3. Remove the carburetor assembly.
4. Using a drill, drill a hole through the sealing plug covering the idle mixture screw and pry the plug from the carburetor.
5. Reinstall the carburetor.
6. Operate the engine until it reaches normal operating temperatures. Be sure the choke is fully open and the air cleaner is installed. If equipped, turn the air conditioning **OFF**.
7. Disconnect and plug the distributor vacuum, the canister purge and EGR vacuum lines. Shut off the vacuum to the idle compensator by bending the rubber hose.
8. Connect a dwell meter (4 cyl. scale) or duty meter to the duty monitor lead.
9. Turn the idle mixture screw all the way in and back out 1½ turns.
10. Turn the throttle adjusting screw until the engine speed is 950 rpm (1986–87) or 900 rpm (1988–90). Also refer to the "Tune-up" specification chart in this Chapter.
11. Adjust the idle mixture screw to achieve an average dwell of 36° or duty of 40 percent.
   NOTE: *The dwell or duty reading specified is the average of the most constant variation.*
12. Reset the throttle adjusting screw until the engine speed is 850–950 rpm.
13. Reinstall a mixture adjustment plug.

GASOLINE FUEL INJECTION SYSTEMS

IDLE SPEED ADJUSTMENT

All 4-CYL. Engines, Except 4XE1 Impulse

1. Firmly set the parking brake and block the drive wheels.
2. Place the transmission in **N**.
3. Set the engine tachometer.
4. Make sure the throttle valve is fully closed.
5. If equipped with air conditioning, turn **OFF** the air conditioning.
6. Place the manual transmission in **N** or the automatic transmission in **P**.
7. Disconnect the electrical connector from the vacuum switching valve (VSV) on the pressure regulator; the idle speed should 850–950 rpm.
8. If the idle speed is not correct, turn the adjusting screw **A** on the throttle body.

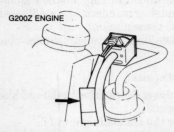

Before checking idle, disconnect the VSV pressure regulator—1983–88 EFI Impulse

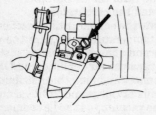

Idle speed adjusting screw—1983–88 Impulse with G200Z, 4ZD1 and 4ZC1-T

Before checking the idle speed, disconnect the VSV pressure regulator—EFI 4ZD1 and 4ZE1 engines

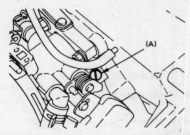

Idle adjustment screw—EFI 4ZD1 and 4ZE1 engines

4XE1 and V6 Engines

The idle speed is controlled by the ECM and IAC (idle air control) valve. No adjustment is necessary or possible.

DASH POT TOUCH ROTATION SPEED

1. This system is used in the 1983–88 EFI Impulse with automatic transmission.
2. Push the accelerator pedal fully to the floor. Allow the engine speed to increase and then release the pedal.
3. Check to make sure that the engine speed returns to 2000 ± 100 rpm and then continues to slowly drop towards the correct idling speed.
4. If not, set the engine speed to 2000 rpm with the throttle lever.
5. Tighten the adjusting screw until it just makes contact with the dash pot shaft head.
6. Lock the adjusting screw in position with the lock nut.
7. Repeat the dash pot touch rotation speed check procedure as described above.

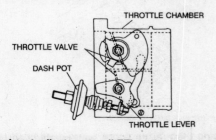

Dash pot adjustment—all EFI engines except 4XE1

IDLE MIXTURE ADJUSTMENT

No idle mixture adjustment is necessary or possible.

DIESEL ENGINE FUEL SYSTEM

IDLE SPEED ADJUSTMENT

NOTE: *The idle speed should be adjusted every 30,000 miles (48,000 km).*

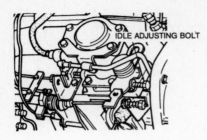

Location of the diesel idle adjustment screw

1. Set the parking brake and block the drive wheels.
2. Place the transmission in **NEUTRAL**.
3. Start the engine and allow it to warm up to operating temperature.
4. Connect a tachometer according to the manufacturer's instructions.
5. If the idle speed deviates from the specified range, loosen the idle adjusting screw lock nut and turn the screw in or out until the idle speed is correct.

FAST IDLE SPEED ADJUSTMENT

1. Start and warm up the engine.
2. Connect a tachometer according to the manufacturer's instructions.
3. Disconnect the hoses from the vacuum switch valve, then connect a pipe (4mm diameter) in position between the hoses.
4. Loosen the adjusting nut and adjust the idle speed. Fast idle should be around 900–950 rpm.
5. Tighten the adjusting nut and remove the tachometer.

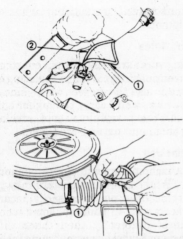

Disconnect the hoses 1 and 2 from the vacuum switch valve, then connect a pipe in position between the hoses 1 and 2

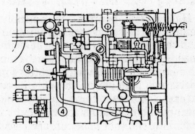

3 and 4, fast idle adjusting bolt and nut

Engine and Engine Overhaul

3

ENGINE ELECTRICAL

The engine electrical system can be broken down into three separate and distinct systems:

1. The ignition system
2. The charging system
3. The starting system.

High Energy Ignition (HEI) System

The HEI system operates in basically the same manner as the conventional ignition system, with the exception of the type of switching device used. A toothed iron timer core is mounted on the distributor shaft which rotates inside of an electronic pole piece. The pole piece has internal teeth (corresponding to those on the timer core) which contains a permanent magnet and pick-up coil (not to be confused with the ignition coil). The pole piece senses the magnetic field of the timer core teeth and sends a signal to the ignition module which electronically controls the primary coil voltage. The ignition coil operates in basically the same manner as a conventional ignition coil (though the ignition coils DO NOT interchange).

NOTE: *The HEI systems uses a capacitor which is primarily used for radio interference purposes. Do not confuse the capacitor as a tune-up component.*

PRECAUTIONS

Before troubleshooting the systems, it might be a good idea to take note of the following precautions:

Timing Light Use

Inductive pick-up timing lights are the best kind to use. Timing lights which connect between the spark plug and the spark plug wire occasionally give false readings.

Some engines incorporate a magnetic timing probe terminal (at the damper pulley) for use of special electronic timing equipment. Refer to the manufacturer's instructions when using this equipment.

Spark Plug Wires

The plug wires are of a different construction than conventional wires. When replacing them, make sure to use the correct wires, since conventional wires won't carry the higher voltage. Also, handle them carefully to avoid cracking or splitting them and never pierce them.

Tachometer Use

Not all tachometers will operate or indicate correctly. While some tachometers may give a reading, this does not necessarily mean the reading is correct. In addition, some tachometers connect differently than others. If you can't figure out whether or not your tachometer will work on your vehicle, check with the tachometer manufacturer.

System Testers

Instruments designed specifically for testing the electronic ignition system are available from several tool manufacturers. Some of these will even test the module.

The Charging System

The charging system provides electrical power for operation of the vehicle's ignition, starting system and all of the electrical accessories. The battery serves as an electrical surge or storage tank, storing (in chemical form) the energy originally produced by the alternator. The system also provides a means of regulating the alternator output to protect the battery from being overcharged and the accessories from being destroyed.

The storage battery is a chemical device incorporating parallel lead plates in a tank containing a sulfuric acid-water solution. Adjacent plates are slightly dissimilar and the chemical reaction of the two dissimilar plates produces electrical energy when the battery is connected to a load such as the starter motor. The chemical reaction is reversible, so that when the alternator is producing a voltage (electrical pressure) greater than that produced by the battery, electricity is forced into the battery and it is returned to it's fully charged state.

Alternators are used on the modern vehicle for they are lighter, more efficient, rotate at higher speeds and have fewer brush problems. In an alternator, the field rotates while all of the current produced passes only through the stator windings. The brushes bear against the continuous slip rings; this causes the current produced to periodically reverse the direction of it's flow. Diodes (electrical one-way switches) block the flow of current from traveling in the wrong direction. A series of diodes are wired together to permit the alternating flow of the stator to be converted to a pulsating but unidirectional flow at the alternator output. The alternator's field is wired in series with the voltage regulator.

Battery and Starting System

The battery is the first link in the chain of mechanisms which work together to provide cranking of the engine. In most modern vehicles, the battery is a lead-acid electrochemical device consisting of six 2 volt (2V) subsections connected in series so the unit is capable of producing approximately 12V of electrical pressure. Each subsection (cell) consists of a series of positive and negative plates held a short distance apart in a solution of sulfuric acid and water. The two types of plates are of dissimilar metals. A chemical reaction takes place which produces current flow from the battery, when it's positive and negative terminals are connected to an electrical appliance such as a lamp or motor. The continued transfer of electrons would eventually convert the sulfuric acid in the electrolyte to water and make the two plates identical in chemical composition. As electrical energy is removed from the battery, it's voltage output tends to drop. Thus, measuring battery voltage and battery electrolyte composition are two ways of checking the ability of the unit to supply power. During the starting of the engine, electrical energy is removed from the battery. However, if the charging circuit is in good condition and the operating conditions are normal, the power removed from the battery will be replaced by the alternator which will force electrons back into the battery, reversing the normal flow and restoring the battery to it's original chemical state.

The battery and starting motor are linked by very heavy electrical cables designed to minimize resistance to the flow of current. Generally, the major power supply cable that leaves the battery goes directly to the starter, while other electrical system needs are supplied by a smaller cable. During the starter operation, power flows from the battery to the starter, then is grounded through the vehicle's frame and the battery's negative ground strap.

The starting motor is a specially designed, direct current electric motor capable of producing a very great amount of power for it's size. One thing that allows the motor to produce a great deal of power is it's tremendous rotating speed. It drives the engine through a tiny pinion gear (attached to the starter's armature), which drives the very large flywheel ring gear at a greatly reduced speed. Another factor allowing it to produce so much power is that only intermittent operation is required of it. Thus, little allowance for air circulation is required and the windings can be built into a very small space.

The starter solenoid is a magnetic device which employs the small current supplied by the starting switch circuit of the ignition switch. This magnetic action moves a plunger, which mechanically engages the starter and electrically closes the heavy switch which connects it to the battery. The starting switch circuit consists of the starting switch (contained within the ignition switch), a transmission neutral safety switch or clutch pedal switch and wiring necessary to connect these with the starter solenoid or relay.

The pinion (small gear) is mounted to a one-way drive clutch. This clutch is splined to the starter armature shaft. When the ignition switch is moved to the Start position, the solenoid plunger slides the pinion toward the flywheel ring rear via a collar and spring. If the teeth on the pinion and flywheel match properly, the pinion will engage the flywheel immediately. If the gear teeth butt one another, the spring will be compressed and will force the gears to mesh as soon as the starter turns far enough to allow them to do so. As the solenoid plunger reaches the end of its travel, it closes the contacts that connect the battery to the starter, then the engine is cranked.

As soon as the engine starts, the flywheel ring gear begins turning fast enough to drive the pinion at an extremely high rate of speed. At this point, the one-way clutch allows the pinion to spin faster than the starter shaft so that the starter will not operate at excessive speed(s). When the ignition switch is released from the starter position, the solenoid is de-energized, the spring (contained within the solenoid assembly) pulls the pinion out of mesh and interrupts the current flow to the starter.

Ignition Coil

TESTING

Use an ohmmeter to test the ignition coil primary and secondary circuits.

G180Z, G200Z and 4ZC1-T Engines

INPUT VOLTAGE TEST

1. Place the ignition switch in the **ON** position.
2. Using a suitable voltmeter, measure the voltage between the positive (+) terminal of the coil and a ground.
3. The standard voltage should be approximately 12 volts. If the voltage is not within specification, check the wiring and connectors. Replace the coil if found defective if the wiring and connectors are found OK.

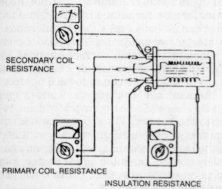

SECONDARY COIL RESISTANCE

PRIMARY COIL RESISTANCE

INSULATION RESISTANCE

Testing ignition coil—early model conventional externally mounted coils

PRIMARY COIL RESISTANCE TEST

1. Place the ignition switch in the **OFF** position.
2. Disconnect the ignition coil terminals.
3. Using a suitable ohmmeter, measure the resistance between the ignition coil positive (+) terminal and the ignition coil negative (−) terminal.
4. The standard resistance should be 1.130–1.529Ω. If the resistance is not within specification, check the wiring and connectors. Replace the coil if found defective.

SECONDARY COIL RESISTANCE TEST

1. Place the ignition switch in the **OFF** position.
2. Disconnect the ignition coil terminals.
3. Using a suitable ohmmeter, measure the resistance between the ignition coil positive (+) terminal and the high voltage terminal.
4. The standard resistance should be 10.20–13.80 kΩ. If the resistance is not within specification, check the wiring and connectors. Replace the coil if found defective.

INSULATION RESISTANCE TEST

1. Place the ignition switch in the **OFF** position.
2. Disconnect the ignition coil terminals.
3. Using a suitable ohmmeter, measure the resistance between the ignition coil positive (+) terminal and the body of the coil.
4. The standard resistance should be more than 10 mΩ. If the resistance is not within specification, check the wiring and connectors. Replace the coil if found defective.

1986–89 I-Mark Non-Turbo (4XC1-U)

INPUT VOLTAGE TEST

1. Place the ignition switch in the **ON** position.
2. Using a suitable voltmeter, measure the voltage between the positive (+) terminal of the coil and a ground.
3. The standard voltage should be approximately 12 volts. If the voltage is not within specification, check the wiring and connectors. Replace the coil if found defective.

PRIMARY COIL RESISTANCE TEST

1. Place the ignition switch in the **OFF** position.
2. Disconnect the ignition coil terminals.
3. Using a suitable ohmmeter, measure the resistance between the ignition coil positive (+) terminal and the ignition coil negative (−) terminal.
4. The standard resistance should be 1.2–1.5Ω. If the resistance is not within specification, check the wiring and connectors. Replace the coil if found defective.

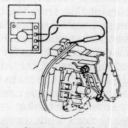

Ignition coil input voltage test—I-Mark (non-Turbo)

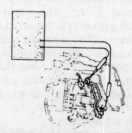

Primary coil resistance test—I-Mark (non-Turbo)

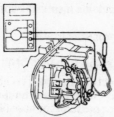

Secondary coil resistance test—I-Mark (non-Turbo)

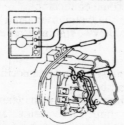

Insulator resistance test—I-Mark (non-Turbo)

SECONDARY COIL RESISTANCE TEST

1. Place the ignition switch in the **OFF** position.

2. Disconnect the ignition coil terminals.

3. Using a suitable ohmmeter, measure the resistance between the ignition coil positive (+) terminal and the high voltage terminal.

4. The standard resistance should be 10.2–13.8 kΩ. If the resistance is not within specification, check the wiring and connectors. Replace the coil if found defective.

INSULATION RESISTANCE TEST

1. Place the ignition switch in the **OFF** position.

2. Disconnect the ignition coil terminals.

3. Using a suitable ohmmeter, measure the resistance between the ignition coil positive (+) terminal and the body of the coil.

4. The standard resistance should be more than 10 mΩ. If the resistance is not within specification, check the wiring and connectors. Replace the coil if found defective.

I-Mark Turbo

CHECKING FOR OPENS AND GROUNDS

1. Using the high scale on the ohmmeter, check the ignition coil resistance by positioning the ohmmeter probes as shown. It should read infinite resistance.

2. Switch the ohmmeter to the low scale and check the resistance across the coil terminals. It should read very low or zero resistance.

3. Now, switch to the high scale and perform a second resistance test by placing the ohmmeter probes as shown. Infinite resistance should be read.

4. If the resistance readings are not as described, replace the ignition coil.

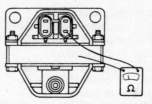

Checking ignition coil resistance—I-Mark (non-Turbo). When the ohmmeter is connected as shown, infinite resistance should be read

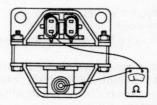

Checking ignition coil resistance—I-Mark (Turbo). When the ohmmeter is connected as shown, infinite resistance should be read

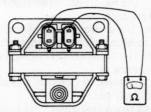

Checking ignition coil resistance—I-Mark (Turbo). When the ohmmeter is connected as shown, very low or zero resistance should be read

4XE1 DOHC Turbo Impulse

Refer to the Electronic Ignition Diagnosis section in this Chapter for "Direct Ignition System" diagnosis procedures.

Amigo, P'UP, Trooper, Trooper II with 4ZD1 and 4ZE1 Engines

RESISTANCE TESTS

1. Disconnect the wiring along with the ignition coil and high tension cable at the connector.

2. Using a suitable ohmmeter, measure the resistance of the coil across the appropriate coil terminals. The resistance should be as follows:

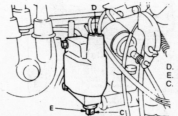

D. High tension lead
E. Positive lead
C. Negative lead

Testing the ignition coil—Trooper, Amigo and P'up with the 4ZD1 and 4ZE1 engines

- Primary coil resistance
  4ZD1 engines (C–E) – 1.2–1.4Ω
  4ZE1 engines (C–E) – 0.81–0.99Ω
- Secondary coil resistance
  4ZD1 engines (C–D) – 8.6–13.0 kΩ
  4ZE1 engines (C–D) – 7.5–13.5 kΩ
- Insulation resistance
  4ZD1 and 4ZE1 engines (C-Body) – more than 10 mΩ.

Trooper, Trooper II and Rodeo with V6 Engine

1. Disconnect the distributor wire and wiring from the coil.
2. Make sure the metal ground surface is clean.
3. Connect an ohmmeter as shown in position **1**. Set the ohmmeter to the high ohms scale and measure the resistance. It should read infinite resistance.
4. Connect an ohmmeter as shown in position **2**. Set the ohmmeter to the low ohms scale and measure the resistance. It should read very low or zero resistance.
5. Connect an ohmmeter as shown in position **3**. Set the ohmmeter to the high ohms scale and measure the resistance. It should *not* read infinite resistance.
6. If the resistance is not as described, replace the ignition coil.
7. Connect the coil wiring.

COIL REMOVAL AND INSTALLATION

G180Z, G200Z and 4ZC1-T Engines

1. Disconnect the negative (–) battery cable.
2. Disconnect the ignition coil, condenser and transistor leads.
3. Remove the coil and bracket assembly. Remove the bracket assembly from the the coil.

To install:

1. Install the bracket to the coil and tighten the retaining screw.
2. Install the assembly to the vehicle and torque the mounting bolts to 15 ft. lbs. (20 Nm).

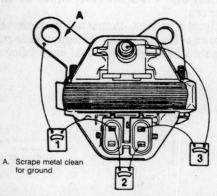

A. Scrape metal clean
for ground

Ignition coil test on the Trooper and Rodeo with V6 engines

3. Reconnect all electrical connectors and battery cable.
4. Check for proper operation.

1986–89 I-Mark Non-Turbo (4XC1-U)

1. Disconnect the negative (–) battery cable.
2. Mark the distributor housing, cylinder block and rotor position for ease of installation.
3. Remove the distributor cap and disconnect the electrical connectors.
4. Remove the distributor from the vehicle.
5. Remove the two retaining screws and ignition coil.

To install:

1. Remove any sealing and packing adhering to the coil and housing.
2. Wash the coil clean with cleaning solvent.
3. Lightly apply RTV sealer to the areas around the coil.
4. Install the coil and tighten the retaining bolts.
5. Install the distributor as outlined in this Section.
6. Connect all electrical connectors and check operation.

I-Mark Turbo

1. Disconnect the negative (–) battery cable.
2. Disconnect the ignition coil electrical connectors.
3. Remove the mounting bolts and coil assembly.

To install:

1. Install the coil and mounting bolts. Torque the bolts to 20 ft. lbs. (27 Nm).
2. Connect all electrical connectors and battery cable. Check for proper operation.

4XE1 DOHC Turbo Impulse

1. Disconnect the negative (–) battery cable.
2. Remove the intercooler and cover.
3. Label and mark the spark plug wires before removal. Remove the ignition coil cover and spark plug wires.
4. Remove the ignition coil by removing the two retaining screws from the module. Be careful not to damage the module.

To install:

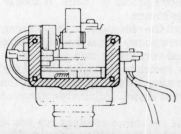

RTV sealer application—I-Mark (non-Turbo)

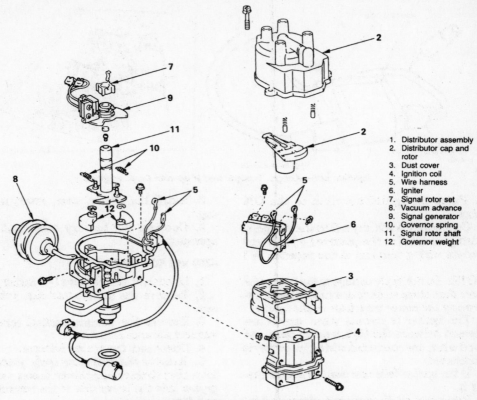

1. Distributor assembly
2. Distributor cap and rotor
3. Dust cover
4. Ignition coil
5. Wire harness
6. Igniter
7. Signal rotor set
8. Vacuum advance
9. Signal generator
10. Governor spring
11. Signal rotor shaft
12. Governor weight

Distributor assembly—I-Mark (non-Turbo) 4XC1-U engine

1. Install the coil and torque the screws to 40 inch lbs. (4.5 Nm).
2. Install the spark plug wires to their original locations.
3. Install the coil cover and intercooler.
4. Connect the negative battery cable and check operation.

Amigo, P'UP, Trooper, Trooper II with 4ZD1 and 4ZE1 Engines

1. Disconnect the negative (−) battery cable and coil connectors.

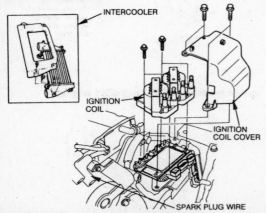

Ignition coil removal—4XE1 DOHC Turbo

2. Remove the two retaining screws and coil assembly.
3. Install the assembly and tighten the bolts.
4. Reconnect the electrical connectors and battery cable.

Trooper, Trooper II and Rodeo with V6 Engine

1. Disconnect the negative (−) battery cable.
2. Disconnect the ignition coil electrical connectors.
3. Remove the mounting bolts and coil assembly.

To install:
1. Install the coil and mounting bolts. Torque the bolts to 20 ft. lbs. (27 Nm).
2. Connect all electrical connectors and battery cable. Check for proper operation.

Igniter

ON-VEHICLE INSPECTION

Amigo, P'up, Trooper II, Rodeo With 4ZD1 and 4ZE1 Engines Only

1. Remove the distributor cap.
2. Disconnect the ignition coil high tension cable at the distributor side. Move the high tension cable end to the coil fixing screw and maintain a 5mm clearance.

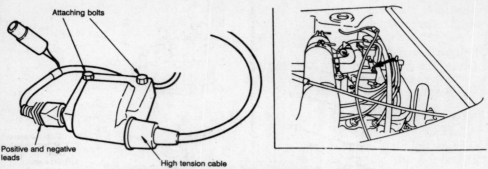

Ignition coil—Amigo, Trooper and P'up with 4-cyl. engines

3. Place the ignition switch to the **ON** position.

4. Connect a 1.5 volt dry cell to the red igniter wiring terminal at the positive (+) side and the white wiring terminal at the negative (−) side.

NOTE: *Do not apply voltage to the igniter for more than three seconds at a time to avoid destroying the power transistor in the igniter.*

5. The igniter is normal when sparks are generated between the high tension cable and ground when one connected wiring (or probe) is disconnected.

6. If the igniter fails this test (no sparks), replace it.

7. Reconnect all disconnected wiring and install all removed parts.

REMOVAL AND INSTALLATION

G180Z, G200Z Engines

1. Disconnect the negative (−) battery cable.
2. Remove the distributor cap, seal and rotor.
3. Remove the igniter cover and igniter assembly.
To install:
1. Install the igniter and adjust the gap between the pick-up coil and coil projections with a feeler gauge. The measurement should be between 0.008–0.016 in. (0.2–0.4mm).

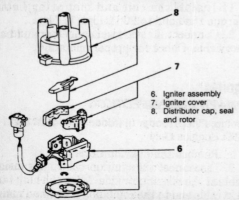

6. Igniter assembly
7. Igniter cover
8. Distributor cap, seal and rotor

Igniter assembly—G180Z and G200Z engines

2. Install the igniter cover, rotor, seal and cap.
3. Connect the battery cable and check operation.

4ZD1 and 4ZE1 Engines

1. Disconnect the negative (−) battery cable.
2. Remove the distributor cap, rotor and seal.
3. Remove the vacuum control screw and vacuum advance canister.
4. Disconnect the wiring harness.
5. Remove the retractor (pole piece). Pry loose the retractor outer cover, insert a suitable prybar into the lower side of the retractor and pull free.
6. Remove the igniter and breaker plate assembly. Remove the stator, magnet and igniter.
To install:
1. Install the igniter, stator and magnet.
2. Carefully align the scribe marks on the breaker plate assembly and the housing.

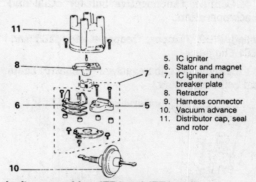

5. IC igniter
6. Stator and magnet
7. IC igniter and breaker plate
8. Retractor
9. Harness connector
10. Vacuum advance
11. Distributor cap, seal and rotor

Igniter assembly—4ZD1 and 4ZE1 engines

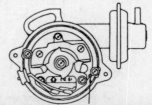

Align the breaker plate with housing at arrow

3. Install the retractor with the roll pin notch and retractor notch in parallel alignment.

4. Install the harness connector, vacuum advance, distributor cap, seal and rotor.

5. Check the vacuum canister by applying vacuum to the vacuum port. The breaker plate should move freely and hold vacuum.

I-Mark (Non-Turbo) 4XC1-U

1. Remove the distributor cap.

2. Remove the rotor and dust cover.

3. Disconnect the ignition coil wiring harness, remove the ignition coil retaining screws and remove the coil along with the wire harness.

4. Remove the screws retaining the igniter and remove the igniter.

5. Install the igniter and tighten the retaining screws.

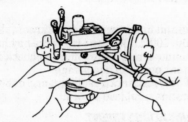

Removing the igniter on the I-Mark (non-Turbo)

6. When installing the ignition coil, remove any sealing and packing adhering to the ignition coil and the housing. Apply silicone gasket compound to the area where the coil seats on the body of the distributor housing.

7. Route the coil wiring harness and position the coil against the distributor housing.

8. Install the coil retaining screws.

9. Install the dust cover, rotor and distributor cap.

I-Mark (Turbo), Impulse DOHC and Stylus

1. Disconnect the negative (–) battery cable.

2. Remove the distributor cap retaining screws and cap.

3. Remove the rotor.

4. Disconnect the module electrical connectors.

5. Remove the module retaining screws and module.

To install:

1. Clean the module mating surfaces. Apply a coat of dielectric compound to both module and mating surfaces. This compound helps absorb heat and is essential for long module life.

2. Tighten the retaining screws.

3. Connect the electrical connectors.

4. Install the rotor and distributor cap.

5. Connect the battery cable and check operation.

4XE1 DOHC Turbo Impulse

1. Disconnect the negative (–) battery cable.

2. Remove the intercooler, coil cover and disconnect module wiring.

3. Label and disconnect the spark plug wires from the ignition coils.

4. Remove the DIS assembly from the vehicle.

To install:

1. Remove the coils from the module.

2. Install the coils onto the new module.

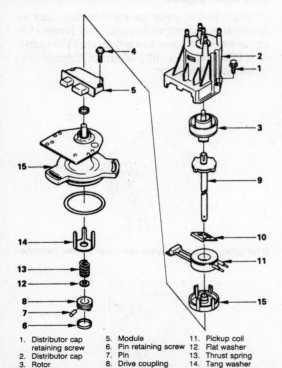

1. Distributor cap retaining screw
2. Distributor cap
3. Rotor
4. Module retaining screw
5. Module
6. Pin retaining screw
7. Pin
8. Drive coupling
9. Shaft assembly
10. Pickup coil retainer
11. Pickup coil
12. Flat washer
13. Thrust spring
14. Tang washer
15. Housing assembly

Exploded view of the distributor used on the I-Mark (Turbo) 4XC1-T

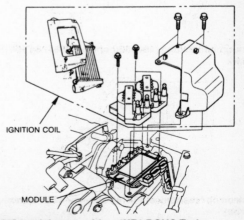

IGNITION COIL

MODULE

DIS module assembly—4XE1 DOHC Turbo

3. Install the assembly onto the vehicle and torque to 19 ft. lbs. (26 Nm).

4. Connect the spark plug wires to their original location.

5. Connect the DIS electrical connectors.

6. Install the coil cover and intercooler.

7. Connect the negative battery cable and check operation.

Pick-up Coil

TESTING

G180Z and G200Z

Using an ohmmeter, check the resistance at the connector. The reading should be between 140–180Ω.

I-Mark Non-Turbo

1. Place the ignition switch in the **OFF** position.

2. Disconnect the ignition coil terminals.

3. Using a suitable ohmmeter, measure the pick-up coil resistance between the 2 pick-up coil terminals.

4. The standard resistance should be 140–180Ω. If the resistance is not within specification, check the wiring and connectors. Replace the pick-up coil if found defective.

I-Mark Turbo, Impulse, Stylus and V6 Engines

1. Disconnect the pick-up coil wiring.

2. Switch the ohmmeter to the middle ohms scale.

3. Measure the coil resistance between either of the pick-up coil leads and the housing. Infinite resistance should be read.

4. Connect the ohmmeter probes across the

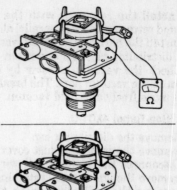
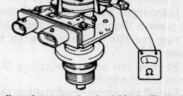

Pick-up coil resistance check—I-Mark (Turbo), Impulse, Stylus and V6 engines

coil leads and measure the resistance. It should read 500–1000Ω. Flex the lead wires by hand at the coil and connector by hand to check for intermittent opens in the wiring.

5. If the resistance readings are not within specifications, replace the coil.

AIR GAP ADJUSTMENT

Early Model Engines

Using a feeler gauge, measure the air gap between the pick-up coil projection. Loosen the two screws and move the igniter until the gap is at 0.008–0.016 in. (0.2–0.4mm). Tighten the screws and install cap.

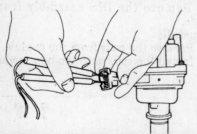

Pick-up coil testing, 140–180 ohms—1981–84 RWD I-Mark

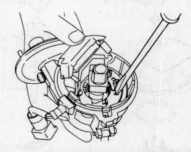

Distributor air gap adjustment—early model engines

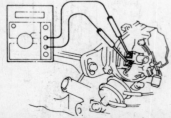

Pick-up coil resistance, 140–180 ohms—4XC1-U (non-Turbo)

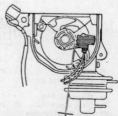

Distributor air gap adjustment—I-Mark (non-Turbo) 4XC1-U

I-Mark Non-Turbo

Inspect the air gap, by using a non-magnetic feeler gauge. Measure the gap between the signal rotor and the pick-up coil projection. You should be able to insert the feeler gauge with a slight drag. The air gap should be 0.008–0.0016 in. (0.2–0.4mm).

Camshaft Angle Sensor
4XE1 DOHC Turbo Only
REMOVAL AND INSTALLATION

1. Rotate the engine and bring up the No. 1 cylinder to top dead center of its compression stroke.
NOTE: *To bring the engine to TDC of the No. 1 compression stroke, remove the spark plug for the No. cylinder. With the engine cool, turn the crankshaft over until compression is forced out of the spark plug hole. Watch the crankshaft damper while feeling for compression. When compression is felt, align the mark on the crankshaft damper with the 0° mark on the timing cover.*
2. Disconnect the negative battery cable. Disconnect and tag (if necessary) all the electrical connectors along with the spark plug wires from the distributor.
3. Remove the intercooler and disconnect the sensor electrical connector.
4. Remove the mounting bolt and camshaft angle sensor.
To install:
1. Install the sensor to its original position and install the mounting bolt.
2. Connect the wiring connectors.
3. Install the intercooler and connect the battery cable.
4. Start the engine and adjust the timing as outlined in the ''Ignition Timing'' section in Chapter 2.

Distributor
REMOVAL AND INSTALLATION

All Models

UNDISTURBED ENGINE

1. Rotate the engine and bring up the No. 1 cylinder to top dead center of its compression stroke.
NOTE: *To bring the engine to TDC of the No. 1 compression stroke, remove the spark plug for the No. cylinder. With the engine cool, turn the crankshaft over until compression is forced out of the spark plug hole. Watch the crankshaft damper while feeling for compression. When compression is felt, align the mark on the crankshaft damper with the 0° mark on the timing cover.*

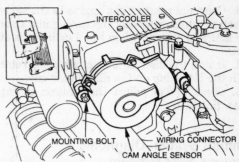

Camshaft angle sensor—4XE1 DOHC Turbo

2. Disconnect the negative battery cable. Disconnect and tag (if necessary) all the electrical connectors along with the spark plug wires from the distributor.
3. Disconnect the wiring harness from the distributor lead wire. Disconnect the vacuum hoses from the vacuum advance if so equipped.
4. Using a scribe tool or a marker, scribe or mark an alignment mark on the base of the distributor and the cylinder head or engine block. Also mark the position of the rotor to the distributor housing. This can be used for an easier installation procedure.
5. Remove the distributor clamp bolt and bracket and lift out the distributor assembly from the engine cylinder head. Remove the distributor housing seal and discard it. Lubricate the new seal with clean engine oil prior to installation.
To install:
6. Install the distributor assembly into the cylinder block, be sure to align the scribe marks made previously. Lightly tighten the distributor mounting bolt.
7. Connect the wiring harness to the distributor lead wire. Connect the vacuum hoses to the vacuum controller.
8. Connect all the electrical connectors along with the spark plug wires to the distributor.
9. Connect the negative battery cable. Start the engine, set the timing and check the idle speed as outlined in Chapter 2. Tighten the distributor mounting bolt.

DISTURBED ENGINE

NOTE: *Disconnecting the negative battery cable on some vehicles may interfere with the functions of the on board computer systems and may require the computer to undergo a relearning process, once the negative battery cable is reconnected.*
1. If the engine was disturbed while the distributor was removed, remove the No. 1 spark plug.
2. Rotate the crankshaft in the normal direction of rotation until compression is felt at the spark plug hole.

3. Continue rotating the engine in the same direction while observing the timing marks at the indicator line up when No. 1 cylinder is at TDC.

4. Install the distributor and align the rotor with the No. 1 lug on the distributor cap.

5. Check and/or adjust the ignition timing when finished.

Ignition System Diagnosis
SERVICE PRECAUTIONS

Be careful not to get water on any fuel injection system component. Pay close attention to the relay box and throttle valve switch connector. The connector is not water proofed and will be damaged by water.

When charging the battery be sure to remove it from the vehicle first. Never disconnect the battery cable from the battery when the engine is running. The generation of surge voltage may damage the control unit harness connector, disconnect all the control unit harnesses first, then set the starter switch to the ON position.

When replacing parts or checking the system, make sure to set the starter switch to the OFF position. When measuring voltage at the control unit harness connector, disconnect all the control unit harnesses first, then set the starter switch to the ON position.

The wiring connectors for the fuel injector, throttle valve switch, air regulator and water temperature sensor are provided with locked wires. To unlock the connector, pull and shake it gently.

System cables must be placed at least four inches away from the tension cables. Be careful not to apply and shock to the system components such as the air flow sensor, crank angle sensor and control unit. Component parts of the fuel injection system are precisely set. Even a slight distortion or dent will seriously affect performance.

The fuel pump must not be operated without fuel. Since fuel lubricates the pump, noise or other serious problems such as parts seizure will result. It is also prohibited to use any fuel other than gasoline.

NOTE: *For wiring diagrams not found in this section, refer to Chapter 6.*

**G180Z, G200Z, 4ZC1-T and 1985 4XC1-U
Diagnostic Charts 1–4**

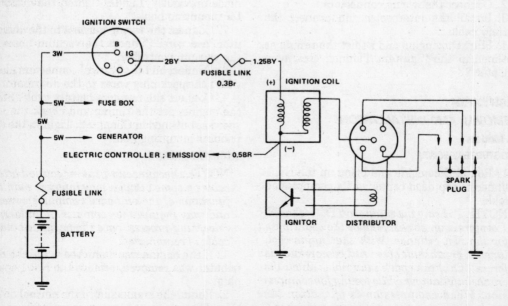

Ignition system wiring—RWD I-Mark

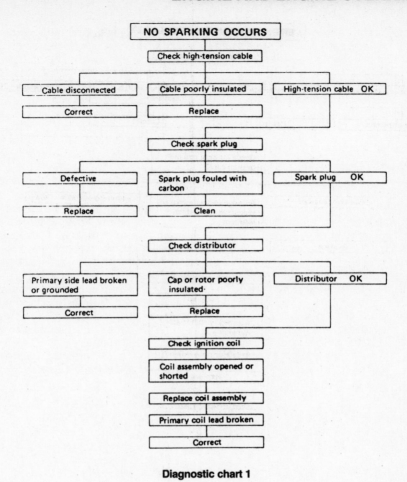

Diagnostic chart 1

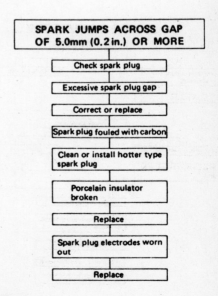

Diagnostic chart 2

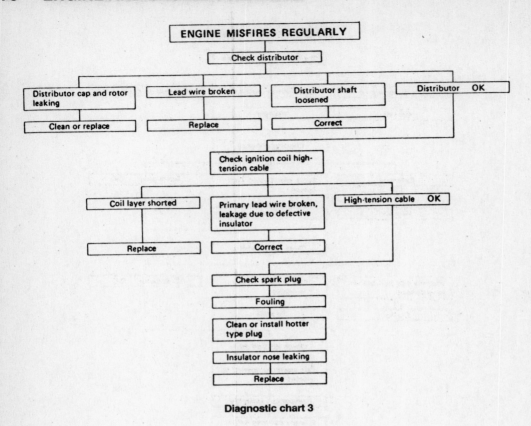

Diagnostic chart 3

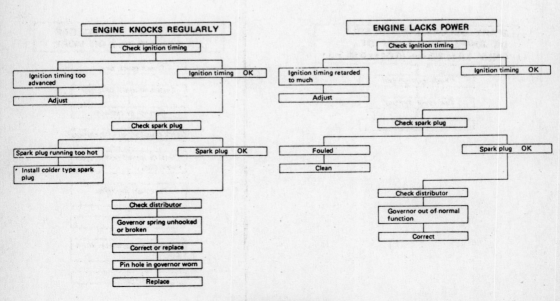

Diagnostic chart 4

**1986–89 4XC1-U and 4XC1-T I-Mark
Diagnostic Charts 5 and 6**

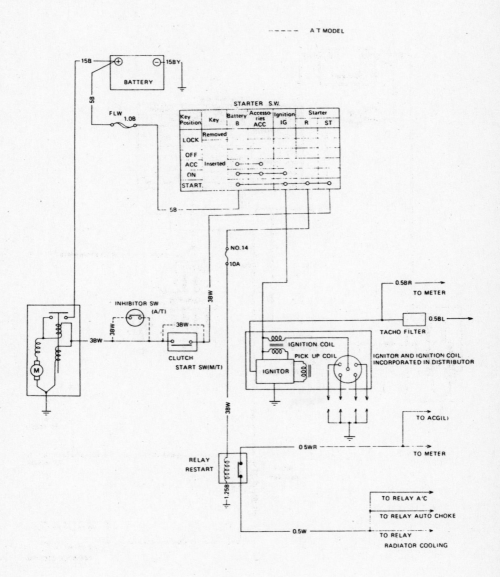

Wiring diagram—1986–89 I-Mark (non-Turbo) 4XC1-U

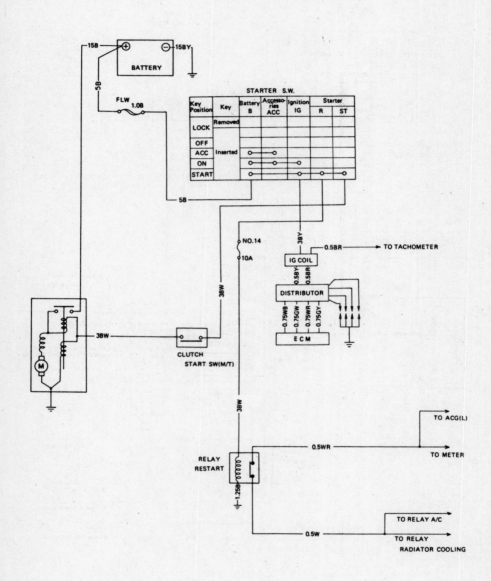

Wiring diagram—1988–89 I-Mark (Turbo) 4XC1-T

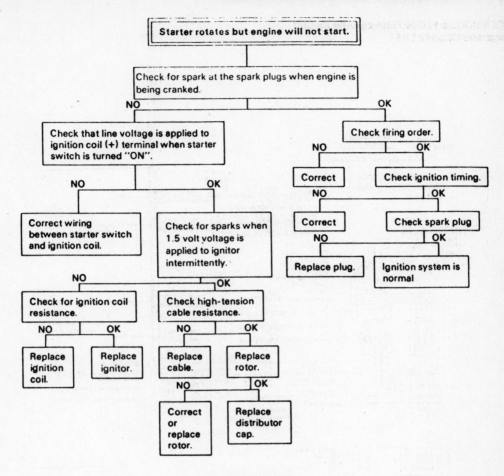

Diagnostic chart 5

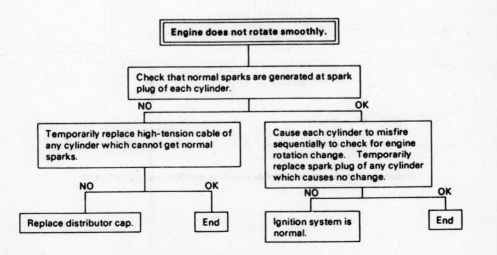

Diagnostic chart 6

4XE1 SOHC and DOHC Impulse and Stylus
Diagnostic Charts 11-15

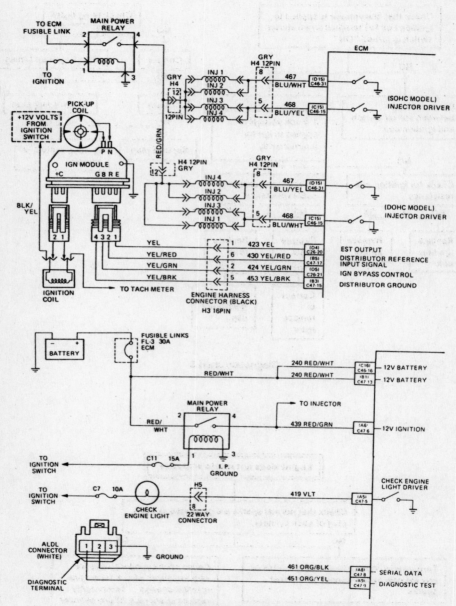

Ignition wiring diagram—Impulse and Stylus SOHC and DOHC 4XE1

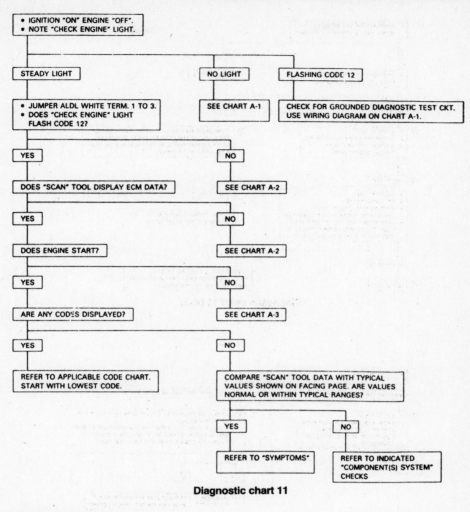

Diagnostic chart 11

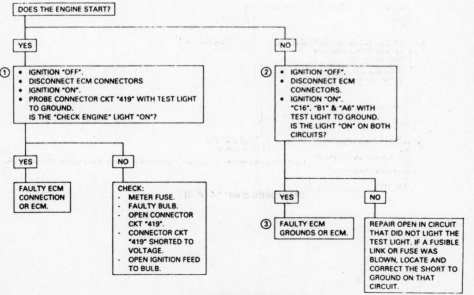

Diagnostic chart 12 (A-1)

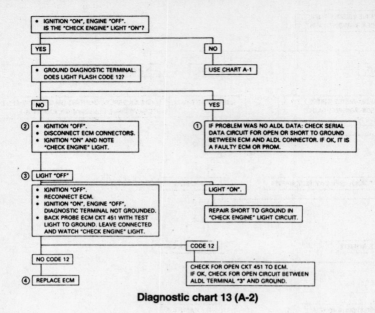

Diagnostic chart 13 (A-2)

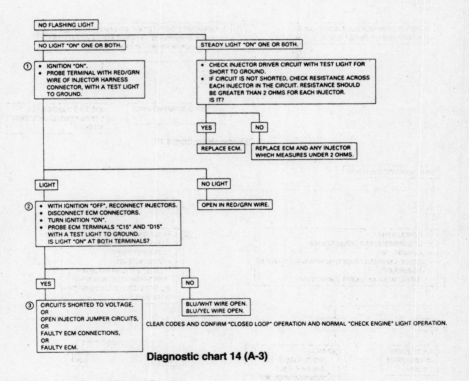

Diagnostic chart 14 (A-3)

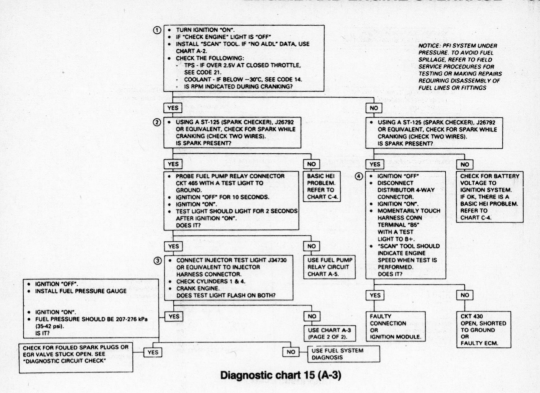

Diagnostic chart 15 (A-3)

4XE1 DOHC Turbo Impulse Diagnostic Charts 16-23

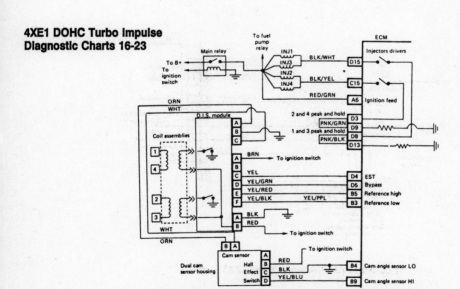

Ignition system wiring diagram—Impulse Turbo DOHC 4XE1

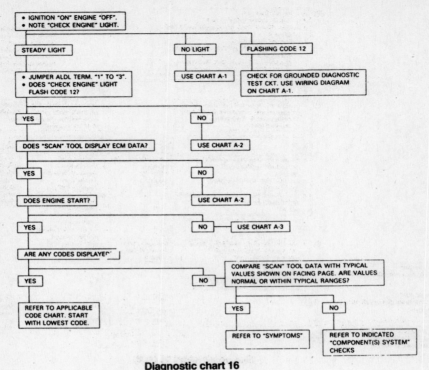

Diagnostic chart 16

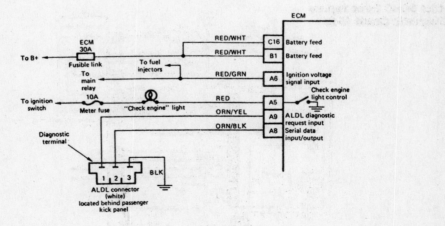

ECM and ALDL wiring—DOHC 4XE1 Turbo

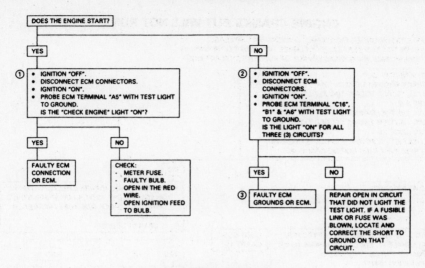

Diagnostic chart 17 (A-1)

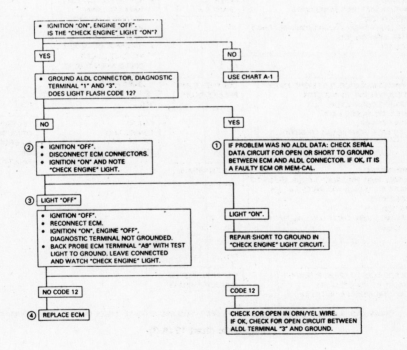

Diagnostic chart 18 (A-2)

ENGINE CRANKS BUT WILL NOT RUN

NOTE: PFI SYSTEM UNDER PRESSURE. TO AVOID FUEL SPILLAGE,
      REFER TO FIELD SERVICE PROCEDURES FOR TESTING OR MAKING
      REPAIRS REQUIRING DISASSEMBLY OF FUEL LINES OR FITTINGS

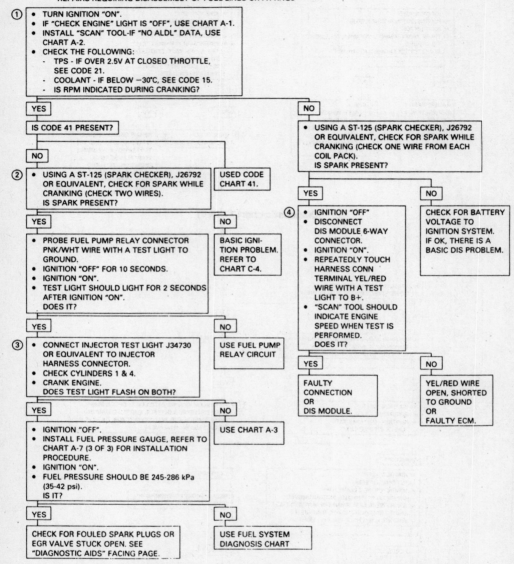

① • TURN IGNITION "ON".
   • IF "CHECK ENGINE" LIGHT IS "OFF", USE CHART A-1.
   • INSTALL "SCAN" TOOL-IF "NO ALDL" DATA, USE
     CHART A-2.
   • CHECK THE FOLLOWING:
     - TPS - IF OVER 2.5V AT CLOSED THROTTLE,
       SEE CODE 21.
     - COOLANT - IF BELOW −30°C, SEE CODE 15.
     - IS RPM INDICATED DURING CRANKING?

YES

NO

IS CODE 41 PRESENT?

• USING A ST-125 (SPARK CHECKER), J26792
  OR EQUIVALENT, CHECK FOR SPARK WHILE
  CRANKING (CHECK ONE WIRE FROM EACH
  COIL PACK).
  IS SPARK PRESENT?

NO

② • USING A ST-125 (SPARK CHECKER), J26792
   OR EQUIVALENT, CHECK FOR SPARK WHILE
   CRANKING (CHECK TWO WIRES).
   IS SPARK PRESENT?

USED CODE
CHART 41.

YES

NO

YES

NO

• PROBE FUEL PUMP RELAY CONNECTOR
  PNK/WHT WIRE WITH A TEST LIGHT TO
  GROUND.
• IGNITION "OFF" FOR 10 SECONDS.
• IGNITION "ON".
• TEST LIGHT SHOULD LIGHT FOR 2 SECONDS
  AFTER IGNITION "ON".
  DOES IT?

BASIC IGNI-
TION PROBLEM.
REFER TO
CHART C-4.

④ • IGNITION "OFF"
   • DISCONNECT
     DIS MODULE 6-WAY
     CONNECTOR.
   • IGNITION "ON".
   • REPEATEDLY TOUCH
     HARNESS CONN
     TERMINAL YEL/RED
     WIRE WITH A TEST
     LIGHT TO B+.
   • "SCAN" TOOL SHOULD
     INDICATE ENGINE
     SPEED WHEN TEST IS
     PERFORMED.
     DOES IT?

CHECK FOR BATTERY
VOLTAGE TO
IGNITION SYSTEM.
IF OK, THERE IS A
BASIC DIS PROBLEM.

YES

NO

③ • CONNECT INJECTOR TEST LIGHT J34730
   OR EQUIVALENT TO INJECTOR
   HARNESS CONNECTOR.
   • CHECK CYLINDERS 1 & 4.
   • CRANK ENGINE.
   DOES TEST LIGHT FLASH ON BOTH?

USE FUEL PUMP
RELAY CIRCUIT

YES

NO

FAULTY
CONNECTION
OR
DIS MODULE.

YEL/RED WIRE
OPEN, SHORTED
TO GROUND
OR
FAULTY ECM.

YES

NO

• IGNITION "OFF".
• INSTALL FUEL PRESSURE GAUGE, REFER TO
  CHART A-7 (3 OF 3) FOR INSTALLATION
  PROCEDURE.
• IGNITION "ON".
• FUEL PRESSURE SHOULD BE 245-286 kPa
  (35-42 psi).
  IS IT?

USE CHART A-3

YES

NO

CHECK FOR FOULED SPARK PLUGS OR
EGR VALVE STUCK OPEN. SEE
"DIAGNOSTIC AIDS" FACING PAGE.

USE FUEL SYSTEM
DIAGNOSIS CHART

CLEAR CODES AND CONFIRM "CLOSED LOOP" OPERATION AND NORMAL "CHECK ENGINE" LIGHT OPERATION.

Diagnostic chart 19 (A-3)

ENGINE CRANKS BUT WILL NOT RUN

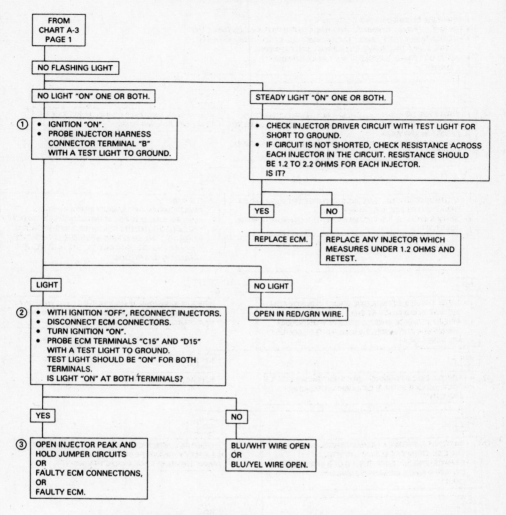

CLEAR CODES AND CONFIRM "CLOSED LOOP" OPERATION AND NORMAL "CHECK ENGINE" LIGHT OPERATION.

Diagnostic chart 20 (A-3)

DIS MISFIRE AT IDLE

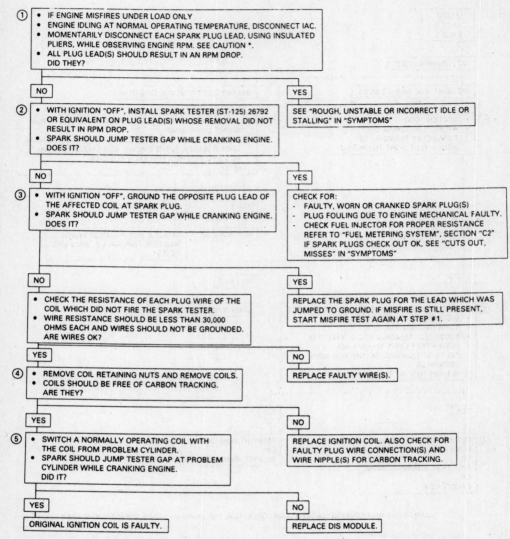

① • IF ENGINE MISFIRES UNDER LOAD ONLY
   • ENGINE IDLING AT NORMAL OPERATING TEMPERATURE, DISCONNECT IAC.
   • MOMENTARILY DISCONNECT EACH SPARK PLUG LEAD, USING INSULATED PLIERS, WHILE OBSERVING ENGINE RPM. SEE CAUTION *.
   • ALL PLUG LEAD(S) SHOULD RESULT IN AN RPM DROP. DID THEY?

NO

YES

② • WITH IGNITION "OFF", INSTALL SPARK TESTER (ST-125) 26792 OR EQUIVALENT ON PLUG LEAD(S) WHOSE REMOVAL DID NOT RESULT IN RPM DROP.
   • SPARK SHOULD JUMP TESTER GAP WHILE CRANKING ENGINE. DOES IT?

SEE "ROUGH, UNSTABLE OR INCORRECT IDLE OR STALLING" IN "SYMPTOMS"

NO

YES

③ • WITH IGNITION "OFF", GROUND THE OPPOSITE PLUG LEAD OF THE AFFECTED COIL AT SPARK PLUG.
   • SPARK SHOULD JUMP TESTER GAP WHILE CRANKING ENGINE. DOES IT?

CHECK FOR:
- FAULTY, WORN OR CRANKED SPARK PLUG(S)
- PLUG FOULING DUE TO ENGINE MECHANICAL FAULTY.
- CHECK FUEL INJECTOR FOR PROPER RESISTANCE REFER TO "FUEL METERING SYSTEM", SECTION "C2" IF SPARK PLUGS CHECK OUT OK, SEE "CUTS OUT, MISSES" IN "SYMPTOMS"

NO

YES

   • CHECK THE RESISTANCE OF EACH PLUG WIRE OF THE COIL WHICH DID NOT FIRE THE SPARK TESTER.
   • WIRE RESISTANCE SHOULD BE LESS THAN 30,000 OHMS EACH AND WIRES SHOULD NOT BE GROUNDED. ARE WIRES OK?

REPLACE THE SPARK PLUG FOR THE LEAD WHICH WAS JUMPED TO GROUND. IF MISFIRE IS STILL PRESENT, START MISFIRE TEST AGAIN AT STEP #1.

YES

NO

④ • REMOVE COIL RETAINING NUTS AND REMOVE COILS.
   • COILS SHOULD BE FREE OF CARBON TRACKING. ARE THEY?

REPLACE FAULTY WIRE(S).

YES

NO

⑤ • SWITCH A NORMALLY OPERATING COIL WITH THE COIL FROM PROBLEM CYLINDER.
   • SPARK SHOULD JUMP TESTER GAP AT PROBLEM CYLINDER WHILE CRANKING ENGINE. DID IT?

REPLACE IGNITION COIL. ALSO CHECK FOR FAULTY PLUG WIRE CONNECTION(S) AND WIRE NIPPLE(S) FOR CARBON TRACKING.

YES

NO

ORIGINAL IGNITION COIL IS FAULTY.

REPLACE DIS MODULE.

*CAUTION: When handling secondary spark plug leads with engine running, insulted pliers must be used and care exercised to prevent a possible electrical shock.

CLEAR CODES AND CONFIRM "CLOSED LOOP" OPERATION AND NORMAL "CHECK ENGINE" LIGHT OPERATION.

Diagnostic chart 21

DIS MISFIRE UNDER LOAD

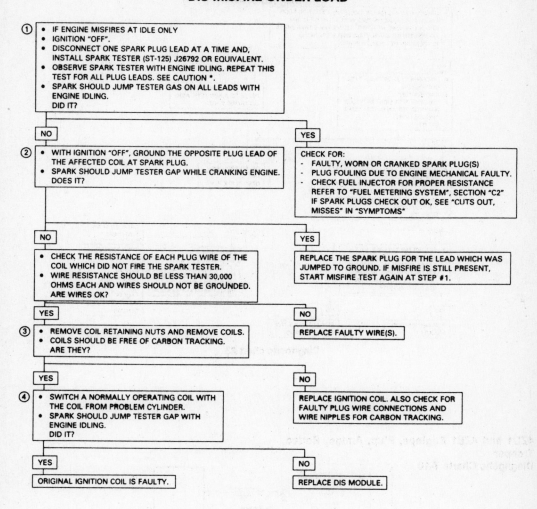

① • IF ENGINE MISFIRES AT IDLE ONLY
   • IGNITION "OFF".
   • DISCONNECT ONE SPARK PLUG LEAD AT A TIME AND,
     INSTALL SPARK TESTER (ST-125) J26792 OR EQUIVALENT.
   • OBSERVE SPARK TESTER WITH ENGINE IDLING. REPEAT THIS
     TEST FOR ALL PLUG LEADS. SEE CAUTION *.
   • SPARK SHOULD JUMP TESTER GAS ON ALL LEADS WITH
     ENGINE IDLING.
     DID IT?

NO | **YES**

② • WITH IGNITION "OFF", GROUND THE OPPOSITE PLUG LEAD OF
   THE AFFECTED COIL AT SPARK PLUG.
   • SPARK SHOULD JUMP TESTER GAP WHILE CRANKING ENGINE.
     DOES IT?

CHECK FOR:
- FAULTY, WORN OR CRANKED SPARK PLUG(S)
- PLUG FOULING DUE TO ENGINE MECHANICAL FAULTY.
- CHECK FUEL INJECTOR FOR PROPER RESISTANCE
  REFER TO "FUEL METERING SYSTEM", SECTION "C2"
  IF SPARK PLUGS CHECK OUT OK, SEE "CUTS OUT,
  MISSES" IN "SYMPTOMS"

NO | **YES**

• CHECK THE RESISTANCE OF EACH PLUG WIRE OF THE
  COIL WHICH DID NOT FIRE THE SPARK TESTER.
• WIRE RESISTANCE SHOULD BE LESS THAN 30,000
  OHMS EACH AND WIRES SHOULD NOT BE GROUNDED.
  ARE WIRES OK?

REPLACE THE SPARK PLUG FOR THE LEAD WHICH WAS
JUMPED TO GROUND. IF MISFIRE IS STILL PRESENT,
START MISFIRE TEST AGAIN AT STEP #1.

YES | **NO**

③ • REMOVE COIL RETAINING NUTS AND REMOVE COILS.
   • COILS SHOULD BE FREE OF CARBON TRACKING.
     ARE THEY?

REPLACE FAULTY WIRE(S).

YES | **NO**

④ • SWITCH A NORMALLY OPERATING COIL WITH
   THE COIL FROM PROBLEM CYLINDER.
   • SPARK SHOULD JUMP TESTER GAP WITH
     ENGINE IDLING.
     DID IT?

REPLACE IGNITION COIL. ALSO CHECK FOR
FAULTY PLUG WIRE CONNECTIONS AND
WIRE NIPPLES FOR CARBON TRACKING.

YES | **NO**

ORIGINAL IGNITION COIL IS FAULTY. | REPLACE DIS MODULE.

*CAUTION: When handling secondary spark plug leads with engine running, insulted pliers must be used and care exercised to prevent a possible electrical shock.

Diagnostic chart 22

"DIS" NO SPARK

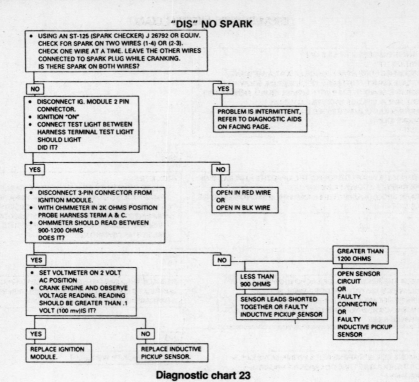

- USING AN ST-125 (SPARK CHECKER) J 26792 OR EQUIV. CHECK FOR SPARK ON TWO WIRES (1-4) OR (2-3). CHECK ONE WIRE AT A TIME. LEAVE THE OTHER WIRES CONNECTED TO SPARK PLUG WHILE CRANKING. IS THERE SPARK ON BOTH WIRES?

NO

YES

- DISCONNECT IG. MODULE 2 PIN CONNECTOR.
- IGNITION "ON"
- CONNECT TEST LIGHT BETWEEN HARNESS TERMINAL TEST LIGHT SHOULD LIGHT DID IT?

PROBLEM IS INTERMITTENT, REFER TO DIAGNOSTIC AIDS ON FACING PAGE.

YES

NO

- DISCONNECT 3-PIN CONNECTOR FROM IGNITION MODULE.
- WITH OHMMETER IN 2K OHMS POSITION PROBE HARNESS TERM A & C.
- OHMMETER SHOULD READ BETWEEN 900-1200 OHMS DOES IT?

OPEN IN RED WIRE OR OPEN IN BLK WIRE

YES

NO

GREATER THAN 1200 OHMS

- SET VOLTMETER ON 2 VOLT AC POSITION
- CRANK ENGINE AND OBSERVE VOLTAGE READING. READING SHOULD BE GREATER THAN .1 VOLT (100 mv)IS IT?

LESS THAN 900 OHMS

OPEN SENSOR CIRCUIT OR FAULTY CONNECTION OR FAULTY INDUCTIVE PICKUP SENSOR

SENSOR LEADS SHORTED TOGETHER OR FAULTY INDUCTIVE PICKUP SENSOR

YES

NO

REPLACE IGNITION MODULE.

REPLACE INDUCTIVE PICKUP SENSOR.

Diagnostic chart 23

4ZD1 and 4ZE1 Engines, P'up, Amigo, Rodeo, Trooper
Diagnostic Charts 7-10

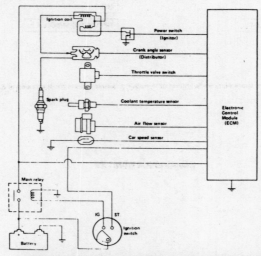

Ignition system diagram—4ZD1 and 4ZE1 engines

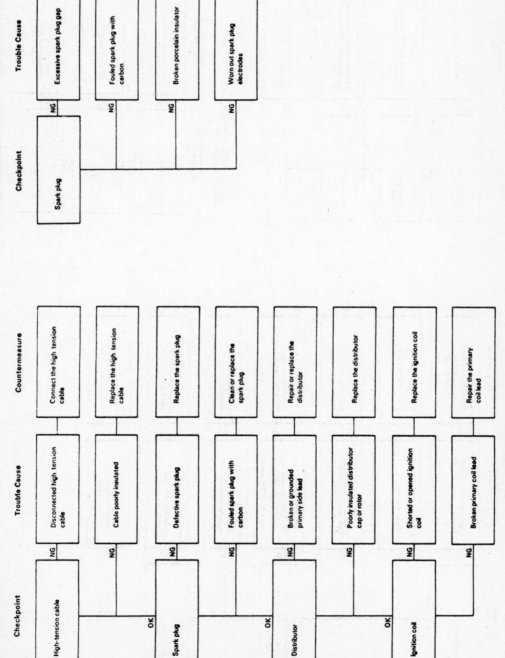

SPARK JUMPS ACROSS GAP OF 5 mm (0.2 in) OR MORE

Checkpoint	Trouble Cause	Countermeasure
Spark plug	Excessive spark plug gap	Adjust or replace the spark plug
	Fouled spark plug with carbon	Clean or replace with hotter type spark plug
	Broken porcelain insulator	Replace the spark plug
	Worn out spark plug electrodes	Replace the spark plug

Diagnostic chart 8

NO SPARK OCCURS

Checkpoint	Trouble Cause	Countermeasure
High-tension cable	Disconnected high tension cable	Connect the high tension cable
	Cable poorly insulated	Replace the high tension cable
Spark plug	Defective spark plug	Replace the spark plug
	Fouled spark plug with carbon	Clean or replace the spark plug
Distributor	Broken or grounded primary side lead	Repair or replace the distributor
	Poorly insulated distributor cap or rotor	Replace the distributor
Ignition coil	Shorted or opened ignition coil	Replace the ignition coil
	Broken primary coil lead	Repair the primary coil lead

Diagnostic chart 7

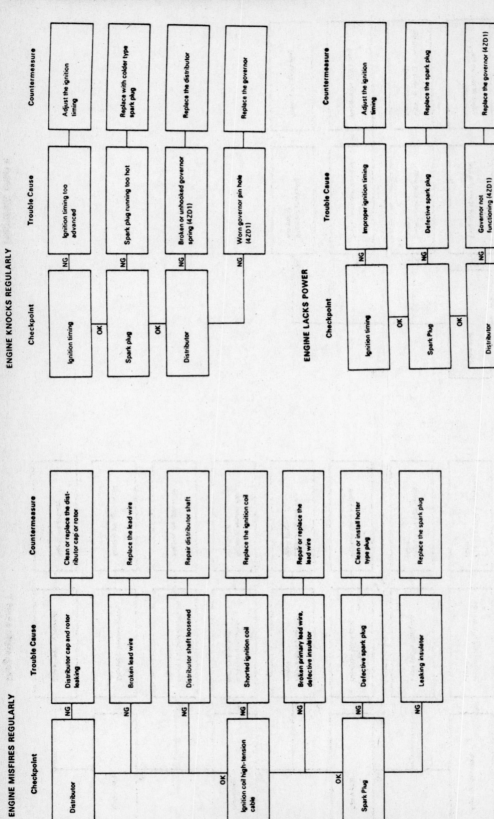

ENGINE KNOCKS REGULARLY

Checkpoint		Trouble Cause		Countermeasure
Ignition timing	NG	Ignition timing too advanced		Adjust the ignition timing
Spark plug	OK / NG	Spark plug running too hot		Replace with colder type spark plug
Distributor	OK / NG	Broken or unhooked governor spring (4ZD1)		Replace the distributor
	NG	Worn governor pin hole (4ZD1)		Replace the governor

ENGINE LACKS POWER

Checkpoint		Trouble Cause		Countermeasure
Ignition timing	NG	Improper ignition timing		Adjust the ignition timing
Spark Plug	OK / NG	Defective spark plug		Replace the spark plug
Distributor	OK / NG	Governor not functioning (4ZD1)		Replace the governor (4ZD1)

Diagnostic chart 10

ENGINE MISFIRES REGULARLY

Checkpoint		Trouble Cause		Countermeasure
Distributor	NG	Distributor cap and rotor leaking		Clean or replace the distributor cap or rotor
	NG	Broken lead wire		Replace the lead wire
	NG	Distributor shaft loosened		Repair distributor shaft
Ignition coil high-tension cable	NG	Shorted ignition coil		Replace the ignition coil
	NG	Broken primary lead wire, defective insulator		Repair or replace the lead wire
Spark Plug	OK / NG	Defective spark plug		Clean or install hotter type plug
	NG	Leaking insulator		Replace the spark plug

Diagnostic chart 9

V6 Engines, Trooper II and Rodeo
Diagnostic Chart 24

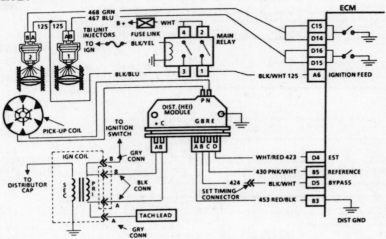

Ignition wiring diagram—V6 Trooper

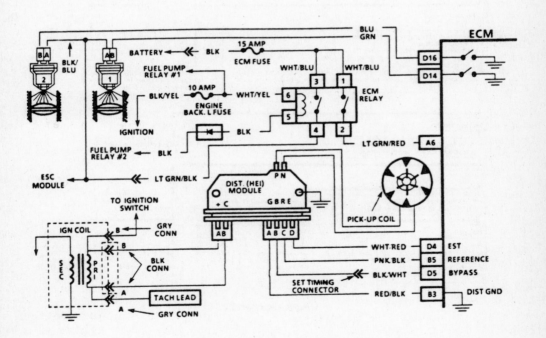

Ignition wiring diagram—V6 Rodeo

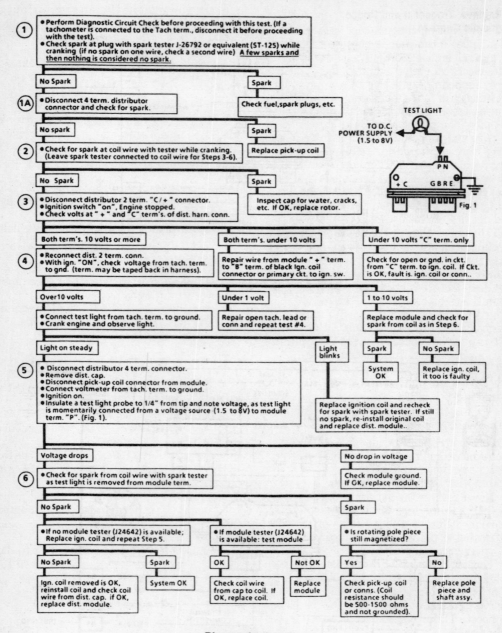

① • Perform Diagnostic Circuit Check before proceeding with this test. (If a tachometer is connected to the Tach term., disconnect it before proceeding with the test).
• Check spark at plug with spark tester J-26792 or equivalent (ST-125) while cranking (if no spark on one wire, check a second wire) A few sparks and then nothing is considered no spark.

| No Spark | | Spark |

①A • Disconnect 4 term. distributor connector and check for spark.

Check fuel, spark plugs, etc.

TEST LIGHT

| No spark | | Spark |

② • Check for spark at coil wire with tester while cranking. (Leave spark tester connected to coil wire for Steps 3-6).

Replace pick-up coil

TO D.C.
POWER SUPPLY
(1.5 to 8V)

| No Spark | | Spark |

③ • Disconnect distributor 2 term. "C / +" connector.
• Ignition switch "on", Engine stopped.
• Check volts at " + " and "C" term's. of dist. harn. conn.

Inspect cap for water, cracks, etc. If OK, replace rotor.

Fig. 1

| Both term's. 10 volts or more | Both term's. under 10 volts | Under 10 volts "C" term. only |

④ • Reconnect dist. 2 term. conn.
• With ign. "ON", check voltage from tach. term. to gnd. (term. may be taped back in harness).

Repair wire from module " + " term. to "B" term. of black Ign. coil connector or primary ckt. to ign. sw.

Check for open or gnd. in ckt. from "C" term. to ign. coil. If Ckt. is OK, fault is. ign. coil or conn..

| Over 10 volts | Under 1 volt | 1 to 10 volts |

• Connect test light from tach. term. to ground.
• Crank engine and observe light.

Repair open tach. lead or conn and repeat test #4.

Replace module and check for spark from coil as in Step 6.

| Light on steady | Light blinks | Spark | No Spark |

⑤ • Disconnect distributor 4 term. connector.
• Remove dist. cap.
• Disconnect pick-up coil connector from module.
• Connect voltmeter from tach. term. to ground.
• Ignition on.
• Insulate a test light probe to 1/4" from tip and note voltage, as test light is momentarily connected from a voltage source (1.5 to 8V) to module term. "P". (Fig. 1).

System OK

Replace ign. coil, it too is faulty

Replace ignition coil and recheck for spark with spark tester. If still no spark, re-install original coil and replace dist. module..

| Voltage drops | No drop in voltage |

⑥ • Check for spark from coil wire with spark tester as test light is removed from module term.

Check module ground. If OK, replace module.

| No Spark | Spark |

• If no module tester (J24642) is available; Replace ign. coil and repeat Step 5.

• If module tester (J24642) is available: test module

• Is rotating pole piece still magnetized?

| No Spark | Spark | OK | Not OK | Yes | No |

Ign. coil removed is OK, reinstall coil and check coil wire from dist. cap. if OK, replace dist. module.

System OK

Check coil wire from cap to coil. If OK, replace coil.

Replace module

Check pick-up coil or conns. (Coil resistance should be 500-1500 ohms and not grounded).

Replace pole piece and shaft assy.

Diagnostic chart 24

Alternator

The alternating current generator (alternator) supplies a continuous output of electrical energy at all engine speeds. The alternator generates electrical energy and recharges the battery by supplying it with electrical current. This unit consists of four main assemblies: two end-frame assemblies, a rotor assembly and a stator assembly. The rotor assembly is supported in the drive end-frame by a roller bearing. These bearings are lubricated during assembly and require no maintenance. There are six diodes in the end-frame assembly. These diodes are electrical check valves that also change the alternating current developed within the stator windings to a direct current (DC) at the output (BAT) terminal. Three of these diodes are negative and are mounted flush with the end-frame, while the other three are positive and are mounted into a strip called a heat sink. The positive diodes are easily identified as the ones within the small cavities or depressions.

The V6 engines experienced engineering changes, which are: The elimination of the diode trio and the reduction of the external wiring connectors from three-to-two wires.

NOTE: *The new alternators are not serviceable and no periodic maintenance is required.*

ALTERNATOR PRECAUTIONS

To prevent damage to the on-board computer, alternator and regulator, the following precautionary measures must be taken when working with the electrical system.

• Never reverse the battery connections. Always check the battery polarity visually. This is to be done before any connections are made to be sure that all of the connections correspond to the battery ground polarity.

• Booster batteries for starting must be connected properly. Make sure that the positive cable of the booster battery is connected to the positive terminal of the battery that is getting the boost. This applies to both negative and ground cables.

• Make sure the ignition switch is OFF when connecting or disconnecting any electrical component, especially on trucks equipped with an on-board computer control system.

• Disconnect the battery cables before using a fast charger; the charger has a tendency to force current through the diodes in the opposite direction for which they were designed. This burns out the diodes.

• Never use a fast charger as a booster for starting the vehicle.

• Never disconnect the voltage regulator while the engine is running.

• Do not ground the alternator output terminal.

• Do not operated the alternator on an open circuit with the field energized.

• Do not attempt to polarize an alternator.

REMOVAL AND INSTALLATION

Except V6 Engine and FWD Vehicles

1. **Disconnect the negative battery cable.** If equipped with an air pump, it may be necessary to remove it.
2. Disconnect and label the alternator wiring.
3. Remove the alternator pivot bolt on the lower part of the alternator. Remove the drive belt from the pulley.
4. Remove the alternator mounting bolt(s) and the alternator from the engine.

To install:

5. Install the alternator.
6. Adjust the belt tension and tighten the alternator mounting bolts.
7. Reconnect the alternator's wiring connectors. Connect the negative battery cable.

V6 Engine

1. **Disconnect the negative battery cable.**
2. Remove the terminal plug and the battery lead from the rear of the alternator.
3. Remove the drive belt.
4. Remove the air pump bracket bolt from the rear of the alternator.
5. Remove the mounting bolts from the front of the alternator and the alternator from the vehicle.

To install:

6. Install the alternator and the mounting bolts.
7. Install the drive belt.
8. Torque the lower mounting bolt to 26 ft. lbs. (35 Nm), the upper mounting bolt to 18 ft.

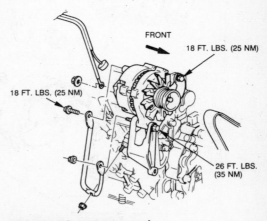

FRONT

18 FT. LBS. (25 NM)

18 FT. LBS. (25 NM)

26 FT. LBS. (35 NM)

V6 engine alternator removal

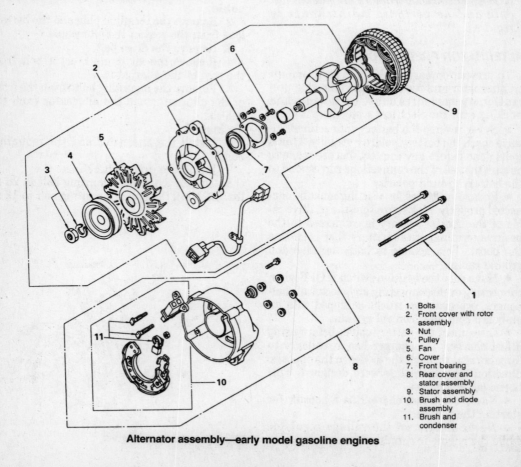

Installation steps
To install, follow the removal steps in the reverse order.

Removal steps
1. Right tie-rod end (4WD only)
2. Right lower ball joint (4WD only)
3. Right drive shaft (4WD only)
4. Bolt, adjust plate
5. Wiring connector
6. Bolts, bracket
7. Generator and bracket
8. Generator

Alternator removal—FWD vehicles

lbs. (25 Nm) and the air pump bracket bolt to 18 ft. lbs. (25 Nm).

9. Connect the terminal connector and the battery lead to the rear of the alternator. Reconnect the negative battery cable.

Front Wheel Drive (FWD) Vehicles

1. **Disconnect the negative (−) battery cable.**

2. Remove the right tie rod end, lower ball joint and driveshaft (4WD only).

3. Remove the adjuster plate bolt.

4. Disconnect the electrical connector.

5. Remove the alternator bracket bolts, alternator and bracket.

To install:

1. Install the alternator bracket bolts, alternator and bracket.

2. Connect the electrical connector.

3. Install the adjuster plate bolt.

4. Install the right tie rod end, lower ball joint and driveshaft (4WD only).

5. Connect the negative (−) battery cable.

OVERHAUL AND TESTING

Early Model Engines with External Voltage Regulator

1. Remove the alternator from the vehicle.

2. Remove the through bolts and front cover.

3. Remove the shaft nut, pulley and fan.

4. Remove the cover and front bearing.

1. Bolts
2. Front cover with rotor assembly
3. Nut
4. Pulley
5. Fan
6. Cover
7. Front bearing
8. Rear cover and stator assembly
9. Stator assembly
10. Brush and diode assembly
11. Brush and condenser

Alternator assembly—early model gasoline engines

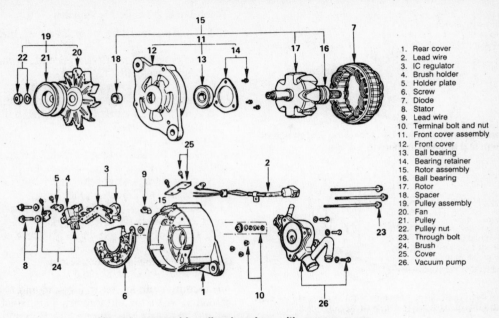

1. Rear cover
2. Lead wire
3. IC regulator
4. Brush holder
5. Holder plate
6. Screw
7. Diode
8. Stator
9. Lead wire
10. Terminal bolt and nut
11. Front cover assembly
12. Front cover
13. Ball bearing
14. Bearing retainer
15. Rotor assembly
16. Ball bearing
17. Rotor
18. Spacer
19. Pulley assembly
20. Fan
21. Pulley
22. Pulley nut
23. Through bolt
24. Brush
25. Cover
26. Vacuum pump

Alternator assembly—diesel engines with vacuum pump

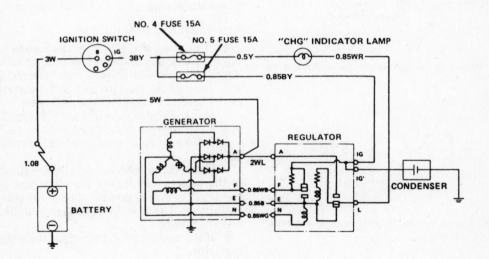

Alternator electrical wiring—early model gasoline engines with external regulator

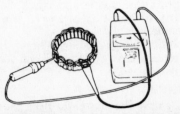

Measure the resistance between stator coils—standard, 1 mΩ or above

Measure resistance between each diode terminal and holder—nearly zero ohms in one direction and infinite in the other direction

Check the rotor opens by measuring resistance between slip rings—standard is 4 ohms

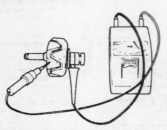

Checking resistance between rotor core and (+) side of slip ring—standard, 1 mΩ or above

Check continuity across stator coils—should be continuity

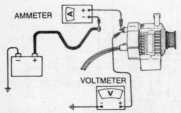

Charging circuit check—internal voltage regulator, except V6 engines

5. Remove the rear cover and stator assembly.

6. Remove the brush and diode assembly.

7. Test the rotor for an open circuit by measuring the resistance between the slip rings. The normal resistance is 4Ω.

8. Check the resistance between the rotor core and the positive side of the slip ring. The resistance should be 1 mΩ or above.

9. Make a continuity test across the stator coil. There should be continuity.

10. Check the resistance between the stator coils and the core using an ohmmeter. The resistance should be 1 mΩ.

11. Measure the resistance between each di-

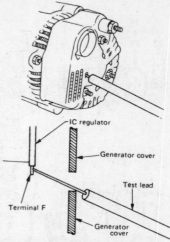

Grounding F terminal to check voltage

ode terminal and holder in forward and reverse direction with an ohmmeter. The resistance should be nearly zero in one direction and infinite in the other.

**Internally Mounted Voltage Regulator
Except V6 Engines**

CHARGING CIRCUIT CHECK

1. Disconnect the wire from the battery terminal at the alternator and connect it to the negative terminal of a circuit tester (ammeter).

2. Connect the positive lead of the ammeter to the battery terminal of the alternator.

3. Run the engine from idle to 1900 rpm. The standard amperage should be less than 10.

4. If the reading is larger, replace the voltage regulator.

5. Connect the positive lead of the voltmeter to the battery terminal of the alternator and the negative lead to ground. Run the engine at 1900 rpm. The standard voltage should be 14.2–14.8 volts.

6. If the reading is larger, replace the voltage regulator.

7. If the reading is smaller, check the regulator and alternator.

8. Ground the F (field) terminal of the regulator by inserting a tool through the alternator cover.

9. Start the engine and check the voltage reading of the battery terminal of the alternator.

10. If the voltage reading is larger than specified, replace the regulator. If not, inspect the alternator.

DISASSEMBLY

1. Remove the alternator from the vehicle.

2. Remove the long through bolts, nut and pulley.

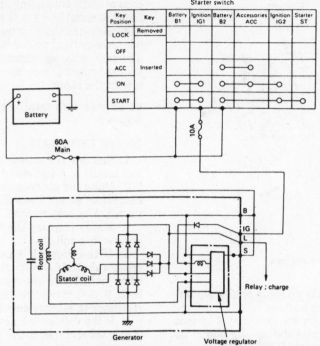

Key Position	Key	Battery B1	Ignition IG1	Battery B2	Accessories ACC	Ignition IG2	Starter ST
LOCK	Removed						
OFF							
ACC	Inserted				○——○		
ON		○——○		○——○		○——○	
START		○——○		○			○——○

Starter switch

Wiring for internal mounted voltage regulator—except V6 engines

3. Remove the rotor assembly, bearing retainer and front bearing.

4. Remove the front cover and rectifier retaining nuts.

5. Remove the rear cover, stator assembly and nuts.

6. Remove the fan guide, battery terminal and condenser.

7. Remove the diode assembly and brush/regulator assembly.

8. **Test the following components using an ohmmeter.**

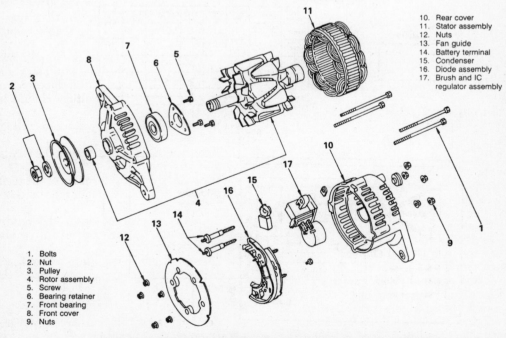

10. Rear cover
11. Stator assembly
12. Nuts
13. Fan guide
14. Battery terminal
15. Condenser
16. Diode assembly
17. Brush and IC regulator assembly

1. Bolts
2. Nut
3. Pulley
4. Rotor assembly
5. Screw
6. Bearing retainer
7. Front bearing
8. Front cover
9. Nuts

Alternator disassembly—internal mounted regulator, except V6 engines

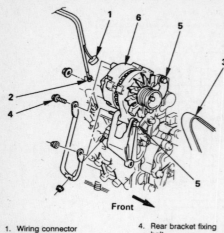

Front

1. Wiring connector
2. Battery lead wire
3. Drive belt
4. Rear bracket fixing bolt
5. Mounting bolts
6. Alternator

Alternator removal—V6 engines

NOTE: *Refer to the previous section for testing procedure illustrations.*

9. Test the rotor for an open circuit by measuring the resistance between the slip rings. The normal resistance is 2.63Ω or less.

10. Check the resistance between the rotor core and the positive side of the slip ring. The resistance should be 1 mΩ or above.

11. Make a continuity test across the stator coil. There should be continuity.

12. Check the resistance between the stator coils and the core using an ohmmeter. The resistance should be 1 mΩ or more.

13. Measure the resistance between each diode terminal and holder in forward and reverse direction with an ohmmeter. The resistance should be nearly zero in one direction and infinite in the other.

V6 Engine with Internally Mounted Voltage Regulator

CHARGING CIRCUIT CHECK

1. Remove the alternator from the vehicle and install in a test stand.

2. Make the connections as shown in the illustration, except leave the carbon pile disconnected. The battery must be fully charged.

3. Slowly increase the alternator speed and observe the voltage.

4. If the voltage is uncontrolled and increases above 16.0 volts, the rotor field is shorted or grounded or the regulator is defective, or both. A defective rotor field coil can cause the regulator to become defective.

5. If the voltage is below 16.0 volts, increase the speed and adjust the carbon pile to obtain maximum amperes output. Maintain a voltage above 13.0 volts.

6. If the output is within 15 amperes of the rated output, the alternator is good. If the output is not within 15 amperes of rated output, the alternator is defective and requires replacement. The CS-130 alternator is not serviceable.

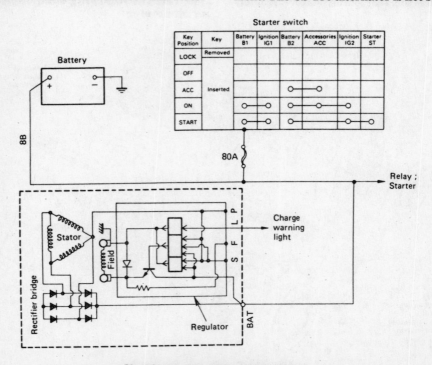

Charging system wiring—V6 engines

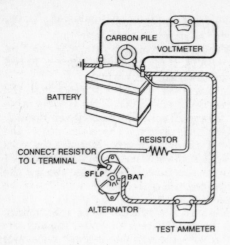

Testing charging system—V6 engines

TABLE 1

TESTER LIGHTS			INSTRUMENT PANEL CHARGE INDICATOR LIGHT	CONDITION
RED	YELLOW	GREEN		
OFF	OFF	ON	OFF	Normal
ON	ON	OFF	ON	Bad positive diode.
ON	ON	OFF	OFF	Bad negative diode.
ON	ON	OFF	DIM LIGHT or OFF	Bad auxiliary diode.
ON	OFF	OFF	ON	Bad rotor coil.
ON	OFF	OFF	OFF	Bad internal (IC) regulator.
ON or OFF	ON	ON	DIM LIGHT or OFF	Bad stator coil.
OFF	ON	ON	DIM LIGHT or OFF	Bad auxiliary diode. Bad stator coil. Bad negative diode.

TABLE 2

TESTER LIGHTS			INSTRUMENT PANEL CHARGE INDICATOR LIGHT	CONDITION
RED	YELLOW	GREEN		
OFF	OFF	ON	OFF	Bad positive diode.
ON	OFF	OFF	OFF	Bad rotor coil. Bad internal (IC) regulator. Poor or no brush contact.

Charging system diagnosis tables—V6 engines

DISASSEMBLY

No periodic maintenance on the alternator is required. The CS-130 alternator is serviced as a complete assembly ONLY. No internal repair parts are available.

External Voltage Regulator

An external voltage regulator is used with the early model engine. The regulator is mounted on the left inner fender.

ADJUSTMENT

1. Remove the regulator from the vehicle and remove the regulator cover.

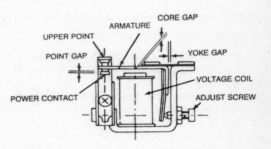

Voltage regulator adjustment—external type

Troubleshooting Basic Charging System Problems

Problem	Cause	Solution
Noisy alternator	• Loose mountings • Loose drive pulley • Worn bearings • Brush noise • Internal circuits shorted (High pitched whine)	• Tighten mounting bolts • Tighten pulley • Replace alternator • Replace alternator • Replace alternator
Squeal when starting engine or accelerating	• Glazed or loose belt	• Replace or adjust belt
Indicator light remains on or ammeter indicates discharge (engine running)	• Broken fan belt • Broken or disconnected wires • Internal alternator problems • Defective voltage regulator	• Install belt • Repair or connect wiring • Replace alternator • Replace voltage regulator
Car light bulbs continually burn out—battery needs water continually	• Alternator/regulator overcharging	• Replace voltage regulator/alternator
Car lights flare on acceleration	• Battery low • Internal alternator/regulator problems	• Charge or replace battery • Replace alternator/regulator
Low voltage output (alternator light flickers continually or ammeter needle wanders)	• Loose or worn belt • Dirty or corroded connections • Internal alternator/regulator problems	• Replace or adjust belt • Clean or replace connections • Replace alternator or regulator

2. If the points are pitted, clean them carefully with fine emery paper.

3. Check and adjust the core gap first and then the point gap.

4. Adjust the core gap by loosening the screws attaching the contact set to the yoke. Move the contact set up or down as required. The standard core gap is 0.6–1.0 mm (0.024–0.039 in.). Tighten the attaching screw.

5. Adjust the point gap by loosening the screw attaching the upper contact. Move the upper contact up or down as required. The standard point gap is 0.3–0.4mm (0.012–0.016 in.).

6. Adjust the regulated voltage by turning the adjusting screw. Turn the adjusting screw in to increase voltage and out to reduce voltage. When the correct adjustment is obtained, secure the adjusting screw by tig'..cening the locknut. The regulated voltage is 13.8–14.8V.

7. Install the regulator cover, reconnect the electrical leads and install the regulator.

REMOVAL AND INSTALLATION

1. Disconnect the negative battery cable.

2. Disconnect and label the electrical leads at the regulator.

3. Remove the 2 regulator mounting screws and remove the regulator.

To install:

4. Install the voltage regulator.

5. Connect the electrical leads to the regulator.

6. Connect the negative battery cable.

Internal Regulator, Except V6

TESTING

1. Disconnect the negative (–) battery cable.

2. Remove the alternator from the vehicle.

3. Connect a variable resistor, two 12V batteries, a fixed resistor and a voltmeter to the regulator as shown in the illustration.

4. Measure the voltage V1 across the first battery BAT1. If the reading is between 10 and 13 volts, the battery is normal.

5. Measure the voltage V3 across both the batteries BAT1 and BAT2. If the reading is between 20 and 26 volts, the batteries air normal.

6. Gradually increase the resistance of the variable resistor from zero. Measure the voltage V2. Check to see that the voltage across V1 changes at this time. If there is no change, the voltage regulator is faulty and must be replaced.

7. Measure the voltage at V4 (the voltage across the variable resistor center tap and terminal E with the variable resistor resistance held constant. The measured voltage should be within the specified 14.0–14.6 volts. If not, the regulator must be replaced.

REMOVAL AND INSTALLATION

1. Remove the alternator from the vehicle.

2. Remove the through bolts and pry case apart.

3. Remove the mounting nuts holding the BAT terminal, the diode and brush holder. Separate the rear cover from the stator.

4. Remove the stator assembly. Cut the diode soldering points, then remove the stator.

5. Remove the nut, fan guide, battery terminal, condenser, diode bridge and voltage regulator. Use a drill press to remove the staked rivet attaching the diode and the brush holder terminal. Break the solder connection between the diode L terminal and the brush holder.

Battery

REMOVAL AND INSTALLATION

1. Disconnect the negative battery terminal, then the positive battery terminal.

2. Remove the battery holddown retainer.

3. Remove the battery from the vehicle.

4. Inspect the battery, the cables and the battery carrier for damage.

5. To install, reverse the removal procedures. Torque the battery retainer to 11 ft. lbs. (15 Nm), the top bar to 96 inch lbs. (11 Nm), if so equipped and the battery cable terminals to 120 inch lbs. (14 Nm).

Starter

REMOVAL AND INSTALLATION

4-Cylinder Engines

1. Disconnect the negative battery cable.

2. If equipped, it may be necessary to disconnect and remove the EGR pipe.

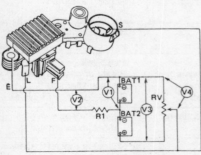

1. Fixed resistor (R1): 10Ω/3W
2. Variable resistor (Rv): 0-300Ω/12W
3. Batteries (BAT1, BAT2): 12V (2 batteries)
4. DC voltmeter: 0-50V/ 0.5 steps (4 check points)

Voltage regulator test leads—internal regulator, except V6 engines

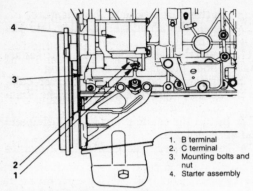

1. B terminal
2. C terminal
3. Mounting bolts and nut
4. Starter assembly

Starter motor removal—4-cyl. engines

3. Disconnect and label the starter wiring at the starter.

4. Remove the starter-to-engine bolts and the starter from the vehicle.

To install:

4. Installation the starter to the engine.

5. Connect the electrical connectors to the starter.

6. If the EGR pipe was removed, install it.

7. Connect the negative battery cable.

V6 Engine

1. Disconnect the negative battery cable.

2. Raise and safely support the vehicle.

3. Label and disconnect the electrical connectors from the starter.

4. Remove the starter-to-engine mounting bolts.

5. Lower the starter from the engine. If any shims are present, keep them for reinstallation purposes.

To install:

6. Install the starter and shims, if equipped, to the engine. Torque the bolts to 30 ft. lbs. (40 Nm).

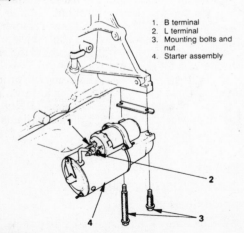

1. B terminal
2. L terminal
3. Mounting bolts and nut
4. Starter assembly

Starter motor removal—V6 engine

7. Reconnect the electrical connectors to the starter.

8. Lower the vehicle.

9. Connect the negative battery cable.

SOLENOID REPLACEMENT

1. Disconnect the negative (−) battery cable.

2. Remove the starter motor from the vehicle.

3. Disconnect the solenoid-to-starter lead wire.

4. Remove the solenoid mounting bolts and solenoid. Pull out the torsion spring of the solenoid switch, if so equipped. On some models, it may be necessary to remove the starter assembly through bolts from the yoke to remove the solenoid.

To install:

1. Install the solenoid with any adjustment shims.

2. Torque the bolts to 15 ft. lbs. (20 Nm).

3. Connect the starter-to-solenoid electrical lead.

4. Install the starter through bolts if removed.

5. Install the starter motor with an shims, connect the wiring and battery cable.

6. Check for proper operation.

OVERHAUL

Non-Reduction Type

DISASSEMBLY AND ASSEMBLY

1. Position the starter in a soft jawed vise. Disconnect the field coil wire from the solenoid terminal.

2. Remove the solenoid mounting screws and work the solenoid from the shift fork. Remove the bearing cover, the armature shaft lock, the washer, the spring and the seal.

3. Remove the commutator end frame cover through bolts, the cover, the brushes and the brush plate.

4. Slide the field frame from over the armature. Remove the shift lever pivot bolt, the rubber gasket and the metal plate.

5. Remove the armature assembly and the shift lever from the drive end housing. Press the stop collar from the snapring, then remove the snapring, the stop collar and the clutch assembly.

6. If the brushes are worn more than ½ the length of new brushes or are oil-soaked, should be replaced; the new brushes are 16mm (0.630 in.) long.

7. Do not immerse the starter clutch unit in cleaning solvent as the solvent will wash the lubricant from the clutch. Place the drive unit on the armature shaft, then, while holding the armature, rotate the pinion.

NOTE: *The drive pinion should rotate smoothly in one direction only. The pinion may not rotate easily but as long as it rotates smoothly it is in good condition. If the clutch unit does not function properly or if the pinion is worn, chipped or burred, replace the unit.*

To Assemble:

8. Lubricate the armature shaft and splines with lubricant.

9. Install the clutch, the stop collar, the lock ring and the shift fork onto the armature.

10. Install the armature assembly into the drive end housing.

11. Install the field frame housing over the armature and onto the drive end housing.

12. Position the brushes into the brush holder and position the brush holder over the armature's commutator.

13. Install the commutator end housing and the through bolts.

14. Install the cap end gasket, the armature

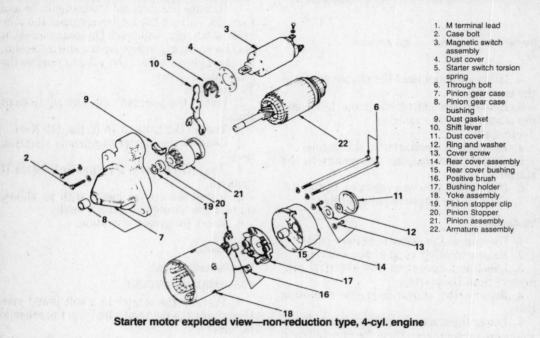

1. M terminal lead
2. Case bolt
3. Magnetic switch assembly
4. Dust cover
5. Starter switch torsion spring
6. Through bolt
7. Pinion gear case
8. Pinion gear case bushing
9. Dust gasket
10. Shift lever
11. Dust cover
12. Ring and washer
13. Cover screw
14. Rear cover assembly
15. Rear cover bushing
16. Positive brush
17. Bushing holder
18. Yoke assembly
19. Pinion stopper clip
20. Pinion Stopper
21. Pinion assembly
22. Armature assembly

Starter motor exploded view—non-reduction type, 4-cyl. engine

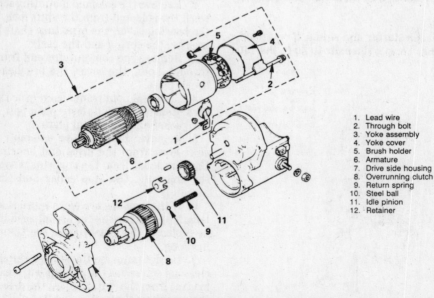

1. Lead wire
2. Through bolt
3. Yoke assembly
4. Yoke cover
5. Brush holder
6. Armature
7. Drive side housing
8. Overrunning clutch
9. Return spring
10. Steel ball
11. Idle pinion
12. Retainer

Starter motor exploded view—reduction gear type

brake spring, the armature plate and the commutator end cap.

Reduction Gear Type

DISASSEMBLY AND ASSEMBLY

1. Position the starter in a soft jawed vise. Remove the nut and disconnect the motor wire from the magnetic switch terminal.

2. Remove the through bolts and pull the field frame (with the armature) from the magnetic switch assembly.

3. Remove the starter housing to magnetic switch assembly bolts and separate the housing from the assembly. Remove the pinion gear, the pinion retainer/bearings and the clutch assembly.

4. Using a magnetic finger, remove the spring and the steel ball from the hole in the clutch assembly shaft. Remove the field frame end cover.

5. Using a small pry bar, separate the brush springs, then remove the brushes from the brush holder and pull the brush holder from the field frame.

6. Remove the armature from the field frame. Using an ohmmeter, make sure there is no continuity between the commutator and the armature coil core. If there is continuity, replace the armature.

7. Using an ohmmeter, check for continuity between the commutator segments. If there is no continuity between any of the segments, replace the armature.

8. If the commutator is dirty, burnt or the runout exceeds 0.05mm (0.002 in.), use a lathe to reface the surface; do not machine the diameter to less than 29mm (1.140 in.) diameter.

9. Using an ohmmeter, make sure there is continuity between the lead wire and the brush lead of the field coil. If there is no continuity, replace the field frame.

10. Using an ohmmeter, make sure there is no continuity between the field coil and the field frame. If there is continuity, replace the field frame.

11. If the brush length is less than 10mm (0.394 in.), replace the brush and dress with emery cloth.

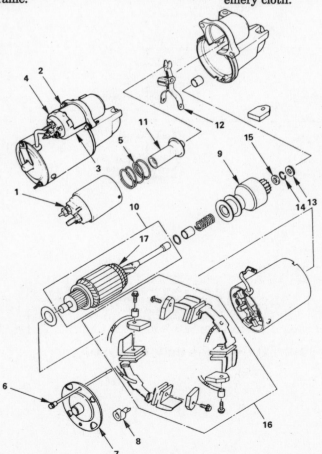

1. Nut
2. Solenoid bolt
3. Solenoid bracket
4. Solenoid
5. Plunger return spring
6. Through bolt
7. Commutator end frame
8. Brush hold spring
9. Field and frame assembly
10. Armature
11. Plunger
12. Shift lever
13. Thrust collar
14. Retaining ring
15. Pinion stop collar
16. Drive assembly
17. Armature

Starter motor exploded view—non-reduction type, V6 engine

DIAGNOSIS

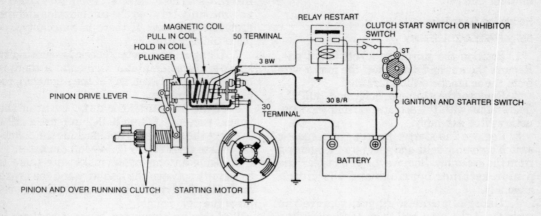

V6 starter motor circuit

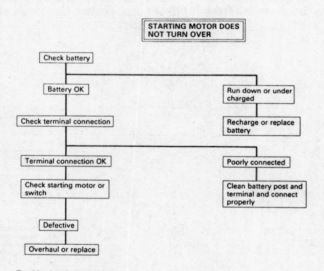

Trouble shooting procedure

Turn on headlights and starter switch.

Headlights go out or dim considerably.	a) Battery undercharged. b) Starting motor oil circuit shorted. c) Starting motor parts defective.
Headlights stay bright.	a) Starting motor circuit open. b) Starting motor coil open. c) Starting switch defective.

Diagnosis chart 1—V6 engine starter, others similar

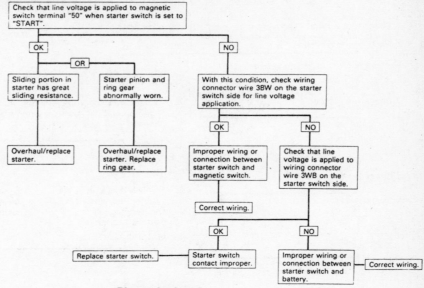

Pinion gear-ring gear engagement is improper.

Check that line voltage is applied to magnetic switch terminal "50" when starter switch is set to "START".

OK — OR

Sliding portion in starter has great sliding resistance.

Starter pinion and ring gear abnormally worn.

NO

With this condition, check wiring connector wire 3BW on the starter switch side for line voltage application.

Overhaul/replace starter.

Overhaul/replace starter. Replace ring gear.

OK

Improper wiring or connection between starter switch and magnetic switch.

NO

Check that line voltage is applied to wiring connector wire 3WB on the starter switch side.

Correct wiring.

OK

Replace starter switch.

Starter switch contact improper.

NO

Improper wiring or connection between starter switch and battery.

Correct wiring.

Diagnosis chart 2

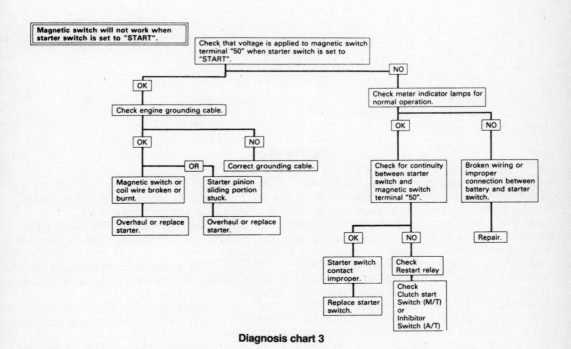

Magnetic switch will not work when starter switch is set to "START".

Check that voltage is applied to magnetic switch terminal "50" when starter switch is set to "START".

NO

Check meter indicator lamps for normal operation.

OK

Check engine grounding cable.

OK — OR

Magnetic switch or coil wire broken or burnt.

Starter pinion sliding portion stuck.

NO

Correct grounding cable.

Overhaul or replace starter.

Overhaul or replace starter.

OK

Check for continuity between starter switch and magnetic switch terminal "50".

NO

Broken wiring or improper connection between battery and starter switch.

OK

Starter switch contact improper.

NO

Check Restart relay

Check Clutch start Switch (M/T) or Inhibitor Switch (A/T)

Replace starter switch.

Repair.

Diagnosis chart 3

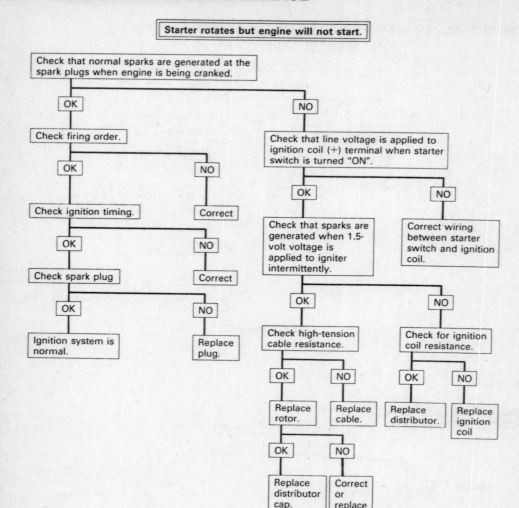

Diagnosis chart 4

12. Check the gear teeth for wear or damage, if damaged, replace them. Turn the clutch assembly pinion clockwise and make sure it rotates freely, try to turn the pinion counterclockwise and make sure it locks. If the pinion does not respond correctly, replace it.

13. While applying inward force on the bearings, turn each by hand; if resistance or sticking is noticed, replace the bearings. To replace the bearings, use the tool 09286–46011 or equivalent, to pull the bearing(s) from the armature shaft. Using the tool 09285–76010 or equivalent, and an arbor press, press the new bearing(s) onto the armature shaft.

14. Using an ohmmeter, check for continuity between the grounded terminal and the insulated terminal, then between the grounded terminal and the housing. If there is no continuity in either case, replace the magnetic switch assembly.

To Assemble:

15. Lubricate the gears, the shafts and bearings with high temperature grease.

16. Install the over-running clutch, the pinion and the retainers with the rollers into the housing.

17. Install the spring to the magnetic switch and assembly the housing and the magnetic switch.

18. Install the brushes into the brush holder; make sure the positive brush leads are not grounded.

19. Install the rear end frame to the yoke, engage the tab with the wire grommet and install the cover.

20. Install the yoke to the magnetic switch, engage the tab on the yoke with the magnetic switch notch.

21. To complete the installation, reverse the removal procedures.

ENGINE MECHANICAL

NOTE: *Disconnecting the negative battery cable on some vehicles may interfere with the functions of the on board computer systems and may require the computer to undergo a relearning process, once the negative battery cable is reconnected.*

Engine Overhaul Tips

Most engine overhaul procedures are fairly standard. In addition to specific parts replacement procedures and complete specifications for your individual engine, this Section also is a guide to accept rebuilding procedures. Examples of standard rebuilding practice are shown and should be used along with specific details concerning your particular engine.

Competent and accurate machine shop services will ensure maximum performance, reliability and engine life.

On most instances it is more profitable for the do-it-yourself mechanic to remove, clean and inspect the component(s), buy the necessary parts and deliver these to a shop for actual machine work.

On the other hand, much of the rebuilding work (crankshaft, block, bearings, piston rods, and other components) is well within the scope of the do-it-yourself mechanic.

TOOLS

The tools required for an engine overhaul or parts replacement will depend on the depth of your involvement. With a few exceptions, they will be the tools found in a mechanic's tool kit (see Chapter 1). More in-depth work will require any or all of the following:
- A dial indicator (reading in thousandths) mounted on a universal base
- Micrometers and telescope gauges
- Jaw and screw-type pullers
- Scraper
- Valve spring compressor
- Ring groove cleaner
- Piston ring expander and compressor
- Ridge reamer
- Cylinder hone or glaze breaker
- Plastigage®
- Engine stand

Use of most of these tools is illustrated in this Section. Many can be rented for a one-time use from a local parts jobber or tool supply house specializing in automotive work.

Occasionally, the use of special tools is called for. See the information on Special Tools and Safety Notice in the front of this book before substituting another tool.

INSPECTION TECHNIQUES

Procedures and specifications are given in this Section for inspecting, cleaning and assessing the wear limits of most major components. Other procedures such as Magnaflux® and Zyglo® can be used to locate material flaws and stress cracks. Magnaflux® is a magnetic process applicable only to ferrous materials. The Zyglo® process coats the material with a fluorescent dye penetrant and can be used on any material. Check for suspected surface cracks can be more readily made using spot check dye. The dye is sprayed onto the suspected area, wiped off and the area sprayed with a developer. Cracks will show up brightly.

OVERHAUL TIPS

Aluminum has become extremely popular for use in engines, due to its low weight. Observe the following precautions when handling aluminum parts:
- Never hot tank aluminum parts (the caustic hot tank solution will eat the aluminum.
- Remove all aluminum parts (identification tag, etc.) from engine parts prior to the tanking.
- Always coat threads lightly with engine oil or anti-seize compounds before installation, to prevent seizure.
- Never over-torque bolts or spark plugs especially in aluminum for you may strip the threads.

Stripped threads in any component can be repaired using any of several commercial repair kits (Heli-Coil®, Microdot®, Keenserts®, etc.).

When assembling the engine, any parts that will have frictional contact must be prelubed to provide lubrication at initial start-up. Any product specifically formulated for this purpose can be used, but engine oil is not recommended as a prelube.

When semi-permanent (locked, but removable) installation of bolts or nuts is desired, threads should be cleaned and coated with Loctite® or other similar, commercial non-hardening sealant.

REPAIRING DAMAGED THREADS

Several methods of repairing damaged threads are available. Heli-Coil® (shown here), Keenserts® and Microdot® are among the most widely used. All involve basically the same principle—drilling out stripped threads, tapping the hole and installing a prewound insert—making welding, plugging and oversize fasteners unnecessary.

Two types of thread repair inserts are usually supplied—a standard type for most Inch Coarse, Inch Fine, Metric Course and Metric Fine thread sizes and a spark lug type to fit

Troubleshooting Basic Starting System Problems

Problem	Cause	Solution
Starter motor rotates engine slowly	• Battery charge low or battery defective	• Charge or replace battery
	• Defective circuit between battery and starter motor	• Clean and tighten, or replace cables
	• Low load current	• Bench-test starter motor. Inspect for worn brushes and weak brush springs.
	• High load current	• Bench-test starter motor. Check engine for friction, drag or coolant in cylinders. Check ring gear-to-pinion gear clearance.
Starter motor will not rotate engine	• Battery charge low or battery defective	• Charge or replace battery
	• Faulty solenoid	• Check solenoid ground. Repair or replace as necessary.
	• Damage drive pinion gear or ring gear	• Replace damaged gear(s)
	• Starter motor engagement weak	• Bench-test starter motor
	• Starter motor rotates slowly with high load current	• Inspect drive yoke pull-down and point gap, check for worn end bushings, check ring gear clearance
	• Engine seized	• Repair engine
Starter motor drive will not engage (solenoid known to be good)	• Defective contact point assembly	• Repair or replace contact point assembly
	• Inadequate contact point assembly ground	• Repair connection at ground screw
	• Defective hold-in coil	• Replace field winding assembly
Starter motor drive will not disengage	• Starter motor loose on flywheel housing	• Tighten mounting bolts
	• Worn drive end busing	• Replace bushing
	• Damaged ring gear teeth	• Replace ring gear or driveplate
	• Drive yoke return spring broken or missing	• Replace spring
Starter motor drive disengages prematurely	• Weak drive assembly thrust spring	• Replace drive mechanism
	• Hold-in coil defective	• Replace field winding assembly
Low load current	• Worn brushes	• Replace brushes
	• Weak brush springs	• Replace springs

most spark plug port sizes. Consult the individual manufacturer's catalog to determine exact applications. Typical thread repair kits will contain a selection of prewound threaded inserts, a tap (corresponding to the outside diameter threads of the insert) and an installation tool.

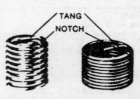

Standard thread repair insert (left) and the spark plug repair insert (right)

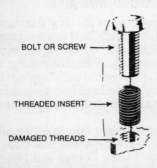

Using the thread repair insert to fix a damaged hole

Using a specified drill to drill out the damaged thread. Drill completely through the hole or to the bottom of a blind hole

Standard Torque Specifications and Fastener Markings

In the absence of specific torques, the following chart can be used as a guide to the maximum safe torque of a particular size/grade of fastener.

- There is no torque difference for fine or coarse threads.
- Torque values are based on clean, dry threads. Reduce the value by 10% if threads are oiled prior to assembly.
- The torque required for aluminum components or fasteners is considerably less.

U.S. Bolts

SAE Grade Number	1 or 2			5			6 or 7		
Number of lines always 2 less than the grade number.									
Bolt Size (Inches)—(Thread)	Maximum Torque			Maximum Torque			Maximum Torque		
	Ft./Lbs.	Kgm	Nm	Ft./Lbs.	Kgm	Nm	Ft./Lbs.	Kgm	Nm
¼ — 20	5	0.7	6.8	8	1.1	10.8	10	1.4	13.5
— 28	6	0.8	8.1	10	1.4	13.6			
5/16 — 18	11	1.5	14.9	17	2.3	23.0	19	2.6	25.8
— 24	13	1.8	17.6	19	2.6	25.7			
3/8 — 16	18	2.5	24.4	31	4.3	42.0	34	4.7	46.0
— 24	20	2.75	27.1	35	4.8	47.5			
7/16 — 14	28	3.8	37.0	49	6.8	66.4	55	7.6	74.5
— 20	30	4.2	40.7	55	7.6	74.5			
½ — 13	39	5.4	52.8	75	10.4	101.7	85	11.75	115.2
— 20	41	5.7	55.6	85	11.7	115.2			
9/16 — 12	51	7.0	69.2	110	15.2	149.1	120	16.6	162.7
— 18	55	7.6	74.5	120	16.6	162.7			
5/8 — 11	83	11.5	112.5	150	20.7	203.3	167	23.0	226.5
— 18	95	13.1	128.8	170	23.5	230.5			
¾ — 10	105	14.5	142.3	270	37.3	366.0	280	38.7	379.6
— 16	115	15.9	155.9	295	40.8	400.0			
7/8 — 9	160	22.1	216.9	395	54.6	535.5	440	60.9	596.5
— 14	175	24.2	237.2	435	60.1	589.7			
1 — 8	236	32.5	318.6	590	81.6	799.9	660	91.3	894.8
— 14	250	34.6	338.9	660	91.3	849.8			

Metric Bolts

Relative Strength Marking	4.6, 4.8			8.8		
Bolt Markings						
Bolt Size Thread Size x Pitch (mm)	Maximum Torque			Maximum Torque		
	Ft./Lbs.	Kgm	Nm	Ft./Lbs.	Kgm	Nm
6 x 1.0	2–3	.2–.4	3–4	3–6	.4–.8	5–8
8 x 1.25	6–8	.8–1	8–12	9–14	1.2–1.9	13–19
10 x 1.25	12–17	1.5–2.3	16–23	20–29	2.7–4.0	27–39
12 x 1.25	21–32	2.9–4.4	29–43	35–53	4.8–7.3	47–72
14 x 1.5	35–52	4.8–7.1	48–70	57–85	7.8–11.7	77–110
16 x 1.5	51–77	7.0–10.6	67–100	90–120	12.4–16.5	130–160
18 x 1.5	74–110	10.2–15.1	100–150	130–170	17.9–23.4	180–230
20 x 1.5	110–140	15.1–19.3	150–190	190–240	26.2–46.9	160–320
22 x 1.5	150–190	22.0–26.2	200–260	250–320	34.5–44.1	340–430
24 x 1.5	190–240	26.2–46.9	260–320	310–410	42.7–56.5	420–550

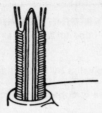

With the tap supplied, tap the hole to receive the thread insert. Keep the tap well oiled and back it out frequently to avoid clogging the threads

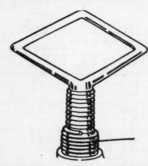

Screw the threaded insert onto the installation tool until the tang engages the slot. Screw the insert into the tapped hole until it is ¼–½ turn below the top surface. After installation, break off the tang with a hammer and a punch

The screw-in type compression gauge is more accurate

Spark plug inserts usually differ because they require a tap equipped with pilot threads and a combined reamer/tap section. Most manufacturers also supply blister-packed thread repair inserts separately in addition to a master kit containing a variety of taps and inserts plus installation tools.

Before effecting a repair to a threaded hole, remove any snapped, broken or damaged bolts or studs. Penetrating oil can be used to free frozen threads; the offending item can be removed with locking pliers or with a screw or stud extractor. After the hole is clear, the thread can be repaired, as follows:

CHECKING ENGINE COMPRESSION

A noticeable lack of engine power, excessive oil consumption and/or poor fuel mileage measured over an extended period are all indicators of internal engine wear. Worn piston rings, scored or worn cylinder bores, blown head gaskets, sticking or burnt valves and worn valve seats are all possible culprits here. A check of each cylinder's compression will help you locate the problems.

As mentioned in the "Tools and Equipment" section of Chapter 1, a screw-in type compression gauge is more accurate that the type you simply hold against the spark plug hole, although it takes slightly longer to use. It's worth it to obtain a more accurate reading. Follow the procedures below for gasoline and diesel engine vehicles.

Gasoline Engines

1. Warm up the engine to normal operating temperature.
2. Remove all spark plugs.
3. Disconnect the high tension lead from the ignition coil.
4. Fully open the throttle, either by operating the throttle linkage by hand or by having an assistant floor the accelerator pedal.
5. Screw the compression gauge into the No. 1 spark plug hole until the fitting is snug.
   WARNING: *Be careful not to crossthread the plug hole. On aluminum cylinder heads use extra care, as the threads in these heads are easily ruined.*
6. Ask an assistant to depress the accelerator pedal fully on both carbureted and fuel injected vehicles. Then, while reading the compression gauge, ask the assistant to crank the engine two or three times in short bursts using the ignition switch.
7. Read the compression gauge at the end of each series of cranks, and record the highest of these readings. Repeat this procedure for each of the engine's cylinders. Compare the highest reading of each cylinder to the compression pressure specification in the "Tune-Up Specifications" chart in Chapter 2. The specs in this chart are maximum values.
   NOTE: *A cylinder's compression pressure is usually acceptable if it is not less than 80% of maximum. The difference between each cylinder should be no more than 12–14 pounds.*
8. If a cylinder is unusually low, pour a tablespoon of clean engine oil into the cylinder through the spark plug hole and repeat the compression test. If the compression rises after adding the oil, it appears that the cylinder's piston rings or bore are damaged or worn. If the pressure remains low, the valves may not be seating properly (a valve job is needed), or the head gasket may be blown near that cylinder. If compression in any two adjacent cylinders is low and if the addition of oil does not help the

GENERAL ENGINE SPECIFICATIONS

Year	Model	Engine Displacement cu. in. (cc)	Fuel System Type	Net Horsepower @ rpm	Net Torque @ rpm (ft. lbs.)	Bore × Stroke (in.)	Com-pression Ratio	Oil Pressure @ rpm
1981–82	I-Mark	110 (1816)	2 bbl	80 @ 4800	95 @ 3000	3.31 × 3.23	8.5:1	57 @ 1400
	I-Mark	111 (1817)	Diesel	51 @ 5000	72 @ 3000	3.31 × 3.23	22.0:1	64 @ 1400
	Pick-up	110 (1816)	2 bbl	80 @ 4800	95 @ 3000	3.31 × 3.23	8.5:1	57 @ 1400
	Pick-up	136 (2238)	Diesel	58 @ 4300	93 @ 2200	3.46 × 3.62	21.0:1	57 @ 1400
1983–84	I-Mark	110.8 (1816)	2 bbl	80 @ 4800	95 @ 3000	3.31 × 3.23	8.5:1	57 @ 1400
	I-Mark	111 (1817)	Diesel	51 @ 5000	72 @ 3000	3.31 × 3.23	22.0:1	64 @ 1400
	Impulse	118.9 (1949)	EFI	90 @ 5000	108 @ 3000	3.43 × 3.29	9.2:1	57 @ 1400
	Pick-up	119 (2049)	2 bbl	82 @ 4600	101 @ 3000	3.42 × 3.23	8.4:1	56 @ 1400
	Pick-up	136 (2238)	Diesel	58 @ 4300	93 @ 2200	3.46 × 3.62	21.1:1	55 @ 1400
	Pick-up	136 (2238)	TD	80 @ 4000	128 @ 2200	3.46 × 3.62	21.1:1	55 @ 1400
1985	I-Mark (FWD)	90 (1471)	2 bbl	70 @ 5400	87 @ 3400	3.03 × 3.11	9.6:1	49 @ 5200
	I-Mark (RWD)	110.8 (1816)	2 bbl	80 @ 4800	95 @ 3000	3.31 × 3.23	8.5:1	57 @ 1400
	I-Mark (RWD)	111 (1817)	Diesel	51 @ 5000	72 @ 3000	3.31 × 3.23	22.0:1	64 @ 1400
	Impulse	118.9 (1949)	EFI	90 @ 5000	146 @ 3000	3.43 × 3.29	9.2:1	57 @ 1400
	Impulse (Turbo)	121 (1994)	EFI	140 @ 5400	166 @ 3000	3.47 × 3.29	7.9:1	57 @ 1400
	Pick-up	119 (2049)	2 bbl	82 @ 4600	101 @ 3000	3.42 × 3.23	8.4:1	56 @ 1400
	Pick-up	136 (2238)	Diesel	58 @ 4300	93 @ 2200	3.46 × 3.62	21.1:1	55 @ 1400
	Pick-up	136 (2238)	TD	80 @ 4000	128 @ 2200	3.46 × 3.62	21.1:1	55 @ 1400
1986	I-Mark	90 (1471)	2 bbl	70 @ 5400	87 @ 3400	3.03 × 3.11	9.6:1	49 @ 5200
	Impulse	118.9 (1949)	EFI	90 @ 5000	146 @ 3000	3.43 × 3.29	9.2:1	57 @ 1400
	Impulse (Turbo)	121.7 (1994)	EFI	140 @ 5400	166 @ 3000	3.47 × 3.29	7.9:1	57 @ 1400
	Pick-up	119 (2049)	2 bbl	82 @ 4600	101 @ 3000	3.42 × 3.23	8.4:1	56 @ 1400
	Pick-up	137 (2250)	2 bbl	96 @ 4600	123 @ 3000	3.52 × 3.54	8.3:1	57 @ 1400
	Pick-up	136 (2238)	Diesel	58 @ 4300	93 @ 2200	3.46 × 3.62	21.1:1	55 @ 1400
	Trooper II	136 (2238)	TD	80 @ 4000	128 @ 2200	3.46 × 3.62	21.1:1	55 @ 1400
	Trooper II	138 (2250)	2 bbl	96 @ 4600	123 @ 3000	3.52 × 3.54	8.3:1	57 @ 1400
1987	I-Mark	90 (1471)	2 bbl	70 @ 5400	87 @ 3400	3.03 × 3.11	9.6:1	49 @ 5200
	Impulse	118.9 (1949)	EFI	90 @ 5000	146 @ 3000	3.43 × 3.29	9.2:1	57 @ 1400
	Impulse (Turbo)	121.7 (1994)	EFI	140 @ 5400	166 @ 3000	3.47 × 3.29	7.9:1	57 @ 1400
	Pick-up	119 (2049)	2 bbl	82 @ 4600	101 @ 3000	3.42 × 3.23	8.4:1	56 @ 1400
	Pick-up	137 (2250)	2 bbl	96 @ 4600	123 @ 3000	3.52 × 3.54	8.3:1	57 @ 1400
	Pick-up	136 (2238)	Diesel	58 @ 4300	93 @ 2200	3.46 × 3.62	21.1:1	55 @ 1400
	Pick-up	136 (2238)	TD	80 @ 4000	128 @ 2200	3.46 × 3.62	21.1:1	55 @ 1400
	Trooper II	156 (2559)	EFI	120 @ 4600	146 @ 2600	3.65 × 3.74	8.3:1	57 @ 1400
1988	I-Mark	90 (1471)	2 bbl	70 @ 5400	87 @ 3400	3.03 × 3.11	9.6:1	49 @ 5200
	I-Mark (Turbo)	90 (1471)	EFI	110 @ 5400	120 @ 3400	3.03 × 3.11	8.0:1	49 @ 5200
	Impulse (Turbo)	121.7 (1994)	EFI	140 @ 5400	166 @ 3000	3.46 × 3.29	7.9:1	57 @ 1400
	Impulse	138 (2254)	EFI	110 @ 5000	127 @ 3000	3.52 × 3.54	8.6:1	57 @ 1400
	Pick-up	119 (1949)	2 bbl	82 @ 4600	101 @ 3000	3.42 × 3.23	8.4:1	56 @ 1400
	Pick-up	137 (2250)	2 bbl	96 @ 4600	123 @ 3000	3.52 × 3.54	8.3:1	57 @ 1400
	Pick-up	136 (2238)	Diesel	58 @ 4300	93 @ 2200	3.46 × 3.62	21.1:1	55 @ 1400
	Pick-up	136 (2238)	TD	80 @ 4000	128 @ 2200	3.46 × 3.62	21.1:1	55 @ 1400
	Trooper II	156 (2559)	EFI	120 @ 4600	146 @ 2600	3.65 × 3.74	8.3:1	57 @ 1400
1989	I-Mark	90 (1471)	2 bbl	70 @ 5400	87 @ 3400	3.03 × 3.11	9.6:1	49 @ 5200
	I-Mark (Turbo)	90 (1471)	EFI	110 @ 5400	120 @ 3400	3.03 × 3.11	8.0:1	49 @ 5200
	I-Mark (DOHC)	92 (1588)	EFI	125 @ 6800	138 @ 5400	3.15 × 3.11	9.8:1	49 @ 5200
	Impulse (Turbo)	121.7 (1994)	EFI	140 @ 5400	166 @ 3000	3.46 × 3.29	7.9:1	57 @ 1400
	Impulse	138 (2254)	EFI	110 @ 5000	127 @ 3000	3.52 × 3.54	8.6:1	57 @ 1400

GENERAL ENGINE SPECIFICATIONS (cont.)

Year	Model	Engine Displacement cu. in. (cc)	Fuel System Type	Net Horsepower @ rpm	Net Torque @ rpm (ft. lbs.)	Bore × Stroke (in.)	Compression Ratio	Oil Pressure @ rpm
1989	Amigo	138 (2254)	2 bbl	96 @ 4600	123 @ 2600	3.52 × 3.54	8.3:1	57 @ 3000
	Amigo	156 (2559)	MPFI	120 @ 4600	146 @ 2600	3.65 × 3.74	8.3:1	57–71 @ 4000
	Pick-up	138 (2254)	2 bbl	96 @ 4600	123 @ 2600	3.52 × 3.54	8.3:1	57 @ 3000
	Pick-up	156 (2559)	MPFI	120 @ 4600	146 @ 2600	3.65 × 3.74	8.3:1	57–71 @ 4000
	Trooper/Trooper II	156 (2559)	MPFI	120 @ 4600	146 @ 2600	3.65 × 3.74	8.3:1	57–71 @ 4000
	Trooper/Trooper II	173 (2828)	TBI	125 @ 4800	150 @ 2400	3.50 × 2.99	8.9:1	30–55 @ 2000
1990–91	Stylus	92 (1588)	EFI	95 @ 5800	97 @ 3400	3.15 × 3.11	9.1:1	49 @ 5200
	Stylus (DOHC)	92 (1588)	EFI	130 @ 6600	102 @ 4600	3.15 × 3.11	9.8:1	49 @ 5200
	Impulse	92 (1588)	EFI	130 @ 6600	102 @ 4600	3.15 × 3.11	9.8:1	49 @ 5200
	Impulse (Turbo)	92 (1588)	EFI Turbo	160 @ 6600	150 @ 4800	3.15 × 3.11	8.5:1	49 @ 5200
	Amigo	138 (2254)	2 bbl	96 @ 4600	123 @ 2600	3.52 × 3.54	8.3:1	57 @ 3000
	Amigo	156 (2559)	MPFI	120 @ 4600	146 @ 2600	3.65 × 3.74	8.3:1	57–71 @ 4000
	Pick-up	138 (2254)	2 bbl	96 @ 4600	123 @ 2600	3.52 × 3.54	8.3:1	57 @ 3000
	Pick-up	156 (2559)	MPFI	120 @ 4600	146 @ 2600	3.65 × 3.74	8.3:1	57–71 @ 4000
	Trooper/Trooper II	156 (2559)	MPFI	120 @ 4600	146 @ 2600	3.65 × 3.74	8.3:1	57–71 @ 4000
	Trooper/Trooper II	173 (2828)	TBI	125 @ 4800	150 @ 2400	3.50 × 2.99	8.9:1	30–55 @ 2000
	Rodeo	156 (2559)	MPFI	120 @ 4600	146 @ 2600	3.65 × 3.74	8.3:1	57–71 @ 4000
	Rodeo	189 (3100)	TBI	120 @ 4200	175 @ 2200	3.50 × 3.40	8.5:1	30–55 @ 2000

EFI—Electronic Fuel Injection MPFI—Multi Port Fuel Injection
TD—Turbo Diesel TBI—Throttle Body Injection

VALVE SPECIFICATIONS

Year	Engine Displacement cu. in. (cc)	Seat Angle (deg.)	Face Angle (deg.)	Spring Test Pressure (lbs.)	Spring Installed Height (in.)	Stem-to-Guide Clearance (in.) Intake	Exhaust	Stem Diameter (in.) Intake	Exhaust
1981–84	110.8 (1816)	45 ①	45	53 @ 160	③	0.0009–0.0022	0.0015–0.0031	0.3150	0.3150
	111 (1817)	45 ①	45	②	④	0.0015–0.0027	0.0020–0.0030	0.3130	0.3130
	118.9 (1949)	45	45	55 @ 1.60	1.60	0.0009–0.0022	0.0015–0.0031	0.3150	0.3150
	137 (2238) ①	45	45	③	④	0.0015–0.0027	0.0025–0.0037	0.3150	0.3150
	137 (2238) ②	45	45	③	④	0.0015–0.0027	0.0025–0.0037	0.3150	0.3150
1985–87	90 (1471)	45	45	49 @ 1.57	1.57	0.0009–0.0022	0.0012–0.0025	0.2740–0.2750	0.2740–0.2744
	118.9 (1949)	45	45	55 @ 1.60	1.60	0.0009–0.0022	0.0015–0.0031	0.3150	0.3150
	121.7 (1994)	45	45	55 @ 1.62	1.62	0.0009–0.0022	0.0015–0.0031	0.3150	0.3150
	137 (2238) ①	45	45	③	④	0.0015–0.0027	0.0025–0.0037	0.3150	0.3150
	137 (2238) ②	45	45	③	④	0.0015–0.0027	0.0025–0.0037	0.3150	0.3150
	138 (2254)	45	45	55.3 @ 1.62	1.62	0.0009–0.0022	0.0015–0.0031	0.3150	0.3150
	156 (2559)	45	45	56 @ 1.61	1.62	0.0009–0.0022	0.0015–0.0031	0.3150	0.3150

VALVE SPECIFICATIONS (cont.)

Year	Engine Displacement cu. in. (cc)	Seat Angle (deg.)	Face Angle (deg.)	Spring Test Pressure (lbs.)	Spring Installed Height (in.)	Stem-to-Guide Clearance (in.)		Stem Diameter (in.)	
						Intake	Exhaust	Intake	Exhaust
1988–89	90 (1471)	45	45	47 @ 1.57	1.57	0.0009–0.0022	0.0012–0.0025	0.2740–0.2750	0.2740–0.2744
	92 (1588)	45	45	47 @ 1.57	1.52	0.0009–0.0022	0.0018–0.0025	0.2340–0.2350	0.2340–0.2350
	119 (1950)	45	45	56 @ 1.61	1.60	0.0009–0.0022	0.0015–0.0031	0.3150	0.3150
	121.7 (1994)	45	45	55.3 @ 1.62	1.62	0.0009–0.0022	0.0015–0.0031	0.3150	0.3150
	137 (2238)	45	45	③	④	0.0015–0.0027	0.0025–0.0037	0.3150	0.3150
	138 (2254)	45	45	56 @ 1.61	1.62	0.0009–0.0022	0.0015–0.0031	0.3150	0.3150
	156 (2559)	45	45	56 @ 1.61	1.62	0.0009–0.0022	0.0015–0.0031	0.3150	0.3150
	173 (2828)	45	45	175 @ 1.26	1.72	0.0010–0.0027	0.0010–0.0027	0.3410–0.3420	0.3410–0.3420
1990–91	92 (1588) SOHC	45	45	⑤	1.52	0.0009–0.0022	0.0018–0.0025	0.2340–0.2350	0.2340–0.2350
	92 (1588) DOHC	45	45	44 @ 1.50	1.50	0.0009–0.0022	0.0018–0.0025	0.2340–0.2350	0.2340–0.2350
	138 (2254)	45	45	56 @ 1.61	1.62	0.0009–0.0022	0.0015–0.0031	0.3150	0.3150
	156 (2559)	45	45	56 @ 1.61	1.62	0.0009–0.0022	0.0015–0.0031	0.3150	0.3150
	173 (2828)	46	45	175 @ 1.26	1.72	0.0010–0.0027	0.0010–0.0027	0.3410–0.3420	0.3410–0.3420
	189 (3100)	46	46	191 @ 1.18	1.57	0.0010–0.0027	0.0010–0.0027	0.3410–0.3420	0.3410–0.3420

① Because of the aluminum head and valve seat inserts, cut the valve seat with 15, 45 or 75 degree cutters. Use the minimum necessary to remove dents or damage, leaving the contact width inside the 0.0472–0.063 range.

② Outer—34.5 @ 1.614
   Inner—20 @ 1.516

③ Outer—1.61
   Inner—1.51

④ Outer—1.85
   Inner—1.51

⑤ Intake—45
   Exhaust—55

CAMSHAFT SPECIFICATIONS

All measurements given in inches.

Year	Engine Displacement cu. in. (cc)	Journal Diameter					Lobe Lift		Bearing Clearance	Camshaft End Play
		1	2	3	4	5	In.	Ex.		
1981–84	110.8 (1816)	1.3362–1.3368	1.3362–1.3368	1.3362–1.3368	1.3362–1.3368	1.3362–1.3368	1.451	1.451	0.0016–0.0035	0.0020–0.0059
	111 (1817) Diesel	1.1004–1.1010	1.1004–1.1010	1.1004–1.1010	1.1004–1.1010	1.1004–1.1010	1.451	1.451	0.0008–0.0035	—
	118.9 (1949)	1.3390	1.3390	1.3390	1.3390	1.3390	1.451	1.451	0.0030–0.0043	0.0020–0.0060
	137 (2238)	1.8900	1.8900	1.8900	—	—	NA	NA	0.0020	0.0080
1985–88	90 (1471)	1.0210–1.0220	1.0210–1.0220	1.0210–1.0220	1.0210–1.0220	1.0210–1.0220	1.426	1.426	0.0024–0.0044	0.0039–0.0071
	110.8 (1816)	1.3362–1.3368	1.3362–1.3368	1.3362–1.3368	1.3362–1.3368	1.3362–1.3368	1.451	1.451	0.0016–0.0035	0.0020–0.0059

CAMSHAFT SPECIFICATIONS (cont.)

All measurements given in inches.

Year	Engine Displacement cu. in. (cc)	Journal Diameter					Lobe Lift		Bearing Clearance	Camshaft End Play
		1	2	3	4	5	In.	Ex.		
1985–88	111 (1817)	1.1004–1.1010	1.1004–1.1010	1.1004–1.1010	1.1004–1.1010	1.1004–1.1010	1.451	1.451	0.0008–0.0035	—
	118.9 (1949)	1.3390	1.3390	1.3390	1.3390	1.3390	1.451	1.451	0.0030–0.0043	0.0020–0.0060
	137 (2238)	1.8900	1.8900	1.8900	—	—	NA	NA	0.0020	0.0080
	121 (1983)	1.3390	1.3390	1.3390	1.3390	1.3390	1.451	1.451	0.0026–0.0043	0.0026–0.0056
	138 (2250)	1.3390	1.3390	1.3390	1.3390	1.3390	1.451	1.451	0.0033–0.0051	0.0020–0.0059
	156 (2559)	1.3390	1.3390	1.3390	1.3390	1.3390	NA	NA	0.0026–0.0043	0.0080
1989–91	90 (1471)	1.0210–1.0220	1.0210–1.0220	1.0210–1.0220	1.0210–1.0220	1.0210–1.0220	1.426	1.426	0.0024–0.0044	0.0039–0.0071
	92 (1588)	1.0210–1.0220	1.0210–1.0220	1.0210–1.0220	1.0210–1.0220	1.0210–1.0220	1.536	1.536	0.0024–0.0044	0.0039–0.0071
	138 (2254)	1.3390	1.3390	1.3390	1.3390	1.3390	1.451	1.451	0.0033–0.0051	0.0002–0.0059
	156 (2559)	1.3390	1.3390	1.3390	1.3390	1.3390	NA	NA	0.0026–0.0043	0.0080
	171 (2800)	1.8670–1.8810	1.8670–1.8810	1.8670–1.8810	1.8670–1.8810	—	0.262	0.273	0.0010–0.0040	NA
	189 (3100)	1.8670–1.8810	1.8670–1.8810	1.8670–1.8810	1.8670–1.8810	—	0.230	0.267	0.0010–0.0040	NA

CRANKSHAFT AND CONNECTING ROD SPECIFICATIONS

All measurements are given in inches.

Year	Engine Displacement cu. in. (cc)	Crankshaft				Connecting Rod		
		Main Brg. Journal Dia.	Main Brg. Oil Clearance	Shaft End-play	Thrust on No.	Journal Diameter	Oil Clearance	Side Clearance
1981–84	110.8 (1816) G180Z	2.2016–2.2022	0.0008–0.0025	0.0024–0.0094	3	1.9290	0.0007–0.0030	0.0137
	111 (1817) 4FB1	2.2016–2.2022	0.0012–0.0027	0.0024–0.0094	3	1.9250	0.0016–0.0027	0.0137
	118.9 (1949) G200Z	2.2016–2.2022	0.0008–0.0025	0.0024–0.0094	3	1.9290	0.0007–0.0029	0.0078–0.0130
	137 (2238) C223	2.3591–2.3594	0.0011–0.0033	0.0039	3	2.0835–2.0839	0.0016	NA
1985–87	90 (1471) 4XC1-U	1.8865–1.8873	0.0008–0.0020	0.0024–0.0099	2	1.5720–1.5726	0.0010–0.0023	0.0079–0.0138
	110.8 (1816) G180Z	2.2016–2.2022	0.0008–0.0025	0.0024–0.0094	3	1.9290	0.0007–0.0030	0.0137
	111 (1817) 4FB1	2.2016–2.2022	0.0012–0.0027	0.0024–0.0094	3	1.9250	0.0016–0.0027	0.0137
	118.9 (1949) G200Z	2.2016–2.2022	0.0008–0.0025	0.0024–0.0094	3	1.9290	0.0007–0.0029	0.0078–0.0130
	121.7 (1994) 4ZC1-T	2.2032–2.2038	0.0009–0.0020	0.0024–0.0099	3	1.9276–1.9282	0.0012–0.0024	0.0078–0.0130
	137 (2238) C223	2.3591–2.3594	0.0011–0.0033	0.0039	3	2.0835–2.0839	0.0016	NA
	138 (2254) 4ZD1	2.2032–2.2038	0.0006–0.0026	0.0024–0.0099	3	1.9276–1.9282	0.0004–0.0026	NA

CRANKSHAFT AND CONNECTING ROD SPECIFICATIONS (cont.)

All measurements are given in inches.

Year	Engine Displacement cu. in. (cc)	Crankshaft				Connecting Rod		
		Main Brg. Journal Dia.	Main Brg. Oil Clearance	Shaft End-play	Thrust on No.	Journal Diameter	Oil Clearance	Side Clearance
1988–89	90 (1471) 4XC1-U	1.8865– 1.8873	0.0008– 0.0020	0.0024– 0.0095	2	1.5720– 1.5726	0.0010– 0.0023	0.0079– 0.0138
	118.9 (1949) G200Z	2.2016– 2.2022	0.0008– 0.0025	0.0024– 0.0094	3	1.9290	0.0007– 0.0029	0.0078– 0.0130
	121.7 (1994) 4ZC1-T	2.2032– 2.2038	0.0009– 0.0020	0.0024– 0.0099	3	1.9276– 1.9282	0.0012– 0.0024	0.0078– 0.0130
	138 (2254) 4ZD1	2.2032– 2.2038	0.0006– 0.0026	0.0024– 0.0099	3	1.9276– 1.9282	0.0004– 0.0026	0.0078– 0.0130
	156 (2559) 4ZE1	2.2032– 2.2038	0.0009– 0.0020	0.0024– 0.0099	3	1.9276– 1.9282	0.0008– 0.0020	0.0078– 0.0130
	173 (2828) 2.8L	2.6473– 2.6483	0.0016– 0.0033	0.0020– 0.0080	3	1.9983– 1.9993	0.0013– 0.0026	0.0060– 0.0170
1989–91	92 (1588) 4XE1	1.8861– 1.9171	0.0008– 0.0020	0.0024– 0.0095	2	1.7193– 1.7197	0.0013– 0.0024	0.0079– 0.0138
	121.7 (1994) 4ZC1-T	2.2032– 2.2038	0.0009– 0.0020	0.0024– 0.0099	3	1.9276– 1.9282	0.0012– 0.0024	0.0078– 0.0130
	138 (2254) 4ZD1	2.2032– 2.2038	0.0009– 0.0020	0.0024– 0.0099	3	1.9276– 1.9282	0.0012– 0.0024	0.0078– 0.0130
	156 (2559) 4ZE1	2.2032– 2.2038	0.0009– 0.0020	0.0024– 0.0099	3	1.9276– 1.9282	0.0008– 0.0020	0.0078– 0.0130
	173 (2828) 2.8L	2.6473– 2.6483	0.0016– 0.0033	0.0020– 0.0080	3	1.9983– 1.9993	0.0013– 0.0026	0.0060– 0.0170
	189 (3100) 3.1L	2.6473– 2.6483	0.0012– 0.0027	0.0024– 0.0083	3	1.9983– 1.9993	0.0011– 0.0032	0.0014– 0.0267

PISTON AND RING SPECIFICATIONS

All measurements are given in inches.

Year	Engine Displacement cu. in. (cc)	Piston Clearance	Ring Gap			Ring Side Clearance		
			Top Compression	Bottom Compression	Oil Control	Top Compression	Bottom Compression	Oil Control
1981–84	110.8 (1816)	0.0018– 0.0026	0.0120– 0.0180	0.0120– 0.0180	0.0080– 0.0350	0.0059	0.0059	0.0059
	111 (1817)	0.0002– 0.0017	0.0078– 0.0157	0.0078– 0.0157	0.0078– 0.0157	0.0035– 0.0049	0.0015– 0.0019	0.0012– 0.0027
	118.9 (1949)	0.0018– 0.0026	0.0140– 0.0190	0.0140– 0.0190	0.0080– 0.0350	0.0010– 0.0024	0.0010– 0.0024	0.0008
	137 (2238)	0.0014– 0.0022	0.0079– 0.0158	0.0079– 0.0158	0.0079– 0.0158	0.0018– 0.0028	0.0012– 0.0021	0.0008– 0.0021
1985–87	90 (1471)	0.0110– 0.0190	0.0098– 0.0138	NA	0.0039– 0.0236	0.0010– 0.0026	NA	NA
	110.8 (1816)	0.0018– 0.0026	0.0120– 0.0180	0.0120– 0.0180	0.0080– 0.0350	0.0059	0.0059	0.0059
	111 (1817)	0.0002– 0.0010	0.0078– 0.0157	0.0078– 0.0157	0.0078– 0.0157	0.0035– 0.0049	0.0015– 0.0019	0.0012– 0.0027
	118.9 (1949)	0.0018– 0.0026	0.0140– 0.0190	0.0140– 0.0190	0.0080– 0.0350	0.0010– 0.0024	0.0010– 0.0024	0.0008
	121.7 (1994)	0.0018– 0.0026	0.0120– 0.0180	0.0100– 0.0160	0.0080– 0.0280	0.0010– 0.0024	0.0010– 0.0024	NA
	137 (2238)	0.0014– 0.0022	0.0079– 0.0158	0.0079– 0.0158	0.0079– 0.0158	0.0018– 0.0028	0.0012– 0.0021	0.0008– 0.0021

PISTON AND RING SPECIFICATIONS (cont.)

All measurements are given in inches.

Year	Engine Displacement cu. in. (cc)	Piston Clearance	Ring Gap			Ring Side Clearance		
			Top Compression	Bottom Compression	Oil Control	Top Compression	Bottom Compression	Oil Control
1985–87	138 (2254)	0.0008–0.0016	0.0120–0.0180	0.0100–0.0160	0.008–0.028	0.0010–0.0024	0.0010–0.0024	—
	156 (2559)	0.0010–0.0018	0.0120–0.0180	0.0240–0.0280	0.008–0.028	0.0010–0.0024	0.0008–0.0022	—
1988–89	90 (1471)	0.0011–0.0019	0.0098–0.0138	NA	0.0039–0.0236	0.0010–0.0025	NA	NA
	90 (1471) Turbo	0.0011–0.0019	0.0106–0.0153	0.0098–0.0145	0.0039–0.0236	0.0010–0.0026	0.0008–0.0024	NA
	92 (1588)	0.0011–0.0019	0.0110–0.0157	0.0177–0.0236	0.0039–0.0236	0.0018–0.0032	0.0008–0.0024	NA
	118.9 (1949)	0.0018–0.0026	0.0120–0.0180	0.0100–0.0160	0.0080–0.0280	0.0010–0.0024	0.0010–0.0024	0.0008
	121.7 (1994)	0.0018–0.0026	0.0120–0.0180	0.0100–0.0160	0.0080–0.0280	0.0010–0.0024	0.0010–0.0024	NA
	137 (2238)	0.0014–0.0022	0.0079–0.0158	0.0079–0.0158	0.0079–0.0158	0.0018–0.0028	0.0012–0.0021	0.0008–0.0021
	138 (2254)	0.0008–0.0016	0.0120–0.0180	0.0240–0.0280	0.008–0.028	0.0010–0.0024	0.0010–0.0024	—
	156 (2559)	0.0010–0.0018	0.0120–0.0180	0.0240–0.0280	0.008–0.028	0.0010–0.0024	0.0010–0.0024	—
	173 (2828)	0.0170–0.0430	0.0098–0.0196	0.0098–0.0196	0.0020–0.0550	0.0011–0.0027	0.0015–0.0037	0.0078 MAX
1990–91	92 (1588)	0.0011–0.0019	0.0110–0.0157	0.0177–0.0236	0.0039–0.0236	0.0018–0.0032	0.0008–0.0024	NA
	138 (2254)	0.0008–0.0016	0.0120–0.0180	0.0240–0.0280	0.008–0.028	0.0010–0.0024	0.0010–0.0024	—
	156 (2559)	0.0010–0.0018	0.0120–0.0180	0.0240–0.0280	0.008–0.028	0.0010–0.0024	0.0010–0.0024	—
	173 (2828)	0.0170–0.0430	0.0098–0.0196	0.0098–0.0196	0.0020–0.0550	0.0011–0.0027	0.0015–0.0037	0.0078 MAX
	189 (3100)	0.0009–0.0022	0.0010–0.0200	0.0200–0.0280	0.0100–0.0300	0.0020–0.0035	0.0020–0.0035	0.0080

compression, there is leakage past the head gasket. Oil and coolant water in the combustion chamber can result from this problem. There may be evidence of water droplets on the engine dipstick when a head gasket has blown.

Diesel Engines

Checking the cylinder compression on diesel engines is basically the same procedures as on gasoline engines, except for the following:

1. A special compression gauge adaptor suitable for diesel engines (because these engines have much greater compression pressures) must be used.

2. Remove the injector tubes and the injectors from each cylinder.

NOTE: *Don't forget to remove the washer beneath each injector; otherwise, it may get lost when the engine is cranked.*

3. When fitting the compression gauge adap-

tor to the cylinder head, make sure the bleeder of the gauge (if equipped) is closed.

4. When reinstalling the injector assemblies, install new washers beneath each injector.

Engine

REMOVAL AND INSTALLATION

Rear Wheel, 2WD Vehicles

1. Disconnect both battery cables, the negative cable first.

2. Matchmark the hood-to-hinges and remove the hood.

3. Remove the undercover, if equipped. Open the drain plugs on the radiator and the cylinder and drain the cooling system.

CAUTION: *When draining the coolant, keep in mind that cats and dogs are attracted by the ethylene glycol antifreeze, and are quite*

TORQUE SPECIFICATIONS
All readings in ft. lbs.

Year	Engine Displacement cu. in. (cc)	Cylinder Head Bolts	Main Bearing Bolts	Rod Bearing Bolts	Crankshaft Pulley Bolts	Flywheel Bolts	Manifold		Spark Plugs
							Intake	Exhaust	
1981–84	110.8 (1816)	①	72	43	87	69	13	15	11–14
	111 (1817)	②	65–72	54–61	108	36–43	25–32	11–18	NA
	118.9 (1949)	①	65–79	42–45	87	72–79	13–18	13–18	11–14
	137 (2238) ③	⑤	116–130	58–65	124–151	83–90	10–17	10–17	—
	137 (2238) ④	⑥	116–130	58–65	124–151	83–90	13–17	13–17	—
1985–87	90 (1471)	⑦	68	25	108	22 ⑧	17	17	11–14
	110.8 (1816)	①	72	43	87	76	13	15	11–14
	111 (1817)	②	65–72	54–61	108	36–43	25–32	11–18	NA
	118.9 (1949)	①	65–79	42–45	87	72–79	13–18	13–18	11–14
	121.7 (1994)	①	72	43	87	43	13–18	16	11–14
	137 (2238) ③	⑤	116–130	58–65	124–151	83–90	10–17	10–17	—
	137 (2238) ④	⑥	116–130	58–65	124–151	83–90	13–17	13–17	—
	138 (2254)	⑨	65–80	42–45	76–98	40–47	14–18	14–18	10–17
	156 (2559)	⑨	65–80	42–45	79–102	40–47	14–18	14–18	10–17
1988–89	90 (1471)	⑦	68	25	108	22 ⑧	17	17	11–14
	92 (1588)	⑦	65	⑩	123	⑪	17	30	11–14
	121.7 (1994)	①	72	43	87	40	13–18	16	11–14
	137 (2238) ③	⑤	116–130	58–65	124–151	83–90	10–17	10–17	—
	137 (2238) ④	⑥	116–130	58–65	124–151	83–90	13–17	13–17	—
	138 (2254)	⑨	65–80	42–45	76–98	40–47	14–18	14–18	10–17
	156 (2559)	⑨	65–80	42–45	79–102	40–47	14–18	14–18	10–17
	173 (2828)	⑫	70	39	70	52	23	25	22
1990–91	92 (1588)	⑦	65	⑩	123	⑪	17	30	11–14
	138 (2254)	⑨	65–80	42–45	76–98	40–47	14–18	14–18	10–17
	156 (2559)	⑨	65–80	42–45	79–102	40–47	14–18	14–18	10–17
	173 (2828)	⑫	70	39	70	52	23	25	22
	189 (3100)	⑫	72	39	85	52	19	19	25

① 1st step: 62 ft. lbs.
  2nd step: 72 ft. lbs.
② Tighten in sequence
  New bolts: 90 ft. lbs.
  Old bolts: 97 ft. lbs.
③ Diesel
④ Turbocharged Diesel
⑤ 1st step: 40–47 ft. lbs.
  2nd step: 54–61 ft. lbs.
⑥ 1st step: 33–40 ft. lbs.
  2nd step: 120–150 degrees
⑦ 1st step: 29 ft. lbs.
  2nd step: 58 ft. lbs.

⑧ Turn the bolt an additional 45 degrees
⑨ 1st step: 58 ft. lbs.
  2nd step: 65 ft. lbs.
  3rd step: 80 ft. lbs.
⑩ 1st step: 11 ft. lbs.
  2nd step: Turn an additional 45–60 degrees
⑪ 1st step: 22 ft. lbs.
  2nd step: Turn an additional 45–60 degrees
⑫ 1st step: 40 ft. lbs.
  2nd step: Turn an additional 90 degrees
  (¼ turn)

likely to drink any that is left in an uncovered container or in puddles on the ground. This will prove fatal in sufficient quantity. Always drain the coolant into a sealable container. Coolant should be reused unless it is contaminated or several years old.

4. Remove the air cleaner by performing the following procedures:

a. Disconnect the air duct and PCV hose from the air cleaner.

b. Disconnect the air hose from the AIR pump.

c. Remove the air cleaner-to-bracket bolts and wing nut.

d. Lift the air cleaner, disconnect the vacuum hose(s) from the under side and remove the air cleaner.

e. Using a clean shop cloth, cover the air cleaner port to prevent dirt from entering the engine.

Engine removal—P'up similar

5. Disconnect the TCA hot air hose and remove the manifold cover.

6. Label and disconnect the electrical connector(s) from the alternator.

7. Remove the exhaust pipe-to-exhaust manifold nuts and separate the pipe from the manifold.

8. Loosen the clutch cable adjusting nut and relieve the tension, if equipped with a manual transmission.

9. Disconnect the heater hoses from the heater core.

10. If equipped with an oxygen sensor, disconnect the electrical connector.

11. If equipped with a vacuum switching valve, disconnect the rubber hose from the valve.

12. Disconnect the engine-to-chassis ground cable.

13. Disconnect the fuel hoses from the carburetor.

14. Disconnect the high-tension wire from the ignition coil, the vacuum hose from the rear connector of the intake manifold and the rubber hoses from the canister.

15. Disconnect the accelerator cable from the carburetor. Disconnect the electrical connectors from the starter, the thermo-unit, the oil pressure switch and distributor harness.

16. Disconnect the hose from the vacuum switch, if equipped, and the solenoid valve.

17. Disconnect the electrical connectors from the EFE heater, the carburetor solenoid valve and the electric choke.

18. From the rear of the engine, disconnect the back-up light switch and transmission wiring at the connector.

19. Using an engine hoist, connect it to the engine hangers and support the engine.

20. Remove the engine-to-mount nut. Raise the engine slightly and remove the left side engine mount stopper plate.

21. If equipped with air conditioning, remove the compressor from the engine and move it aside; do not disconnect the pressure hoses.

22. Disconnect the upper and lower radiator hoses and the reservoir tank hose.

23. Remove the radiator and fan blade assembly.

24. Raise and safely support the vehicle. Drain the oil from the engine.

CAUTION: *The EPA warns that prolonged contact with used engine oil may cause a number of skin disorders, including cancer! You should make every effort to minimize your exposure to used engine oil. Protective gloves should be worn when changing the oil. Wash your hands and any other exposed skin areas as soon as possible after exposure to used engine oil. Soap and water, or waterless hand cleaner should be used.*

25. Remove the clutch return spring and the clutch cable, if equipped with a manual transmission.

26. Remove the starter motor. Disconnect the speedometer from the transmission.

27. Matchmark and remove the driveshaft. Remove the transmission mount bolts. Remove gearshift lever assembly.

28. Lift the engine slightly. Remove the exhaust pipe bracket from the transmission and the engine-to-mount nuts.

29. Make certain that all lines, hoses, cables and wires have been disconnected from the engine and frame.

30. Lift the engine/transmission assembly from the vehicle with the front of the engine raised slightly.

31. Remove the transmission-to-engine bolts and the transmission from the engine.

To install:

32. Lower the engine/transmission assembly into the vehicle, align it with the mounts and install the nuts/bolts.

33. Install the gearshift lever assembly and the driveshaft.

34. Connect the speedometer cable to the transmission. Install the starter motor.

35. If equipped with a manual transmission, install the clutch cable and clutch return spring.

36. Lower the vehicle. Install the fan blade assembly and the radiator.

37. Connect the upper and lower radiator hoses and the reservoir tank hose.

38. If equipped with air conditioning, install the compressor to the engine.

39. Install the left side engine mount stopper plate, lower the engine slightly and install the engine-to-mount nut.

40. Remove the engine hoist.

41. Connect the electrical connector to the back-up light switch and transmission wiring connector at the rear of the engine.

42. Connect the electrical connectors to the EFE heater, the carburetor solenoid valve and the electric choke.

43. Connect the hose to the vacuum switch, if equipped, and the solenoid valve.

44. Connect the accelerator cable to the carburetor. Connect the electrical connectors to the starter, the thermo-unit, the oil pressure switch and distributor harness.

45. Connect the high-tension wire to the ignition coil, the vacuum hose to the rear connector of the intake manifold and the rubber hoses to the canister.

46. Connect the fuel hoses to the carburetor.

47. Connect the engine-to-chassis ground cable.

48. If equipped with a vacuum switching valve, connect the rubber hose to the valve.

49. If equipped with an oxygen sensor, connect the electrical connector.

50. Connect the heater hoses to the heater core.

51. Tension the clutch cable and tighten the adjusting nut, if equipped with a manual transmission.

52. Install the exhaust pipe-to-exhaust manifold nuts.

53. Connect the electrical connector(s) to the alternator.

54. Install the manifold cover and connect the TCA hot air hose.

55. Install the air cleaner by performing the following procedures:

    a. Lower the air cleaner and connect the vacuum hose(s) to the underside.

    b. Install the air cleaner-to-bracket bolts and wing nut.

    c. Connect the air hose to the AIR pump.

    d. Connect the air duct and PCV hose to the air cleaner.

56. Refill the cooling system with the proper coolant and the crankcase with engine oil. Check and adjust the clutch pedal freeplay, if equipped with a manual transmission.

57. Install the hood and connect both battery cables, the positive cable first.

58. Adjust the belt tension. Start the engine, check for leaks.

59. Check and/or adjust the idle speed and ignition timing.

Rear Wheel Drive Impulse

1. Relieve the fuel pressure. Disconnect both battery cables, the negative cable first. Remove the battery.

2. Matchmark the hood-to-hinges and remove the hood.

3. Remove the undercover, if equipped. Open the drain plugs on the radiator and the cylinder and drain the cooling system.

CAUTION: *When draining the coolant, keep in mind that cats and dogs are attracted by the ethylene glycol antifreeze, and are quite likely to drink any that is left in an uncovered container or in puddles on the ground. This will prove fatal in sufficient quantity. Always drain the coolant into a sealable container. Coolant should be reused unless it is contaminated or several years old.*

4. Remove the air cleaner (4ZD1 engine) or air cleaner duct and hose (4ZE1 engine). Using a clean shop cloth, cover the air cleaner port to prevent dirt from entering the engine.

5. Label and disconnect the necessary hoses, electrical connectors, control cables and control rods from the engine.

6. Label and disconnect the following items:

    a. Air switch valve hose.

    b. Oxygen sensor wire.

    c. Vacuum switch valve hose.

    d. Thermal vacuum switching valve hose.

    e. Pressure regulator vacuum hose.

    f. Canister hose.

    g. ECM harness.

    h. Fuel hose(s).

7. Remove the clutch return spring (if equipped), the clutch control cable (if equipped), the back-up light switch connector and the speedometer cable from the transmission.

8. Remove the radiator grille from the deflector panel.

9. Disconnect the upper and lower radiator hoses and the reservoir tank hose.

10. Remove the fan shroud, fan blade assembly and the radiator.

11. If equipped with air conditioning, remove the compressor from the engine and move it aside; do not disconnect the pressure hoses.

12. Remove the gear shift lever by performing the following procedures:

    a. Place the gear shift lever in N.

    b. Remove the front console from the floor panel.

    c. Pull the shift lever boot and grommet upward.

    d. Remove the shift lever cover bolts and the shift lever.

13. Raise and safely support the vehicle. Remove the front wheels.

14. Drain the engine oil and the transmission fluid.

CAUTION: *The EPA warns that prolonged contact with used engine oil may cause a number of skin disorders, including cancer! You should make every effort to minimize your exposure to used engine oil. Protective gloves should be worn when changing the oil. Wash your hands and any other exposed skin areas as soon as possible after exposure to used engine oil. Soap and water, or waterless hand cleaner should be used.*

15. If equipped with an automatic transmission, perform the following procedures:

    a. Remove the oil level gauge and the tube.

    b. Disconnect the shift select control link rod from the select lever.

    c. Disconnect the downshift cable from the transmission.

    d. Disconnect and plug the fluid coolant lines from the transmission.

16. If equipped with a 1-piece driveshaft, remove the driveshaft flange-to-pinion nuts, lower the driveshaft and pull it from the transmission.

17. If equipped with a 2-piece driveshaft, perform the following procedures:

    a. Remove the rear driveshaft flange-to-pinion nuts.

    b. Remove the rear driveshaft flange-to-front driveshaft flange bolts and the rear driveshaft.

    c. Remove the center bearing-to-chassis bolts, move the front driveshaft rearward and from the transmission.

18. Remove the starter-to-engine bolts and the starter.

19. Remove the exhaust pipe-to-exhaust manifold nuts, the exhaust pipe bracket-to-transmission bolts, the front exhaust pipe-to-2nd exhaust pipe bolts and the front exhaust pipe from the vehicle.

20. Attach an engine hanger to the rear of the exhaust manifold.

21. Using an engine hoist, connect it to the engine hangers and support the engine.

22. If equipped with a manual transmission, perform the following procedures:

    a. Using a transmission jack, place it under the transmission; do not support it.

    b. Remove the rear mount-to-transmission nuts.

    c. Remove the rear mount-to-crossmember nuts/bolts and the mount.

NOTE: *Further removal of the transmission may require an assistant.*

    d. Remove the clutch cover and the transmission-to-engine bolts.

    e. Move the transmission rearward into the crossmember and floor pan area; the transmission may rest on the crossmember.

    f. Lower the front of the transmission toward the jack.

    g. Firmly, grasp the transmission the rear cover while the assistant raises the jack toward the transmission.

    h. Carefully lower the transmission onto the jack and center it.

    i. Lower the jack and move the transmission rearward.

23. If equipped with an automatic transmission, perform the following procedures:

NOTE: *Removal of the transmission will require an assistant.*

    a. Remove the torque converter-to-flex plate bolts through the starter hole.

    b. Using a transmission jack, place it under the transmission; do not support it.

    c. Remove the rear mount-to-transmission nuts.

    d. Remove the rear mount-to-crossmember nuts/bolts and the mount.

    e. Remove the transmission-to-engine bolts.

    f. Move the transmission rearward into the crossmember and floor pan area; the transmission may rest on the crossmember.

    g. Lower the front of the transmission toward the jack.

    h. Firmly, grasp the transmission the rear cover while the assistant raises the jack toward the transmission.

    i. Carefully, lower the transmission onto the jack and center it.

    j. Lower the jack and move the transmission rearward.

24. Remove the engine-to-mount nuts/bolts.

25. Using the hoist, slowly, lift the engine; be sure to hold the front of the engine higher than the rear.

26. Place the engine on a work stand.

To install:

27. Using the hoist, slowly, lower the engine into the vehicle; be sure to hold the front of the engine higher than the rear.

28. Install the engine-to-mount nuts/bolts.

29. If equipped with an automatic transmission, perform the following procedures:

NOTE: *Installation of the transmission will require an assistant.*

    a. Raise the transmission into position.

    b. Raise the rear of the transmission and move it into position on the crossmember.

    c. Move the transmission forward and engage it with the engine.

    d. Install the engine-to-transmission bolts.

    e. Install the mount and the rear mount-to-crossmember nuts/bolts.

    f. Install the rear mount-to-transmission nuts.

    g. Install the torque converter-to-flex plate bolts through the starter hole.

30. If equipped with a manual transmission, perform the following procedures:

NOTE: *Installation of the transmission may require an assistant.*

    a. Raise the transmission into position.

    b. Raise the rear of the transmission and move it into position on the crossmember.

    c. Move the transmission forward and engage it with the engine.

d. Install the engine-to-transmission bolts.

e. Install the mount and the rear mount-to-crossmember nuts/bolts.

f. Install the rear mount-to-transmission nuts.

31. Remove the engine hoist and the engine hanger from the rear of the exhaust manifold.

32. Install the front exhaust pipe, exhaust pipe-to-exhaust manifold nuts, the exhaust pipe bracket-to-transmission bolts, the front exhaust pipe-to-2nd exhaust pipe bolts.

33. Install the starter and the starter-to-engine bolts.

34. If equipped with a 2-piece driveshaft, perform the following procedures:

a. Install the front driveshaft into the transmission and the center bearing-to-chassis bolts.

b. Install the rear driveshaft and the rear driveshaft flange-to-front driveshaft flange bolts.

c. Install the rear driveshaft flange-to-pinion nuts.

35. If equipped with a 1-piece driveshaft, install the driveshaft into the transmission and the driveshaft flange-to-pinion nuts.

36. If equipped with an automatic transmission, perform the following procedures:

a. Connect the fluid coolant lines to the transmission.

b. Connect the downshift cable to the transmission.

c. Connect the shift select control link rod to the select lever.

d. Install the oil level gauge and the tube.

37. Install the front wheels and lower the vehicle.

38. Install the gear shift lever by performing the following procedures:

a. Install the shift lever and the shift lever cover bolts.

b. Push the grommet and shift lever boot downward.

c. Install the front console to the floor panel.

39. If equipped with air conditioning, install the compressor to the engine.

40. Install the radiator, the fan blade assembly and the fan shroud.

41. Connect the upper and lower radiator hoses and the reservoir tank hose.

42. Install the radiator grille to the deflector panel.

43. Install the clutch return spring (if equipped), the clutch control cable (if equipped), the back-up light switch connector and the speedometer cable to the transmission.

44. Connect the following items:

a. Air switch valve hose.

b. Oxygen sensor wire.

c. Vacuum switch valve hose.

d. Thermal vacuum switching valve hose.

e. Pressure regulator vacuum hose.

f. Canister hose.

g. ECM harness.

h. Fuel hose(s).

45. Connect the necessary hoses, electrical connectors, control cables and control rods to the engine.

46. Install the air cleaner (2.3L) or air cleaner duct and hose (2.6L).

47. Refill the engine, the transmission and the cooling system. Install the undercover, if equipped.

48. Install the hood.

49. Install the battery and connect both battery cables, the positive cable first.

50. Adjust the belt tension. Start the engine, check for leaks.

51. Check and/or adjust the idle speed and ignition timing.

Diesel Engines

P'UP

1. Matchmark hinges to the hood and remove the hood.

2. Disconnect the battery cables, negative first and remove the battery from the vehicle.

3. Drain the cooling system.

CAUTION: *When draining the coolant, keep in mind that cats and dogs are attracted by the ethylene glycol antifreeze, and are quite likely to drink any that is left in an uncovered container or in puddles on the ground. This will prove fatal in sufficient quantity. Always drain the coolant into a sealable container. Coolant should be reused unless it is contaminated or several years old.*

4. Remove the air cleaner assembly as follows: Remove the intake silencer. Remove the bolts mounting the air cleaner and loosen the clamp bolt. Lift the air cleaner slightly and disconnect the breather hose. Remove the air cleaner assembly.

5. Disconnect the upper radiator hose at the engine.

6. Loosen the air conditioning compressor drive belts by moving the power steering pump or idler.

7. Remove the cooling fan and fan shroud.

8. Disconnect the lower radiator hose at the engine.

9. Remove the radiator grille.

10. Remove the radiator attaching bolts and remove the radiator.

11. Disconnect the accelerator control cable from the injection pump.

12. If equipped with air conditioning, discon-

nect the air conditioning compressor control cable.

13. Disconnect and plug the fuel hoses from the injection pump.

14. Disconnect the ground cable from the engine.

15. Raise and safely support the vehicle. Disconnect and label the transmission wiring. Drain the engine oil.

CAUTION: *The EPA warns that prolonged contact with used engine oil may cause a number of skin disorders, including cancer! You should make every effort to minimize your exposure to used engine oil. Protective gloves should be worn when changing the oil. Wash your hands and any other exposed skin areas as soon as possible after exposure to used engine oil. Soap and water, or waterless hand cleaner should be used.*

16. Disconnect the vacuum hose from the fast idle actuator.

17. Disconnect the fuel cut solenoid wiring.

18. Disconnect the air conditioning compressor wiring, sensing resistor and thermoswitch connectors.

19. Disconnect the heater hoses extending from the heater unit from the dash panel side.

20. Disconnect the hose for power brake booster from the vacuum pump.

21. Disconnect vacuum hose from the vacuum pump.

22. Disconnect the alternator wiring.

23. Disconnect the exhaust pipe from the exhaust manifold at the flange.

24. Remove the exhaust pipe mounting bracket from the engine.

25. Disconnect and label the starter motor wiring.

26. Pull the gearshift lever boot upwards on the lever. Remove the 2 gearshift lever bolts and the lever.

27. Disconnect speedometer and ground cables from the transmission.

28. Matchmark and remove the driveshaft.

29. Remove the clutch fork return spring from the clutch fork.

30. Disconnect clutch cable from the hooked portion of clutch fork and pull it out forward through the stiffener bracket.

31. Remove 2 bracket-to-transmission rear mount bolts and nuts.

32. Raise the engine and transmission and remove the crossmember-to-frame bracket bolts.

33. Remove the rear mounting nuts from the transmission rear extension.

34. Disconnect electrical connectors at CRS switch and back-up lamp switch.

35. Raise the engine and remove the engine mounting bolts and nuts.

36. Remove the engine towards the front of the vehicle making sure the front of the engine is slightly above the level.

To install:

37. Install the engine towards the front of the vehicle making sure the front of the engine is slightly above the level.

38. Lower the engine and install the engine mounting bolts and nuts.

39. Connect electrical connectors at CRS switch and back-up lamp switch.

40. Install the rear mounting nuts to the transmission rear extension.

41. Lower the engine and transmission and install the crossmember-to-frame bracket bolts.

42. Install 2 bracket-to-transmission rear mount bolts and nuts.

43. Connect clutch cable to the hooked portion of clutch fork.

44. Install the clutch fork return spring to the clutch fork.

45. Install the driveshaft.

46. Connect speedometer and ground cables to the transmission.

47. Install the 2 gearshift lever bolts and the lever.

48. Connect the starter motor wiring.

49. Install the exhaust pipe mounting bracket to the engine.

50. Connect the exhaust pipe to the exhaust manifold at the flange.

51. Connect the alternator wiring.

52. Connect vacuum hose to the vacuum pump.

53. Connect the hose for power brake booster to the vacuum pump.

54. Connect the heater hoses extending to the heater unit to the dash panel side.

55. Connect the air conditioning compressor wiring, sensing resistor and thermoswitch connectors.

56. Connect the fuel cut solenoid wiring.

57. Connect the vacuum hose to the fast idle actuator.

58. Lower the vehicle. Connect the transmission wiring. Refill the engine oil.

59. Connect the ground cable to the engine.

60. Connect and plug the fuel hoses to the injection pump.

61. If equipped with air conditioning, connect the air conditioning compressor control cable.

62. Connect the accelerator control cable to the injection pump.

63. Install the radiator attaching bolts and radiator.

64. Install the radiator grille.

65. Connect the lower radiator hose at the engine.

66. Install the cooling fan and fan shroud.

67. Tighten the air conditioning compressor drive belts by moving the power steering pump or idler.

68. Connect the upper radiator hose at the engine.

69. Install the air cleaner assembly.

70. Refill the cooling system with antifreeze.

71. Install the battery. Connect the battery cables, positive first.

72. With the help of an assistant, install the hood to the matchmarked locations.

73. Start the engine, allow to reach operating temperature and check for leaks and proper performance.

74. Check and adjust the clutch pedal freeplay.

4-Wheel Drive Vehicles
1981–87 GASOLINE ENGINES

1. Disconnect both battery cables, the negative cable first.

2. Matchmark the hood-to-hinges and remove the hood.

3. Remove the undercover. Open the drain plugs on the radiator and the cylinder and drain the cooling system.

CAUTION: *When draining the coolant, keep in mind that cats and dogs are attracted by the ethylene glycol antifreeze, and are quite likely to drink any that is left in an uncovered container or in puddles on the ground. This will prove fatal in sufficient quantity. Always drain the coolant into a sealable container. Coolant should be reused unless it is contaminated or several years old.*

4. Remove the air cleaner by performing the following procedures:

    a. Disconnect the air duct and PCV hose from the air cleaner.

    b. Disconnect the air hose from the AIR pump.

    c. Remove the air cleaner-to-bracket bolts and wing nut.

    d. Lift the air cleaner, disconnect the vacuum hose(s) from the underside and remove the air cleaner.

    e. Using a clean shop cloth, cover the air cleaner port to prevent dirt from entering the engine.

5. Disconnect the TCA hot air hose and remove the manifold cover.

6. Label and disconnect the electrical connector(s) from the alternator.

7. Remove the exhaust pipe-to-exhaust manifold nuts and separate the pipe from the manifold.

8. Loosen the clutch cable adjusting nut and relieve the tension, if equipped with a manual transmission.

9. Disconnect the heater hoses from the heater core.

10. If equipped with an oxygen sensor, disconnect the electrical connector.

11. If equipped with a vacuum switching valve, disconnect the rubber hose from the valve.

12. Disconnect the engine-to-chassis ground cable.

13. Disconnect the fuel hoses from the carburetor.

14. Disconnect the high-tension wire from the ignition coil, the vacuum hose from the rear connector of the intake manifold and the rubber hoses from the canister.

15. Disconnect the accelerator cable from the carburetor. Disconnect the electrical connectors from the starter, the thermo-unit, the oil pressure switch and distributor harness.

16. Disconnect the hose from the vacuum switch, if equipped, and the solenoid valve.

17. Disconnect the electrical connectors from the EFE heater, the carburetor solenoid valve and the electric choke.

18. From the rear of the engine, disconnect the back-up light switch and transmission wiring at the connector.

19. Using an engine hoist, connect it to the engine hangers and support the engine.

20. Remove the engine-to-mount nut. Raise the engine slightly and remove the left side engine mount stopper plate.

21. If equipped with air conditioning, remove the compressor from the engine and move it aside; do not disconnect the pressure hoses.

22. Disconnect the upper and lower radiator hoses and the reservoir tank hose.

23. Remove the radiator and fan blade assembly.

24. Raise and support the vehicle safely. Drain the oil from the engine.

CAUTION: *The EPA warns that prolonged contact with used engine oil may cause a number of skin disorders, including cancer! You should make every effort to minimize your exposure to used engine oil. Protective gloves should be worn when changing the oil. Wash your hands and any other exposed skin areas as soon as possible after exposure to used engine oil. Soap and water, or waterless hand cleaner should be used.*

25. Remove the starter motor and the flywheel cover pan.

26. Remove the bell housing-to-engine bolts and support the transmission.

27. Lift the engine slightly. Remove the exhaust pipe bracket from the transmission and the engine-to-mount nuts.

NOTE: *Make certain that all lines, hoses, ca-*

bles and wires have been disconnected from the engine and frame.

28. Lift the engine from the vehicle with the front of the engine raised slightly to clear the transmission input shaft.

To install:

29. Lower the engine into the vehicle, align it transmission assembly and install the nuts/bolts.

30. Install the starter motor and the flywheel cover pan.

31. If equipped with a manual transmission, install the clutch cable and clutch return spring.

32. Lower the vehicle. Install the fan blade assembly and the radiator.

33. Connect the upper and lower radiator hoses and the reservoir tank hose.

34. If equipped with air conditioning, install the compressor to the engine.

35. Install the left side engine mount stopper plate, lower the engine slightly and install the engine-to-mount nut.

36. Remove the engine hoist.

37. Connect the electrical connector to the back-up light switch and transmission wiring connector at the rear of the engine.

38. Connect the electrical connectors to the EFE heater, the carburetor solenoid valve and the electric choke.

39. Connect the hose to the vacuum switch, if equipped, and the solenoid valve.

40. Connect the accelerator cable to the carburetor. Connect the electrical connectors to the starter, the thermo-unit, the oil pressure switch and distributor harness.

41. Connect the high-tension wire to the ignition coil, the vacuum hose to the rear connector of the intake manifold and the rubber hoses to the canister.

42. Connect the fuel hoses to the carburetor.

43. Connect the engine-to-chassis ground cable.

44. If equipped with a vacuum switching valve, connect the rubber hose to the valve.

45. If equipped with an oxygen sensor, connect the electrical connector.

46. Connect the heater hoses to the heater core.

47. Tension the clutch cable and tighten the adjusting nut, if equipped with a manual transmission.

48. Install the exhaust pipe-to-exhaust manifold nuts.

49. Connect the electrical connector(s) to the alternator.

50. Install the manifold cover and connect the TCA hot air hose.

51. Install the air cleaner by performing the following procedures:

a. Lower the air cleaner and connect the vacuum hose(s) to the underside.

b. Install the air cleaner-to-bracket bolts and wing nut.

c. Connect the air hose to the AIR pump.

d. Connect the air duct and PCV hose to the air cleaner.

52. Refill the cooling system with the proper coolant and the crankcase with engine oil. Check and adjust the clutch pedal freeplay, if equipped with a manual transmission.

53. Install the hood and connect both battery cables, the positive cable first.

54. Adjust the belt tension. Start the engine, check for leaks.

55. Check and/or adjust the idle speed and ignition timing.

1988–91 GASOLINE ENGINES

1. Relieve the fuel pressure. Disconnect both battery cables, the negative cable first. Remove the battery.

2. Matchmark the hood-to-hinges and remove the hood.

3. Remove the undercover, if equipped. Open the drain plugs on the radiator and the cylinder and drain the cooling system.

CAUTION: *When draining the coolant, keep in mind that cats and dogs are attracted by the ethylene glycol antifreeze, and are quite likely to drink any that is left in an uncovered container or in puddles on the ground. This will prove fatal in sufficient quantity. Always drain the coolant into a sealable container. Coolant should be reused unless it is contaminated or several years old.*

4. Remove the air cleaner (2.3L engine) or air cleaner duct and hose (2.6L engine). Using a clean shop cloth, cover the air cleaner port to prevent dirt from entering the engine.

5. Label and disconnect the necessary hoses, electrical connectors, control cables and control rods from the engine.

6. Label and disconnect the following items:

a. Air switch valve hose.

b. Oxygen sensor wire.

c. Vacuum switch valve hose.

d. Thermal vacuum switching valve hose.

e. Pressure regulator vacuum hose.

f. Canister hose.

g. ECM harness.

h. Fuel hose(s).

7. Remove the clutch return spring (if equipped), the clutch control cable (if equipped), the back-up light switch connector and the speedometer cable from the transmission.

8. Remove the radiator grille from the deflector panel.

9. Disconnect the upper and lower radiator hoses and the reservoir tank hose.

10. Remove the fan shroud, fan blade assembly and the radiator.

11. If equipped with air conditioning, remove the compressor from the engine and move it aside; do not disconnect the pressure hoses.

12. If equipped with a V6 engine, perform the following procedures:

a. Remove the power steering pump-to-engine brackets and move the pump aside.

b. Remove the spark plug wire from the No. 1 spark plug.

c. Remove the distributor cap with the No. 1 spark plug wire.

d. Remove the ignition coil.

13. Remove the gear shift lever by performing the following procedures:

a. Place the gear shift lever in **N**.

b. Remove the front console from the floor panel.

c. Pull the shift lever boot and grommet upward.

d. Remove the shift lever cover bolts and the shift lever.

14. Remove the transfer shift lever by performing the following procedures:

a. Place the transfer shift lever in **H** (except V6 engine) or **2H** (V6 engine).

b. Pull the shift lever boot and dust cover upward.

c. Remove the shift lever retaining bolts.

d. Pull the shift lever from the transfer case.

15. Raise and safely support the vehicle. Remove the front wheels. Drain the oil from the engine.

CAUTION: *The EPA warns that prolonged contact with used engine oil may cause a number of skin disorders, including cancer! You should make every effort to minimize your exposure to used engine oil. Protective gloves should be worn when changing the oil. Wash your hands and any other exposed skin areas as soon as possible after exposure to used engine oil. Soap and water, or waterless hand cleaner should be used.*

16. Drain the transmission and transfer case fluid.

17. If equipped with an automatic transmission, perform the following procedures:

a. Remove the oil level gauge and the tube.

b. Disconnect the shift select control link rod from the select lever.

c. Disconnect the downshift cable from the transmission.

d. Disconnect and plug the fluid coolant lines from the transmission.

18. If equipped with a 1-piece driveshaft, remove the driveshaft flange-to-pinion nuts, lower the driveshaft and pull it from the transmission.

19. If equipped with a 2-piece driveshaft, perform the following procedures:

a. Remove the rear driveshaft flange-to-pinion nuts.

b. Remove the rear driveshaft flange-to-front driveshaft flange bolts and the rear driveshaft.

c. Remove the center bearing-to-chassis bolts, move the front driveshaft rearward and from the transmission.

20. Remove the front driveshaft's splinded yoke flange-to-transfer case bolts and separate the front driveshaft from the transfer case; do not allow the splined flange to fall away from the driveshaft.

21. Remove the starter-to-engine bolts and the starter.

22. If equipped with a clutch slave cylinder, remove it from the transmission and move it aside.

23. Remove the exhaust pipe-to-exhaust manifold nuts, the exhaust pipe bracket-to-transmission bolts, the front exhaust pipe-to-2nd exhaust pipe bolts and the front exhaust pipe from the vehicle.

24. Attach an engine hanger to the rear of the exhaust manifold.

25. Using an engine hoist, connect it to the engine hangers and support the engine.

26. If equipped with a V6 engine, remove the catalytic converter and the parking brake cable bracket.

27. Remove the transmission/transfer case assembly by performing the following procedures:

a. Using a transmission jack, place it under the transmission and support the assembly.

b. Remove the rear mount-to-transmission nuts.

c. Remove the rear mount-to-side mount member nuts/bolts and the mount.

d. Remove the transmission-to-engine bolts.

e. Move the transmission assembly rearward.

f. Carefully lower the transmission.

28. Remove the engine-to-mount nuts/bolts.

29. Using the hoist, slowly, lift the engine; be sure to hold the front of the engine higher than the rear.

30. Place the engine on a work stand.

To install:

31. Using the hoist, slowly, lower the engine into the vehicle; be sure to hold the front of the engine higher than the rear.

32. Install the engine-to-mount nuts/bolts.

33. Install the transmission/transfer assem-

bly by performing the following procedures:

a. Raise the transmission into position.

b. Move the transmission forward and engage it with the engine.

c. Install the engine-to-transmission bolts.

d. Install the rear mount and the rear mount-to-side mount member nuts/bolts.

e. Install the rear mount-to-transmission nuts.

f. Remove the transmission jack.

34. If equipped with a V6 engine, install the catalytic converter and the parking brake cable bracket.

35. Remove the engine hoist and the engine hanger from the rear of the exhaust manifold.

36. Install the front exhaust pipe, exhaust pipe-to-exhaust manifold nuts, the exhaust pipe bracket-to-transmission bolts, the front exhaust pipe-to-2nd exhaust pipe bolts.

37. If equipped with a clutch slave cylinder, install it onto the transmission.

38. Install the starter and the starter-to-engine bolts.

39. Install the front driveshaft's splined yoke flange-to-transfer case bolts.

40. If equipped with a 2-piece driveshaft, perform the following procedures:

a. Install the front driveshaft into the transmission and the center bearing-to-chassis bolts.

b. Install the rear driveshaft and the rear driveshaft flange-to-front driveshaft flange bolts.

c. Install the rear driveshaft flange-to-pinion nuts.

41. If equipped with a 1-piece driveshaft, install the driveshaft into the transmission and the driveshaft flange-to-pinion nuts.

42. If equipped with an automatic transmission, perform the following procedures:

a. Connect the fluid coolant lines to the transmission.

b. Connect the downshift cable to the transmission.

c. Connect the shift select control link rod to the select lever.

d. Install the oil level gauge and the tube.

43. Install the front wheels and lower the vehicle.

44. Install the transfer shift lever by performing the following procedures:

a. Position the shift lever into the transfer case.

b. Install the shift lever retaining bolts.

c. Push the dust cover and the shift lever boot downward.

45. Install the gear shift lever by performing the following procedures:

a. Install the shift lever and the shift lever cover bolts.

b. Push the grommet and shift lever boot downward.

c. Install the front console to the floor panel.

46. If equipped with a V6 engine, perform the following procedures:

a. Install the ignition coil.

b. Install the distributor cap with the No. 1 spark plug wire.

c. Install the spark plug wire from the No. 1 spark plug and reconnect the wires to the distributor cap.

d. Install the power steering pump-to-engine brackets.

47. If equipped with air conditioning, install the compressor to the engine.

48. Install the radiator, the fan blade assembly and the fan shroud.

49. Connect the upper and lower radiator hoses and the reservoir tank hose.

50. Install the radiator grille to the deflector panel.

51. Install the clutch return spring (if equipped), the clutch control cable (if equipped), the back-up light switch connector and the speedometer cable to the transmission.

52. Connect the following items:

a. Air switch valve hose.

b. Oxygen sensor wire.

c. Vacuum switch valve hose.

d. Thermal vacuum switching valve hose.

e. Pressure regulator vacuum hose.

f. Canister hose.

g. ECM harness.

h. Fuel hose(s).

53. Connect the necessary hoses, electrical connectors, control cables and control rods to the engine.

54. Install the air cleaner (2.3L engine) or air cleaner duct and hose (2.6L engine).

55. Refill the engine, the transmission, the transfer case and the cooling system. Install the undercover, if equipped.

56. Install the hood.

57. Install the battery and connect both battery cables, the positive cable first.

58. Adjust the belt tension. Start the engine, check for leaks.

59. Check and/or adjust the idle speed and ignition timing.

Rocker Arm Cover

REMOVAL AND INSTALLATION

4-Cylinder SOHC Engine

1. Disconnect the negative ($-$) battery cable.

2. Remove the air cleaner (carbureted) and air inlet hose (EFI).

3. Remove the PCV hose.

4. Label and remove the spark plug wires.

1. PCV valve
2. Spark plug wire
3. Timing belt cover bolts
4. Cylinder head cover bolts
5. Cylinder head cover

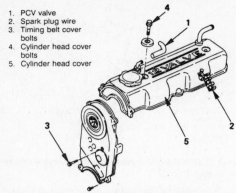

Rocker arm cover removal—SOHC engines

1. PCV valve
2. Center cover
3. Spark plug wires
4. Upper timing cover
5. Cylinder head cover

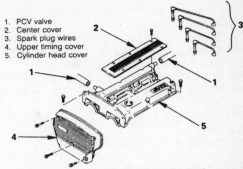

Rocker arm cover removal—DOHC engines

5. Remove the timing belt cover attaching bolts, if so equipped.

6. Disconnect the power brake booster hose and throttle cable if in the way.

7. Remove the rocker arm cover bolts and cover.

8. If the cover will not come loose, tap the sides with a rubber hammer to dislodge.

To install:

1. Clean the gasket mating surfaces with a scraper and solvent.

2. Install a new gasket and apply a 0.08–0.12 in. (2–3mm) bead of RTV sealer around the gasket surface.

3. Install the rocker arm cover and torque the bolts to 89 inch lbs. (10 Nm).

4. Install the spark plug wires, PCV hose, brake booster hose and throttle cable if removed.

5. Install the air cleaner or air inlet hose.

6. Connect the battery cable, start the engine and check for leaks.

4-Cylinder DOHC Engines

1. Disconnect the negative (−) battery cable.

2. Remove the and air inlet hose (EFI).

3. Remove the PCV hose. Remove the center cover.

4. Label and remove the spark plug wires.

5. Remove the upper timing belt cover attaching bolts.

6. Remove the rocker arm cover bolts and cover.

7. If the cover will not come loose, tap the sides with a rubber hammer to dislodge.

To install:

1. Clean the gasket mating surfaces with a scraper and solvent. Be careful not to damage aluminum surfaces.

2. Install a new gasket and apply a 0.08–0.12 in. (2–3mm) bead of RTV sealer around the gasket surface.

3. Install the rocker arm cover and torque the bolts to 53 inch lbs. (6 Nm).

4. Install the spark plug wires, center cover and PCV hose.

5. Install the air cleaner or air inlet hose.

6. Connect the battery cable, start the engine and check for leaks.

V6 Engines

1. Disconnect the negative (−) battery cable.

2. Remove the air cleaner.

3. Remove the ignition coil and bracket (RH) or the crankcase ventilation valve (LH).

4. Label and remove the spark plug wires from the bracket at the rocker arm cover stud.

5. Remove the PCV valve (RH).

6. Remove the throttle cable and alternator (RH only).

7. Remove the rocker arm cover nuts, reinforcements, cover and gasket. If the cover sticks to the head, bump the end of the cover with a rubber hammer. Do NOT damage the sealing flange.

To install:

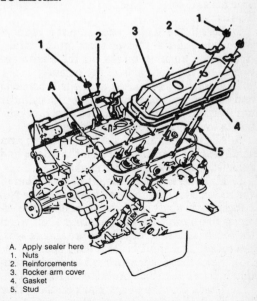

A. Apply sealer here
1. Nuts
2. Reinforcements
3. Rocker arm cover
4. Gasket
5. Stud

Rocker arm cover removal—V6 engines

1. Clean the gasket mating surfaces with a scraper and solvent.

2. Install the rocker arm cover with a new gasket. Apply RTV sealer to the cylinder head-to-intake manifold contact points.

3. Install the rocker arm cover nuts and reinforcements. Torque the cover bolts to 72 inch lbs. (8 Nm).

4. Install the throttle cable and alternator (RH only).

5. Install the PCV valve (RH).

6. Install the spark plug wires to the bracket at the rocker arm cover stud.

7. Install the ignition coil and bracket (RH) or the crankcase ventilation valve (LH).

8. Install the air cleaner.

9. Connect the negative (−) battery cable, start the engine and check for leaks.

Rocker Arms/Shafts

REMOVAL AND INSTALLATION

4-Cylinder Gasoline Engines, Except DOHC

1. Disconnect the negative battery cable. Remove the rocker cover.

2. Loosen the rocker arm shaft bracket nuts a little at a time, in sequence, starting with the outer nuts.

3. Remove the nuts from the rocker arm shaft brackets. Remove shaft assembly.

4. To disassemble the rockers and shafts; remove the spring from the rocker arm shaft, the rocker brackets and arms. Keep parts in order for reassembly.

5. Before installing apply a generous amount of clean engine oil to the rocker arm shaft, rocker arms and valve stems.

To install:

6. Install the longer shaft on the exhaust valve side and the shorter shaft on the intake side so the aligning marks on the shafts are turned on the front side of the engine.

7. Assemble the rocker arm shaft brackets and rocker arms to the shafts so the cylinder number, on the upper face of the brackets, points toward the front of the engine.

8. Align the mark on the No. 1 rocker arm shaft bracket with the mark on the intake and exhaust valve side rocker arm shaft.

9. Make certain the amount of projection of the rocker arm shaft beyond the face of the No. 1 rocker arm shaft bracket, is longer on the exhaust side shaft than on the intake shaft when the rocker arm shaft stud holes are aligned with the rocker arm shaft bracket stud holes.

10. Place the rocker arm shaft springs in position between the shaft bracket and rocker arm.

11. Check that the punch mark on the rocker arm shaft is facing upward, then, install the rocker arm shaft bracket assembly onto the cyl-

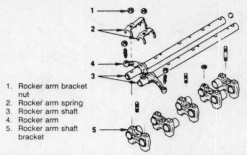

1. Rocker arm bracket nut
2. Rocker arm spring
3. Rocker arm shaft
4. Rocker arm
5. Rocker arm shaft bracket

Rocker arm and shaft assembly—gasoline 4-cyl. engine, except DOHC

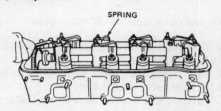

Rocker arm assembly—gasoline 4-cyl. engine, except DOHC

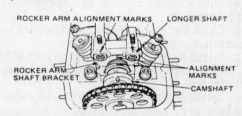

Rocker arm shaft installation—gasoline 4-cyl. engine, except DOHC

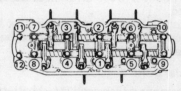

Rocker arm bolt torque sequence—gasoline 4-cyl. engine, except DOHC

inder head studs. Align the mark on the camshaft with the mark on the No. 1 rocker arm shaft bracket.

12. Torque the rocker arm shaft brackets-to-cylinder head nuts to 16 ft. lbs. (21 Nm) and bolts to 72 inch lbs. (8 Nm).

NOTE: *Hold the rocker arm springs while torquing the nuts to prevent damage to the spring. Start with the center nut and work outward.*

13. Adjust the valves as outlined in Chapter 2. Install the rocker arm cover, with a new gasket and sealer. Check the ignition timing.

Diesel Engine

1. Disconnect the negative (−) battery cable. Remove the cam cover.

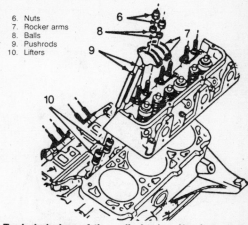

6. Nuts
7. Rocker arms
8. Balls
9. Pushrods
10. Lifters

Bolt loosening sequence for removing rocker arm assembly—diesel engine

2. Loosen the rocker arm shaft bracket nuts a little at a time, in sequence, commencing with the outer brackets.

3. Remove the nuts from the rocker arm shaft brackets.

4. Disassemble the rocker arm shaft assembly by removing the spring from the rocker arm shaft and then removing the rocker arm brackets and arms.

5. Inspect the rocker arm shaft for runout. Support the shaft on V-blocks at each end and check runout by slowly turning it with the probe of a dial indicator. Replace the shaft with a new one if the runout exceeds 0.4mm (0.0156 in.). Runout should not exceed 0.2mm (0.0079 in.).

6. Inspect the rocker arm shaft for wear, replace the shaft if obvious signs of wear are encountered.

To install:

7. Use a liberal amount of clean engine oil to coat the shaft, rocker arms and valve stems. Install the longer shaft on the exhaust valve side, shorter shaft on the intake side, so that the aligning marks on the shafts are turned to the front of the engine.

8. Torque the rocker arm shaft bracket and stud nuts to 15–22 ft. lbs. (20–27 Nm). Hold the rocker arm springs with an adjustable wrench while torquing the nuts to prevent damage to the springs. Torque the nuts a little at a time in sequence, beginning with the center bracket and working outward.

9. Adjust valve clearances, reinstall the cam cover and check for leaks.

V6 Engine

1. Disconnect the negative battery cable.

2. Remove the rocker arm covers.

3. Remove the rocker arm nut, the pivot balls, the rocker arm and the pushrods. Keep all components separated so they may be reinstalled in the same location.

NOTE: *The intake and exhaust pushrods are of different lengths.*

To install:

4. Install the pushrods in their original location; be sure the lower ends are seated in the lifter.

5. Coat the bearing surfaces of the rocker arms and pivot balls with Molykote or equivalent.

Exploded view of the cylinder head/rocker arm assembly—V6 engine

6. Install the rocker arm nuts and torque them to 14–20 ft. lbs. (20–27 Nm).

7. Adjust the valve lash as outlined in Chapter 2.

Thermostat

REMOVAL AND INSTALLATION

Gasoline Engine

The thermostat is located, under the thermostat housing, on top of the intake manifold at the front of the engine. The diesel and 4XE1 engine have the thermostat located in front of the intake manifold.

1. Disconnect the negative battery cable.

2. Drain the cooling system. Disconnect the upper radiator hose from the thermostat housing.

CAUTION: *When draining the coolant, keep in mind that cats and dogs are attracted by the ethylene glycol antifreeze, and are quite likely to drink any that is left in an uncovered container or in puddles on the ground. This will prove fatal in sufficient quantity. Always drain the coolant into a sealable container. Coolant should be reused unless it is contaminated or several years old.*

3. Remove the air cleaner assembly.

4. Remove the thermostat housing from the intake manifold.

Thermostat—typical for all models

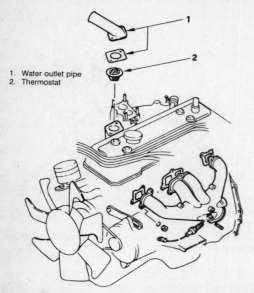

1. Water outlet pipe
2. Thermostat

Thermostat housing—carbureted G180Z and G200Z engines

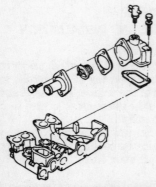

Exploded view of thermostat and housing—FWD I-Mark

Exploded view of thermostat and housing—late model Impulse

5. Remove the gasket and the thermostat.
To install:
6. Install the thermostat, with the spring facing the engine.
7. Using a new gasket, install the thermostat housing. Torque the bolts to 15 ft. lbs. (20 Nm).

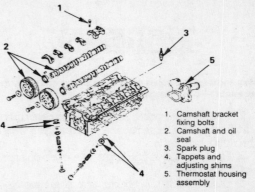

1. Camshaft bracket fixing bolts
2. Camshaft and oil seal
3. Spark plug
4. Tappets and adjusting shims
5. Thermostat housing assembly

Thermostat assembly—DOHC 4XE1 engine, SOHC similar

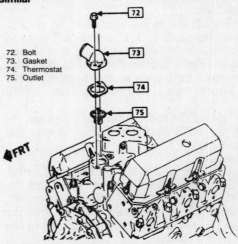

72. Bolt
73. Gasket
74. Thermostat
75. Outlet

FRT

Thermostat assembly—V6 engine

8. Connect the radiator hose to the thermostat housing and refill the cooling system.
9. Install the air cleaner.
10. Connect the negative battery cable.
11. Operate the engine until normal operating temperatures are reached and check the thermostat operation.

Diesel Engine

The thermostat is located, under the thermostat housing, at upper front of the engine.
1. Disconnect the negative battery cable.
2. Drain the cooling system.
CAUTION: *When draining the coolant, keep in mind that cats and dogs are attracted by the ethylene glycol antifreeze, and are quite likely to drink any that is left in an uncovered container or in puddles on the ground. This will prove fatal in sufficient quantity. Always drain the coolant into a sealable container. Coolant should be reused unless it is contaminated or several years old.*
3. Disconnect the electrical connectors from the thermostat housing.

4. Remove the upper thermostat housing-to-lower housing bolts and the upper housing.

5. Remove the gasket and the thermostat.

6. Clean the gasket mounting surfaces.

To install:

7. Install the thermostat, with the spring facing the engine.

8. Using a new gasket, install the upper thermostat housing and torque the upper housing-to-lower housing bolts to 10–17 ft. lbs. (14–24 Nm).

9. Connect the electrical connectors.

10. Connect the radiator hose to the thermostat housing and refill the cooling system.

11. Connect the negative battery cable.

12. Operate the engine until normal operating temperatures are reached and check the thermostat operation.

Intake Manifold

REMOVAL AND INSTALLATION

Carbureted Engines

1. Drain the cooling system and disconnect the battery cables.

CAUTION: *When draining the coolant, keep in mind that cats and dogs are attracted by the ethylene glycol antifreeze, and are quite likely to drink any that is left in an uncovered container or in puddles on the ground. This will prove fatal in sufficient quantity. Always drain the coolant into a sealable container.*

Coolant should be reused unless it is contaminated or several years old.

NOTE: *Before removing the intake manifold, check to make certain the engine coolant is completely drained. If any water remains in the block it will flow into the cylinders when the intake manifold is removed.*

2. Remove the air cleaner assembly.

3. Disconnect the radiator hose from the front part of the intake manifold.

4. Disconnect the fuel lines, all vacuum lines and the carburetor control cable.

5. Disconnect the heater hoses from the rear part of the manifold and from the connector under the dashboard.

6. Disconnect the distributor vacuum hose and all thermo-valve wiring. Disconnect the electric choke or solenoid wires.

NOTE: *Tag all wires before disconnecting them.*

7. Disconnect the PCV hose from the rocker cover. Disconnect the EGR valve from the EGR pipe and disconnect the air injection vacuum hose from the three-way connector.

8. Remove the eight nuts attaching the intake manifold and lift it clear, being careful not to snag any loose lines.

To install:

9. Check the manifold for cracks or damage. The manifold head surfaces can be checked for distortion by using a straight edge and a feeler gauge. Distortion should be no more than

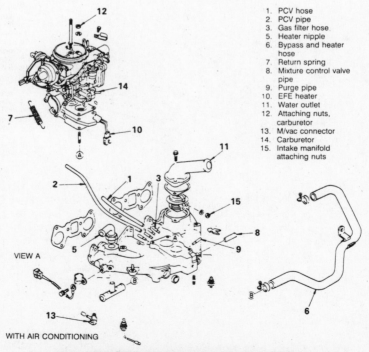

1. PCV hose
2. PCV pipe
3. Gas filter hose
5. Heater nipple
6. Bypass and heater hose
7. Return spring
8. Mixture control valve pipe
9. Purge pipe
10. EFE heater
11. Water outlet
12. Attaching nuts, carburetor
13. M/vac connector
14. Carburetor
15. Intake manifold attaching nuts

VIEW A

WITH AIR CONDITIONING

Intake manifold assembly—4-cyl. carbureted engines

0.4mm (0.0157 in.), if it is beyond the limit, the distortion has to be corrected with a surface grinder.

10. Clean all gasket mating surfaces with a scraper and solvent.

11. Replace all gaskets and torque all nuts in sequence to 25–32 ft. lbs. (34–43 Nm).

12. Connect the PCV hose to the rocker cover. Connect the EGR valve to the EGR pipe and connect the air injection vacuum hose to the three-way connector.

13. Connect the distributor vacuum hose and all thermo-valve wiring. Connect the electric choke or solenoid wires.

14. Connect the heater hoses to the rear part of the manifold and to the connector under the dashboard.

15. Connect the fuel lines, all vacuum lines and the carburetor control cable.

16. Connect the radiator hose to the front part of the intake manifold.

17. Install the air cleaner assembly.

18. Refill the cooling system, connect the battery cables and check for leaks.

G200Z, 4ZD1, 4ZC1-T EFI Engines

1. Relieve the fuel pressure. Disconnect the negative battery cable and remove the air cleaner assembly.

2. Remove the EGR pipe clamp bolt at the rear of the cylinder head.

3. Raise and support the vehicle safely. Remove the EGR pipe from the intake and exhaust manifolds.

4. Remove the EGR valve and bracket assembly from the intake manifold.

5. Lower the vehicle and drain the cooling system.

CAUTION: *When draining the coolant, keep in mind that cats and dogs are attracted by the ethylene glycol antifreeze, and are quite likely to drink any that is left in an uncovered container or in puddles on the ground. This will prove fatal in sufficient quantity. Always drain the coolant into a sealable container. Coolant should be reused unless it is contaminated or several years old.*

6. Remove the upper coolant hoses from the manifold.

7. Disconnect the accelerator linkage, vacuum lines, electrical wiring and fuel line from the intake manifold.

8. Remove the intake manifold mounting nuts and remove the manifold from the cylinder head.

9. Remove the lower heater hose while holding the manifold away from the engine. Remove the manifold from the vehicle.

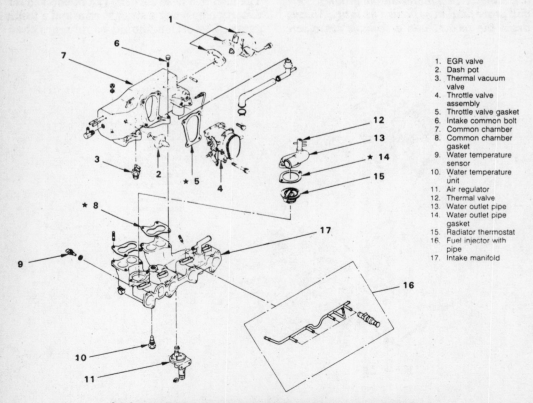

1. EGR valve
2. Dash pot
3. Thermal vacuum valve
4. Throttle valve assembly
5. Throttle valve gasket
6. Intake common bolt
7. Common chamber
8. Common chamber gasket
9. Water temperature sensor
10. Water temperature unit
11. Air regulator
12. Thermal valve
13. Water outlet pipe
14. Water outlet pipe gasket
15. Radiator thermostat
16. Fuel injector with pipe
17. Intake manifold

Intake manifold and common chamber—G200Z, 4ZD1 and 4ZC1-T

To install:

10. Connect the lower heater hose to the manifold. Using a new gasket, install the intake manifold. Torque the bolts to 16 ft. lbs. (21 Nm).

11. Connect the accelerator linkage, vacuum lines, electrical wiring and fuel line to the intake manifold.

12. Connect the upper coolant hose to the intake manifold.

13. Install the EGR valve and bracket assembly to the intake manifold.

14. Install the EGR pipe to the intake and exhaust manifolds. Lower the vehicle.

15. Install the EGR pipe clamp bolt to the rear of the cylinder head.

16. Install the air cleaner and connect the negative battery cable.

4ZE1 Engine

1. Relieve the fuel pressure. Disconnect the negative battery cable and remove the air duct.

2. Drain the cooling system. Remove the upper coolant hoses from the manifold.

CAUTION: *When draining the coolant, keep in mind that cats and dogs are attracted by the ethylene glycol antifreeze, and are quite likely to drink any that is left in an uncovered container or in puddles on the ground. This will prove fatal in sufficient quantity. Always drain the coolant into a sealable container. Coolant should be reused unless it is contaminated or several years old.*

3. Remove the air regulator rubber hose from the intake plenum.

4. Remove the EGR valve and bracket assembly from the intake manifold.

5. Disconnect the accelerator linkage, vacuum lines, electrical wiring and fuel line from the throttle body.

6. Remove the throttle body-to-plenum nuts and the throttle body.

7. Remove the plenum-to-intake manifold bolts and the plenum.

8. Remove the intake manifold-to-cylinder head nuts and the manifold from the cylinder head.

To install:

9. Using a new gasket, install the intake manifold to the cylinder head.

10. Using a new gasket, install the plenum to the intake manifold. Torque the bolts to 14–18 ft. lbs. (20–25 Nm).

11. Using a new gasket, install the throttle body to the plenum.

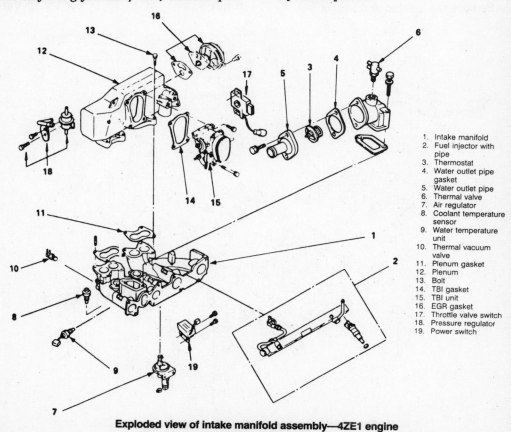

1. Intake manifold
2. Fuel injector with pipe
3. Thermostat
4. Water outlet pipe gasket
5. Water outlet pipe
6. Thermal valve
7. Air regulator
8. Coolant temperature sensor
9. Water temperature unit
10. Thermal vacuum valve
11. Plenum gasket
12. Plenum
13. Bolt
14. TBI gasket
15. TBI unit
16. EGR gasket
17. Throttle valve switch
18. Pressure regulator
19. Power switch

Exploded view of intake manifold assembly—4ZE1 engine

12. Connect the accelerator linkage, vacuum lines, electrical wiring and fuel line.

13. Install the EGR valve and bracket assembly to the intake manifold.

14. Install the air regulator rubber hose to the intake plenum.

15. Install the upper coolant hoses to the manifold.

16. Install the air duct. Connect the negative battery cable. Refill the cooling system.

4XC1-U and 4XC1-T Engines

1. Disconnect the negative (−) battery cable.

2. Release the fuel pressure and remove the pressure regulator.

CAUTION: *When draining the coolant, keep in mind that cats and dogs are attracted by the ethylene glycol antifreeze, and are quite likely to drink any that is left in an uncovered container or in puddles on the ground. This will prove fatal in sufficient quantity. Always drain the coolant into a sealable container. Coolant should be reused unless it is contaminated or several years old.*

3. Drain the engine coolant.

4. Remove the Vacuum Switching Valve (VSV).

5. Remove the bracket and hanger.

6. Remove the throttle body assembly and disconnect the engine harness assembly.

7. Disconnect the IAC valve and remove the relief valve.

8. Disconnect the MAP sensor and back pressure transducer.

9. Remove the EGR valve and adapter.

10. Remove the fuel injectors with pipe.

11. Remove the manifold attaching bolts and manifold.

To install:

12. Clean the gasket mating surfaces with a scraper and solvent. Do NOT damage the aluminum surfaces. Inspect the components for distortion and damage.

13. Using new gaskets, install the manifold attaching bolts and manifold. Torque the bolts and nuts to 17 ft. lbs. (25 Nm).

14. Install the fuel injectors with pipe.

15. Install the EGR valve and adapter.

16. Connect the MAP sensor and back pressure transducer.

17. Connect the IAC valve and install the relief valve.

18. Install the throttle body assembly and connect the engine harness assembly.

19. Install the bracket and hanger.

20. Install the Vacuum Switching Valve (VSV).

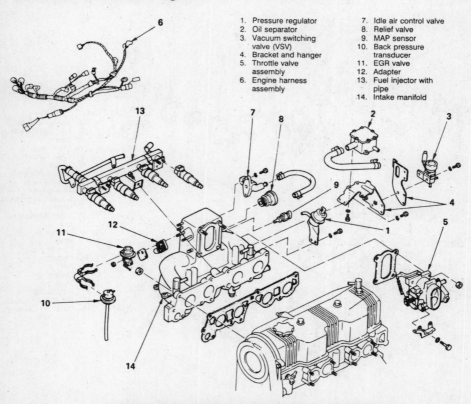

1. Pressure regulator
2. Oil separator
3. Vacuum switching valve (VSV)
4. Bracket and hanger
5. Throttle valve assembly
6. Engine harness assembly
7. Idle air control valve
8. Relief valve
9. MAP sensor
10. Back pressure transducer
11. EGR valve
12. Adapter
13. Fuel injector with pipe
14. Intake manifold

Intake manifold assembly—4XC1-U and 4XC1-T engines

21. Refill the engine with coolant.

22. Install the pressure regulator.

23. Connect the negative (−) battery cable, start the engine and check for leaks.

4XE1 SOHC and DOHC Engine

1. Disconnect negative battery cable and drain cooling system. Remove the air cleaner duct hose from the common chamber.

CAUTION: *When draining the coolant, keep in mind that cats and dogs are attracted by the ethylene glycol antifreeze, and are quite likely to drink any that is left in an uncovered container or in puddles on the ground. This will prove fatal in sufficient quantity. Always drain the coolant into a sealable container. Coolant should be reused unless it is contaminated or several years old.*

2. Disconnect and tag the following vacuum lines and wiring harness:

  a. Fast idle vacuum hose from the air duct hose.

  b. The MAP sensor vacuum hose from the common chamber.

  c. Disconnect the TPC valve vacuum hose from the common chamber.

  d. Disconnect the canister vacuum hose from the common chamber.

  e. Electronic control gas injection harness, disconnect the 2 ECM ground connectors from the bracket located on top of the common chamber. Disconnect the 2 green and black multi-pin connectors on the top of the common chamber.

  f. Remove the MAT sensor conector.

3. Disconnect the accelerator cable from the throttle body and at the common chamber. Disconnect the PCV valve hose from the valve cover.

4. Disconnect the master vacuum hose from the master vacuum tube at the common chamber side.

5. Disconnect the induction valve vacuum hose from the common chamber. Disconnect the EGR valve and the throttle valve.

6. Remove the fuel hose clips from the common chamber. Remove the bolt and nuts retaining the common (intake) chamber to the en-

gine. Remove the common (intake) chamber and gasket from the engine.

To install:

7. Clean the gasket mating with a scraper and solvent. Be sure to use a new gasket and torque the common chamber retaining bolts and nuts to 18 ft. lbs. (25 Nm).

8. Install the common (intake) chamber and gasket to the engine. Install the fuel hose clips to the common chamber. Install the bolt and nuts retaining the common (intake) chamber to the engine. Torque the bolts to 17 ft. lbs. (21 Nm).

9. Connect the induction valve vacuum hose to the common chamber. Connect the EGR valve and the throttle valve.

10. Connect the master vacuum hose to the master vacuum tube at the common chamber side.

11. Connect the accelerator cable to the throttle body and at the common chamber. Connect the PCV valve hose to the valve cover.

  a. Install the MAT sensor connector.

  b. Electronic control gas injection harness, connect the 2 ECM ground connectors to the bracket located on top of the common chamber. Connect the 2 green and black multi-pin connectors on the top of the common chamber.

  c. Connect the canister vacuum hose to the common chamber.

  d. Connect the TPC valve vacuum hose to the common chamber.

  e. The MAP sensor vacuum hose to the common chamber.

  f. Fast idle vacuum hose to the air duct hose.

12. Connect negative battery cable and fill cooling system. Install the air cleaner duct hose to the common chamber.

4FB1 Diesel Engine

1. Open the hood and disconnect the battery. Remove the air cleaner assembly.

2. Remove the connecting hose and PCV hose.

3. Remove the sensing resistor assembly.

4. Remove the 6 screws attaching the injec-

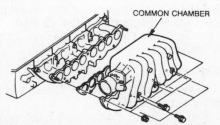

Intake manifold and common chamber—4XE1 SOHC and DOHC engines

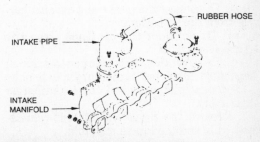

Intake manifold—4FB1 diesel engine

tion pipe clips and remove the injection pipe.

5. Remove the 10 bolts attaching the upper dust cover and remove the upper dust cover.

6. Remove the 2 bolts attaching the engine hanger and remove the engine hanger.

7. Remove the 2 bolts attaching the stay and remove the stay. Remove the three bolts and two nuts attaching the intake manifold and lift off the manifold.

To install:

8. Clean the gasket mating surfaces with a scraper and solvent. Inspect the components for warpage, distortion and damage.

9. Using a new manifold gasket, install the manifold and torque the bolts to 25–32 ft. lbs. (34–44 Nm).

10. Install the 2 bolts attaching the engine hanger and hanger.

11. Install the 10 bolts attaching the upper dust cover and the upper dust cover.

12. Install the 6 screws attaching the injection pipe clips and the injection pipe.

13. Install the sensing resistor assembly.

14. Install the connecting hose and PCV hose.

15. Connect the battery cable, install the air cleaner assembly, start the engine and check for leaks.

Combination Manifold

REMOVAL AND INSTALLATION

C223 and C223-T Diesel Engine

Although the intake and exhaust manifolds are individual parts, they must be remove at the same time so the 1-piece gasket may be replaced.

1. Disconnect the negative battery cable.

2. Remove the air cleaner and air duct, if necessary.

3. Disconnect the accelerator cable from the throttle body.

4. Label and disconnect the necessary vacuum hoses and electrical connectors.

5. If not equipped with a turbocharger, disconnect the exhaust manifold from the exhaust pipe.

6. If equipped with a turbocharger, perform the following procedures:

    a. Disconnect the intake and exhaust hoses from the turbocharger.

    b. Disconnect the oil lines from the turbocharger.

    c. Remove the turbocharger-to-exhaust manifold nuts, the turbocharger assembly-to-exhaust pipe nuts and the turbocharger assembly.

7. Remove the intake manifold-to-cylinder head bolts and the intake manifold.

8. Remove the exhaust manifold-to-cylinder

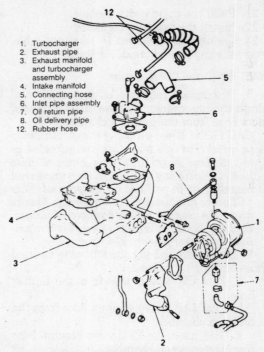

1. Turbocharger
2. Exhaust pipe
3. Exhaust manifold and turbocharger assembly
4. Intake manifold
5. Connecting hose
6. Inlet pipe assembly
7. Oil return pipe
8. Oil delivery pipe
12. Rubber hose

Combination manifold assembly—C223 and C223-T engines

head bolts, the exhaust manifold and discard the gasket.

9. Clean the gasket mounting surfaces.

To install:

10. Using a new gasket, install it onto the cylinder head with the center mark facing outward and upward.

11. Install the exhaust and intake manifolds onto the cylinder head and torque the nuts/bolts to 10–17 ft. lbs. (14–25 Nm) [non-turbocharged engine] or 13–17 ft. lbs. (17–25 Nm) [turbocharged engine].

12. If not equipped with a turbocharger, install the exhaust manifold to the exhaust pipe.

13. If equipped with a turbocharger, perform the following procedures:

    a. Refill the turbocharger with clean engine oil.

    b. Install the turbocharger-to-exhaust manifold nuts to 16–23 ft. lbs. (24–32 Nm) and the turbocharger assembly-to-exhaust pipe nuts to 16–23 ft. lbs. (24–32 Nm).

    c. Connect the oil feed lines to the turbocharger.

V6 Engine

1. Relieve the fuel pressure. Disconnect the negative battery cable.

2. Remove the air cleaner. Drain the cooling system.

CAUTION: *When draining the coolant, keep*

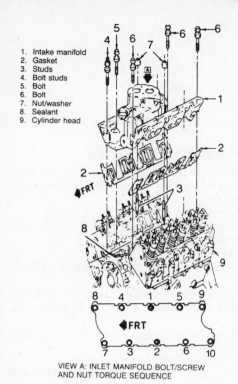

1. Intake manifold
2. Gasket
3. Studs
4. Bolt studs
5. Bolt
6. Bolt
7. Nut/washer
8. Sealant
9. Cylinder head

VIEW A: INLET MANIFOLD BOLT/SCREW
AND NUT TORQUE SEQUENCE

Intake manifold assembly—V6 engines

in mind that cats and dogs are attracted by the ethylene glycol antifreeze, and are quite likely to drink any that is left in an uncovered container or in puddles on the ground. This will prove fatal in sufficient quantity. Always drain the coolant into a sealable container. Coolant should be reused unless it is contaminated or several years old.

3. Label and disconnect the wires and hoses from the TBI unit and the intake manifold.

4. Disconnect and plug the fuel lines from the TBI unit.

5. Disconnect the accelerator cables from the TBI unit.

6. Disconnect the ignition wires from the spark plugs and the wires from the coil.

7. Remove the distributor cap with the wires.

8. Mark the location of the rotor to the distributor housing and the distributor housing to the intake manifold.

9. Remove the distributor hold-down clamp and the distributor.

10. Label and disconnect the EGR vacuum line and the emission hoses.

11. Remove the pipe brackets from the rocker arm covers.

12. Remove the rocker arm covers.

13. Remove the upper radiator hose and the heater hose.

14. Disconnect the electrical connectors from the coolant sensors.

15. Remove the intake manifold nuts/bolts, the manifold and gaskets.

16. Clean the gasket mounting surfaces.

To install:

17. Using RTV sealant, apply an 3mm (⅛ in.) bead to the front and rear of the block; make sure no water or oil is present.

18. Using new gaskets, marked right and left side, apply a 6mm (¼ in.) bead of sealant to hold them in place and install them onto the cylinder heads; the gaskets may have to be cut to be installed around the pushrods.

19. Install the intake manifold and torque the nuts/bolts, in sequence, to 23 ft. lbs. (31 Nm) and retorque using the same sequence.

NOTE: *Make sure the areas between the case ridges and the intake manifold are completely sealed.*

20. Install the heater hose and the radiator to the manifold.

21. Using new gaskets, install the rocker arm covers.

22. Connect the electrical connectors to the coolant sensors.

23. Install the pipe brackets.

24. Align the matchmarks and install the distributor and the distributor cap.

25. Connect the fuel lines and the accelerator cables to the TBI unit.

26. Connect all the wires and vacuum hoses.

27. Install the air cleaner. Connect the negative battery cable. Refill the cooling system.

Exhaust Manifold

REMOVAL AND INSTALLATION

G180Z, G200Z and 4ZD1 Engines

1. Disconnect the negative battery cable and remove the air cleaner assembly.

2. Remove the EGR pipe clamp bolt at the rear of the cylinder head.

3. Raise and safely support the vehicle. Remove the EGR pipe from the intake and exhaust manifolds.

4. Disconnect the exhaust pipe from the exhaust manifold. Disconnect the electrical connector from the oxygen sensor.

5. Remove the manifold shield and heat stove.

6. Remove the manifold retaining nuts and remove the manifold from the engine.

To install:

7. Using a new gasket, install the exhaust manifold and torque the nuts to 14–18 ft. lbs. (20–25 Nm).

8. Install the heat stove and shield.

9. Connect the exhaust pipe to the exhaust

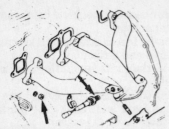

Exhaust manifold assembly showing oxygen sensor—G180Z, G200Z and 4ZD1 engines

Exhaust manifold—4XC1-U engine

manifold. Connect the electrical connector to the oxygen sensor.

10. Install the EGR pipe to the intake and exhaust manifolds and lower the vehicle.

11. Install the EGR pipe clamp bolt to the rear of the cylinder head.

12. Install the air cleaner. Connect the negative battery cable.

4XC1–U and 4XE1 SOHC/DOHC Engine

1. Disconnect the negative (−) battery cable.

2. Disconnect the oxygen sensor connector and remove the exhaust pipe from the exhaust manifold.

3. Remove the heat protector and EGR pipe with clip.

4. Remove the manifold retaining bolts and manifold.

To install:

1. Make sure the sealing surfaces are clean.

2. Install the manifold with a new gasket and torque the bolts to 30 ft. lbs. (39 Nm).

3. Install the EGR pipe with the clip. Torque the bolt to 32 ft. lbs. (44 Nm).

4. Install the heat protector and connect the oxygen sensor.

5. Reconnect the exhaust pipe to the manifold.

6. Start the engine and check for leaks.

4XC1-T and 4ZC1-T (Turbo) Engine

1. Disconnect the negative (−) battery cable.

2. Remove the lower and upper heat protectors.

3. Remove the wastegate manifold.

4. Remove the turbocharger assembly and manifold heat protector.

To install:

1. Clean all gasket mating surfaces with a scraper.

2. Using new gaskets, install the exhaust manifold and torque the bolts to 15 ft. lbs. (21 Nm).

3. Install the turbocharger assembly and manifold heat protector.

4. Install the wastegate manifold.

5. Install the lower and upper heat protectors.

6. Connect the negative (−) battery cable, start the engine and check for leaks.

4ZE1 Engine

1. Disconnect the negative battery cable and remove the air duct.

2. Remove the hoses from the air pump.

3. Remove the air pump bolts, remove the drive belt and the air pump.

4. Remove the EGR pipe clamp bolt at the rear of the cylinder head.

5. Raise and safely support the vehicle. Remove the EGR pipe from the intake and ex-

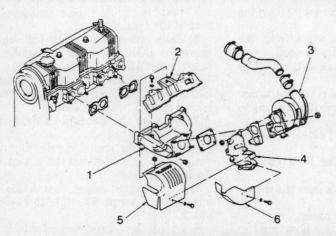

1. Exhaust manifold and hanger
2. Heat protector
3. Turbocharger assembly
4. Wastegate manifold
5. Upper heat protector
6. Lower heat protector

Exhaust manifold and turbocharger assembly—4XC1-T engine

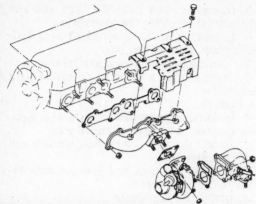

Exhaust manifold and turbocharger assembly—4ZC1-T engine

haust manifolds. If necessary, remove the dipstick and tube.

6. Disconnect the exhaust pipe from the exhaust manifold. Disconnect the electrical connector from the oxygen sensor.

7. Remove the manifold shield.

8. Remove the manifold-to-cylinder head nuts and the manifold from the engine.

To install:

9. Using a new gasket, install the exhaust manifold and torque the nuts to 16 ft. lbs. (22 Nm).

10. Install the heat shield. If the dipstick was removed, install the tube and the dipstick.

11. Connect the exhaust pipe to the exhaust manifold. Connect the electrical connector to the oxygen sensor.

12. Install the EGR pipe to the intake and exhaust manifolds and lower the vehicle.

13. Install the EGR pipe clamp bolt to the rear of the cylinder head.

14. Install the air duct. Connect the negative battery cable.

V6 Engine

1. Disconnect the negative battery cable.

2. Raise and safely support the vehicle.

3. Remove the exhaust pipe from the manifold.

4. Lower the vehicle and remove the rear manifold bolts.

5. On the right side, remove the diverter valve, the heat shield, the AIR pump bracket and alternator bracket.

6. On the left side, remove the heat stove tube and the power steering bracket.

7. Remove the exhaust manifold-to-cylinder head bolts and the manifold.

8. Clean the gasket mounting surfaces.

To install:

9. Using a new gasket, install the exhaust

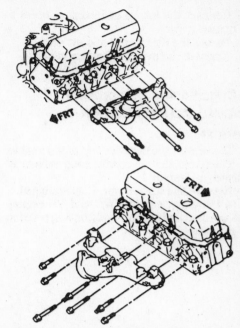

Exhaust manifold assembly—V6 engine

manifold-to-cylinder head bolts and torque the bolts to 25 ft. lbs. (34 Nm).

10. On the left side, install the power steering bracket and heat stove tube.

11. On the right side, install the AIR pump bracket, the alternator bracket, the diverter valve and the heat shield.

12. Raise and safely support the vehicle.

13. Install the exhaust pipe-to-manifold bolts.

14. Lower the vehicle and connect the negative battery cable.

Turbocharger

REMOVAL AND INSTALLATION

1. Disconnect the negative battery cable.

2. Remove the air cleaner and air duct.

3. Disconnect the intake and exhaust hoses from the turbocharger.

4. Disconnect the oil lines from the turbocharger.

5. Remove the turbocharger-to-exhaust manifold nuts, the turbocharger assembly-to-exhaust pipe nuts and the turbocharger assembly.

6. Clean the gasket mounting surfaces. Refill the turbocharger with clean engine oil.

To install:

7. Using a new gasket, install the turbocharger-to-exhaust manifold nuts to 16–23 ft. lbs. (21–33 Nm) and the turbocharger assembly-to-exhaust pipe nuts to 16–23 ft. lbs. (21–33 Nm).

8. Connect the oil feed lines to the turbocharger.

9. Connect the intake and exhaust hoses to the turbocharger.

10. Install the air cleaner and air duct.

11. Connect the negative battery cable.

Air Conditioning Compressor

REMOVAL AND INSTALLATION

All Vehicles

1. Disconnect the negative (−) battery cable.

2. Discharge the air conditioning system as outlined in Chapter 1.

3. Remove the undercover, if so equipped.

4. All engines, except FWD and V6 engine, mark the distributor rotor and housing position and remove.

5. Disconnect and plug the high and low pressure fittings from the compressor.

6. Loosen the belt tension center bolt and adjusting bolt. Remove the belt.

7. Disconnect the clutch electrical wire.

8. Remove the retaining bolts and compressor.

To install:

9. Install the compressor and retaining bolts.

10. Connect the clutch electrical wire.

11. Install the belt, adjust belt tension and tighten center bolt.

12. Connect the high and low pressure fittings to the compressor.

13. Install the distributor.

14. Evacuate, leak test and charge the air conditioning system as outlined in Chapter 1.

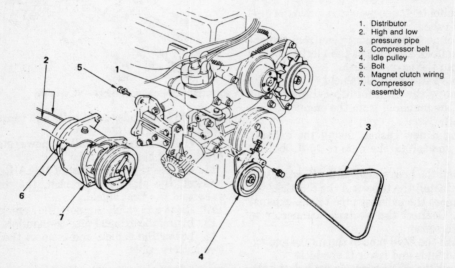

1. Distributor
2. High and low pressure pipe
3. Compressor belt
4. Idle pulley
5. Bolt
6. Magnet clutch wiring
7. Compressor assembly

Air conditioning compressor assembly—all engines, except FWD vehicles and V6 engines

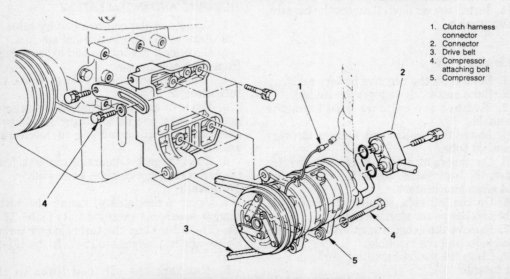

1. Clutch harness connector
2. Connector
3. Drive belt
4. Compressor attaching bolt
5. Compressor

Air conditioning compressor assembly—FWD I-Mark

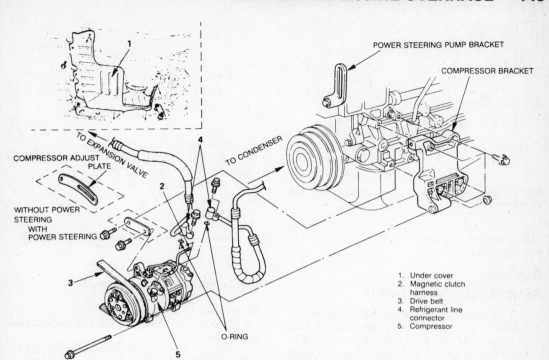

POWER STEERING PUMP BRACKET

COMPRESSOR BRACKET

TO EXPANSION VALVE

TO CONDENSER

COMPRESSOR ADJUST PLATE

WITHOUT POWER STEERING

WITH POWER STEERING

O-RING

1. Under cover
2. Magnetic clutch harness
3. Drive belt
4. Refrigerant line connector
5. Compressor

Air conditioning compressor assembly—FWD Stylus and Impulse

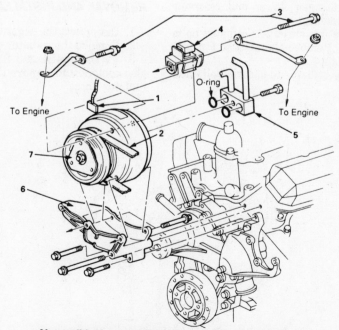

To Engine

O-ring

To Engine

1. Magnetic clutch harness
2. Drive belt
3. Bolt
4. Dynamic damper
5. Refrigerant line connector
6. Bracket
7. Compressor

Air conditioning compressor assembly—V6 engines

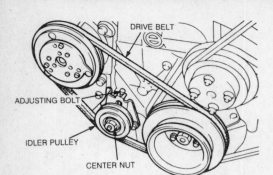

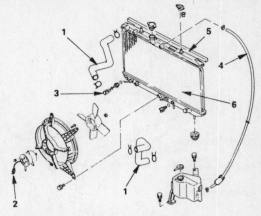

Belt adjusting pulley—all engines, except FWD and V6 engines

1. Radiator hoses
2. Fan motor cable connector
3. Thermo switch cable connector
4. Coolant recovery tank
5. Upper end panel
6. Radiator and cooling fan

Radiator assembly—Cars with electric fans

15. Connect the negative (−) battery cable and check operation.

Radiator

REMOVAL AND INSTALLATION

1. Disconnect the negative battery cable.
CAUTION: *When draining the coolant, keep in mind that cats and dogs are attracted by the ethylene glycol antifreeze, and are quite likely to drink any that is left in an uncovered container or in puddles on the ground. This will prove fatal in sufficient quantity. Always drain the coolant into a sealable container. Coolant should be reused unless it is contaminated or several years old.*
2. Drain the cooling system.
3. Remove the upper, lower and reservoir hoses from the radiator.
4. Remove the fan shroud-to-radiator bolts and the shroud. Remove the electric fan and shroud, if so equipped.
5. Remove the radiator-to-chassis bolts and the radiator.

To install:
6. Install the radiator and the radiator-to-chassis bolts.
7. Install the fan shroud and the shroud-to-radiator bolts. Install and connect the electric fan, if so equipped.
8. Reconnect the radiator hoses.
9. Refill the cooling system.
10. Connect the negative battery cable.

Electric Cooling Fan

REMOVAL AND INSTALLATION

1. Disconnect the negative (−) battery cable.
2. Remove the radiator dynamic damper.
3. FWD Impulse and Stylus; drain the engine coolant and remove the upper and lower radiator hoses.

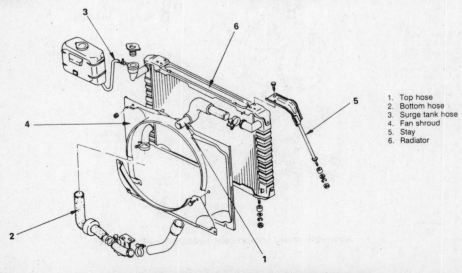

1. Top hose
2. Bottom hose
3. Surge tank hose
4. Fan shroud
5. Stay
6. Radiator

Radiator assembly—Trucks, cars with mechanical fan similar

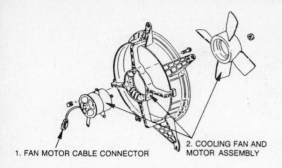

1. FAN MOTOR CABLE CONNECTOR
2. COOLING FAN AND MOTOR ASSEMBLY

Electric cooling fan—FWD Impulse and Stylus

CAUTION: *When draining the coolant, keep in mind that cats and dogs are attracted by the ethylene glycol antifreeze, and are quite likely to drink any that is left in an uncovered container or in puddles on the ground. This will prove fatal in sufficient quantity. Always drain the coolant into a sealable container. Coolant should be reused unless it is contaminated or several years old.*

4. Disconnect the fan electrical connector.

5. Remove the fan guide, fan and motor assembly.

To install:

6. Install the fan guide, fan and motor assembly.

7. Connect the fan electrical connector.

8. FWD Impulse and Stylus; install the radiator hoses and refill the engine coolant.

9. Install the radiator dynamic damper.

10. Connect the negative (−) battery cable, start the engine and check for leaks.

Water Pump
REMOVAL AND INSTALLATION
G180Z and G200Z Engine

NOTE: *This procedure may be easier if the radiator and shroud is removed. If the radiator is not removed, place cardboard in front so not to damage the radiator core*

1. Open the hood and disconnect the battery. Remove the lower engine cover.

2. Drain the cooling system.

CAUTION: *When draining the coolant, keep in mind that cats and dogs are attracted by the ethylene glycol antifreeze, and are quite likely to drink any that is left in an uncovered container or in puddles on the ground. This will prove fatal in sufficient quantity. Always drain the coolant into a sealable container. Coolant should be reused unless it is contaminated or several years old.*

3. On cars without air conditioning, remove the fan.

4. On cars with air conditioning, remove the air pump and generator mounting bolts, then remove the fan and air pump drive belt (pivot the generator and air pump in toward the engine). Remove the fan and pulley with set plate. Remove the hoses to the pump.

5. Remove the 6 bolts attaching the water pump and remove the water pump assembly. Clean all gasket surfaces carefully.

To install:

6. Install the 6 bolts attaching the water pump with a new gasket.

7. On cars with air conditioning, install the air pump and generator mounting bolts, then

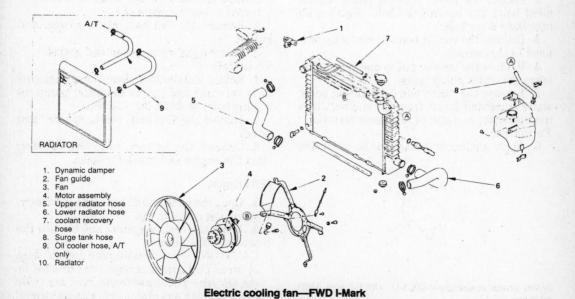

1. Dynamic damper
2. Fan guide
3. Fan
4. Motor assembly
5. Upper radiator hose
6. Lower radiator hose
7. coolant recovery hose
8. Surge tank hose
9. Oil cooler hose, A/T only
10. Radiator

Electric cooling fan—FWD I-Mark

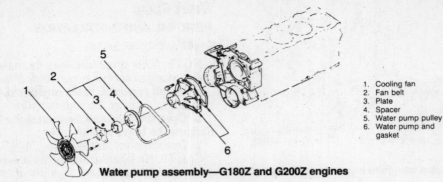

1. Cooling fan
2. Fan belt
3. Plate
4. Spacer
5. Water pump pulley
6. Water pump and gasket

Water pump assembly—G180Z and G200Z engines

install the fan and air pump drive belt (pivot the generator and air pump in toward the engine). Install the fan and pulley with set plate. Install the hoses to the pump.

8. On cars without air conditioning, install the fan.

9. Refill the cooling system.

10. Connect the battery, start the engine and check for leaks.

4XC1-U, 4XC1-T and 4XE1 DOHC Engines

1. Disconnect the negative battery cable and drain the coolant into a suitable drain pan.

CAUTION: *When draining the coolant, keep in mind that cats and dogs are attracted by the ethylene glycol antifreeze, and are quite likely to drink any that is left in an uncovered container or in puddles on the ground. This will prove fatal in sufficient quantity. Always drain the coolant into a sealable container. Coolant should be reused unless it is contaminated or several years old.*

2. Loosen the power steering pump adjustment bolts and remove the belt. (Remove all necessary drive belts).

3. Remove the timing belt as previously outlined in this section.

4. Remove the tension pulley and spring. Remove the water pump pulley.

5. Remove the water pump mounting bolts, water pump and gasket from the engine. Clean the mounting surfaces of all gasket material.

To install:

6. Apply a suitable sealant to the mounting

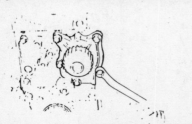

Water pump assembly—4XC1-U, 4XC1-T and 4XE1 engines

surfaces of the pump and torque the pump to 17 ft. lbs. (23 Nm).

7. Install the tension pulley and spring. Install the water pump pulley.

8. Install the timing belt as previously outlined in this section.

9. Install the belt and tighten the power steering pump adjustment bolts.

10. Connect the negative battery cable and refill the coolant. Start the engine and check for leaks.

4ZC1-T and 4ZD1 Engines

1. Disconnect the battery and drain the radiator.

CAUTION: *When draining the coolant, keep in mind that cats and dogs are attracted by the ethylene glycol antifreeze, and are quite likely to drink any that is left in an uncovered container or in puddles on the ground. This will prove fatal in sufficient quantity. Always drain the coolant into a sealable container. Coolant should be reused unless it is contaminated or several years old.*

2. Remove the fan belt, plate, spacer, and pulley.

3. Remove the water pump and gasket.

To install:

4. Before installation, clean the gasket surfaces carefully and torque the water pump retaining bolts to 18 ft. lbs. (25 Nm).

5. Install the fan belt, plate, spacer, and pulley.

6. Connect the battery, refill the radiator, start the engine and check for leaks.

4FB1 Engine

1. Open the hood and disconnect the battery. Remove the radiator cap.

2. Drain the cooling system and remove the hoses from the pump.

CAUTION: *When draining the coolant, keep in mind that cats and dogs are attracted by the ethylene glycol antifreeze, and are quite likely to drink any that is left in an uncovered*

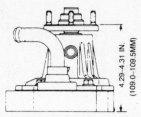

4.29–4.31 IN.
(109.0–109.5MM)

Water pump assembly—4FB1 diesel engine

container or in puddles on the ground. This will prove fatal in sufficient quantity. Always drain the coolant into a sealable container. Coolant should be reused unless it is contaminated or several years old.

3. Remove the fan and pulley.

4. Remove the four attaching bolts holding the damper pulley. Remove the damper pulley.

5. Remove the engine dust covers.

6. Remove the bypass hose.

7. Remove the five bolts attaching the water pump and remove the pump and gasket.

To install:

8. Clean all gasket surfaces carefully and inspect for nicks, cracks or deep scratches.

9. Use a new gasket. Torque all water pump mounting bolts to 11–18 ft. lbs. (15–23 Nm).

10. Install the bypass hose.

11. Install the engine dust covers.

12. Install the four attaching bolts holding the damper pulley and damper pulley.

13. Install the fan and pulley.

14. Install the hoses to the water pump and refill the cooling system.

15. Connect the battery, install the radiator cap, start the engine and check for leaks.

4ZE1 Engine

1. Disconnect the negative battery cable.

2. Remove the undercover, if equipped, and drain the cooling system.

CAUTION: *When draining the coolant, keep in mind that cats and dogs are attracted by the ethylene glycol antifreeze, and are quite likely to drink any that is left in an uncovered container or in puddles on the ground. This will prove fatal in sufficient quantity. Always drain the coolant into a sealable container. Coolant should be reused unless it is contaminated or several years old.*

3. Remove the drive belt from the water pump pulley.

4. Remove the coolant hose from the pump body, if so equipped.

5. Remove the fan blade and pulley from the pump hub.

6. Remove the water pump-to-engine bolts, the water pump and gasket.

7. Clean and inspect the mounting surfaces of the water pump and engine.

To install:

8. Install a new gasket and the water pump; torque the water pump-to-engine bolts to 24–38 ft. lbs. (33–52 Nm).

9. Install the fan blade and pulley to the water pump.

10. Connect the water hose to the pump, if so equipped.

11. Install and adjust the drive belt.

12. Refill the cooling system and install the undercover, if equipped.

13. Connect the negative battery cable.

14. Operate the engine to normal operating temperatures and check for leaks.

V6 Engine

1. Disconnect the negative battery terminal.

2. Drain the cooling system.

CAUTION: *When draining the coolant, keep in mind that cats and dogs are attracted by the ethylene glycol antifreeze, and are quite likely to drink any that is left in an uncovered container or in puddles on the ground. This will prove fatal in sufficient quantity. Always drain the coolant into a sealable container. Coolant should be reused unless it is contaminated or several years old.*

3. Remove the fan shroud and/or radiator support, as applicable.

4. Remove all drive belts.

5. Remove the fan and pulley from the water pump.

6. Remove the alternator upper and lower brackets. Remove the power steering pump lower bracket and swing aside.

7. Remove the bottom radiator hose and heater hose from the pump.

8. Remove the water pump.

To install:

1. Clean the gasket mating surfaces with solvent and a scraper.

2. Coat the new gasket with RTV Sealer.

3. Install the gasket, pump and bolts. Torque the pump bolts 15–25 ft. lbs. (20–34 Nm).

4. Install the bottom radiator hose and heater hose to the pump.

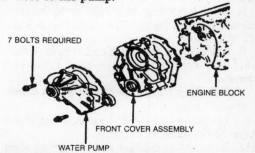

7 BOLTS REQUIRED

ENGINE BLOCK

FRONT COVER ASSEMBLY

WATER PUMP

Water pump assembly—V6 engine

5. Install the alternator upper and lower brackets. Install the power steering pump lower bracket.

6. Install the fan and pulley to the water pump.

7. Install all drive belts.

8. Install the fan shroud and/or radiator support, as applicable.

9. Refill the cooling system.

10. Connect the negative battery terminal. Start the engine and check for leaks.

Cylinder Head

REMOVAL AND INSTALLATION

G180Z and G200Z Engine

1. Disconnect the negative battery cable and drain the engine coolant. Remove the rocker cover.

CAUTION: *When draining the coolant, keep in mind that cats and dogs are attracted by the ethylene glycol antifreeze, and are quite likely to drink any that is left in an uncovered container or in puddles on the ground. This will prove fatal in sufficient quantity. Always drain the coolant into a sealable container. Coolant should be reused unless it is contaminated or several years old.*

2. Remove the EGR pipe clamp bolt at the rear of the cylinder head.

3. Raise and support the vehicle safely. Disconnect the exhaust pipe at the exhaust manifold.

4. Lower the vehicle.

5. Disconnect the heater hoses at the intake manifold and at the rear of the cylinder head. Remove the air conditioning compressor and/or power steering pump with hoses attached and support them aside.

6. Disconnect the accelerator linkage and fuel line at the carburetor. Disconnect and label the electrical connections, spark plug wires and vacuum lines at the cylinder head.

7. Rotate the engine until the No. 4 cylinder is in the firing position. Remove the distributor cap and mark the rotor to housing relationship. Remove distributor and the fuel pump.

8. Lock the timing chain adjuster by depressing and turning the automatic adjuster side pin 90° clockwise.

9. Remove the timing sprocket-to-camshaft bolt and remove the sprocket from the camshaft.

NOTE: *Keep the sprocket on the chain damper and chain.*

10. Disconnect the AIR hose and the check valve at the exhaust manifold.

11. Remove the cylinder head to timing cover bolts.

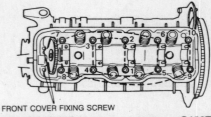

FRONT COVER FIXING SCREW

Cylinder head bolt torque sequence—G180Z and G200Z engines

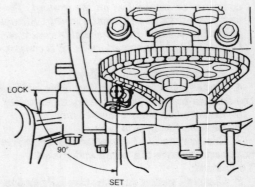

LOCK

90°

SET

Locking the timing chain adjuster—G180Z engine

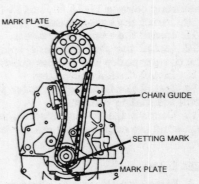

MARK PLATE

CHAIN GUIDE

SETTING MARK

MARK PLATE

Keeping the timing sprocket attached to the chain while aligning or removing

12. Starting with the outer bolts and working inward, remove the cylinder head bolts.

13. Remove the cylinder head, intake and exhaust manifold as a unit. Remove all accessories if the manifold has to be serviced.

To install:

14. Clean the gasket mating surfaces with scraper and solvent. Check the cylinder head and block for warpage using a straight edge and feeler gauge. Refer to "Cylinder Head Inspection" section in this Chapter.

15. Use a new gasket and install the cylinder head on the engine.

16. Torque the bolts to specifications. Refer to the "Torque" specification chart in the beginning of this Chapter.

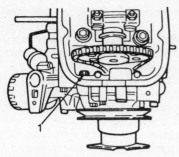

Locking the timing chain adjuster—G200Z engine

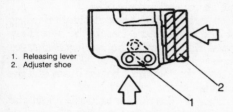

1. Releasing lever
2. Adjuster shoe

Push in on the automatic adjuster shoe 1 and lock it in the retracted position by releasing the lever 2— G200Z engine

17. Install the timing chain by performing the following procedures:

a. Install the timing sprocket and pinion gear with the groove side toward the front cover. Align the key grooves with the key on the crankshaft, then drive into position.

b. Confirm that the No. 1 piston is at TDC. If not, turn the crankshaft so the key is turned toward the cylinder head side (No. 1 and No. 4 pistons at top dead center).

c. Install the timing chain by aligning the mark plate on the chain with the mark on the crankshaft timing sprocket. The side of the chain with the mark plate is on the front side and the side of the chain with the most links between the mark plates is on the chain guide side.

d. Install the camshaft timing sprocket so the mark side of the sprocket faces forward and so the triangular mark aligns with the chain mark plate.

NOTE: *Keep the timing chain engaged with the camshaft timing sprocket until the sprocket is installed on the camshaft.*

18. Install the front cover assembly, using a new gasket and sealer.

19. Connect the AIR hose and the check valve at the exhaust manifold.

20. Connect the accelerator linkage and fuel line to the carburetor. Connect the electrical connections, the spark plug wires and the vacuum lines.

21. Connect the heater hoses to the intake manifold and the rear of the cylinder head. In-

stall the air conditioner compressor and/or power steering pump.

22. Connect the exhaust pipe to the exhaust manifold.

23. Install the EGR pipe clamp bolt to the rear of the cylinder head.

24. Install the rocker arm cover and connect the negative battery cable.

25. Refill the engine with coolant. Start the engine and check for leaks.

4XC1-U and 4XC1-T Engines

1. Disconnect the negative battery cable and drain the cooling system into a suitable drain pan.

CAUTION: *When draining the coolant, keep in mind that cats and dogs are attracted by the ethylene glycol antifreeze, and are quite likely to drink any that is left in an uncovered container or in puddles on the ground. This will prove fatal in sufficient quantity. Always drain the coolant into a sealable container. Coolant should be reused unless it is contaminated or several years old.*

2. Remove the air cleaner assembly and disconnect the flex hose along with the oxygen sensor at the exhaust manifold.

3. Disconnect the exhaust pipe bracket at the block and the exhaust pipe at the manifold. On turbocharged model remove exhaust pipe at wastegate manifold, and remove vacuum line for turbocharger control.

4. Disconnect the spark plug wires and remove the thermostat housing.

5. Rotate the engine until the engine is at TDC on the compression stroke of the No. 1 cylinder. Remove distributor cap and mark the distributor rotor to housing position and housing to cylinder head. Remove the distributor hold down bolt and remove the distributor.

6. Remove the vacuum advance hoses and the ground cable at the cylinder head.

7. Disconnect the fuel lines at the fuel pump

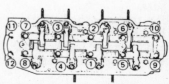

Rocker arm shaft torque sequence—4XC1-U and 4XC1-T, to 16 ft. lbs. (22 Nm)

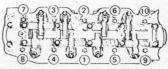

Cylinder head torque sequence—4XC1-U and 4XC1-T engines

and at the carburetor, remove the secondary hoses and throttle cable on non-turbocharged model.

8. Remove engine wiring harness assembly from fuel injectors and fuel line from fuel injector pipe on turbocharged model.

9. Disconnect the vacuum switching valve electrical connector and the heater hoses.

10. Remove the alternator, power steering pump and air conditioning adjusting bolts, brackets and drive belts. Remove and tag all necessary electrical and vacuum lines.

11. Support the engine using a suitable vertical hoist. Remove the right hand motor mount and the bracket at the front cover.

12. Remove the crankshaft bolt and remove the boss and the crank pulley.

13. Remove the timing cover and be sure the mark on the cam pulley is aligned with the upper surface of the cylinder head. Also the dowel pin on the camshaft should be positioned at the top.

14. Disconnect the PCV hoses and remove the valve cover. If the cover sticks to the head, carefully strike the valve cover with a soft mallet.

15. Insert a hex wrench into the tension pulley hexagonal hole. Loosen the timing belt tension by rotating the tension pulley clockwise and remove the timing belt.

16. Remove the fuel pump (non-turbocharged model) and disconnect the intake manifold coolant hoses.

17. Remove the cylinder head bolts, remove the bolts from both ends at the same time, working toward the middle and remove the cylinder head.

To install:

18. To install, use new seals and gaskets, apply oil to the head bolt threads and torque the head bolts.

NOTE: *When torquing the cylinder head bolts, work from the middle toward both ends at the same time. The torque should be 29 ft. lbs. on the first pass and 58 ft. lbs. on the second pass.*

19. After torquing the head bolts, adjust the valve clearance.

20. Install the fuel pump (non-turbocharged model) and connect the intake manifold coolant hoses.

21. Install the timing belt. Insert a hex wrench into the tension pulley hexagonal hole. tighten the timing belt tension by rotating the tension pulley counterclockwise.

22. Connect the PCV hoses and install the valve cover with new gasket.

23. Install the timing cover and be sure the mark on the cam pulley is aligned with the upper surface of the cylinder head. Also the dowel

pin on the camshaft should be positioned at the top.

24. Install the crankshaft pulley and bolt.

25. Install the right hand motor mount and the bracket at the front cover.

26. Install the alternator, power steering pump and air conditioning adjusting bolts, brackets and drive belts. Connect all necessary electrical and vacuum lines.

27. Connect the vacuum switching valve electrical connector and the heater hoses.

28. Install engine wiring harness assembly from fuel injectors and fuel line from fuel injector pipe on turbocharged model.

29. Connect the fuel lines at the fuel pump and at the carburetor, install the secondary hoses and throttle cable on non-turbocharged model.

30. Install the vacuum advance hoses and the ground cable at the cylinder head.

31. Install the distributor hold down bolt and distributor to the marked position.

32. Connect the spark plug wires and install the thermostat housing.

33. Connect the exhaust pipe bracket at the block and the exhaust pipe at the manifold. On turbocharged model install exhaust pipe at wastegate manifold, and connect vacuum line for turbocharger control.

34. Install the air cleaner assembly and connect the flex hose along with the oxygen sensor at the exhaust manifold.

35. Connect the negative battery cable and refill the cooling system.

4ZD1, 4ZC1-T, 4XE1 (SOHC) Engines

1. Disconnect negative battery cable and drain cooling system.

CAUTION: *When draining the coolant, keep in mind that cats and dogs are attracted by the ethylene glycol antifreeze, and are quite*

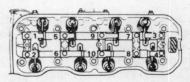

Rocker arm shaft torque sequence—torque nuts 1-8 to 16 ft. lbs. (22 Nm) and 9 and 10 to 60 inch lbs. (7 Nm), 4ZD1 and 4ZC1-T engines

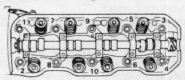

Cylinder head torque sequence—4ZD1 and 4ZC1-T engine

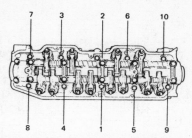

Cylinder head torque sequence—4XE1 SOHC engine

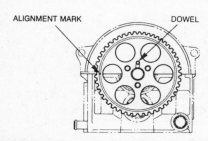

Camshaft pulley alignment marks—4XE1 SOHC engine

likely to drink any that is left in an uncovered container or in puddles on the ground. This will prove fatal in sufficient quantity. Always drain the coolant into a sealable container. Coolant should be reused unless it is contaminated or several years old.

2. Rotate the engine until the engine is at TDC on the compression stroke of the No. 1 cylinder, make sure timing mark is on the scale. Remove distributor cap and mark the distributor rotor to housing position and housing to cylinder head. Remove the distributor hold down bolt and remove the distributor.

3. Disconnect radiator inlet and outlet hoses and remove the radiator.

4. Remove the alternator and the air conditioner drive belts. Remove engine fan.

5. Remove the crankshaft pulley center bolt and remove the pulley and hub assembly.

6. Remove the air pump belt and move the air pump out of the way. Remove the air conditioning compressor and lay it to one side (if equipped with air conditioning). Remove the compressor mounting bracket.

7. Remove the water pump pulley. Remove the top section of the front cover and the water pump.

8. Remove the lower section of the front cover.

9. Remove the tension spring. Loosen the top bolt of the tension pulley and draw the tension pulley fully to the water pump side.

10. Remove the timing belt.

11. Remove cam cover.

12. Sequentially loosen and remove the rocker arm shaft tightening nuts from the outermost one and remove the rocker arm shaft with the bracket as an assembly.

13. Raise vehicle and disconnect the exhaust pipe at the exhaust manifold. On turbocharged model disconnect exhaust pipe from wastegate manifold and remove control cable for turbocharger.

14. Lower vehicle disconnect all lines, hoses, electrical connections and spark plug wires.

NOTE: *Tag all wires and hoses before disconnecting them from the engine.*

15. Disconnect the accelerator linkage, on turbocharged model remove engine wiring harness assembly from fuel injectors and fuel line from fuel injector pipe.

16. Remove the cylinder head bolts using an extension bar with socket. Remove bolts in progressive sequence, beginning with the outer bolts.

NOTE: *Use light oil to free frozen bolts.*

17. With the aid of an assistant, remove the cylinder head, intake and exhaust manifolds as an assembly.

To install:

18. Clean all gasket material from the cylinder head and block surfaces. Check for nicks or heavy scratches on the mating surfaces.

19. Cylinder bolt threads in the block and threads on the bolts must be cleaned. Dirt will affect head torque.

20. Match up the old gasket with the new gasket to make sure it is an exact fit.

21. Install the gasket and cylinder head with the help of an assistant. Torque in sequence and 2 steps first step 57 ft. lbs. (76 Nm) and second step 72 ft. lbs. (96 Nm).

22. Connect the accelerator linkage, on turbocharged model install engine wiring harness assembly to fuel injectors and fuel line to fuel injector pipe.

23. Connect all lines, hoses, electrical connections and spark plug wires.

24. Raise vehicle and connect the exhaust pipe at the exhaust manifold. On turbocharged model connect exhaust pipe to wastegate manifold and install control cable for turbocharger.

25. Sequentially install and torque the rocker arm shaft tightening nuts from the outermost one and install the rocker arm shaft with the bracket as an assembly. Refer to the appropriate illustration.

26. Install the rocker arm cover.

27. Install the timing belt.

28. Install the tension spring. Tighten the top bolt of the tension pulley.

29. Install the lower section of the front cover.

30. Install the water pump pulley. Install the top section of the front cover and the water pump.

31. Install the air pump and belt. Install the air conditioning compressor bracket and compressor.

32. Install the crankshaft pulley and center bolt.

33. Install the alternator and the air conditioner drive belts. Install engine fan.

34. Connect radiator inlet and outlet hoses and after installing the radiator.

35. Install the distributor, hold down bolt and cap.

36. Connect negative battery cable, refill the cooling system and check for leaks.

4XE1 DOHC Engine

NOTE: *The following procedure is the long version of cylinder head removal for I-Mark, Stylus and Impulse equipped with the 4XE1 DOHC engine. The instruction below may be altered as seen fit by the technician using this procedure. It may also be necessary to remove the engine from the vehicle in order to remove the cylinder head.*

1. Disconnect negative battery cable and drain cooling system. Remove the air cleaner duct hose from the common chamber.

CAUTION: *When draining the coolant, keep in mind that cats and dogs are attracted by the ethylene glycol antifreeze, and are quite likely to drink any that is left in an uncovered container or in puddles on the ground. This will prove fatal in sufficient quantity. Always drain the coolant into a sealable container. Coolant should be reused unless it is contaminated or several years old.*

2. Rotate the engine until the engine is at TDC on the compression stroke of the No. 1 cylinder, make sure timing mark is on the scale. Remove distributor cap and mark the distributor rotor to housing position and housing to cylinder head. Remove the distributor hold down bolt and remove the distributor.

3. Disconnect radiator inlet and outlet hoses along with transmission oil cooler lines, if so equipped and remove the radiator.

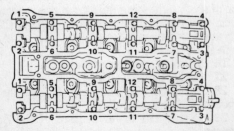
Camshaft bearing cap torque sequence—4XE1 DOHC engine

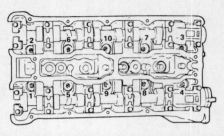
Cylinder head bolt REMOVAL sequence—4XE1 DOHC engine

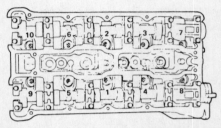
Cylinder head bolt torque sequence—4XE1 DOHC engine

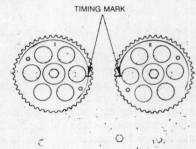
Camshaft timing marks—4XE1 DOHC engine

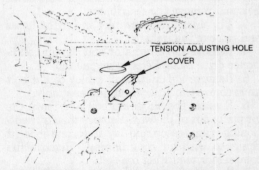
Timing belt tension adjuster—4XE1 DOHC engine

4. Remove the power steering pump drive belt, for vehicles with air conditioners, remove the power steering pump and compressor drive belt. Loosen the 2 power steering pump adjust plates bolts.

5. Remove the alternator drive belt from the crank pulley side. Disconnect the clip securing the high pressure air conditioning line to the strut tower.

6. Disconnect and tag the following vacuum lines and wiring harness:

a. Fast idle vacuum hose from the air duct hose.

b. The MAP sensor vacuum hose from the common chamber.

c. Disconnect the TPC valve vacuum hose from the common chamber.

d. Disconnect the canister vacuum hose from the common chamber.

e. Electronic control gas injection harness, disconnect the 2 ECM ground connectors from the bracket located on top of the common chamber. Disconnect the 2 green and black multi-pin connectors on the top of the common chamber.

f. Remove the MAT sensor connector.

7. Disconnect the accelerator cable from the throttle body and at the common chamber. Disconnect the PCV valve hose from the valve cover.

8. Disconnect the master vacuum hose from the master vacuum tube at the common chamber side.

9. Disconnect the induction valve vacuum hose from the common chamber. Disconnect the EGR valve and the throttle valve.

10. Remove the fuel hose clips from the common chamber. Remove the common (intake) chamber retaining bolts and remove the chamber. Disconnect the fuel injection harness from the fuel injector.

11. Remove the fuel rail assembly. Disconnect the induction control vacuum switching valve harness connection. Disconnect the idle air control valve connector and vacuum hose. Remove the air induction control valve assembly.

12. Disconnect the center (valve)' cover and disconnect (and tag) the high tension cables from the spark plugs and clips.

13. Remove the pulse air bracket with pipe. Remove the heat protector and the EGR pipe.

14. Disconnect the exhaust pipe from the exhaust manifold and remove the exhaust hanger. Remove the exhaust manifold bolts along with the manifold.

15. Remove the coolant bypass line and the thermostat housing.

16. Remove the engine mounting bridge.

17. Remove the upper timing belt cover.

18. Using a suitable engine hoist, slightly raise and support the engine safely.

19. Remove the passenger side engine mount from the engine. Disconnect the torque rod at the firewall.

20. Remove the passenger side engine mounting bracket from the engine. Using special crank pulley tool J-37988 or equivalent, remove the crank pulley bolt.

21. Raise the passenger side of the engine, be sure that the front wheels remain on the ground while lifting the engine. Raise the engine too high will left the front wheels off the ground and may cause damage to the drive shaft universal joint.

22. Remove the timing belt lower cover. Remove the cranking pulley and extract up through the engine compartment. Refit the crank pulley bolt. Align the crank pulley timing gear to top dead center.

23. Loosen the tension pulley bolt a ½ turn counterclockwise. If the pulley bolt is loosened more than ½ a turn, the pulley will swing too far out of adjustment and may be difficult to readjust.

24. Mark the direction of rotation of the timing mark with a piece of chalk and remove the timing belt.

25. Loosen and remove the cylinder head bolts from the outermost one and remove the cylinder head from the engine.

To install:

26. Clean all gasket material from the cylinder head and block surfaces. Check for nicks or heavy scratches on the mating surfaces.

27. Cylinder bolt threads in the block and threads on the bolts must be cleaned. Dirt will affect head torque.

28. Torque in sequence and 2 steps first step 29 ft. lbs. (40 Nm) and second step 58 ft. lbs. (80 Nm).

29. Install the timing belt as outlined in the "Timing Belt" section in this Chapter.

30. Tighten the tension pulley bolt a ½ turn clockwise.

31. Install the timing belt lower cover. Install the cranking pulley. Refit the crank pulley bolt. Align the crank pulley timing gear to top dead center.

32. Lower passenger side of the engine.

33. Install the passenger side engine mounting bracket to the engine. Install the crank pulley bolt.

34. Install the passenger side engine mount to the engine. Connect the torque rod at the firewall.

35. Install the upper timing belt cover.

36. Install the engine mounting bridge.

37. Install the coolant bypass line and the thermostat housing.

38. Install the exhaust manifold bolts along with the manifold. Connect the exhaust pipe to the exhaust manifold and install the exhaust hanger.

39. Install the pulse air bracket with pipe. Install the heat protector and the EGR pipe.

40. Connect the high tension cables to the spark plugs and clips and install the center cover.

41. Connect the induction control vacuum

switching valve harness connection. Install the fuel rail assembly. Connect the idle air control valve connector and vacuum hose. Install the air induction control valve assembly.

42. Install the common (intake) chamber and retaining bolts. Install the fuel hose clips to the common chamber. Connect the fuel injection harness to the fuel injector.

43. Connect the induction valve vacuum hose to the common chamber. Connect the EGR valve and the throttle valve.

44. Connect the master vacuum hose to the master vacuum tube at the common chamber side.

45. Connect the accelerator cable to the throttle body and at the common chamber. Connect the PCV valve hose to the valve cover.

46. Connect the following vacuum lines and wiring harness:

    a. Install the MAT sensor connector.

    b. Electronic control gas injection harness, connect the 2 ECM ground connectors to the bracket located on top of the common chamber. Connect the 2 green and black multi-pin connectors on the top of the common chamber.

    c. Connect the canister vacuum hose to the common chamber.

    d. Connect the TPC valve vacuum hose to the common chamber.

    e. Connect MAP sensor vacuum hose to the common chamber.

    f. Connect the fast idle vacuum hose to the air duct hose.

47. Install the alternator drive belt to the crank pulley side.

48. Install the power steering pump drive belt, for vehicles with air conditioners, install the power steering pump and compressor drive belt. Tighten the 2 power steering pump adjust plates bolts.

49. Install the radiator and connect radiator inlet and outlet hoses along with transmission oil cooler lines, if so equipped.

50. Install the distributor, hold down bolt and cap.

51. Connect negative battery cable and refill the cooling system. Install the air cleaner duct hose to the common chamber.

52. Start the engine and check for leaks.

4ZE1 Engine

1. Relieve the fuel pressure. Disconnect the negative battery cable. Drain the cooling system.

    CAUTION: *When draining the coolant, keep in mind that cats and dogs are attracted by the ethylene glycol antifreeze, and are quite likely to drink any that is left in an uncovered container or in puddles on the ground. This*

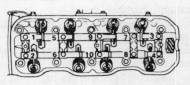

Rocker arm shaft torque sequence—4ZE1 engine

will prove fatal in sufficient quantity. Always drain the coolant into a sealable container. Coolant should be reused unless it is contaminated or several years old.

2. Remove the drive belts from the power steering pump, the air pump, the air conditioning compressor (if equipped) and the cooling fan.

3. Rotate the engine to position the No. 1 cylinder on TDC.

4. Remove the distributor cap, high tension cables and the distributor.

5. Remove the exhaust manifold-to-exhaust pipe bolts.

6. Label and disconnect the electrical connectors and vacuum hoses which may be in the way.

7. Remove the coolant hoses, the radiator and the cooling fan assembly.

8. Remove the crankshaft pulley bolt and the pulley.

9. Remove the upper and lower timing belt covers, the tension spring and the timing belt.

10. Remove the camshaft pulley bolt, the pulley and the camshaft boss.

11. Remove the timing belt guide plate and the cylinder head front plate.

12. Remove the rocker arm cover and gasket.

13. Remove the cylinder head-to-engine bolts, the cylinder head and gasket.

14. Clean the gasket mounting surfaces.

To install:

15. Using a new gasket, install the cylinder head and torque the bolts, in sequence to 57 ft. lbs. (76 Nm) in the 1st step and to 65–79 ft. lbs. (88–108 Nm) in the final step.

16. Install the camshaft pulley.

17. Using a new gasket, install the rocker arm cover.

18. Align the camshaft pulley mark with the mark on the front plate. Make sure the keyway on the crankshaft if facing upward, aimed at the pointer on the engine block.

19. Install the timing belt in the following order: crankshaft pulley, the oil pump pulley, the camshaft and the tensioner.

20. Install the timing belt covers, using a new gasket.

21. Install the crankshaft pulley.

22. Install the cooling fan assembly, the radiator and the coolant hoses.

23. Connect the electrical connectors and vacuum hoses.

24. Install the exhaust manifold-to-exhaust pipe bolts.

25. Install the distributor, the distributor cap, and the high tension cables.

26. Install the drive belts to the power steering pump, the air pump, the air conditioning compressor (if equipped) and the cooling fan.

27. Connect the negative battery cable. Refill the cooling system.

28. Start the engine and check for leaks.

V6 Engine

LEFT SIDE

1. Relieve the fuel pressure. Disconnect the negative battery cable. Drain the cooling system.

CAUTION: *When draining the coolant, keep in mind that cats and dogs are attracted by the ethylene glycol antifreeze, and are quite likely to drink any that is left in an uncovered container or in puddles on the ground. This will prove fatal in sufficient quantity. Always drain the coolant into a sealable container. Coolant should be reused unless it is contaminated or several years old.*

2. Remove the intake manifold.

3. Raise and safely support the vehicle.

4. Disconnect the exhaust pipe from the exhaust manifold and remove the exhaust manifold-to-cylinder head bolts.

5. Remove the dipstick tube from the engine.

6. Lower the vehicle.

7. Loosen the rocker arm nuts, turn the rocker arms and remove the pushrods; keep the pushrods in the same order as removed.

8. Remove the cylinder head bolts in stages and in the reverse order of torquing.

9. Remove the cylinder head; do not pry on the head to loosen it.

10. Clean the gasket mounting surfaces.

To install:

11. Position a new cylinder head gasket over the dowel pins with the words **This Side Up**

facing upwards. Carefully, guide the cylinder head into place.

12. Install the pushrods; make sure the lower ends are in the lifter heads. Torque the rocker arm nuts to 14–20 ft. lbs. (20–27 Nm).

13. Install the intake manifold.

14. Install the dipstick tube to the engine.

15. Install the exhaust manifold-to-cylinder head bolts and the exhaust pipe-to-exhaust manifold nuts.

16. Refill the cooling system. Start the engine and check for leaks.

RIGHT SIDE

1. Relieve the fuel pressure. Disconnect the negative battery cable. Drain the cooling system.

CAUTION: *When draining the coolant, keep in mind that cats and dogs are attracted by the ethylene glycol antifreeze, and are quite likely to drink any that is left in an uncovered container or in puddles on the ground. This will prove fatal in sufficient quantity. Always drain the coolant into a sealable container. Coolant should be reused unless it is contaminated or several years old.*

2. Remove the intake manifold.

3. If equipped, remove the cruise control servo bracket, the air management valve and hose.

4. Raise and safely support the vehicle.

5. Disconnect the exhaust pipe from the exhaust manifold and remove the exhaust manifold-to-cylinder head bolts.

6. Remove the exhaust pipe at crossover, the crossover and the heat shield, if equipped.

7. Lower the vehicle.

8. Label and disconnect the electrical wiring and vacuum hoses that may interfere with the removal of the right cylinder head.

9. Loosen the rocker arm nuts, turn the rocker arms and remove the pushrods; keep the pushrods in the same order as removed.

10. Remove the cylinder head bolts in stages and in the reverse order of torquing.

11. Remove the cylinder head; do not pry on the head to loosen it.

12. Clean the gasket mounting surfaces.

To install:

13. Position a new cylinder head gasket over the dowel pins with the words **This Side Up** facing upwards. Carefully, guide the cylinder head into place.

14. Install the pushrods; make sure the lower ends are in the lifter heads. Torque the rocker arm nuts to 14–20 ft. lbs. (20–27 Nm).

15. Install the intake manifold.

16. Install the exhaust pipe at crossover, the crossover and the heat shield, if equipped.

17. Install the exhaust manifold-to-cylinder

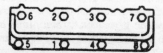

Cylinder head torque sequence—V6 engine

head bolts and the exhaust pipe-to-exhaust manifold nuts.

19. Connect the electrical wiring and vacuum hoses to the right cylinder head.

20. If equipped, install the cruise control servo bracket, the air management valve and hose.

21. Refill the cooling system. Start the engine and check for leaks.

C223 and C223-T Engine

1. Relieve the fuel pressure. Disconnect the negative battery cable. Drain the cooling system.

CAUTION: *When draining the coolant, keep in mind that cats and dogs are attracted by the ethylene glycol antifreeze, and are quite likely to drink any that is left in an uncovered container or in puddles on the ground. This will prove fatal in sufficient quantity. Always drain the coolant into a sealable container. Coolant should be reused unless it is contaminated or several years old.*

2. Remove the cooling fan assembly and the drive belt. Remove the alternator and bracket.

3. Remove the upper radiator hose and heater hose(s).

4. Remove the air cleaner and intake duct.

5. Label and disconnect the necessary vacuum hoses and electrical connectors.

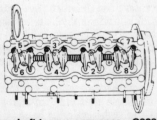

Rocker arm shaft torque sequence—C223 diesel engine, 15 ft. lbs. (20 Nm)

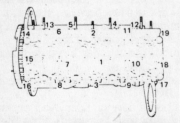

Cylinder head torque sequence—C223 diesel engine

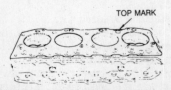

TOP MARK

Head gasket positioning—C223 diesel engine

6. Remove the fuel injector pipe, the clip and the nozzle holder assembly.

7. Remove the glow plugs and sensing resister.

8. If equipped with a turbocharger, remove the turbocharger cover and the turbocharger.

9. Remove the intake and exhaust manifolds from the cylinder head; discard the gaskets.

10. Remove the rocker arm cover, the valve tappet chamber cover and rocker oil feed pipe.

11. Back off the rocker arm adjustments. Remove the rocker arm assembly-to-cylinder head bolts and the rocker arm assembly.

12. Remove the pushrods and keep them in order for reinstallation purposes.

13. Remove the cylinder head-to-engine bolts, a little at a time, by reversing the torquing sequence. Remove the cylinder head; it may be necessary to use a mallet to tap the cylinder head loose from the engine.

14. Match the old gasket to the new cylinder head gasket and clean the gasket mounting surfaces.

To install:

15. Using a new gasket, position it onto the engine with the work **TOP** facing upwards.

16. Refill the turbocharger with clean engine oil before installation.

17. Install the cylinder head onto the engine. Lubricate the cylinder head bolts with engine oil and torque them, in sequence, using the following procedure:
- Turbocharged Engine
  1st step: 33–40 ft. lbs. (45–54 Nm)
  2nd step: 120–150°
- Non-turbocharged Engine
  1st step: 40–47 ft. lbs. (54–63 Nm)
  2nd step: 54–61 ft. lbs. (74–81 Nm) [new bolt] or 61–69 ft. lbs. (81–95 Nm) [used bolt]

18. Install the pushrods and make sure they are positioned in the tappets.

19. Install the rocker arm assembly and torque the rocker arm-to-cylinder head bolts to 10–17 ft. lbs. (14–24 Nm) Adjust the valve lash.

20. Using new gaskets, reverse the removal procedures.

21. Refill the cooling system. Connect the negative battery cable. Start the engine and check for leaks.

4FB1 Engine

1. Drain the cooling system by opening the drain plug on the cylinder block.

CAUTION: *When draining the coolant, keep in mind that cats and dogs are attracted by the ethylene glycol antifreeze, and are quite likely to drink any that is left in an uncovered container or in puddles on the ground. This will prove fatal in sufficient quantity. Always*

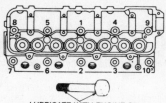

LUBRICATE WITH ENGINE OIL

Cylinder head torque sequence—4FB1 diesel engine

1 AND 3 CHECK DIAGONALLY
2 CHECK ACROSS CENTER

Check the cylinder head for warpage

drain the coolant into a sealable container. Coolant should be reused unless it is contaminated or several years old.

2. Remove the camshaft.

3. Remove the sensing resistor assembly.

4. Remove the six screws attaching the injection pipe clip and remove the injection pipe clip.

5. Remove the eight sleeve nuts attaching the injection pipes and separate the infection pipes.

6. Remove the clip attaching the fuel leak off hose and separate the hose from the return pipe.

7. Remove the two nuts connecting the exhaust manifold to the exhaust pipe and separate the pipe from the manifold.

8. Disconnect the joint bolt attaching the oil feed line to the head side.

9. Disconnect the heater hose at the thermostat housing pipe.

10. Remove the cylinder head bolts by loosening them in sequence, then remove the cylinder head and gasket.

NOTE: *Use light oil to free stubborn bolts.*

11. Clean the head and block of all gasket material before reassembly.

To install:

12. Match up the old gasket to the new to ensure an exact fit. Install the gasket and cylinder head.

13. Torque all bolts in the sequence given at the front of this section. Apply oil to the bolt threads and clean them thoroughly before reinstalling them in the head. Torque the cylinder head bolts in 2 passes the first pass to 21–36 ft. lbs. (27–48 Nm) and the second pass to 83–98 ft. lbs. (112–135 Nm). Torque the reused bolts to 90–105 ft. lbs. (122–140 Nm).

NOTE: *Make sure that the cylinder head*

gasket is properly placed before lowering the head. Look for the TOP mark to assure proper placement.

14. Reinstall the camshaft and rocker arm assembly. Reinstall the timing belt and adjust the valve clearance.

15. Start the engine and check for leaks.

CLEANING AND INSPECTION

Chip carbon away from the valve heads, combustion chambers, and ports, using a chisel made of hardwood. Remove the remaining deposits with a stiff wire brush.

NOTE: *Be sure that the deposits are actually removed, rather than burnished.*

Have the cylinder head hot-tanked to remove grease, corrosion, and scale from the water passages. Clean the remaining cylinder head parts in an engine cleaning solvent. Do not remove the protective coating from the springs.

WARNING: *Aluminum cylinder head can not be hot-tanked in the same solution that is used for cast iron. Make sure the machine shop knows if the cylinder heads are aluminum.*

Place a straightedge across the gasket surface of the cylinder head. Using feeler gauges, determine the clearance at the center of the straightedge. If warpage exceeds 0.08mm (0.003 in.) in a 152mm (6 in.) span, or 0.15mm (0.006 in.) over the total length, the cylinder head must be resurfaced.

NOTE: *If warpage exceeds the manufacturer's maximum tolerance for material removal, the cylinder head must be replaced.*

When milling the cylinder heads of V-type engines, the intake manifold mounting position is altered, and must be corrected by milling the manifold flange a proportionate amount.

RESURFACING

This procedure should be performed only by a machine shop.

Valves and Springs

REMOVAL AND INSTALLATION

NOTE: *Invert the cylinder head, and number the valve faces front to rear, using a permanent felt-tip marker.*

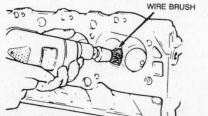

WIRE BRUSH

Remove the carbon from the cylinder head with a wire brush and electric drill

Removing the valve springs

PROPER TIP PATTERN	NO ROTATION PATTERN	PARTIAL ROTATION PATTERN
ROTATOR FUNCTIONING PROPERLY	REPLACE ROTATOR AND CHECK ROTATION	REPLACE ROTATOR AND CHECK ROTATION

Valve stem wear

Compressing the valve springs

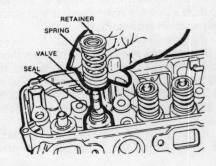

Install valve stem seals

Using an appropriate valve spring compressor, compress the valve springs. Lift out the keepers with needlenosed pliers, release the compressor, and remove the valve, spring, and spring retainer. Clean the valve stem with lacquer thinner or a similar solvent to remove any gum and varnish. Clean the valve guides using solvent and an expanding wire-type valve guide cleaner. Replace any parts that are damaged or worn.

REFACING

NOTE: *This procedure should only be performed by a qualified machine shop.*

CHECK SPRINGS

Place the spring on a flat surface nest to a square. Measure the height of the spring, and rotate it against the edge of the square to measure distortion. If spring height varies (by comparison) by more than 1.5mm ($\frac{1}{16}$ in.), or, if distortion exceeds 1.5mm ($\frac{1}{16}$ in.), replace the spring.

In addition to evaluating the spring as above, test the spring pressure at the installed and compressed (installed height minus valve lift) height using a valve spring tester. Springs used on small displacement engines (up to 3 liters) should be ± 1 lb. of all other springs in either

Check the valve spring test pressure

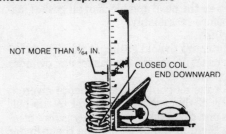

NOT MORE THAN $\frac{5}{64}$ IN.

CLOSED COIL END DOWNWARD

Check the valve spring free length and squareness

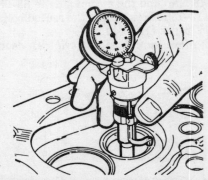

Have the valve seat concentricity checked at a machine shop

position. A tolerance of ± 5 lbs. is permissible on larger engines.

Valve Guides

NOTE: *The valve guides are not removable, they are an integral part of the cylinder head. Any cutting or grinding operation performed on the valve guides, should be done by a qualified machine shop.*

KNURLING

Valve guides which are not excessively worn or distorted may, in some cases, be knurled. Knurling is a process in which metal is displaced and raised, thereby reducing clearance. Knurling also provides excellent oil control.

This procedure should only be performed by a qualified machine shop.

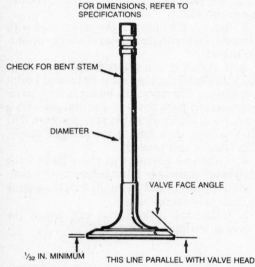

FOR DIMENSIONS, REFER TO SPECIFICATIONS

CHECK FOR BENT STEM

DIAMETER

VALVE FACE ANGLE

¹/₃₂ IN. MINIMUM   THIS LINE PARALLEL WITH VALVE HEAD

Critical valve dimensions

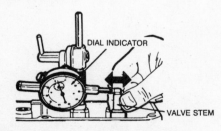

DIAL INDICATOR

VALVE STEM

Checking the valve stem-to-guide clearance

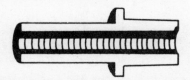

Cutaway of a knurled valve guide

Valve Seats

NOTE: *The valve seats are not removable, they are an integral part of the cylinder head. Any cutting or grinding operation performed on the valve guides, should be done by a qualified machine shop.*

LAPPING THE VALVES

When valve faces and seats have been refaced and re-cut, or if they are determined to be in good condition, the valves must the "lapped in" to ensure efficient sealing when the valve closes against the seat.

1. Invert the cylinder head so that the combustion chambers are facing up.

2. Lightly lubricate the valve stems with clean oil, and coat the valve seats with valve grinding compound. Install the valves in the head as numbered.

3. Attach the suction cup of a valve lapping tool to a valve head. You'll probably have to moisten the cup to securely attach the tool to the valve.

4. Rotate the tool between the palms, changing position and lifting the tool often to prevent grooving. Lap the valve until a smooth, polished seat is evident (you may have to add a bit more compound after some lapping is done).

5. Remove the valve and tool, and remove ALL traces of grinding compound with solvent-soaked rag, or rinse the head with solvent.

NOTE: *Valve lapping can also be done by*

Lapping the valves by hand

HAND DRILL

ROD

SUCTION CUP

Home made valve lapping tool

fastening a suction cup to a piece of drill rod in a hand "eggbeater" type drill. Proceed as above, using the drill as a lapping tool. Due to the higher speeds involved when using the hand drill, care must be exercised to avoid grooving the seat. Lift the tool and change direction of rotation often.

Valve Lifters (Tappet)

REMOVAL AND INSTALLATION

C223 Diesel Engine

1. Disconnect the negative (−) battery cable.
2. Remove the engine from the vehicle as outlined in this Section.
3. Remove the rocker arm cover and rocker arm assembly.
4. Label and remove the pushrods.
5. Remove the tappet chamber cover and oil feed pipe.
6. Remove the camshaft oil seal retainer.
7. Remove the timing pulley housing.
8. Remove the camshaft as outlined in this Section.
9. Remove and label the tappets.

To install:

10. Install the tappets into their original locations.
11. Install the camshaft as outlined in this Section.
12. Install the timing pulley housing.
13. Install the camshaft oil seal retainer.
14. Install the tappet chamber cover and oil feed pipe.
15. Install the pushrods into their original locations.
16. Install the rocker arm assembly and cover.

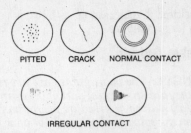

PITTED   CRACK   NORMAL CONTACT

IRREGULAR CONTACT

Tappet wear indicators—C223 diesel engines

17. Install the engine into the vehicle as outlined in this Section.
18. Connect the negative (−) battery cable, refill all engine fluids, start the engine and check for leaks.

V6 Engine

1. Disconnect the negative (−) battery cable. Remove the intake manifold and valve cover. Label and remove the rocker arms and remove the push rods.
2. Remove the lifters. If they are coated with varnish, clean with carburetor cleaning solvent.

To install:

3. If installing new lifters or you have disassembled the lifters, they must be primed before installation. Submerge the lifters in SAE 10 oil and carefully push down on the plunger with a 3mm (⅛ in.) drift. Hold the plunger down (DO NOT pump), then release the plunger slowly. The lifter is now primed.
4. **Coat the bottoms of the lifters with** Molykote® (assembly lube) before installation. Install the lifters and pushrods into the engine in their original position.
5. Install the rocker arms and adjust the valves as outlined in Chapter 2.

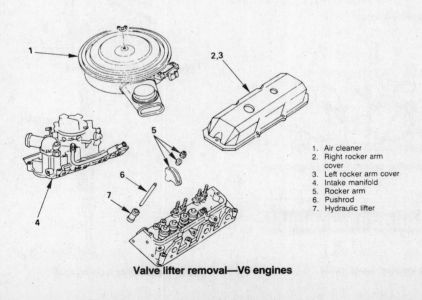

1. Air cleaner
2. Right rocker arm cover
3. Left rocker arm cover
4. Intake manifold
5. Rocker arm
6. Pushrod
7. Hydraulic lifter

Valve lifter removal—V6 engines

Oil Pan

REMOVAL AND INSTALLATION

4-Cylinder Gasoline Engines with Rear Wheel Drive

NOTE: *Isuzu recommends removing the engine (or at least raising it up) to service the oil pan. There is not sufficient clearance to remove the pan with the engine bolted down.*

1. Remove or raise the engine to allow sufficient room to clear the oil pan.

NOTE: *On the 4XC1-U engine, disconnect the exhaust pipe bracket and the exhaust pipe at the manifold. Disconnect the right hand tension rod located under the front bumper to gain access to the oil pan.*

2. Remove the bolts and nuts attaching the oil pan to the engine block. Remove the oil pan and gasket.

3. Clean the oil pan and engine block gasket surface carefully to remove all traces of the old gasket.

To install:

4. Using a thin coat of Permatex® No. 2 or equivalent to hold the gasket in place while installing the bolts and to prevent any oil leaks.

NOTE: *If using a silicone sealant, apply the correct width bead of the sealant to the contact surfaces of the oil pan. There must be no gaps in the bead. The oil pan must be installed within 30 minutes after the sealant application*

5. Torque the all the oil pan bolts evenly. Check the edges of the gasket to ensure that it is sealed properly. If the gasket projects unevenly around the oil pan flange, remove the gasket and reinstall carefully.

NOTE: *Do not overtighten the oil pan bolts. Bolts that are too tight cause as many leaks as bolts that are too loose.*

6. Start the engine and check for leaks.

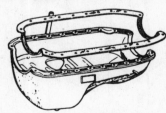

Oil pan assembly—G180Z, others similar

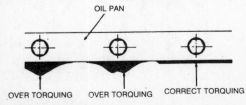

OIL PAN

OVER TORQUING   OVER TORQUING   CORRECT TORQUING

Oil pan gasket compression

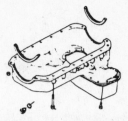

Exploded view of the oil pan used with 4WD—4ZD1 and 4ZE1 engines

4ZD1 and 4ZE1 Engines

NOTE: *On 4WD gasoline engines, the engine must be removed before removing the oil pan.*

1. Disconnect the negative battery cable.
2. Raise and safely support the vehicle.
3. Drain the engine oil.

CAUTION: *The EPA warns that prolonged contact with used engine oil may cause a number of skin disorders, including cancer! You should make every effort to minimize your exposure to used engine oil. Protective gloves should be worn when changing the oil. Wash your hands and any other exposed skin areas as soon as possible after exposure to used engine oil. Soap and water, or waterless hand cleaner should be used.*

4. Remove the front splash shield, if equipped.
5. If equipped with a crossmember, remove it.
6. Disconnect the relay rod at the idler arm and lower the relay rod.
7. Remove the left side bellhousing bracket.
8. Disconnect the vacuum line from the oil pan.
9. Remove the oil pan bolts and remove the oil pan.

To install:

10. Clean the gasket mounting surfaces.
11. Using a new gasket and sealant, install the oil pan. Torque the oil pan-to-engine bolts to 35–51 inch lbs. (4–6 Nm).
12. Connect the vacuum line to the oil pan.
13. Install the left side bellhousing bracket.
14. Connect the relay rod at the idler arm and lower the relay rod.
15. If equipped with a crossmember, install it.
16. Install the front splash shield, if equipped.
17. Refill the engine oil.
18. Lower the vehicle.
19. Connect the negative battery cable, start the engine and check for leaks.

Diesel Engine

UPPER OIL PAN

1. Disconnect the negative battery cable.
2. Remove the engine from the vehicle.

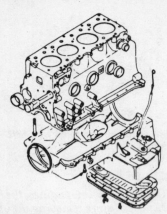

Exploded view of the upper and lower oil pans—diesel engines

3. Drain the engine oil. Remove the dipstick and the dipstick tube.

CAUTION: *The EPA warns that prolonged contact with used engine oil may cause a number of skin disorders, including cancer! You should make every effort to minimize your exposure to used engine oil. Protective gloves should be worn when changing the oil. Wash your hands and any other exposed skin areas as soon as possible after exposure to used engine oil. Soap and water, or waterless hand cleaner should be used.*

4. Remove the upper oil pan-to-engine bolts and the oil pan.

To install:

5. Clean the gasket mounting surfaces.

6. Using a new gasket and sealant, install the oil pan. Torque the oil pan-to-engine bolts to 120–185 inch lbs. (14–18 Nm).

7. Install the engine into the vehicle as outlined in this Section.

8. Connect the battery cable, start the engine and check for leaks.

LOWER OIL PAN

1. Raise and safely support the vehicle.
2. Drain the crankcase.

CAUTION: *The EPA warns that prolonged contact with used engine oil may cause a number of skin disorders, including cancer! You should make every effort to minimize your exposure to used engine oil. Protective gloves should be worn when changing the oil. Wash your hands and any other exposed skin areas as soon as possible after exposure to used engine oil. Soap and water, or waterless hand cleaner should be used.*

3. Remove the lower oil pan-to-upper oil pan bolts and the lower pan.

To install:

4. Clean the gasket mounting surfaces.

5. Using a new gasket and sealant, install the lower oil pan and torque the bolts to 24–96 inch lbs. (3–11 Nm).

6. Refill the crankcase, connect the negative the battery cable, start the engine and check for leaks.

V6 Engine

1. Disconnect the negative battery cable.

2. Remove the dipstick. Raise and safely support the vehicle. Drain the crankcase.

CAUTION: *The EPA warns that prolonged contact with used engine oil may cause a number of skin disorders, including cancer! You should make every effort to minimize your exposure to used engine oil. Protective gloves should be worn when changing the oil. Wash your hands and any other exposed skin areas as soon as possible after exposure to used engine oil. Soap and water, or waterless hand cleaner should be used.*

3. Remove the front skid plate and the crossmember.

4. Remove the exhaust pipe-to-catalytic converter bolts, the exhaust pipe-to-manifolds bolts and the Y-exhaust pipe.

5. Remove the front driveshaft from the front differential.

6. Remove the braces from the flywheel cover.

7. Disconnect the electrical connectors from the starter. Remove the starter-to-engine bolts and the starter.

8. Remove the flywheel inspection cover.

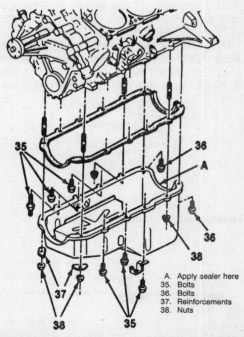

A. Apply sealer here
35. Bolts
36. Bolts
37. Reinforcements
38. Nuts

Exploded view of the oil pan assembly—V6 engines

9. Matchmark the pitman arm-to-pitman shaft for reassembly. Remove the pitman arm-to-pitman arm shaft nut and separate the pitman arm from the pitman shaft.

10. Remove the idler arm-to-shaft nut and separate the idler arm from the shaft.

11. Remove the rubber hose from the front axle vent and support the axle housing assembly.

12. Remove both bolts from the left axle housing isolator and the right axle housing isolator, then, lower the front axle housing assembly.

13. Remove the oil pan-to-engine bolts, the oil pan and discard the gasket.

14. Clean the gasket mounting surfaces.

To install:

15. Using a new gasket and sealant, install the oil pan. Torque both rear pan-to-engine bolts to 18 ft. lbs. (25 Nm) and the other bolts/nuts/studs to 7 ft. lbs. (10 Nm).

16. To complete the installation, reverse the removal procedures. Torque the following fasteners:

• Pitman arm-to-pitman shaft nut – 159 ft. lbs. (215 Nm)

• Idler arm-to-shaft nut – 86 ft. lbs. (117 Nm)

• Front drive axle shaft bolts – 46 ft. lbs. (62 Nm)

17. Refill the crankcase. Connect the negative battery cable.

18. Start the engine and check for leaks.

Oil Pump

REMOVAL AND INSTALLATION

G180Z and G200Z Engine

The oil pump is located in the oil pan and is attached to the front cover.

1. Disconnect the negative battery cable. Raise and safely support the vehicle.

2. Rotate the crankshaft to position the No. 1 or No. 4 cylinder at the TDC of its compression stroke.

3. Drain the crankcase and remove the oil pan as outlined in this Section.

CAUTION: *The EPA warns that prolonged contact with used engine oil may cause a number of skin disorders, including cancer! You should make every effort to minimize your exposure to used engine oil. Protective gloves should be worn when changing the oil. Wash your hands and any other exposed skin areas as soon as possible after exposure to used engine oil. Soap and water, or waterless hand cleaner should be used.*

4. Remove the oil pick-up-to-engine bolt and the oil pick-up tube from the oil pump.

5. Remove the oil pump-to-front cover bolts and the oil pump.

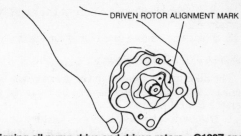

Aligning oil pump drive and driven rotors—G180Z and G200Z engines

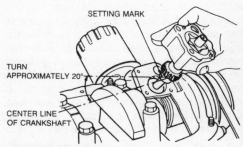

Installing the oil pump

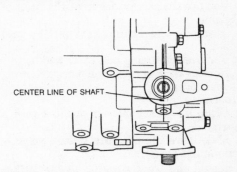

Oil pump shaft alignment—G180Z and G200Z engines

To install:

6. Turn the punch mark on the oil pump drive gear toward the oil filter and align the center of the oil pump's drive gear with the mark on the oil pump case.

7. Insert the oil pump into the front cover.

NOTE: *When installing the oil pump, turn the oil pump shaft so the drive gear engages with the drive pinion. When installed, the punch mark on the drive gear should be facing the main bearings and the shaft tang must be engaged with the distributor shaft.*

8. Install the oil pump and pump-to-front cover bolts.

9. Remove the oil pick-up-to-engine bolt and the oil pick-up tube from the oil pump.

10. Install the oil pan as outlined in this Section.

11. Connect the negative battery cable. Lower the vehicle.

12. Refill the crankcase. Connect the negative battery cable.

13. Start the engine and check for leaks.

4XC1-U, 4XC1-T, 4XE1 Engine

The oil pump is located in the front cover assembly. The engine may have to be removed to service the oil pump.

1. Disconnect the negative (−) battery cable.

2. Drain the engine oil into a suitable container.

CAUTION: *The EPA warns that prolonged contact with used engine oil may cause a number of skin disorders, including cancer! You should make every effort to minimize your exposure to used engine oil. Protective gloves should be worn when changing the oil. Wash your hands and any other exposed skin areas as soon as possible after exposure to used engine oil. Soap and water, or waterless hand cleaner should be used.*

3. Rotate the crankshaft to the No. 4 cylinder is at top dead center on the compression stroke and align the timing marks.

4. Remove the accessories from the front of the engine.

5. Remove the crankshaft pulley and damper.

6. Remove the timing belt cover and belt.

7. Remove the front cover/oil pump retaining bolts and cover.

To install:

1. Clean all gasket mating surfaces with a scraper.

2. Make sure the pressure release valve is functioning properly.

3. Install the front cover/oil pump, gasket and retaining bolts.

4. Install the timing belt and cover.

5. Install the crankshaft pulley and damper.

6. Install the accessories to the front of the engine.

7. Install the engine, if removed.

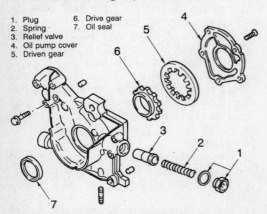

1. Plug
2. Spring
3. Relief valve
4. Oil pump cover
5. Driven gear
6. Drive gear
7. Oil seal

Oil pump—4XC1 and 4XE1 engines

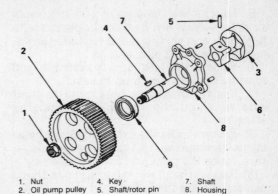

1. Nut
2. Oil pump pulley
3. Outer rotor
4. Key
5. Shaft/rotor pin
6. Inner rotor
7. Shaft
8. Housing
9. Oil seal

Oil pump assembly—4ZD1 and 4ZE1 engines

8. Refill the engine with engine oil.

9. Connect the negative (−) battery cable, start the engine and check for leaks.

4ZC1-T, 4ZD1 and 4ZE1 Engine

The oil pump is attached to the front, lower right side of the engine and is driven by the timing belt.

1. Remove the upper and lower timing belt covers.

2. Remove the timing belt from the crankshaft and oil pump sprockets.

3. Remove the oil pump sprocket-to-oil pump nut and the sprocket from the oil pump.

4. Using a 6mm Allen wrench, remove the oil pump-to-engine bolts and the oil pump.

To install:

5. Using petroleum jelly, pack the oil pump.

6. Using a new O-ring, install the oil pump and torque the bolts to 10–17 ft. lbs. (14–22 Nm).

7. Install the sprocket to the oil pump and torque the nut to 48–62 ft. lbs. (63–86 Nm).

8. Align the timing marks on the camshaft and crankshaft sprockets and install the timing belt.

9. Fill the engine with oil, start the engine and check for leaks.

V6 Engine

The oil pump is attached to the cylinder block and is located in the oil pan.

1. Disconnect the negative battery cable. Raise and safely support the vehicle.

2. Drain the crankcase. Remove the oil pan as outlined in this Section.

CAUTION: *The EPA warns that prolonged contact with used engine oil may cause a number of skin disorders, including cancer! You should make every effort to minimize your exposure to used engine oil. Protective gloves should be worn when changing the oil. Wash your hands and any other exposed skin*

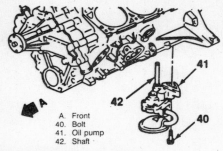

A. Front
40. Bolt
41. Oil pump
42. Shaft

Oil pump assembly—V6 engines

areas as soon as possible after exposure to used engine oil. Soap and water, or waterless hand cleaner should be used.

3. Remove the oil pump-to-engine bolts and the oil pump.

To install:

4. Align the oil pump shaft with the hexagon socket and install the pump. Torque the oil pump-to-engine bolts to 30 ft. lbs. (41 Nm).

5. Install the oil pan.

6. Connect the negative battery cable. Start the engine and check for leaks.

4FB1 Diesel Engine

1. Disconnect the negative (−) battery cable. Remove the timing belt.

2. Remove the Allen bolts attaching the oil pump and remove the pump together with the pulley.

NOTE: *The special tool for the Allen bolts is J-29767*

3. Disassemble the oil pump on the workbench. A gear puller may be necessary to remove the pulley.

To install:

4. Apply generous amounts of clean engine oil to all components before installation. Install the vane with the taper side toward the cylinder body.

5. Install a new O-ring into the groove in the housing. Lubricate with oil. Install the rotor

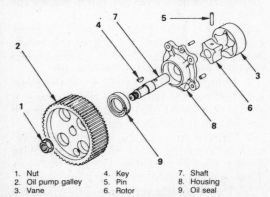

1. Nut
2. Oil pump galley
3. Vane
4. Key
5. Pin
6. Rotor
7. Shaft
8. Housing
9. Oil seal

Oil pump assembly—4FB1 diesel engine

and then the pump body together with the pulley. Torque the Allen bolts to 11–18 ft. lbs. (14–25 Nm).

6. Install the timing bolt and covers as outlined in this Section.

7. Connect the battery cable, refill engine with oil, start the engine and check for leaks.

C223 and C223-T Diesel Engine

1. Disconnect the negative battery cable and drain the engine oil.

CAUTION: *The EPA warns that prolonged contact with used engine oil may cause a number of skin disorders, including cancer! You should make every effort to minimize your exposure to used engine oil. Protective gloves should be worn when changing the oil. Wash your hands and any other exposed skin areas as soon as possible after exposure to used engine oil. Soap and water, or waterless hand cleaner should be used.*

2. Remove the engine from the vehicle as outlined in this Section.

3. Remove the oil pan as outlined in this Section.

4. Remove the oil pipe from the oil pump. Remove the oil pump-to-engine bolts and the oil pump.

To install:

5. Clean the gasket mounting surfaces.

6. Using a new gasket, install the oil pump and connect the oil pipe to the oil pump. Install and torque the oil pan-to-engine bolts to 10–17 ft. lbs. (14–22 Nm).

7. Install the oil pan.

8. Install the engine into the vehicle.

9. Connect the negative battery cable, refill the engine oil, start the engine and check for leaks.

CHECKING OIL PUMP

G180Z, G200Z Engine

1. Visually inspect the oil pump for wear, damage or other abnormal conditions.

2. Remove the oil pump cover from the bottom of the oil pump.

3. Using a feeler gauge, measure the clearance between the pump body and the vane; it should be 0.16–0.22mm (0.0063–0.0086 in.), if not, replace the entire pump assembly.

4. Using a feeler gauge, measure the clearance between the rotor and the vane; it should be 0.13–0.15mm (0.0051–0.0059 in.), if not, replace the rotor set: pin, shaft, rotor and vane.

5. Place a straight edge across the bottom of the oil pump and a feeler gauge between the straight edge and the rotor; the clearance between the rotor/vane-to-cover should be 0.03–0.09mm (0.0011–0.0035 in.), if not, replace the rotor set: pin, shaft, rotor and vane.

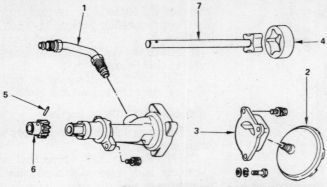

1. Oil line
2. Strainer
3. Cover
4. Vane
5. Pinion/shaft pin
6. Pinion
7. Rotor with shaft

Oil pump assembly—C223 diesel engine

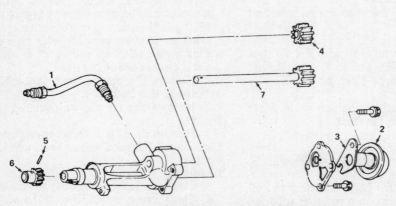

1. Oil line
2. Strainer
3. Cover
4. Driven gear
5. Pinion/shaft pin
6. Pinion
7. Drive gear with shaft

Oil pump assembly—C223-Turbo diesel engine

6. Using a feeler gauge, measure the clearance between the pump body and the rotor shaft; it should be less than 0.2mm (0.0079 in.), if not, replace the entire pump assembly.

4ZC1-T, 4ZD1 and 4ZE1 Engine

1. Visually inspect the oil pump for wear, damage or other abnormal conditions.

2. Insert the oil pump vane into the cylinder block.

3. Place a straight edge across the oil pump opening and a feeler gauge between the straight edge and the vane; the clearance between the vane-to-cylinder block surface should be 0.05–0.10mm (0.002–0.004 in.), if not, replace the vane.

4. Using a feeler gauge, measure the side clearance between the cylinder block and the vane; it should be 0.23–0.36mm (0.009–0.014 in.), if not, replace the vane.

5. Position the vane onto the rotor shaft.

6. Using a feeler gauge, measure the clearance between the rotor and the vane; it should be 0.13–0.15mm (0.005–0.006 in.), if not, replace the rotor and/or vane.

C223 Diesel Engine

1. Visually inspect the oil pump for wear, damage or other abnormal conditions.

2. Remove the oil pump cover from the bottom of the oil pump.

3. Place a straight edge across the bottom of the oil pump and a feeler gauge between the straight edge and the rotor; the clearance between the rotor/vane-to-cover should be 0.02–0.07mm (0.0008–0.0028 in.), if not, replace the rotor set: pin, shaft, rotor and vane.

4. Using a feeler gauge, measure the clearance between the rotor and the vane; it should be less than 0.14mm (0.0055 in.), if not, replace the rotor set: pin, shaft, rotor and vane.

5. Using a feeler gauge, measure the clearance between the pump body and the vane; it should be 0.20–0.27mm (0.0079–0.0106 in.), if not, replace the entire pump assembly.

6. Using a feeler gauge, measure the clearance between the pump body and the rotor shaft; it should be less than 0.2mm (0.0079 in.), if not, replace the entire pump assembly.

NOTE: *When necessary to replace the pinion and shaft, install the shaft in the pump body and set the pinion on the shaft. Drill a hole through the pinion and shaft using a 5mm drill, then, install and stake the pin.*

Timing Chain Front Cover
REMOVAL AND INSTALLATION

G180Z and G200Z Engine

1. Disconnect the negative battery cable.
2. Drain the cooling system.

CAUTION: *When draining the coolant, keep in mind that cats and dogs are attracted by the ethylene glycol antifreeze, and are quite likely to drink any that is left in an uncovered container or in puddles on the ground. This will prove fatal in sufficient quantity. Always drain the coolant into a sealable container. Coolant should be reused unless it is contaminated or several years old.*

3. Disconnect the radiator hoses and remove the radiator.
4. Remove the air cleaner and the rocker arm cover.
5. Remove the alternator and air conditioning compressor drive belts.
6. Remove the cooling fan.
7. Raise and safely support the vehicle. Drain the engine oil.

CAUTION: *The EPA warns that prolonged contact with used engine oil may cause a number of skin disorders, including cancer! You should make every effort to minimize your exposure to used engine oil. Protective gloves should be worn when changing the oil. Wash your hands and any other exposed skin areas as soon as possible after exposure to used engine oil. Soap and water, or waterless hand cleaner should be used.*

8. Remove the crankshaft pulley center bolt, the pulley and balancer assembly.
9. Remove the oil pan-to-engine bolts and the oil pan.
10. Remove the oil pump pick-up tube, the oil pump-to-front cover bolts and the oil pump.
11. Remove the front cover-to-engine bolts and the front cover from the engine and discard the gasket.
12. Clean the gasket mounting surfaces.

NOTE: *When the front cover is removed, replace the oil seal.*

To install:
13. Using a new gasket and sealant, install the front cover to the engine and torque the bolts to 18 ft. lbs. (25 Nm).
14. Align the oil pump's slotted shaft with the tip of the distributor and install the oil pump. Install the oil pick-up tube to the oil pump.
15. Using a new gasket, install the oil pan.
16. Install the crankshaft balancer assembly, pulley and bolt. Lower the vehicle.

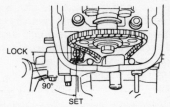

Locking the timing chain adjuster—G180Z engine

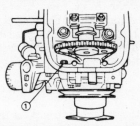

Locking the timing chain adjuster—G200Z engine

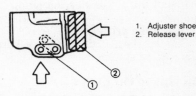

1. Adjuster shoe
2. Release lever

Timing chain adjuster—G200Z engine

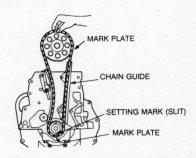

Timing chain alignment—G180Z and G200Z engines

17. Install the cooling fan assembly.
18. Install the alternator and compressor drive belts and adjust the tension.
19. Using a new gasket, install the rocker arm cover. Install the air cleaner.
20. Refill the crankcase and the cooling system.
21. Connect the negative battery cable.

V6 Engine

1. Disconnect the negative battery cable.
2. Drain the cooling system. Remove the lower radiator hose from the front cover.

CAUTION: *When draining the coolant, keep in mind that cats and dogs are attracted by the ethylene glycol antifreeze, and are quite likely to drink any that is left in an uncovered container or in puddles on the ground. This will prove fatal in sufficient quantity. Always drain the coolant into a sealable container. Coolant should be reused unless it is contaminated or several years old.*

3. Remove the water pump.

4. Remove the power steering bracket, if equipped.

5. Remove the crankshaft pulley.

6. Remove the front cover-to-engine bolts and the cover and discard the gasket.

7. Clean the gasket mounting surfaces.

NOTE: *When the front cover is removed, replace the oil seal.*

To install:

8. Using a new gasket and sealant, install the front cover.

9. Install the water pump and the lower radiator hose.

10. Install the crankshaft pulley.

11. Install the power steering pump bracket, if equipped.

12. Install the drive belt(s).

13. Connect the negative battery cable and refill the cooling system.

Front Cover Oil Seal

REMOVAL AND INSTALLATION

1. Disconnect the negative battery cable.

2. Drain the cooling system.

CAUTION: *When draining the coolant, keep in mind that cats and dogs are attracted by the ethylene glycol antifreeze, and are quite likely to drink any that is left in an uncovered container or in puddles on the ground. This will prove fatal in sufficient quantity. Always drain the coolant into a sealable container. Coolant should be reused unless it is contaminated or several years old.*

3. Disconnect the radiator hoses and remove the radiator (RWD only).

4. Remove the alternator and compressor drive belts.

5. Remove the cooling fan.

6. Remove the crankshaft pulley center bolt, the pulley and balancer assembly.

7. Using a small pry bar and care not to damage the crankshaft and cover sealing surfaces, carefully, pry out the timing cover seal.

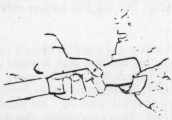

Front cover oil seal installation

To install:

8. Using engine oil, lubricate the new seal and tap it into the front cover.

9. Install the balancer assembly, the pulley and the center bolt.

10. Install the cooling fan and the drive belts.

11. Install the radiator and connect the hoses.

12. Refill the cooling system and connect the negative battery cable.

Timing Chain and Sprockets

REMOVAL AND INSTALLATION

G180Z and G200Z Engine

1. Disconnect the negative battery cable. Rotate the engine until No. 1 piston is at TDC on the compression stroke.

2. Remove the rocker arm cover, the front cover and the oil pan.

3. Depress or lock the shoe of the automatic chain adjuster in the retracted position.

4. Remove the camshaft sprocket-to-camshaft bolts and the sprocket.

5. Remove the timing chain from the timing sprockets.

6. Using a puller, remove the sprocket and the pinion gear from the crankshaft.

7. Remove the bolt or E-clip and remove the automatic chain adjuster.

8. Inspect the adjuster pin, arm, wedge and rack teeth. Replace assembly if worn. Remove the chain tensioner.

9. Check the timing chain for wear.

10. Check the tensioner pins for wear or damage and replace if necessary.

11. Replace the chain tensioner and adjuster using the E-clips or bolt.

To install:

12. Install the timing sprocket and pinion gear with the groove side toward the front cover. Align the key grooves with the key on the crankshaft, then, drive into position.

13. Confirm the No. 1 piston is at TDC; if not, turn the crankshaft so the key is turned toward the cylinder head side (No. 1 and No. 4 pistons at top dead center).

14. Install the timing chain by aligning the mark plate on the chain with the mark on the crankshaft timing sprocket. The side of the chain with the mark plate is on the front side and the side of the chain with the most links between the mark plates is on the chain guide side.

15. Install the camshaft timing sprocket so the mark side of the sprocket faces forward and so the triangular mark aligns with the chain mark plate.

NOTE: *Keep the timing chain engaged with the camshaft timing sprocket until the sprocket is installed on the camshaft.*

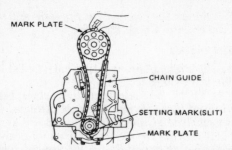

Timing chain positioning—G180Z and G200Z engines

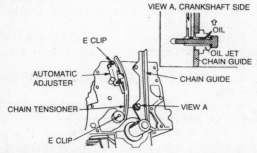

Remove the E-clip to remove the adjuster—G180Z and G200Z engines

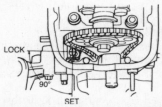

Locking the timing chain adjuster—G180Z engine, G200Z similar

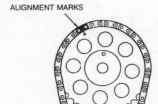

Aligning the timing chain with the camshaft sprocket—G180Z and G200Z engine

16. Using a new gasket and sealant, install the front cover assembly.

17. Install the rocker arm cover and oil pan.

18. Refill the cooling system and the crankcase.

19. Connect the negative battery cable.

V6 Engine

1. Disconnect the negative battery cable.

2. Rotate the crankshaft to position the No. 1 cylinder at the TDC of its compression stroke.

3. Remove the front cover.

4. Inspect the sprocket for chipped teeth and wear.

5. Inspect the timing chain for wear; if the chain can be pulled out more than 9.5mm (0.374 in.) from the damper, replace the chain.

6. Remove camshaft sprocket-to-camshaft bolts, the sprocket and the timing chain; if necessary, use a mallet to tap the sprocket from the camshaft.

7. Using a puller tool, press the crankshaft sprocket from the crankshaft.

To install:

8. Using an installation tool and a hammer, drive the crankshaft sprocket onto the crankshaft; make sure the timing mark faces outward.

9. Using Molykote or equivalent, lubricate the camshaft sprocket thrust surface and install the timing chain onto the sprocket.

10. While holding the camshaft sprocket and chain vertically, align the marks on the camshaft and crankshaft sprockets.

11. Align the camshaft dowel with the camshaft sprocket hole. Install the camshaft sprocket and torque the bolts to 17 ft. lbs. (23 Nm).

12. Lubricate the timing chain with engine oil.

13. Install the front cover and crankshaft pulley.

14. Connect the negative battery cable.

15. Start the engine, then, check and/or adjust the timing.

Timing Belt Front Cover

REMOVAL AND INSTALLATION

4XC1-U and 4XC1-T Engine

1. Disconnect the negative (−) battery cable.

2. Rotate the crankshaft to position the No. 1 cylinder at the TDC of its compression stroke.

3. Remove the alternator assembly.

4. Remove the crankshaft pulley bolt and

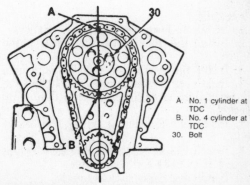

A.	No. 1 cylinder at TDC
B.	No. 4 cylinder at TDC
30.	Bolt

Timing chain alignment marks—V6 engines

pulley. Remove the crankshaft damper with a Harmonic Balancer puller, if so equipped.

5. Remove the timing cover. Be sure the mark on the cam pulley is aligned with the upper surface of the cylinder head and the camshaft dowel pin is positioned at the top.

To install:

6. Install the timing cover.

7. Install the crankshaft damper, pulley and bolt, if removed.

8. Install the alternator assembly.

9. Connect the negative (−) battery cable and check operation.

4ZC1-T, 4ZD1 and 4ZE1 Engine

NOTE: *The engine may be set up with the No. 4 cylinder at TDC on its compression stroke, at the start of this procedure.*

1. Disconnect the negative battery cable and drain the coolant into a suitable drain pan.

CAUTION: *When draining the coolant, keep in mind that cats and dogs are attracted by the ethylene glycol antifreeze, and are quite likely to drink any that is left in an uncovered container or in puddles on the ground. This will prove fatal in sufficient quantity. Always drain the coolant into a sealable container. Coolant should be reused unless it is contaminated or several years old.*

2. Disconnect the radiator inlet and outlet hoses and remove the radiator.

3. Remove alternator and the air conditioning drive belts. Remove the engine fan.

4. Remove the crankshaft pulley center bolt and remove the pulley and hub assembly.

5. Remove the air pump belt and move the air pump out of the way. Remove the air conditioning compressor and lay it to one side (if equipped with air conditioning). Remove the compressor mounting bracket.

6. Remove the distributor (if it is necessary).

7. Remove the water pump pulley. Remove the top section of the front cover and the water pump.

8. Remove the lower section of the front cover.

To install:

1. Install the lower section of the front cover.

2. Install the upper cover and water pump pulley.

3. Install the distributor (if it was removed).

4. Install the air pump and belt. Install the air conditioning compressor and mounting bracket.

5. Install the crankshaft pulley and center bolt.

6. Install the alternator and the air conditioning drive belts and engine fan.

7. Install and connect the radiator.

8. Connect the negative battery cable and refill the coolant. Check for leaks.

Diesel Engines

1. Disconnect the negative battery cable. Drain the cooling system.

CAUTION: *When draining the coolant, keep in mind that cats and dogs are attracted by the ethylene glycol antifreeze, and are quite likely to drink any that is left in an uncovered container or in puddles on the ground. This will prove fatal in sufficient quantity. Always drain the coolant into a sealable container. Coolant should be reused unless it is contaminated or several years old.*

2. Remove the cooling fan assembly and the drive belt(s). Remove the alternator and bracket.

3. Remove the radiator hoses and the radiator.

4. Label and disconnect the necessary vacuum hoses and electrical connectors.

5. Remove the crankshaft pulley.

6. Remove the timing belt cover-to-engine bolts and the cover.

To install:

7. Install the timing belt cover-to-engine bolts and the cover.

8. Install the crankshaft pulley.

9. Connect the necessary vacuum hoses and electrical connectors.

10. Install the radiator hoses and the radiator.

11. Install the cooling fan assembly and the drive belt(s). Install the alternator and bracket.

12. Connect the negative battery cable.

13. Refill the cooling system.

14. Start the engine, allow it to reach normal operating temperatures and check for leaks.

Front Oil Seal

REMOVAL AND INSTALLATION

Gasoline Engine

1. Disconnect the negative battery cable. Remove the crankshaft pulley.

2. Remove the upper and lower timing belt covers.

3. Rotate the crankshaft to align the camshaft sprocket with the mark on the rear timing cover and the crankshaft sprocket keyway with the mark on the oil seal retainer cover.

NOTE: *With the timing marks aligned, the engine is positioned on the TDC of the No. 4 cylinder's compression stroke.*

4. Loosen the timing belt tensioner and relax the tension and remove the timing belt from the crankshaft sprocket.

5. Remove the crankshaft sprocket bolt, the sprocket, the key and deflector shield.

6. Using a small pry bar, pry the oil seal from the oil seal retainer.

To install:

7. Using a new oil seal, lubricate it with engine oil and tap it into the retainer with an oil seal installation tool.

8. Install the deflector, the key, the crankshaft sprocket and bolt.

9. With the crankshaft sprocket aligned with the timing mark, install the timing belt.

10. Apply the tensioner pulley spring pressure to the timing belt.

11. Rotate the crankshaft 2 complete revolutions in the opposite direction of rotation and realign the timing marks.

12. Loosen the tensioner pulley bolt to allow the spring to adjust the correct tension. Torque the tensioner pulley bolt to 14 ft. lbs. (20 Nm).

13. Install the timing covers and the crankshaft pulley.

14. To complete the installation, reverse the removal procedures.

Diesel Engines

1. Disconnect the negative battery terminal. Drain the cooling system.

CAUTION: *When draining the coolant, keep in mind that cats and dogs are attracted by the ethylene glycol antifreeze, and are quite likely to drink any that is left in an uncovered container or in puddles on the ground. This will prove fatal in sufficient quantity. Always drain the coolant into a sealable container. Coolant should be reused unless it is contaminated or several years old.*

2. Remove the timing belt.

3. Remove the crankshaft sprocket bolt.

NOTE: *To remove the crankshaft sprocket bolt, it may be necessary to remove the starter or the flywheel cover plate to lock the flywheel; otherwise, it may be difficult to keep the crankshaft from turning.*

4. Using a puller tool press the crankshaft center and timing sprocket from the crankshaft.

5. Remove the oil seal retainer-to-rear timing cover bolts and the retainer.

6. Using a small pry bar, pry the oil seal from engine housing; be careful not to damage the crankshaft or the oil seal mounting surface.

To install:

7. Using a new oil seal, lubricate the seal lips with engine oil and install it into the engine using a seal installation tool.

8. Install the oil seal retainer.

9. Install the crankshaft center and timing sprocket to the crankshaft.

10. Install the timing belt.

11. Refill the cooling system. Start the engine, check and/or adjust the timing and check for leaks.

Timing Belt and Tensioner

ADJUSTMENT

Gasoline Engine

1. Disconnect the negative battery cable. Remove the crankshaft pulley.

2. Remove the upper and lower timing belt covers.

3. Loosen the timing belt tensioner and relax the belt tension.

4. Apply the tensioner pulley spring pressure to the timing belt.

5. Rotate the crankshaft 2 complete revolutions in the opposite direction of rotation and realign the timing marks.

6. Loosen the tensioner pulley bolt to allow the spring to adjust the correct tension. Torque the tensioner pulley bolt to 14 ft. lbs. (20 Nm).

7. Install the timing covers and the crankshaft pulley.

Diesel Engines

1. Disconnect the negative battery cable. Drain the cooling system.

CAUTION: *When draining the coolant, keep in mind that cats and dogs are attracted by the ethylene glycol antifreeze, and are quite likely to drink any that is left in an uncovered container or in puddles on the ground. This will prove fatal in sufficient quantity. Always drain the coolant into a sealable container. Coolant should be reused unless it is contaminated or several years old.*

2. Remove the timing belt cover and temporarily install the crankshaft pulley.

3. Rotate the crankshaft until the No. 1 cylinder is at the TDC of its compression stroke; make sure the alignment mark on the crankshaft pulley is aligned with timing indicator. Make sure the timing marks on the camshaft sprocket and the injection pump sprocket are facing each other at their closest point.

NOTE: *Any timing belt slack will be absorbed between the injection pump sprocket and camshaft sprocket.*

4. Adjust the timing belt tensioner pulley so the end of the tension center is fitted against the 2 pins on the timing pulley housing; hand tighten the nut, so the tension pulley can be rotated freely.

5. Make sure the tension spring is installed correctly. Torque the tension pulley nut to 22–36 ft. lbs. (29–47 Nm).

6. Rotate the crankshaft 2 complete revolu-

Timing belt alignment—4XC1-U and 4XC1-T, camshaft sprocket dowel pin and crankshaft woodruff key at 12 o:clock

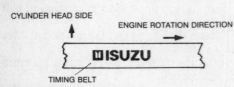

Timing belt positioning—all engines

tions in the clockwise direction. Further, turn the crankshaft 90° beyond TDC to settle the injection pump.

7. Loosen the tension pulley nut to allow the timing belt slackness to be taken up, then, tighten the tension pulley nut to 79–94 ft. lbs. (108–135 Nm).

NOTE: *Never attempt to rotate the crankshaft counterclockwise.*

8. Using a belt tension gauge, measure the belt tension between the injection pump sprocket and the crankshaft sprocket; it should be 33–55 lbs. (45–75 Nm).

REMOVAL AND INSTALLATION

1985–87 4XC1-U and 4XC1-T Engines

1. Remove the engine by referring to the Engine Removal and Installation procedure in this section. Mount the engine to an engine stand.

2. Remove the accessory drive belts.

3. Remove the engine mounting bracket from the timing cover.

4. Rotate the crankshaft until the notch on the crankshaft pulley aligns with the **0** mark on the timing cover and the No. 4 cylinder is on TDC of the compression stroke.

5. Remove the starter and install the flywheel holding tool (J–35271).

6. Remove the crankshaft bolt, boss and pulley.

7. Remove the timing cover bolts and the timing cover.

8. Loosen the tension pulley bolt.

9. Insert an allen wrench into the tension pulley hexagonal hole and loosen the timing belt by turning the tension pulley clockwise.

10. Remove the timing belt.

NOTE: *Inspect the timing belt for signs of cracking, abnormal wear and hardening. Never expose the belt to oil, sunlight or heat.*

Avoid excessive bending, twisting or stretching.

To install:

11. Position the woodruff key on the crankshaft followed by the crankshaft timing gear. Align the groove on the timing gear with the mark on the oil pump.

12. Align the timing gear mark with the upper surface of the cylinder head and the dowel pin in its uppermost position.

13. Place the timing belt arrow in the direction of the engine rotation and install the timing belt. Tighten the tension pulley bolt.

14. Insert a hex wrench into the tension pulley hexagonal hole and hold the pulley stationary while tightening the bolt temporarily.

15. Turn the crankshaft two complete reverse revolutions and align the crankshaft timing pulley groove with the mark on the oil pump. Loosen the tension pulley bolt and apply tension to the timing belt.

16. Insert a hex wrench into the tension pulley hexagonal hole and hold the pulley stationary while torquing the bolt to 37 ft. lbs. (49 Nm).

17. Move the crankshaft back to about 50° before TDC and re-adjust the timing belt. Use a drive belt tension gauge to check the timing belt tension. The tension should be 38 ± 4 ft. lbs.; if the belt is not at the proper tension it must be re-adjusted.

18. Adjust the valve clearance and to complete the installation. Install the engine and check for proper operation.

1988–90 4XC1-U, 4XC1-T and 4XE1 Engines

1. Disconnect the negative battery cable. Drain the radiator coolant into a suitable drain pan.

CAUTION: *When draining the coolant, keep in mind that cats and dogs are attracted by the ethylene glycol antifreeze, and are quite likely to drink any that is left in an uncovered container or in puddles on the ground. This will prove fatal in sufficient quantity. Always drain the coolant into a sealable container. Coolant should be reused unless it is contaminated or several years old.*

2. Place a wooden block on a suitable floor jack and place the jack under the strongest point of the oil pan, slightly raise the engine.

3. Remove the rear side torque rod while the engine is slightly lifted.

4. Remove the right side engine mount, then remove the body side mount and the engine side mount.

5. Loosen the power steering oil pump retaining bolt and remove the V-belt.

6. Remove the 4 crank pulley bolts with the engine slightly lifted.

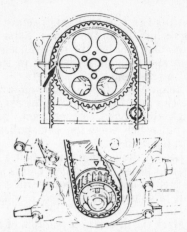

Camshaft and crankshaft timing belt alignment marks—4XC1-U and 4XC1-T engines

7. Remove the 6 timing cover bolts and remove the timing belt cover.

8. Be sure that the crankshaft timing mark on the crankshaft pulley hub is aligned with the top dead center mark.

9. Use special crankshaft bolt tool (J-37376 or equivalent) to turn and stop the crankshaft, then remove the bolt on the end part of the crank shaft and remove the pulley.

10. Confirm the crankshaft is at top dead center, prior to removing the timing belt. In this state, if the notch on the camshaft pulley hub is aligned with the left upper corner of the cylinder head, the number 4 cylinder is at top dead center. If the notch on the camshaft pulley is aligned with the right upper corner of the cylinder head, the No. 1 cylinder is at top dead center.

11. Loosen the bolts fixing the tension pulley. Turn the tension pulley clockwise with the allen wrench, then remove the timing belt.

NOTE: *Remove the camshaft pulley and make sure that there are no oil leaks or bolts on the oil seal section. Make sure that there are no water leaks from the water pump or oil leaks from the crankshaft oil seal. If water leaks or oil leaks appear, replace the oil seal or water pack packing with a new part.*

To install:

12. Install the camshaft pulley and be sure that the camshaft pulley timing mark is aligned with the upper surface of the cylinder head and the dowel pin is in the up position. Torque the retaining bolt to 84 inch lbs. (10 Nm).

13. Install the crankshaft timing pulley, making sure that the woodruff key is positioned correctly.

14. Install the tension spring and position the long part of the tension spring to the rear of the timing case and the short end to the rear of the tension spring retaining bolt.

15. Install the timing belt. Be sure that the belt is installed correctly, the lettering mark in the direction of the engine rotation and install the belt in the following order; over the crankshaft timing gear, camshaft timing pulley, water pump pulley and tensioner pulley.

NOTE: *There must be no slack in the timing belt after it has been installed. The teeth of the belt and the teeth of the pulley must be in perfect alignment.*

16. Loosen the tension pulley bolt. Insert an allen wrench into the tension pulley hexagonal hole. Hold the pulley stationary and temporarily tighten the bolt.

17. Turn the crankshaft 2 complete reverse revolutions and align the crankshaft timing pulley groove with the mark on the oil pump.

18. Loosen the tension pulley bolt and apply tension to the belt. Insert an allen wrench into the tension pulley hexagonal hole. Hold the pulley stationary and torque the bolt to 37 ft. lbs. (49 Nm).

19. Move the crankshaft back to approximately 50° BTDC. Once again adjust the timing belt. Set the crankshaft at that position, use a belt tension gauge to check the timing belt tension. The belt tension should be 44 lbs.

20. Attach the taper face of the crankshaft pulley to the timing belt. Fasten the crankshaft pulley center bolt and torque it to 108 ± 11 ft. lbs.

21. Install the timing cover and torque the bolts to 84 inch lbs. (10 Nm). Be sure to pay attention to the timing belt cover bolt length. Use the following torque specifications:

   a. Crank pulley — 5.4–9.5 inch lbs. (7–10 Nm).

   b. Engine mount bracket body side — 30 ft. lbs. (41 Nm).

   c. Engine mount bracket engine side — 45 ft. lbs. (61 Nm).

   d. Torque rod — 42 ft. lbs. (56 Nm).

4XE1 DOHC Engine

1. Disconnect negative battery cable and drain cooling system. Remove the air cleaner duct hose from the common chamber.

CAUTION: *When draining the coolant, keep in mind that cats and dogs are attracted by the ethylene glycol antifreeze, and are quite likely to drink any that is left in an uncovered container or in puddles on the ground. This will prove fatal in sufficient quantity. Always drain the coolant into a sealable container. Coolant should be reused unless it is contaminated or several years old.*

2. Rotate the engine until the engine is at TDC on the compression stroke of the No. 1 cylinder, make sure timing mark is on the scale.

3. Remove the power steering pump drive

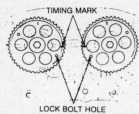

Camshaft sprocket alignment marks—4XE1 DOHC engine

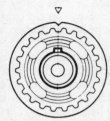

Crankshaft sprocket alignment marks—4XE1 DOHC engine

1. Crankshaft timing gear
2. Water pump
3. Idler pulley
4. Exhaust camshaft pulley
5. Intake camshaft pulley
6. Tensioner pulley

Timing belt routing—4XE1 DOHC engine

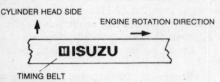

Timing belt positioning

belt, for vehicles with air conditioners, remove the power steering pump and compressor drive belt. Loosen the 2 power steering pump adjust plates bolts.

4. Remove the alternator drive belt from the crank pulley side. Disconnect the clip securing the high pressure air conditioning line to the strut tower.

5. Remove the upper timing belt cover.

6. Using a suitable engine hoist, slightly raise and support the engine safely.

7. Remove the passenger side engine mount from the engine. Disconnect the torque rod at the firewall.

8. Remove the passenger side engine mounting bracket from the engine. Using special crank pulley tool J-37988 or equivalent, remove the crank pulley bolt.

9. Raise the passenger side of the engine, be sure that the front wheels remain on the ground while lifting the engine. Raise the engine too high will left the front wheels off the ground and may cause damage to the drive shaft universal joint.

10. Remove the timing belt lower cover. Remove the cranking pulley and extract up through the engine compartment. Refit the crank pulley bolt. Align the crank pulley timing gear to top dead center.

11. Loosen the tension pulley bolt a ½ turn counterclockwise. If the pulley bolt is loosened more than ½ a turn, the pulley will swing too far out of adjustment and may be difficult to readjust.

12. Mark the direction of rotation of the timing mark with a piece of chalk and remove the timing belt. Using and open end wrench, hole the camshaft from turning and remove the camshaft pulley(s).

NOTE: *Inspect the timing belt for signs of cracking, abnormal wear and hardening. Never expose the belt to oil, sunlight or heat. Avoid excessive bending, twisting or stretching.*

To install:

13. Install the camshaft pulley(s) and torque the retaining bolts to 43 ft. lbs. (59 Nm). Align the camshaft pulley timing marks. Lock the camshaft pulley in position by inserting a 6mm bolt through the camshaft pulleys and into the cylinder head.

NOTE: *The camshaft timing pulleys have and identification mark, the I mark for the intake side and the E mark for the exhaust side.*

14. Align the crank pulley timing gear to top dead center.

15. Install the timing belt. Be sure that the belt is installed correctly, the lettering must be able to be read while viewing it from the passenger side fender.

16. The belt must be installed in the following order; over the crankshaft timing gear, water pump pulley, idle pulley, exhaust camshaft pulley, intake camshaft pulley and tensioner pulley.

NOTE: *There must be no slack in the timing belt after it has been installed. The teeth of the belt and the teeth of the pulley must be in perfect alignment.*

17. Loosen the tensioner bolt and apply spring force to the belt. If reusing the old belt, do not tension the belt with more than spring force applied. When a new belt is being used, push the tension pulley in the direction of the belt tension. The tensioner pulley retaining bolt should be torqued to 17 ft. lbs. (24 Nm).

18. Keep the tension pulley from turning while fastening the fixing bolt in order to pre-

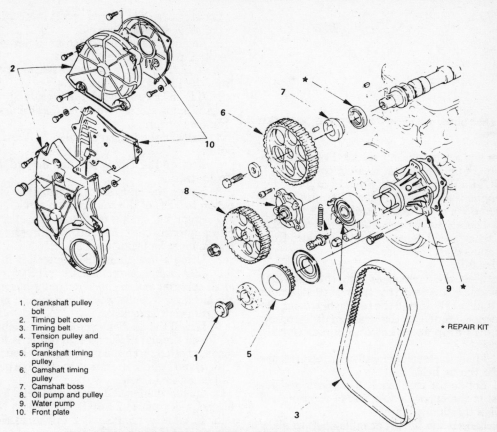

1. Crankshaft pulley bolt
2. Timing belt cover
3. Timing belt
4. Tension pulley and spring
5. Crankshaft timing pulley
6. Camshaft timing pulley
7. Camshaft boss
8. Oil pump and pulley
9. Water pump
10. Front plate

★ REPAIR KIT

Timing belt and tensioner assembly—4ZC1-T, 4ZD1 and 4ZE1 engines

vent excessively high low tension of the timing belt.

19. Rotate the crankshaft 2 turns normally and make sure that the notch on cylinder number 1 matches the scale on the timing cover match as well as the mark on the cam pulley. If it does not match them, repeat this procedure again from Step number 1.

20. Turn the crankshaft by 60° normally and measure the deflection of the timing belt. Be sure that it is within the specified range. If the deflection is not within the specified values, repeat the this procedure from Step 4. The belt tension should be as follows:

    a. New belt — 0.28–0.33 lbs.
    a. Old belt — 0.35–0.41 lbs.

21. Attach the taper face of the crankshaft pulley to the timing belt. Fasten the crankshaft pulley center bolt and torque it to 123 ft. lbs. (170 Nm).

22. Install the timing cover and torque the bolts to 84 inch lbs. (9.5 Nm).

4ZD1 and 4ZE1 Engines

1. Disconnect the negative battery cable. Remove the crankshaft pulley.

2. Remove the upper and lower timing belt covers.

3. Rotate the crankshaft to align the camshaft sprocket with the mark on the rear timing

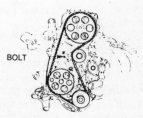

BOLT

Timing belt tensioner—loosen bolt and then tighten

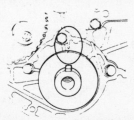

Crankshaft pulley alignment—4ZC1-T, 4ZD1 and 4ZE1 engines

Camshaft pulley alignment—4ZC1-T, 4ZD1 and 4ZE1 engines

cover and the crankshaft sprocket keyway with the mark on the oil seal retainer cover.

NOTE: *With the timing marks aligned, the engine is positioned on the TDC of the No. 4 cylinder's compression stroke.*

4. Loosen the timing belt tensioner and relax the tension and remove the timing belt from the crankshaft sprocket.

To install:

5. With the crankshaft and the camshaft sprockets aligned with the timing marks, install the timing belt. Install the timing belt using the following sequence: the crankshaft sprocket, the oil pump sprocket and the camshaft sprocket.

6. Apply the tensioner pulley spring pressure to the timing belt.

7. Rotate the crankshaft 2 complete revolutions in the opposite direction of rotation and realign the timing marks.

8. Loosen the tensioner pulley bolt to allow the spring to adjust the correct tension. Torque the tensioner pulley bolt to 14 ft. lbs. (20 Nm).

9. Install the timing covers and the crankshaft pulley.

10. Connect the negative battery cable. Start the engine and check for leaks.

C223 and C223-T Engines

1. Disconnect the negative battery cable. Drain the cooling system.

CAUTION: *When draining the coolant, keep in mind that cats and dogs are attracted by the ethylene glycol antifreeze, and are quite likely to drink any that is left in an uncovered container or in puddles on the ground. This will prove fatal in sufficient quantity. Always drain the coolant into a sealable container.*

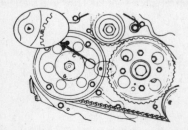

Injection pump and camshaft alignment marks—C223 diesel

Coolant should be reused unless it is contaminated or several years old.

2. Remove the timing belt cover. Remove the injection pump sprocket flange.

3. Using a prybar, remove the tension spring from the timing belt tensioner.

NOTE: *When removing the tension spring, avoid using excessive force for the spring may become distorted.*

4. Remove the tensioner pulley bolt and the pulley.

5. Remove the timing belt and discard it.

To install:

6. Rotate the crankshaft to bring the No. 1 piston to TDC of the compression stroke.

7. Align the timing marks on the injection pump sprocket with the camshaft sprocket; the marks must be facing each other.

8. Using a new timing belt, install it in the following sequence: crankshaft sprocket, camshaft sprocket and the injection pump sprocket; the slack must be between the injection pump and camshaft sprockets.

9. Install the tension center and the tension pulley so the end of the tension center is fitted against both pins on the timing pulley housing.

10. Hand tighten the nut so the tension pulley can be rotated freely.

11. Install the tension spring and semi-tighten the pulley nut to 22–36 ft. lbs. (30–48 Nm).

12. Rotate the crankshaft 2 full turns clockwise to seat the belt and further turn the crankshaft 90° beyond TDC to settle the injection pump.

13. Loosen the tension pulley nut to take up the timing belt slack. Tighten the tension pulley nut to 79–94 ft. lbs. (108–128 Nm).

14. Install the injection pump sprocket flange; the hole in the outer circumference of the flange should be aligned with the triangular timing mark on the injection pump sprocket.

15. Rotate the crankshaft 2 full turns clockwise to bring the No. 1 piston to TDC of the compression stroke. Make sure the triangular timing mark on the timing sprocket is aligned with the hole in the flange, then, measure the timing belt tension; it should be 33–55 lbs.

16. Install the timing belt cover.

17. Connect the negative battery cable.

4FB1 Diesel Engine

1. Open the hood and disconnect the battery. Drain the radiator system.

CAUTION: *When draining the coolant, keep in mind that cats and dogs are attracted by the ethylene glycol antifreeze, and are quite likely to drink any that is left in an uncovered container or in puddles on the ground. This will prove fatal in sufficient quantity. Always drain the coolant into a sealable container.*

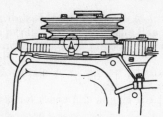

After removing the timing cover, make sure the crankshaft is in the No. 1 cyl. TDC position

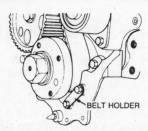

Remove the timing belt holder—C223 diesel engine

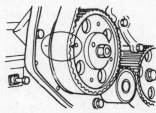

Injection pump alignment marks—C223 diesel engine

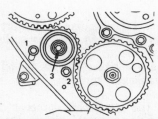

Tensioner pulley bolt sequence—C223 diesel engine

Coolant should be reused unless it is contaminated or several years old.

2. Remove the lower engine shrouds.

3. Remove the fan shroud, V-belt, cooling fan and pulley.

4. Remove the 10 retaining bolts on the upper dust cover and remove the cover.

5. Remove the bypass hose.

6. With the piston in the No. 1 cylinder at TDC, make sure the setting mark on the pump pulley is in alignment with the front plate, then lock the pulley with an 8mm 1.25 pitch bolt.

7. Remove the cam cover. Loosen the adjusting screws so that the rocker arms are held in a free state. Lock the camshaft by fitting a plate to the slit in the rear end of the camshaft.

8. Remove the damper pulley after making sure the piston in No. 1 is at TDC.

9. Remove the lower dust cover, then remove the timing belt holder.

10. Remove the tension spring. Loosen the tension pulley and plate bolts and remove the timing belt.

To install:

11. Remove the bolt locking the camshaft pulley and remove the pulley from the camshaft. Put the pulley back on the shaft, but only tighten the bolts enough to allow the pulley to be turned by hand.

12. Install the new timing belt, making sure the cogs on the pulley and the belt are engaged properly. The crankshaft should not be turned.

13. Concentrate belt looseness on the tension pulley, then depress the tension pulley with your fingers and install the tension spring. Semi-tighten the bolts in numerical sequence to prevent movement of the tension pulley.

14. Tighten the camshaft pulley bolts.

15. Remove the injection pump pulley lock bolt.

16. Remove the locking plate on the end of the camshaft.

17. Install the damper pulley on the hub and make sure the No. 1 piston is still at TDC.

CAUTION: *Do not turn the crankshaft in an attempt to make an adjustment.*

18. Make sure the injection pump pulley mark is in alignment with the mark on the plate.

19. Loosen the tensioner pulley and plate bolts. Concentrate the looseness of the belt on the tensioner, then tighten the bolts on numerical sequence. Torque the bolts to:

    a. Bolt No. 1 to 11–18 ft. lbs. (15–25 Nm)
    b. Bolt No. 2 to 11–18 ft. lbs. (15–25 Nm)
    c. Bolt No. 3 to 47–61 ft. lbs. (63–83 Nm)

20. Check valve adjustment and install the cam cover.

21. Remove the damper pulley and install the belt holder in position away from the timing belt.

22. Install the bypass hose and dust covers.

23. Install the damper pulley and reverse removal Steps 1–5.

24. Refill the cooling system.

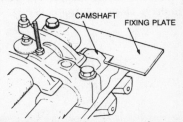

Install a camshaft fixing plate to the slit in the end of the camshaft—4FB1 diesel engine

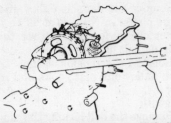

Camshaft sprocket removal, torque to 55 ft. lbs. (75 Nm)—G180Z and G200Z engines

Gasoline Engine Timing Sprockets

REMOVAL AND INSTALLATION

G180Z and G200Z Engines

CAMSHAFT

1. Disconnect the negative (−) battery cable.
2. Remove the rocker arm cover as outlined in this Chapter.
3. Remove the rubber half plug in front of the camshaft sprocket.
4. Using a suitable prybar, insert it through one of the sprocket holes and remove the retaining bolt.
5. Release the timing chain tensioner as outlined in the Timing Chain section of this Chapter.
6. Wiggle the sprocket off of the camshaft. Use a small rubber hammer for assistance in removal if necessary.
7. Use a piece of wire to keep the timing chain from falling into the engine.

To install:

1. Install the sprocket with the timing marks aligned as shown in the Timing Chain section of this Chapter. Install the bolt and washer, torque the bolt to 55 ft. lbs. (75 Nm).
2. Install the rocker arm cover, connect the battery cable and, start the engine and check for leaks.

CRANKSHAFT

1. Disconnect the negative (−) battery cable.
2. Remove the timing cover as outlined in this Chapter.
3. Using a gear puller, remove the oil pump drive and crankshaft sprocket.

To install:

1. Install the crankshaft sprocket and oil pump drive using a suitable driver. Be careful

Crankshaft and oil pump sprocket removal—G180Z and G200Z engines

not to damage the crankshaft. Install the timing chain and align the timing marks as illustrated in the Timing Chain section of this Chapter.
2. Install the timing cover and connect the negative battery cable.
3. Start the engine and check for leaks.

4XC1-U, 4XC1-T and 4XE1 SOHC Engines

CAMSHAFT

1. Disconnect the negative (−) battery cable.
2. Remove the rocker arm cover as outlined in this Chapter.
3. Remove the upper timing belt cover in front of the camshaft sprocket. Release the tension and remove the timing belt as outlined in the Timing Belt section of this Chapter.
4. Using a suitable prybar, insert it through one of the sprocket holes and remove the retaining bolt.
5. Wiggle the sprocket off of the camshaft. Use a small rubber hammer for assistance in removal if necessary.

To install:

1. Install the sprocket with the timing marks aligned as shown in the Timing Bent section of this Chapter. Install the bolt and washer, torque the bolt to 55 ft. lbs. (75 Nm).
2. Install the rocker arm and timing cover, connect the battery cable and, start the engine and check for leaks.

CRANKSHAFT

1. Disconnect the negative (−) battery cable.
2. Remove the timing cover as outlined in this Section.
3. Using a gear puller, remove the oil pump drive and crankshaft sprocket.

To install:

1. Install the crankshaft sprocket and oil pump drive using a suitable driver. Be careful not to damage the crankshaft. Install the timing chain and align the timing marks as illustrated in the Timing Belt section of this Chapter.
2. Install the timing cover and connect the negative battery cable.
3. Start the engine and check for leaks.

4ZC1-T, 4ZD1 and 4ZE1 Engines

CAMSHAFT SPROCKET

1. Disconnect the negative battery cable.
2. Remove the timing belt.
3. Remove the camshaft sprocket-to-camshaft bolt and the sprocket.

NOTE: *It may be necessary to use a mallet to tap the sprocket from the camshaft.*

4. Remove and replace the camshaft oil seal.

To install:

5. Align the camshaft sprocket-to-rear plate

Camshaft sprocket removal—4ZC1-T, 4ZD1 and 4ZE1 engines

timing marks. With the crankshaft sprocket aligned with the timing mark, install the timing belt.

6. Apply the tensioner pulley spring pressure to the timing belt.

7. Rotate the crankshaft 2 complete revolutions in the opposite direction of rotation and realign the timing marks.

8. Loosen the tensioner pulley bolt to allow the spring to adjust the correct tension. Torque the tensioner pulley bolt to 14 ft. lbs. (19 Nm).

9. Install the timing covers and the crankshaft pulley.

10. Connect the battery cable, start the engine and check for leaks.

CRANKSHAFT SPROCKET

1. Disconnect the negative battery cable.
2. Remove the timing belt.
3. Remove the crankshaft sprocket-to-crankshaft bolt. Using a puller, pull the sprocket from the crankshaft.
4. Remove and replace the crankshaft oil seal.

To install:

5. Align the crankshaft sprocket-to-oil seal retainer plate timing marks.

6. With the camshaft sprocket aligned with its timing mark, install the timing belt.

7. Apply the tensioner pulley spring pressure to the timing belt.

8. Rotate the crankshaft 2 complete revolutions in the opposite direction of rotation and realign the timing marks.

9. Loosen the tensioner pulley bolt to allow

the spring to adjust the correct tension. Torque the tensioner pulley bolt to 14 ft. lbs. (22 Nm).

10. Install the timing covers and the crankshaft pulley.

11. To complete the installation, reverse the removal procedures.

4XE1 DOHC Engine

CAMSHAFT

1. Disconnect the negative (−) battery cable.
2. Remove the cylinder head cover as outlined in this Section.
3. Rotate the crankshaft to the No. 1 TDC position on the compression stroke by aligning the camshaft pulleys' timing marks as indicated in the Timing Belt section of this Chapter.
4. Remove the right hand engine mounting rubber.
5. Remove the tension adjusting hole cover, loosen the tension pulley lock bolt and turn the tension pulley clockwise with a hex wrench and remove the belt.
6. Remove the camshaft pulley bolts by holding the camshaft from turning with a suitable tool inserted through the pulley hole.

To install:

7. Install the pulley and torque the bolt to 43 ft. lbs. (59 Nm).

8. Install the timing belt as outlined in the Timing Belt section in this Chapter.

9. Adjust the belt tension and install the hole cover.

10. Install the right side engine mount and cylinder head cover.

11. Connect the battery cable, start the engine and check for leaks.

Diesel Engine Timing Sprockets
REMOVAL AND INSTALLATION

Injection Pump Sprocket

1. Disconnect the negative battery cable. Drain the cooling system.

CAUTION: *When draining the coolant, keep in mind that cats and dogs are attracted by*

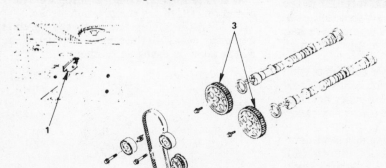

1. Tension adjusting hole cover
2. Timing belt
3. Camshaft pulley

Camshaft pulley removal—4XE1 DOHC engine

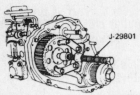

Injection pump sprocket—diesel engine

the ethylene glycol antifreeze, and are quite likely to drink any that is left in an uncovered container or in puddles on the ground. This will prove fatal in sufficient quantity. Always drain the coolant into a sealable container. Coolant should be reused unless it is contaminated or several years old.

2. Remove the timing belt cover. Remove the injection pump sprocket flange.

3. Using a pry bar, remove the tension spring from the timing belt tensioner.

NOTE: When removing the tension spring, avoid using excessive force for the spring may become distorted.

4. Remove the tensioner pulley bolt and the pulley.

5. Remove the timing belt and discard it.

6. Using a 6mm, 1.25 pitch bolt, install the threaded portion into the threaded hole in the timing sprocket housing through the hole in the sprocket to prevent the sprocket from turning.

7. Remove the injection pump sprocket-to-shaft bolts.

8. Using a wheel puller, connect it to the injection pump sprocket and press it from the shaft.

To install:

9. Install the injection pump sprocket by aligning it with the key groove and torque the bolt to 42–52 ft. lbs. (56–70 Nm)

10. Rotate the crankshaft to bring the No. 1 piston to TDC of the compression stroke.

11. Align the timing marks on the injection pump sprocket with the camshaft sprocket; the marks must be facing each other.

12. Using a new timing belt, install it in the following sequence: crankshaft sprocket, camshaft sprocket and the injection pump sprocket; the slack must be between the injection pump and camshaft sprockets.

13. Install the tension center and the tension pulley so the end of the tension center is fitted against both pins on the timing pulley housing.

14. Hand tighten the nut so the tension pulley can be rotated freely.

15. Install the tension spring and semi-tighten the pulley nut to 22–36 ft. lbs. (30–48 Nm).

16. Rotate the crankshaft 2 full turns clockwise to seat the belt and further turn the crank-

shaft 90° beyond TDC to settle the injection pump.

17. Loosen the tension pulley nut to take up the timing belt slack. Tighten the tension pulley nut to 79–94 ft. lbs. (108–130 Nm).

18. Install the injection pump sprocket flange; the hole in the outer circumference of the flange should be aligned with the triangular timing mark on the injection pump sprocket.

19. Rotate the crankshaft 2 full turns clockwise to bring the No. 1 piston to TDC of the compression stroke. Make sure the triangular timing mark on the timing sprocket is aligned with the hole in the flange, then, measure the timing belt tension; it should be 33–55 lbs.

20. Install the timing belt cover.

21. To complete the installation, reverse the removal procedures.

22. Connect the negative battery cable. Refill the cooling system.

Camshaft Sprocket

1. Disconnect the negative battery cable.

2. Remove the timing belt cover. Remove the injection pump sprocket flange.

3. Using a pry bar, remove the tension spring from the timing belt tensioner.

NOTE: When removing the tension spring, avoid using excessive force for the spring may become distorted.

4. Remove the tensioner pulley bolt and the pulley.

5. Remove the timing belt and discard it.

6. Using a 6mm, 1.25 pitch bolt, install the threaded portion into the threaded hole in the camshaft sprocket housing through the hole in the sprocket to prevent the sprocket from turning.

7. Using a wheel puller, connect it to the camshaft sprocket and press it from the camshaft.

To install:

8. Install the camshaft sprocket and torque the camshaft sprocket-to-camshaft bolt to 72–87 ft. lbs. (96–115 Nm).

9. Rotate the crankshaft to bring the No. 1 piston to TDC of the compression stroke.

10. Align the timing marks on the injection pump sprocket with the camshaft sprocket; the marks must be facing each other.

Camshaft sprocket—diesel engine

11. Using a new timing belt, install it in the following sequence: crankshaft sprocket, camshaft sprocket and the injection pump sprocket; the slack must be between the injection pump and camshaft sprockets.

12. Install the tension center and the tension pulley so the end of the tension center is fitted against both pins on the timing pulley housing.

13. Hand tighten the nut so the tension pulley can be rotated freely.

14. Install the tension spring and semi-tighten the pulley nut to 22–36 ft. lbs. (29–48 Nm).

15. Rotate the crankshaft 2 full turns clockwise to seat the belt and further turn the crankshaft 90° beyond TDC to settle the injection pump.

16. Loosen the tension pulley nut to take up the timing belt slack. Tighten the tension pulley nut to 79–94 ft. lbs. (108–130 Nm).

17. Install the injection pump sprocket flange; the hole in the outer circumference of the flange should be aligned with the triangular timing mark on the injection pump sprocket.

18. Rotate the crankshaft 2 full turns clockwise to bring the No. 1 piston to TDC of the compression stroke. Make sure the triangular timing mark on the timing sprocket is aligned with the hole in the flange, then, measure the timing belt tension; it should be 33–55 lbs.

19. Install the timing belt cover.

20. To complete the installation, reverse the removal procedures.

21. Connect the negative battery cable. Refill the cooling system.

Crankshaft Sprocket

1. Disconnect the negative battery cable. Drain the cooling system.

CAUTION: *When draining the coolant, keep in mind that cats and dogs are attracted by the ethylene glycol antifreeze, and are quite likely to drink any that is left in an uncovered container or in puddles on the ground. This will prove fatal in sufficient quantity. Always drain the coolant into a sealable container. Coolant should be reused unless it is contaminated or several years old.*

2. Remove the timing belt cover.

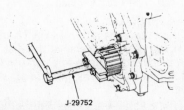

J-29752

Crankshaft sprocket—diesel engine

3. Using a pry bar, remove the tension spring from the timing belt tensioner.

NOTE: *When removing the tension spring, avoid using excessive force for the spring may become distorted.*

4. Remove the tensioner pulley bolt and the pulley.

5. Remove the timing belt and discard it.

6. Remove the crankshaft sprocket bolt.

NOTE: *To remove the crankshaft sprocket bolt, it may be necessary to remove the starter or the flywheel cover plate to lock the flywheel; otherwise, it may be difficult to keep the crankshaft from turning.*

7. Using a puller tool press the crankshaft center and timing sprocket from the crankshaft.

To install:

8. Install the crankshaft center and timing sprocket to the crankshaft and install the bolt.

9. Rotate the crankshaft to bring the No. 1 piston to TDC of the compression stroke.

10. Align the timing marks on the injection pump sprocket with the camshaft sprocket; the marks must be facing each other.

11. Using a new timing belt, install it in the following sequence: crankshaft sprocket, camshaft sprocket and the injection pump sprocket; the slack must be between the injection pump and camshaft sprockets.

12. Install the tension center and the tension pulley so the end of the tension center is fitted against both pins on the timing pulley housing.

13. Hand tighten the nut so the tension pulley can be rotated freely.

14. Install the tension spring and semi-tighten the pulley nut to 22–36 ft. lbs. (28–48 Nm).

15. Rotate the crankshaft 2 full turns clockwise to seat the belt and further turn the crankshaft 90° beyond TDC to settle the injection pump.

16. Loosen the tension pulley nut to take up the timing belt slack. Tighten the tension pulley nut to 79–94 ft. lbs. (108–130 Nm).

17. Install the injection pump sprocket flange; the hole in the outer circumference of the flange should be aligned with the triangular timing mark on the injection pump sprocket.

18. Rotate the crankshaft 2 full turns clockwise to bring the No. 1 piston to TDC of the compression stroke. Make sure the trangular timing mark on the timing sproket is aligned with the hole in the flange, then, measure the timing belt tension; it should be 33–55 lbs.

19. Install the timing belt cover.

20. To complete the installation, reverse the removal procedures.

21. Connect the negative battery cable. Refill the cooling system.

Camshaft

REMOVAL AND INSTALLATION

G180Z and G200Z Engine

1. Disconnect the negative battery cable.
2. Remove the rocker arm cover.
3. Rotate the engine until the No. 4 cylinder is at TDC (top dead center) on the compression stroke. Remove the distributor cap and mark the rotor to housing position.
4. Release the tension on the automatic timing chain adjuster by performing the following procedures:

 a. Using a small pry bar, depress the lock lever on the automatic adjuster rearward.

 b. Push on the automatic adjuster shoe and lock it into the retracted position by releasing the lever.

5. Remove the camshaft sprocket-to-camshaft bolt, the sprocket and suspend the assembly on the wire; allow the chain to remain on the sprocket.
6. Remove the rocker arm brackets-to-cylinder head bolts and the rocker arm bracket assembly from the cylinder head.
7. Remove the camshaft from the cylinder head.

To install:

8. Lubricate the camshaft with engine oil and install it onto the cylinder head.
9. Install the rocker arm assembly onto the cylinder head and torque the bolts to 16 ft. lbs. (21 Nm).
10. Align the camshaft sprocket hole with camshaft dowel pin and install the sprocket.

ROCKER ARM ALIGNMENT MARKS

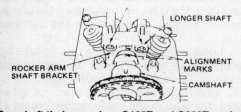

Camshaft timing marks—G180Z and G200Z engines

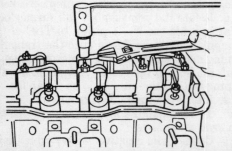

Tightening rocket arm retainers—G180Z and G200Z engines

Torque the camshaft sprocket-to-camshaft bolt to 50–65 ft. lbs. (68–88 Nm).

11. Set the automatic adjuster by turning the adjuster slide pin 90° counterclockwise with a small pry bar.
12. Adjust the valve lash.
13. Install the rocker arm cover and make sure the alignment marks are aligned.
14. To complete the installation, reverse the removal procedures. Start the engine and check and/or adjust the timing.

4XC1-U, 4XC1-T and 4XE1 SOHC Engines

1. Disconnect the negative battery cable.
2. Align the crankshaft pulley notch with the 0 mark on the timing cover.
3. Remove the cylinder head cover.
4. Remove the timing cover.
5. Loosen the camshaft timing gear bolts (DO NOT rotate the engine).
6. Loosen the timing belt tensioner and remove the timing belt from the camshaft timing gear.
7. Remove the rocker arm shaft/rocker arm assembly.
8. Remove the distributor bolt and the distributor.
9. Remove the camshaft and the camshaft seal.

To install:

10. Drive a new camshaft seal onto the camshaft using seal installation tool No. J–35268 or equivalent. Place the camshaft in the cylinder head with the dowel pin in the camshaft facing forward.
11. Install the distributor and hold down bolt.
12. Install the rocker arm shaft/rocker arm assembly.
13. Install the timing belt to the camshaft timing gear and adjust tensioner.
14. Tighten the camshaft timing gear bolts (DO NOT rotate the engine).
15. Install the timing cover.
16. Install the cylinder head cover.
17. Align the crankshaft pulley notch with the 0 mark on the timing cover.
18. Connect the negative battery cable, start the engine and check for leaks.

4ZC1-T, 4ZD1 and 4ZE1 Engines

1. Remove the cam cover.
2. Rotate the camshaft until the No. 4 cyl. is in the firing position. Remove the distributor cap and mark the rotor-to-housing position.
3. Remove the timing belt as previously outlined.
4. Apply a detention to the camshaft pulley by placing a T-bar or equivalent over the front plate fitting bolt and loosen the pulley fitting

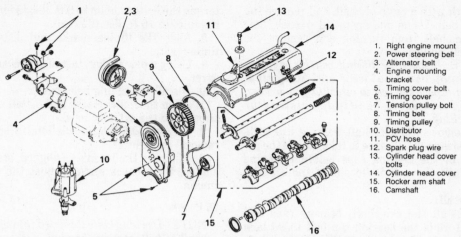

Camshaft and related components—4XC1-U, 4XC1-T and 4XE1 engines

1. Right engine mount
2. Power steering belt
3. Alternator belt
4. Engine mounting bracket
5. Timing cover bolt
6. Timing cover
7. Tension pulley bolt
8. Timing belt
9. Timing pulley
10. Distributor
11. PCV hose
12. Spark plug wire
13. Cylinder head cover bolts
14. Cylinder head cover
15. Rocker arm shaft
16. Camshaft

bolt. Remove the camshaft pulley, do not lose the camshaft boss or key.

5. Sequentially loosen and remove the outermost one and remove the rocker arm shaft with the bracket as an assembly.

6. Remove the camshaft.

To install:

7. Use a liberal amount of oil to coat the camshaft before installing it. Be sure that the mark on the camshaft is facing upward when it is being installed.

8. Use the timing belt removal and installation procedure previously outlined in this section to finish the installation.

9. Install the rocker arm shaft with the bracket as an assembly.

10. Install the camshaft pulley and bolt.

11. Install the distributor and cap to the marked position.

12. Install the cam cover.

13. Connect the battery cable, start the engine and check for leaks.

4XE1 DOHC Engine

1. Disconnect the negative battery cable. Remove the engine center (head) cover from the engine.

2. Rotate the engine until the engine is at TDC on the compression stroke of the No. 1 cylinder, make sure timing mark is on the scale.

3. Remove the power steering pump drive belt, for vehicles with air conditioners, remove the power steering pump and compressor drive belt. Loosen the 2 power steering pump adjust plates bolts.

4. Remove the alternator drive belt from the crank pulley side. Disconnect the clip securing the high pressure air conditioning line to the strut tower.

5. Remove the upper timing belt cover.

6. Using a suitable engine hoist, slightly raise and support the engine safely.

7. Remove the passenger side engine mount from the engine. Disconnect the torque rod at the firewall.

8. Remove the passenger side engine mounting bracket from the engine. Using special crank pulley tool J-37988 or equivalent, remove the crank pulley bolt.

9. Raise the passenger side of the engine, be sure that the front wheels remain on the ground while lifting the engine. Raise the engine too high, it will lift the front wheels off the ground and may cause damage to the drive shaft universal joint.

10. Remove the timing belt lower cover. Remove the cranking pulley and extract up through the engine compartment. Refit the crank pulley bolt. Align the crank pulley timing gear to top dead center.

11. Loosen the tension pulley bolt a ½ turn counterclockwise. If the pulley bolt is loosened more than ½ a turn, the pulley will swing too far out of adjustment and may be difficult to readjust.

12. Mark the direction of rotation of the tim-

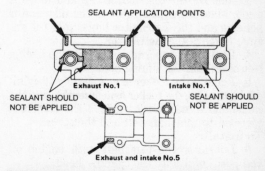

Camshaft sealant locations—4XE1 DOHC engine

ing mark with a piece of chalk and remove the timing belt. Using and open end wrench, hole the camshaft from turning and remove the camshaft pulley(s).

NOTE: *Inspect the timing belt for signs of cracking, abnormal wear and hardening. Never expose the belt to oil, sunlight or heat. Avoid excessive bending, twisting or stretching.*

13. Remove the camshaft bearing cap bolts and bearing caps. Be sure to take note of the positions of the bearing caps before removing them. Lift the camshafts out of the cylinder head.

To install:

14. Install the camshaft, bearing caps and bolts. Torque the bearing cap bolt to 96 inch lbs. (11 Nm). Be sure to install the camshaft bearing caps in their proper position.

15. Using and open end wrench, hold the camshaft from turning and install the camshaft pulley(s).

16. Tighten the tension pulley bolt.

17. Install the timing belt lower cover.

18. Lower the passenger side of the engine.

19. Install the passenger side engine mounting bracket to the engine. Install the crank pulley bolt.

20. Connect the torque rod at the firewall.

21. Install the upper timing belt cover.

22. Install the alternator drive belt to the crank pulley side. Connect the clip securing the high pressure air conditioning line to the strut tower.

23. Install the power steering pump and air compressor drive belt.

24. Connect the negative battery cable. Install the engine center (head) cover to the engine. Start the engine and check for leaks.

4ZD1 and 4ZE1 Engines

1. Disconnect the negative battery cable.

2. Rotate the crankshaft to position the No. 4 cylinder on the TDC of its compression stroke.

3. Remove the distributor cap and move it aside. Matchmark the rotor to the distributor housing and the distributor housing to the engine. Remove the distributor.

4. Remove the rocker arm cover, the timing belt cover and the timing belt.

5. Remove the rocker arm assembly-to-cylinder head bolts, the rocker arm assembly and the camshaft. If necessary, remove the camshaft sprocket-to-camshaft bolt and the sprocket.

To install:

6. Lubricate the camshaft with engine oil and position it onto the cylinder head.

7. Install the rocker arm assembly and

torque the bolts to bolts to 6 ft. lbs. (8 Nm) and the nuts to 16 ft. lbs. (22 Nm).

8. Align the timing marks and install the timing belt.

9. Using a new gasket, install the rocker arm cover.

10. Install the timing belt cover.

11. Align the matchmarks and install the distributor to the cylinder head.

12. To complete the installation, reverse the removal procedures.

13. With the timing marks aligned, start the engine, then, check and/or adjust the engine timing.

V6 Engine

NOTE: *Use long bolts threaded into the camshaft to help remove the shaft without damaging the camshaft bearings. Remove the camshaft slowly while supporting the weight with the long bolt.*

1. Relieve the fuel pressure. Disconnect the negative battery cable.

2. Remove the timing cover and the camshaft sprocket.

3. Remove the upper fan shroud and the radiator.

4. Disconnect the fuel line(s), the accelerator linkage, the vacuum hoses and electrical connectors from the throttle body unit.

5. Remove the rocker arm covers.

6. Loosen the valves, rotate them 90° and remove the pushrods; be sure to keep them aligned so they may be installed in their original positions.

7. Remove the intake manifold.

8. Using a hydraulic lifter removal tool, pull the valve lifters from the engine.

9. Using 3 long bolts, thread them into the camshaft holes. Grasp the bolts and carefully, pull the camshaft from the front of the engine.

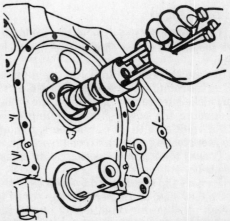

Removing the camshaft—V6 and C223 diesel engines

NOTE: *All the camshaft bearing journals are the same diameter; exercise care in removing the camshaft so the bearings do not become damaged.*

To install:

10. Lubricate the camshaft with engine oil and install it into the engine.

11. Using a hydraulic lifter installation tool, install the hydraulic lifters into the engine.

12. Using new gaskets and sealant, install the intake manifold.

13. Install the pushrods and the rocker arms.

14. Install the camshaft sprocket, the timing chain and the front cover; be sure the timing marks are aligned.

15. Adjust the valves.

16. Using new gaskets, install the rocker arm covers.

17. To complete the installation, reverse the removal procedures. Refill the cooling system.

18. Start the engine and allow it to reach normal operating temperatures. Check and/or adjust the timing.

4FB1 Diesel Engine

1. Remove the cam cover.

2. Remove the timing belt.

3. Remove the rear plug and hold the shaft by attaching the fixing plate (J–29761 or equivalent) into the slit at the rear of the camshaft.

4. Remove the camshaft pulley bolt, then remove the pulley with a gear puller.

5. Remove the rocker arms and shaft.

6. Remove the bolts attaching the front head plate and remove the plate.

7. Remove the bolts attaching the camshaft bearing caps. Remove the caps and bearings.

8. Remove the camshaft oil seal, then remove the camshaft.

To install:

9. Use a liberal amount of clean oil to coat the camshaft and journals during assembly. Install the camshaft and torque the rocker arm assembly to 18 ft. lbs. (25 Nm).

10. Install a new oil seal and apply Permatex® or equivalent gasket compound to the cylinder head fitting face of the No. 1 camshaft bearing cap.

11. Install the rocker arm cover and complete installation procedures.

C223, C223-T Diesel Engine

1. Disconnect the negative battery cable.

2. Drain the crankcase. Remove the oil pan and the oil pump.

CAUTION: *The EPA warns that prolonged contact with used engine oil may cause a number of skin disorders, including cancer! You should make every effort to minimize your exposure to used engine oil. Protective*

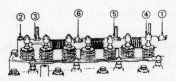

Bolt loosening sequence for removing rocker arm assembly—4FB1 diesel engine

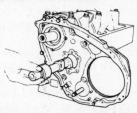

Camshaft removal—C223 and C223-T diesel engines

gloves should be worn when changing the oil. Wash your hands and any other exposed skin areas as soon as possible after exposure to used engine oil. Soap and water, or waterless hand cleaner should be used.

3. Remove the timing belt cover, the timing belt, the camshaft sprocket.

4. Remove the rocker arm assembly, the pushrods and the valve lifters; be sure to keep the parts in order for reinstallation purposes.

5. Remove the camshaft retainer-to-engine bolts and the retainer. Using a small prybar, pry the oil seal from the cylinder block.

6. Screw a bolt into the camshaft and carefully remove the camshaft from the front of the engine; be careful not to damage the bearing surfaces.

7. Inspect the camshaft for wear, scoring and/or damage; if necessary, replace it.

To install:

8. Lubricate the camshaft with engine oil and insert it into the front of the engine.

9. Using a new oil seal, lubricate the seal lips with engine oil and install it into the engine.

10. Install the camshaft retainer and the camshaft sprocket.

11. Install the oil pump and the oil pan.

12. Install the valve lifters, the pushrods and the rocker arm assembly.

13. Install and adjust the timing belt. Install the timing belt cover.

14. Rotate the crankshaft to bring the No. 1 piston to TDC of the compression stroke and adjust the valve lash.

15. To complete the installation, reverse the removal procedures.

16. Refill the cooling system and the crankcase.

17. Connect the negative battery cable. Start the engine, allow it to reach normal operating temperatures.

18. Check and/or adjust the idle speed and timing.

CAMSHAFT BEARING REMOVAL AND INSTALLATION

NOTE: *The V6 and C223 diesel engines are equipped with removeable camshaft bearings. The remaining engines do not have removeable camshaft bearings. The journal is cast into the head and acts as the bearing also.*
NOTE:
It is recommended that the engine be removed from the vehicle before attempting this procedure.

The camshaft, lifters, flywheel and the expansion plug (at the rear of the camshaft) must be removed. Drive the expansion plug out from the inside of the engine block.

ALL V6 AND C223 DIESEL ENGINES

To remove the camshaft bearings, the camshaft, lifters, flywheel, rear camshaft expansion plug, and crankshaft must be removed.

Camshaft bearings can be replaced with engine completely or partially disassembled. To replace bearings without complete disassembly remove the camshaft and crankshaft leaving cylinder heads attached and pistons in place. Before removing crankshaft, install rubber fuel hoses on the threads of connecting rod bolts to prevent damage to crankshaft. Fasten connecting rods against sides of engine so they will not be in the way while replacing camshaft bearings. Use rubber bands and the oil pan bolts to

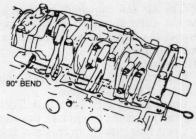

Aligning the camshaft bearing oil holes with a piece of wire bent at a 90 degree angle. The holes MUST be in alignment

hold the connecting rods away from the crankshaft during removal.

If excessive wear is indicated, or if the engine is being completely rebuilt, camshaft bearings should be replaced as follows: Drive the camshaft rear plug from the block. Assemble the removal puller with its shoulder on the bearing to be removed. Gradually tighten the puller nut until bearing is removed. Remove remaining bearings, leaving the front and rear for last. To remove front and rear bearings, reverse position of the tool, so as to pull the bearings in toward the center of the block. Leave the tool in this position, pilot the new front and rear bearings on the installer, and pull them into position: Return the tool to its original position and pull remaining bearings into position.

NOTE: *Ensure that oil holes align when installing bearings.*

Replace camshaft rear plug, and stake it into position to aid retention.

INSPECTION

Using solvent, degrease the camshaft and clean out all of the oil holes. Visually inspect the cam lobes and bearing journals for excessive wear. If a lobe is questionable, check all of the lobes as indicated. If a journal or lobe is worn, the camshaft MUST BE reground or replaced.

NOTE: *If a journal is worn, there is a good chance that the bearings or journals are worn and need replacement.*

If the lobes and journals appear intact, place the front and rear journals in V-blocks and rest a dial indicator on the center journal. Rotate the camshaft to check the straightness. If devi-

Make sure the oil ports are aligned with the bearing ports in the block—C223 diesel engine

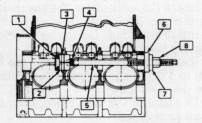

1.	Backup nut	5.	Two piece puller
2.	Expanding collet	6.	Pulling plate
3.	Bearing	7.	Thrust gearing
4.	Expanding mandrel	8.	Pulling nut

Removal and installation of the camshaft bearings—V6 engine

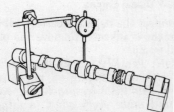

Camshaft run-out check

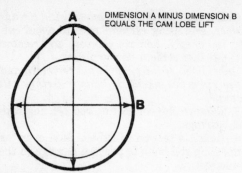

DIMENSION A MINUS DIMENSION B
EQUALS THE CAM LOBE LIFT

Measuring camshaft lift

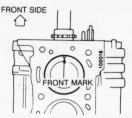

FRONT SIDE

FRONT MARK

Position mark towards the front of the engine

ation exceeds 0.001″ (0.0254mm), replace the camshaft.

Check the camshaft lobes with a micrometer, by measuring the lobes from the nose to the base and again at 90° (see illustration). The lobe lift is determined by subtracting the second measurement from the first. If all of the exhaust and intake lobes are not identical, the camshaft must be reground or replace.

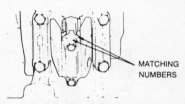

MATCHING
NUMBERS

Connecting rod and cap positioning—both marks go on the same side

Piston and Connecting Rod
REMOVAL AND INSTALLATION

It is not advisable to remove the piston from the connecting rod unless part replacement is necessary. Whenever a piston is removed, the piston pin should be replaced. When examining a piston, look for scuffs, cracking or wear. The rings should be removed with a ring expander and should be kept separately to avoid interchanging parts. All clearances should be checked with a micrometer or comparable precision gauge. Assemble the piston rings to the piston so that the NPR or TOP marks are turned up. Every piston has a mark to designate proper installation, this **FRONT MARK** is located on the top edge, in line with the piston pin bore. In addition, the cylinder number that the piston came from is stamped on the connecting rod and the bearing cap.

Before removal of connecting rod(s) and cap(s), mark them with their respective cylinder number. This will insure a proper match during reinstallation.

Cylinder Bore Ridge

NOTE: *This procedure is easily completed if the engine has been removed from the car. If the oil pan can be removed without removing the engine assembly from the vehicle, the piston/connecting rod can be removed with the engine in the vehicle.*

1. Remove the cylinder head(s), intake manifold, exhaust manifold, oil pan, and oil pump as outlined in this Section.
2. Mount the engine on a stand. In order to

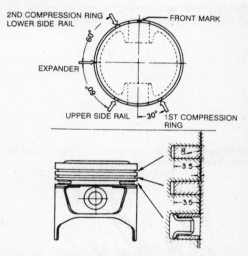

2ND COMPRESSION RING
LOWER SIDE RAIL

FRONT MARK

60°

EXPANDER

60°

UPPER SIDE RAIL — 30° 1ST COMPRESSION
RING

Piston ring positioning—all 4-cyl. gasoline engines

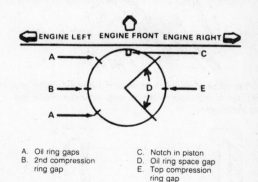

ENGINE LEFT ENGINE FRONT ENGINE RIGHT

A
B
A
D
C
E

A. Oil ring gaps
B. 2nd compression ring gap
C. Notch in piston
D. Oil ring space gap
E. Top compression ring gap

Piston ring positioning—V6 engines

facilitate removal of the piston and connecting rod, the ridge at the top of the cylinder (unworn area; see illustration) must be removed. Place the piston at the bottom of the bore, and cover

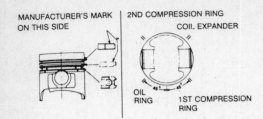

MANUFACTURER'S MARK ON THIS SIDE | 2ND COMPRESSION RING | COIL EXPANDER | OIL RING | 1ST COMPRESSION RING

Piston ring positioning—diesel engines

RING COMPRESSOR

Installing piston and connecting rod assembly—always use a ring compressor, all engines

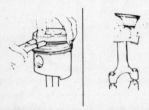

Installing piston rings—always use ring expander for compression ring, all engines

USE A SHORT PIECE OF ¾ IN. HOSE AS A GUIDE

Use lengths of vacuum hose or rubber tubing to protect the crankshaft journals and cylinder walls during installation

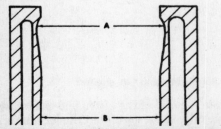

Cylinder wear patterns measuring points—ridge must be removed to remove the pistons

it with a rag. *Cut the ridge away using a ridge reamer*, exercising extreme care to avoid cutting too deeply. Remove the rag, and remove cuttings that remain on the piston.

CAUTION: *If the ridge is not removed, and new rings are installed, damage to rings will result.*

3. Remove the connecting rod bearing caps and bearings.

4. Install a section of rubber hose over the connecting rod bolts to prevent damage to the crankshaft.

5. Slide the piston/connecting rod assembly through the top of the cylinder block.

CAUTION: *Do not attempt to force the piston past the cylinder ridge (see above).*

POSITIONING

NOTE: *Most pistons are notched or marked to indicate which way they should be installed. If your pistons are not marked, mark them before removal. The pistons should be installed with the aligning mark facing front.*

CLEANING AND INSPECTING

A piston ring expander is necessary for removing piston rings without damaging them; any other method (screwdriver blades, pliers, etc.) usually results in the rings being bent, scratched or distorted, or the piston itself being damaged. When the rings are removed, clean the ring grooves using an appropriate ring groove cleaning tool, using care not to cut too deeply. Thoroughly clean all carbon and varnish from the piston with solvent.

CAUTION: *Do not use a wire brush or caustic solvent (acids, etc.) on piston.*

Inspect the pistons for scuffing, scoring, cracks, pitting, or excessive ring groove wear. If these are evident, the piston must be replaced.

The piston should also be checked in relation to the cylinder diameter. Using a telescoping gauge and micrometer, or a dial gauge, measure the cylinder bore diameter perpendicular (90°) to the piston pin, 64mm (2½ in.) below the cylinder block deck (surface where the block mates with the heads). Then, with the micrometer, measure the piston perpendicular to its wrist pin on the skirt. The difference between the two measurements is the piston clearance.

If the clearance is within specifications or slightly below (after the cylinders have been bored or honed), finish honing is all that is necessary. If the clearance is excessive, try to obtain a slightly larger piston to bring clearance to within specifications. If this is not possible obtain the first oversize piston and hone (or if necessary, bore) the cylinder to size. Generally, if the cylinder bore is tapered 0.127mm (0.005

in.) or more or is out-of-round 0.076mm (0.003 in.) or more, it is advisable to rebore for the smallest possible oversize piston and rings. After measuring mark pistons with a felt-tip pen for reference and for assembly.

NOTE: *Cylinder block boring should be performed by a reputable machine shop with the proper equipment. in some cases, "clean-up" honing can be done with the cylinder block in the car, but most excessive honing and all cylinder boring must be done with the block stripped and removed from the car.*

PISTON PIN
REMOVAL AND INSTALLATION

Use care at all times when handling and servicing connecting rods and pistons. To prevent

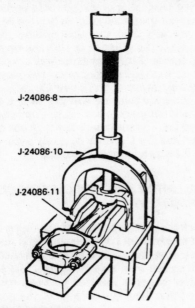

J-24086-8
J-24086-10
J-24086-11

Removing the piston pin

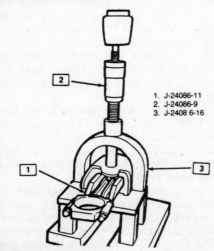

2
1. J-24086-11
2. J-24086-9
3. J-2408 6-16
1
3

Installing the piston pin

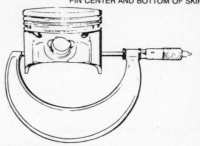

PISTON TAPER–MEASURE AT PISTON PIN CENTER AND BOTTOM OF SKIRT

PISTON SIZE–MEASURE ¾ IN. BELOW CENTER LINE OF PISTON PIN HOLE

Piston skirt measurement

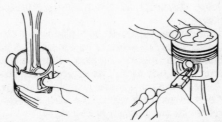

Installing piston pin and snapring—diesel engines

possible damage to these units, do not clamp the rod or piston in a vise since they may become distorted. Do not allow the pistons to strike against one another, against hard objects or bench surfaces, since distortion of the piston contour or nicks in the soft aluminum material may result.

1. Remove the piston rings using a suitable piston ring remover.

2. Install the guide bushing of the piston pin removing and installing tool.

NOTE: *The front mark on the piston and the capital letter ISUZU mark on the connecting rod should face the same direction for the four cylinder engines.*

3. Install the piston and connecting rod assembly on a support, and place the assembly in an arbor press. Press the pin out of the connecting rod, using the appropriate piston pin tool.

4. When installing the new piston, apply clean engine oil to the pin and press in with a piston pin installing tool. Make sure the connecting rod moves freely without binding after pin is installed. If not, reaming the pin hole may have to be performed.

MEASURING THE OLD PISTONS

Check used piston-to-cylinder bore clearance as follows:

1. Measure the cylinder bore diameter with a telescope gauge.

2. Measure the piston diameter. When measuring the pistons for size or taper, measure-

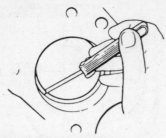

Measuring piston ring gap—typical

ments must be made with the piston pin removed.

3. Subtract the piston diameter from the cylinder bore diameter to determine piston-to-bore clearance.

4. Compare the piston-to-bore clearances obtained with those clearances recommended in the "Piston and Connecting Rod" chart in the beginning of this Section. Determine if the piston-to-bore clearance is in the acceptable range.

5. When measuring taper, the largest reading must be at the bottom of the skirt.

6. If the measurement is not within specifications, the cylinders should be bored and new oversize pistons should be installed.

SELECTING NEW PISTONS

1. If the used piston is not acceptable, check the service piston size and determine if a new piston can be selected. (Service pistons are available in standard, high limit and standard 0.254mm (0.010 in.) oversize.).

2. If the cylinder bore must be reconditioned, measure the new piston diameter, then hone the cylinder bore to obtain the preferred clearance.

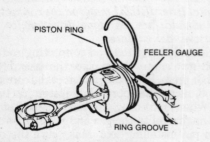

Measuring piston ring side clearance

Installing a piston using a piston ring compressor

3. Select a new piston and mark the piston to identify the cylinder for which it was fitted. (On some cars, oversize pistons may be found. These pistons will be 0.254mm (0.010 in.) oversize). After market piston manufactures supply oversized pistons 0.030 in., 0.040 in., and 0.060 in. in most cases.

4. After the cylinder has been reconditioned and new pistons purchased, remeasure bore and piston to ensure proper piston fit.

CHECKING RING END GAP

Piston ring end gap should be checked while the rings are removed from the pistons. Incorrect end gap indicates that the wrong size rings are being used; ring breakage could occur.

Compress the piston rings to be used in a cylinder, one at a time, into that cylinder. Squirt clean oil into the cylinder, so that the rings and the top 50mm (2 in.) of cylinder wall are coated. Using an inverted piston, press the rings approximately 25mm (1 in.) below the deck of the block. Measure the ring end gap with a feeler gauge, and compare to the "Ring Gap" chart in this Section. Carefully pull the ring out of the cylinder and file the ends squarely with a fine file to obtain the proper clearance.

INSTALLATION AND SIDE CLEARANCE MEASUREMENT

Check the pistons to see that the ring grooves and oil return holes have been properly cleaned. Slide a piston ring into its groove and check the side clearance with a feeler gauge. Make sure the feeler gauge is inserted between the ring and its lower land (lower edge of the groove), because any wear that occurs forms a step at the inner portion of the lower land. If the piston grooves have worn to the extent that relatively high steps exist on the lower land, the piston should be replaced, because these will interfere with the operation of the new rings and ring clearances will be excessive. Piston rings are not furnished in oversize widths to compensate for ring groove wear.

Install the rings on the piston, lowest ring first (oil ring), using a piston ring expander for the compression rings. There is a high risk of breaking or distorting the rings, or scratching the piston, if the compression rings are installed by hand or other means.

Position the rings on the piston as illustrated; spacing of the various piston ring gaps is crucial to proper oil retention and even cylinder wear. When installing new rings, refer to the installation diagram furnished with the new parts.

Connecting Rod Bearings

Connecting rod bearings for the engines covered in this guide consist of two halves or shells. Some are interchangeable in the rod and cap and others have oil holes in the rod shell. When the shells are placed in position, the ends extend slightly beyond the rod and cap surfaces so that when the rod bolts are torqued, the shells will be clamped tightly in place to insure positive seating and to prevent turning. A tang holds the shells in place.

NOTE: *The ends of the bearing shells must never be filed flush with the mating surface of the rod and cap.*

If a rod bearing becomes noisy or is worn so that its clearance on the crank journal is excessive, a new bearing of the correct undersize must be selected and installed since there is no provision for adjustment.

CAUTION: *Under no circumstances should the rod end or cap be filed to adjust the bearing clearance, nor should shims of any kind be used.*

Inspect the rod bearings while the rod assemblies are out of the engine. If the shells are scored or show flaking, they should be replaced. If they are in good shape check for proper clearance on the crank journal (see below). Any scoring or ridges on the crank journal means the crankshaft must be replaced, or reground and fitted with undersized bearings.

NOTE: *If journals are deeply scored or ridged the crankshaft must be replaced, as regrinding will reduce the durability of the crankshaft*

ROD BEARING INSPECTION AND REPLACEMENT

NOTE: *Make sure connecting rods and their caps are kept together, and that the caps are installed in the proper direction. Match up the markings on the rod and cap. Make sure they face the same direction.*

Replacement bearings are available in standard size, and in undersizes for reground crankshafts. Connecting rod-to-crankshaft bearing clearance is checked using Plastigage® at either the top or bottom of each crank journal.

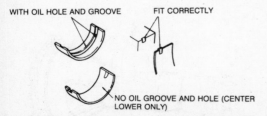

Connecting rod bearings—4FB1 diesel engine, other engines similar

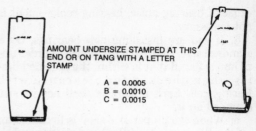

AMOUNT UNDERSIZE STAMPED AT THIS END OR ON TANG WITH A LETTER STAMP

A = 0.0005
B = 0.0010
C = 0.0015

Bearing insert size marking

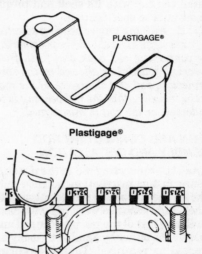

PLASTIGAGE®

Plastigage®

Use the Plastigage® package to measure the bearing clearance (check crankshaft specification chart for specs)

nal. The Plastigage® has a range of 0.025–0.080mm (0.001–0.003 in.).

1. Remove the rod cap with the bearing shell. Completely clean the bearing shell and the crank journal, and blow any oil from the oil hole in the crankshaft; Plastigage® lengthwise along the bottom center of the lower bearing shell, then install the cap with shell and torque the bolt or nuts to specification. DO NOT turn the crankshaft with Plastigage® in the bearing.

2. Remove the bearing cap with the shell. The flattened Plastigage® will be found sticking to either the bearing shell or crank journal. DO NOT REMOVE IT YET.

3. Use the scale printed on the Plastigage® envelope to measure the flattened material at its widest point. The number within the scale which most closely corresponds to the width of the Plastigage® indicates bearing clearance in hundreths of a millimeter (thousandths of an inch).

4. Check the specifications chart in this Section for the desired clearance. It is advisable to install a new bearing if clearance exceeds 0.076mm (0.003 in.); however, if the bearing is in good condition and is not being checked be-

cause of bearing noise, bearing replacement is not necessary.

5. If you are installing new bearings, try a standard size, then each undersize in order until one is found that is within the specified limits when checked for clearance with Plastigage®. Each undersize shell has its size stamped on it.

6. When the proper size shell is found, clean off the Plastigage®, oil the bearing thoroughly, reinstall the cap with its shell and torque the rod bolt nuts to specification.

NOTE: *With the proper bearing selected and the nuts torqued, it should be possible to move the connecting rod back and forth freely on the crank journal as allowed by the specified connecting rod end clearance. If the rod cannot be moved, either the rod bearing is too far undersize or the rod is misaligned.*

PISTON AND CONNECTING ROD ASSEMBLY AND INSTALLATION

Install the connecting rod to the piston, making sure piston installation notches and any marks on the rod are in proper relation to one another. Lubricate the wrist pin with clean engine oil, and install the pin into the rod and piston assembly, either by hand or by using a wrist pin press as required. Install snaprings if equipped, and rotate them in their grooves to make sure they are seated. To install the piston and connecting rod assembly:

1. Make sure connecting rod big-end bearings (including end cap) are of the correct size and properly installed.

2. Fit rubber hoses over the connecting rod bolts to protect the crankshaft journals, as in the "Piston Removal" procedure. Coat the rod bearings with Assembly Lube.

3. Using the proper ring compressor, insert the piston assembly into the cylinder so that the notch in the top of the piston faces the front of the engine (this assumes that the dimple(s) or other markings on the connecting rods are in correct relation to the piston notch(es).

4. From beneath the engine, coat each crank journal with Assembly Lube or clean oil. Pull the connecting rod, with the bearing shell in place, into position against the crank journal.

5. Remove the rubber hoses. Install the bearing cap and cap nuts and torque to specification.

NOTE: *When more than one rod and piston assembly is being installed, the connecting rod cap attaching nut should only be tightened enough to keep each rod in position until all have been installed. This will ease the installation of the remaining piston assemblies.*

6. Check the clearance between the sides of the connecting rods and the crankshaft using a feeler gauge. Spread the rods slightly with a small prybar to insert the gauge. If clearance is below the minimum tolerance, the rod may be machined to provide adequate clearance. If clearance is excessive, substitute an unworn rod, and recheck. If clearance is still outside specifications, the crankshaft must be welded and reground, or replaced.

7. Replace the oil pump, if removed, and the oil pan.

8. Install the cylinder head(s) and intake manifold, as previously described.

Rear Main Bearing Oil Seal

REMOVAL AND INSTALLATION

One Piece Seal

NOTE: *All engines, except the 4ZC1, 4ZD1 and 4ZE1 have one piece rear crankshaft oil seals. The oil pan does not have to be remove to access the seal.*

1. Disconnect the negative battery cable. Raise and safely support the vehicle.

2. Drain the engine oil and remove the oil pan.

CAUTION: *The EPA warns that prolonged contact with used engine oil may cause a number of skin disorders, including cancer! You should make every effort to minimize your exposure to used engine oil. Protective gloves should be worn when changing the oil. Wash your hands and any other exposed skin areas as soon as possible after exposure to used engine oil. Soap and water, or waterless hand cleaner should be used.*

3. If equipped with an automatic transmission, remove the transmission. If equipped with a manual transmission, remove the transmission and clutch assembly.

4. Remove the starter without disconnecting the wires and secure it aside.

5. Remove the flywheel-to-crankshaft bolts and the flywheel.

6. Carefully, remove the oil seal, using a small pry bar; work the tool around the diameter of the seal until the seal begins to lift out. Use care not to damage the seat and area around the seal.

7. Fill the space between the seal lips with

One piece rear crankshaft oil seal

grease and lubricate the seal lips with clean engine oil. Install the new oil seal.

8. Install the flywheel, transmission and starter motor.

9. Connect the battery cable, start the engine and check for leaks.

Two Piece Seal

Both halves of the rear main oil seal can be replaced without removing the crankshaft. Always replace the upper and lower seal together. The lip should face the front of the engine. Be very careful that you do not break the sealing bead in the channel on the outside portion of the seal while installing it. An installation tool can be fabricated to protect the seal bead.

1. Remove the oil pan and rear main bearing cap.

2. Remove the oil seal from the bearing cap by prying it out.

3. Remove the upper half of the seal with a small punch. Drive it around far enough to be gripped with pliers. **Be very careful not to damage the crankshaft sealing surface.**

To install:

4. Clean the crankshaft and bearing cap.

5. Coat the lips and bead of the seal with light engine oil, keeping oil from the ends of the seal.

6. Position the a suitable tool between the crankshaft and seal seat.

7. Position the seal between the crankshaft and tip of the tool so that the seal bead contacts the tip of the tool. The oil seal lip should face forward.

8. Roll the seal around the crankshaft using the tool to protect the seal bead from the sharp corners of the crankcase.

9. The installation tool should be left installed until the seal is properly positioned with both ends flush with the block.

10. Remove the tool.

11. Install the other half of the seal in the bearing cap using the tool in the same manner as before. Light thumb pressure should install the seal.

12. Install the bearing cap with sealant applied to the mating areas of the cap and block. Keep sealant from the ends of the seal.

13. Torque the rear main bearing cap to specifications.

14. Install the oil pan and refill the engine with oil. Start the engine and check for leaks.

Crankshaft and Main Bearings

Crankshaft servicing literally makes or breaks any engine; especially a high performance one.

The most critical maintenance operation is the replacement of the crankshaft main bearings. These bearings are of the precision insert design and do not require adjustment through shims. They are offered in undersizes of 0.001 in., 0.002 in., 0.009 in., 0.010 in., 0.020 in., and 0.030 in., depending on the engine.

Despite the advent of these inserts and accompanying precision machine work, it does happen that sizing mistakes are made and no crankshaft should be installed in a block without checking clearances. One of the simplest means of doing so is to use Plastigage®. This is a wax-like plastic material that is formed into precision threads. It will compress evenly between two surfaces, without damage, and when measured, will indicate the actual clearance.

It is easiest to check bearing clearance with the engine removed from the car and the block inverted. This ensures that the crank is resting against the upper bearing shells. If Plastigage® is to be used on an engine still in the vehicle, it will be necessary to support the crankshaft at both ends so that clearance between the crankshaft and the upper bearing shells is eliminated.

REMOVAL

1. Drain the engine oil and remove the engine from the car. Mount the engine on a work stand in a suitable working area. Invert the engine, so the oil pan is facing up.

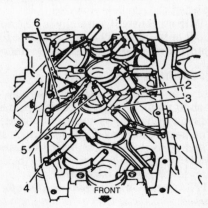

1. Rubber hose
2. No. 4 rod
3. No. 3 rod
4. Oil pan bolt
5. Note overlap of adjacent rods
6. Rubber bands

Crankshaft removal showing hose lengths and rubber bands on rod bolts

NO. 5 BEARING CAP

Two piece rear crankshaft oil seal—apply sealer at arrowed areas

CAUTION: *The EPA warns that prolonged contact with used engine oil may cause a number of skin disorders, including cancer! You should make every effort to minimize your exposure to used engine oil. Protective gloves should be worn when changing the oil. Wash your hands and any other exposed skin areas as soon as possible after exposure to used engine oil. Soap and water, or waterless hand cleaner should be used.*

2. Remove the engine water pump and front (timing) cover.

3. Remove the timing chain (if equipped) and gears.

4. Remove the oil pan.

5. Remove the oil pump, if in the way.

6. If not marked, stamp or mark the cylinder number on the machined surfaces of the bolt bosses of the connecting rods and caps for identification when reinstalling. If the pistons are to be removed from the connecting rod, mark the cylinder number on the pistons with silver paint or felt-tip pen for proper cylinder identification and cap-to-rod location.

7. Remove the connecting rod caps. install lengths of rubber hose on each of the connecting rod bolts, to protect the crank journals when the crank is removed.

8. If not marked, mark the main bearing caps with a number punch or punch so that they can be reinstalled in their original positions.

9. Remove all main bearing caps.

10. Note the position of the keyway in the crankshaft so it can be installed in the same position.

11. Install rubber bands between a bolt on each connecting rod and oil pan bolts that have been reinstalled in the block (see illustration). This will keep the rods from banging on the block when the crank is removed.

12. With an assistant, carefully lift the crankshaft out of the block. The rods will pivot to the center of the engine when the crank is removed.

MAIN BEARING INSPECTION

Like connecting rod big-end bearings, the crankshaft main bearings are shell-type inserts that do not utilize shims and cannot be adjusted. The bearings are available in various standard and undersizes; if main bearing clearance is found to be excessive, a new bearing (both upper and lower halves) is required.

NOTE: *Factory-undersized crankshafts are marked, sometimes with a "9" and/or a large spot of light green paint; the bearing caps also will have the paint on each side of the undersized journal.*

Generally, the lower half of the bearing shell (except No. 1 bearing) shows greater wear and fatigue. If the lower half only shows the effects of normal wear (no heavy scoring or discoloration), it can usually be assumed that the upper half is also in good shape; conversely, if the lower half is heavily worn or damaged, both halves should be replaced. NEVER REPLACE ONE BEARING HALF WITHOUT REPLACING THE OTHER!

MEASURING MAIN BEARING CLEARANCE

Main bearing clearance can be checked both with the crankshaft in the car and with the engine out of the car. If the engine block is still in the car, the crankshaft should be supported both front and rear (by the damper and the transmission) to remove clearance from the upper bearing. Total clearance can then be measured between the lower bearing and journal. If the block has been removed from the car, and is inverted, the crank will rest on the upper bearings and the total clearance can be measured between the lower bearing and journal. Clearance is checked in the same manner as the connecting rod bearings, with Plastigage®.

NOTE: *Crankshaft bearing caps and bearing shells should NEVER be filed flush with the cap-to-block mating surface to adjust for*

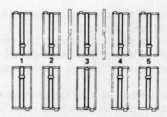

Crankshaft bearing inserts—G180Z, G200Z, 4ZD1 and 4ZC1 engines

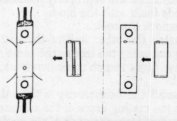

Crankshaft bearing inserts—4XC1, 4XE1 and 4ZE1 engines

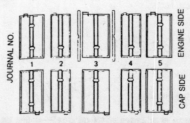

Crankshaft bearing inserts—diesel engines

wear in the old bearings. Always install new bearings.

1. If the crankshaft has been removed, install it (block removed from car). If the block is still in the car, remove the oil pan and oil pump. Starting with the rear bearing cap, remove the cap and wipe all oil from the crank journal and bearing cap.

2. Place a strip of Plastigage® the full width of the bearing, (parallel to the crankshaft), on the journal.

NOTE: *Plastigage® is soluble in oil; therefore, oil on the journal or bearing could result in erroneous readings.*

CAUTION: *Do not rotate the crankshaft while the gaging material is between the bearing and the journal.*

3. Install the bearing cap and evenly torque the cap bolts to specification.

4. Remove the bearing cap. The flattened Plastigage® will be sticking to either the bearing shell or the crank journal.

5. Use the graduated scale on the Plastigage® envelope to measure the material at its widest point. If the flattened Plastigage® tapers toward the middle or ends, there is a difference in clearance indicating the bearing or journal has a taper, low spot or other irregularity. If this is indicated, measure the crank journal with a micrometer.

6. If bearing clearance is within specifications, the bearing insert is in good shape. Replace the insert if the clearance is not within specifications. Always replace both upper and lower inserts as a unit.

7. Standard, 0.001 in. or 0.002 in. undersize bearings should produce the proper clearance. If these sizes still produce too sloppy a fit, the crankshaft must be reground for use with the next undersize bearing. Recheck all clearances after installing new bearings.

8. Replace the rest of the bearings in the same manner. After all bearings have been checked, rotate the crankshaft to make sure there is no excessive drag. When checking the No. 1 main bearing, loosen the accessory drive belts (engine in car) to prevent a tapered reading with the Plastigage®.

MAIN BEARING REPLACEMENT

Engine Out of Car

1. Remove and inspect the crankshaft.

2. Remove the main bearings from the bearing saddles in the cylinder block and main bearing caps.

3. Coat the bearing surfaces of the new, correct size main bearings with clean engine oil and install them in the bearing saddles in the block and in the main bearing caps.

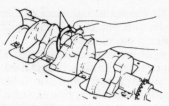

Crankshaft thrust bearing

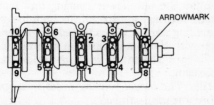

Crankshaft bearing cap torque sequence

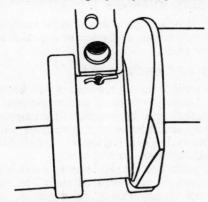

Removing the upper crankshaft bearing

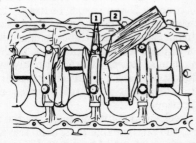

Seating the crankshaft thrust bearing. (1) center main bearing thrust flange. (2) wood block

4. Install the crankshaft. See "Crankshaft Installation".

Engine In Car

1. With the oil pan, oil pump and spark plugs removed, remove the cap from the main bearing needing replacement and remove the bearing from the cap.

2. Make a bearing roll-out pin, using a bent cotter pin as shown in the illustration. Install the end of the pin in the oil hole in the crankshaft journal.

3. Rotate the crankshaft clockwise as viewed from the front of the engine. This will roll the upper bearing out of the block.

4. Lube the new upper bearing with clean engine oil and insert the plain (unnotched) end between the crankshaft and the indented or notched side of the block. Roll the bearing into place, making sure that the oil holes are aligned. Remove the roll pin from the oil hole.

5. Lube the new lower bearing and install the main bearing cap. Install the main bearing cap, making sure it is positioned in proper direction with the matchmarks in alignment.

6. Torque the main bearing cap bolts to specification.

NOTE: *The thrust bearing must be aligned before torquing cap bolts.*

REGRINDING JOURNALS

NOTE: *Regrinding rod and/or main bearing journals should be performed by a qualified machine shop.*

CRANKSHAFT INSTALLATION

When main bearing clearance has been checked, bearings examined and/or replaced, the crankshaft can be installed. Thoroughly clean the upper and lower bearing surfaces, and lube them with clean engine oil. Install the crankshaft and main bearing caps.

Dip all main bearing cap bolts in Assembly Lube or clean oil, and torque all main bearing caps, except thrust bearing, in sequence, to specifications (see the "Crankshaft and Connecting Rod" chart in this Section to determine which bearing is the thrust bearing). Tighten the thrust bearing bolts finger tight. To align the thrust bearing, pry the crankshaft the extent of its axial travel several times, holding the last movement toward the front of the engine. Add thrust washers if required for proper alignment. Torque the thrust bearing cap to specifications.

To check crankshaft end-play, pry the crankshaft to the extreme rear of its axial travel, then to the extreme front of its travel. Using a feeler gauge, measure the end-play at the front of the rear main bearing. End play may also be measured at the thrust bearing. Install a new rear main bearing oil seal in the cylinder block and main bearing cap. Continue to reassemble the engine in reverse of disassembly procedures.

Flywheel and Ring Gear
REMOVAL AND INSTALLATION

The ring gear is an integral part of the automatic flywheel and is not replaceable. The manual transmission ring gear is removeable. The ring has to be heated with a torch and stetched

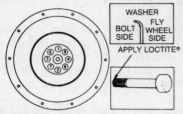

Flywheel torque sequence

onto the flywheel. This procedure should be performed by a qualified machine shop.

1. Remove the transmission as outlined in Chapter 7.

2. Remove the six or eight bolts attaching the flywheel to the crankshaft flange. Remove the flywheel.

3. Inspect the flywheel for cracks, and inspect the ring gear for burrs or worn teeth. Replace the flywheel if any damage is apparent. Remove burrs with a mill file.

4. Install the flywheel. The flywheel will only attach to the crankshaft in one position, as the bolt holes are unevenly spaced. Install the bolts and torque to specification found in the beginning of this Section. Tighten bolts in crisscross pattern.

EXHAUST SYSTEM

Safety Precautions

For a number of reasons, exhaust system work can be the most dangerous type of work you can do on your car. Always observe the following precautions:

• Support the car extra securely. Not only will you often be working directly under it, but you'll frequently be using a lot of force, say, heavy hammer blows, to dislodge rusted parts. This can cause a car that's improperly supported to shift and possibly fall.

• Wear goggles. Exhaust system parts are always rusty. Metal chips can be dislodged, even when you're only turning rusted bolts. Attempting to pry pipes apart with a chisel makes the chips fly even more frequently.

• If you're using a cutting torch, keep it a great distance from either the fuel tank or lines. Stop what you're doing and feel the temperature of the fuel bearing pipes on the tank frequently. Even slight heat can expand and/or vaporize fuel, resulting in accumulated vapor, or even a liquid leak, near your torch.

• Watch where your hammer blows fall and make sure you hit squarely. You could easily tap a brake or fuel line when you hit an exhaust system part with a glancing blow. Inspect all lines and hoses in the area where you've been working.

Special Tools

A number of special exhaust system tools can be rented from auto supply houses or local stores that rent special equipment. A common one is a tail pipe expander, designed to enable you to join pipes of identical diameter.

It may also be quite helpful to use solvents designed to loosen rusted bolts or flanges. Soaking rusted parts the night before you do the job can speed the work of freeing rusted parts considerably. Remember that these solvents are often flammable. Apply only to parts after they are cool!

Checking

Check complete exhaust system and nearby body areas and trunk lid for broken, damaged, missing or mispositioned parts, open seams, holes, loose connections or other deterioration which could permit exhaust fumes to seep into the trunk or passenger compartment. Dust or water in the trunk may be an indication of a problem in one of these areas. Any defects should be corrected immediately. To help insure continued integrity, the exhaust system pipe rearward of the muffler must be replaced whenever a new muffler is installed.

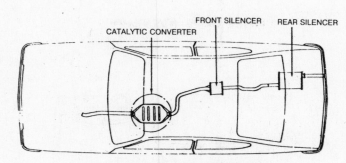

Exhaust system—RWD I-Mark

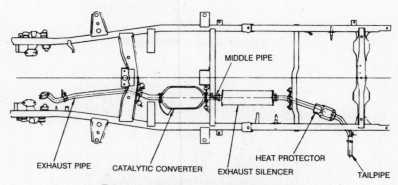

Exhaust system—early model gasoline P'up

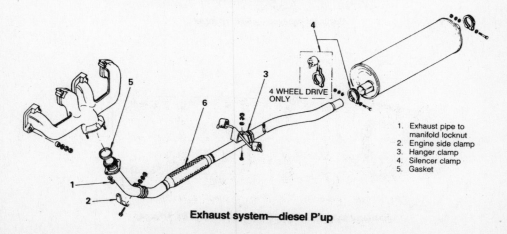

1. Exhaust pipe to manifold locknut
2. Engine side clamp
3. Hanger clamp
4. Silencer clamp
5. Gasket

Exhaust system—diesel P'up

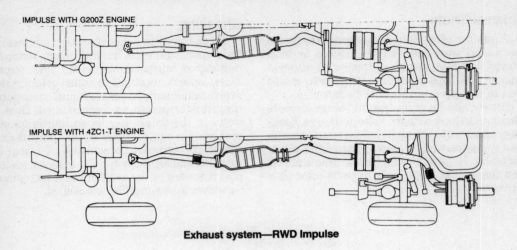

IMPULSE WITH G200Z ENGINE

IMPULSE WITH 4ZC1-T ENGINE

Exhaust system—RWD Impulse

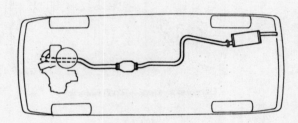

Exhaust system—FWD I-Mark

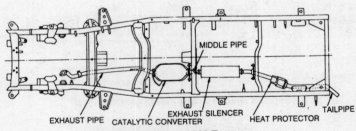

MIDDLE PIPE

EXHAUST PIPE   CATALYTIC CONVERTER   EXHAUST SILENCER   HEAT PROTECTOR   TAILPIPE

Exhaust system—1986 Trooper

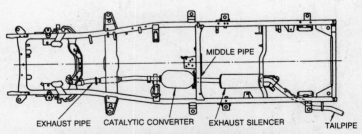

MIDDLE PIPE

EXHAUST PIPE   CATALYTIC CONVERTER   EXHAUST SILENCER   TAILPIPE

Exhaust system—P'up, Amigo and 1987–91 Trooper

Exhaust Pipe

The exhaust manifold-to-crossover pipe connections are of the flange and gasket type, except V6 engine. The V6 engine uses flange and donut gaskets. the need for gaskets.

Muffler

The mufflers are a tri-flow design. Some muffler installations have a slot in the inlet and/or outlet pipe which indexes to a key (tab) welded on the exhaust and/or tail pipe to help maintain alignment.

Resonator

A resonator is used on some series exhaust systems. It allows the use of mufflers with less back pressure and provides for optimum tuning characteristics of the exhaust system.

Catalytic Converter

The catalytic converter is an emission control device added to the exhaust system to reduce pollutants from the exhaust gas stream.

Periodic maintenance of the exhaust system is not required, however, if the car is raised for other service, it is advisable to check the general condition of the catalytic converter, pipes and mufflers.

Check the exhaust system hangers for damage and deterioration. Replace any hardware if necessary. System damage may occur if broken hangers exist.

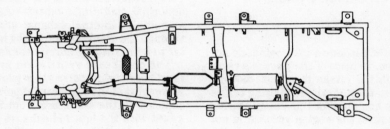

Exhaust system—Rodeo, Trooper with V6 engine

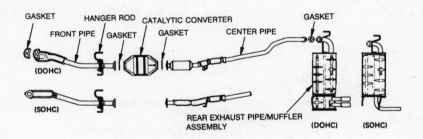

Exhaust system—Stylus and Impulse with 4XE1 engine

Emission Controls

EMISSION CONTROLS

Crankcase Ventilation System

OPERATION

Gasoline

The carbureted gasoline 4-cyl. engines do not use a PCV valve. In place of the valve is a regulating orifice in the intake manifold. Blow-by gases are drawn through the regulating orifice into the intake manifold for reburning. During wide open throttle, the engine vacuum is not sufficient to draw enough vapor through the manifold, allowing part to be drawn into the air cleaner via the rear end of the rocker arm cover.

The fuel injected gasoline 4-cyl. and V6 engines use a PCV valve. The PCV valve meters the flow at a rate depending upon the manifold vacuum. If the manifold vacuum is high, the PCV restricts the flow to the intake manifold. If abnormal, operating conditions occur, excessive amounts of internal exhaust gases back flow through the crankcase vent tube into the air filter to be burned by normal combustion.

The crankcase ventilation system (PCV) must be operating correctly to provide complete scavenging of the crankcase vapors. Fresh air is supplied to the crankcase from the air filter, mixed with the internal exhaust gases, passed through the PCV valve or orifice and into the intake manifold.

If the engine is idling roughly, a quick check of the PCV valve can be made. While the engine is idling, pull the PCV valve from the valve cov-

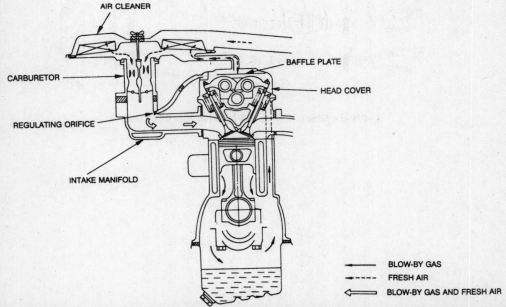

PCV system—carbureted 4-cylinder gas engines do not use a valve. They use a regulating orifice located in the intake manifold

er, place your thumb over the end of the PCV valve and check for vacuum. If no vacuum exists, check for a plugged PCV valve, manifold port, hoses or deteriorated hoses. Turn the engine "OFF", remove the PCV valve and shake it. Listen for the rattle of the check needle inside the valve. If it does not rattle, replace the valve.

The PCV system should be checked at every oil change and serviced every 30,000 miles.

NOTE: *Never operate an engine without a*

PCV valve or a ventilation system, for it can become damaged.

Diesel Engine

The crankcase ventilation system is a closed type, and is designed to force blow-by gas generated in the engine crankcase back into the intake manifold to return with the fresh air back into the combustion chamber.

When the engine is running at high speed, the high negative pressure from the intake

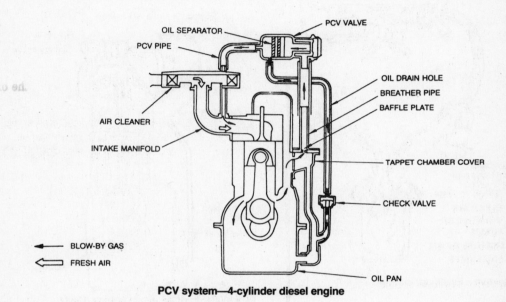

PCV system—4-cylinder diesel engine

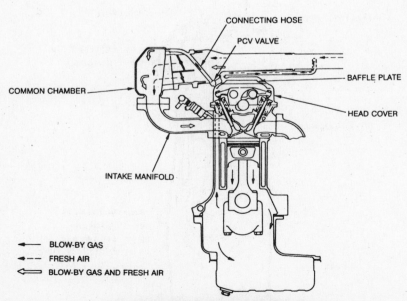

PCV system—4-cylinder gas EFI 4ZEI engine

manifold makes the diaphragm valve close, as a result, the blow-by gas passes through the regulating orifice. When the engine is running at low speed, the negative pressure from the intake manifold is so small that the cylinder head cover pressure makes the diaphragm valve open. As a result, the blow-by gas passes through both the regulating orifice and the dia-

phragm passage opened by the diaphragm valve.

SERVICE

PCV Valve

Check the diaphragm valve for damage and adhesion to the seating surface. Check the oil

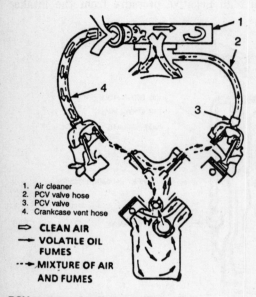

1. Air cleaner
2. PCV valve hose
3. PCV valve
4. Crankcase vent hose

⇨ CLEAN AIR

➤ VOLATILE OIL FUMES

--➤ MIXTURE OF AIR AND FUMES

PCV system—6-cylinder engine

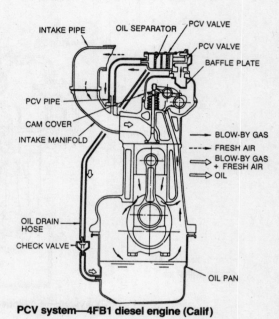

PCV system—4FB1 diesel engine (Calif)

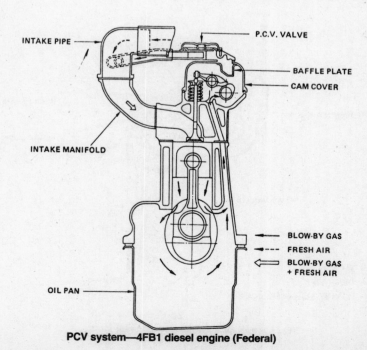

PCV system—4FB1 diesel engine (Federal)

separator element for wear if any abnormal conditions are found, replace the PCV valve assembly.

Check Valve

Using a vacuum pump, check the valve function. If the air flows in the wrong direction or if the valve is plugged, replace the check valve.

Hoses

Check the rubber hoses for deterioration and damage. Also check for proper routing. Refer to the vacuum diagrams at the end of this Chapter.

REMOVAL AND INSTALLATION

Label the PCV valve hoses before removing. Disconnect the hoses and remove the valve. Re-

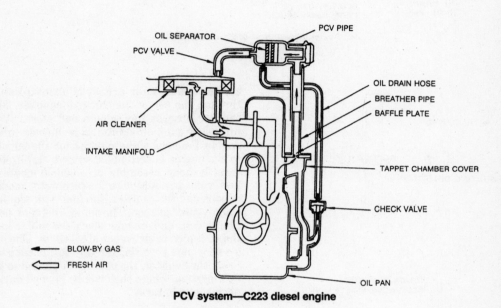

PCV system—C223 diesel engine

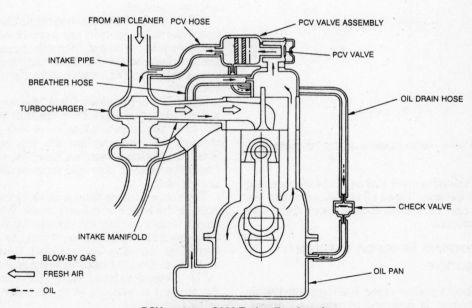

PCV system—C223 Turbo diesel engine

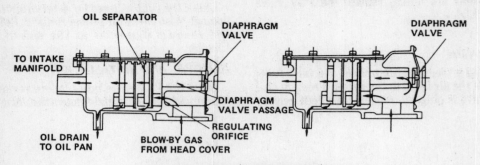

PCV valve operation—4FB1 diesel (Calif)

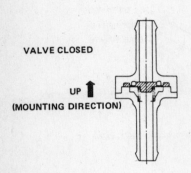

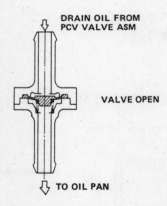

Check valve—4FB1 (Calif) and C223 Turbo diesel

move the valve cover and clean the oil separator and diaphragm. Clean all components with solvent and reinstall. Replace any defective components.

Evaporative Emission Controls
OPERATION

To limit gasoline vapor discharge into the air this system is designed to trap fuel vapors, which normally escape from the fuel tank and carburetor. Vapor arrest is accomplished through the use of the charcoal canister. This canister absorbs fuel vapors and stores them until they can be removed to be burned in the engine. Removal of the vapors from the canister to the engine is accomplished by a carburetor, throttle body assembly or solenoid operated bowl vent. In addition to the carburetor modifications and the canister, the fuel tank requires a non-vented gas cap. The domed fuel tank positions a vent high enough above the fuel to keep the vent pipe in the vapor at all times. The single vent pipe is routed directly to the canister. From the canister, the vapors are routed to the PCV system, where they will be burned during normal combustion.

SERVICING

Make sure the hoses are connected properly and not damaged.

G180Z and G200Z Carbureted: The check and relief valve controls the amount of vapor that goes into the engine. When the pressure in the tank becomes 0.2–0.6 in. Hg the check valve opens, allowing the vapor into the engine crankcase.

4XC1-U carbureted: When the engine is not running, fuel vapor from the tank reaches the tank pressure control valve and passes through the bypass orifice into the canister. When the engine is running, manifold vacuum forces the valve to open and vapor is stored in the canister.

The vent switching valve is an electrically operated valve built into the carburetor. When the engine is not running, the valve opens to introduce vapor into the canister. When the engine is running, the valve closes to block the flow of ambient air from the canister to the carburetor.

The thermal vacuum valve (TVV) controls the amount of vacuum to the canister purge valve.

4XC1-T Fuel Injected: The vacuum switching valve and vacuum reservoir tank are connected in series on the vacuum line to keep the tank pressure control valve opening under the condition of positive common chamber boost. It prevents vapor purge during engine warm-up and cold driving conditions.

Check the vacuum reservoir tank by disconnecting the two vacuum hoses. Blow air into the hose at the A side of the tank, and confirm that

the air flows to the B port. Confirm that the air does not flow to the A port when blowing in the B port. If a problem is found, replace the tank.

4ZD1 engine: The roll over valve and float valve is designed to prevent fuel leaks when the vehicle has turned over. The relief valve is intended to relieve the tank internal pressure to avoid tank damage.

All Vehicles, except V6 engines: Inspect

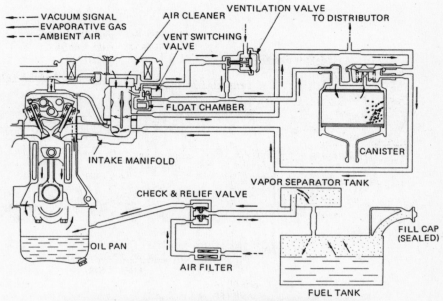

Evaporative emission control—G180Z and G200Z with carburetor

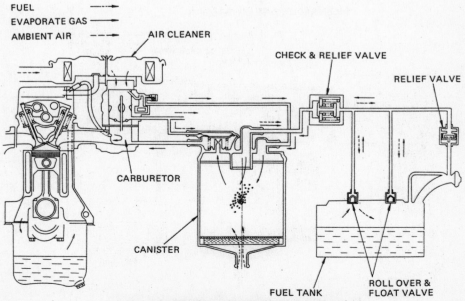

Evaporative emission control—4ZD1 carb. engine

the charcoal canister for cracks and other damage. Remove the canister from the vehicle to test. Apply about 7.5 psi positive pressure to the port marked VC. There should be no air leakage from the diaphragm. Apply about 15.0 in. Hg of vacuum to the port marked PURGE and gradually apply a negative pressure to the port marked VC. If the purge control valve begins to open at between 1.6 and 3.2 in. Hg of pressure as the negative gauge reading falls, the control

valve is functioning normally. If not, the canister assembly must be replaced.

FUNCTIONAL TEST — V6 ONLY

Canister Purge Valve

1. Apply a short length of hose to the lower tube of the purge valve and attempt to blow through the hose. Little or no air should pass through into the canister.

2. With a hand vacuum pump, apply 15 in.

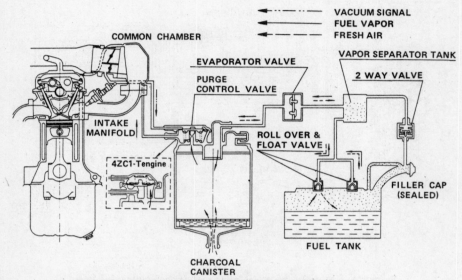

Evaporative emission control—G200Z and 4ZC1-T EFI engine

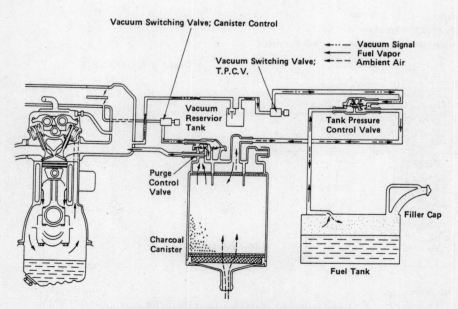

Evaporative emission control—4XC1-Turbo engine

Hg (51 kPa) of vacuum through the control valve tube (upper tube). The diaphragm should hold vacuum for at least 20 seconds, if not the canister has to be replaced.

Fuel Tank Pressure Control Valve

1. Apply 15 in. Hg (51 kPa) of vacuum to the control vacuum tube. The diaphragm should hold vacuum for at least 20 seconds. If it does not, the diaphragm is leaking and the valve must be replaced.

2. With the vacuum applied to the control vacuum tube, apply a short hose to the valve's tank tube side and blow into the tube. The air should pass through the valve. If no air passes through the valve, the valve should be replaced.

REMOVAL AND INSTALLATION

Label and disconnect the fuel canister hoses from the canister, remove the bracket bolt and canister.

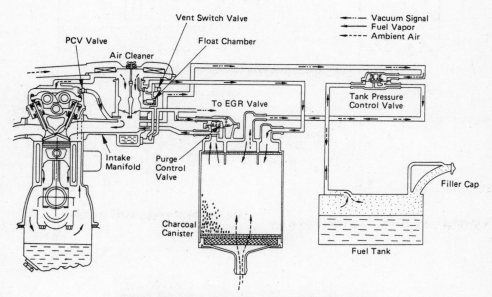

Evaporative emission control—4XC1-U carb. engine

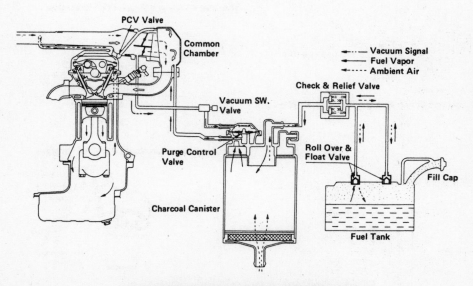

Evaporative emission control—4ZE1 EFI engine

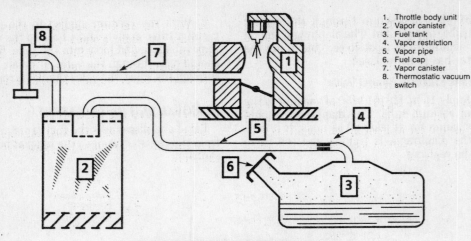

1. Throttle body unit
2. Vapor canister
3. Fuel tank
4. Vapor restriction
5. Vapor pipe
6. Fuel cap
7. Vapor canister
8. Thermostatic vacuum switch

Evaporative emission control—V6 engines

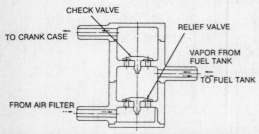

Check and relief valve—G180Z and G200Z carb. engine

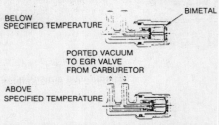

Vent switching valve—4XC1-U engine

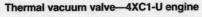

Thermal vacuum valve—4XC1-U engine

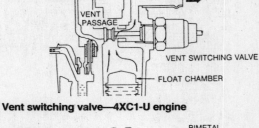

Ventilation valve—G180Z and G200Z carb. engine

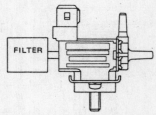

Vacuum switching valve—4XC1-U engine

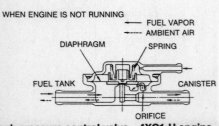

Tank pressure control valve—4XC1-U engine

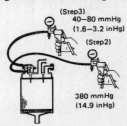

Checking canister

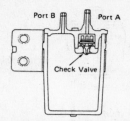

Vacuum reservoir tank—4XC1-T engine

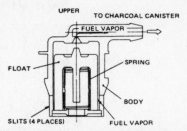

Roll-over and relief valve—4ZD1 engine

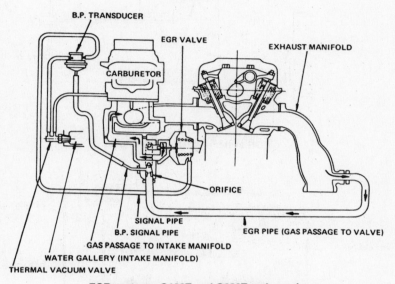

EGR system—G180Z and G200Z carb. engine

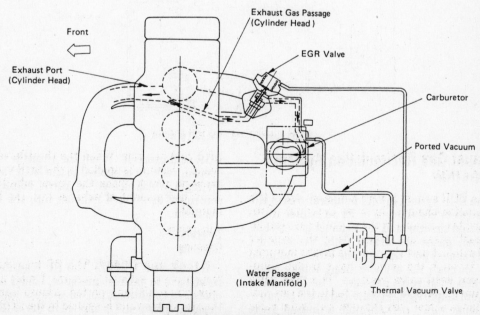

EGR system—4XC1-U engine

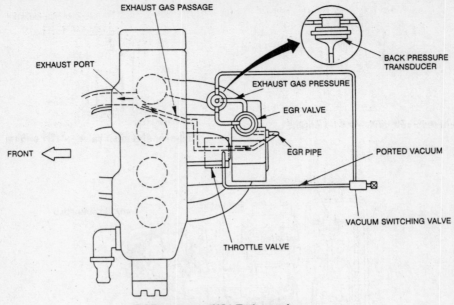

EGR system—4XC1-Turbo engine

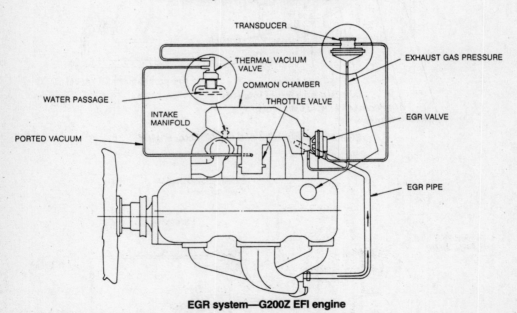

EGR system—G200Z EFI engine

Exhaust Gas Recirculation System
OPERATION

The EGR system lowers temperatures in the combustion chamber in order to reduce nitrogen oxide emissions in the exhaust gas stream. Exhaust gases are drawn from the cylinder head exhaust port through the intake manifold riser through the cylinder head, intake manifold and EGR valve passages. The EGR valve vacuum diaphragm is connected to the carburetor flange signal port through a thermal valve vacuum valve. The configuration controls the EGR cold override. When the throttle valve is opened, vacuum is applied to the EGR valve diaphragm which opens the valve, admitting a controlled amount of exhaust into the intake manifold.

SERVICE
Gasoline

G180Z and G200Z: The BP transducer is responsive to exhaust pressure. Under normal operating conditions, ported vacuum leaks into the atmosphere and is applied to the EGR valve under high pressure conditions.

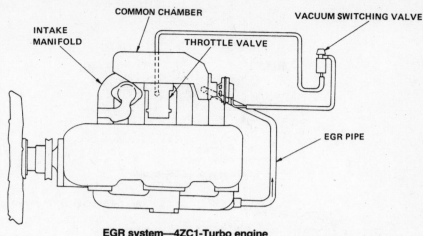

EGR system—4ZC1-Turbo engine

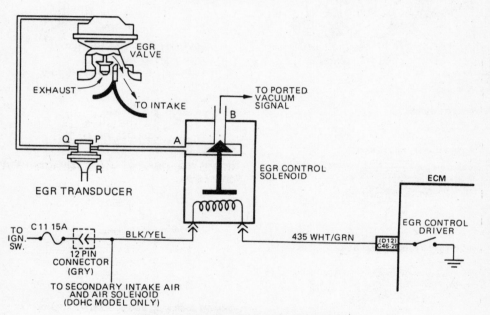

EGR system—4XE1 DOHC and SOHC engine

To test the BPT, disconnect the hoses, blow air into the black colored hose at the lower side of the BPT, should be closed. Check to see if air passes through the signal hose on the opposite side and air filter side of BPT when tested by blowing air into the EGR side signal hose.

The thermal vacuum valve is mounted on the intake manifold and is connected in series between the vacuum port in the carburetor and EGR valve. While the coolant temperature is below 115–129°F (46–54°C) the valve is closed. Above that temperature, the valve is open.

To test the thermal vacuum valve; disconnect hoses, check that no continuity exists between the hoses when the engine is cold and that the passage opens after engine warm up.

4XC1-T: The vacuum switching valve overrides the EGR system when the engine is started cold. The valve blocks the vacuum signal to protect the EGR valve from excessive pressure from the turbocharger. The valve is controlled by the ECM (electronic control module).

The 4XC1-T engine uses the same BP transducer as does the G180Z and G200Z carbureted engine.

To test the EGR system, connect a tachometer to the engine and connect a vacuum gauge to the BPT, location A. Start the engine when cold — below 176°F (80°C). The vacuum gauge should read 0 at all engine speeds. Allow the engine to warm. The gauge should read 0 at idle and raise at 3500 rpm. Disconnect the vacuum

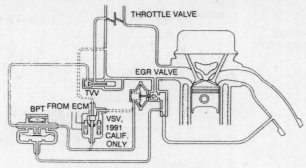

EGR system—4ZE1 engine

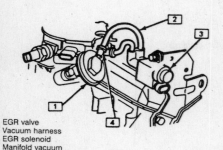

1. EGR valve
2. Vacuum harness
3. EGR solenoid
4. Manifold vacuum

EGR valve—V6 engine

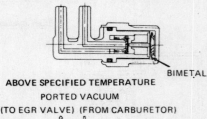

BELOW SPECIFIED TEMPERATURE

BIMETAL

ABOVE SPECIFIED TEMPERATURE

PORTED VACUUM

(TO EGR VALVE) (FROM CARBURETOR)

Thermal vacuum valve—G180Z, G200Z and 4XC1-U carb. engine

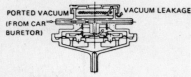

NORMAL OPERATING CONDITION

PORTED VACUUM
(FROM CAR-
BURETOR)

VACUUM LEAKAGE

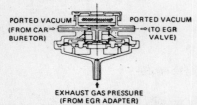

HIGH EXHAUST PRESSURE CONDITION

PORTED VACUUM
(FROM CAR-
BURETOR)

PORTED VACUUM
(TO EGR
VALVE)

EXHAUST GAS PRESSURE
(FROM EGR ADAPTER)

Backpressure transducer—G180Z, G200Z and 4XC1-T carb. engine, others similar

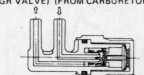

FILTER

Vacuum switching valve—4XC1-T engine

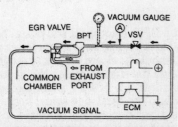

VACUUM GAUGE

EGR VALVE
BPT
VSV

COMMON
CHAMBER

FROM
EXHAUST
PORT

VACUUM SIGNAL
ECM

Checking the EGR system—4XC1-T engine

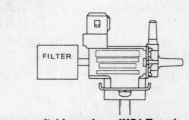

gauge and connect it to the BPT. Make sure the EGR diaphragm operates properly when racing the engine up to 2000 rpm.

Diesel

4FB1 diesel (Calif.) engine: The EGR controller is mounted with the UQOS controller. The controller sends electrical ON-OFF signal to the vacuum switching valve according to coolant temperature, engine speed and injection pump control lever angle.

The engine speed sensor is mounted on the right side of the injection pump. The control lever position sensor is mounted on the front upper part of the injection pump. The resistance changes depending of lever position. The

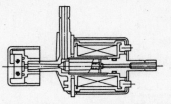

Vacuum switching valve—4ZC1-Turbo engine

thermoswitch is mounted on the thermostat housing.

Testing: The EGR valve should hold constant vacuum at 13.8 in. Hg with a vacuum pump. Test the vacuum switching valve by applying 12V to the electrical terminals. Listen for plunger noise that is accompanied with electrical operation of the plunger. Connect a volt-

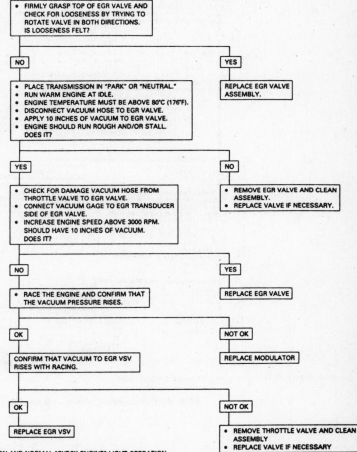

- FIRMLY GRASP TOP OF EGR VALVE AND CHECK FOR LOOSENESS BY TRYING TO ROTATE VALVE IN BOTH DIRECTIONS. IS LOOSENESS FELT?

NO →
- PLACE TRANSMISSION IN "PARK" OR "NEUTRAL."
- RUN WARM ENGINE AT IDLE.
- ENGINE TEMPERATURE MUST BE ABOVE 80°C (176°F).
- DISCONNECT VACUUM HOSE TO EGR VALVE.
- APPLY 10 INCHES OF VACUUM TO EGR VALVE.
- ENGINE SHOULD RUN ROUGH AND/OR STALL. DOES IT?

YES → REPLACE EGR VALVE ASSEMBLY.

YES →
- CHECK FOR DAMAGE VACUUM HOSE FROM THROTTLE VALVE TO EGR VALVE.
- CONNECT VACUUM GAGE TO EGR TRANSDUCER SIDE OF EGR VALVE.
- INCREASE ENGINE SPEED ABOVE 3000 RPM. SHOULD HAVE 10 INCHES OF VACUUM. DOES IT?

NO →
- REMOVE EGR VALVE AND CLEAN ASSEMBLY.
- REPLACE VALVE IF NECESSARY.

NO →
- RACE THE ENGINE AND CONFIRM THAT THE VACUUM PRESSURE RISES.

YES → REPLACE EGR VALVE

OK → CONFIRM THAT VACUUM TO EGR VSV RISES WITH RACING.

NOT OK → REPLACE MODULATOR

OK → REPLACE EGR VSV

NOT OK →
- REMOVE THROTTLE VALVE AND CLEAN ASSEMBLY
- REPLACE VALVE IF NECESSARY

CLEAR CODES AND CONFIRM "CLOSED LOOP" OPERATION AND NORMAL "CHECK ENGINE" LIGHT OPERATION.

EGR troubleshooting chart—4XE1 engine

Thermal Vacuum Valve	Throttle Valve Opening Angle	Back Pressure Transducer (BPT)		EGR Valve	Exhaust Gas
Close Below 50°C	—	Signal port close		Closed	Not recirculated
Open Above 50°C	Positioned below EGR port	Signal port close		Closed	Not recirculated
	Positioned above EGR port	(1) Low	Signal port partially open	Partially open	Partially recirculated
		(2) High	Signal port open	Open	Recirculated

EGR system check—4ZE1 engine

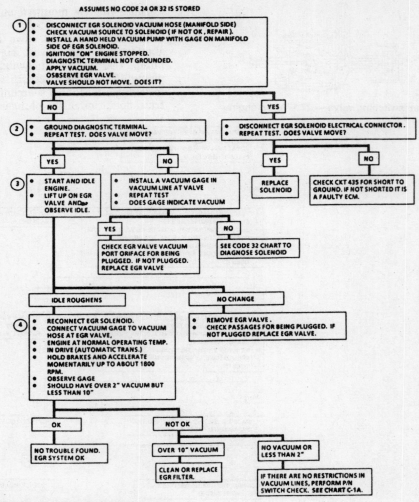

ASSUMES NO CODE 24 OR 32 IS STORED

① • DISCONNECT EGR SOLENOID VACUUM HOSE (MANIFOLD SIDE)
 • CHECK VACUUM SOURCE TO SOLENOID (IF NOT OK , REPAIR).
 • INSTALL A HAND HELD VACUUM PUMP WITH GAGE ON MANIFOLD SIDE OF EGR SOLENOID.
 • IGNITION "ON" ENGINE STOPPED.
 • DIAGNOSTIC TERMINAL NOT GROUNDED.
 • APPLY VACUUM.
 • OSBSERVE EGR VALVE.
 • VALVE SHOULD NOT MOVE. DOES IT?

NO → **YES**

② • GROUND DIAGNOSTIC TERMINAL.
 • REPEAT TEST. DOES VALVE MOVE?

• DISCONNECT EGR SOLENOID ELECTRICAL CONNECTOR .
 • REPEAT TEST. DOES VALVE MOVE?

YES / **NO** **YES** / **NO**

③ • START AND IDLE ENGINE.
 • LIFT UP ON EGR VALVE AND OBSERVE IDLE.

• INSTALL A VACUUM GAGE IN VACUUM LINE AT VALVE
 • REPEAT TEST
 • DOES GAGE INDICATE VACUUM

REPLACE SOLENOID

CHECK CKT 435 FOR SHORT TO GROUND. IF NOT SHORTED IT IS A FAULTY ECM.

YES / **NO**

CHECK EGR VALVE VACUUM PORT ORIFACE FOR BEING PLUGGED. IF NOT PLUGGED. REPLACE EGR VALVE

SEE CODE 32 CHART TO DIAGNOSE SOLENOID

IDLE ROUGHENS / **NO CHANGE**

④ • RECONNECT EGR SOLENOID.
 • CONNECT VACUUM GAGE TO VACUUM HOSE AT EGR VALVE,
 • ENGINE AT NORMAL OPERATING TEMP.
 • IN DRIVE (AUTOMATIC TRANS.)
 • HOLD BRAKES AND ACCELERATE MOMENTARILY UP TO ABOUT 1800 RPM.
 • OBSERVE GAGE
 • SHOULD HAVE OVER 2" VACUUM BUT LESS THAN 10"

• REMOVE EGR VALVE .
 • CHECK PASSAGES FOR BEING PLUGGED. IF NOT PLUGGED REPLACE EGR VALVE.

OK / **NOT OK**

NO TROUBLE FOUND. EGR SYSTEM OK

OVER 10" VACUUM / **NO VACUUM OR LESS THAN 2"**

CLEAN OR REPLACE EGR FILTER.

IF THERE ARE NO RESTRICTIONS IN VACUUM LINES, PERFORM P/N SWITCH CHECK. SEE CHART C-1A.

CONFIRM "CLOSED LOOP" OPERATION AND NO "CHECK ENGINE" LIGHT.

EGR troubleshooting chart—V6 engine

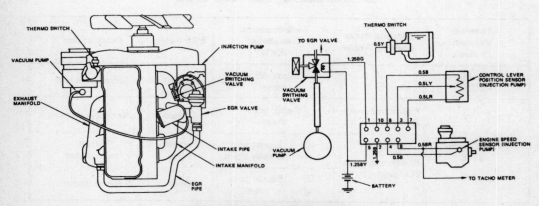

EGR system—4FB1 diesel (Calif)

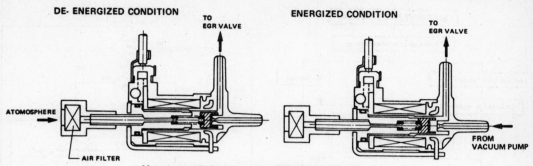

DE- ENERGIZED CONDITION

TO EGR VALVE

ENERGIZED CONDITION

TO EGR VALVE

ATOMOSPHERE

AIR FILTER

FROM VACUUM PUMP

Vacuum switching valve—4FB1 diesel (Calif. only)

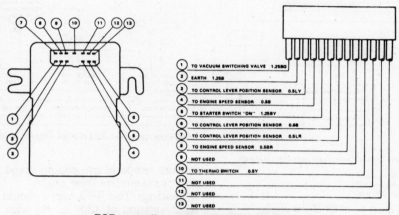

1	TO VACUUM SWITCHING VALVE	1.25BG
2	EARTH	1.25B
3	TO CONTROL LEVER POSITION SENSOR	0.5LY
4	TO ENGINE SPEED SENSOR	0.5B
5	TO STARTER SWITCH "ON"	1.25BY
6	TO CONTROL LEVER POSITION SENSOR	0.5B
7	TO CONTROL LEVER POSITION SENSOR	0.5LR
8	TO ENGINE SPEED SENSOR	0.5BR
9	NOT USED	
10	TO THERMO SWITCH	0.5Y
11	NOT USED	
12	NOT USED	
13	NOT USED	

EGR controller—4FB1 diesel (Calif. only)

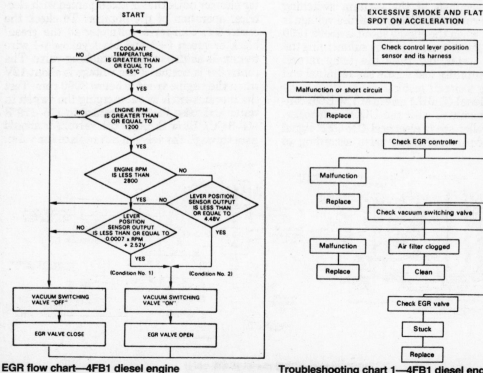

EGR flow chart—4FB1 diesel engine

Troubleshooting chart 1—4FB1 diesel engine

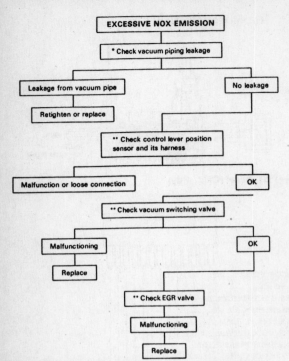

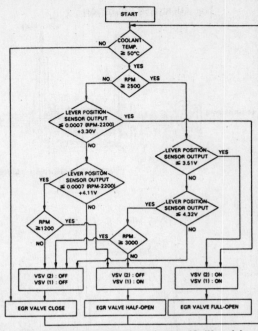

EGR flow chart—C233 diesel engine (Calif. only)

* This vacuum leakage also causes excessive brake pedal effort or fast idle malfunction.
** Check in the condition as follows:
1) Coolant temp is higher than 55°C.
2) Engine speed is over 1200 rpm.

Troubleshooting chart 2—4FB1 diesel engine

meter to the black/green (+) and black/yellow (–) wire terminals at the vacuum switching valve. The controller is normal if the voltage is about 12V when the engine speed is above 1200 rpm. Test the thermo switch by submerging the switch in water and raise the temperature. Make a continuity test across the terminal and body using a circuit tester.

C223 diesel (Calif.) engine: The EGR controller is mounted with the UQOS controller. The controller sends electrical ON-OFF signal to the vacuum switching valve according to

coolant temperature, engine speed and injection pump control lever angle.

Testing: The EGR valve should hold constant vacuum at 13.8 in. Hg with a vacuum pump. Test the vacuum switching valve by applying 12V to the electrical terminals. Listen for plunger noise that is accompanied with electrical operation of the plunger. To check the controller; connect a voltmeter to the green/black or green (+) and black/yellow (–) wire terminals at the vacuum switching valve. The controller is normal if the voltage is about 12V when the engine speed is below 3000 rpm. Test the thermoswitch by submerging the switch in water and raise the temperature to 115–129°F (46–54°C). Blow through the valve. Air should pass through the valve, if not replace the valve.

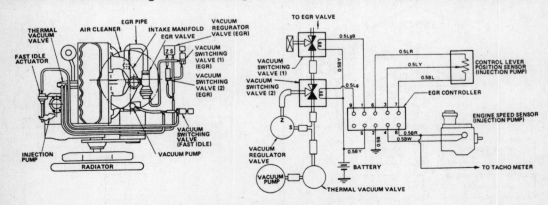

EGR system—C223 diesel (Calif. only)

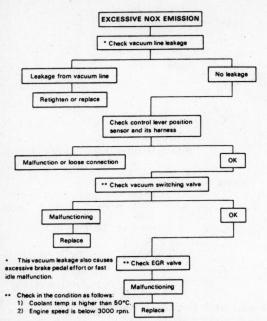

Troubleshooting chart 1—C233 diesel engine (Calif. only)

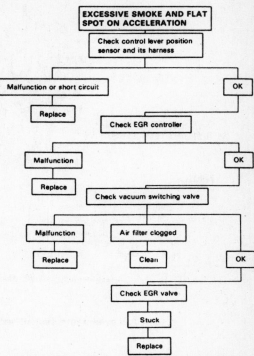

Troubleshooting chart 2—C223 diesel engine (Calif. only)

Early Fuel Evaporation System

The early fuel evaporation system consists of the EFE heater, electronic control module, coolant temperature sensor and the EFE relay.

The EFE heater is equipped with a ceramic ring which is located below the primary carburetor bore. The ring is an internal part of the carburetor gasket.

The EFE heats the incoming air charge to improve atomization. This offers better cold start and drive–away performance.

The coolant temperature sensor is activated when the ignition switch is turned to the **ON** position and the engine is started. If the engine coolant temperature is below the specified value, the ECM will supply current from the battery to the coils in the EFE heater to heat the incoming fuel/air charge.

REMOVAL AND INSTALLATION

1. Disconnect the negative (–) battery cable.
2. Remove the air cleaner assembly.

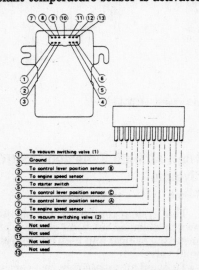

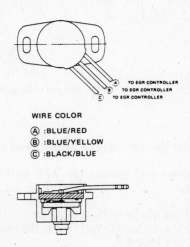

EGR controller and control lever position sensor—C223 diesel (Calif. only)

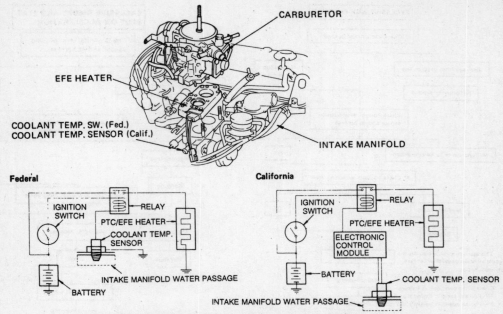

Early fuel evaporative system—after 1988, all systems are ECM controlled

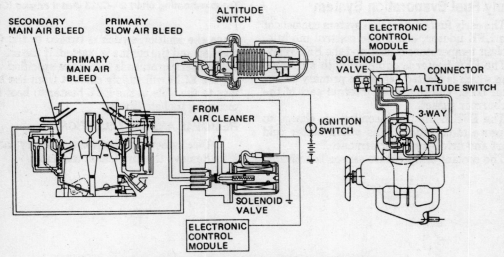

High altitude emission control system—RWD I-Mark

3. Remove the carburetor as outlined in Chapter 5.

4. Disconnect and remove the EFE heater and gaskets.

To install:

5. Install the heater with new gaskets.

6. Install the carburetor and torque the nuts as outlined in Chapter 5.

7. Install the air cleaner, connect the battery cable, start the engine and check operation.

High Altitude Emission Control System

I-Mark

This system consists of the altitude sensing switch, solenoid valve, air cleaner, 3 carburetor metering orifices and high altitude idle-up solenoid valve.

To avoid an excessively rich carburetor mixture at high altitudes due to decreased air den-

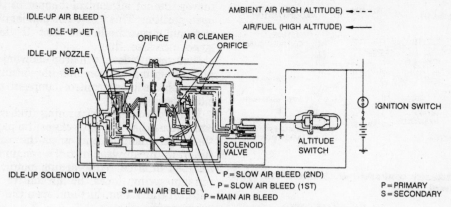

High altitude emission control system—FWD I-Mark

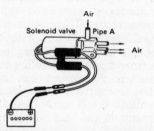

Check high altitude solenoid valve—FWD I-Mark

sity, the system functions to supply additional air through the carburetor metering orifices.

In addition, in order to stabilize the idle speed during high altitude operation, the system adjusts the fuel/air mixture according to signals from the idle-up solenoid valve.

At a certain altitude, the altitude sensing switch will close the circuit between the battery and the idle-up solenoid valve. The solenoid valve will open the passage between the air cleaner and the carburetor. Fresh air is then admitted through the 3 metering orifices and is supplied to the idle, off idle, primary and secondary main metering systems. Also, the idle

up solenoid valve will open the passage to the port downstream of the throttle valve, providing additional fuel/air mixtures for stable idle speed at high altitude.

Inspection: Disconnect the three rubber hoses at the carburetor, blow air from inlet pipe A and supply electricity to the valve. Check to see that the valve is open. If the valve is open, air will be felt from all three pipes. Disconnect the electric supply and check to see that the valve is closed.

Amigo and P'up

On the 1988 Pick-Up, the major component of the system is the altitude switch which is installed on the right side of the dash panel. This switch senses altitude to the height of 2000 meters. The switch is connected to the ECM and makes the "System Malfunction Indicator" lamp inoperable in case of a "Rich Oxygen Sensor Error" at or above the designated altitude. There is no interaction between the altitude switch and the emission control system and the system does not require adjustment.

On 1989–90 Amigo and Pick-Up, a MAP sensor is used to measure atmospheric pressure

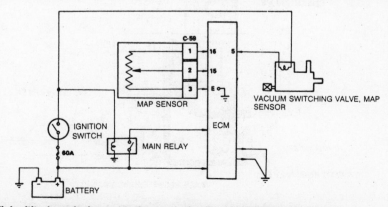

High altitude emission control system circuit—1989–90 Amigo and P'up

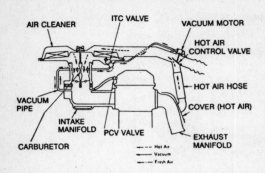

Thermostatically controlled air cleaner (TCA) system—Typical

though a vacuum switching valve. The system prevents the vehicle's self-diagnostic system from generating a false "Rich Fuel Metering Error" at altitudes higher than the system's set point.

Thermostatically Controlled Air (TCA) Cleaner System

The TCA functions to maintain ambient air air temperature at an optimum level so that the fuel/air ratio remains constant. This ensures fuel combustion and reduces pollutant emissions.

The TCA system is mounted on the air cleaner. It consists of a vacuum motor, hot air control damper and an inlet temperature compensator (ITC) valve.

When the engine is running, there is no vacuum signal at either the vacuum motor or the ITC valve. In this condition the vacuum motor spring closes off the passage from the hot air duct.

On a cold start, the ITC valve delivers maximum vacuum to the vacuum motor which moves the hot air control damper to the fully open position. This closes the ambient air passage and opens the hot air duct. If the engine speed increases, the system vacuum level will drop allowing the diaphragm spring to overcome the vacuum force and push the hot air control damper to the fully closed position.

When the engine is running under normal conditions, the ITC valve closes the passage to the intake manifold and opens the passage to the from the air cleaner to the vacuum motor. As fresh air is fed to the vacuum motor, the diaphragm spring forces the air control valve to close off the hot air duct and open the ambient air passage.

During conditions of extended idling, hill climbing or high speed driving, there is a substantial increase in engine and engine compartment temperatures. This results in an excessive amount of fuel vapor entering the intake manifold, causing an over-rich mixture. The over-rich mixture causes rough idling and increased CO emissions. To prevent this, the ITC valve opens the passage from the air cleaner to the intake manifold. Fresh air is allowed to enter the intake manifold and lean out the mixture.

3–Way Catalytic Converter System

The 3–way catalytic converter functions to reduce nitrogen oxides and oxidizes hydrocarbons and carbon monoxide.

The converter is mounted directly to the exhaust manifold. The converter unit houses a "honeycomb" type catalyst with bonding material inside a cast iron casing. A ceramic type seal is employed to prevent exhaust leakage between the case and the outer wall of the catalyst.

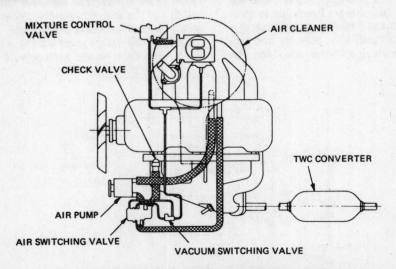

Air injection reaction system—RWD I-Mark (G180Z)

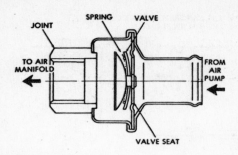

AIR system check valve

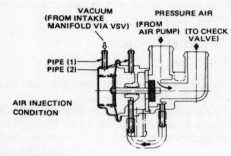

AIR switching valve

Air Injection Reactor System

OPERATION

The air injection reactor system is used on RWD I-Mark, 1986–90 Amigo, Pick-Up and Trooper.

In gasoline engine, it is difficult to burn the air-fuel mixture completely through combustion that takes place with the combustion chambers. In order to reduce HC and CO emissions, the system draws air into the exhaust ports to speed up oxidation. The air management valve switches air passage from the air pump through a vacuum management valve which is actuated by an electric signal supplied from the ECM.

The air pump is belt driven by the pulley mounted on the water pump shaft of the engine. Air is drawn through the air cleaner and suction hose into the outlet chamber, where it is trapped between two vanes and the pump body. As the rotor turns, these vanes carry the air to the outlet chamber and then to the air manifold.

SERVICE

G180Z and G200Z Inspection: The check valve should only allow air to flow in one direction. If air does not flow or in both directions, the valve is defective and must be replaced.

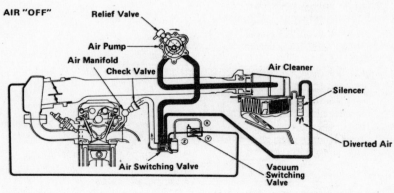

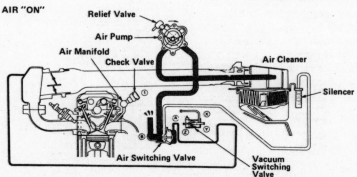

Air injection reaction system—4ZE 1 engines

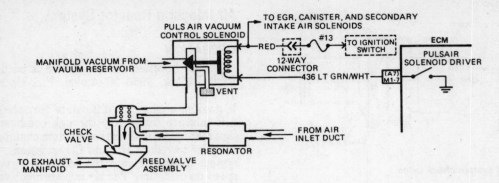

Air injection system—4XE1 DOHC engine

The air switching valve is designed to switch air flow from the air pump. When the manifold vacuum flows to the pipe, the air switching valve allows air from the pump to flow to the check valve.

4ZE1 engine: With the engine at normal operating temperature and at idle, disconnect the vacuum signal hose (Y) from the VSV and vacuum hose (X and Z) from the ASV. Disconnect the air hose 1 at the check valve and plug the valve. Connect the vacuum signal hose (Y) directly to the pipe A of the ASV. Secondary air should continue to blow out from pipe B of the ASV. If a problem is found, replace the ASV (air switching valve).

Air Induction System
OPERATION

The air induction system is used on late 1988 and all 1989–90 I-Mark models.

The air induction system reduces HC and CO emissions by admitting filtered air through the air induction valves into the exhaust manifold

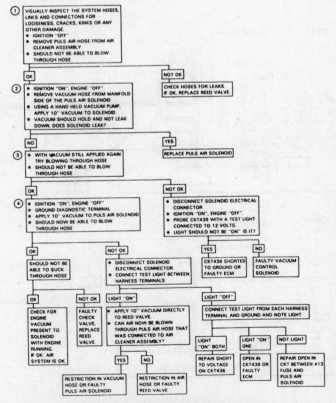

Air injection diagnosis chart—4XE1 engine

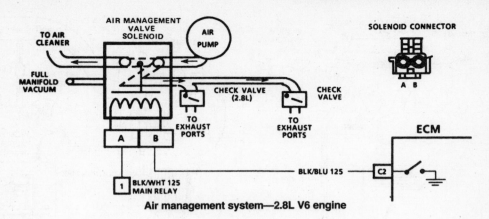

Air management system—2.8L V6 engine

to cool the exhaust gas stream before the gases enter the catalytic converter.

In warm conditions, after the engine is started, the system introduces air into the exhaust manifold for 3 seconds then cuts it off.

In cold starts with an engine idle speed greater than 4000 rpm, induction is always cut off.

While the engine is running at normal operating temperature, the air induction system admits cooling air according to rpm, water temperature and throttle position.

SERVICE

4XC1-U engine: Inspect the air induction valve by removing the air cleaner and element. Disconnect the hose to the suction pipe. Apply vacuum to the diaphragm, check that air flows from the filter side to the outlet pipe. Check that air does not flow from the outlet pipe to the filter side. Release the vacuum and check that hardly any air flows from the filter side to the outlet side. Connect the rubber hoses and reinstall the air cleaner.

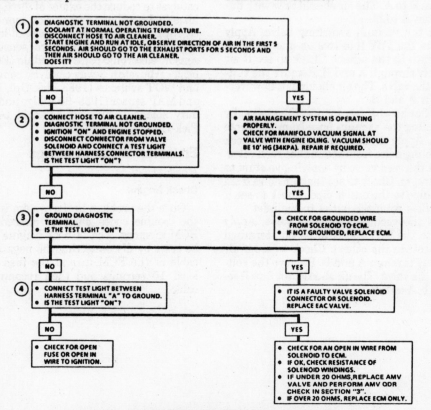

Air management system diagnosis chart—2.8L V6 engine

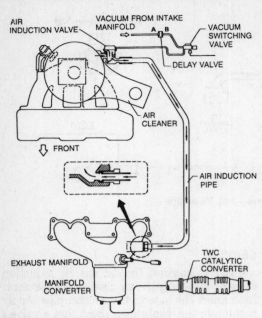

Air induction system—4XC1-U engine

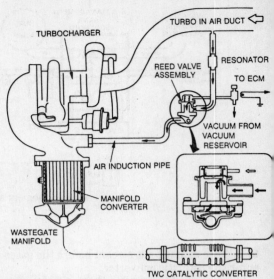

Air induction system—4XC1-Turbo engine

Inspect the delay valve by blowing air into each side. The air should flow without resistance from **B** to **A**. The air should flow with difficulty from **A** to **B**.

Inspect the vacuum switching valve. Apply 12 volts to the VSV (positive on one terminal and negative to the other). Check to see if air flows freely through **A** and **B**. Remove the voltage from the valve. The air should not flow freely through **A** and **B**.

4XC1-Turbo engine: Inspect the system by disconnecting the vacuum hose from the three way tube. Apply vacuum to the hose and check for a bubbling noise from around the reed valve.

Inspect the reed valve by applying vacuum to the diaphragm. Check to see that air flows from the inlet pipe to the outlet pipe. Check to see if does not flow from the outlet to the inlet.

Inspect the vacuum switching valve. Apply 12 volts to the VSV (positive on one terminal and negative to the other). Check to see if air flows freely through **A** and **B**. Remove the voltage from the valve. The air should not flow freely through **A** and **B**.

Closed Loop Emission Control System

The closed loop emission control system precisely controls the air/fuel ratio near the optimum mixture and allows the use of the 3-way catalyst to reduce the oxides of nitrogen and oxidize hydrocarbons and carbon monoxide. The essential components of the closed loop system are the coolant temperature sensor, oxygen sensor, electronic control module (ECM), feedback carburetor, 3-way catalytic converter, idle and WOT switches (1988 Pick-Up), idle switch and MAP sensor (1989–90 Amigo and Pick-Up), duty solenoid, fuel cut solenoid (Amigo and Pick-Up).

Emission Warning Lamps
RESETTING
Check Engine

Once the problem in the system is corrected, the trouble codes must be cleared from the ECM memory. The "Check Engine" light can be reset by disconnecting the negative battery cable or the ECM fuse at the fuse box for at least 10 seconds and then reconnecting the cable.

VACUUM DIAGRAMS

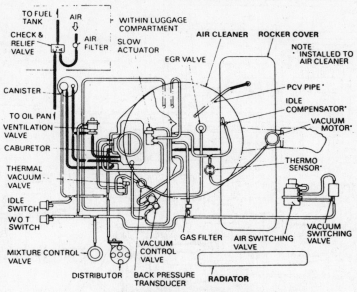

1981—85 RWD I-Mark (Federal)

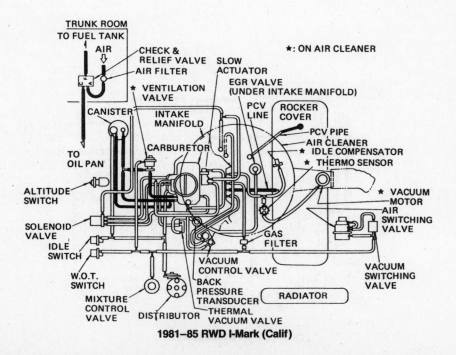

1981—85 RWD I-Mark (Calif)

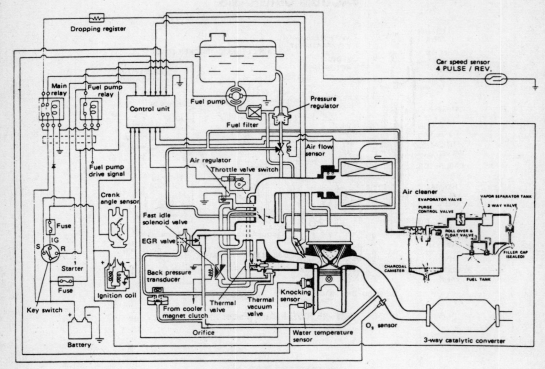

1983–87 Impulse G200Z

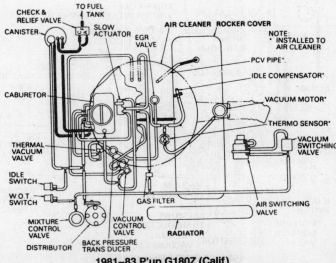

1981–83 P'up G180Z (Calif)

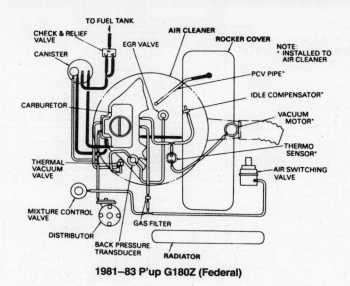

CHECK & RELIEF VALVE

TO FUEL TANK

AIR CLEANER

ROCKER COVER

EGR VALVE

CANISTER

NOTE:
* INSTALLED TO AIR CLEANER

CARBURETOR

PCV PIPE*

IDLE COMPENSATOR*

VACUUM MOTOR*

THERMO SENSOR*

THERMAL VACUUM VALVE

AIR SWITCHING VALVE

MIXTURE CONTROL VALVE

DISTRIBUTOR

GAS FILTER

BACK PRESSURE TRANSDUCER

RADIATOR

1981—83 P'up G180Z (Federal)

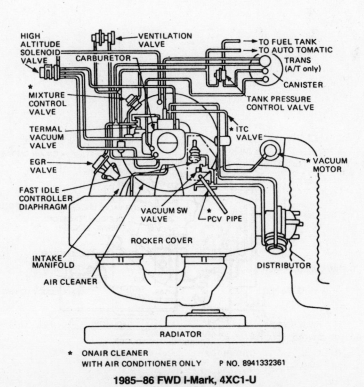

HIGH ALTITUDE SOLENOID VALVE

VENTILATION VALVE

CARBURETOR

TO FUEL TANK

TO AUTO TOMATIC TRANS (A/T only)

CANISTER

* MIXTURE CONTROL VALVE

TANK PRESSURE CONTROL VALVE

TERMAL VACUUM VALVE

* ITC VALVE

EGR VALVE

* VACUUM MOTOR

FAST IDLE CONTROLLER DIAPHRAGM

VACUUM SW VALVE

* PCV PIPE

ROCKER COVER

INTAKE MANIFOLD

DISTRIBUTOR

AIR CLEANER

RADIATOR

* ONAIR CLEANER WITH AIR CONDITIONER ONLY   P NO. 8941332361

1985—86 FWD I-Mark, 4XC1-U

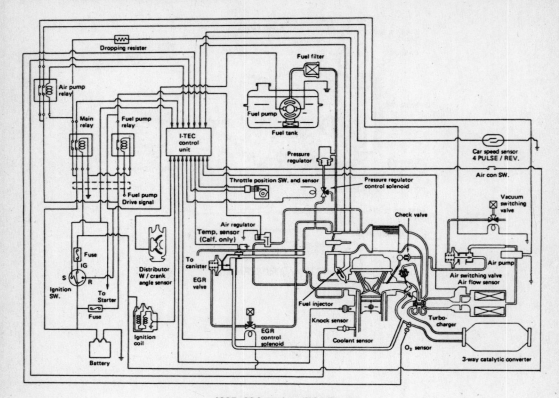

1985—88 Impulse 4ZC1-Turbo

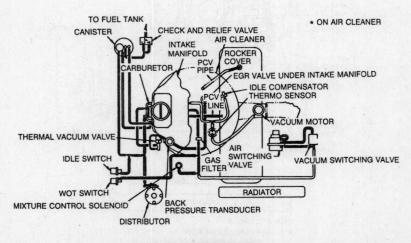

1984 P'up G180Z (Calif)

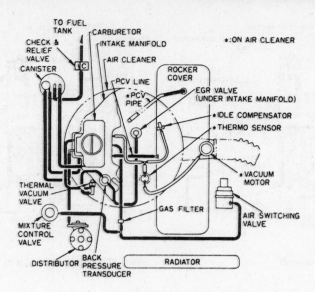

1984 P'up G180Z (Federal)

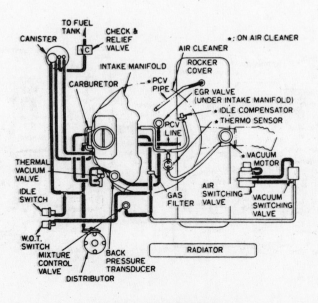

1985–87 P'up G200Z (Calif)

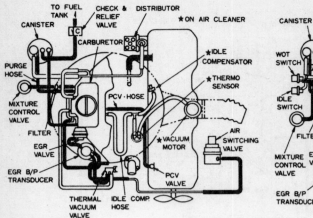

1985–88 P'up G200Z (Federal)

1986–87 Trooper 4ZD1 (Calif)

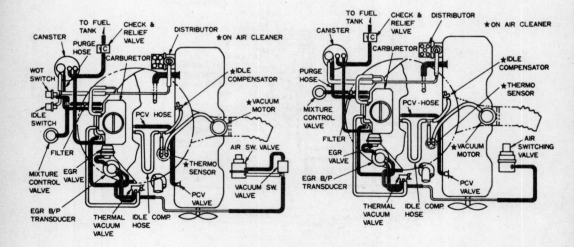

1985–88 P'up 4ZD1 (Calif)

1986–87 Trooper 4ZD1 (Federal)

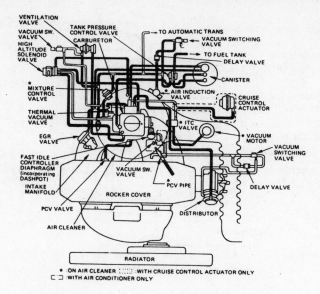

1987–89 FWD I-Mark, 4XC1-U with auto transaxle

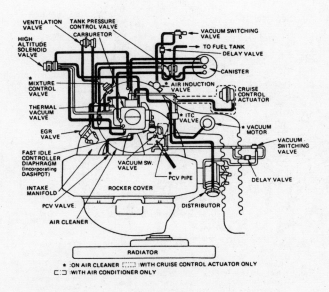

1987–89 FWD I-Mark, 4XC1-U with manual transaxle

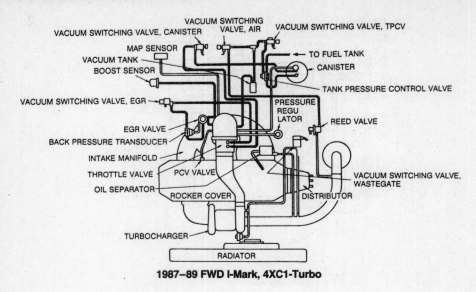

VACUUM SWITCHING
VALVE, AIR
VACUUM SWITCHING VALVE, CANISTER
VACUUM SWITCHING VALVE, TPCV
MAP SENSOR
VACUUM TANK
BOOST SENSOR
← TO FUEL TANK
CANISTER
TANK PRESSURE CONTROL VALVE
VACUUM SWITCHING VALVE, EGR
PRESSURE REGU LATOR
EGR VALVE
REED VALVE
BACK PRESSURE TRANSDUCER
INTAKE MANIFOLD
THROTTLE VALVE
PCV VALVE
OIL SEPARATOR
VACUUM SWITCHING VALVE, WASTEGATE
ROCKER COVER
DISTRIBUTOR
TURBOCHARGER
RADIATOR

1987–89 FWD I-Mark, 4XC1-Turbo

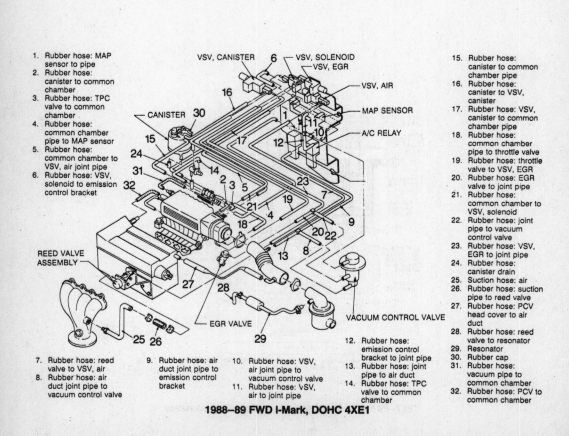

1. Rubber hose: MAP sensor to pipe
2. Rubber hose: canister to common chamber
3. Rubber hose: TPC valve to common chamber
4. Rubber hose: common chamber pipe to MAP sensor
5. Rubber hose: common chamber to VSV, air joint pipe
6. Rubber hose: VSV, solenoid to emission control bracket

7. Rubber hose: reed valve to VSV, air
8. Rubber hose: air duct joint pipe to vacuum control valve
9. Rubber hose: air duct joint pipe to emission control bracket
10. Rubber hose: VSV, air joint pipe to vacuum control valve
11. Rubber hose: VSV, air to joint pipe
12. Rubber hose: emission control bracket to joint pipe
13. Rubber hose: joint pipe to air duct
14. Rubber hose: TPC valve to common chamber

15. Rubber hose: canister to common chamber pipe
16. Rubber hose: canister to VSV, canister
17. Rubber hose: VSV, canister to common chamber pipe
18. Rubber hose: common chamber pipe to throttle valve
19. Rubber hose: throttle valve to VSV, EGR
20. Rubber hose: EGR valve to joint pipe
21. Rubber hose: common chamber to VSV, solenoid
22. Rubber hose: joint pipe to vacuum control valve
23. Rubber hose: VSV, EGR to joint pipe
24. Rubber hose: canister drain
25. Suction hose: air
26. Rubber hose: suction pipe to reed valve
27. Rubber hose: PCV head cover to air duct
28. Rubber hose: reed valve to resonator
29. Resonator
30. Rubber cap
31. Rubber hose: vacuum pipe to common chamber
32. Rubber hose: PCV to common chamber

VSV, CANISTER
VSV, SOLENOID
VSV, EGR
VSV, AIR
MAP SENSOR
CANISTER
A/C RELAY
REED VALVE ASSEMBLY
EGR VALVE
VACUUM CONTROL VALVE

1988–89 FWD I-Mark, DOHC 4XE1

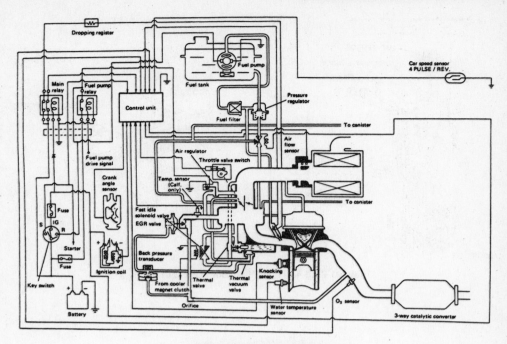

1988–89 FWD Impulse 4ZD1

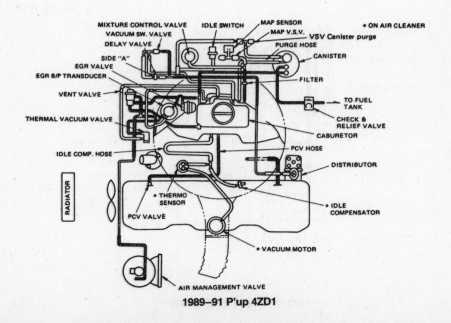

1989–91 P'up 4ZD1

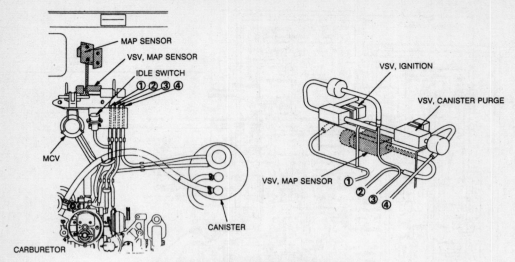

1989–91 P'up 4ZD1, MAP sensor hose routing

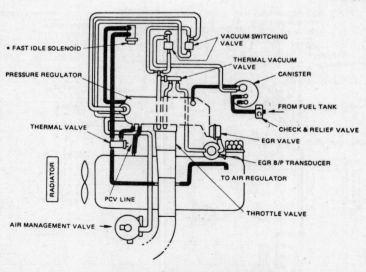

1990–91 P'up 4ZE1 (Federal)

*: IF SO EQUIPPED

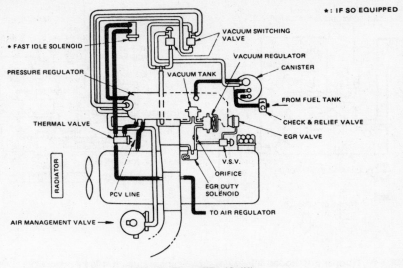

1990-91 P'up 4ZE1 (Calif)

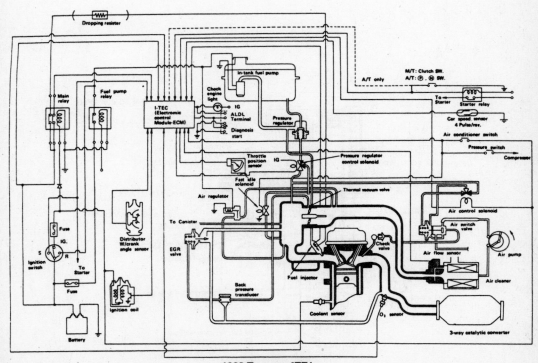

1988 Trooper 4ZE1

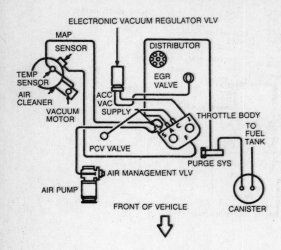

1989–91 Trooper and Rodeo V6

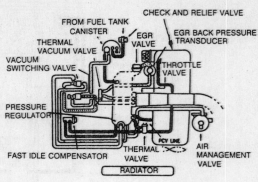

1991 Rodeo 4ZE1

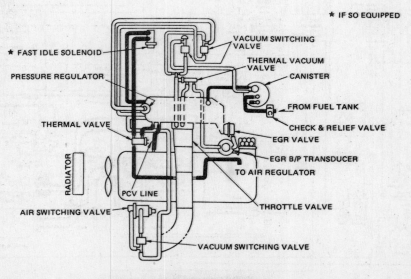

1990–91 Trooper 4ZE1 (Federal)

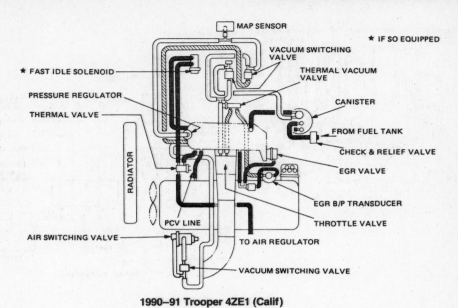

1990–91 Trooper 4ZE1 (Calif)

MAP SENSOR

★ IF SO EQUIPPED

VACUUM SWITCHING VALVE

★ FAST IDLE SOLENOID

THERMAL VACUUM VALVE

PRESSURE REGULATOR

CANISTER

THERMAL VALVE

FROM FUEL TANK

CHECK & RELIEF VALVE

EGR VALVE

RADIATOR

EGR B/P TRANSDUCER

THROTTLE VALVE

PCV LINE

AIR SWITCHING VALVE

TO AIR REGULATOR

VACUUM SWITCHING VALVE

INTAKE MANIFOLD

THERMAL VACUUM VALVE

AIR CLEANER

EGR PIPE

EGR VALVE

VACUUM SWITCHING VALVE (EGR)

FAST IDLE ACTUATOR

TO EGR VALVE

CONTROL LEVER POSITION SENSOR (INJECTION PUMP)

VACUUM SWITCHING VALVE

THERMAL VACUUM VALVE

EGR CONTROLLER

VACUUM PUMP

VACUUM SWITCHING VALVE (FAST IDLE)

INJECTION PUMP

VACUUM PUMP

RADIATOR

ENGINE SPEED SENSOR (INJECTION PUMP)

BATTERY

1981–83 P'up diesel (Calif)

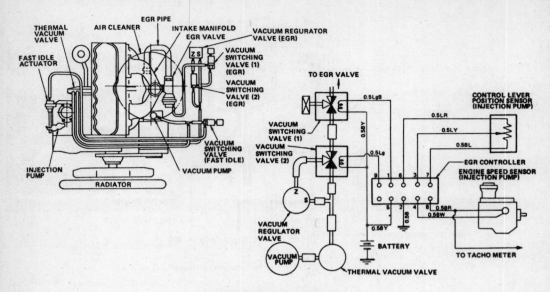

1984–86 P'up diesel (Calif)

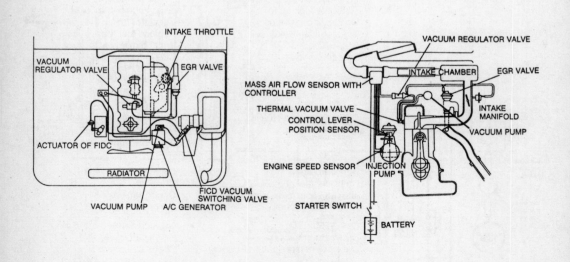

1987–88 P'up diesel (Calif)

Fuel System

5

GASOLINE FUEL SYSTEM

Fuel System Service Precaution

Disconnect the negative battery cable. Keep a Class B dry chemical fire extinguisher available. Always relieve the fuel pressure before disconnecting a fuel line. Wrap a shop cloth around the fuel line when disconnecting a fuel line. Always use new O-rings. Do not replace the fuel pipes with fuel hoses. Always us a back-up wrench when opening or closing a fuel line.

Relieving Fuel System Pressure

Carbureted Engine

1. Release the fuel vapor pressure in the fuel tank by removing the fuel tank cap and reinstalling it.

2. Cover the fuel line with an absorbent shop cloth and loosen the connection slowly to release the fuel pressure gradually.

Fuel Injected Engine

1. Allow the engine to cool. Then, remove the fuel pump fuse from the fuse block or disconnect the fuel pump relay connector.

Troubleshooting Basic Fuel System Problems

Problem	Cause	Solution
Engine cranks, but won't start (or is hard to start) when cold	• Empty fuel tank • Incorrect starting procedure • Defective fuel pump • No fuel in carburetor • Clogged fuel filter • Engine flooded • Defective choke	• Check for fuel in tank • Follow correct procedure • Check pump output • Check for fuel in the carburetor • Replace fuel filter • Wait 15 minutes; try again • Check choke plate
Engine cranks, but is hard to start (or does not start) when hot— (presence of fuel is assumed)	• Defective choke	• Check choke plate
Rough idle or engine runs rough	• Dirt or moisture in fuel • Clogged air filter • Faulty fuel pump	• Replace fuel filter • Replace air filter • Check fuel pump output
Engine stalls or hesitates on acceleration	• Dirt or moisture in the fuel • Dirty carburetor • Defective fuel pump • Incorrect float level, defective accelerator pump	• Replace fuel filter • Clean the carburetor • Check fuel pump output • Check carburetor
Poor gas mileage	• Clogged air filter • Dirty carburetor • Defective choke, faulty carburetor adjustment	• Replace air filter • Clean carburetor • Check carburetor
Engine is flooded (won't start accompanied by smell of raw fuel)	• Improperly adjusted choke or carburetor	• Wait 15 minutes and try again, without pumping gas pedal • If it won't start, check carburetor

2. Crank the engine, it will start and run until the fuel supply remaining in the fuel lines is exhausted. When the engine stops, engage the starter again for 3.0 seconds to assure dissipation of any remaining pressure.

3. With the ignition **OFF**, replace the fuel pump fuse or connect the fuel pump relay.

Mechanical Fuel Pump

REMOVAL AND INSTALLATION

G180Z and G200Z Engine with Mechanical Pump

The fuel pump is located beside the distributor at the right, front side of the engine.

1. Relieve the fuel pressure.
2. Disconnect the negative battery cable.
3. Mark the distributor rotor and housing location before removing distributor. Remove the distributor cap, with the wires attached and the distributor assembly.
4. Disconnect and plug the fuel lines from the fuel pump.
5. Remove the engine hanger.
6. Remove the fuel pump-to-engine bolts and remove the pump assembly.

To install:

7. Using a new gasket, install the fuel pump on the engine.
8. Install the engine hanger.
9. Unplug and connect the fuel lines to the fuel pump.
10. Install the distributor and the distributor cap.
11. Connect the negative battery cable.
12. Start the engine and check for fuel leaks.

4XC1-U Engine

1. Disconnect the negative (–) battery cable.
2. Relieve the fuel system pressure.
3. Disconnect the fuel hoses.
4. Remove the retaining bolts, pump and gasket.

To install:

5. Clean the gasket mating surfaces and install the pump with a new gasket.
6. Tighten the retaining bolts.
7. Connect the pump hoses and negative battery cable.
8. Start the engine and check for leaks.

4ZD1 Carb. Engine

The fuel pump is located at the right side of the engine, directly under the intake manifold.

1. Relieve the fuel pressure.
2. Disconnect the negative battery cable.
3. Remove the air cleaner assembly.
4. Remove the intake manifold assembly.
5. Disconnect and plug the fuel lines at the fuel pump.

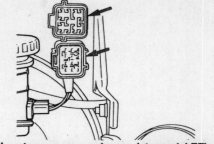

Fuel system pressure release—late model EFI cars

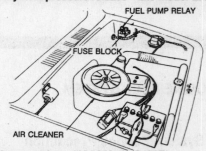

Fuel pump relay—1981 I-Mark, G180Z

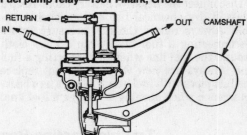

Mechanical fuel pump

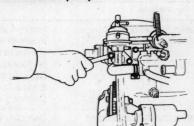

Fuel pump—4XC1-U engines

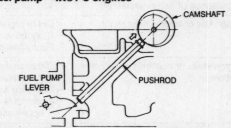

Fuel pump and pushrod—4ZD1 carb. engine

6. Remove the fuel pump-to-engine bolts and the pump assembly.

To install:

7. Remove the cylinder head cover.

8. Rotate the engine to position the No. 4 cylinder at TDC.

9. Lift the fuel pump pushrod toward the camshaft and hold it in the raised position.

10. Using a new gasket, install the fuel pump on the engine; torque the bolts to 15–25 ft. lbs. (20–34 Nm).

11. Connect the fuel hoses to the fuel pump.

12. Using a new gasket, install the intake manifold.

13. Install the air cleaner assembly.

14. Connect the negative battery cable.

15. Start the engine and check for fuel leaks.

TESTING

1. Remove the fuel pump from the vehicle.

2. Check the outside of the pump for cracks, leakage and other damage, replace if necessary.

3. Check for excessive wear between the rocker arm and camshaft contact surfaces.

4. Check the inlet valve by moving the rocker arm to the pump side and hold it in this position. Shut both the return and outlet pipes with your fingers. When the rocker arm has returned to its original position, there should show a marked increase in the amount of play. If no increase, replace the pump.

5. Check the outlet valve by closing the inlet pipe. The rocker arm must not move when the pipe is closed. Do not use excessive force.

6. Check the diaphragm. The rocker arm must not move when the inlet, outlet and return pipes are shut, if so replace the pump.

Electric Fuel Pump

PRESSURE TESTING

1. Relieve the fuel pressure.

2. Disconnect the fuel line near the engine and install fuel pressure gauge T-connector in the line.

3. Connect the fuel pressure gauge to the T-connector.

4. Start the engine and check the fuel pressure, it should be:

- 1981 I-Mark G180Z — 2.4–3.3 psi, carburetor inlet hose.
- 4XC1-Turbo and DOHC I-Mark, G200Z Impulse — 35.6 psi with the vacuum hose of the

pressure regulator disconnected and plugged. 28.4 psi with the vacuum hose connected and at idle.

- 4ZC1-Turbo, 4ZD1 Impulse and 4ZE1 engine — 42.6 psi with the vacuum hose at the pressure regulator disconnected and plugged. 35.6 psi with the vacuum hose connected at idle. Disconnect the VSV before checking pressure.
- V6 engine — 9–13 psi at the fuel pressure line after the fuel filter.
- 4XE1 SOHC and DOHC engine — Flow test, disconnect the hose from the EFI fuel feed line at the engine and place in a suitable container. Apply battery voltage to the fuel pump. Pump should supply ¼ quart (0.24L) within 15 seconds. Pressure test, connect a pressure gauge in the fuel pressure line after the fuel filter, located at the driver's side frame rail. Disconnect the vacuum hose from the pressure regulator. Apply battery voltage to the pump. After the pump stabilizes, the pressure should be 35-38 psi (245-256 kPa) and hold steady.

REMOVAL AND INSTALLATION

1981 I-Mark, G180Z Engine

The 1981 I-Mark has an electric fuel pump located in the rear of the vehicle. Disconnect the negative (–) battery cable and release the fuel pressure. Disconnect the fuel lines and electrical connectors. Remove the retaining bolts and pump.

In-tank Fuel Pump

NOTE: *Fuel is under high pressure, if the following steps are not followed the fuel could spray out and result in a fire hazard or possible injury. The fuel pump is located inside the gas tank.*

1. Relieve fuel pressure then disconnect negative battery cable.

2. Raise and support the vehicle safely.

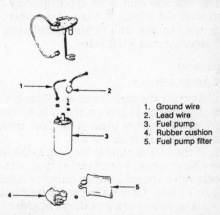

1. Ground wire
2. Lead wire
3. Fuel pump
4. Rubber cushion
5. Fuel pump filter

Exploded view of the electric fuel pump—except V6 engine

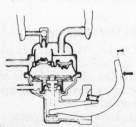

Check fuel pump

Drain fuel tank. Remove the undercover screws and undercover, if so equipped.

3. Remove all gas line hose connections and fuel pump ground wire.

4. Remove filler neck hose and clamp.

5. Remove breather hose and clamp.

6. Disconnect fuel tank hose to evaporator pipe. Place a suitable floor jack with a piece of wood on it under the fuel tank.

7. Remove fuel tank mounting bolts and lower tank from car. At this point remove hose from pump to fuel filter.

8. Remove fuel pump bracket plate and fuel pump as an assembly.

9. Remove pump bracket, rubber cushion and fuel pump filter.

To install:

10. Install the pump to the bracket and rubber cushion. Install the fuel pump filter.

11. Install fuel pump bracket plate and fuel pump as an assembly.

12. Raise the tank and connect the hoses. Tighten the tank straps.

13. Connect fuel tank hose to evaporator pipe.

14. Install the breather hose and clamp.

15. Connect the fuel pump ground wire. Install the undercover and screws.

16. Lower the vehicle safely. Refill fuel tank and check for leaks.

17. Connect negative battery cable and check operation.

Carburetor

ADJUSTMENT

Fast Idle

The automatic choke fast idle is adjusted by the opening angle of the throttle valve on the carburetor, not by engine speed. Adjusted throttle valve opening at the 1st step of the fast idle cam is 16° (MT) and 18° (AT).

The fast idle should be approximately 3200 rpm after the engine is warm. Disconnect and plug the vacuum line to the distributor, idle compensator and EGR valve.

Float Level

RWD I-MARK AND P'UP

1. Remove the carburetor and float cover.

2. The fuel level is normal if it is within the mark on the window glass of the float chamber when the engine is stationary.

3. If the level is outside the line, make necessary adjustments by bending the float seat. The needle valve should have an effective stroke of about 1.5mm. Check this measurement between the valve stem and the float seat.

4. Do not bend the needle valve rod when installing the float.

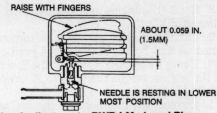

Float level adjustment—RWD I-Mark and P'up

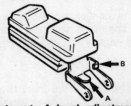

Float adjustment—A level adjustment, B drop adjustment

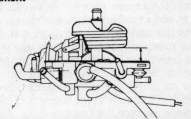

Float level adjustment—FWD I-Mark and P'up

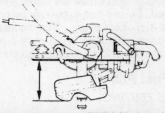

Float drop adjustment—FWD I-Mark and P'up

FWD I-MARK

1. Remove the carburetor and float cover.

2. Check the clearance between the float top and gasket. The measurement should be 1.5mm.

3. Bend tab (A) to adjust the float level.

4. Check the clearance between the float top and gasket at the lowered position of the float.

5. The level should be 44.3mm.

6. Bend tab (B) to adjust the float drop.

Primary Throttle Valve Adjustment

The primary throttle valve is opened by means of the fast idle adjusting screw to an angle of 16° when the choke valve is completely closed. The primary throttle valve opening angle may be checked as follows:

1. Close the choke valve completely and measure the clearance between the center of the

throttle valve and the wall of the throttle valve chamber. Standard clearance is 1.3–1.5mm.

2. Adjust the throttle valve opening angle with the fast idle adjusting screw.

NOTE: *Be sure to turn the throttle stop screw all the way in before measuring the clearance.*

Kick Lever Adjustment

1. Turn out the throttle valve adjusting screw to completely close the primary side of the throttle valve.

2. Loosen the locknut on the kick lever screw and turn the screw until it is in contact with the return plate.

3. Tighten the locknut.

Choke Valve Opening Adjustment

1988-91 P'UP AND AMIGO

1. Move the fast idle screw tip against the 2nd step of the fast idle cam.

2. Measure the clearance between the choke valve and the choke valve chamber wall.

3. If the clearance measured is not between 0.8–1.3mm, bend the counter lever tang to adjust.

Unloader Adjustment

1988-91 P'up AND AMIGO

1. Open the primary valve fully.

2. Measure the clearance between the choke valve and the choke valve chamber wall.

3. If the clearance measured is not between

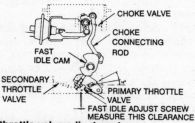

Primary throttle valve adjustment

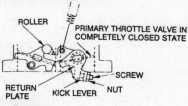

Kick lever adjustment

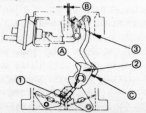

Choke valve opening—1988–91 P'up and Amigo

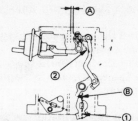

Unloader adjustment—1988–91 P'up and Amigo

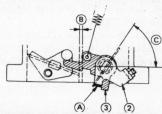

Primary and secondary valve adjustment—1988–91 P'up and Amigo

2.5–3.3mm, bend the adjusting lever tang to adjust.

Primary and Secondary Throttle Valve Adjustment

1988-91 P'up AND AMIGO

1. Slowly open the primary throttle valve until the kick lever tang contacts the return plate.

2. Measure the clearance between the choke valve and the choke valve chamber wall.

3. If the clearance measured is not between 7.0–8.5mm, bend the kick lever tang to adjust.

CARBURETOR REMOVAL AND INSTALLATION

I-Mark

1. Disconnect the negative battery cable.

2. Remove the air cleaner wing nut and disconnect the rubber hoses from the clips on the air cleaner cover.

3. Remove the bracket bolts, if equipped, at the air cleaner and remove the air cleaner cover and filter element.

4. Disconnect the hot air hose (to the hot air duct), the air hose to the air pump at the air cleaner and the vacuum hose at the joint nipple side of the intake manifold.

5. Loosen the bolt clamping the air cleaner to the carburetor. Separate the air cleaner body from the carburetor but do not remove it completely.

6. Disconnect the PCV hose (to the camshaft cover), the rubber hoses to the check and relief valve. Remove the air cleaner body.

7. Disconnect the vacuum hoses from the EGR valve.

8. Disconnect the choke control wire.

9. Disconnect the lead from the throttle solenoid.

10. Disconnect the throttle linkage return spring.

11. Disconnect the accelerator linkage and detent cable, if so equipped.

12. Disconnect the fuel line at the carburetor.

13. Remove the carburetor-to-manifold nuts and the carburetor.

To install:

14. Using a new gasket, install the carburetor to the intake manifold.

15. Connect the fuel line and the accelerator linkage to the carburetor.

16. Connect the throttle linkage return spring, the throttle solenoid lead, the choke control wire and the vacuum hoses to the EGR and the PCV.

17. Install the air cleaner and any necessary hoses.

18. Start the engine and check for fuel leaks.

P'up, Amigo and Trooper

1. Disconnect the negative (–) battery cable.

2. Disconnect the PCV and AIR hose.

3. Remove the air cleaner assembly with the TCA vacuum hose and air duct.

4. Remove the throttle return spring.

5. Label and disconnect the emission control vacuum hoses.

6. Disconnect the lead wire connectors and accelerator cable.

7. Release the fuel pressure and disconnect the fuel pipes.

8. Remove the carburetor retaining nuts and carburetor.

To install:

9. Install the carburetor, gaskets and retaining nuts.

10. Connect the fuel pipes.

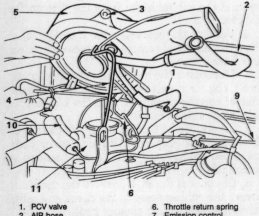

1. PCV valve
2. AIR hose
3. Air cleaner attaching bolts
4. TCA vacuum hose and air duct
5. Air cleaner
6. Throttle return spring
7. Emission control vacuum hoses
8. Lead wire connector
9. Accelerator cable
10. Fuel pipes
11. Carburetor assembly

Carburetor removal—P'up, Amigo and Trooper

11. Connect the lead wire connectors and accelerator cable.

12. Connect the emission control vacuum hoses.

13. Install the throttle return spring.

14. Install the air cleaner assembly with the TCA vacuum hose and air duct.

15. Connect the PCV and AIR hose.

16. Connect the negative (–) battery cable, start the engine and check for leaks.

Idle Speed Adjustment

Refer to the "Idle Speed" section in Chapter 2.

Idle Mixture Adjustment

Refer to the "Idle Mixture" section in Chapter 2.

Carburetor Overhaul

Efficient carburetion depends greatly on careful cleaning and inspection during overhaul, since dirt, gum, water, or varnish in or on the carburetor parts are often responsible for poor performance.

Overhaul your carburetor in a clean, dustfree area. Carefully disassembly the carburetor, referring often to the exploded views and directions packaged with the rebuilding kit. Keep all similar and look alike parts segregated during disassembly and cleaning to avoid accidental interchange during assembly. Make a note of all jet sizes.

NOTE: *Before performing any service on the carburetor, it is recommended that it be placed on a suitable holding fixture, such as Tool J–9789–118, BY–30–15 or equivalent. Without the use of the holding fixture, it is possible to damage throttle valves or other parts of the carburetor.*

When the carburetor is disassembled, wash all parts (except diaphragms, electric choke units, pump plunger, and any other plastic, leather, fiber, or rubber parts) in clean carburetor solvent. Do not leave parts in the solvent any longer than is necessary to sufficiently loosen the deposits. Excessive cleaning may remove the special finish from the float bowl and choke valve bodies, leaving these parts unfit for service. Soak all parts in clean solvent and blow them dry with compressed air or allow them to air dry. Wipe clean all cork, plastic, leather, and fiber parts with a clean, lint free cloth.

Blow out all passages and jets with compressed air and be sure that there are no restrictions or blockages. Never use wire or similar tools to clean jets, fuel passages, or air bleeds. Clean all jets and valves separately to avoid accidental interchange.

1. chamber assembly
2. Counter lever
3. Solenoid switch valve
4. Float chamber assembly
5. Slow cut solenoid valve
6. Throttle chamber assembly
7. Throttle adjusting screw
8. Throttle adjusting spring
9. Idle adjusting screw
10. Idle adjusting spring
11. Idle adjusting washer
12. Idle adjusting rubber seal
13. Diaphragm chamber
14. Diaphragm
15. Diaphragm spring
16. Gasket kit
17. Washer and screw kit A
18. Washer and screw kit B
19. Actuator bracket
20. Rubber hose A
21. Hose clamp A
22. Rubber hose B
23. Fuel nipple
24. Stopping plate
25. Fast idle cam
26. Float fuel level
27. Drain plug lock plate
28. Rubber mount
29. Plate
30. Collar
31. Main actuator
32. Slow actuator
33. Harness assembly
34. Pump lever spring
35. Lock lever
36. Pump lever
37. Throttle return plate
38. Secondary throttle spring
39. Throttle lever
40. Throttle adjusting lever
41. Throttle sleeve A
42. Fast lever adjuster
43. Fast idle screw
44. Pump rod
45. Fast idle cam spring
46. Throttle sleeve B
47. Throttle kick lever
48. Piston return spring
49. Hose clamp B
50. Lead wire holder
51. Injector weight
52. Pump jet screw
53. Injector spring
54. Float set collar
55. Level gauge seal
56. Cylinder plate
57. Dust cover
58. Pump piston
59. Nipple set screw
60. Drain plug
61. Slow jet plug

62. Needle valve filter
63. Slow jet spring
64. Lead wire connector
65. Packing O-ring
66. Needle valve
67. Primary main jet
68. Secondary main jet
69. Primary main air bleed
70. Secondary main air bleed

71. Primary slow jet
72. Secondary slow jet
73. Primary slow air bleed
74. Secondary slow air bleed
75. Collar
76. Down shift lever
77. Connecting lever
78. Rubber cap

Carburetor exploded view—RWD I-Mark and 1981–87 P'up

Check all parts for wear or damage. If wear or damage is found, replace the defective parts.

Especially check the following:

1. Check the float needle and seat for wear. If wear is found, replace the complete assembly.

2. Check the float hinge pin for wear and the floats for dents or distortion. Replace the float if fuel has leaked into it.

3. Check the throttle and choke shaft bores for wear or an out-of-round condition. Damage or wear to the throttle arm, shaft, or shaft bore will often require replacement of the throttle body. These parts require a close tolerance of fit; wear may allow air leakage, which could affect starting and idling.

NOTE: *Throttle shafts and bushings are not included in overhaul kits. They can be purchased separately.*

4. Inspect the idle mixture adjusting needles for burrs or grooves. Any such condition requires replacement of the needle, since you will not be able to obtain a satisfactory idle.

39. Throttle adjust screw spring
40. Throttle adjust arm
41. Throttle assist return spring
42. Throttle assist return spring bushing
43. Mixture bypass solenoid
44. Throttle sensor arm
45. Primary throttle arm
46. Throttle switch

66. Engine control cable bracket
67. Link assembly
68. Throttle return spring
69. Clamp
70. Clamp
71. Clamp
72. Rubber clamp
73. TPS bracket
74. FICD lever spring
75. FICD and nut
76. FICD bracket
77. Level gauge gasket
78. Small venturi gasket
79. Diaphragm chamber gasket
80. Level gauge cover gasket
81. Body gasket
82. Insulator flange
83. Small venturi rubber
84. Idle screw seal
85. Mixture bypass screw O-ring
86. Feed back solenoid O-ring
87. Feed back solenoid O-ring
88. Cotter pin
89. Check ball
90. E-clip
91. E-clip
92. E-clip
93. Nut
94. Nut
95. Nut
96. Main jet packing
97. Solenoid valve packing
98. Main jet passage packing
99. Float valve seat packing
100. TPS arm pin
101. Screw
102. Screw and washer
103. Screw and washer
104. Screw and washer
105. Screw and washer
106. Screw and washer
107. Screw and washer
108. Screw and washer
109. Screw and washer
110. Screw and washer
111. Spring washer
112. Spring washer
113. Washer
114. Washer
115. Washer
116. Washer
117. Screw
118. Screw and washer
119. Screw, spring washer
120. Screw, spring washer
121. Screw
122. Screw
123. Bolt and washer
124. Pump air washer
125. Solenoid packing
126. Mixture bypass solenoid
127. Throttle opener

1. Body
2. Slow jet
3. Step jet
4. Primary main jet
5. Secondary main jet
6. Primary main air bleed
7. Secondary main air bleed
8. Mixture bypass jet
9. Small primary venturi
10. Small secondary venturi
11. Pump weight
12. Pump injector spring
13. Pump strainer
14. Pump strainer clip
15. Pump return spring
16. Flat screw plug
17. Main passage plug
18. Glass level gauge
19. Level gauge cover
20. Slow cut solenoid
21. Diaphragm chamber
22. Diaphragm spring
23. Diaphragm assembly

24. Plunger
25. 2nd lock spring hanger
26. Mixture bypass screw
27. Complete flange
28. Complete flange
29. Lever assembly
30. Plate return collar
31. Return plate assembly
32. Lever
33. Throttle lever
34. FICD lever
35. Spring
36. Idle mixture adjust screw
37. Idle mixture adjust screw spring
38. Throttle adjust screw

47. Throttle sensor
48. Air horn
49. Air horn
50. Housing
51. Housing
52. Secondary slow air bleed
53. Pump plunger bellows
54. Rubber pipe
55. Choke piston link
56. Float valve
57. Float assembly
58. Float pin
59. Choke piston
60. Air vent solenoid
61. Feedback solenoid
62. Pump arm
63. Pump arm spring
64. Pump rod
65. Secondary lock spring

Carburetor exploded view—FWD I-Mark 4XC1-U

5. Test the accelerator pump check valves. They should pass air one way but not the other. Test for proper seating by blowing and sucking on the valve. Replace the valve as necessary. If the valve is satisfactory, wash the valve again to remove breath moisture.

6. Check the bowl cover for warped surfaces with a straightedge.

7. Closely inspect the valves and seats for wear and damage, replacing as necessary.

8. After the carburetor is assembled, check the choke valve for freedom of operation.

Carburetor overhaul kits are recommended for each overhaul. These kits contain all gaskets and new parts to replace those which deteriorate most rapidly. Failure to replace all parts supplied with the kit (especially gaskets) can result in poor performance later.

Some carburetor manufacturers supply overhaul kits of three basic types: minor repair; major repair; and gasket kits. Basically, they contain the following:

Minor Repair Kits:
- All gasket
- Float needle valve
- Volume control screw
- All diaphragms
- Spring for the pump diaphragm

Major Repair Kits:
- All jets and gaskets

- All diaphragms
- Float needle valve
- Volume control screw
- Pump ball valve
- Float
- Complete intermediate rod
- Intermediate pump lever
- Some cover holddown screws and washers

Gasket Kits:
- All gaskets

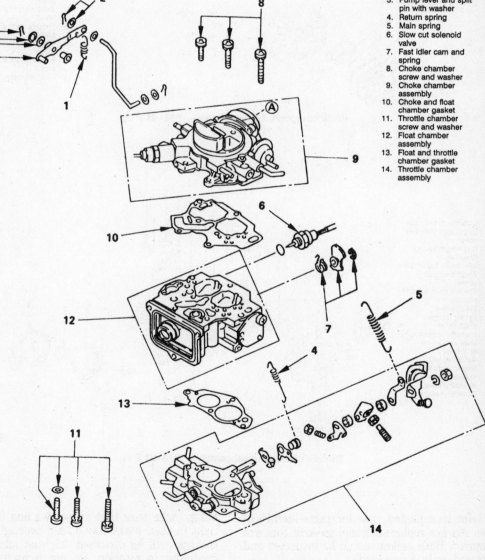

1. Assist spring
2. Pump rod split pin with washer
3. Pump lever and split pin with washer
4. Return spring
5. Main spring
6. Slow cut solenoid valve
7. Fast idler cam and spring
8. Choke chamber screw and washer
9. Choke chamber assembly
10. Choke and float chamber gasket
11. Throttle chamber screw and washer
12. Float chamber assembly
13. Float and throttle chamber gasket
14. Throttle chamber assembly

Major component disassembly—1988–91 P'up

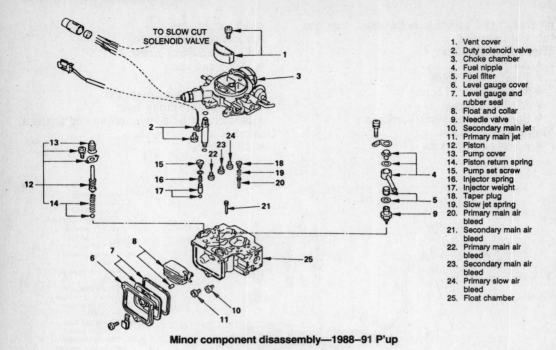

TO SLOW CUT
SOLENOID VALVE

1. Vent cover
2. Duty solenoid valve
3. Choke chamber
4. Fuel nipple
5. Fuel filter
6. Level gauge cover
7. Level gauge and rubber seal
8. Float and collar
9. Needle valve
10. Secondary main jet
11. Primary main jet
12. Piston
13. Pump cover
14. Piston return spring
15. Pump set screw
16. Injector spring
17. Injector weight
18. Taper plug
19. Slow jet spring
20. Primary main air bleed
21. Secondary main air bleed
22. Primary main air bleed
23. Secondary main air bleed
24. Primary slow air bleed
25. Float chamber

Minor component disassembly—1988–91 P'up

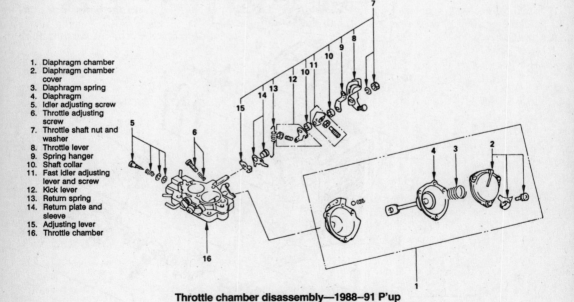

1. Diaphragm chamber
2. Diaphragm chamber cover
3. Diaphragm spring
4. Diaphragm
5. Idler adjusting screw
6. Throttle adjusting screw
7. Throttle shaft nut and washer
8. Throttle lever
9. Spring hanger
10. Shaft collar
11. Fast idler adjusting lever and screw
12. Kick lever
13. Return spring
14. Return plate and sleeve
15. Adjusting lever
16. Throttle chamber

Throttle chamber disassembly—1988–91 P'up

Refer to exploded view for parts identification. Always replace internal gaskets that are removed. Base gasket should be inspected and replaced, only if damaged.

After cleaning and checking all components, reassemble the carburetor, using new parts and referring to the exploded view. When reassembling, make sure that all screws and jets are tight in their seats, buy do not overtighten as the tips will be distorted. Tighten all screws gradually, in rotation. Do not tighten needle valves into their seats; uneven jetting will result. Always use new gaskets. Be sure to adjust the float level when reassembling.

GASOLINE FUEL INJECTION

Throttle Body

REMOVAL AND INSTALLATION

Except V6 Engine

1. Disconnect the negative (–) battery cable.
2. Remove the air intake duct.
3. Drain the engine coolant below the throttle body assembly.
4. Disconnect accelerator cable, vacuum and coolant hoses.
5. Remove the four throttle body attaching bolts and throttle body assembly.

To install:

6. Clean the gasket mating surfaces with a scraper and solvent.
7. Install the four throttle body attaching bolts and throttle body assembly.
8. Connect accelerator cable, vacuum and coolant hoses.
9. Refill the engine coolant.
10. Install the air intake duct.
11. Connect the negative (–) battery cable and check for leaks.

V6 Engine

1. Disconnect the negative (–) battery cable.
2. Relieve the fuel pressure and remove the air cleaner.

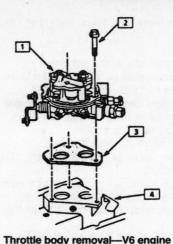

1. TBI unit
2. Bolt, 18 ft. lbs. (25 Nm)
3. Gasket
4. Intake manifold

Throttle body removal—V6 engine

3. Disconnect the throttle body electrical connectors.
4. Disconnect the throttle cable, transmission cable and cruise control cable.
5. Remove the cable support brackets.
6. Label and disconnect the vacuum hoses.
7. Using a backup wrench, disconnect the fuel pressure and return lines.
8. Remove the TBI attaching bolts, TBI unit and gasket.
9. Place a shop towel in the intake manifold

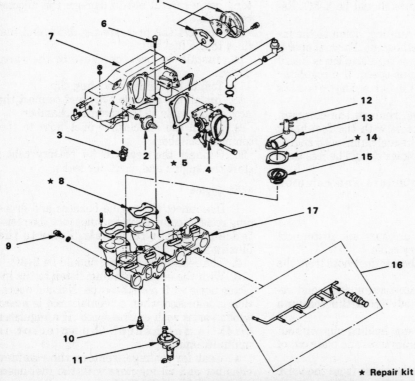

1. EGR valve
2. Dashpot
3. Thermal vacuum valve
4. Throttle valve assembly
5. Throttle valve gasket
6. Intake bolt
7. Common chamber
8. Common chamber gasket
9. Water temperature sensor
10. Water temperature unit
11. Air regulator
12. Thermal valve
13. Water outlet pipe
14. Gasket
15. Thermostat
16. Fuel injector with pipe
17. Intake manifold

★ **Repair kit**

Intake manifold and throttle body assembly—G200Z and 4ZC1-T engine

openings to prevent dirt from entering the engine.

To install:

10. Clean the gasket mating surfaces.

11. Install the new gasket, TBI unit and bolts. Torque the bolts to 18 ft. lbs. (25 Nm).

12. Install the fuel lines with new O-ring gaskets. Torque the lines to 20 ft. lbs. (27 Nm).

13. Connect the vacuum hoses.

14. Install the cable support bracket.

15. Install the throttle, transmission and cruise control cables.

16. Connect all electrical wiring. Make sure the connectors are fully seated and latched.

17. Install the air cleaner and connect the battery cable.

18. Reset the IAC pintle by depressing the accelerator pedal slightly, start the engine and run for three seconds, turn the ignition OFF for ten seconds, restart the engine and check for proper idle.

Fuel Injector

INSPECTION, REMOVAL AND INSTALLATION

4XC1-T I-Mark
Impulse G200Z and 4ZC1-T engine

1. Disconnect the injector harness connector and measure the resistance between the injector terminals. Resistance should be 2–3Ω. Reconnect the harness.

2. With the engine running, listen to the injector noise with a stethoscope. Normal operation is indicated when a regular click is heard which varies with engine speed. If a regulator click is not heard, the injector is malfunctioning.

3. Test for leakage, remove the common chamber and all injectors with the fuel hoses connected. Turn ON the fuel pump with engine NOT running. The leakage should be less than 2 drops per minute.

4. Install the injectors and common chamber.

4XE1 Engine

1. Release the fuel pressure and disconnect the negative (–) battery cable.

2. Remove the air cleaner duct hose from the common chamber.

3. Disconnect the accelerator cable and remove the throttle body from the common chamber.

4. Release the canister holding clip without disconnecting the vacuum lines and place out of the way.

5. Remove the breather hose from the valve cover.

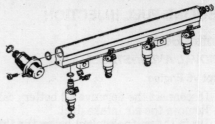

Fuel rail and injectors—4XE1 engine

6. Disconnect the pressure regulator and fuel lines from the fuel rail.

7. Disconnect the injection harness from the injectors, being careful not to damage the injector terminals.

8. Remove the two fuel rail attaching bolts.

9. Disconnect the fuel lines and remove the fuel rail assembly with the injectors.

10. Release the injector retaining clips and remove the injectors.

To install:

11. Lubricate the injector seals with motor oil and install the injector into the fuel rail. Lock the retaining clip.

12. Install the fuel rail assembly and connect the fuel lines. Make sure all seals are positioned properly and use backup wrenches on the fuel lines.

13. Install the two fuel rail attaching bolts.

14. Connect the injection harness to the injectors, being careful not to damage the injector terminals.

15. Connect the pressure regulator and fuel lines to the fuel rail.

16. Install the breather hose to the valve cover.

17. Install the canister holding clip.

18. Install the throttle body and connect the accelerator cable to the common chamber.

19. Install the air cleaner duct hose to the common chamber.

20. Connect the negative (–) battery cable, start the engine and check for leaks.

4ZE1 Engine

1. Disconnect the engine harness and dropping resistor connectors and measure the resistance across the terminals. Refer to the illustration.

2. The resistance reading should be 2–3Ω.

3. With the engine running, listen to the injector noise with a stethoscope. Normal operation is indicated when a regular click is heard which varies with engine speed. If a regulator click is not heard, the injector is malfunctioning.

4. Test for leakage, remove the common chamber and all injectors with the fuel hoses connected. Turn ON the fuel pump with engine

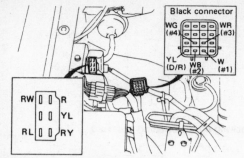

Fuel injector check—4ZE1 engine

CYL No.	Dropping resistor connector	Engine harness connector
1	R (Red) ——————————	W (White)
2	RW (Red/White) ————	WB (White/Black)
3	RY (Red/Yellow) ————	WR (White/Red)
4	RL (Red/Blue) —————	WG (White/Green)

Injector harness connector wiring

NOT running. The leakage should be less than 2 drops per minute.

The engine is equipped 4 fuel injectors, with one located at each cylinder.

1. Relieve the fuel pressure.
2. Disconnect the negative battery cable.
3. Label and disconnect the electrical connectors from the fuel injectors.
4. Disconnect the fuel rail from the fuel system.
5. Remove the fuel rail from the intake manifold; pull the fuel rail with the injectors connected from the intake manifold.
6. Separate the fuel injectors from the fuel rail.

To install:

7. Replace the fuel injector O-rings.
8. Install the fuel injectors to the fuel rail.
9. Lubricate the fuel injector O-rings with automatic transmission fluid and press them, with the fuel rail, into the intake manifold.
10. Install the fuel rail-to-intake manifold bolts.
11. Connect the fuel rail to the fuel system.
12. Connect the electrical connectors to the fuel injectors.
13. Connect the negative battery cable.
14. Turn the ignition switch **ON** and check for fuel leaks at the fuel rail.

V6 Engine

The engine is equipped with 2 fuel injectors, both are located in the throttle body.

1. Relieve the fuel pressure.
2. Disconnect the negative battery cable.
3. Remove the air cleaner.
4. At the injector electrical connectors,

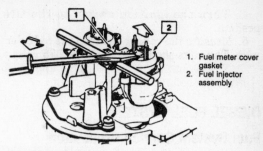

1. Fuel meter cover gasket
2. Fuel injector assembly

Fuel injector removal—V6 engine

squeeze the 2 tabs together and pull them straight upward.

5. Remove the fuel meter cover and leave the cover gasket in place.
6. Using a small pry bar, carefully pry the injectors upward until they are free of the throttle body.
7. Remove the small O-ring from the nozzle end of the injector. Carefully rotate the injector's fuel filter back-and-forth to remove it from the base of the injector.
8. Discard the fuel meter cover gasket.
9. Remove the large O-ring and back-up washer from the top of the counterbore of the fuel meter body injector cavity.

To install:

10. Lubricate the O-rings with automatic transmission fluid and push them into the fuel injector cavities.
11. Install the new fuel meter cover gasket and cover.
12. Install the electrical connectors to the injectors.
13. Install the air cleaner and connect the negative battery cable.

Throttle Valve Switch (Throttle Position Sensor)

INSPECTION, REMOVAL AND INSTALLATION

G200Z, 4XC1-Turbo and 4ZC1-Turbo Engine

The throttle position sensor is mounted on the throttle body assembly at the opposite side of the throttle cable.

NOTE: *The throttle valve stopper screw is factory set and sealed with paint. Setting of the screw should not be disturbed unless absolutely necessary.*

1. **Adjustment**: check that the throttle valve is completely closed. Loosen the throttle position sensor (TPS) mounting screws slightly.
2. Remove the water shield cover but do not remove the connector.
3. Place the circuit tester positive probe in the red color wire (No. 5 pin).

4. Turn the ignition switch to the ON position.

5. Measure the voltage between the red color wire. The volts should be 3.75 ± 0.075 volts.

DIESEL FUEL SYSTEM

Fuel System Service Precaution

Disconnect the negative battery cable. Keep a Class B dry chemical fire extinguisher available. Always relieve the fuel pressure before disconnecting a fuel line. Wrap a shop cloth around the fuel line when disconnecting a fuel line. Always use new O-rings. Do not replace the fuel pipes with fuel hoses. Always us a back-up wrench when opening or closing a fuel line.

Injection Lines

Use backup and flarenut wrenches to remove the pump-to-injector nozzle lines. These lines may be damaged if the proper wrenches are not used.

Fuel Injector

REMOVAL AND INSTALLATION

1. Relieve the fuel system pressure.
2. Remove the fuel pressure line(s) and return line(s) from the fuel injector(s).
3. Remove the fuel injector(s) from the engine.
4. Remove the O-rings from the fuel injector.
To install:
5. Using new O-rings, lubricate them in diesel fuel and install them onto the fuel injector(s).
6. Install the fuel injector(s) into the engine.
7. Using new O-rings, install the fuel pressure line(s) and return line(s) onto the fuel injector(s).

INSPECTION

CAUTION: *When using the injector tester, test fluid will spray out of the injector nozzle at great pressure which can easily puncture the skin or eyes. Since a defective injector may spray in any direction, make sure the hands and eyes are placed away from the injector outlet and protective clothing and safety glasses are used.*

Injector Opening Pressure Test

Remove the injector and install a injector tester J-28829 or equivalent. Measure the injector pressure.
- 4FB1 engine – 1706 psi (120 kg/cm²)
- C223 engine – 1493 psi (105 kg/cm²)
- C223-T engine –1920 psi (135 kg/cm²)

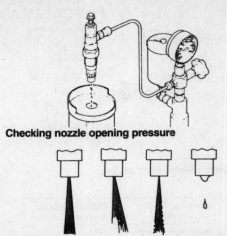

Checking nozzle opening pressure

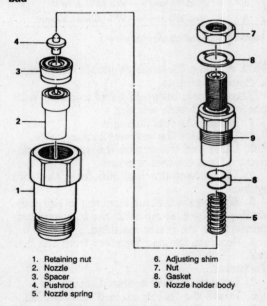

Injector spray pattern—1st pattern is good, rest is bad

1. Retaining nut	6. Adjusting shim
2. Nozzle	7. Nut
3. Spacer	8. Gasket
4. Pushrod	9. Nozzle holder body
5. Nozzle spring	

Injector nozzle—4FB1 diesel engine

Injector Leakage Test

Using the injector tester J-28829, maintain a pressure of 284 psi (20 kg/cm²). If there is no leakage, the injector is satisfactory.

Injector Spray Pattern

Observe the spray pattern coming from the outlet. It should be a fine uniform spray. If not, clean or replace injector.

DISASSEMBLY AND ASSEMBLY

4FB1 Engine

1. Remove the injector from the vehicle.
2. Place the injector in a vise clamping the hexagonal portion in the vise. Loosen the retaining nut and remove it.

CHILTON'S
FUEL ECONOMY
& TUNE-UP TIPS

55 WAYS TO IMPROVE FUEL ECONOMY

Tune-up • Spark Plug Diagnosis • Emission Controls

Fuel System • Cooling System • Tires and Wheels

General Maintenance

CHILTON'S FUEL ECONOMY & TUNE-UP TIPS

Fuel economy is important to everyone, no matter what kind of vehicle you drive. The maintenance-minded motorist can save both money and fuel using these tips and the periodic maintenance and tune-up procedures in this Repair and Tune-Up Guide.

There are more than 130,000,000 cars and trucks registered for private use in the United States. Each travels an average of 10-12,000 miles per year, and, and in total they consume close to 70 billion gallons of fuel each year. This represents nearly ⅔ of the oil imported by the United States each year. The Federal government's goal is to reduce consumption 10% by 1985. A variety of methods are either already in use or under serious consideration, and they all affect you driving and the cars you will drive. In addition to "down-sizing", the auto industry is using or investigating the use of electronic fuel delivery, electronic engine controls and alternative engines for use in smaller and lighter vehicles, among other alternatives to meet the federally mandated Corporate Average Fuel Economy (CAFE) of 27.5 mpg by 1985. The government, for its part, is considering rationing, mandatory driving curtailments and tax increases on motor vehicle fuel in an effort to reduce consumption. The government's goal of a 10% reduction could be realized — and further government regulation avoided — if every private vehicle could use just 1 less gallon of fuel per week.

How Much Can You Save?

Tests have proven that almost anyone can make at least a 10% reduction in fuel consumption through regular maintenance and tune-ups. When a major manufacturer of spark plugs sur-

TUNE-UP

1. Check the cylinder compression to be sure the engine will really benefit from a tune-up and that it is capable of producing good fuel economy. A tune-up will be wasted on an engine in poor mechanical condition.

2. Replace spark plugs regularly. New spark plugs alone can increase fuel economy 3%.

3. Be sure the spark plugs are the correct type (heat range) for your vehicle. See the Tune-Up Specifications.

Heat range refers to the spark plug's ability to conduct heat away from the firing end. It must conduct the heat away in an even pattern to avoid becoming a source of pre-ignition, yet it must also operate hot enough to burn off conductive deposits that could cause misfiring.

The heat range is usually indicated by a number on the spark plug, part of the manufacturer's designation for each individual spark plug. The numbers in bold-face indicate the heat range in each manufacturer's identification system.

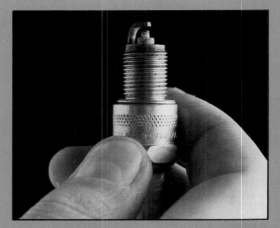

Periodically, check the spark plugs to be sure they are firing efficiently. They are excellent indicators of the internal condition of your engine.

Manufacturer	Typical Designation
AC	R **45** TS
Bosch (old)	WA **145** T30
Bosch (new)	HR **8** Y
Champion	RBL **15** Y
Fram/Autolite	4**15**
Mopar	P-**62** PR
Motorcraft	BRF-**42**
NGK	BP **5** ES-15
Nippondenso	W **16** EP
Prestolite	14GR **5** 2A

On AC, Bosch (new), Champion, Fram/Autolite, Mopar, Motorcraft and Prestolite, a higher number indicates a hotter plug. On Bosch (old), NGK and Nippondenso, a higher number indicates a colder plug.

4. Make sure the spark plugs are properly gapped. See the Tune-Up Specifications in this book.

5. Be sure the spark plugs are firing efficiently. The illustrations on the next 2 pages show you how to "read" the firing end of the spark plug.

6. Check the ignition timing and set it to specifications. Tests show that almost all cars have incorrect ignition timing by more than 2°.

veyed over 6,000 cars nationwide, they found that a tune-up, on cars that needed one, increased fuel economy over 11%. Replacing worn plugs alone, accounted for a 3% increase. The same test also revealed that 8 out of every 10 vehicles will have some maintenance deficiency that will directly affect fuel economy, emissions or performance. Most of this mileage-robbing neglect could be prevented with regular maintenance.

Modern engines require that all of the functioning systems operate properly for maximum efficiency. A malfunction anywhere wastes fuel. You can keep your vehicle running as efficiently and economically as possible, by being aware of your vehicle's operating and performance characteristics. If your vehicle suddenly develops performance or fuel economy problems it could be due to one or more of the following:

PROBLEM	POSSIBLE CAUSE
Engine Idles Rough	Ignition timing, idle mixture, vacuum leak or something amiss in the emission control system.
Hesitates on Acceleration	Dirty carburetor or fuel filter, improper accelerator pump setting, ignition timing or fouled spark plugs.
Starts Hard or Fails to Start	Worn spark plugs, improperly set automatic choke, ice (or water) in fuel system.
Stalls Frequently	Automatic choke improperly adjusted and possible dirty air filter or fuel filter.
Performs Sluggishly	Worn spark plugs, dirty fuel or air filter, ignition timing or automatic choke out of adjustment.

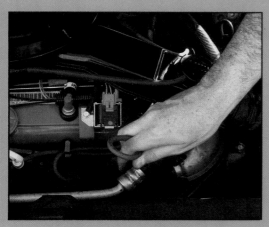

Check spark plug wires on conventional point type ignition for cracks by bending them in a loop around your finger.

Be sure that spark plug wires leading to adjacent cylinders do not run too close together. (Photo courtesy Champion Spark Plug Co.)

7. If your vehicle does not have electronic ignition, check the points, rotor and cap as specified.

8. Check the spark plug wires (used with conventional point-type ignitions) for cracks and burned or broken insulation by bending them in a loop around your finger. Cracked wires decrease fuel efficiency by failing to deliver full voltage to the spark plugs. One misfiring spark plug can cost you as much as 2 mpg.

9. Check the routing of the plug wires. Misfiring can be the result of spark plug leads to adjacent cylinders running parallel to each other and too close together. One wire tends to pick up voltage from the other causing it to fire "out of time".

10. Check all electrical and ignition circuits for voltage drop and resistance.

11. Check the distributor mechanical and/or vacuum advance mechanisms for proper functioning. The vacuum advance can be checked by twisting the distributor plate in the opposite direction of rotation. It should spring back when released.

12. Check and adjust the valve clearance on engines with mechanical lifters. The clearance should be slightly loose rather than too tight.

SPARK PLUG DIAGNOSIS

Normal

APPEARANCE: This plug is typical of one operating normally. The insulator nose varies from a light tan to grayish color with slight electrode wear. The presence of slight deposits is normal on used plugs and will have no adverse effect on engine performance. The spark plug heat range is correct for the engine and the engine is running normally.

CAUSE: Properly running engine.

RECOMMENDATION: Before reinstalling this plug, the electrodes should be cleaned and filed square. Set the gap to specifications. If the plug has been in service for more than 10-12,000 miles, the entire set should probably be replaced with a fresh set of the same heat range.

Oil Deposits

APPEARANCE: The firing end of the plug is covered with a wet, oily coating.

CAUSE: The problem is poor oil control. On high mileage engines, oil is leaking past the rings or valve guides into the combustion chamber. A common cause is also a plugged PCV valve, and a ruptured fuel pump diaphragm can also cause this condition. Oil fouled plugs such as these are often found in new or recently overhauled engines, before normal oil control is achieved, and can be cleaned and reinstalled.

RECOMMENDATION: A hotter spark plug may temporarily relieve the problem, but the engine is probably in need of work.

Incorrect Heat Range

APPEARANCE: The effects of high temperature on a spark plug are indicated by clean white, often blistered insulator. This can also be accompanied by excessive wear of the electrode, and the absence of deposits.

CAUSE: Check for the correct spark plug heat range. A plug which is too hot for the engine can result in overheating. A car operated mostly at high speeds can require a colder plug. Also check ignition timing, cooling system level, fuel mixture and leaking intake manifold.

RECOMMENDATION: If all ignition and engine adjustments are known to be correct, and no other malfunction exists, install spark plugs one heat range colder.

Photos Courtesy Fram Corporation

Carbon Deposits

APPEARANCE: Carbon fouling is easily identified by the presence of dry, soft, black, sooty deposits.

CAUSE: Changing the heat range can often lead to carbon fouling, as can prolonged slow, stop-and-start driving. If the heat range is correct, carbon fouling can be attributed to a rich fuel mixture, sticking choke, clogged air cleaner, worn breaker points, retarded timing or low compression. If only one or two plugs are carbon fouled, check for corroded or cracked wires on the affected plugs. Also look for cracks in the distributor cap between the towers of affected cylinders.

RECOMMENDATION: After the problem is corrected, these plugs can be cleaned and reinstalled if not worn severely.

MMT Fouled

APPEARANCE: Spark plugs fouled by MMT (Methycyclopentadienyl Maganese Tricarbonyl) have reddish, rusty appearance on the insulator and side electrode.

CAUSE: MMT is an anti-knock additive in gasoline used to replace lead. During the combustion process, the MMT leaves a reddish deposit on the insulator and side electrode.

RECOMMENDATION: No engine malfunction is indicated and the deposits will not affect plug performance any more than lead deposits (see Ash Deposits). MMT fouled plugs can be cleaned, regapped and reinstalled.

High Speed Glazing

APPEARANCE: Glazing appears as shiny coating on the plug, either yellow or tan in color.

CAUSE: During hard, fast acceleration, plug temperatures rise suddenly. Deposits from normal combustion have no chance to fluff-off; instead, they melt on the insulator forming an electrically conductive coating which causes misfiring.

RECOMMENDATION: Glazed plugs are not easily cleaned. They should be replaced with a fresh set of plugs of the correct heat range. If the condition recurs, using plugs with a heat range one step colder may cure the problem.

Ash (Lead) Deposits

APPEARANCE: Ash deposits are characterized by light brown or white colored deposits crusted on the side or center electrodes. In some cases it may give the plug a rusty appearance.

CAUSE: Ash deposits are normally derived from oil or fuel additives burned during normal combustion. Normally they are harmless, though excessive amounts can cause misfiring. If deposits are excessive in short mileage, the valve guides may be worn.

RECOMMENDATION: Ash-fouled plugs can be cleaned, gapped and reinstalled.

Detonation

APPEARANCE: Detonation is usually characterized by a broken plug insulator.

CAUSE: A portion of the fuel charge will begin to burn spontaneously, from the increased heat following ignition. The explosion that results applies extreme pressure to engine components, frequently damaging spark plugs and pistons.

Detonation can result by over-advanced ignition timing, inferior gasoline (low octane) lean air/fuel mixture, poor carburetion, engine lugging or an increase in compression ratio due to combustion chamber deposits or engine modification.

RECOMMENDATION: Replace the plugs after correcting the problem.

EMISSION CONTROLS

13. Be aware of the general condition of the emission control system. It contributes to reduced pollution and should be serviced regularly to maintain efficient engine operation.

14. Check all vacuum lines for dried, cracked or brittle conditions. Something as simple as a leaking vacuum hose can cause poor performance and loss of economy.

15. Avoid tampering with the emission control system. Attempting to improve fuel econ-

FUEL SYSTEM

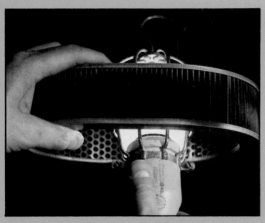

Check the air filter with a light behind it. If you can see light through the filter it can be reused.

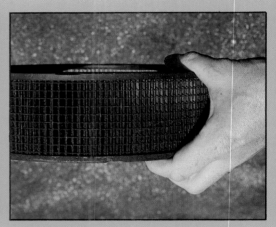

Extremely clogged filters should be discarded and replaced with a new one.

18. Replace the air filter regularly. A dirty air filter richens the air/fuel mixture and can increase fuel consumption as much as 10%. Tests show that ⅓ of all vehicles have air filters in need of replacement.

19. Replace the fuel filter at least as often as recommended.

20. Set the idle speed and carburetor mixture to specifications.

21. Check the automatic choke. A sticking or malfunctioning choke wastes gas.

22. During the summer months, adjust the automatic choke for a leaner mixture which will produce faster engine warm-ups.

COOLING SYSTEM

29. Be sure all accessory drive belts are in good condition. Check for cracks or wear.

30. Adjust all accessory drive belts to proper tension.

31. Check all hoses for swollen areas, worn spots, or loose clamps.

32. Check coolant level in the radiator or expansion tank.

33. Be sure the thermostat is operating properly. A stuck thermostat delays engine warm-up and a cold engine uses nearly twice as much fuel as a warm engine.

34. Drain and replace the engine coolant at least as often as recommended. Rust and scale

TIRES & WHEELS

38. Check the tire pressure often with a pencil type gauge. Tests by a major tire manufacturer show that 90% of all vehicles have at least 1 tire improperly inflated. Better mileage can be achieved by over-inflating tires, but never exceed the maximum inflation pressure on the side of the tire.

39. If possible, install radial tires. Radial tires deliver as much as ½ mpg more than bias belted tires.

40. Avoid installing super-wide tires. They only create extra rolling resistance and decrease fuel mileage. Stick to the manufacturer's recommendations.

41. Have the wheels properly balanced.

omy by tampering with emission controls is more likely to worsen fuel economy than improve it. Emission control changes on modern engines are not readily reversible.

16. Clean (or replace) the EGR valve and lines as recommended.

17. Be sure that all vacuum lines and hoses are reconnected properly after working under the hood. An unconnected or misrouted vacuum line can wreak havoc with engine performance.

23. Check for fuel leaks at the carburetor, fuel pump, fuel lines and fuel tank. Be sure all lines and connections are tight.

24. Periodically check the tightness of the carburetor and intake manifold attaching nuts and bolts. These are a common place for vacuum leaks to occur.

25. Clean the carburetor periodically and lubricate the linkage.

26. The condition of the tailpipe can be an excellent indicator of proper engine combustion. After a long drive at highway speeds, the inside of the tailpipe should be a light grey in color. Black or soot on the insides indicates an overly rich mixture.

27. Check the fuel pump pressure. The fuel pump may be supplying more fuel than the engine needs.

28. Use the proper grade of gasoline for your engine. Don't try to compensate for knocking or "pinging" by advancing the ignition timing. This practice will only increase plug temperature and the chances of detonation or pre-ignition with relatively little performance gain.

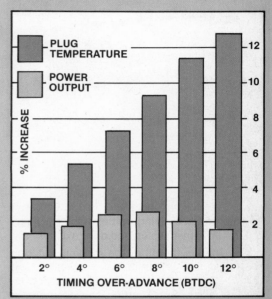

Increasing ignition timing past the specified setting results in a drastic increase in spark plug temperature with increased chance of detonation or preignition. Performance increase is considerably less. (Photo courtesy Champion Spark Plug Co.)

that form in the engine should be flushed out to allow the engine to operate at peak efficiency.

35. Clean the radiator of debris that can decrease cooling efficiency.

36. Install a flex-type or electric cooling fan, if you don't have a clutch type fan. Flex fans use curved plastic blades to push more air at low speeds when more cooling is needed; at high speeds the blades flatten out for less resistance. Electric fans only run when the engine temperature reaches a predetermined level.

37. Check the radiator cap for a worn or cracked gasket. If the cap does not seal properly, the cooling system will not function properly.

42. Be sure the front end is correctly aligned. A misaligned front end actually has wheels going in differed directions. The increased drag can reduce fuel economy by .3 mpg.

43. Correctly adjust the wheel bearings. Wheel bearings that are adjusted too tight increase rolling resistance.

Check tire pressures regularly with a reliable pocket type gauge. Be sure to check the pressure on a cold tire.

GENERAL MAINTENANCE

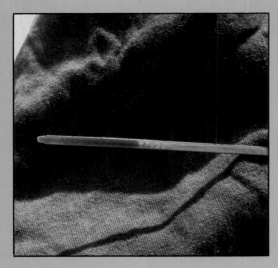

Check the fluid levels (particularly engine oil) on a regular basis. Be sure to check the oil for grit, water or other contamination.

A vacuum gauge is another excellent indicator of internal engine condition and can also be installed in the dash as a mileage indicator.

44. Periodically check the fluid levels in the engine, power steering pump, master cylinder, automatic transmission and drive axle.

45. Change the oil at the recommended interval and change the filter at every oil change. Dirty oil is thick and causes extra friction between moving parts, cutting efficiency and increasing wear. A worn engine requires more frequent tune-ups and gets progressively worse fuel economy. In general, use the lightest viscosity oil for the driving conditions you will encounter.

46. Use the recommended viscosity fluids in the transmission and axle.

47. Be sure the battery is fully charged for fast starts. A slow starting engine wastes fuel.

48. Be sure battery terminals are clean and tight.

49. Check the battery electrolyte level and add distilled water if necessary.

50. Check the exhaust system for crushed pipes, blockages and leaks.

51. Adjust the brakes. Dragging brakes or brakes that are not releasing create increased drag on the engine.

52. Install a vacuum gauge or miles-per-gallon gauge. These gauges visually indicate engine vacuum in the intake manifold. High vacuum = good mileage and low vacuum = poorer mileage. The gauge can also be an excellent indicator of internal engine conditions.

53. Be sure the clutch is properly adjusted. A slipping clutch wastes fuel.

54. Check and periodically lubricate the heat control valve in the exhaust manifold. A sticking or inoperative valve prevents engine warm-up and wastes gas.

55. Keep accurate records to check fuel economy over a period of time. A sudden drop in fuel economy may signal a need for tune-up or other maintenance.

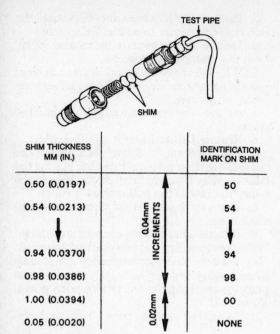

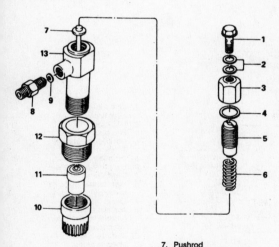

SHIM THICKNESS MM (IN.)	IDENTIFICATION MARK ON SHIM
0.50 (0.0197)	50
0.54 (0.0213)	54
↓	↓
0.94 (0.0370)	94
0.98 (0.0386)	98
1.00 (0.0394)	00
0.05 (0.0020)	NONE

Injector nozzle adjuster

1. Eye bolt
2. Gasket
3. Cap nut
4. Gasket
5. Adjusting screw
6. Nozzle spring
7. Pushrod
8. Inlet connector
9. Gasket
10. Retaining nut
11. Nozzle
12. Setting screw
13. Nozzle holding body

Injector nozzle—C223 and C223-T diesel engine

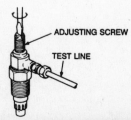

Injector nozzle adjuster—C223 and C223-T engine

3. Remove the nozzle, spacer and pushrod.

4. Remove the nozzle spring, adjusting shim and nut.

5. Remove the gasket from the nozzle body.

6. **Injector opening pressure adjustment:**

a. Using the injector holder and injector tester. Adjust the opening pressure by setting pressure adjusting shim until desired pressure is obtained.

b. The injector pressure can be at a rate of 68 psi (4.8 kg/cm^2) every thickness change of the shim by 0.04mm. Add one 0.05mm to increase the pressure by 85 psi (6 kg/cm^2).

7. Install the injector components and torque the retaining nut to 65 ft. lbs. (88 Nm).

C223 and C223-T Engine

1. Remove the injector from the vehicle.

2. Place the injector in a vise clamping the hexagonal portion in the vise. Loosen the retaining nut and remove it.

3. Remove the eye bold, gasket, cap nut and gasket.

4. Remove the adjusting screw, nozzle spring and pushrod.

5. Remove the inlet connector, gasket and retaining nut.

6. Remove the setting screw and nozzle holding body.

7. **Injector opening pressure adjust-**

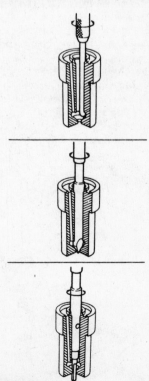

Injector cleaning

ment: Using the injector holder and injector tester. Adjust the opening pressure by setting pressure adjusting screw until desired pressure is obtained.

8. Install the cap nut and torque to 22–29 ft. lbs. (3–4 Nm).

9. Assembly the injector and torque the retaining nut to 65 ft. lbs. (88 Nm).

CLEANING

Remove the carbon from the outside of the nozzle body with a soft brush. Clean the sac portion of the body with a rod J-28826-2. Clean the nozzle seat of the body with a cleaning tool J-28826. Clean the injection hole of the body with a rod J-28826-4.

Diesel Injection Pump
REMOVAL AND INSTALLATION

1. Disconnect the negative battery cable.
2. Remove the timing belt cover.

3. Remove the fuel lines and disconnect the electrical connectors from the fuel injector.

4. Using a pry bar, remove the tension spring from the timing belt tensioner.

NOTE: *When removing the tension spring, avoid using excessive force for the spring may become distorted.*

5. Remove the tensioner pulley bolt and the pulley.

6. Remove the timing belt and discard it.

7. Using a 6mm, 1.25 pitch bolt, install the threaded portion into the threaded hole in the timing pulley housing through the hole in the pulley to prevent the pulley from turning.

8. Remove the injection pump pulley-to-shaft bolts.

9. Using a wheel puller, connect it to the injection pump pulley and press it from the shaft.

10. Remove the injection pump bracket-to-timing pulley housing bolts, the rear injection pump-to-bracket bolts and the injection pump.
To install:

11. Install the injection pump. Tighten the in-

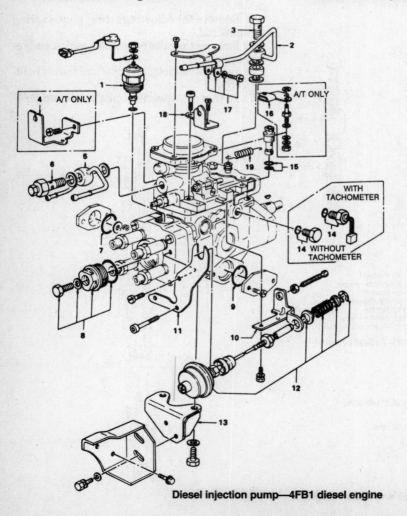

1. Fuel cut solenoid valve assembly
2. Fuel pipe
3. Fuel pipe joint bolt
4. Governor bracket, A/T only
5. Over flow pipe
6. Over flow pipe bolt
7. Timer O-ring
8. High pressure plug assembly
9. O-ring
10. Actuator bracket
11. Actuator to distributor head bracket
12. Fast idle actuator
13. Injection pump housing bracket
14. Tachometer pickup or plug and O-ring
15. Regulating valve O-ring
16. Plate assembly, A/T only
17. Fuel pipe bracket
18. Lever spring

WITH TACHOMETER

WITHOUT TACHOMETER

A/T ONLY

A/T ONLY

Diesel injection pump—4FB1 diesel engine

jection pump-to-timing pulley housing bolts and leave the rear pump-to-bracket bolts semi-tight.

12. Install the injection pump pulley by aligning it with the key groove and torque the bolt to 42–52 ft. lbs. (57–70 Nm).

13. Rotate the crankshaft to bring the No. 1 piston to TDC of the compression stroke.

14. Align the timing marks on the injection pump pulley with the camshaft pulley; the marks must be facing each other.

15. Using a new timing belt, install it in the following sequence: crankshaft pulley, camshaft pulley and the injection pump pulley; the slack must be between the injection pump and camshaft pulleys.

16. Install the tension center and the tension pulley so the end of the tension center is fitted against both pins on the timing pulley housing.

17. Hand tighten the nut so the tension pulley can be rotated freely.

18. Install the tension spring and semi-tighten the pulley nut to 22–36 ft. lbs. (29–48 Nm).

19. Rotate the crankshaft 2 full turns clockwise to seat the belt and further turn the crankshaft 90° beyond TDC to settle the injection pump.

20. Loosen the tension pulley nut to take up the timing belt slack. Tighten the tension pulley nut to 79–94 ft. lbs. (108–130 Nm).

21. Install the injection pump pulley flange; the hole in the outer circumference of the flange should be aligned with the triangular timing mark on the injection pump pulley.

22. Rotate the crankshaft 2 full turns clockwise to bring the No. 1 piston to TDC of the compression stroke. Make sure the triangular timing mark on the timing pulley is aligned with the hole in the flange, then, measure the timing belt tension; it should be 33–55 lbs.

23. Install the timing belt cover.

24. Connect the negative battery cable.

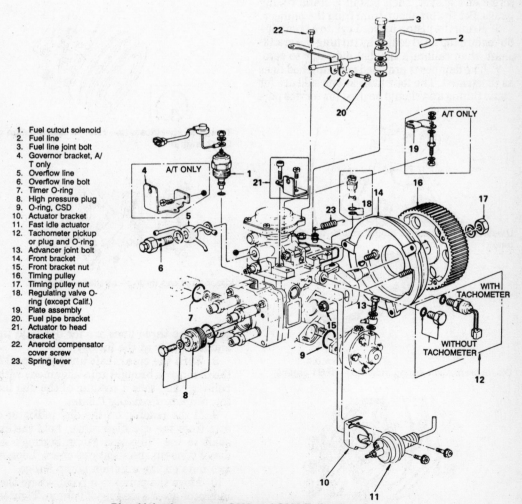

1. Fuel cutout solenoid
2. Fuel line
3. Fuel line joint bolt
4. Governor bracket, A/T only
5. Overflow line
6. Overflow line bolt
7. Timer O-ring
8. High pressure plug
9. O-ring, CSD
10. Actuator bracket
11. Fast idle actuator
12. Tachometer pickup or plug and O-ring
13. Advancer joint bolt
14. Front bracket
15. Front bracket nut
16. Timing pulley
17. Timing pulley nut
18. Regulating valve O-ring (except Calif.)
19. Plate assembly
20. Fuel pipe bracket
21. Actuator to head bracket
22. Aneroid compensator cover screw
23. Spring lever

Diesel injection pump—C223 and C223-T diesel engine

Idle Speed

Refer to the "Idle Speed" procedures for diesel engines in Chapter 2.

INJECTION TIMING

1. Check to see if the notched line on the injection pump and mounting plate are aligned.

2. Bring the No. 1 piston to top dead center on the compression stroke by turning the crankshaft. The correct notch must be used for alignment as the damper pulley is provided with a total of seven notches.

3. Remove the front upper timing belt cover, check the timing belt for proper tension and alignment of the timing marks.

4. Remove the cam cover and rear plug, then check that the fixing plate fits smoothly into the slit at the rear end of the camshaft, then remove the fixing plate J–29761.

5. Disconnect the injection pipe from the injection pump and remove the distributor head screw and gasket, then install a static timing gauge. Set the lift about 1mm from the plunger.

6. Bring the piston in No. 1 cyl. to a point 45–60° before top dead center by turning the crankshaft, then calibrate the dial indicator to zero.

7. The damper is provided with notched lines as illustrated. The four lines at one side are for static timing and should be used for service pur-

Diesel injection pump timing mark—all diesel engines

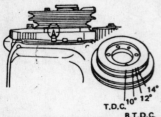

Diesel crankshaft timing indicator—4FB1 engine

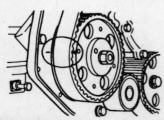

Timing marks—4FB1 engine

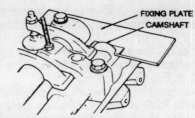

Camshaft fixing plate—4FB1 engine

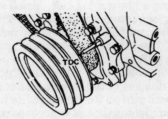

Timing indicator—C223 diesel engine

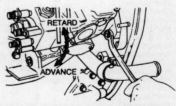

Timing to specifications—refer to specification chart, C223 engine

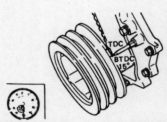

Injection pump timing—all diesel engines

poses. The three lines are for dynamic timing and used only at the factory.

8. Turn the crankshaft until the line 12° on the damper is brought into alignment with the pointer, then take a reading of the dial indicator. *Standard reading 0.5mm.*

9. If the reading on the dial indicator deviates from the specified range, hold the crankshaft to the "Injection Pump Setting" in the diesel tune-up specifications chart. Loosen the two nuts on the injection pump flange.

10. Move the pump to a point where the dial indicator gives a reading of 0.5mm. Tighten the flange nuts.

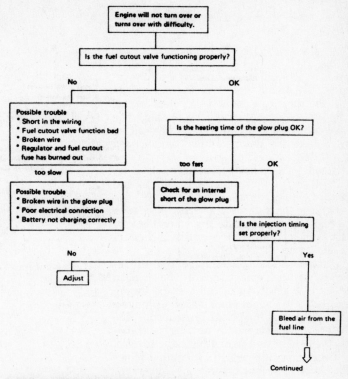

General conditions
* Fuel in the vehicle.
* Starter operation is normal.
* Battery condition is normal.

Engine will not turn over or turns over with difficulty.

Is the fuel cutout valve functioning properly?

No

Possible trouble
* Short in the wiring
* Fuel cutout valve function bad
* Broken wire
* Regulator and fuel cutout fuse has burned out

OK

Is the heating time of the glow plug OK?

too slow

Possible trouble
* Broken wire in the glow plug
* Poor electrical connection
* Battery not charging correctly

too fast

Check for an internal short of the glow plug

OK

Is the injection timing set properly?

No

Adjust

Yes

Bleed air from the fuel line

Continued

Diesel fuel system diagnosis—Chart 1

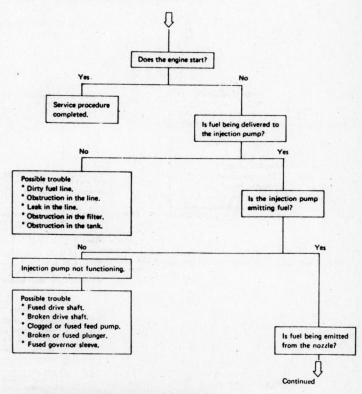

Does the engine start?

Yes

Service procedure completed.

No

Is fuel being delivered to the injection pump?

No

Possible trouble
* Dirty fuel line.
* Obstruction in the line.
* Leak in the line.
* Obstruction in the filter.
* Obstruction in the tank.

Yes

Is the injection pump emitting fuel?

No

Injection pump not functioning.

Possible trouble
* Fused drive shaft.
* Broken drive shaft.
* Clogged or fused feed pump.
* Broken or fused plunger.
* Fused governor sleeve.

Yes

Is fuel being emitted from the nozzle?

Continued

Diesel fuel system diagnosis—Chart 2

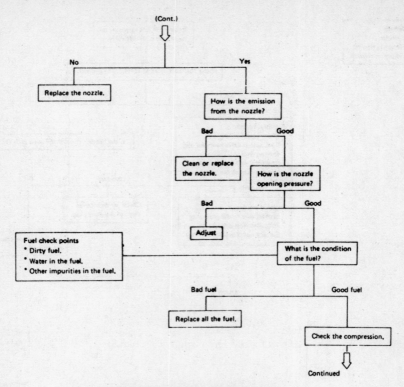

Diesel fuel system diagnosis—Chart 3

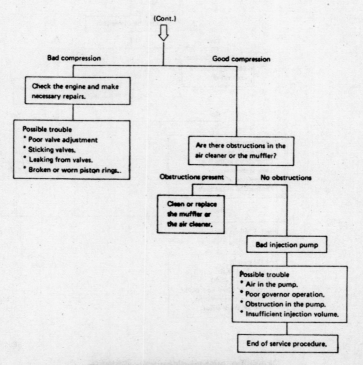

Diesel fuel system diagnosis—Chart 4

General conditions
* Engine is warm

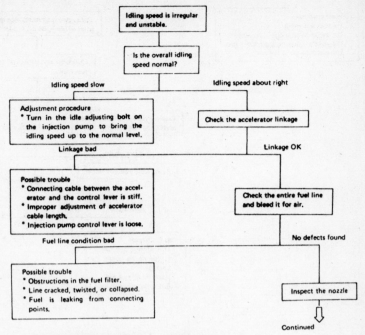

Idling speed is irregular and unstable.

Is the overall idling speed normal?

Idling speed slow

Idling speed about right

Adjustment procedure
* Turn in the idle adjusting bolt on the injection pump to bring the idling speed up to the normal level.

Check the accelerator linkage

Linkage bad

Linkage OK

Possible trouble
* Connecting cable between the accelerator and the control lever is stiff.
* Improper adjustment of accelerator cable length.
* Injection pump control lever is loose.

Check the entire fuel line and bleed it for air.

Fuel line condition bad

No defects found

Possible trouble
* Obstructions in the fuel filter.
* Line cracked, twisted, or collapsed.
* Fuel is leaking from connecting points.

Inspect the nozzle

Continued

Diesel fuel system diagnosis—Chart 5

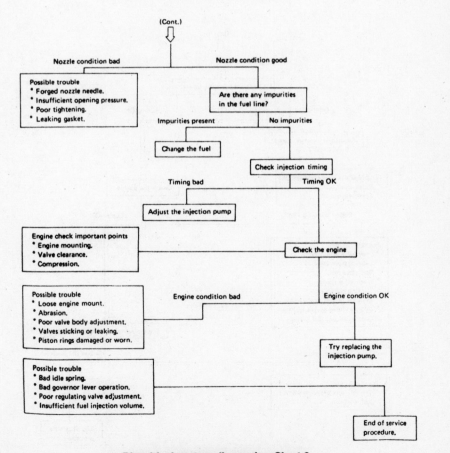

(Cont.)

Nozzle condition bad

Nozzle condition good

Possible trouble
* Forged nozzle needle.
* Insufficient opening pressure.
* Poor tightening.
* Leaking gasket.

Are there any impurities in the fuel line?

Impurities present

No impurities

Change the fuel

Check injection timing

Timing bad

Timing OK

Adjust the injection pump

Engine check important points
* Engine mounting.
* Valve clearance.
* Compression.

Check the engine

Possible trouble
* Loose engine mount.
* Abrasion.
* Poor valve body adjustment.
* Valves sticking or leaking.
* Piston rings damaged or worn.

Engine condition bad

Engine condition OK

Try replacing the injection pump.

Possible trouble
* Bad idle spring.
* Bad governor lever operation.
* Poor regulating valve adjustment.
* Insufficient fuel injection volume.

End of service procedure.

Diesel fuel system diagnosis—Chart 6

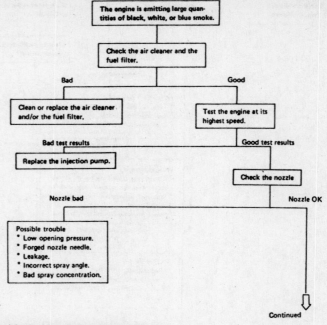

General conditions
* The engine is warm.
* The transmission is operating properly.
* The vehicle is burning the correct fuel.
* The turbocharger is normal.

The engine is emitting large quantities of black, white, or blue smoke.

Check the air cleaner and the fuel filter.

Bad — Good

Clean or replace the air cleaner and/or the fuel filter.

Test the engine at its highest speed.

Bad test results — Good test results

Replace the injection pump.

Check the nozzle

Nozzle bad — Nozzle OK

Possible trouble
* Low opening pressure.
* Forged nozzle needle.
* Leakage.
* Incorrect spray angle.
* Bad spray concentration.

Continued

Diesel fuel system diagnosis—Chart 7

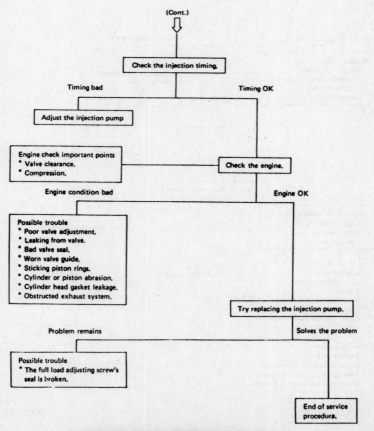

(Cont.)

Check the injection timing.

Timing bad — Timing OK

Adjust the injection pump

Engine check important points
* Valve clearance.
* Compression.

Check the engine.

Engine condition bad — Engine OK

Possible trouble
* Poor valve adjustment.
* Leaking from valve.
* Bad valve seal.
* Worn valve guide.
* Sticking piston rings.
* Cylinder or piston abrasion.
* Cylinder head gasket leakage.
* Obstructed exhaust system.

Try replacing the injection pump.

Problem remains — Solves the problem

Possible trouble
* The full load adjusting screw's seal is broken.

End of service procedure.

Diesel fuel system diagnosis—Chart 8

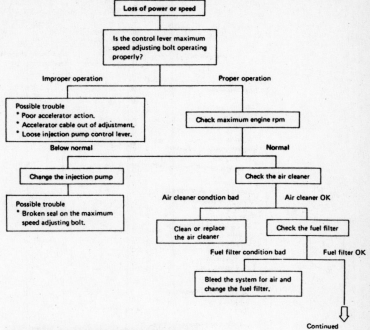

General conditions
* Maximum speed is normal.
* Tires are normal.
* Clutch function is normal.
* The turbocharger is normal.

Loss of power or speed

Is the control lever maximum speed adjusting bolt operating properly?

Improper operation

Possible trouble
* Poor accelerator action.
* Accelerator cable out of adjustment.
* Loose injection pump control lever.

Below normal

Change the injection pump

Possible trouble
* Broken seal on the maximum speed adjusting bolt.

Proper operation

Check maximum engine rpm

Normal

Check the air cleaner

Air cleaner condtion bad

Clean or replace the air cleaner

Air cleaner OK

Check the fuel filter

Fuel filter condition bad

Bleed the system for air and change the fuel filter.

Fuel filter OK

Continued

Diesel fuel system diagnosis—Chart 9

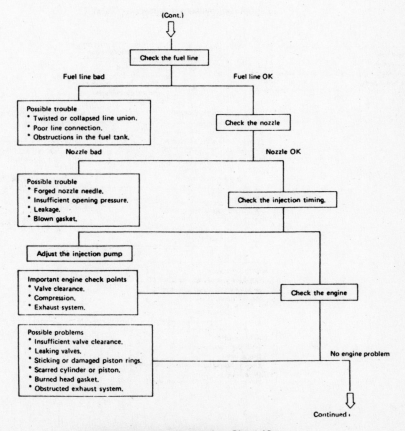

(Cont.)

Check the fuel line

Fuel line bad

Possible trouble
* Twisted or collapsed line union.
* Poor line connection.
* Obstructions in the fuel tank.

Fuel line OK

Check the nozzle

Nozzle bad

Possible trouble
* Forged nozzle needle.
* Insufficient opening pressure.
* Leakage.
* Blown gasket.

Adjust the injection pump

Nozzle OK

Check the injection timing.

Important engine check points
* Valve clearance.
* Compression.
* Exhaust system.

Check the engine

Possible problems
* Insufficient valve clearance.
* Leaking valves.
* Sticking or damaged piston rings.
* Scarred cylinder or piston.
* Burned head gasket.
* Obstructed exhaust system.

No engine problem

Continued

Diesel fuel system diagnosis—Chart 10

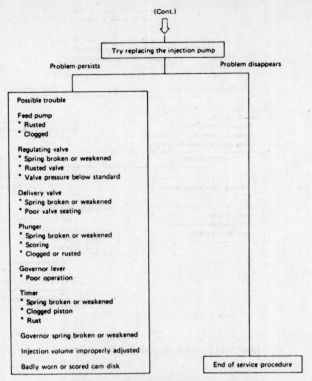

(Cont.)

Try replacing the injection pump

Problem persists

Problem disappears

Possible trouble

Feed pump
* Rusted
* Clogged

Regulating valve
* Spring broken or weakened
* Rusted valve
* Valve pressure below standard

Delivery valve
* Spring broken or weakened
* Poor valve seating

Plunger
* Spring broken or weakened
* Scoring
* Clogged or rusted

Governor lever
* Poor operation

Timer
* Spring broken or weakened
* Clogged piston
* Rust

Governor spring broken or weakened

Injection volume improperly adjusted

Badly worn or scored cam disk

End of service procedure

Diesel fuel system diagnosis—Chart 11

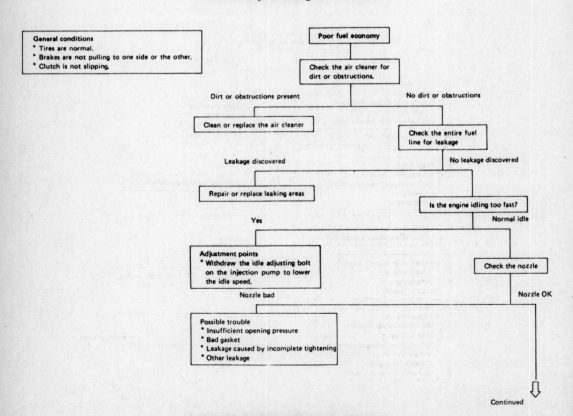

General conditions
* Tires are normal.
* Brakes are not pulling to one side or the other.
* Clutch is not slipping.

Poor fuel economy

Check the air cleaner for dirt or obstructions.

Dirt or obstructions present

No dirt or obstructions

Clean or replace the air cleaner

Check the entire fuel line for leakage

Leakage discovered

No leakage discovered

Repair or replace leaking areas

Is the engine idling too fast?

Yes

Normal idle

Adjustment points
* Withdraw the idle adjusting bolt on the injection pump to lower the idle speed.

Check the nozzle

Nozzle bad

Nozzle OK

Possible trouble
* Insufficient opening pressure
* Bad gasket
* Leakage caused by incomplete tightening
* Other leakage

Continued

Diesel fuel system diagnosis—Chart 12

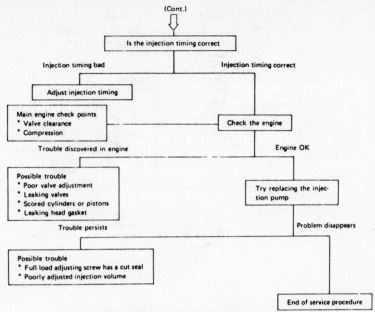

(Cont.)

Is the injection timing correct

Injection timing bad ← → Injection timing correct

Adjust injection timing

Main engine check points
* Valve clearance
* Compression

Check the engine

Trouble discovered in engine   Engine OK

Possible trouble
* Poor valve adjustment
* Leaking valves
* Scored cylinders or pistons
* Leaking head gasket

Try replacing the injec-
tion pump

Trouble persists   Problem disappears

Possible trouble
* Full load adjusting screw has a cut seal
* Poorly adjusted injection volume

End of service procedure

Diesel fuel system diagnosis—Chart 13

Quick-On Start System (Glow Plugs)
INSPECTION

4FB1 I-Mark

4FB1 I-Mark Component Location: the controller unit is located beneath the glove compartment. The glow plug relay unit is located in the relay box at the right side of the engine compartment. The dropping resistor is located near the fuel inlet pipe of the engine. The glow plugs and sensing resistor is located on the right side of the engine installed in the cylinder head. The fusible link is located near the battery and relay box at the left side of the engine compartment. The thermo switch is located in the thermostat housing of the engine.

Dropping resistor check: check for continuity across the terminals. If no continuity exists, replace the unit.

Thermo switch check: submerge the end of the switch in water and raise the temperature gradually. The switch should be OFF between 126–140°F (53–60°C) or lower. The switch should be ON between 134–145°F (57–63°C) or higher. If no, replace the switch.

REMOVAL AND INSTALLATION

The glow plugs are located under the injection nozzles.
1. Disconnect the negative (–) battery cable.
2. Disconnect the dropping resistor for the I-Mark.
3. Disconnect the glow plug and remove from the engine. The plug is threaded into the cylinder head.

To install:
4. Lubricate with anti-seize compound before installing the plug.
5. Install and torque the plug to 65 ft. lbs. (88 Nm).
6. Reconnect the plug and dropping resistor.
7. Connect the battery cable and check operation.

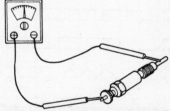

Checking glow plug continuity voltage of 5V, resistance 0.1 ohm

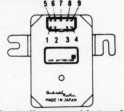

1. Starter switch ON position
2. Sensing resistor
3. Thermo switch
4. Starter switch START position
5. Sensing resistor
6. Glow plug relay 1
7. Ground
8. Glow indicator lamp
9. Not applicable

Controller assembly terminals—P'up and Trooper

Glow plug location

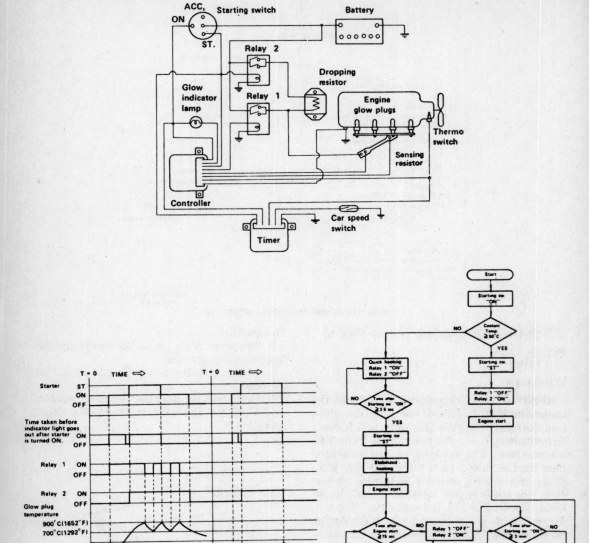

Glow plug system—1981–82 4FB1 diesel engine

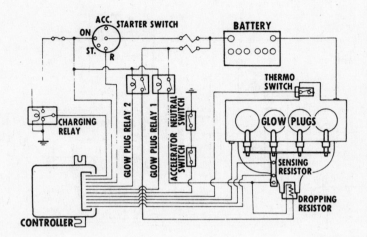

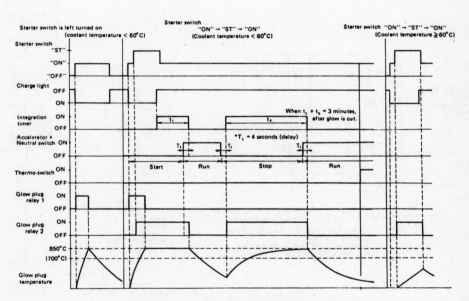

Glow plug system—1982–85 4FB1 diesel engine

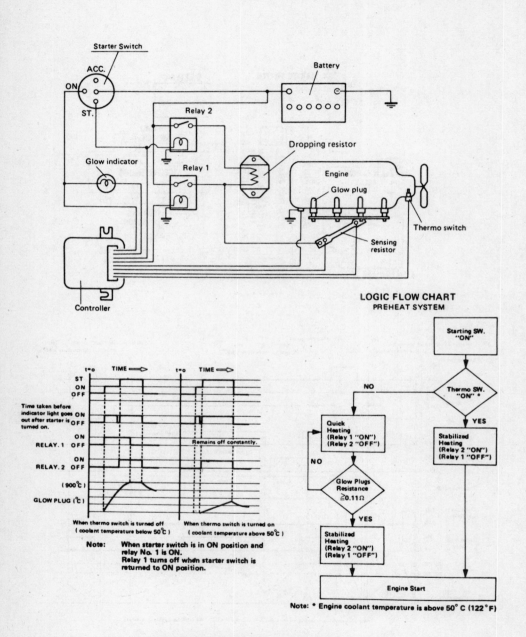

Glow plug system—C223 and C223-T diesel engine

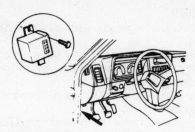

Controller unit—P'up and Trooper

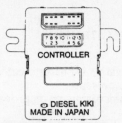

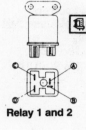

1. Starter switch ON position
2. Sensing resistor
3. Sensing resistor
4. Sensing resistor
5. Glow plug relay 1
6. Charging relay
7. Fast idle circuit
8. Thermo switch
9. Accelerator switch
10. Grounding
11. Starter switch R
12. Glow plug relay 2

Controller unit—I-Mark

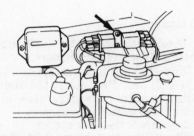

Glow plug relay (arrow) and dropping resistor (to left)—P'up and Trooper

With a circuit tester make a continuity test across Ⓒ and Ⓓ with the battery voltage applied to Ⓐ and Ⓑ Replace the parts if the tester does not indicate a continuity.

Relay 1 and 2

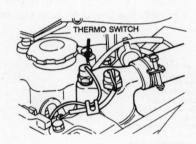

THERMO SWITCH

Thermo switch location—P'up and Trooper

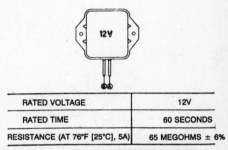

RATED VOLTAGE	12V
RATED TIME	60 SECONDS
RESISTANCE (AT 76°F [25°C], 5A)	65 MEGOHMS ± 6%

Dropping resistor check—P'up and Trooper

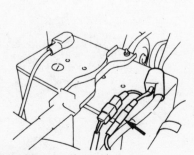

Fusible link—P'up and Trooper

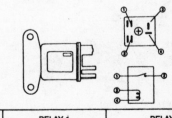

	RELAY 1	RELAY 2
1	FROM BATTERY	FROM BATTERY
2	TO SENSING RESISTOR	TO DROPPING RESISTOR
3	FROM CONTROLLER	FROM STARTER SWITCH
4	GROUND	GROUND

Relay check—P'up and Trooper

FUEL TANK

REMOVAL AND INSTALLATION

RWD I-Mark

1. Disconnect the negative (–) battery cable. Release the fuel system pressure.
2. Drain the fuel tank using an approved pump.
3. Disconnect the fuel return and drain the remaining fuel.
4. Remove the filler cap and tank cover.
5. Label and disconnect all fuel and vapor lines.
6. Disconnect the electrical connectors.
7. Remove the tank retaining bolts and fuel tank with the filler neck seal ring.
8. Remove the seal ring from the tank.
9. Remove the pump and gauge unit if needed.

To install:

1. Install the pump and gauge unit if removed.
2. Insert the end of the fuel filler neck into the fitting hole, then install and hand tighten the retaining bolts.
3. Move the tank all the way in toward the filler cap side.
4. Apply soapy water to the seal ring. Using a small prybar, work the lipped portion of the seal ring into the flange at the filler neck recess.
5. Fully tighten the retaining bolts, connect all wiring and fuel lines.
6. Connect the battery cable and check for leaks.

FWD I-Mark

1. Disconnect the negative (–) battery cable. Release the fuel system pressure.
2. Drain the fuel using an approved pump.
3. Label and disconnect the fuel filler, breather, tank to evaporator, tank to return pipe and tank to fuel pipe hoses.
4. Disconnect the tank wiring.
5. Place a floor jack under the tank, remove the retaining bolts and lower the tank.

To install:

1. Raise the tank with the jack and install the retaining bolts.
2. Connect the wiring and fuel hoses.
3. Connect the breather hose and fuel filler hose.

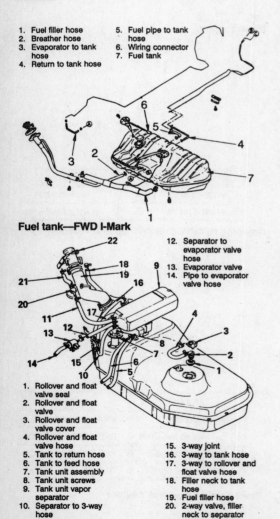

1. Fuel filler hose
2. Breather hose
3. Evaporator to tank hose
4. Return to tank hose
5. Fuel pipe to tank hose
6. Wiring connector
7. Fuel tank

Fuel tank—FWD I-Mark

1. Rollover and float valve seal
2. Rollover and float valve
3. Rollover and float valve cover
4. Rollover and float valve hose
5. Tank to return hose
6. Tank to feed hose
7. Tank unit assembly
8. Tank unit screws
9. Tank unit vapor separator
10. Separator to 3-way hose
11. Separator to 2-way valve hose
12. Separator to evaporator valve hose
13. Evaporator valve
14. Pipe to evaporator valve hose
15. 3-way joint
16. 3-way to tank hose
17. 3-way to rollover and float valve hose
18. Filler neck to tank hose
19. Fuel filler hose
20. 2-way valve, filler neck to separator
21. 2-way valve hose
22. Fuel filler neck

Fuel tank—RWD Impulse

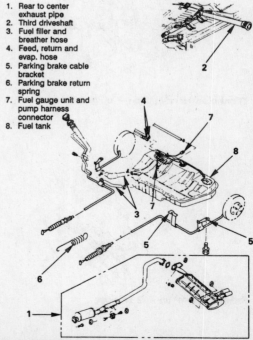

1. Rear to center exhaust pipe
2. Third driveshaft
3. Fuel filler and breather hose
4. Feed, return and evap. hose
5. Parking brake cable bracket
6. Parking brake return spring
7. Fuel gauge unit and pump harness connector
8. Fuel tank

Fuel tank—FWD Impulse and Stylus

4. Connect the battery cable, fill the tank with fuel and check for leaks.

RWD Impulse

1. Disconnect the negative (–) battery cable. Release the fuel system pressure.

2. Drain the fuel tank using an approved pump.

3. Disconnect the tank harness connectors.

4. Disconnect the fuel filler assembly and remove the hose guard.

5. Remove the fuel filler guard.

6. Position a floor jack under the tank and remove the tank strap.

7. Lower the tank and disconnect any wiring or hoses.

To install:

1. Raise the tank and connect any wiring or hoses.

2. Install the tank straps and retainers.

3. Install the fuel filler guard.

4. Connect the fuel filler assembly and install the hose guard.

5. Connect the tank harness connectors.

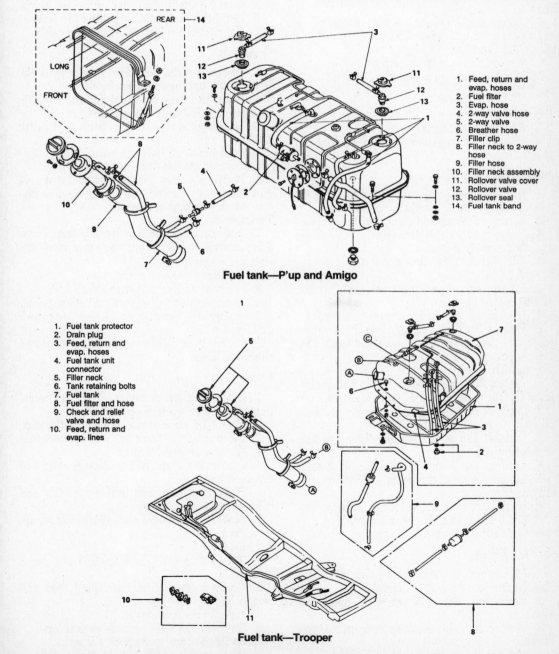

1. Feed, return and evap. hoses
2. Fuel filter
3. Evap. hose
4. 2-way valve hose
5. 2-way valve
6. Breather hose
7. Filler clip
8. Filler neck to 2-way hose
9. Filler hose
10. Filler neck assembly
11. Rollover valve cover
12. Rollover valve
13. Rollover seal
14. Fuel tank band

Fuel tank—P'up and Amigo

1. Fuel tank protector
2. Drain plug
3. Feed, return and evap. hoses
4. Fuel tank unit connector
5. Filler neck
6. Tank retaining bolts
7. Fuel tank
8. Fuel filter and hose
9. Check and relief valve and hose
10. Feed, return and evap. lines

Fuel tank—Trooper

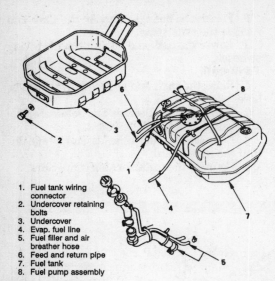

1. Fuel tank wiring connector
2. Undercover retaining bolts
3. Undercover
4. Evap. fuel line
5. Fuel filler and air breather hose
6. Feed and return pipe
7. Fuel tank
8. Fuel pump assembly

Rodeo fuel tank

6. Refill the fuel tank.
7. Connect the negative (–) battery cable and check for leaks.

FWD Impulse and Stylus

1. Disconnect the negative (–) battery cable.
2. Drain the tank with a suitable pump.
3. Remove the rear and center exhaust pipes.
4. Remove the third driveshaft, fuel filler and air breather hose.
5. Disconnect the feed, return and evap. hoses.
6. Disconnect the parking brake cable bracket and return spring.
7. Disconnect the tank harness connectors.
8. Place a floor jack under the tank and remove the tank retainers. Lower the tank and disconnect any wiring or hoses.

To install:

1. Place a floor jack under the tank and raise it into position. Install the tank retainers.
2. Connect the tank harness connectors and hoses.
3. Connect the parking brake cable bracket and return spring.
4. Connect the feed, return and evap. hoses.
5. Install the third driveshaft, fuel filler and air breather hose.
6. Install the rear and center exhaust pipes.
7. Refill the tank and check for leaks.
8. Connect the negative (–) battery cable.

P'up and Amigo

1. Disconnect the negative (–) battery cable. Release the fuel system pressure.
2. Drain the fuel tank using an approved pump.
3. Disconnect the feed, return and evap. hoses.
4. Disconnect all vapor and fuel hoses.

5. Remove the fuel tank band, long bed only.
6. Disconnect the filler neck.
7. Place a floor jack under the tank.
8. Remove the retainers, lower the tank far enough to disconnect any hoses or wires not already disconnected.

To install:

1. Raise the tank far enough to connect any hoses or wires. Install the tank retainers.
2. Connect the filler neck.
3. Install the fuel tank band, long bed only.
4. Connect all vapor and fuel hoses.
5. Connect the feed, return and evap. hoses.
6. Refill the fuel tank and check for leaks.
7. Connect the negative (–) battery cable.

Trooper

1. Disconnect the negative (–) battery cable. Release the fuel system pressure.
2. Drain the tank using an approved pump. Remove the fuel tank undercover.
3. Disconnect the feed, return and evap. hoses.
4. Disconnect all harness connectors.
5. Disconnect the filler neck.
6. Position a floor jack under the tank, remove the retainers and lower far enough to disconnect any wiring or hoses.

To install:

1. Position a floor jack under the tank, raise it far enough to connect any wiring or hoses. Install the retainers.
2. Connect the filler neck.
3. Connect all harness connectors.
4. Connect the feed, return and evap. hoses.
5. Refill the tank. Install the fuel tank undercover.
6. Connect the negative (–) battery cable and check for leaks.

Rodeo

1. Disconnect the negative (–) battery cable. Release the fuel system pressure.
2. Drain the tank using an approved pump.
3. Disconnect the tank harness connectors.
4. Remove the undercover.
5. Disconnect evap., filler, breather, feed and return hoses.
6. Position a floor jack under the tank and remove the tank retainers.
7. Lower the tank and remove the fuel pump, if needed.

To install:

1. Raise the tank and install the tank retainer.
2. Connect evap., filler, breather, feed and return hoses.
3. Install the undercover.
4. Connect the tank harness connectors.
5. Refill the tank and check for leaks.
6. Connect the negative (–) battery cable.

Chassis Electrical

HEATING AND AIR CONDITIONING

Heater and Air Conditioner Blower Motor

REMOVAL AND INSTALLATION

RWD I-Mark

The blower motor is located inside the engine compartment on the fire wall. The blower relay is attached to the blower assembly. The resistor assembly is located under the outer blower case cover.

1. Disconnect the negative (−) battery cable.
2. Disconnect the motor harness connector.
3. Remove the retaining screws and pull the motor and cage out of the housing.
4. Remove the retaining clip or nut and remove the cage from the motor.

To install:

5. Install the cage onto the motor and install the clip or retaining nut.
6. Install the motor and tighten the retaining screws.
7. Connect the wiring and battery cable.

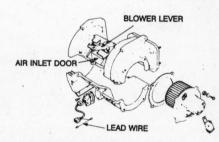

Blower motor and high blower relay

Trouble	Possible Cause and Correction
Blower Motor Inoperative	1. Look for burned, broken, or incorrect fuse. 2. Look for loose connectors or broken wires. 3. Visually inspect the resistor assembly. Look for broken or melted coils. 4. Test for continuity. 5. Test for a malfunctioned blower switch.
Insufficient Heating	1. Partially plugged heater core. 2. Malfunctioning water valve. 3. Improperly adjusted temperature lever cable. 4. Test engine thermostat for opening too soon, stuck open, or held open by foreign material. 5. Visually inspect radiator coolant level and add if necessary. 6. Pinched or plugged heater hose.
Inadequate Defrosting	1. Partially plugged heater core. 2. Malfunctioning water valve. 3. Improperly adjusted selector and/or temperature lever cable. 4. Mispositioned defroster outlets and/or hoses. 5. Obstructed defroster outlets and/or hoses. 6. Visually inspect the coolant level in radiator. Add coolant if necessary.

Heater diagnosis chart—RWD I-Mark

All Others

The blower motor is located under the instrument panel next to the right side kick panel.

1. Disconnect the negative (−) battery cable.
2. Remove the instrument panel trim panel, if so equipped.
3. Disconnect the blower motor wiring.
4. Remove the retaining screws and motor assembly.

5. Remove the cage retaining clip and cage from the motor.

To install:

6. Install the cage onto the motor and install the clip.
7. Install the motor, retaining screws and wiring connector.
8. Connect the battery cable and check operation.

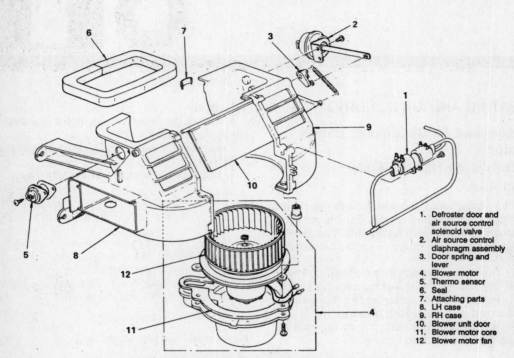

1. Defroster door and air source control solenoid valve
2. Air source control diaphragm assembly
3. Door spring and lever
4. Blower motor
5. Thermo sensor
6. Seal
7. Attaching parts
8. LH case
9. RH case
10. Blower unit door
11. Blower motor core
12. Blower motor fan

Blower motor—P'up and Trooper shown, others similar

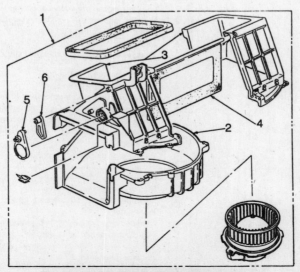

1. Blower assembly
2. Lower case
3. Upper case
4. Mode door
5. Sub lever
6. Door lever

Blower motor—Rodeo shown, others similar

Auxiliary Heater and Air Conditioner Unit Blower Motor

REMOVAL AND INSTALLATION

Trooper

1. Disconnect the negative (−) battery cable.
2. Drain the cooling system into a suitable container.

CAUTION: *When draining the coolant, keep in mind that cats and dogs are attracted by the ethylene glycol antifreeze, and are quite likely to drink any that is left in an uncovered container or in puddles on the ground. This will prove fatal in sufficient quantity. Always drain the coolant into a sealable container. Coolant should be reused unless it is contaminated or several years old.*

3. Remove the rear seat as outlined in Section 10.
4. Disconnect the coolant hoses at the heater assembly.
5. Remove the mounting bolts and disconnect the electrical connector.
6. Remove the heater unit.
7. Disassembly the heater unit to remove the blower motor.
8. Remove the housing retaining screws and clips.
9. Carefully disassembly the housing being careful not to damage the assembly. Remove the blower motor and cages.

To install:

10. If the seals are damaged, install new seals before assembly.
11. Install the blower motor and cage assembly. Assemble the housing.
12. Install the housing and reconnect the coolant hoses.
13. Refill the engine with coolant, connect the battery cable and check for leaks.

Heater Core

REMOVAL AND INSTALLATION

RWD I-Mark

The heater core is located inside the heater system under the instrument panel. The steering column and instrument panel have to be removed.

1. Disconnect the negative (−) battery cable.
2. Drain the radiator coolant into a suitable container.

CAUTION: *When draining the coolant, keep in mind that cats and dogs are attracted by the ethylene glycol antifreeze, and are quite likely to drink any that is left in an uncovered container or in puddles on the ground. This will prove fatal in sufficient quantity. Always drain the coolant into a sealable container. Coolant should be reused unless it is contaminated or several years old.*

3. Disconnect the hoses at the core connections and plug the hoses. They are located inside the engine compartment.

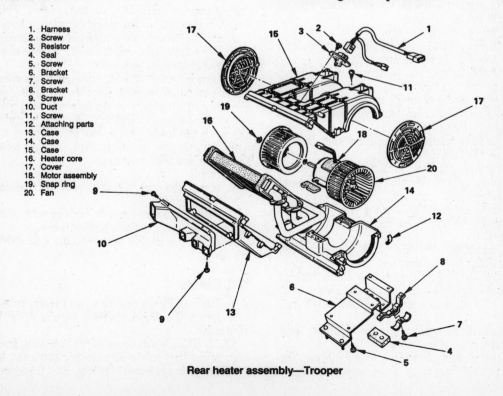

1. Harness
2. Screw
3. Resistor
4. Seal
5. Screw
6. Bracket
7. Screw
8. Bracket
9. Screw
10. Duct
11. Screw
12. Attaching parts
13. Case
14. Case
15. Case
16. Heater core
17. Cover
18. Motor assembly
19. Snap ring
20. Fan

Rear heater assembly—Trooper

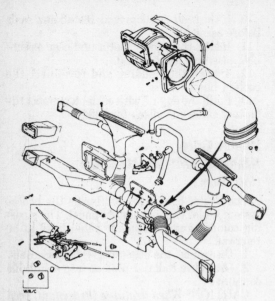

Heater core—RWD I-Mark

4. Remove the outer blower unit case cover and disconnect the fresh air door cable. Disconnect the temperature cable at the water valve.

5. Remove the steering column as outlined in Chapter 8.

6. Remove the instrument cluster as outlined in this Chapter.

7. Disconnect the console wiring and remove the console as outlined in this Chapter.

8. Remove the heater control and plate as outlined in this Chapter.

9. Remove the glove box.

10. Disconnect the selector mode cable from the driver side of the heater unit.

11. Carefully pull the temperature and fresh air door cables through the cowl and remove the control panel through the cluster opening.

12. Remove instrument panel assembly as outlined in this Chapter.

13. Remove the heater unit through bolt located at the rear of the unit.

14. Remove the four attaching nuts holding the heater unit to the blower unit and remove the heater unit.

15. Remove the bolts holding the heater unit case halves together and remove heater core.

To install:

16. Install the core and bolts holding the heater unit case halves together.

17. Install the heater unit and four attaching nuts holding the heater unit to the blower unit. Make sure the seal is in place. Water will leak, if not.

18. Install the heater unit through bolt located at the rear of the unit.

19. Install instrument panel assembly as outlined in this Chapter.

20. Carefully thread the temperature and fresh air door cables through the cowl and install the control panel through the cluster opening.

21. Connect the selector mode cable to the driver side of the heater unit.

22. Install the glove box.

23. Install the heater control and plate as outlined in this Chapter.

24. Connect the console wiring and install the console as outlined in this Chapter.

25. Install the instrument cluster as outlined in this Chapter.

26. Install the steering column as outlined in Chapter 8.

27. Install the outer blower unit case cover and connect the fresh air door cable. Connect the temperature cable at the water valve.

28. Connect the hoses at the core connections. Do not overtighten the hose clamps.

29. Refill the radiator with coolant.

30. Connect the negative (−) battery cable and check for leaks.

FWD I-Mark

1. Disconnect the negative (−) battery cable.

2. Drain the engine coolant into a suitable container.

CAUTION: *When draining the coolant, keep in mind that cats and dogs are attracted by the ethylene glycol antifreeze, and are quite likely to drink any that is left in an uncovered container or in puddles on the ground. This will prove fatal in sufficient quantity. Always drain the coolant into a sealable container. Coolant should be reused unless it is contaminated or several years old.*

3. Disconnect the heater hoses from the core. Be careful not to damage the core by pulling on the hose to remove. Cut the hoses if they will not come off easily. Use a prybar to carefully pry open the lower part of the unit case.

4. Remove the retaining clips, lower heater unit case and core assembly.

To install:

5. Install the core, being careful not to damage the assembly.

6. Install the lower heater unit case, retaining clips and connect the heater hoses.

7. Refill the engine with coolant and check for leaks.

RWD Impulse

1. Disconnect the negative (−) battery cable.

2. Drain the engine coolant into a suitable container.

CAUTION: *When draining the coolant, keep in mind that cats and dogs are attracted by the ethylene glycol antifreeze, and are quite*

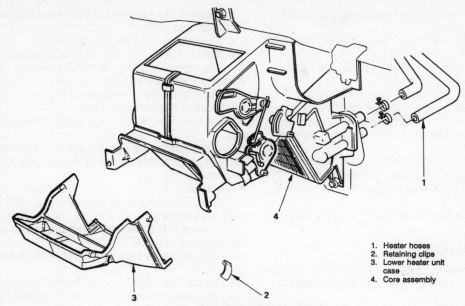

1. Heater hoses
2. Retaining clips
3. Lower heater unit case
4. Core assembly

Heater core—FWD I-Mark

likely to drink any that is left in an uncovered container or in puddles on the ground. This will prove fatal in sufficient quantity. Always drain the coolant into a sealable container. Coolant should be reused unless it is contaminated or several years old.

3. Remove the instrument panel and glove compartment as outlined in this Chapter.

4. Remove the air conditioning line and plug so contamination does not enter the system.

5. Disconnect the heater hoses. Be careful not to damage the core by pulling on the hose to remove. Cut the hoses if they will not come off easily.

6. Remove the evaporator assembly, blower assembly and heater unit.

7. Disassembly the heater unit be prying the retaining clips and split the unit in half. Remove the heater core from the unit.

To install:

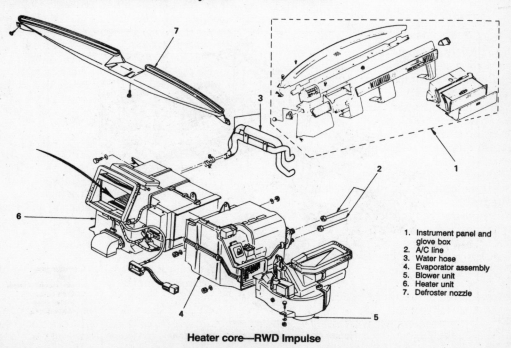

1. Instrument panel and glove box
2. A/C line
3. Water hose
4. Evaporator assembly
5. Blower unit
6. Heater unit
7. Defroster nozzle

Heater core—RWD Impulse

8. Install the heater core, making sure all the seals are in place.

9. Assemble the heater unit, making sure all the seals are in place.

10. Install the evaporator assembly, blower assembly and heater unit.

11. Connect the heater hoses. Be careful not to damage the core by pulling on the hoses.

12. Install the air conditioning line, evacuate, leak test and recharge the air conditioning system.

13. Install the instrument panel and glove compartment as outlined in this Chapter.

14. Refill the engine coolant into a suitable container.

15. Connect the negative (−) battery cable.

FWD Impulse and Stylus

1. Disconnect the negative (−) battery cable.

2. Drain the engine coolant into a suitable container.

CAUTION: *When draining the coolant, keep in mind that cats and dogs are attracted by the ethylene glycol antifreeze, and are quite likely to drink any that is left in an uncovered container or in puddles on the ground. This will prove fatal in sufficient quantity. Always drain the coolant into a sealable container. Coolant should be reused unless it is contaminated or several years old.*

3. Disconnect the heater hoses. Be careful not to damage the core by pulling on the hose to remove. Cut the hoses if they will not come off easily.

4. Remove the instrument panel as outlined in this Chapter.

5. Disconnect the resistor assembly.

6. Remove the duct (non air conditioning) or the evaporator housing (air conditioning). If equipped with air conditioning, refer to Chapter 1 for discharging, evacuating and recharging the air conditioning system.

7. Remove the center vent duct and heater unit.

8. Disassemble the heater unit by removing the duct, mode control case, core assembly and heater core.

To install:

9. Install the heater core, making sure all the seals are in place.

10. Assemble the heater unit, making sure all the seals are in place.

11. Install the center vent duct and heater unit.

12. Install the duct (non air conditioning) or the evaporator housing (air conditioning). If equipped with air conditioning, refer to Chapter 1 for discharging, evacuating and recharging the air conditioning system.

13. Connect the resistor assembly.

14. Install the instrument panel as outlined in this Chapter.

15. Connect the heater hoses. Be careful not to damage the core by pulling on the hose to remove. Cut the hoses if they will not come off easily.

16. Refill the engine coolant.

17. Connect the negative (−) battery cable and check for leaks.

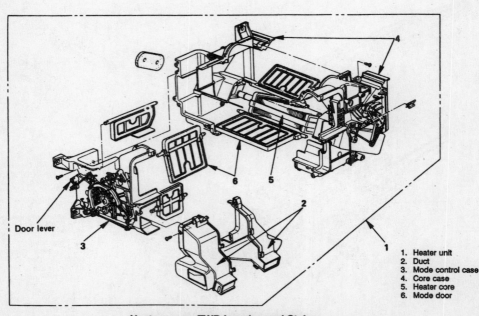

1. Heater unit
2. Duct
3. Mode control case
4. Core case
5. Heater core
6. Mode door

Door lever

Heater core—FWD Impulse and Stylus

P'up, Amigo, Rodeo and Trooper

1. Disconnect the negative (−) battery cable.
2. Drain the engine coolant into a suitable container.

CAUTION: *When draining the coolant, keep in mind that cats and dogs are attracted by the ethylene glycol antifreeze, and are quite likely to drink any that is left in an uncovered container or in puddles on the ground. This will prove fatal in sufficient quantity. Always drain the coolant into a sealable container.*

Coolant should be reused unless it is contaminated or several years old.

3. Disconnect the heater hoses. Be careful not to damage the core by pulling on the hose to remove. Cut the hoses if they will not come off easily.
4. Remove the instrument panel as outlined in this Chapter.
5. Disconnect the resistor assembly.
6. If possible, disconnect and move the duct (non air conditioning) or the evaporator hous-

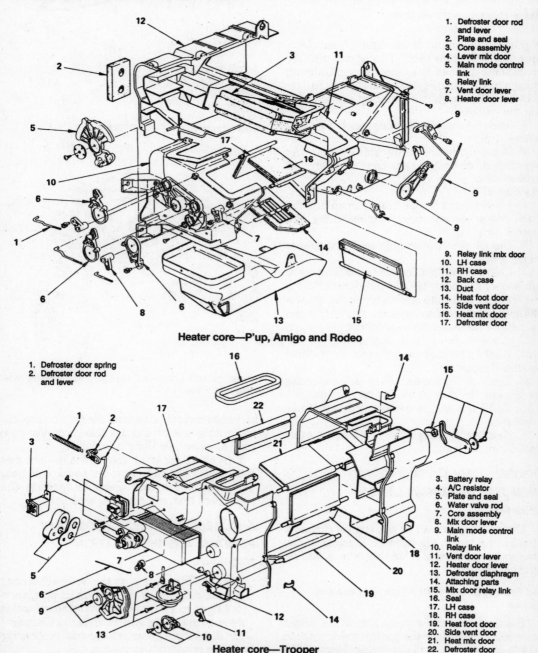

1. Defroster door rod and lever
2. Plate and seal
3. Core assembly
4. Lever mix door
5. Main mode control link
6. Relay link
7. Vent door lever
8. Heater door lever

9. Relay link mix door
10. LH case
11. RH case
12. Back case
13. Duct
14. Heat foot door
15. Side vent door
16. Heat mix door
17. Defroster door

Heater core—P'up, Amigo and Rodeo

1. Defroster door spring
2. Defroster door rod and lever

3. Battery relay
4. A/C resistor
5. Plate and seal
6. Water valve rod
7. Core assembly
8. Mix door lever
9. Main mode control link
10. Relay link
11. Vent door lever
12. Heater door lever
13. Defroster diaphragm
14. Attaching parts
15. Mix door relay link
16. Seal
17. LH case
18. RH case
19. Heat foot door
20. Side vent door
21. Heat mix door
22. Defroster door

Heater core—Trooper

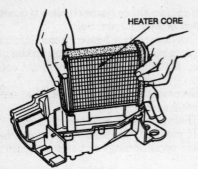

Heater core removal from case

ing (air conditioning) to the right to gain clearance for the heater unit. If equipped with air conditioning, do not disconnect air conditioning system until absolutely necessary. Refer to Section 1 for discharging, evacuating and recharging the system.

7. Remove the instrument panel stay and heater unit.

8. Disassemble the heater unit by removing the duct, mode control case, core assembly and heater core.

To install:

9. Assemble the heater unit by installing the duct, mode control case, core assembly and heater core.

10. Install the heater unit and instrument panel stay.

11. Connect the duct (non air conditioning) or the evaporator housing (air conditioning) to the heater unit. Evacuate and recharge the air conditioning system if the system was discharged to remove the evaporator assembly.

12. Connect the resistor assembly.

13. Install the instrument panel as outlined in this Chapter.

14. Connect the heater hoses. Be careful not to damage the core by pulling on the hose.

15. Refill the engine coolant into a suitable container.

16. Connect the negative (−) battery cable and check for leaks.

Heater Water Control Valve

REMOVAL AND INSTALLATION

RWD I-Mark

The valve is located in the engine compartment, attached to the firewall. Disconnect the heater hoses, control cable and remove the retaining screws.

All Others, Except FWD I-Mark, Impulse and Stylus

The heater control valve is part of the heater core inlet. To replace the control valve, remove the heater core as outlined in this Chapter. Re-

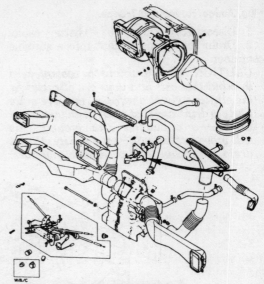

Heater control valve—RWD I-Mark

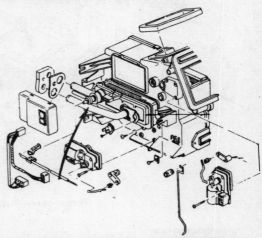

Heater control valve—all except, FWD I-Mark, Impulse and Stylus

move the control valve from the heater core, being careful not to damage the core. Use new gaskets when installing new valves.

The remainder of the vehicles are not equipped with heater water control valves. They use heater unit doors to regulate the amount of heat entering the vehicle.

Air Conditioner Expansion Valve

REMOVAL AND INSTALLATION

RWD I-Mark

NOTE: *When servicing the air conditioning system, always cap the disconnected refrigerant lines to prevent dirt and contamination from entering the system. Refer to Chapter 1 for discharging, evacuating and recharging the air conditioning system.*

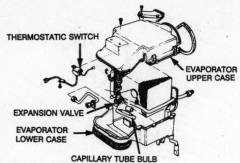

THERMOSTATIC SWITCH

EVAPORATOR UPPER CASE

EXPANSION VALVE

EVAPORATOR LOWER CASE

CAPILLARY TUBE BULB

Expansion valve—RWD I-Mark

1. Disconnect the negative (−) battery cable.
2. Discharge the air conditioning system.
3. Disconnect and cap the liquid and suction line from the evaporator. Can use tape to cap the open lines.
4. Disconnect the retaining band from the passenger compartment intake duct.
5. Disconnect the electrical connectors from the thermostatic switch. Reach through air intake duct in the passenger compartment.
6. Remove the glove box assembly and the two evaporator housing retaining bolts in back of the glove box.
7. Remove the one retaining bolt at the bottom the the evap. housing in the engine compartment and carefully lift out the assembly.
8. Remove the thermostatic switch cover and switch.
9. Remove the case screws and clips. Separate the two halves carefully.
10. Remove the capillary bulb, external equalizer line and expansion valve. Plug all open ends.

To install:

11. Install the capillary bulb, external equalizer line and expansion valve.
12. Install the case screws and clips. Make sure the seals are in place and secure.
13. Install the thermostatic switch cover and switch.
14. Install the assembly and one retaining bolt at the bottom the the evap. housing in the engine compartment.
15. Install the two evaporator housing retaining bolts in back of the glove box and glove box assembly.
16. Connect the electrical connectors to the thermostatic switch. Reach through air intake duct in the passenger compartment.
17. Connect the retaining band to the passenger compartment intake duct.
18. Connect the liquid and suction line to the evaporator.
19. Evacuate and recharge the air conditioning system as outlined in Chapter 1.

20. Connect the negative (−) battery cable and check operation.

FWD I-Mark, P'up, Amigo, Trooper and Rodeo

1. Disconnect the negative (−) battery cable.
2. Discharge the air conditioning system as outlined in Chapter 1.
3. Disconnect and plug the inlet and outlet pipe from the evaporator.
4. Remove the glove box and disconnect the thermoswitch wire.
5. Disconnect the defroster hose and remove the evap. housing retaining nuts and bolts. Remove the evaporator assembly, being careful not to damage the seals.
6. Remove the housing retaining clips and split the housing in two. Be careful not to damage the seals.
7. Using a backup and flarenut wrench, remove the expansion valve.

To install:

8. Using a backup and flarenut wrench, install the expansion valve.
9. Install the housing halves and retaining clips. Be careful not to damage the seals.
10. Install the evap. housing and connect the defroster hose. Be careful not to damage the seals.
11. Install the glove box and connect the thermoswitch wire.
12. Connect the inlet and outlet pipe to the evaporator.
13. Evacuate and recharge the air conditioning system as outlined in Chapter 1.
14. Connect the negative (−) battery cable, check for leaks and operation.

RWD Impulse

1. Disconnect the negative (−) battery cable.
2. Discharge the air conditioning system as outlined in Chapter 1.
3. Remove the glove box and disconnect the air conditioning lines to the evaporator. Plug the lines so contamination does not enter the system.
4. Remove the evaporator housing.
5. Remove the housing retaining clips and split the housing in two. Be careful not to damage the seals.
6. Using a backup and flarenut wrench, remove the expansion valve.

To install:

7. Using a backup and flarenut wrench, install the expansion valve.
8. Install the housing halves and retaining clips. Be careful not to damage the seals.
9. Install the evaporator housing.
10. Install the glove box and connect the air conditioning lines to the evaporator.

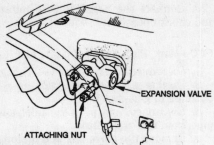

Expansion valve—FWD Impulse and Stylus

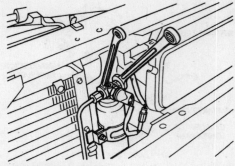

Receiver/drier assembly

11. Evacuate and recharge the air conditioning system as outlined in Chapter 1.

12. Connect the negative (−) battery cable, check for leaks and operation.

FWD Impulse and Stylus

1. Disconnect the negative (−) battery cable.

2. Discharge the air conditioning system as outlined in Chapter 1.

3. Remove the clamp and loosen the retaining nuts at the expansion valve.

4. Remove the clip and expansion valve.

To install:

5. Install the expansion valve with new O-rings with a coating of refrigerant oil applied.

6. Torque the nuts to 48 inch lbs. (6 Nm).

7. Evacuate and recharge the air conditioning system as outlined in Chapter 1.

Air Conditioner Receiver/Drier
REMOVAL AND INSTALLATION

RWD I-Mark

The receiver/drier is located next to the ignition coil on the right side inner fender. It is a tall can like assembly with an inlet and outlet pipe.

1. Disconnect the negative (−) battery cable.

2. Discharge the air conditioning system as outlined in Chapter 1.

3. Using a backup and flarenut wrench, remove the inlet and outlet pipes. Be careful not to damage the pipe fittings.

4. Immediately cap the open refrigerant lines to prevent contamination.

5. Remove the retaining clamp bolts and remove the receiver/drier.

To install:

6. Install the receiver using new O-rings. Make sure the direction of flow is facing towards the evaporator. The refrigerant flows from the condenser to the receiver to the evaporator. Tighten the fittings to 15 ft. lbs. (20 Nm).

7. Evacuate and recharge the air conditioning system as outlined in Chapter 1.

All Except RWD I-Mark

1. Disconnect the negative (−) battery cable.

2. Discharge the air conditioning system as outlined in Chapter 1.

3. On some vehicles, the front grille assembly has to be removed to access the receiver/drier assembly.

4. Disconnect the pressure switch, if so equipped.

5. Use a backup and flarenut wrench to remove the inlet and outlet pipes.

6. Plug all open refrigerant pipes to prevent contamination to sytstem.

7. Remove the bracket bolt and receiver/drier.

To install:

8. Install the unit and bracket bolt.

9. Unplug all refrigerant pipes, install new O-rings and lubricate with refrigerant oil.

10. Use a backup and flarenut wrench to install the inlet and outlet pipes. Torque to 15 ft. lbs. (20 Nm).

11. Connect the pressure switch, if so equipped.

12. On some vehicles, install the front grille assembly.

13. Evacuate and recharge the air conditioning system as outlined in Chapter 1.

14. Connect the negative (−) battery cable, check for leaks and proper operation.

Evaporator Assembly and Core
REMOVAL AND INSTALLATION

RWD I-Mark

NOTE: *When servicing the air conditioning system, always cap the disconnected refrigerant lines to prevent dirt and contamination from entering the system. Refer to Chapter 1 for discharging, evacuating and recharging the air conditioning system.*

1. Disconnect the negative (−) battery cable.

2. Discharge the air conditioning system as outlined in Chapter 1.

3. Disconnect and cap the liquid and suction

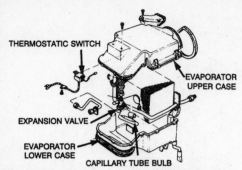

Evaporator housing and core—RWD I-Mark

line from the evaporator. Can use tape to cap the open lines.

4. Disconnect the retaining band from the passenger compartment intake duct.

5. Disconnect the electrical connectors from the thermostatic switch. Reach through air intake duct in the passenger compartment.

6. Remove the glove box assembly and the two evaporator housing retaining bolts in back of the glove box.

7. Remove the one retaining bolt at the bottom the the evap. housing in the engine compartment and carefully lift out the assembly.

8. Remove the thermostatic switch cover and switch.

9. Remove the case screws and clips. Separate the two halves carefully.

10. Remove the capillary bulb, external equalizer line and expansion valve. Plug all open ends.

11. Remove the evaporator from the case, being careful not to damage the seals.

To install:

12. Install the evaporator core into the case, making sure all seals are in place and good condition.

13. Install the capillary bulb, external equalizer line and expansion valve.

14. Install the case screws and clips. Make sure the seals are in place and secure.

15. Install the thermostatic switch cover and switch.

16. Install the assembly and one retaining bolt at the bottom the the evap. housing in the engine compartment.

17. Install the two evaporator housing retaining bolts in back of the glove box and glove box assembly.

18. Connect the electrical connectors to the thermostatic switch. Reach through air intake duct in the passenger compartment.

19. Connect the retaining band to the passenger compartment intake duct.

20. Connect the liquid and suction line to the evaporator.

21. Evacuate and recharge the air conditioning system as outlined in Chapter 1.

22. Connect the negative (−) battery cable and check operation.

FWD I-Mark, P'up, Amigo, Trooper and Rodeo

1. Disconnect the negative (−) battery cable.

2. Discharge the air conditioning system as outlined in Chapter 1.

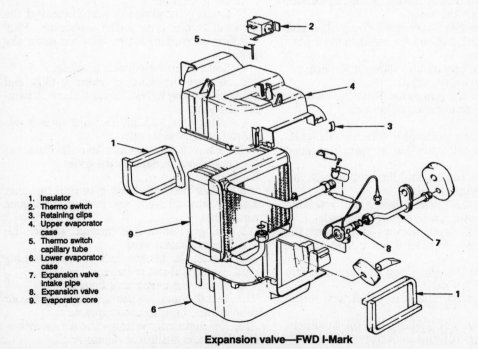

1. Insulator
2. Thermo switch
3. Retaining clips
4. Upper evaporator case
5. Thermo switch capillary tube
6. Lower evaporator case
7. Expansion valve intake pipe
8. Expansion valve
9. Evaporator core

Expansion valve—FWD I-Mark

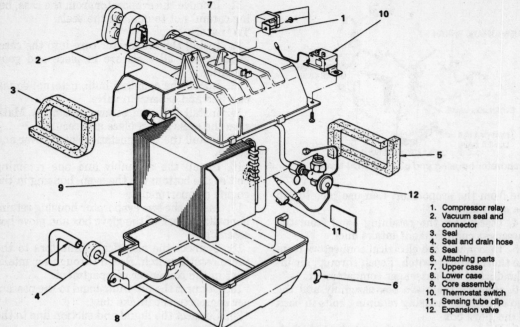

1. Compressor relay
2. Vacuum seal and connector
3. Seal
4. Seal and drain hose
5. Seal
6. Attaching parts
7. Upper case
8. Lower case
9. Core assembly
10. Thermostat switch
11. Sensing tube clip
12. Expansion valve

Expansion valve and housing—Trooper shown, P'up and Rodeo similar

3. Disconnect and plug the inlet and outlet pipe from the evaporator.

4. Remove the glove box and disconnect the thermoswitch wire.

5. Disconnect the defroster hose and remove the evap. housing retaining nuts and bolts. Remove the evaporator assembly, being careful not to damage the seals.

6. Remove the housing retaining clips and split the housing in two. Be careful not to damage the seals.

7. Using a backup and flarenut wrench, remove the expansion valve.

8. Remove the evaporator from the case, being careful not to damage the seals.

To install:

9. Install the evaporator core into the case, making sure all seals are in place and good condition.

10. Using a backup and flarenut wrench, install the expansion valve.

11. Install the housing halves and retaining clips. Be careful not to damage the seals.

12. Install the evap. housing and connect the defroster hose. Be careful not to damage the seals.

13. Install the glove box and connect the thermoswitch wire.

14. Connect the inlet and outlet pipe to the evaporator.

15. Evacuate and recharge the air conditioning system as outlined in Chapter 1.

16. Connect the negative (−) battery cable, check for leaks and operation.

RWD Impulse

1. Disconnect the negative (−) battery cable.

2. Discharge the air conditioning system as outlined in Chapter 1.

3. Remove the glove box and disconnect the air conditioning lines to the evaporator. Plug the lines so contamination does not enter the system.

4. Remove the evaporator housing.

5. Remove the housing retaining clips and split the housing in two. Be careful not to damage the seals.

6. Using a backup and flarenut wrench, remove the expansion valve.

7. Remove the evaporator from the case, being careful not to damage the seals.

To install:

8. Install the evaporator core into the case, making sure all seals are in place and good condition.

9. Using a backup and flarenut wrench, install the expansion valve.

10. Install the housing halves and retaining clips. Be careful not to damage the seals.

11. Install the evaporator housing.

12. Install the glove box and connect the air conditioning lines to the evaporator.

13. Evacuate and recharge the air conditioning system as outlined in Chapter 1.

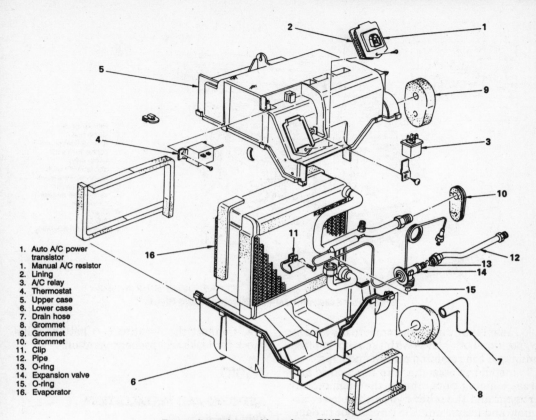

1. Auto A/C power transistor
1. Manual A/C resistor
2. Lining
3. A/C relay
4. Thermostat
5. Upper case
6. Lower case
7. Drain hose
8. Grommet
9. Grommet
10. Grommet
11. Clip
12. Pipe
13. O-ring
14. Expansion valve
15. O-ring
16. Evaporator

Expansion valve and housing—RWD Impulse

14. Connect the negative (−) battery cable, check for leaks and operation.

FWD Impulse and Stylus

1. Disconnect the negative (−) battery cable.
2. Discharge the air conditioning system as outlined in Chapter 1.
3. Disconnect the evaporator drain hose and remove the glove box.
4. Disconnect the air conditioning cut control unit, if equipped with auto. trans.
5. Remove the instrument panel lower reinforcement and disconnect the electro and resistor sensor connectors.
6. Loosen the refrigerant lines at the retaining nuts.
7. Remove the three retaining nuts, one in the engine compartment and the other two in the blower assembly and heater unit. Remove the evaporator assembly, being careful not to damage the seals.
8. Remove the assembly retaining screws and clips. Separate the two halves to remove the evaporator core.

To install:

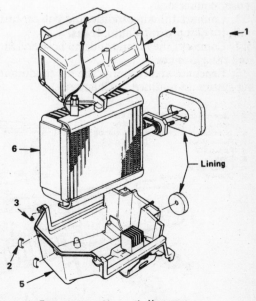

1. Evaporator assembly
2. Clip
3. Attaching screw
4. Upper case
5. Lower case
6. Evaporator core

Lining

Evaporator core—FWD Impulse and Stylus

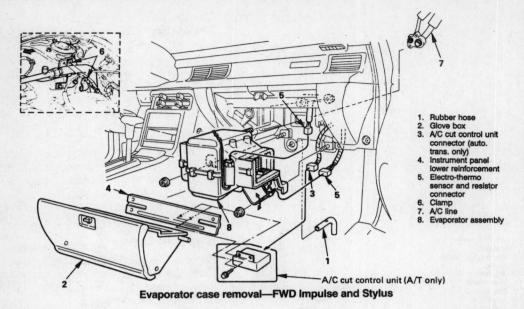

1. Rubber hose
2. Glove box
3. A/C cut control unit connector (auto. trans. only)
4. Instrument panel lower reinforcement
5. Electro-thermo sensor and resistor connector
6. Clamp
7. A/C line
8. Evaporator assembly

A/C cut control unit (A/T only)

Evaporator case removal—FWD Impulse and Stylus

9. Install the evaporator core into the assembly, position both halves with the seals in place and install the retaining screws and clips.

10. Install the assembly into the vehicle and three retaining nuts, one in the engine compartment and the other two in the blower assembly and heater unit. Be careful not to damage the seals.

11. Install and torque the refrigerant line nuts to 53 inch lbs. (6 Nm).

12. Install the instrument panel lower reinforcement and connect the electro and resistor sensor connectors.

13. Connect the air conditioning cut control unit, if equipped with auto. trans.

14. Connect the evaporator drain hose and install the glove box.

15. Evacuate and recharge the air conditioning system as outlined in Chapter 1.

16. Connect the negative (−) battery cable, check for leaks and proper operation.

RADIO

REMOVAL AND INSTALLATION

RWD I-Mark

1. Disconnect the negative (−) battery cable.
2. Remove the radio knobs by pulling off.
3. Remove the ashtray.
4. Remove the air conditioning control knobs by pulling off.
5. Remove the four screws and then the control panel cover.
6. Remove the two screws retaining the radio.
7. Pull the radio out and disconnect the harness connector.

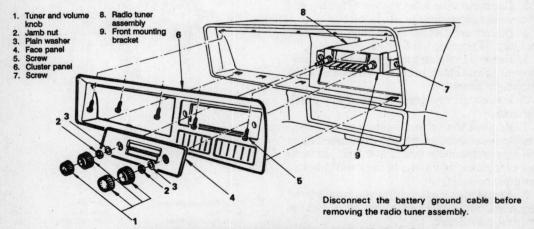

1. Tuner and volume knob
2. Jamb nut
3. Plain washer
4. Face panel
5. Screw
6. Cluster panel
7. Screw
8. Radio tuner assembly
9. Front mounting bracket

Disconnect the battery ground cable before removing the radio tuner assembly.

Radio assembly—early model P'up shown, RWD I-Mark similar

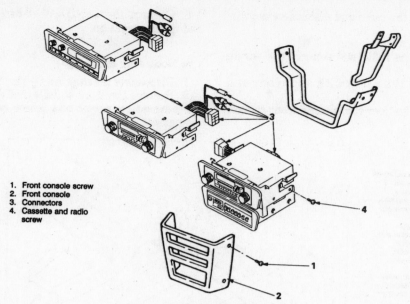

1. Front console screw
2. Front console
3. Connectors
4. Cassette and radio
   screw

Radio—FWD I-Mark

To install:

8. Connect the harness connector and install the radio and screws.

9. Install the panel cover and four screws.

10. Install the air conditioning control knobs by pushing on.

11. Install the ashtray.

12. Install the radio knobs by pushing on.

13. Connect the negative (−) battery cable and check operation.

FWD I-Mark

1. Disconnect the negative (−) battery cable.

2. Remove the front console screws and console.

3. Disconnect the wiring harness and remove the radio and cassette.

To install:

4. Install the radio and connect the wiring harness.

5. Install the front console and screws.

6. Connect the battery cable and check operation.

Early Model P'up

1. Disconnect the negative (−) battery cable.

2. Remove the radio knobs by pulling off.

3. Remove the jamb nuts, washers and face panel.

4. Remove the instrument cluster panel and radio retaining screws.

5. Remove the radio and disconnect the harness connector.

To install:

6. Connect the harness connector, install the radio and screws.

7. Install the instrument cluster panel.

8. Install the jamb nuts, washers and face panel.

9. Install the radio knobs by pushing on.

10. Connect the negative (−) battery cable and check operation.

RWD Impulse

1. Disconnect the negative (−) battery cable.

2. Remove the front console to body and console to bracket.

3. Remove the console assembly.

4. Remove the front console pad and front console screws.

5. Remove the bezel to radio screws, bezel and radio/equalizer assemblies.

6. Disconnect the wiring harnesses while removing.

To install:

7. Connect the wiring harnesses while installing.

8. Install the radio, bezel and radio screws.

9. Install the front console pad and front console.

10. Install the console assembly.

11. Install the front console to body and console to bracket screw.

12. Connect the negative (−) battery cable and check operation.

FWD Impulse and Stylus

1. Disconnect the negative (−) battery cable.

2. Remove the floor console and front console panel.

3. Remove the radio with audio box and bracket.

4. Remove the radio and disconnect the wiring harness.

To install:

5. Install the radio and connect the wiring harness.

6. Install the radio with audio box and bracket.

7. Install the floor console and front console panel.

8. Connect the negative (−) battery cable and check operation.

Late Model P'up and Amigo

1. Disconnect the negative (−) battery cable.

2. Remove the front console and disconnect the harness connector and feeder cable, if so eqiupped.

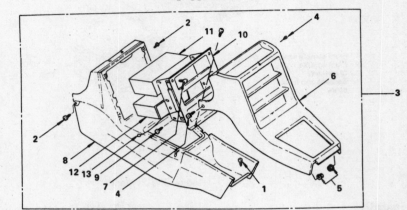

1. Front console screw
2. Front console bracket screw
3. Console assembly
4. Front console pad screws
5. Flange nuts
6. Front console pad
7. Bezel screws
8. Front console
9. Bezel screws
10. Bezel
11. Graphic equalizer or cassette deck
12. Cassette deck with radio
13. Ground cable

Radio and equalizer—RWD Impulse

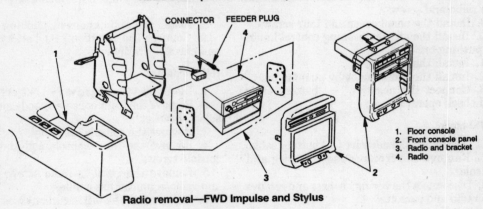

CONNECTOR FEEDER PLUG

1. Floor console
2. Front console panel
3. Radio and bracket
4. Radio

Radio removal—FWD Impulse and Stylus

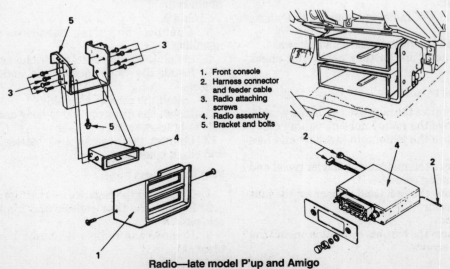

1. Front console
2. Harness connector and feeder cable
3. Radio attaching screws
4. Radio assembly
5. Bracket and bolts

Radio—late model P'up and Amigo

3. Remove the radio retaining screws and radio assembly.

4. Remove the radio bracket and bolts.

To install:

5. Install the radio bracket and bolts.

6. Install the radio retaining screws and radio assembly.

7. Install the front console and connect the harness connector and feeder cable, if so equipped.

8. Connect the negative (−) battery cable and check operation.

Trooper

1. Disconnect the negative (−) battery cable.

2. Remove the radio knobs, nuts and washers.

3. Remove the case, radio and screws.

4. Disconnect the wiring harness and remove the radio retaining screws.

5. Remove the brackets from the radio chassis.

To install:

6. Install the brackets to the radio chassis.

1. Knobs, nuts and washer
2. Panel assembly
3. Radio case screws
4. Harness connector
5. Radio fixing screws
6. Radio
7. Bracket and bolts
8. Antenna screws
9. Antenna assembly
10. Front speaker screws
11. Front speaker
12. Harness connector
13. Rear speaker screws
14. Rear speaker
15. Harness connector

AM/FM RADIO WITH CASSETTE PLAYER

AM/FM RADIO

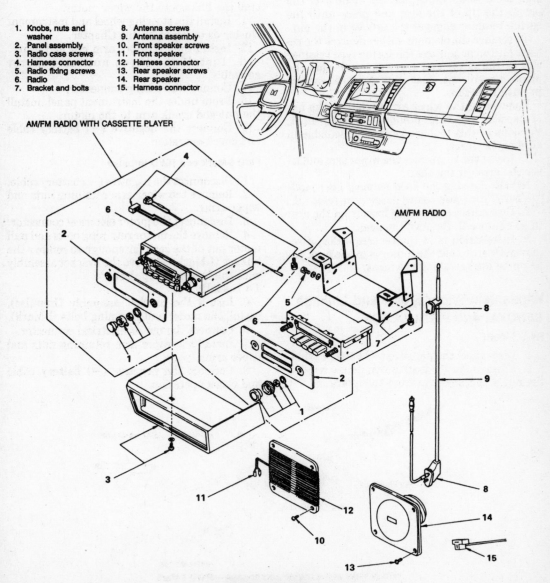

Radio—Trooper

7. Connect the wiring harness and install the radio retaining screws.

8. Install the case, radio and screws.

9. Install the radio washers, nuts and knobs.

10. Connect the negative (−) battery cable.

WINDSHIELD WIPERS

Blade and Arm

REMOVAL AND INSTALLATION

If the wiper assembly has a press type release tab at the center, simply depress the tab and remove the blade. If the blade has no release tab, use a screwdriver to depress the spring at the center. This will release the assembly. To install the assembly, position the blade over the pin at the tip of the arm and press until the spring retainer engages the groove in the pin.

To remove the element, either depress the release button or squeeze the spring type retainer clip at the outer end together, and slide the blade element out. Just slide the new element in until it latches.

Removal of the wiper arms requires the use of a special tool, G.M. J-8966 or its equivalent. Versions of this tool are generally available in auto parts stores.

1. Insert the tool under the wiper arm and lever the arm off the shaft.

NOTE: *Raising the hood on most later models will facilitate easier wiper arm removal.*

2. Disconnect the washer hose from the arm (if so equipped). Remove the arm.

3. Installation is in the reverse order of removal. Be sure that the motor is in the park position before installing the arms.

Windshield Wiper Motor and Linkage

REMOVAL AND INSTALLATION

RWD I-Mark

1. Disconnect the negative (−) battery cable.

2. From under the instrument panel, remove the nut and crank arm from the motor.

3. Disconnect the wiring connector.

4. Remove the three nuts and motor assembly.

5. To remove the left linkage assembly: remove the left wiper arm nut and arm.

6. Remove the steering wheel and instrument cluster as outlined in this Chapter.

7. Reaching through the cluster opening, pry the linkage loose from the wiper transmission, being careful not to damage the nylon bushing.

8. Remove the three bolts and wiper transmission linkage from the cowl.

To install:

9. To install the left left linkage assembly. Install the wiper transmission and three bolts to the cowl.

10. Reaching through the cluster opening, install the linkage to the wiper motor.

11. Install the steering wheel and instrument cluster as outlined in this Chapter.

12. Install the left wiper arm nut and arm.

13. Install the three nuts and motor assembly.

14. Connect the wiring connector.

15. From under the instrument panel, install the nut and crank arm to the motor.

16. Connect the negative (−) battery cable and check operation.

FWD I-Mark and RWD Impulse

1. Disconnect the negative (−) battery cable.

2. Remove the wiper arm retaining nuts and wiper arms.

3. Disconnect the motor electrical connector.

4. Remove the motor retaining bolts and pull motor out of the cowl far enough to remove the linkage (I-Mark). Remove the bracket assembly with the linkage (Impulse).

To install:

5. Install the bracket assembly (Impulse). Install the motor and retaining bolts (I-Mark).

6. Connect the motor electrical connector.

7. Install the wiper arm retaining nuts and wiper arms.

8. Connect the negative (−) battery cable and check operation.

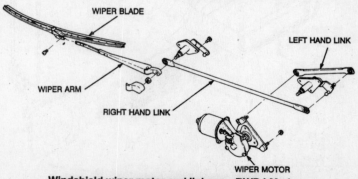

WIPER BLADE

LEFT HAND LINK

WIPER ARM

RIGHT HAND LINK

WIPER MOTOR

Windshield wiper motor and linkage—RWD I-Mark

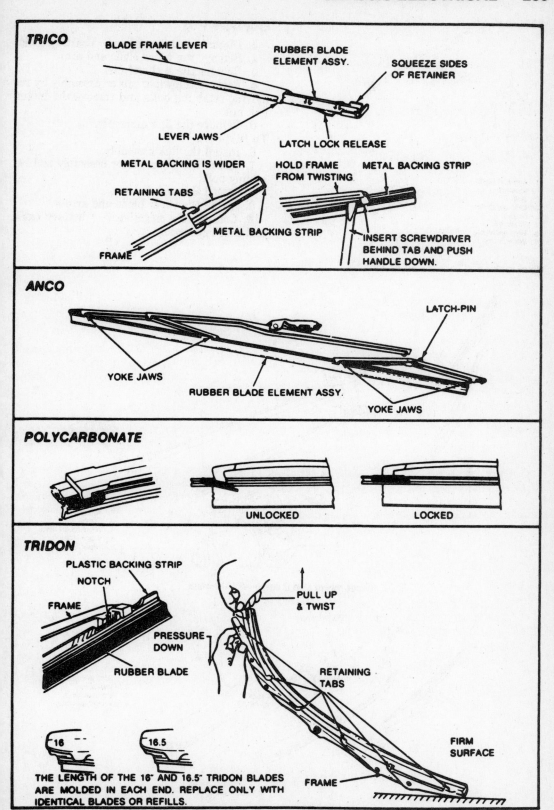

Popular styles of wiper refills

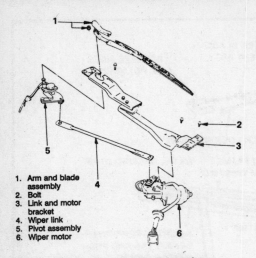

1. Arm and blade assembly
2. Bolt
3. Link and motor bracket
4. Wiper link
5. Pivot assembly
6. Wiper motor

Wiper motor and linkage—RWD Impulse

Early Model P'up

1. Disconnect the negative (−) battery cable.
2. Remove the wiper blade and arm.
3. Remove the seal and nut.
4. Remove the wiper motor assembly by removing retaining bolts and remove the motor link nut.
5. Remove the link assembly.

To install:

6. Install the link assembly.
7. Install the wiper motor assembly and retaining bolts.
8. Install the seal and nut.
9. Install the wiper blade and arm.
10. Connect the negative (−) battery cable and check operation.

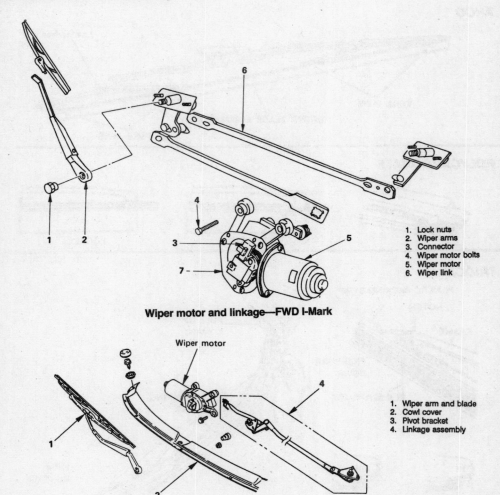

1. Lock nuts
2. Wiper arms
3. Connector
4. Wiper motor bolts
5. Wiper motor
6. Wiper link

Wiper motor and linkage—FWD I-Mark

Wiper motor

1. Wiper arm and blade
2. Cowl cover
3. Pivot bracket
4. Linkage assembly

Wiper motor and linkage—FWD Impulse and Stylus

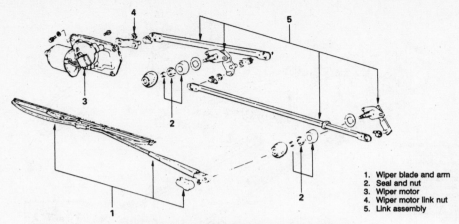

1. Wiper blade and arm
2. Seal and nut
3. Wiper motor
4. Wiper motor link nut
5. Link assembly

Wiper motor and linkage—early model P'up

Late Model P'up, Amigo and Rodeo

1. Disconnect the negative (−) battery cable and wiper motor connector.

2. Remove the wiper motor bracket screws and pull the motor out of the cowl far enough to disconnect the motor from the linkage at the ball joint.

3. Remove the wiper arm cap, nut and arm.

4. Remove the cowl vent cover and linkage from the access hole.

To install:

5. Install the linkage and cowl vent cover.

6. Install the wiper arm cap, nut and arm.

7. Connect the motor to the linkage at the ball joint, install the motor and retaining screws.

8. Connect the negative (−) battery cable and wiper motor connector.

Trooper

1. Disconnect the negative (−) battery cable.

2. Remove the wiper arm assembly from the linkage.

3. Remove the link pivot nut.

4. Remove the center and left work hole covers.

5. Disconnect the motor wiring.

6. Remove the wiper motor assembly with the link assembly intact.

To install:

7. Install the wiper motor assembly with the link assembly intact.

8. Connect the motor wiring.

9. Install the center and left work hole covers.

10. Install the link pivot nut.

11. Install the wiper arm assembly to the linkage.

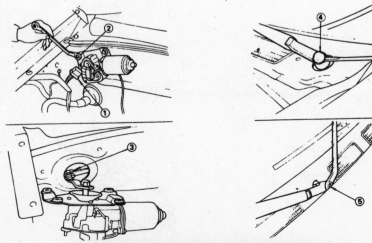

Wiper motor and linkage—P'up, Amigo and Rodeo

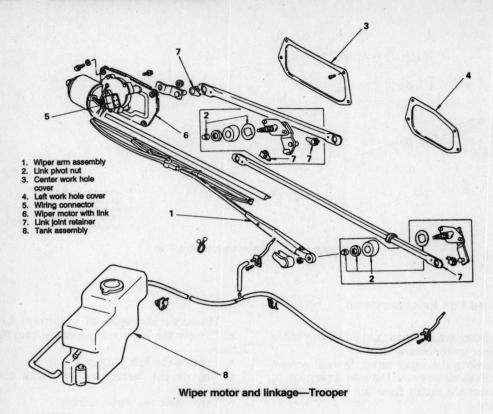

1. Wiper arm assembly
2. Link pivot nut
3. Center work hole cover
4. Left work hole cover
5. Wiring connector
6. Wiper motor with link
7. Link joint retainer
8. Tank assembly

Wiper motor and linkage—Trooper

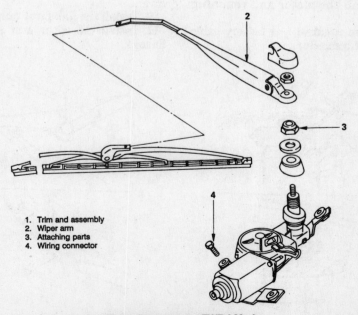

1. Trim and assembly
2. Wiper arm
3. Attaching parts
4. Wiring connector

Rear wiper motor—FWD I-Mark

12. Connect the negative (−) battery cable and check operation.

Rear Window Wiper Motor
REMOVAL AND INSTALLATION

1. Disconnect the negative (−) battery cable.
2. Open the liftgate or hatchback. Remove the trim panel.
3. Remove the wiper arm assembly.

4. Remove the motor shaft nut, motor retaining bolts and disconnect wiring connectors.
5. Remove the motor from the access panel.
To install:
6. Install the motor into the access panel.
7. Install the motor shaft nut, motor retaining bolts and disconnect wiring connectors.
8. Install the wiper arm assembly.
9. Install the trim panel.
10. Connect the negative (−) battery cable and check operation.

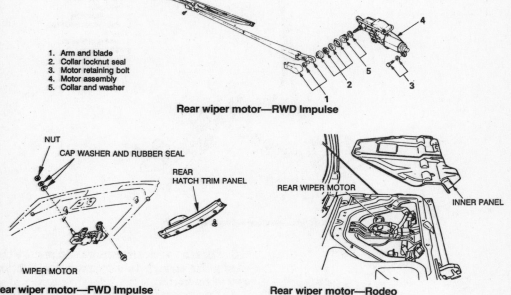

1. Arm and blade
2. Collar locknut seal
3. Motor retaining bolt
4. Motor assembly
5. Collar and washer

Rear wiper motor—RWD Impulse

NUT
CAP WASHER AND RUBBER SEAL

REAR
HATCH TRIM PANEL

WIPER MOTOR

Rear wiper motor—FWD Impulse

REAR WIPER MOTOR

INNER PANEL

Rear wiper motor—Rodeo

INSTRUMENTS AND SWITCHES

Instrument Cluster
REMOVAL AND INSTALLATION

I-Mark

1. Disconnect the negative (−) battery cable.
2. Remove the cluster panel (RWD) and cluster hood (FWD).
3. Remove the cluster retaining screws (RWD). Rotate the cluster outward and disconnect the electrical and speedometer cable connectors.
4. Disconnect the wiper switch (FWD).
5. Remove the cluster screws and disconnect the electrical and speedometer connectors (FWD).
To install:
6. Install the cluster and connect the electrical and speedo connectors.
7. Connect the wiper switch (FWD).

8. Install and tighten the cluster retaining screw.
9. Install the cluster trim panel (RWD) and cluster hood (FWD). Connect the battery cable and check operation.

Impulse and Stylus

1. Disconnect the negative (−) battery cable.
2. Set the ignition switch to LOCK.
3. Remove the steering wheel and column cover as outlined in this Chapter (RWD only).
4. Remove the upper cluster hood.
5. Remove the cluster retaining screw, lift cluster out of instrument panel and disconnect the electrical and speedo connectors. Remove the satellite switch assemblies with the cluster (RWD only).
To install:
6. Install the cluster and retaining screws.
7. Install the upper cluster hood.

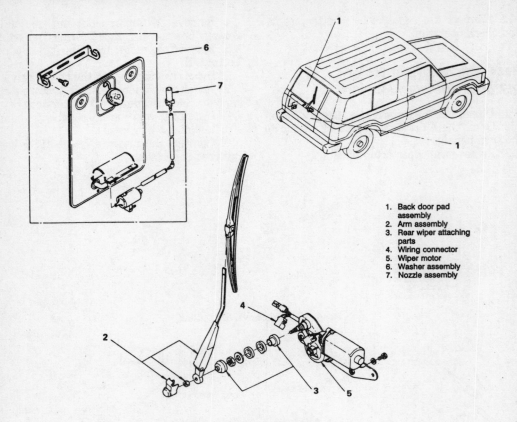

1. Back door pad assembly
2. Arm assembly
3. Rear wiper attaching parts
4. Wiring connector
5. Wiper motor
6. Washer assembly
7. Nozzle assembly

Rear wiper motor—Trooper

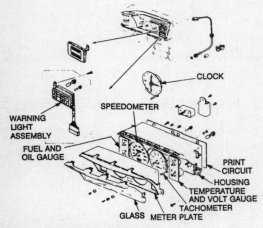

CLOCK

SPEEDOMETER

WARNING
LIGHT
ASSEMBLY

FUEL AND
OIL GAUGE

PRINT
CIRCUIT

HOUSING

TEMPERATURE
AND VOLT GAUGE

TACHOMETER

GLASS   METER PLATE

Instrument cluster—RWD I-Mark

8. Install the steering wheel and column cover as outlined in this Chapter (RWD only).

9. Connect the negative (−) battery cable and check operation.

P'up, Amigo, Rodeo and Trooper

1. Disconnect the negative (−) battery cable.

2. Move the tilt steering wheel to the full down position, if so equipped.

3. Loosen the cluster screws and remove the cluster far enough to disconnect the lighting switch connector.

4. Disconnect the wiper and washer connector from the switch.

5. Remove the cluster from the hood, if needed.

To install:

6. Install the cluster to the hood, if removed.

7. Connect the wiper and washer connector to the switch.

8. Install the cluster and connect the lighting switch connector.

9. Connect the negative (−) battery cable and check operation.

Speedometer

REMOVAL AND INSTALLATION

1. Disconnect the negative (−) battery cable.

2. Remove the instrument cluster from the vehicle as outlined in this Chapter.

3. Remove the housing retaining screws or release the cluster cover snaps. Be careful not to damage the cluster cover during removal.

4. Remove the speedometer assembly from the cluster housing.

To install:

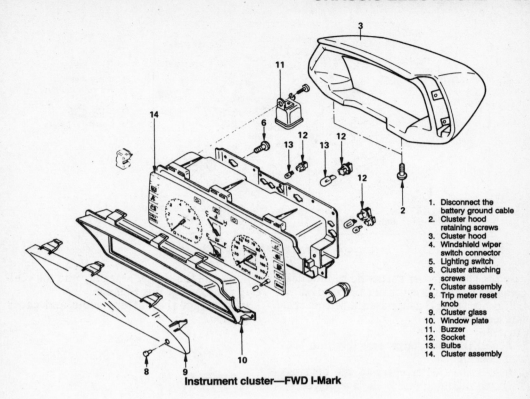

1. Disconnect the battery ground cable
2. Cluster hood retaining screws
3. Cluster hood
4. Windshield wiper switch connector
5. Lighting switch
6. Cluster attaching screws
7. Cluster assembly
8. Trip meter reset knob
9. Cluster glass
10. Window plate
11. Buzzer
12. Socket
13. Bulbs
14. Cluster assembly

Instrument cluster—FWD I-Mark

5. Install the speedometer assembly into the cluster housing.

6. Install the cluster cover to the housing and tighten retaining screws, if so equipped.

7. Install the cluster assembly into the vehicle as outlined in this Chapter.

8. Connect the battery cable and check operation.

Fuel Gauge

REMOVAL AND INSTALLATION

1. Disconnect the negative (−) battery cable.

2. Remove the instrument cluster from the vehicle as outlined in this Chapter.

3. Remove the housing retaining screws or

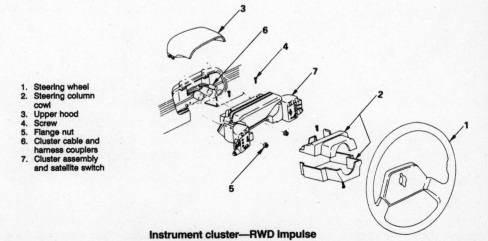

1. Steering wheel
2. Steering column cowl
3. Upper hood
4. Screw
5. Flange nut
6. Cluster cable and harness couplers
7. Cluster assembly and satellite switch

Instrument cluster—RWD Impulse

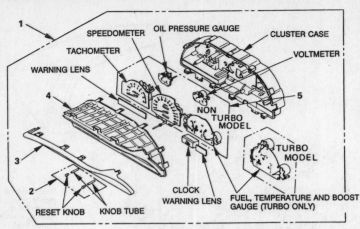

1. Cluster assembly
2. Trip meter and clock reset knob
3. Cluster glass
4. Cluster bezel
5. Cluster and gauges

Instrument cluster—FWD Impulse and Stylus

release the cluster cover snaps. Be careful not to damage the cluster cover during removal.

4. Remove the fuel gauge assembly from the cluster housing.

To install:

5. Install the fuel gauge assembly into the cluster housing.

6. Install the cluster cover to the housing and tighten retaining screws, if so equipped.

7. Install the cluster assembly into the vehicle as outlined in this Chapter.

8. Connect the battery cable and check operation.

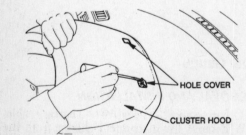

Instrument cluster hood—FWD Impulse and Stylus

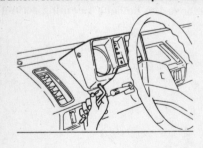

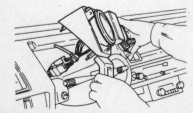

Instrument cluster—Trooper

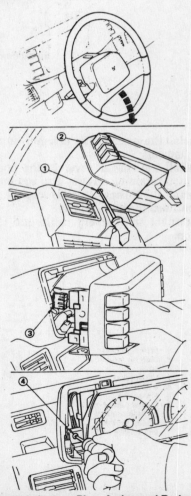

Instrument cluster—P'up, Amigo and Rodeo

Instrument Panel

REMOVAL AND INSTALLATION

RWD I-Mark

1. Disconnect the negative (−) battery cable.
2. Remove the glove box and steering column cover.
3. Remove the gearshift knob, console retaining screws and console.
4. Pull off the radio knobs and remove the radio bezel.
5. Remove the air conditioning control bezel.
6. Remove the radio and disconnect.
7. Remove the ashtray. Remove the four screws retaining the center cluster cover to the instrument panel. Draw the cluster cover out and disconnect the cigar lighter. Remove the center cluster cover.
8. Remove the ashtray support. Remove the air conditioning control unit by lifting the controls through the instrument panel.
9. Remove the fuse box cover and fuse box.
10. Through the fuse box opening, remove the wing nut located behind the switch panel.
11. Remove the cluster panel-to-meter hood screws and draw the cluster panel out. Disconnect the connectors. Remove and disconnect the instrument cluster.
12. Disconnect the headlight switch.
13. Remove both defroster hoses.
14. Remove the front parcel shelf and front cover. Remove the seven hole covers and screws to remove the front cover.

15. Remove the five bolts and five screws securing the lower part of the instrument panel.
16. Remove the two bolts on both sides of the panel.
17. Remove the four upper panel retaining bolts.
18. Remove the instrument panel and grilles.
To install:
19. Install the instrument panel and grilles.
20. Install the four upper panel retaining bolts.
21. Install the two bolts on both sides of the panel.
22. Install the five bolts and five screws securing the lower part of the instrument panel.
23. Install the front parcel shelf and front cover. Install the seven hole covers and screws.
24. Install both defroster hoses.
25. Connect the headlight switch.
26. Install the cluster panel-to-meter hood screws and cluster panel. Connect the connectors.
27. Through the fuse box opening, install the wing nut located behind the switch panel.
28. Install the fuse box cover and fuse box.
29. Install the ashtray support. Install the air conditioning control unit.
30. Install the ashtray.
31. Install the radio.
32. Install the air conditioning control bezel.
33. Install the radio bezel and knobs.
34. Install the gearshift knob, console retaining screws and console.
35. Install the glove box and steering column cover.

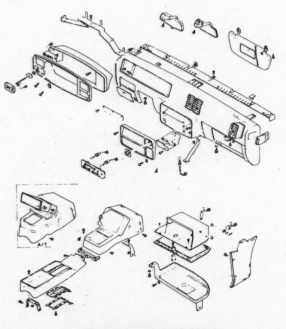

Instrument panel—RWD I-Mark

36. Connect the negative (−) battery cable and check operation.

FWD I-Mark

1. Disconnect the negative (−) battery cable.
2. Remove the glove box and console assembly as outlined in this Chapter.
3. Remove the instrument cluster hood and cluster assembly.
4. Remove the speedometer boss and side trim.
5. Remove the fuse box, right and left air defroster hoses.
6. Remove the steering column-to-instrument panel bolts.
7. Remove the panel screw cover and screws. Remove the instrument panel from the vehicle.
To install:
8. Install the instrument panel. Install the panel screw cover and screws.
9. Remove the steering column-to-instrument panel bolts.
10. Install the fuse box, right and left air defroster hoses.
11. Install the speedometer boss and side trim.
12. Install the instrument cluster hood and cluster assembly.
13. Install the glove box and console assembly as outlined in this Chapter.
14. Connect the negative (−) battery cable.

RWD Impulse

1. Disconnect the negative (−) battery cable.
2. Remove the steering wheel.
3. Remove the lap vent grille, instrument cluster hood and cluster/switch assembly.
4. Remove the console and instrument panel front cover.
5. Remove the front piller trim cover and instrument panel grille.
6. Remove the instrument panel retaining screws and panel.
To install:
7. Install the instrument panel retaining screws and panel.
8. Install the front piller trim cover and instrument panel grille.
9. Install the console and instrument panel front cover.
10. Install the lap vent grille, instrument cluster hood and cluster/switch assembly.
11. Install the steering wheel.
12. Connect the negative (−) battery cable.

FWD Impulse and Stylus

1. Disconnect the negative (−) battery cable.
2. Remove the switch bezel, cigar lighter bezel and engine hood opener cable.
3. Remove the knee pad, glove box and front console bracket.
4. Remove the instrument cluster hood and cluster assembly.

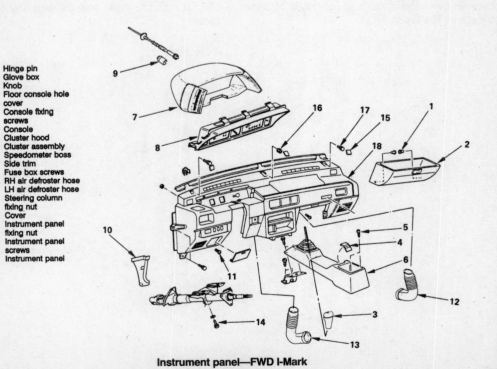

1. Hinge pin
2. Glove box
3. Knob
4. Floor console hole cover
5. Console fixing screws
6. Console
7. Cluster hood
8. Cluster assembly
9. Speedometer boss
10. Side trim
11. Fuse box screws
12. RH air defroster hose
13. LH air defroster hose
14. Steering column fixing nut
15. Cover
16. Instrument panel fixing nut
17. Instrument panel screws
18. Instrument panel

Instrument panel—FWD I-Mark

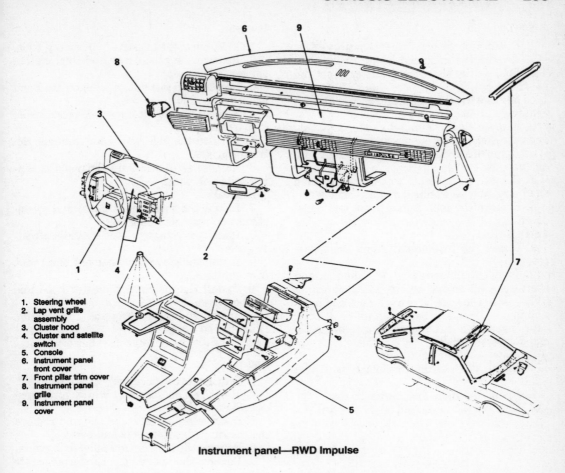

1. Steering wheel
2. Lap vent grille assembly
3. Cluster hood
4. Cluster and satellite switch
5. Console
6. Instrument panel front cover
7. Front pillar trim cover
8. Instrument panel grille
9. Instrument panel cover

Instrument panel—RWD Impulse

5. Remove the front cover hole cover and front cover.

6. Remove the instrument panel assembly.

To install:

7. Install the instrument panel assembly.

8. Install the front cover hole cover and front cover.

9. Install the instrument cluster hood and cluster assembly.

10. Install the knee pad, glove box and front console bracket.

11. Install the switch bezel, cigar lighter bezel and engine hood opener cable.

12. Connect the negative (−) battery cable.

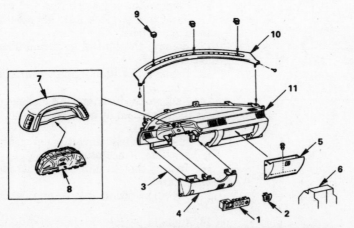

1. Switch bezel
2. Cigar lighter bezel
3. Engine hood cable
4. Knee pad assembly
5. Glove box
6. Front console bracket
7. Cluster hood
8. Cluster assembly
9. Front cover hole cover
10. Front cover
11. Instrument panel

Instrument panel—FWD Impulse and Stylus

Amigo and P'up

1. Disconnect the negative (−) battery cable.
2. Remove the radio and heater knobs.
3. Remove the instrument cluster panel and radio.
4. Remove the side ventilator by prying with a suitable prybar.
5. Remove the instrument cluster assembly and defroster nozzle.
6. Remove the ventilator duct, duct and heater unit.
7. Remove the steering wheel, columns and shaft assembly as outlined in this Chapter.
8. Remove the instrument panel and panel cover.

To install:

9. Install the instrument panel and panel cover.
10. Install the steering wheel, columns and shaft assembly as outlined in this Chapter.
11. Install the ventilator duct, duct and heater unit.
12. Install the instrument cluster assembly and defroster nozzle.
13. Install the side ventilator.
14. Install the instrument cluster panel and radio.
15. Install the radio and heater knobs.
16. Connect the negative (−) battery cable.

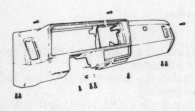

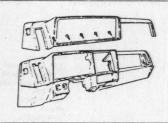

Instrument panel—P'up and Amigo

Trooper

1. Disconnect the negative (−) battery cable.
2. Remove the parcel tray and combination gauges, if so equipped.
3. Remove the instrument cluster hood and cluster assembly.
4. Remove the glove compartment and radio, if so equipped.
5. Remove the side ventilator and side defroster grille.
6. Remove the 10 instrument panel retaining bolts and panel.

To install:

7. Install the instrument panel and 10 instrument panel retaining bolts.
8. Install the side ventilator and side defroster grille.
9. Install the glove compartment and radio, if so equipped.
10. Install the instrument cluster hood and cluster assembly.
11. Install the parcel tray and combination gauges, if so equipped.
12. Connect the negative (−) battery cable.

Rodeo

1. Disconnect the negative (−) battery cable.
2. Remove the steering wheel and cowl assembly.
3. Insert a prybar into the gap and remove the instrument panel grille and bezel.
4. Remove the instrument panel fixing nuts.
5. Remove the instrument cluster assembly as outlined in this Chapter.
6. Remove the cluster hood and engine hood opener cable.
7. Remove the steering lower cover and fuse box.
8. Remove the dash trim panel and ECM (electronic control module).
9. Remove the console and lower reinforcement.
10. Remove the speaker grilles and speakers.
11. Remove the glove box, air conditioning and heater knobs.
12. Remove the control lever and disconnect the cables.
13. Remove the illumination controller and switch bezel.
14. Remove the instrument panel and disconnect the harnesses, if necessary.

To install:

15. Install the instrument panel and connect the harnesses, if necessary.
16. Install the illumination controller and switch bezel.
17. Install the control lever and connect the cables.
18. Install the glove box, air conditioning and heater knobs.

1. Parcel tray
1a. Combination gauges
2. Cluster hood
3. Cluster assembly
4. Glove compartment
5. Radio
6. Ventilator and defroster grille duct
7. Bolts
8. Instrument panel

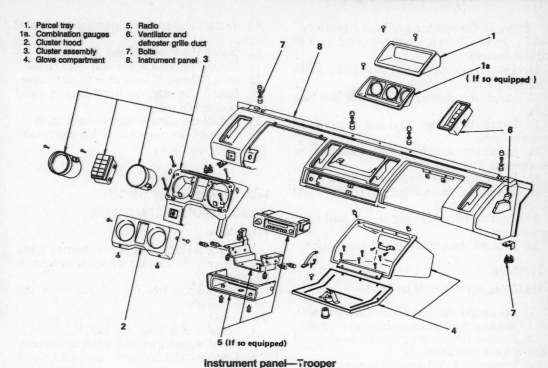

Instrument panel—Trooper

1. Steering wheel and steering cowl
2. Grille and bezel
2a. Driving pattern indicator panel (A/T only)
3. Meter hood
4. Meter cluster assembly
5. Meter complete
6. Engine hood release handle
7. Steering lower cover
8. Fuse box
9. Side trim
10. ECM box
11. Front console
12. Lower reinforcement
13. Speaker grille
14. Glove box
15. Knob
16. Bezel
17. Control lever assembly
18. Illumination controller
19. Instrument panel

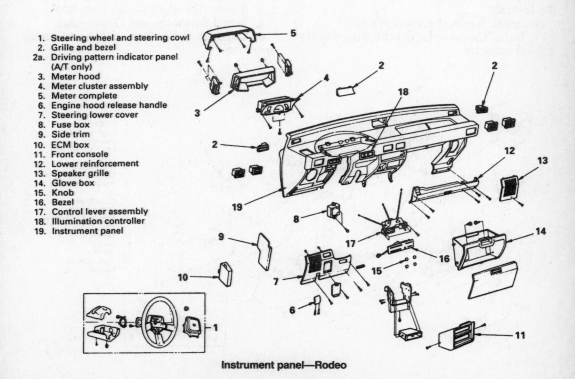

Instrument panel—Rodeo

19. Install the speaker grilles and speakers.
20. Install the console and lower reinforcement.
21. Install the dash trim panel and ECM (electronic control module).
22. Install the steering lower cover and fuse box.
23. Install the cluster hood and engine hood opener cable.
24. Install the instrument cluster assembly as outlined in this Chapter.
25. Install the instrument panel fixing nuts.
26. Install the instrument panel grille and bezel.
27. Install the steering wheel and cowl assembly.
28. Connect the negative (−) battery cable.

Console

REMOVAL AND INSTALLATION

1. Disconnect the negative (−) battery cable.
2. Remove the climate control lever knob.
3. Remove the ashtray, front console panel and console side panel.
4. Remove the shift knob or indicator cover.
5. Remove the console pad and floor panel.
6. Remove the knee pad and glove box.
7. Remove the control lever assembly and radio.
8. Remove the control unit behind the climate control assembly.
9. Remove the front console bracket.

To install:
10. Install the front console bracket.
11. Install the control unit behind the climate control assembly.

12. Install the control lever assembly and radio.
13. Install the knee pad and glove box.
14. Install the console pad and floor panel.
15. Install the shift knob or indicator cover.
16. Install the ashtray, front console panel and console side panel.
17. Install the climate control lever knob.
18. Connect the negative (−) battery cable and check operation.

Windshield Wiper Switch

REMOVAL AND INSTALLATION

RWD I-Mark

1. Disconnect the negative (−) battery cable.
2. Remove the steering wheel as outlined in Chapter 8.
3. Remove the steering column cover and switch assembly.

To install:
4. Install and connect the switch.
5. Install steering column cover and wheel.
6. Connect the battery cable and check operation.

FWD I-Mark, All Impulse and Stylus

1. Disconnect the negative (−) battery cable.
2. Remove the instrument cluster hood retaining screws and lift the hood from the instrument panel.
3. Remove the wiper switch from hood.
4. Install the switch and cluster hood.
5. Connect the battery cable and check operation.

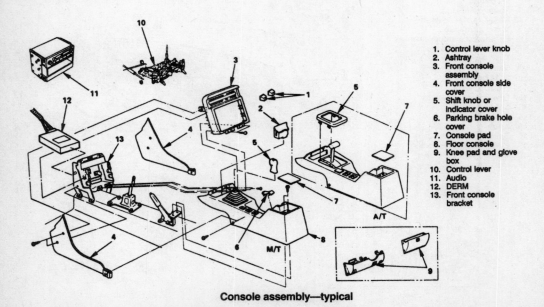

1. Control lever knob
2. Ashtray
3. Front console assembly
4. Front console side cover
5. Shift knob or indicator cover
6. Parking brake hole cover
7. Console pad
8. Floor console
9. Knee pad and glove box
10. Control lever
11. Audio
12. DERM
13. Front console bracket

Console assembly—typical

P'up, Amigo, Trooper and Rodeo

1. Disconnect the negative (−) battery cable.
2. Remove the steering wheel as outlined in Chapter 8.
3. Remove the steering column shroud and disconnect the multi-switch connector.
4. Remove the multi-switch assembly from the steering column.
5. Install the switch, column shroud and steering wheel.
6. Connect the battery cable and check operation.

Rear Window Wiper Switch

REMOVAL AND INSTALLATION

1. Disconnect the negative (−) battery cable.
2. Carefully slide a small prybar under the lower lip of the switch and pry outward. Be careful not to damage the switch or the instrument panel.
3. Remove the switch and disconnect the electrical connector.
4. Install the switch and connect the battery cable.

Headlight Switch

REMOVAL AND INSTALLATION

RWD I-Mark, Early P'up and Trooper

1. Disconnect the negative (−) battery cable.
2. Using a small screwdriver, loosen the knob set screw and remove the switch knob.

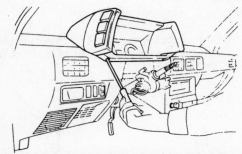

Wiper switch and instrument cluster hood—FWD I-Mark, RWD Impulse similar

Rear wiper switch—typical

3. Remove the retaining nut, being careful not to damage the instrument panel.
4. Remove the switch and disconnect the wiring.

To install:

5. Install the switch and connect the wiring.
6. Install the retaining nut and knob.
7. Connect the battery cable and check operation.

FWD I-Mark, Impulse and Stylus

1. Disconnect the negative (−) battery cable.
2. Remove the instrument cluster hood as outlined in the "Instrument Cluster" section in this Chapter.
3. Remove the headlight switch from the left side of the cluster hood.
4. Install the switch in the hood and reinstall the hood onto the instrument panel.
5. Connect the battery cable and check operation.

Late Model P'up, Amigo and Rodeo

1. Disconnect the negative (−) battery cable.
2. Remove the instrument cluster as outlined in this Chapter.

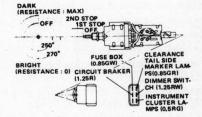

Headlight switch—RWD I-Mark, early P'up and Trooper

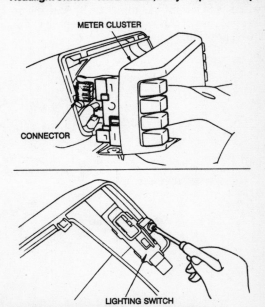

Headlight switch—P'up, Amigo and Rodeo

3. Loosen the switch screws and remove the switch.

4. Install the switch and tighten screws.

5. Install the cluster and connect the negative battery cable.

Clock

REMOVAL AND INSTALLATION

RWD I-Mark

1. Disconnect the negative (−) battery cable.

2. Remove the instrument cluster as outlined in this Chapter.

3. Remove the cluster lens by depressing the tabs.

4. Remove the clock retaining screws and clock.

To install:

5. Install the clock and retaining screws.

6. Install the cluster lens and cluster into the the instrument panel.

7. Connect the battery cable and check operation.

Backup/Neutral Start Switch

REMOVAL AND INSTALLATION

RWD I-Mark, Impulse and Early P'up

1. Disconnect the negative (−) battery cable.

2. Remove the shift console assembly.

3. Remove the switch screws and switch.

4. Disconnect the electrical connector.

To install:

5. Install the switch and retaining screws.

6. **Adjust the switch as follows:** loosen the two screws and set the shift lever in the NEUTRAL position. Bring the center of the switch slide bar into alignment with the line on the steel case of the switch indicating the NEUTRAL position.

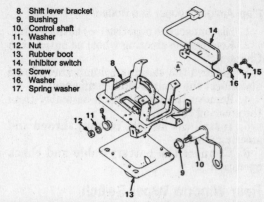

8. Shift lever bracket
9. Bushing
10. Control shaft
11. Washer
12. Nut
13. Rubber boot
14. Inhibitor switch
15. Screw
16. Washer
17. Spring washer

Backup/neutral start switch—RWD I-Mark, Impulse and early P'up

SHIFT LEVER POSITION	COLOR OF CABLE					
	BL	B	RB	RL	LgW	Lg
P, N	O—O					
R			O—O			
D, 1, 2					O—O	

BL, B STARTING CIRCUIT
RB, RL BACKUP LIGHT CIRCUIT
LGW, LG COASTING FUEL CUT CIRCUIT
(GAS ENGINE ONLY)

Backup/neutral start switch terminals—RWD I-Mark

7. When the adjustment is completed, check function of the switch by making a continuity test with shift lever in each position.

Ignition Switch

REMOVAL AND INSTALLATION

1. Disconnect the negative (−) battery cable.

2. Remove the steering wheel as outlined in Chapter 8.

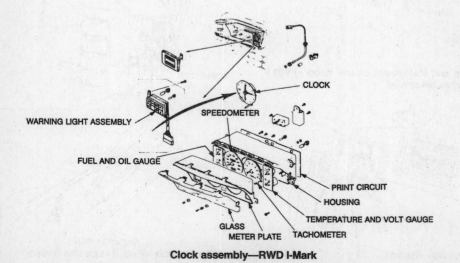

WARNING LIGHT ASSEMBLY

CLOCK

SPEEDOMETER

FUEL AND OIL GAUGE

PRINT CIRCUIT

HOUSING

TEMPERATURE AND VOLT GAUGE

GLASS
METER PLATE   TACHOMETER

Clock assembly—RWD I-Mark

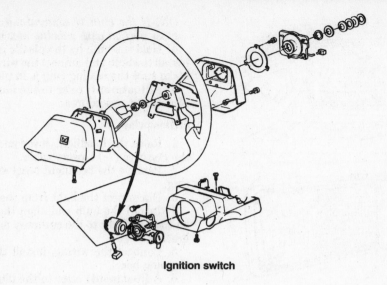

Ignition switch

3. Remove the steering column shroud.
4. Disconnect the switch wiring and remove the switch from the column.
To install:
5. Install the switch and wiring.
6. Install the column shroud and steering wheel.
7. Connect the battery cable and check operation.

Speedometer Cable

REMOVAL AND INSTALLATION

1. Disconnect the negative (−) battery cable.
2. Raise the vehicle and support with jackstands.
3. Loosen the speedometer cable nut at the transmission.
4. If the cable is accessible from under the instrument panel, reach up to the cable and release it from the speedometer head.
5. If not, remove the instrument cluster as outlined in this Chapter.
To install:
6. Connect the speedometer cable and install the instrument cluster as outlined in this Chapter.
7. If the cable is accessible from under the instrument panel, reach up to the cable and connect it to the speedometer head.
8. Tighten the speedometer cable nut at the transmission.
9. Lower the vehicle.
10. Connect the negative (−) battery cable and check operation.

LIGHTING

Headlights

REMOVAL AND INSTALLATION

Non-aerodynamic

1. Disconnect the negative (−) battery cable.
2. Remove the front grille or headlight bezel.
3. Remove the headlight bulb retaining ring, headlight and disconnect the wiring.
4. Before installing, spray some silicone grease into the bulb socket.
5. Connect the wiring and install the bulb.
6. Install the retaining ring and bezel.

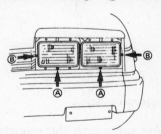

Headlight aiming—RWD Impulse

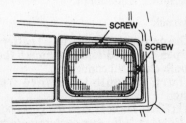

Non-aerodynamic headlight adjustment

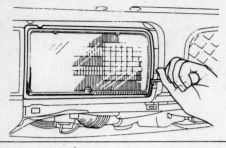

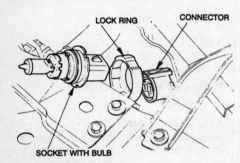

Headlight aiming—Rodeo and Trooper

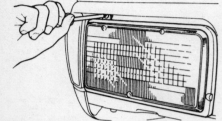

LOCK RING   CONNECTOR

SOCKET WITH BULB

Headlight bulb removal

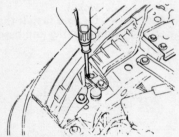

Vertical adjustment—Stylus

7. **Adjustment:** turn the adjusting screw (A) for vertical adjustment. Turn the screw (B) for horizontal adjustment.

Aerodynamic

1. Disconnect the negative (−) battery cable.
2. Open the hood and disconnect the headlight bulb electrical connector.
3. Turn the bulb to remove from the housing.
   CAUTION: *Do not touch the glass portion of the Halogen bulb. Any contamination on the bulb may cause the bulb to burst when turned*

ON. *If the bulb is contaminated, clean the glass portion with rubbing alcohol.*
4. Hold the bulb by the plastic portion only. Install the bulb and connect the wiring harness. Make sure the sealing ring is in place.
5. **Adjustment:** refer to the illustration for adjustment procedures.

FWD Impulse

1. Raise the headlight cover and disconnect the negative (−) battery cable.
2. Remove the headlight bezel and retaining ring.
3. Disconnect the light from the harness.
4. Install the bulb and align the protrusion on the headlight to the cut-away portion of the bracket.
5. Connect the wiring, install the retaining ring and bezel.
6. **Adjustment:** refer to the illustration.

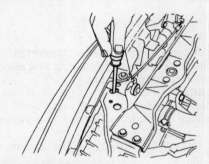

Horizontal adjustment—Stylus

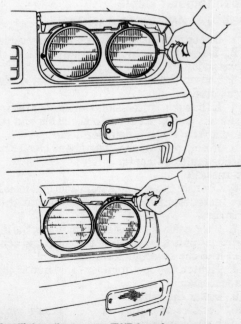

Headlight adjustment—FWD Impulse

Signal and Marker Lights

REMOVAL AND INSTALLATION

Front Turn Signal and Parking

1. Disconnect the negative (−) battery cable.
2. Remove the lens retaining screws.
3. Pull the assembly out of the bumper and remove the bulb.
4. Install the bulb and assembly into the vehicle.
5. Connect the battery cable and check operation.

Side Marker Lights

1. Disconnect the negative (−) battery cable.
2. Remove the lens retaining screws, lens assembly and bulb. Turn the bulb holder out of the lens to remove.
3. Install the bulb, lens assembly and retaining screws.

Rear Turn Signal, Brake and Parking

1. Disconnect the negative (−) battery cable.
2. Remove the lens retaining screws, lens and bulb for the P'up, Amigo, Trooper and Rodeo.
3. Enter the trunk or luggage compartment. Remove the garnish panel and remove the bulb socket for the cars.

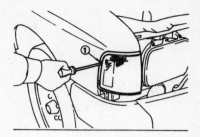

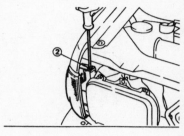

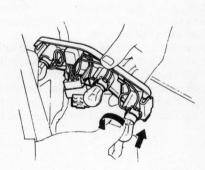

Marker light removal—corner mount type

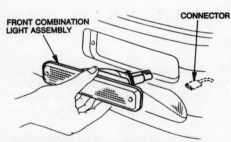

Turn signal and parking light—typical

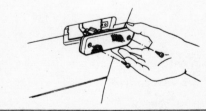

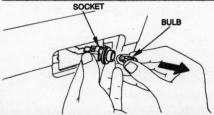

Marker light removal—side mounted type

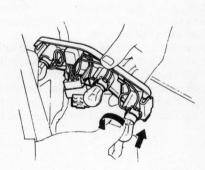

Rear light assembly—cars

4. Install the bulb and install the socket and garnish panel.

TRAILER WIRING

Wiring the car for towing is fairly easy. There are a number of good wiring kits available and these should be used, rather than trying to design your own. All trailers will need brake lights and turn signals as well as tail lights and side marker lights. Most states require extra

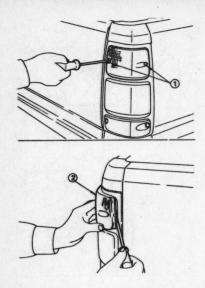

Rear light assembly—P'up, Trooper, Amigo and Rodeo

marker lights for overly wide trailers. Also, most states have recently required back-up lights for trailers, and most trailer manufacturers have been building trailers with back-up lights for several years.

Additionally, some Class I, most Class II and just about all Class III trailers will have electric brakes.

Add to this number an accessories wire, to operate trailer internal equipment or to charge the trailer's battery, and you can have as many as seven wires in the harness.

Determine the equipment on your trailer and buy the wiring kit necessary. The kit will contain all the wires needed, plus a plug adapter set which included the female plug, mounted on the bumper or hitch, and the male plug, wired into, or plugged into the trailer harness.

When installing the kit, follow the manufacturer's instructions. The color coding of the wires is standard throughout the industry.

One point to note: some domestic vehicles, and most imported vehicles, have separate turn signals. On most domestic vehicles, the brake lights and rear turn signals operate with the same bulb. For those vehicles with separate turn signals, you can purchase an isolation unit so that the brake lights won't blink whenever the turn signals are operated, or, you can go to your local electronics supply house and buy four diodes to wire in series with the brake and turn signal bulbs. Diodes will isolate the brake and turn signals. The choice is yours. The isolation units are simple and quick to install, but far more expensive than the diodes. The diodes, however, require more work to install properly, since they require the cutting of each bulb's wire and soldering in place of the diode.

One final point, the best kits are those with a spring loaded cover on the vehicle mounted socket. This cover prevents dirt and moisture from corroding the terminals. Never let the vehicle socket hang loosely; always mount it securely to the bumper or hitch.

CIRCUIT PROTECTION

Fuses

The fuse block on some models is located under the instrument panel next to the steering wheel and is a swing down unit. Other models have the fuse block located on the right side of the dash and access is gained through an opening in the instrument panel.

Each fuse block uses miniature fuses which are designed for increased circuit protection and greater reliability. The compact fuse is a

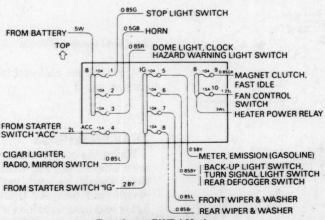

Fuse box—RWD I-Mark

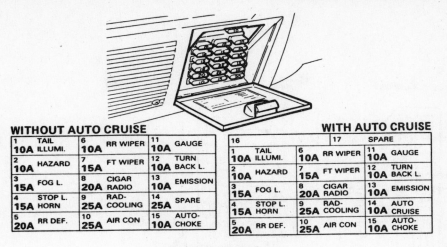

WITHOUT AUTO CRUISE

1 10A	TAIL ILLUMI.	6 10A	RR WIPER	11 10A	GAUGE
2 10A	HAZARD	7 15A	FT WIPER	12 10A	TURN BACK L.
3 15A	FOG L.	8 20A	CIGAR RADIO	13 10A	EMISSION
4 15A	STOP L. HORN	9 25A	RAD- COOLING	14 25A	SPARE
5 20A	RR DEF.	10 25A	AIR CON	15 10A	AUTO- CHOKE

WITH AUTO CRUISE

16		17	SPARE		
1 10A	TAIL ILLUMI.	6 10A	RR WIPER	11 10A	GAUGE
2 10A	HAZARD	7 15A	FT WIPER	12 10A	TURN BACK L.
3 15A	FOG L.	8 20A	CIGAR RADIO	13 10A	EMISSION
4 15A	STOP L. HORN	9 25A	RAD- COOLING	14 10A	AUTO CRUISE
5 20A	RR DEF.	10 25A	AIR CON	15 10A	AUTO- CHOKE

Fuse box—FWD I-Mark

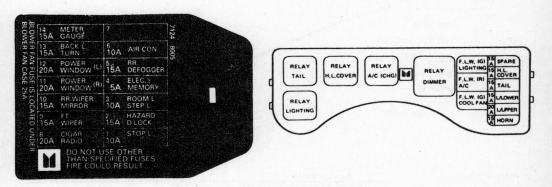

Fuse and relay box—RWD Impulse

blade terminal design which allows fingertip removal and replacement.

Although the fuses are interchangeable, the amperage values are molded in bold, color coded, easy to read numbers on the fuse body. Use only fuses of equal replacement valve.

A blown fuse can easily be checked by visual inspection or by continuity testing.

Fusible Links

In addition to circuit breakers and fuses, the wiring harness incorporates fusible links to protect the wiring. Links are used rather than a fuse, in wiring circuits that are not normally fused, such as the ignition circuit. Isuzu fusible links are color coded and load circuits to match the color coding of the circuits they protect. Each link is four gauges smaller than the cable it protects, and is marked on the insulation with the gauge size because the insulation makes it appear heavier than it really is.

The engine compartment wiring harness has several fusible links. The same size wire with a special hypalon insulation must be used when replacing a fusible link.

The links are located in the following areas:

RWD I-Mark

- At the starter solenoid, red, 0.7
- Between ignition switch and ignition coil, brown, 0.3

P'up

- At the starter solenoid, red, 0.7

REPLACEMENT

1. Determine which circuit is damaged, its location and the cause of the open fuse link. If the damaged fuse link is one of three fed by a common No. 10 or 12 gauge feed wire, determine the specific affected circuit.
2. Disconnect the negative battery cable.
3. Cut the damaged fuse link from the wiring

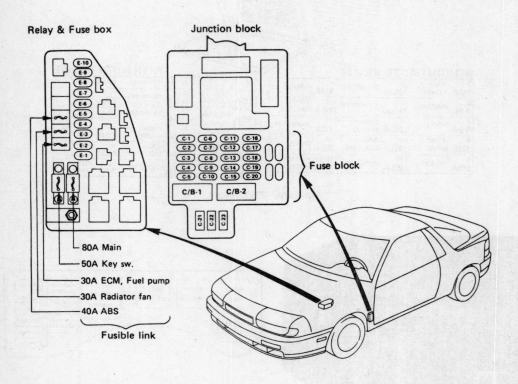

Relay & Fuse box

Junction block

Fuse block

- 80A Main
- 50A Key sw.
- 30A ECM, Fuel pump
- 30A Radiator fan
- 40A ABS

Fusible link

Relay & Fuse box

No.	Usage
80A	Main
50A	Key SW
40A	ABS (only for model with ABS)
30A	ECM Fuel pump
30A	Radiator fan
E-1	Blower motor
E-2	Heater & A/C
E-3	—
E-4	A/C condenser fan
E-5	Headlight cover
E-6	ABS (only for model with ABS)
E-7	Headlight
E-8	Headlight
E-9	—
E-10	—

(Fusible link brace covers rows 80A through 30A Radiator fan)

Junction block

No.	Usage
C-1	Audio Door mirror
C-2	Electrical IG
C-3	RR wiper & washer
C-4	Fog light
C-5	Dome light Clock
C-6	Cigar lighter
C-7	Meter Gauge
C-8	Windshield wiper & washer
C-9	Door lock
C-10	RR Defogger
C-11	Engine
C-12	Backup light Turn signal light
C-13	—
C-14	—
C-15	Tail, illumination

No.	Usage
C-16	IG coil
C-17	—
C-18	—
C-19	Stoplight ECU (A/T)
C-20	Horn Hazard warning
C-21	Starter
C-22	SIR-1
C-23	SIR-2
C/B-1	Power window, Sun roof
C/B-2	—

Fuse, relay and junction box—FWD Impulse

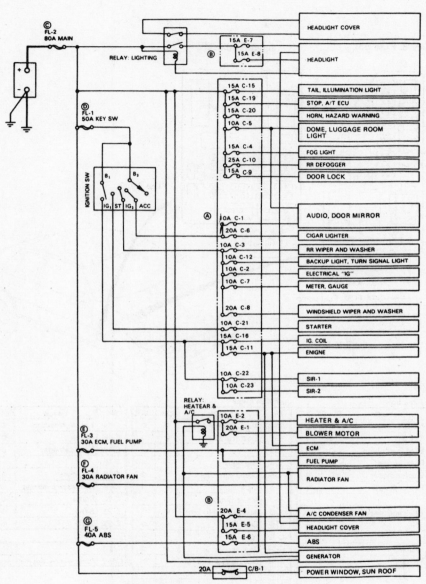

Fuse box circuit diagram—FWD Impulse

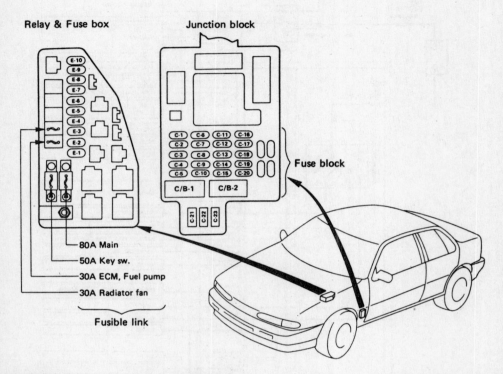

Relay & Fuse box

Junction block

Fuse block

80A Main
50A Key sw.
30A ECM, Fuel pump
30A Radiator fan

Fusible link

Relay & Fuse box

No.		Usage	SOHC	DOHC
Fusible link	80A	Main	o	o
	50A	Key SW	o	o
	30A	ECM Fuel pump	o	o
	30A	Radiator fan	o	o
E-1		Blower motor	o	o
E-2		Heater & A/C	o	o
E-3		—	—	—
E-4		A/C condenser fan	o	o
E-5		—	—	—
E-6		—	—	—
E-7		Headlight	o	o
E-8		Headlight	o	o
E-9		—	—	—
E-10		—	—	—

Junction block

No.	Usage	SOHC	DOHC
C-1	Audio Door mirror	o	o
C-2	Electrical IG	o	o
C-3	—	—	—
C-4	Fog light	—	o
C-5	Dome light Clock	o	o
C-6	Cigar lighter	o	o
C-7	Meter Gauge	o	o
C-8	Windshield wiper & washer	o	o
C-9	Door lock	—	o
C-10		—	—
C-11	Engine	o	o
C-12	Backup light Turn signal light	o	o
C-13	—	—	—
C-14	—	—	—

No.	Usage	SOHC	DOHC
C-15	Tail, illumination	o	o
C-16	IG coil	o	o
C-17	Rear defogger	o	o
C-18	—	—	—
C-19	Stoplight	o	o
C-20	Horn Hazard warning	o	o
C-21	Starter	o	o
C-22	SIR-1	o	o
C-23	SIR-2	o	o
C/B-1	—	—	—
C/B-2	Power window, Sun roof	—	o

Fuse, relay and junction box—Stylus

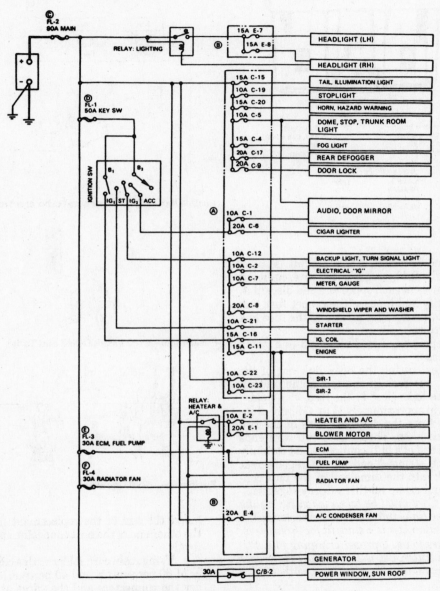

Note: (A) Junction block (Installed at the lower left-hand side of the dash side trim panel.)
(B) Relay and fuse box (Installed at the left hand side of the engine compartment.)
(C) (D) (E) (F) Fusible link (Installed in the relay and fuse box.)

Fuse box circuit diagram—Stylus

1. To test for a blown fuse, pull the fuse out and check visually
2. With the circuit activated, use a test light across the points shown

MINI FUSE COLOR CODES	
5 AMPS	TAN
10 AMPS	RED
20 AMPS	YELLOW
25 AMPS	WHITE

Blown fuse

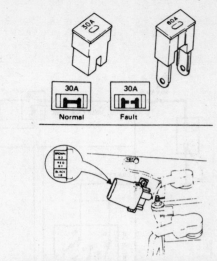

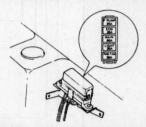

Fusible link—FWD I-Mark non-Turbo and Trooper

harness and discard it. If the fuse link is one of three circuits fed by a single feed wire, cut it out of the harness at each splice end and discard it.

4. Identify and procure the proper fuse link and butt connectors for attaching the fuse link to the harness.

5. To repair any fuse link in a 3-link group with one feed:

a. After cutting the open link out of the harness, cut each of the remaining undamaged fuse links close to the feed wire weld.

b. Strip approximately ½ in. (13mm) of insulation from the detached ends of the two good fuse links, Then insert two wire ends into one end of a butt connector and carefully push one stripped end of the replacement fuse link into the same end of the butt connector and crimp all three firmly together.

NOTE: *Care must be taken when fitting the three fuse links into the butt connector as the internal diameter is a snug fit for three wires. Make sure to use a proper crimping tool. Pliers, side cutter, etc. will not apply the proper crimp to retain the wires and withstand a pull test.*

c. After crimping the butt connector to the three fuse links, cut the weld portion from the feed wire and strip approximately ½ in. (13mm) of insulation from the cut end. Insert the stripped end into the open end of the butt connector and crimp very firmly.

d. To attach the remaining end of the replacement fuse link, strip approximately ½ in. (13mm) of insulation from the wire end of the circuit from which the blown fuse link was removed, and firmly crimp a butt connector or equivalent to the stripped wire. Then,

Fusible link—FWD I-Mark DOHC and Turbo

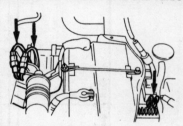

Fusible link—RWD Impulse

insert the end of the replacement link into the other end of the butt connector and crimp firmly.

e. Using rosin core solder with a consistency of 60 percent tin and 40 percent lead, solder the connectors and the wires at the repairs and insulate with electrical tape.

6. To replace any fuse link on a single circuit in a harness, cut out the damaged portion, strip approximately ½ in. (13mm) of insulation from the two wire ends and attach the appropriate replacement fuse link to the stripped wire ends with two proper size butt connectors. Solder the connectors and wires and insulate with tape.

7. To repair any fuse link which has an eyelet terminal on one end such as the charging circuit, cut off the open fuse link behind the weld,

strip approximately ½ in. (13mm) of insulation from the cut end and attach the appropriate new eyelet fuse link to the cut stripped wire with an appropriate size butt connector. Solder

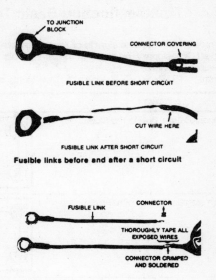

Fusible links before and after a short circuit

New fusible links are spliced to the wire

the connectors and wires at the repair and insulate with tape.

8. Connect the negative battery cable to the battery and test the system for proper operation.

NOTE: *Do not mistake a resistor wire for a fuse link. The resistor wire is generally longer and has print stating, "Resistor-don't cut or splice".*

When attaching a single No. 16, 17, 18 or 20 gauge fuse link to a heavy gauge wire, always double the stripped wire end of the fuse link before inserting and crimping it into the butt connector for positive wire retention.

Circuit Breakers

Various circuit breakers are located under the instrument panel and in the fuse and relay box in the engine compartment. In order to gain access to these components, it may be necessary to first remove the under dash padding. Most of the circuit breakers are located in the fuse and relay box or the fuse panel.

Flashers

The turnsignal and hazard flasher is located under the instrument panel next to the steering column on the early model vehicles. Late model vehicles have the flashers located in the fuse box.

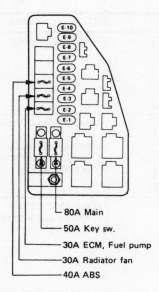

Fusible link—FWD Impulse

- 80A Main
- 50A Key sw.
- 30A ECM, Fuel pump
- 30A Radiator fan
- 40A ABS

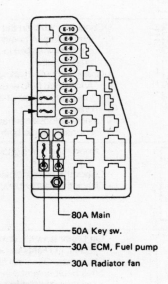

Fusible link—Stylus

- 80A Main
- 50A Key sw.
- 30A ECM, Fuel pump
- 30A Radiator fan

Troubleshooting Basic Turn Signal and Flasher Problems

Most problems in the turn signals or flasher system, can be reduced to defective flashers or bulbs, which are easily replaced. Occasionally, problems in the turn signals are traced to the switch in the steering column, which will require professional service.

F = Front   R = Rear   ● = Lights off   ○ = Lights on

Problem		Solution
Turn signals light, but do not flash		• Replace the flasher
No turn signals light on either side		• Check the fuse. Replace if defective. • Check the flasher by substitution • Check for open circuit, short circuit or poor ground
Both turn signals on one side don't work		• Check for bad bulbs • Check for bad ground in both housings
One turn signal light on one side doesn't work		• Check and/or replace bulb • Check for corrosion in socket. Clean contacts. • Check for poor ground at socket
Turn signal flashes too fast or too slow		• Check any bulb on the side flashing too fast. A heavy-duty bulb is probably installed in place of a regular bulb. • Check the bulb flashing too slow. A standard bulb was probably installed in place of a heavy-duty bulb. • Check for loose connections or corrosion at the bulb socket
Indicator lights don't work in either direction		• Check if the turn signals are working • Check the dash indicator lights • Check the flasher by substitution

One indicator light doesn't light		• On systems with 1 dash indicator: See if the lights work on the same side. Often the filaments have been reversed in systems combining stoplights with taillights and turn signals.
		  Check the flasher by substitution
		• On systems with 2 indicators: Check the bulbs on the same side
		  Check the indicator light bulb
		  Check the flasher by substitution

Troubleshooting Basic Lighting Problems

Problem	Cause	Solution
Lights		
One or more lights don't work, but others do	• Defective bulb(s) • Blown fuse(s) • Dirty fuse clips or light sockets • Poor ground circuit	• Replace bulb(s) • Replace fuse(s) • Clean connections • Run ground wire from light socket housing to car frame
Lights burn out quickly	• Incorrect voltage regulator setting or defective regulator • Poor battery/alternator connections	• Replace voltage regulator • Check battery/alternator connections
Lights go dim	• Low/discharged battery • Alternator not charging • Corroded sockets or connections • Low voltage output	• Check battery • Check drive belt tension; repair or replace alternator • Clean bulb and socket contacts and connections • Replace voltage regulator
Lights flicker	• Loose connection • Poor ground • Circuit breaker operating (short circuit)	• Tighten all connections • Run ground wire from light housing to car frame • Check connections and look for bare wires
Lights "flare"—Some flare is normal on acceleration—if excessive, see "Lights Burn Out Quickly"	• High voltage setting	• Replace voltage regulator
Lights glare—approaching drivers are blinded	• Lights adjusted too high • Rear springs or shocks sagging • Rear tires soft	• Have headlights aimed • Check rear springs/shocks • Check/correct rear tire pressure
Turn Signals		
Turn signals don't work in either direction	• Blown fuse • Defective flasher • Loose connection	• Replace fuse • Replace flasher • Check/tighten all connections
Right (or left) turn signal only won't work	• Bulb burned out • Right (or left) indicator bulb burned out • Short circuit	• Replace bulb • Check/replace indicator bulb • Check/repair wiring
Flasher rate too slow or too fast	• Incorrect wattage bulb • Incorrect flasher	• Flasher bulb • Replace flasher (use a variable load flasher if you pull a trailer)
Indicator lights do not flash (burn steadily)	• Burned out bulb • Defective flasher	• Replace bulb • Replace flasher
Indicator lights do not light at all	• Burned out indicator bulb • Defective flasher	• Replace indicator bulb • Replace flasher

Troubleshooting Basic Dash Gauge Problems

Problem	Cause	Solution
Coolant Temperature Gauge		
Gauge reads erratically or not at all	• Loose or dirty connections • Defective sending unit	• Clean/tighten connections • Bi-metal gauge: remove the wire from the sending unit. Ground the wire for an instant. If the gauge registers, replace the sending unit.
	• Defective gauge	• Magnetic gauge: disconnect the wire at the sending unit. With ignition ON gauge should register COLD. Ground the wire; gauge should register HOT.
Ammeter Gauge—Turn Headlights ON (do not start engine). Note reaction		
Ammeter shows charge Ammeter shows discharge Ammeter does not move	• Connections reversed on gauge • Ammeter is OK • Loose connections or faulty wiring • Defective gauge	• Reinstall connections • Nothing • Check/correct wiring • Replace gauge
Oil Pressure Gauge		
Gauge does not register or is inaccurate	• On mechanical gauge, Bourdon tube may be bent or kinked	• Check tube for kinks or bends preventing oil from reaching the gauge
	• Low oil pressure	• Remove sending unit. Idle the engine briefly. If no oil flows from sending unit hole, problem is in engine.
	• Defective gauge	• Remove the wire from the sending unit and ground it for an instant with the ignition ON. A good gauge will go to the top of the scale.
	• Defective wiring	• Check the wiring to the gauge. If it's OK and the gauge doesn't register when grounded, replace the gauge.
	• Defective sending unit	• If the wiring is OK and the gauge functions when grounded, replace the sending unit
All Gauges		
All gauges do not operate	• Blown fuse • Defective instrument regulator	• Replace fuse • Replace instrument voltage regulator
All gauges read low or erratically	• Defective or dirty instrument voltage regulator	• Clean contacts or replace
All gauges pegged	• Loss of ground between instrument voltage regulator and car • Defective instrument regulator	• Check ground • Replace regulator
Warning Lights		
Light(s) do not come on when ignition is ON, but engine is not started	• Defective bulb • Defective wire	• Replace bulb • Check wire from light to sending unit
	• Defective sending unit	• Disconnect the wire from the sending unit and ground it. Replace the sending unit if the light comes on with the ignition ON.
Light comes on with engine running	• Problem in individual system • Defective sending unit	• Check system • Check sending unit (see above)

Troubleshooting the Heater

Problem	Cause	Solution
Blower motor will not turn at any speed	• Blown fuse • Loose connection • Defective ground • Faulty switch • Faulty motor • Faulty resistor	• Replace fuse • Inspect and tighten • Clean and tighten • Replace switch • Replace motor • Replace resistor
Blower motor turns at one speed only	• Faulty switch • Faulty resistor	• Replace switch • Replace resistor
Blower motor turns but does not circulate air	• Intake blocked • Fan not secured to the motor shaft	• Clean intake • Tighten security
Heater will not heat	• Coolant does not reach proper temperature • Heater core blocked internally • Heater core air-bound • Blend-air door not in proper position	• Check and replace thermostat if necessary • Flush or replace core if necessary • Purge air from core • Adjust cable
Heater will not defrost	• Control cable adjustment incorrect • Defroster hose damaged	• Adjust control cable • Replace defroster hose

Troubleshooting Basic Windshield Wiper Problems

Problem	Cause	Solution
Electric Wipers		
Wipers do not operate— Wiper motor heats up or hums	• Internal motor defect • Bent or damaged linkage • Arms improperly installed on linking pivots	• Replace motor • Repair or replace linkage • Position linkage in park and reinstall wiper arms
Wipers do not operate— No current to motor	• Fuse or circuit breaker blown • Loose, open or broken wiring • Defective switch • Defective or corroded terminals • No ground circuit for motor or switch	• Replace fuse or circuit breaker • Repair wiring and connections • Replace switch • Replace or clean terminals • Repair ground circuits
Wipers do not operate— Motor runs	• Linkage disconnected or broken	• Connect wiper linkage or replace broken linkage
Vacuum Wipers		
Wipers do not operate	• Control switch or cable inoperative • Loss of engine vacuum to wiper motor (broken hoses, low engine vacuum, defective vacuum/fuel pump) • Linkage broken or disconnected • Defective wiper motor	• Repair or replace switch or cable • Check vacuum lines, engine vacuum and fuel pump • Repair linkage • Replace wiper motor
Wipers stop on engine acceleration	• Leaking vacuum hoses • Dry windshield • Oversize wiper blades • Defective vacuum/fuel pump	• Repair or replace hoses • Wet windshield with washers • Replace with proper size wiper blades • Replace pump

Drive Train

7

UNDERSTANDING THE MANUAL TRANSMISSION

Because of the way an internal combustion engine breathes, it can produce torque, or twisting force, only within a narrow speed range. Most modern, overhead valve engines must turn at about 2,500 rpm to produce their peak torque. By 4,500 rpm they are producing so little torque that continued increases in engine speed produce no power increases.

The torque peak on overhead camshaft engines is, generally, much higher, but much narrower.

The manual transmission and clutch are employed to vary the relationship between engine speed and the speed of the wheels so that adequate engine power can be produced under all circumstances. The clutch allows engine torque to be applied to the transmission input shaft gradually, due to mechanical slippage. The truck can, consequently, be started smoothly from a full stop.

The transmission changes the ratio between the rotating speeds of the engine and the wheels by the use of gears. 4-speed or 5-speed transmissions are most common. The lower gears allow full engine power to be applied to the rear wheels during acceleration at low speeds.

The transmission contains a mainshaft which passes all the way through the transmission, from the clutch to the driveshaft. This shaft is separated at one point, so that front and rear portions can turn at different speeds.

Power is transmitted by a countershaft in the lower gears and reverse. The gears of the countershaft mesh with gears on the mainshaft, allowing power to be carried from one to the other. All the countershaft gears are integral with that shaft, while several of the mainshaft gears can either rotate independently of the shaft or be locked to it. Shifting from one gear to the next causes one of the gears to be freed from rotating with the shaft and locks another to it. Gears are locked and unlocked by internal dog clutches which slide between the center of the gear and the shaft. The forward gears usually employ synchronizers; friction members which smoothly bring gear and shaft to the same speed before the toothed dog clutches are engaged.

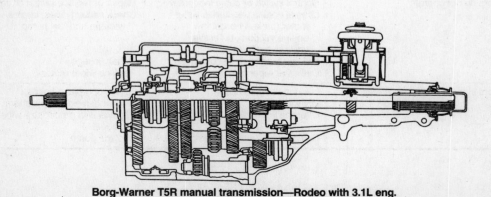

Borg-Warner T5R manual transmission—Rodeo with 3.1L eng.

Troubleshooting the Manual Transmission and Transfer Case

Problem	Cause	Solution
Transmission shifts hard	• Clutch adjustment incorrect • Clutch linkage or cable binding • Shift rail binding	• Adjust clutch • Lubricate or repair as necessary • Check for mispositioned selector arm roll pin, loose cover bolts, worn shift rail bores, worn shift rail, distorted oil seal, or extension housing not aligned with case. Repair as necessary.
	• Internal bind in transmission caused by shift forks, selector plates, or synchronizer assemblies • Clutch housing misalignment • Incorrect lubricant • Block rings and/or cone seats worn	• Remove, dissemble and inspect transmission. Replace worn or damaged components as necessary. • Check runout at rear face of clutch housing • Drain and refill transmission • Blocking ring to gear clutch tooth face clearance must be 0.030 inch or greater. If clearance is correct it may still be necessary to inspect blocking rings and cone seats for excessive wear. Repair as necessary.
Gear clash when shifting from one gear to another	• Clutch adjustment incorrect • Clutch linkage or cable binding • Clutch housing misalignment • Lubricant level low or incorrect lubricant • Gearshift components, or synchronizer assemblies worn or damaged	• Adjust clutch • Lubricate or repair as necessary • Check runout at rear of clutch housing • Drain and refill transmission and check for lubricant leaks if level was low. Repair as necessary. • Remove, disassemble and inspect transmission. Replace worn or damaged components as necessary.
Transmission noisy	• Lubricant level low or incorrect lubricant • Clutch housing-to-engine, or transmission-to-clutch housing bolts loose • Dirt, chips, foreign material in transmission • Gearshift mechanism, transmission gears, or bearing components worn or damaged • Clutch housing misalignment	• Drain and refill transmission. If lubricant level was low, check for leaks and repair as necessary. • Check and correct bolt torque as necessary • Drain, flush, and refill transmission • Remove, disassemble and inspect transmission. Replace worn or damaged components as necessary. • Check runout at rear face of clutch housing
Jumps out of gear	• Clutch housing misalignment • Gearshift lever loose • Offset lever nylon insert worn or lever attaching nut loose • Gearshift mechanism, shift forks, selector plates, interlock plate, selector arm, shift rail, detent plugs, springs or shift cover worn or damaged • Clutch shaft or roller bearings worn or damaged	• Check runout at rear face of clutch housing • Check lever for worn fork. Tighten loose attaching bolts. • Remove gearshift lever and check for loose offset lever nut or worn insert. Repair or replace as necessary. • Remove, disassemble and inspect transmission cover assembly. Replace worn or damaged components as necessary. • Replace clutch shaft or roller bearings as necessary

Troubleshooting the Manual Transmission and Transfer Case (cont.)

Problem	Cause	Solution
Jumps out of gear (cont.)	• Gear teeth worn or tapered, synchronizer assemblies worn or damaged, excessive end play caused by worn thrust washers or output shaft gears • Pilot bushing worn	• Remove, disassemble, and inspect transmission. Replace worn or damaged components as necessary. • Replace pilot bushing
Will not shift into one gear	• Gearshift selector plates, interlock plate, or selector arm, worn, damaged, or incorrectly assembled • Shift rail detent plunger worn, spring broken, or plug loose • Gearshift lever worn or damaged • Synchronizer sleeves or hubs, damaged or worn	• Remove, disassemble, and inspect transmission cover assembly. Repair or replace components as necessary. • Tighten plug or replace worn or damaged components as necessary • Replace gearshift lever • Remove, disassemble and inspect transmission. Replace worn or damaged components.
Locked in one gear—cannot be shifted out	• Shift rail(s) worn or broken, shifter fork bent, setscrew loose, center detent plug missing or worn • Broken gear teeth on countershaft gear, clutch shaft, or reverse idler gear Gearshift lever broken or worn, shift mechanism in cover incorrectly assembled or broken, worn damaged gear train components	• Inspect and replace worn or damaged parts • Inspect and replace damaged part • Disassemble transmission. Replace damaged parts or assemble correctly.
Transfer case difficult to shift or will not shift into desired range	• Vehicle speed too great to permit shifting • If vehicle was operated for extended period in 4H mode on dry paved surface, driveline torque load may cause difficult shifting • Transfer case external shift linkage binding • Insufficient or incorrect lubricant • Internal components binding, worn, or damaged	• Stop vehicle and shift into desired range. Or reduce speed to 3–4 km/h (2–3 mph) before attempting to shift. • Stop vehicle, shift transmission to neutral, shift transfer case to 2H mode and operate vehicle in 2H on dry paved surfaces • Lubricate or repair or replace linkage, or tighten loose components as necessary • Drain and refill to edge of fill hole with SAE 85W-90 gear lubricant only • Disassemble unit and replace worn or damaged components as necessary
Transfer case noisy in all drive modes	• Insufficient or incorrect lubricant	• Drain and refill to edge of fill hole with SAE 85W-90 gear lubricant only. Check for leaks and repair if necessary. Note: If unit is still noisy after drain and refill, disassembly and inspection may be required to locate source of noise.
Noisy in—or jumps out of four wheel drive low range	• Transfer case not completely engaged in 4L position • Shift linkage loose or binding • Shift fork cracked, inserts worn, or fork is binding on shift rail	• Stop vehicle, shift transfer case in Neutral, then shift back into 4L position • Tighten, lubricate, or repair linkage as necessary • Disassemble unit and repair as necessary
Lubricant leaking from output shaft seals or from vent	• Transfer case overfilled • Vent closed or restricted	• Drain to correct level • Clear or replace vent if necessary

Troubleshooting the Manual Transmission and Transfer Case (cont.)

Problem	Cause	Solution
Lubricant leaking from output shaft seals or from vent (cont.)	• Output shaft seals damaged or installed incorrectly	• Replace seals. Be sure seal lip faces interior of case when installed. Also be sure yoke seal surfaces are not scored or nicked. Remove scores, nicks with fine sandpaper or replace yoke(s) if necessary.
Abnormal tire wear	• Extended operation on dry hard surface (paved) roads in 4H range	• Operate in 2H on hard surface (paved) roads

MANUAL TRANSMISSION

Identification

The identification number is stamped into a tag mounted on the shift quadrant box on the left side.

General Description

The Isuzu MUA 4-speed and 5-speed transmissions are a fully synchronized unit with all internal shifting mechanisms. The bell housing and main housing are one piece with a separate rear housing. The reverse gears and shifting mechanisms are located behind the intermediate plate reducing the width of the main housing.

The Isuzu 4WD 5 speed transmission is a fully synchronized unit with all internal shifting mechanisms. The bell housing and main housing are one piece with a separate transfer case built into the rear of the transmission. The reverse gears, 5th gears and shifting mechanisms are located behind the intermediate plate reducing the width of the main housing.

Backup Light Switch
REMOVAL AND INSTALLATION

1. Raise and safely support the vehicle.
2. Disconnect the switch wiring harness.
3. Turn the switch counterclockwise with a wrench.

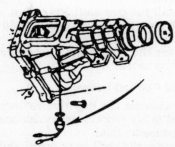

Backup light switch

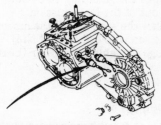

Backup light switch—FWD I-Mark

Backup light switch—FWD Impulse and Stylus

4. Replace the O-ring, install the switch and torque to 15 ft. lbs. (20 Nm).
5. Connect the harness and lower the vehicle.

Driveshaft Seal
REMOVAL AND INSTALLATION

1. Raise and safely support the vehicle.
2. Remove the 4 driveshaft retaining bolts at the differential.
3. For a Pick-Up, remove the center bearing bolts. Mark the differential and driveshaft flanges for proper installation. Remove the driveshaft assembly.
4. For an I-Mark and Impulse, mark the rear U-joint retainer and center bearing flanges, remove the 4 retaining bolts, and slide the driveshaft out of the transmission.
5. Using a suitable prybar, remove the rear housing oil seal.
To install:
6. Install the oil seal using an installer tool J–26508.
7. Lubricate the inside lip with engine oil.

8. Install the driveshaft as marked previously.

9. With the bolt head facing rearward, install the 4 bolts and torque the nuts to 22 ft. lbs. (30 Nm).

10. For a Pick-Up, install the center bearing bolts and torque to 46 ft. lbs. (65 Nm).

Speedometer Gear

REMOVAL AND INSTALLATION

1. Raise and safely support the vehicle.
2. Remove the speedometer cable.
3. Remove the retaining screw and pull the assembly out of the transmission.
4. Replace the seal, install the assembly and torque the screw to 5 ft. lbs. (7 Nm).
5. Engage the cable and tighten the retaining nut.

Transmission

REMOVAL AND INSTALLATION

RWD I-Mark and 2WD P'up

1. Disconnect the negative battery cable.
2. Remove the drain plug and drain the oil.
3. Remove the console, boot and shift lever.
4. Remove the starter and speedometer cable.
5. For a Pick-Up, remove the center bearing retainer bolts.
6. Mark the driveshaft flanges and remove the driveshaft.
7. Remove the clutch cable and flywheel stone guard.
8. Remove the frame-to-transmission mount bolts.
9. Position a jack under the transmission and remove the engine-to-transmission bolts. Turn the transmission 90° clockwise for easier removal.

To install:

1. Using a transmission jack, position the transmission-to-engine and torque the retaining bolts to 40 ft. lbs. (54 Nm).
2. Install the frame-to-rear housing mount bolts and tighten.
3. Install the flywheel stone guard and clutch cable.
4. Install the driveshaft to the mark position. For the Pick-Up, torque the center bearing bolts to 46 ft. lbs. (65 Nm). Position the retaining bolts with the head facing rearward and torque to 22 ft. lbs. (30 Nm).
5. Install the speedometer cable, starter motor, shift lever and boot.
6. Install the drain plug and refill the transmission with 30 SAE engine oil.

RWD Impulse

1. Disconnect the negative battery cable.
2. Raise and safely support the vehicle.
3. Disconnect the slave cylinder.
4. Disconnect the back-up light switch and speedometer cable.
5. Lower the vehicle.
6. Remove the gear shift boot, console and shift lever.
7. Raise and safely support the vehicle.
8. Remove the transmission drain plug and drain the oil.
9. Mark the driveshaft flanges and remove the driveshaft, starter motor, exhaust pipe and hanger.
10. Support the transmission with a jack.
11. Remove the rear transmission mount from the crossmember.
12. Remove the shift quadrant box.
13. Remove the transmission-to-engine bolts.
14. Manually move the transmission as far as possible toward the rear of the vehicle, above the crossmember. Lower the clutch housing end while the rear of the transmission is supported by the crossmember. Lower the transmission jack after the clutch housing has cleared the engine.

To install:

1. Apply axle grease to the top gear shaft spline.
2. Place the transmission on a jack and move into position behind the engine.
3. Raise the jack until the rear of the transmission can be rested on the rear crossmember. Raise the clutch housing and align the top shaft splines with the clutch assembly. Move the transmission into position.

NOTE: *The engine may have to be raised to allow the engine and transmission to be at the same angle.*

4. Install the engine-to-transmission bolts and torque to 28 ft. lbs. (37 Nm).
5. Install the rear mount-to-crossmember, starter motor, exhaust pipe and bracket.
6. Install the driveshaft as previously marked and torque the bolts to 26 ft. lbs. (37 Nm). Torque the center bearing bolts to 45 ft. lbs. (61 Nm).
7. Install the gear shift lever, boot, console and refill the transmission with SAE 30 weight engine oil.
8. Lower the vehicle and connect the negative battery cable.

Early 4WD P'up and Trooper

1. Disconnect the negative battery cable, raise and safely support the vehicle and drain the transmission fluid.
2. Remove the shift lever boots, shift lever and quadrant box.

3. Remove the starter, speedometer cable and center bearing.

4. Mark the driveshaft-to-differential flanges and remove the front and rears driveshafts.

5. Disconnect the clutch cable.

6. Remove the flywheel stone guard, transfer side case and transmission frame member.

7. Install a transmission jack and remove the mount bolts and nuts.

8. Remove the transmission-to-engine bolts, turn the transmission assembly 90° clockwise to ease removal.

To install:

1. Using a transmission jack, position the transmission to the engine and clutch assembly. Torque the retaining bolts to 34 ft. lbs. (46 Nm).

2. Install the frame-to-rear housing mount bolts and tighten.

3. Install the transmission-to-transfer side case. Align the grooves in the shift arms and shift sleeves while held in the 2H position. Torque the retaining bolts to 34 ft. lbs. (46 Nm).

4. Install the flywheel stone guard and clutch cable.

5. Install the driveshafts to the mark position. Torque the center bearing bolts to 46 ft. lbs. (65 Nm). Position the retaining bolts with the head facing rearward and torque to 22 ft. lbs. (30 Nm).

6. Install the speedometer cable, starter motor, shift levers and boots.

7. Install the drain plug and refill the transmission with 30 SAE engine oil. Torque the fill plug to 25 ft. lbs. (34 Nm).

Late 4WD P'up, Amigo and Trooper

1. Disconnect the negative battery cable. Drain the transmission and transfer case oil.

2. Remove the transfer case undercover, starter motor, speedometer cable and gear shift levers.

3. Remove the front exhaust pipes (2.8L V6 only).

4. Mark the driveshaft-to-differential flanges and remove the front and rear driveshafts.

5. Leave the clutch slave cylinder fluid hose connect and remove the cylinder from the transmission and attach out of the way.

6. Remove the transmission-to-engine bolts. Install a jack and slightly raise the the transmission.

7. Remove the crossmember and transmission mount. Support the engine with a jackstand.

8. With an assistant, remove the transmission/transfer case as an assembly.

To install:

1. With an assistant, install the transmission-to-engine. Make sure the input shaft is splined properly into the clutch disc.

2. Install the clutch slave cylinder and crossmember.

3. Install the front exhaust pipe on vehicles equipped with 2.8L engine.

4. Install the front and rear driveshafts in the marked locations.

5. Install the speedometer cable, starter motor and gear shift lever.

6. Refill the transmission and transfer case with the specified amount of SAE 30 oil.

7. Install the undercover and connect the negative battery cable.

Rodeo

1. Disconnect the negative (–) battery cable.

2. Remove the engine hood and cooling fan. Place the fan on the fan guide.

3. Place the shift lever in NEUTRAL, pull up the shift lever grommet and dust cover. Remove the gear shift lever. Cover the opening with a rag to prevent dirt from entering the transmission.

4. Remove the suspension crossmember.

5. Remove the starter motor assembly.

6. Remove the clutch slave cylinder from the transmission. Be careful not to allow the cylinder piston from falling out of the bore.

7. Remove the rear driveshaft.

8. Disconnect the exhaust pipe from the manifold and catalytic converter and remove the pipe.

9. Disconnect all electrical connectors and speedometer cable from the transmission.

10. Remove the flywheel dust cover.

11. Attach an engine lifting cable to the engine hanger and take the engine weight off of the crossmember. Remove the center crossmember.

12. Install a transmission jack under the transmission and remove the retaining nuts and bolts. Remove the assembly from the vehicle.

To install:

1. Install a transmission jack under the transmission and install the transmission into the vehicle. Install the retaining nuts and bolts.

2. Install the center crossmember. Lower the engine onto the crossmember. Install the retaining nuts and bolts.

3. Install the flywheel dust cover.

4. Connect all electrical connectors and speedometer cable to the transmission.

5. Connect the exhaust pipe to the manifold and catalytic converter.

6. Install the rear driveshaft.

7. Install the clutch slave cylinder to the

transmission. Be careful not to allow the cylinder piston from falling out of the bore.

8. Install the starter motor assembly.

9. Install the suspension crossmember.

10. Install the gear shift lever.

11. Install the engine hood and cooling fan.

12. Connect the negative (–) battery cable and check operation.

2-Wheel Drive 4-Speed Overhaul

BEFORE DISASSEMBLY

Cleanliness is an important factor in the overhaul of the manual transmission. Before opening up this unit, the entire outside of the transmission assembly should be cleaned, preferably with a high pressure washer such as a car wash spray unit. Dirt entering the transmission internal parts will negate all the time and effort spent on the overhaul. During inspection and reassembly all parts should be

thoroughly cleaned with solvent then dried with compressed air.

Wheel bearing grease, long used to hold thrust washers and lube parts, should not be used. Lube seals with clean SAE 30 weight engine oil and use ordinary unmedicated petroleum jelly to hold the thrust washers, needle bearings and to ease the assembly of seals, since it will not leave a harmful residue as grease often will. Do not use solvent on neoprene seals, friction plates if they are to be reused, or thrust washers.

Before installing bolts into aluminum parts, always dip the threads into clean transmission fluid. Antiseize compound can also be used to prevent bolts from galling the aluminum and seizing. Always use a torque wrench to keep from stripping the threads. Take care when installing new O-rings, especially the smaller O-rings. The internal snaprings should be expanded and the external rings should be compressed, if they are to be reused. This will help insure proper seating when installed.

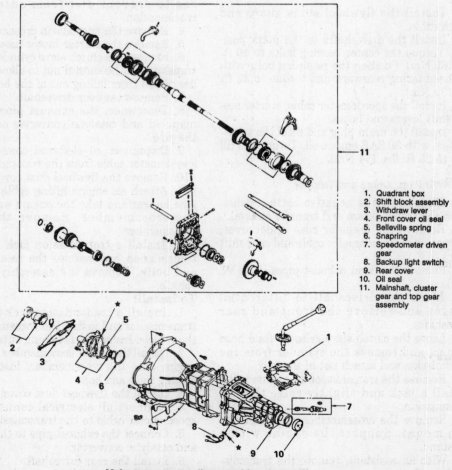

1. Quadrant box
2. Shift block assembly
3. Withdraw lever
4. Front cover oil seal
5. Belleville spring
6. Snapring
7. Speedometer driven gear
8. Backup light switch
9. Rear cover
10. Oil seal
11. Mainshaft, cluster gear and top gear assembly

Major component disassembly—4-speed

MAJOR COMPONENT DISASSEMBLY

1. Remove the shift quadrant box, shift block and withdraw the lever.

2. Remove the front cover retainer, oil seal and Belleville spring.

3. Remove the front bearing snapring.

4. Remove the speedometer driven gear and backup light switch.

5. Remove the rear housing and oil seal.

6. Remove the mainshaft, cluster gear and top gear shaft assemblies.

MAINSHAFT, CLUSTER GEAR AND TOP GEAR SHAFT DISASSEMBLY

1. Remove the reverse idler gear thrust washers and idler gear.

2. Remove the reverse idler shaft retaining bolt, lock plate and shaft.

3. Remove the detent plate, spring and ball.

4. Remove the reverse shift rod and arm.

5. Remove the top/3rd and low/2nd shift rod by driving out the pins.

6. Remove the top/3rd and low/2nd shift arms.

7. Remove the interlock pin.

8. Remove the reverse gear outer snapring, speedometer drive gear, key, inner snapring and reverse gear.

9. Remove the mainshaft locknut and washer.

10. Remove the cluster gear locknut and washer.

11. Slide the intermediate plate off the shaft assemblies.

12. Remove the cluster gear bearing snapring.

13. Remove the mainshaft bearing snapring.

14. From the cluster gear assembly, remove the counter reverse gear, collar, cluster rear bearing, cluster gear and needle bearings.

15. Remove the top gear shaft, press off the bearing and remove the needle bearings.

16. Remove the top/3rd blocker ring, mainshaft snapring and top/3rd synchronizer.

17. Remove the 3rd blocker ring, 3rd gear and needle bearings.

18. Remove the mainshaft bearing, thrust washer, low gear, needle bearings and collar.

19. Remove the outer low/2nd blocker ring, low/2nd synchronizer, inner low/2nd blocker ring, 2nd gear, needle bearings and mainshaft.

INSPECTION

1. Using a micrometer, check the shift arm thickness where it rides on the synchronizer. Low/2nd = 7.8–7.9mm (0.307–0.311 in.), 3rd/4th = 7.1–7.2mm (0.280–0.283 in.) and reverse = 6.8–6.9mm (0.268-0.272 in.).

2. Using a inside caliper, check the free length of the detent springs. Low/2nd and top/3rd = 27.5–30.5mm (1.084–1.201 in.). Reverse = 24.7–27.7mm (0.973–1.091 in.).

3. Using a spring tension tester, check the detent spring tension. Low/2nd and top/3rd = 8.8–9.3 lbs. (4.0–4.2 kg). Reverse = 13.9–14.8 lbs. (6.3–6.7 kg).

4. Using a feeler gauge, check the clearance between the blocker ring and gear. Standard clearance 1.5–0.8mm (0.059–0.031 in.).

5. Using a feeler gauge, check the clearance

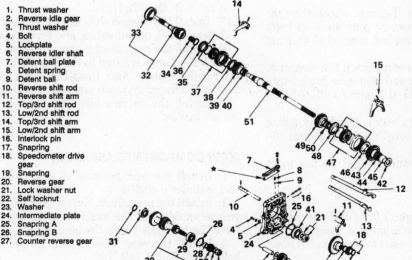

1. Thrust washer
2. Reverse idle gear
3. Thrust washer
4. Bolt
5. Lockplate
6. Reverse idler shaft
7. Detent ball plate
8. Detent spring
9. Detent ball
10. Reverse shift rod
11. Reverse shift arm
12. Top/3rd shift rod
13. Low/2nd shift rod
14. Top/3rd shift arm
15. Low/2nd shift arm
16. Interlock pin
17. Snapring
18. Speedometer drive gear
19. Snapring
20. Reverse gear
21. Lock washer nut
22. Self locknut
23. Washer
24. Intermediate plate
25. Snapring A
26. Snapring B
27. Counter reverse gear

28. Collar
29. Cluster gear bearing
30. Cluster gear
31. Snapring and bearing
32. Top gear shaft
33. Top gear shaft bearing
34. Needle bearing
35. Top/3rd blocker ring
36. Snapring
37. Top/3rd synchronizer
38. 3rd blocker ring
39. 3rd gear
40. Needle bearing
41. Mainshaft bearing
42. Thrust washer
43. Low gear
44. Needle bearing
45. Collar
46. Low/2nd blocker ring
47. Low/2nd synchronizer
48. Low/2nd blocker ring
49. 2nd gear
50. Needle bearing
51. Mainshaft

Mainshaft, cluster gear and top gear assembly—4-speed

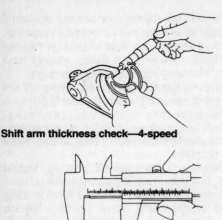

Shift arm thickness check—4-speed

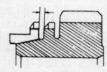

Detent spring check—4-speed

Blocker ring to gear clearance check—4-speed

between the blocker rings and inserts. Standard clearance 3.51–4.00mm (0.138–0.157 in.).

6. Using a feeler gauge, check the clearance between the clutch hub and inserts. Standard clearance 0.01–0.3mm (0.0004–0.012 in.).

7. Using a dial indicator and holding fixture, check the mainshaft run-out. Limit 0.03mm (0.001 in.).

8. Using an inside T-gauge, check the gear inside diameter. Low/rev gear 45.0–45.1mm (1.772–1.776 in.). 2nd/3rd gear 41.0–41.1mm (1.614–1.618 in.).

9. Using a micrometer, check the clearance between the bushing and idler gear shaft. Standard clearance 0.041–0.15mm (0.0016–0.006 in.).

10. Using a dial indicator, check the spline play. Top/3rd and low/2nd 0.0–0.20mm (0–0.0079 in.).

11. Replace components that do not meet specifications.

ASSEMBLY

NOTE: *The mainshaft front and rear needle bearings are interchangeable. Pack the needle bearings with grease to keep them in place during installation.*

1. Install the needle bearings onto the mainshaft. Install the 2nd gear with the taper cone facing rearward.

2. Install the inner low/2nd blocker ring, low/2nd synchronizer assembly, outer low/2nd blocker ring and collar.

3. Install the needle bearing onto the mainshaft and low gear with the taper cone facing forwards.

4. Install the thrust washer with the oil groove facing forward. Press on the mainshaft bearing.

5. Install the needle bearings, 3rd gear, top/3rd blocker ring and top/3rd synchronizer assembly.

6. Install the mainshaft snapring and measure clearance with a feeler gauge. Selective snaprings can be purchased to adjust clearance. Standard clearance is 0.0–0.05mm (0.0–0.0019 in.).

7. Install the top/3rd blocker ring and needle bearings.

8. Using a press install the top shaft bearing so that the snapring groove faces forward. Install the cluster gear rear bearing so the ring groove is facing rearward.

9. Install the needle bearings and intermediate plate.

10. Install the mainshaft bearing snapring.

11. Install the cluster gear bearing snapring.

12. Install the cluster gear collar, reverse counter gear, washer and locknut. Torque the locknut to 72–87 ft. lbs. (100–120 Nm).

13. Install the mainshaft lock washer and nut. Torque to 87–101 ft. lbs. (120–140 Nm).

14. Install the reverse gear, snapring, key, speedometer drive gear and snapring.

15. Install the reverse idler shaft, lock plate and bolt. Torque to 30 ft. lbs. (34 Nm).

16. Install the interlock pin, top/3rd shift arm, low/2nd shift arm and bolt. Torque the bolt to 16 ft. lbs. (22 Nm).

17. Install the reverse shift arm, reverse shift rod, detent ball, detent spring and spring plate.

18. Install the reverse idler gear thrust washer with the flange is fitted to the stopper in the intermediate plate. Also, install the idler gear so that the undercut teeth are turned outward.

19. Install the reverse idler gear and outer thrust washer.

MAIN COMPONENTS ASSEMBLY

1. Install the rear housing oil seal using a seal installer J–26508.

2. Install the mainshaft, cluster gear and top gear assemblies to the main housing. Do not force the mainshaft into the housing.

3. Install the rear housing and torque the bolts to 30 ft. lbs. (42 Nm).

4. Install the backup light switch, speedometer driven gear and mainshaft front bearing snapring.

5. Install the Belleville spring, front cover oil

seal, front cover and torque the bolts to 16 ft. lbs. (22 Nm).

6. Install the clutch fork, shift block and quadrant box assemblies. Make sure the shift lever is fitted into the support properly.

5-Speed Overhaul
2-Wheel Drive P'up
Rear Wheel Drive Impulse and I-Mark

BEFORE DISASSEMBLY

Cleanliness is an important factor in the overhaul of the manual transmission. Before opening up this unit, the entire outside of the transmission assembly should be cleaned, preferably with a high pressure washer such as a car wash spray unit. Dirt entering the transmission internal parts will negate all the time and effort spent on the overhaul. During inspection and reassembly all parts should be thoroughly cleaned with solvent then dried with compressed air. Wiping cloths and rags should not be used to dry parts.

Wheel bearing grease, used to hold thrust washers and lube parts, should not be used. Lube seals with clean SAE 30 weight engine oil and use ordinary unmedicated petroleum jelly to hold the thrust washers, needle bearings and to ease the assembly of seals, since it will not leave a harmful residue as grease often will. Do not use solvent on neoprene seals, friction plates if they are to be reused, or thrust washers.

Before installing bolts into aluminum parts, always dip the threads into clean transmission fluid. Antiseize compound can also be used to prevent bolts from galling the aluminum and seizing. Always use a torque wrench to keep from stripping the threads. Take care when installing new O-rings, especially the smaller O-rings. The internal snaprings should be expanded and the external rings should be compressed, if they are to be reused. This will help insure proper seating when installed.

DISASSEMBLY

1. Remove the clutch shift block and release bearing.
2. Remove the clutch fork, speedometer driven gear and front cover with oil seal.

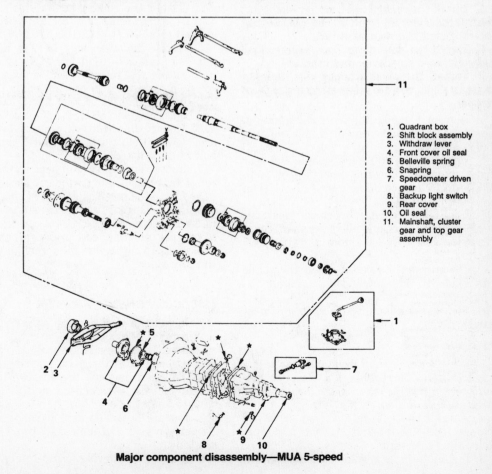

1. Quadrant box
2. Shift block assembly
3. Withdraw lever
4. Front cover oil seal
5. Belleville spring
6. Snaping
7. Speedometer driven gear
8. Backup light switch
9. Rear cover
10. Oil seal
11. Mainshaft, cluster gear and top gear assembly

Major component disassembly—MUA 5-speed

3. Remove the front bearing belleville spring, counter gear snapring and front bearing snapring.

4. Remove the rear housing with oil seal.

5. Pull the intermediate plate with gear assemblies out of the transmission case.

Shift Quadrant and Lever

IMPULSE

1. Remove the upper change lever, spring stopper, retainer and spring.

2. Remove the outer spherical cage, U-bolt nuts and select stop spring.

3. Remove the select stop U-bolt, inner spherical cage from the pivot case.

4. Remove the joint bolt, lock washer and lower change lever.

5. Remove the pivot stopper, reverse select stopper, bracket mounting bolt, pivot stopper bolt and bracket.

6. Remove the dust cover, joint bolt, rear control rod and dust cover boot.

7. Remove the neutral switch, gasket, spring pin, internal lever, front control rod, oil seal and control rod boot.

To assemble

1. Install the control rod boot, oil seal, front control rod, internal lever, spring pin, neutral switch gasket and neutral switch.

2. Install the dust cover boot, rear control rod, joint bolt, dust cover and bracket.

3. Install the pivot stopper bolt, bracket mounting bolt, reverse select stopper and pivot stopper.

4. Install the lower change lever, lock washer, joint bolt and pivot case.

5. Install the inner spherical cage, select stop U-bolt, select stop spring, U-bolt nuts and outer spherical cage.

6. Install the lever spring, retainer, spring stopper and upper change lever.

Detent, Shift Fork and Interlock Pin

DISASSEMBLY

1. Remove the detent spring plate, springs and detent balls using a magnet.

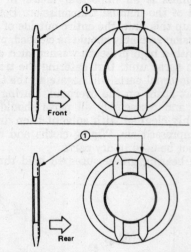

Low/rev thrust washer oil groove position—MUA 5-speed, top is low

1. Upper change lever
2. Change lever stopper
3. Stopper retainer
4. Return spring
5. Outer cage
6. Double U-bolt nut
7. Select stop spring
8. U-bolt stop
9. Inner cage
10. Pivot cage
11. Front to rear bolt
12. Washer lock
13. Change lever
14. Pivot stopper
15. Reverse stopper
16. Mounting bracket bolt
17. Stopper pivot bolt
18. Change lever mounting bracket
19. Dust cover
20. Front to rear bolt
21. Gear control rod
22. Dust cover boot
23. Neutral switch
24. Switch gasket
25. Spring pin
26. Manual lever
27. Gear control rod
28. Oil control box seal
29. Front boot rod

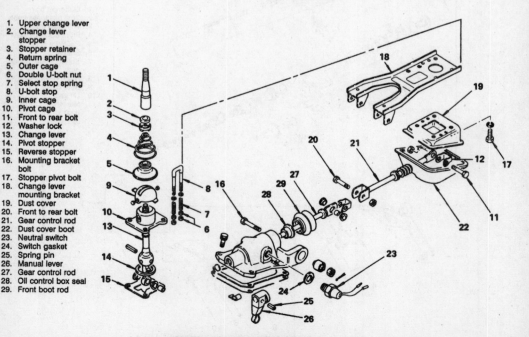

Shift quadrant box—Impulse

2. Remove the 5th/rev shift arm and rod.

3. Remove the 1st/2nd shift rod, 3rd/4th shift rod, 3rd/4th shift arm and 1st/2nd shift arm.

4. Remove the interlock pin.

ASSEMBLY

1. Install the 1st/2nd shift arm, 3rd/4th shift arm, interlock pin, 3rd/4th shift rod and 1st/2nd shift rod. Use a round bar against the shift rods to protect against damage then drive in the spring pins.

2. Install the 5th/rev shift arm and rod. Drive in spring pin.

3. Install the detent balls, springs and spring plate. Torque the retaining bolts to 15 ft. lbs. (20 Nm).

Reverse and 5th Gear

DISASSEMBLY

1. Remove the mainshaft bearing snapring, speedometer drive gear and lock ball, bearing spacer and bearing.

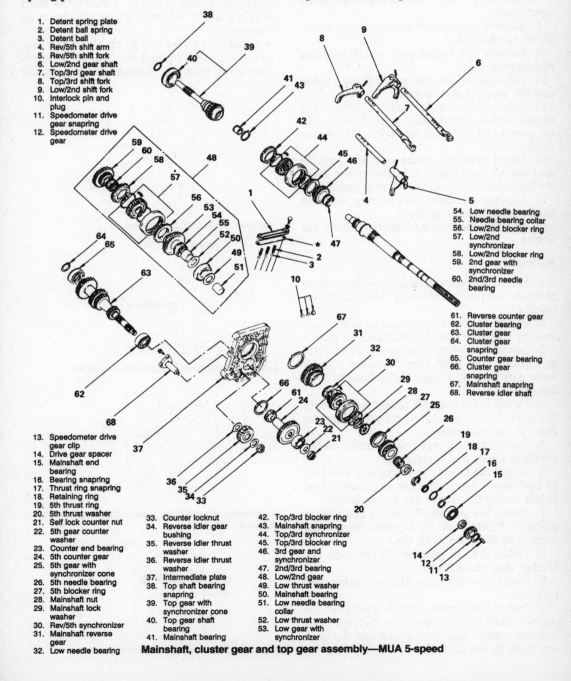

1. Detent spring plate
2. Detent ball spring
3. Detent ball
4. Rev/5th shift arm
5. Rev/5th shift fork
6. Low/2nd gear shaft
7. Top/3rd gear shaft
8. Top/3rd shift fork
9. Low/2nd shift fork
10. Interlock pin and plug
11. Speedometer drive gear snapring
12. Speedometer drive gear

13. Speedometer drive gear clip
14. Drive gear spacer
15. Mainshaft end bearing
16. Bearing snapring
17. Thrust ring snapring
18. Retaining ring
19. 5th thrust ring
20. 5th thrust washer
21. Self lock counter nut
22. 5th gear counter washer
23. Counter end bearing
24. 5th counter gear
25. 5th gear with synchronizer cone
26. 5th needle bearing
27. 5th blocker ring
28. Mainshaft nut
29. Mainshaft lock washer
30. Rev/5th synchronizer
31. Mainshaft reverse gear
32. Low needle bearing

33. Counter locknut
34. Reverse idler gear bushing
35. Reverse idler thrust washer
36. Reverse idler thrust washer
37. Intermediate plate
38. Top shaft bearing snapring
39. Top gear with synchronizer cone
40. Top gear shaft bearing
41. Mainshaft bearing

42. Top/3rd blocker ring
43. Mainshaft snapring
44. Top/3rd synchronizer
45. Top/3rd blocker ring
46. 3rd gear and synchronizer
47. 2nd/3rd bearing
48. Low/2nd gear
49. Low thrust washer
50. Mainshaft bearing
51. Low needle bearing collar
52. Low thrust washer
53. Low gear with synchronizer

54. Low needle bearing
55. Needle bearing collar
56. Low/2nd blocker ring
57. Low/2nd synchronizer
58. Low/2nd blocker ring
59. 2nd gear with synchronizer
60. 2nd/3rd needle bearing

61. Reverse counter gear
62. Cluster bearing
63. Cluster gear
64. Cluster gear snapring
65. Counter gear bearing
66. Cluster gear snapring
67. Mainshaft snapring
68. Reverse idler shaft

Mainshaft, cluster gear and top gear assembly—MUA 5-speed

2. Remove the thrust ring, thrust ring retaining ring, thrust washer and lock ball.

3. Remove the reverse counter gear nut and washer.

4. Remove the counter gear bearing and 5th counter gear using a jaw puller J–22888 or equivalent.

5. Remove the reverse counter gear.

6. From the mainshaft, remove the 5th gear, 5th blocker ring and needle bearings.

7. Remove the mainshaft locknut and washer using a locknut wrench J–29768 or equivalent.

8. Remove the 5th/rev synchronizer assembly as an assembly.

9. Remove the reverse gear, needle bearings and bearing collar.

10. Remove the reverse gear thrust washer and the counter gear locknut.

11. After removing the locknut, remove the thrust washer, reverse idler gear, thrust washer, reverse shaft retaining bolt and reverse shaft.

12. Insert snapring pliers into the counter gear bearing snapring hole located in the intermediate plate. Remove the bearing snapring.

13. Remove the mainshaft bearing snapring in the same fashion as above.

14. Remove the intermediate plate from the shafts.

ASSEMBLY

1. Install the reverse shaft-to-intermediate plate and torque the retaining bolt to 15 ft. lbs. (20 Nm).

2. Install the mainshaft and counter shaft bearing snapring into the intermediate plate.

3. Install the reverse idler gear thrust washer, reverse idler gear, thrust washer and reverse gear locknut. Torque the locknut to 80 ft. lbs. (108 Nm).

4. Install the mainshaft thrust washer onto the mainshaft with the oil groove facing the front of the transmission.

5. Install the reverse gear bearing collar, needle bearings and reverse gear.

6. Install the 5th/rev synchronizer assembly so that sleeve heavy chamfer and insert short side is facing the rear of the transmission.

7. Install the mainshaft locknut and washer using the locknut wrench J–36629. Torque the locknut to 87 ft. lbs. (118 Nm).

8. Install the 5th gear needle bearings, 5th blocker ring and 5th gear.

9. Install the 5th gear thrust washer and lock ball.

10. Install the reverse counter gear onto the counter shaft, 5th counter gear, counter shaft bearing, washer and locknut. Torque the locknut to 80 ft. lbs. (108 Nm).

11. Install the thrust washer thrust ring and thrust ring retaining ring onto the mainshaft.

12. Install the thrust ring snapring onto the mainshaft.

13. Install the mainshaft bearing, bearing spacer, speedometer drive gear and lock ball and bearing snapring.

Top Shaft, Mainshaft and Counter Gear

DISASSEMBLY

1. Remove the top gear shaft snapring, top shaft and needle bearings. Remove the shaft bearing using a bench press and bearing remover.

2. Remove the top gear blocker ring, mainshaft snapring and the 3rd/4th synchronizer as an assembly. Remove the 3rd blocker ring.

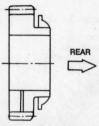

2nd gear positioning—4-speed

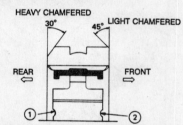

Low/2nd synchronizer assembly—4-speed

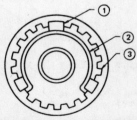

Synchronizer assembly, 1. key, 2. spring, 3. clutch—4-speed

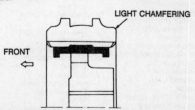

Top/3rd synchronizer assembly—4-speed

3. Remove the 3rd gear and needle bearings.

4. Remove the mainshaft bearing using a press and bearing remover.

5. Remove the 1st gear thrust washer, 1st gear, needle bearings and bearing collar.

6. Remove the 1st blocker ring and 1st/2nd synchronizer as an assembly.

7. Remove the 2nd blocker ring, 2nd gear, and needle bearings from the mainshaft.

8. Remove the front and rear counter shaft bearings with a bench press and bearing remover.

ASSEMBLY

1. Install the 2nd gear needle bearings into the mainshaft. Install the 2nd gear so the teeth face the rear of the transmission.

2. Install the 2nd blocker ring and the 1st/2nd synchronizer as an assembly. The outside sleeve heavy chamfering 30° must face to the rear of the transmission. Install the 1st blocker ring.

3. Using a press and a collar installer J–33851, install the needle bearing collar into the 1st gear.

4. Install the 1st gear needle bearings and 1st gear onto the mainshaft with the teeth facing the front of the transmission.

5. Install the 1st gear thrust washer with the oil groove facing forward.

6. Install the mainshaft bearing using a press and bearing installer.

7. Install the 3rd gear needle bearings and 3rd gear with the teeth facing forward.

8. Install the 3rd blocker ring and 3rd/4th synchronizer as an assembly. The sleeve light chamfer and clutch hub heavy boss must face rearward.

9. Install the mainshaft snapring and measure the clearance between the mainshaft and the snapring. There are four snapring sizes to pick from.

10. Install the top gear shaft needle bearings and top blocker ring onto the top gear shaft.

11. Install the top gear shaft bearing with a press and bearing installer. The snapring groove must face forward.

12. Install the top shaft snapring.

13. Using a press and bearing installer, install the counter shaft front bearing, snapring and rear bearing.

COMPONENT INSPECTION

1. Using a micrometer, check the shift arm thickness where it rides on the synchronizer. 1st/2nd = 0.307–0.276 in. (7.8–7.0mm), 3rd/4th = 0.280–0.256 in. (7.1–6.5mm) and 5th/rev = 0.268-0.248 in. (6.8–6.3mm).

2. Using a inside slide ruler, check the free

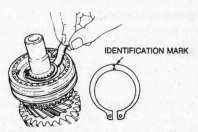

Checking thrust washer clearance—MUA 5-speed

length of the detent springs. 1.01–0.93 in. (25.6–23.6mm).

3. Using a spring tension tester, check the detent spring tension. 14.0–15.0 lbs. (6.3–6.7 kg).

4. Using a feeler gauge, check the clearance between the blocker ring and gear. Standard clearance for 1st/2nd = 0.067–0.032 in. (1.7–0.8mm), 3rd/4th = 0.059–0.032 in. (1.5–0.8mm) and 5th/rev = 0.051–0.032 in. (1.3–0.8mm).

5. Using a feeler gauge, check the clearance between the blocker rings and inserts. Standard clearance 0.138–0.158 in. (3.51–4.00mm).

6. Using a feeler gauge, check the clearance between the clutch hub and inserts. Standard clearance 0.0004–0.012 in. (0.01–0.3mm).

7. Using a dial indicator and holding fixture, check the mainshaft run-out. Limit 0.0012 in. (0.03mm).

8. Using an inside T-gauge, check the gear inside diameter. Low gear 1.773–1.777 in. (45.0–45.1mm). 2nd/3rd gear 1.615–1.619 in. (41.0–41.1mm).

9. Using a micrometer, check the clearance between the bushing and idler gear shaft. Standard clearance 0.0016–0.0059 in. (0.041–0.15mm).

10. Using a dial indicator, check the spline play. Clutch hub 0.0–0.0079 in. (0.0–0.20mm) and reverse gear 0.0024–0.0078 in. (0.062–0.200).

11. Replace components that do not meet specifications.

TRANSMISSION ASSEMBLY

1. Install the intermediate plate with the gear assemblies into the main housing.

2. Install the rear housing with oil seal. Torque the housing bolts to 15 ft. lbs. (20 Nm).

3. Install the top gear shaft and counter shaft snaprings after the gear shafts are installed in the housing.

4. Install the belleville spring and front cover with a new oil seal. Torque the cover retaining bolts to 15 ft. lbs. (20 Nm).

5. Install the speedometer driven gear, clutch shift fork, shift block and release bearing.

5-Speed Overhaul
Early 4-Wheel Drive P'up and Trooper

BEFORE DISASSEMBLY

Cleanliness is an important factor in the overhaul of the Isuzu 5 speed transmission. Before opening up this unit, the entire outside of the transmission assembly should be cleaned, preferably with a high pressure washer such as a car wash spray unit. Dirt entering the transmission internal parts will negate all the time and effort spent on the overhaul. During inspection and reassembly all parts should be thoroughly cleaned with solvent then dried with compressed air.

Wheel bearing grease, used to hold thrust washers and lube parts, should not be used. Lube seals with clean SAE 30 weight engine oil and use ordinary unmedicated petroleum jelly to hold the thrust washers, needle bearings and to ease the assembly of seals, since it will not leave a harmful residue as grease often will.

Before installing bolts into aluminum parts, always dip the threads into clean transmission fluid. Antiseize compound can also be used to prevent bolts from galling the aluminum and seizing. Always use a torque wrench to keep from stripping the threads. The internal snaprings should be expanded and the external rings should be compressed, if they are to be reused. This will help insure proper seating when installed.

TRANSMISSION DISASSEMBLY

1. Remove the backup light switch, transfer case side assembly and shift block if not already done.

2. Remove the clutch release lever, front cov-

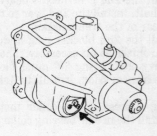

Removing the countershaft lock plate and distance plate

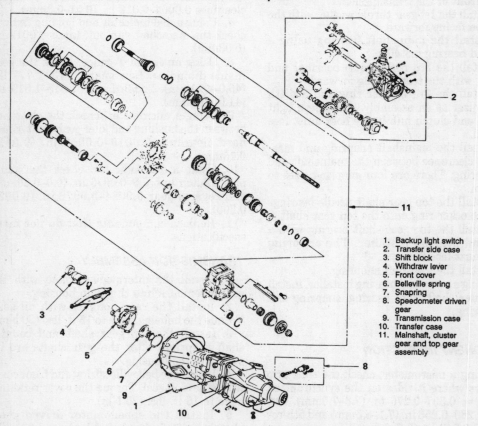

1. Backup light switch
2. Transfer side case
3. Shift block
4. Withdraw lever
5. Front cover
6. Belleville spring
7. Snapring
8. Speedometer driven gear
9. Transmission case
10. Transfer case
11. Mainshaft, cluster gear and top gear assembly

Major component disassembly—early 4WD P'up and Trooper

er, Belleville spring and top shaft bearing snapring.

3. Remove the speedometer driven gear and transfer countershaft lock plate.

4. Remove the transfer housing bolts and pull the mainshaft, counter gear shaft and top gear shaft from the main housing. The intermediate plate and transfer housing will still be attached to the gear shafts.

Mainshaft, Counter and Top Gear Shafts

DISASSEMBLY

1. Remove the detent spring plate, springs and balls using a pencil magnet.

2. Hold a round bar against the ends of the shift rods to prevent damage. Remove the spring pins from the 1st/2nd, 3rd/4th and 5th/ rev shift rods. Remove the rods and arms from the transmission.

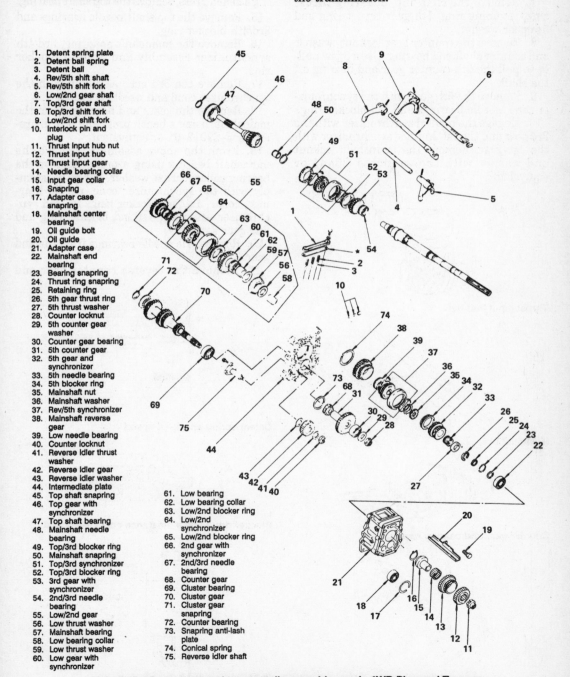

1. Detent spring plate
2. Detent ball spring
3. Detent ball
4. Rev/5th shift shaft
5. Rev/5th shift fork
6. Low/2nd gear shaft
7. Top/3rd gear shaft
8. Top/3rd shift fork
9. Low/2nd shift fork
10. Interlock pin and plug
11. Thrust input hub nut
12. Thrust input hub
13. Thrust input gear
14. Needle bearing collar
15. Input gear collar
16. Snapring
17. Adapter case snapring
18. Mainshaft center bearing
19. Oil guide bolt
20. Oil guide
21. Adapter case
22. Mainshaft end bearing
23. Bearing snapring
24. Thrust ring snapring
25. Retaining ring
26. 5th gear thrust ring
27. 5th thrust washer
28. Counter locknut
29. 5th counter gear washer
30. Counter gear bearing
31. 5th counter gear
32. 5th gear and synchronizer
33. 5th needle bearing
34. 5th blocker ring
35. Mainshaft nut
36. Mainshaft washer
37. Rev/5th synchronizer
38. Mainshaft reverse gear
39. Low needle bearing
40. Counter locknut
41. Reverse idler thrust washer
42. Reverse idler gear
43. Reverse idler washer
44. Intermediate plate
45. Top shaft snapring
46. Top gear with synchronizer
47. Top shaft bearing
48. Mainshaft needle bearing
49. Top/3rd blocker ring
50. Mainshaft snapring
51. Top/3rd synchronizer
52. Top/3rd blocker ring
53. 3rd gear with synchronizer
54. 2nd/3rd needle bearing
55. Low/2nd gear
56. Low thrust washer
57. Mainshaft bearing
58. Low bearing collar
59. Low thrust washer
60. Low gear with synchronizer
61. Low bearing
62. Low bearing collar
63. Low/2nd blocker ring
64. Low/2nd synchronizer
65. Low/2nd blocker ring
66. 2nd gear with synchronizer
67. 2nd/3rd needle bearing
68. Counter gear
69. Cluster bearing
70. Cluster gear
71. Cluster gear snapring
72. Counter bearing
73. Snapring anti-lash plate
74. Conical spring
75. Reverse idler shaft

Mainshaft, cluster gear and top gear disassembly—early 4WD P'up and Trooper

3. Remove the interlock pin and plug.

4. Remove the input hub thrust nut using a wrench J–29041 or equivalent. Remove the thrust input hub, input gear, needle bearings, collar and bearing snapring.

5. Remove the mainshaft bearings snapring, bearing, oil guide bolt and oil guide.

6. Remove the intermediate case from the shafts.

7. Remove the snapring, snapring thrust ring, retaining ring, 5th gear thrust ring and 5th gear washer.

8. Remove the counter gear locknut, washer and counter shaft end bearing. Use a 3 jaw puller to pull the 5th counter gear and bearing off the shaft.

9. Remove the 5th gear with the synchronizer cone, needle bearings and 5th blocker ring.

10. Engage the top/3rd synchronizer with the 3rd gear and the 1st/2nd side synchronizer with the 1st gear. Remove the mainshaft locknut and washer with the wrench J–33441 or equivalent.

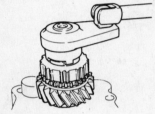

Thrust input hub nut

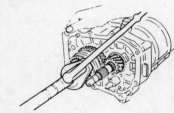

Mainshaft nut

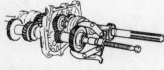

Counter gear and bearing removal

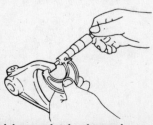

Shift arm thickness check—4-speed

11. Remove the 5th/rev synchronizer assembly, reverse gear and needle bearings.

12. Remove the reverse idler shaft locknut, thrust washer, reverse idler gear and thrust washer.

13. Remove the intermediate plate from the shafts.

14. Remove the top shaft bearings snapring and top shaft with the synchronizer cone. Using a bench press, remove the top shaft bearing.

15. Remove the top shaft needle bearings and 3rd/4th blocker ring.

16. Remove the mainshaft snapring, 3rd/4th synchronizer assembly and 3rd/4th blocker ring.

17. Remove the 3rd gear assembly with the synchronizer cone and needle bearings.

18. Remove the gears and bearings from the mainshaft, using a bench press and bearing remover J–22912–01 or equivalent.

19. From the above assembly, remove the mainshaft bearing using a press. Remove the bearing collar, thrust washer, low gear assembly with the synchronizer cone, needle bearings, collar, 1st/2nd blocker ring, 1st/2nd synchronizer assembly, 1st/2nd blocker ring and 2nd gear assembly.

20. Remove the needle bearings from the 2nd gear.

21. Remove the reverse counter gear and

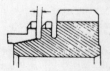

Detent spring check—4-speed

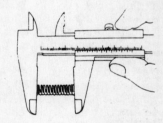

Blocker ring to gear clearance check—4-speed

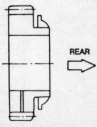

REAR

2nd gear positioning—4-speed

bearing from the counter gear using a press. Remove the front counter shaft bearing snapring, front bearing, rear bearing snapring, conical spring and unbolt the reverse idler shaft.

INSPECTION

1. Using a micrometer, check the shift arm thickness where it rides on the synchronizer. 1st/2nd = 0.276–0.311 in. (7.0–7.9mm), 3rd/4th = 0.256–0.284 in. (6.5–7.2mm), transfer = 0.236-0.268 in. (6.0–6.8mm) and 5th/rev = 0.248–0.272 in. (6.3–6.9mm).

2. Using a inside slide ruler, check the free length of the detent springs. 1st/2nd, 3rd/4th and reverse = 0.985–1.091 in. (25.0–27.7mm) and transfer = 1.615–1.694 in. (41.0–43.0).

3. Using a spring tension tester, check the detent spring tension. 1st/2nd, 3rd/4th and reverse = 13.9–14.7 lbs. (6.3–6.7 kg) and transfer = 19.8–24.3 lbs. (9.0–11 kg).

4. Using a feeler gauge, check the clearance between the blocker ring and gear. 1st/2nd = 0.032–0.067 in. (0.8–1.7mm), 3rd/5th = 0.032–0.059 in. (0.8–1.5mm) and top gear = 0.032–0.051 in. (0.8–1.3mm).

5. Using a feeler gauge, check the clearance between the blocker rings and inserts. Standard clearance 0.138–0.158 in. (3.51–4.00mm).

6. Using a feeler gauge, check the clearance between the clutch hub and inserts. Standard clearance 0.0004–0.012 in. (0.01–0.3mm).

7. Using a dial indicator and holding fixture, check the mainshaft run-out. Limit 0.001 in. (0.05mm).

8. Using an inside T-gauge, check the gear inside diameter. 1st/rev = 1.773–1.777 in. (45.0–45.1mm), 2nd/3rd gear = 1.615–1.619 in. (41.0–41.1mm), transfer idler = 1.300–1.304 in. (33.0–33.1mm) and 5th = 1.261–1.264 in. (32.03–32.10mm).

9. Using a micrometer, check the clearance between the bushing and idler gear shaft. Standard clearance 0.0016–0.0059 in. (0.041–0.150mm).

10. Using a dial indicator, check the spline play. Clutch hub 0.0–0.0079 in. (0.0–0.20mm) and reverse gear 0.0024–0.0078 in. (0.062–0.200mm).

11. Using a dial indicator, check the play in the ball bearings. Limit 0.068 in. (0.2mm).

12. Replace components that do not meet specifications.

ASSEMBLY

1. Onto the mainshaft, install the 2nd gear needle bearings and 2nd gear with synchronizer cone. The taper cone on the gear must face rearward.

2. Install the 1st/2nd blocker ring and 1st/2nd synchronizer assembly. The parallel oil grooves in the clutch hub must be on the same side as the heavy chamfer on the sleeve. Make sure the inserts are fitted into the grooves in the blocker ring. Make sure the sleeve slides smoothly. Install the 1st/2nd blocker ring.

3. Install the needle bearing collar onto the shaft with a press and collar installer J–33851.

4. Install the needle bearings, 1st gear with synchronizer assembly and the low thrust washer with the oil groove facing forward.

5. Install the mainshaft radial bearing with a press and bearing installer. Install the reverse thrust washer with the oil groove facing rearward.

6. Press on the reverse needle bearing collar. Install the needle bearings, 3rd gear with synchronizer cone and 3rd/4th blocker ring.

7. Install the 3rd/4th synchronizer assembly with the side of the hub with the higher boss facing the light chamfer of the sleeve. Install the mainshaft selective snapring after measur-

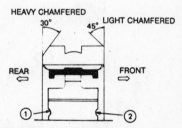

Low/2nd synchronizer assembly—4-speed

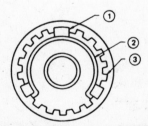

Synchronizer assembly, 1. key, 2. spring, 3. clutch—4-speed

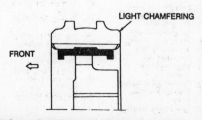

Top/3rd synchronizer assembly—4-speed

ing the distance between the shaft and the 3rd/4th clutch hub.

8. Install the 3rd/4th blocker ring, needle bearings and top gear shaft bearing using a press. Install the bearing snapring.

9. Install the top shaft with synchronizer cone.

10. Install the front and rear counter shaft bearings using a press. Install the snaprings.

11. Install the counter gear shaft, reverse id-ler gear and reverse idler shaft. Torque the idler shaft retaining bolts to 16 ft. lbs. (22 Nm).

12. Install the mainshaft radial bearing snapring and counter gear bearing snapring into the intermediate plate. Use a holding fixture J–29768 or equivalent to align the mainshaft and countershaft with the intermediate plate.

13. Install the reverse idler thrust washer, reverse idler gear with bushing, thrust washer

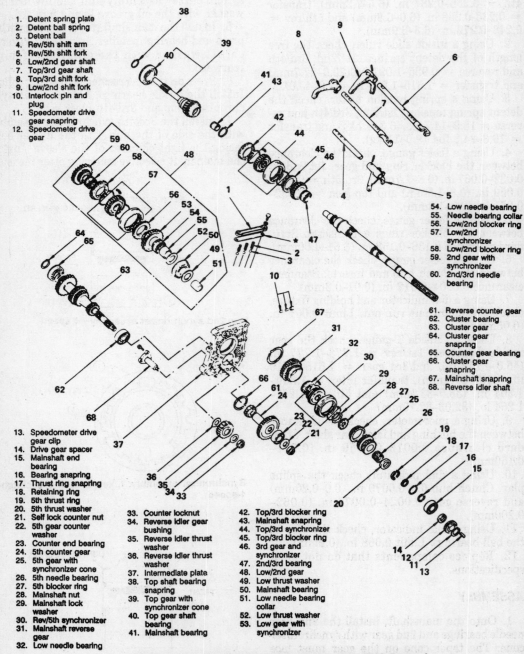

1. Detent spring plate
2. Detent ball spring
3. Detent ball
4. Rev/5th shift arm
5. Rev/5th shift fork
6. Low/2nd gear shaft
7. Top/3rd gear shaft
8. Top/3rd shift fork
9. Low/2nd shift fork
10. Interlock pin and plug
11. Speedometer drive gear snapring
12. Speedometer drive gear

13. Speedometer drive gear clip
14. Drive gear spacer
15. Mainshaft end bearing
16. Bearing snapring
17. Thrust ring snapring
18. Retaining ring
19. 5th thrust ring
20. 5th thrust washer
21. Self lock counter nut
22. 5th gear counter washer
23. Counter end bearing
24. 5th counter gear
25. 5th gear with synchronizer cone
26. 5th needle bearing
27. 5th blocker ring
28. Mainshaft nut
29. Mainshaft lock washer
30. Rev/5th synchronizer
31. Mainshaft reverse gear
32. Low needle bearing

33. Counter locknut
34. Reverse idler gear bushing
35. Reverse idler thrust washer
36. Reverse idler thrust washer
37. Intermediate plate
38. Top shaft bearing snapring
39. Top gear with synchronizer cone
40. Top gear shaft bearing
41. Mainshaft bearing

42. Top/3rd blocker ring
43. Mainshaft snapring
44. Top/3rd synchronizer
45. Top/3rd blocker ring
46. 3rd gear and synchronizer
47. 2nd/3rd bearing
48. Low/2nd gear
49. Low thrust washer
50. Mainshaft bearing
51. Low needle bearing collar
52. Low thrust washer
53. Low gear with synchronizer

54. Low needle bearing
55. Needle bearing collar
56. Low/2nd blocker ring
57. Low/2nd synchronizer
58. Low/2nd blocker ring
59. 2nd gear with synchronizer
60. 2nd/3rd needle bearing
61. Reverse counter gear
62. Cluster bearing
63. Cluster gear
64. Cluster gear snapring
65. Counter gear bearing
66. Cluster gear snapring
67. Mainshaft snapring
68. Reverse idler shaft

Mainshaft, cluster gear and top gear assembly—MUA 5-speed

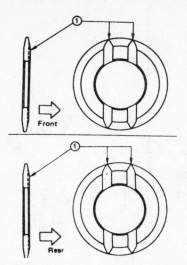

Low/rev thrust washer oil groove position—MUA 5-speed, top is low

and locknut. Torque the locknut to 87 ft. lbs. (120 Nm).

14. Install the needle bearings into the reverse gear and install the assembly onto the mainshaft.

15. Install the 5th/rev synchronizer assembly. The clutch hub with the higher boss must face the heavy chamfer of the sleeve.

16. Install the mainshaft lock washer and nut. Using the nut installer wrench J–33441 or equivalent, torque to 101 ft. lbs. (140 Nm).

17. Install the 5th blocker ring, 5th gear with synchronizer cone, needle bearings and thrust washer. Install the thrust washer and lock ball onto the shaft using the snapring.

18. Install the thrust ring and thrust ring snapring so the opening in the snapring is positioned at a right angle to the opening in the thrust ring. Install the thrust ring retaining ring and bearing snapring.

19. Install the 5th counter gear, counter end bearing, plain washer and locknut. Torque the locknut to 101 ft. lbs. (140 Nm).

20. Install the adapter case, oil guide and oil guide bolt. Torque the guide bolt to 15 ft. lbs. (20 Nm).

21. Install the mainshaft center bearing and snapring.

22. Install the mainshaft snapring, input gear thrust collar, needle bearings, input thrust gear, input thrust hub an input hub nut. Using a nut wrench J–29041 or equivalent, torque the nut to 101 ft. lbs. (140 Nm).

23. Install the interlock pin and plug.

24. Install the 1st/2nd shift arm, 3rd/4th shift arm, 3rd/4th shift rod, 1st/2nd shift rod and spring pins.

25. Install the 5th/rev shift arm and shaft.

26. Install the detent balls, springs, plate and torque the retaining bolts to 16 ft. lbs. (22 Nm).

5-Speed Overhaul Late Model Trooper, Amigo and Rodeo

BEFORE DISASSEMBLY

Cleanliness is an important factor in the overhaul of the manual transmission. Before opening up this unit, the entire outside of the transmission assembly should be cleaned, preferably with a high pressure washer such as a car wash spray unit. Dirt entering the transmission internal parts will negate all the time and effort spent on the overhaul. During inspection and reassembly all parts should be thoroughly cleaned with solvent then dried with compressed air. Wiping cloths and rags should not be used to dry parts.

Wheel bearing grease, used to hold thrust washers and lube parts, should not be used. Lube seals with clean SAE 30 weight engine oil and use ordinary unmedicated petroleum jelly to hold the thrust washers, needle bearings and to ease the assembly of seals, since it will not leave a harmful residue as grease often will.

Before installing bolts into aluminum parts, always dip the threads into clean transmission fluid. Antiseize compound can also be used to prevent bolts from galling the aluminum and seizing. Always use a torque wrench to keep from stripping the threads. Take care when installing new O-rings, especially the smaller O-rings. The internal snaprings should be expanded and the external rings should be compressed, if they are to be reused. This will help insure proper seating when installed.

TRANSMISSION DISASSEMBLY

1. Position the transmission is a suitable holding fixture.

2. Drain the lubricant, as required.

3. Remove the speedometer driven gear and transfer flange using a flange remover J–37221 or equivalent.

4. Remove the front cover with oil seal, countershaft snapring and top gear shaft snapring.

5. Remove the transmission-to-transfer case bolts and separate the assemblies.

UNIT DISASSEMBLY AND ASSEMBLY

Intermediate Plate and Shift Arms

DISASSEMBLY

1. Remove the detent spring plate, springs and balls using a pencil magnet.

2. Remove the spring, 5th/rev shift rod, 5th/rev shift arm and inhibitor by driving out the spring pin.

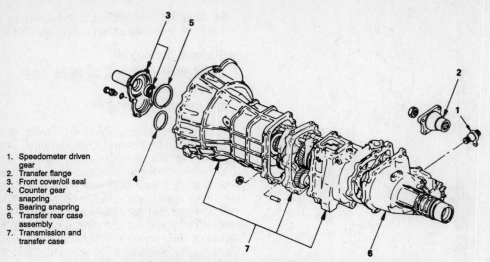

1. Speedometer driven gear
2. Transfer flange
3. Front cover/oil seal
4. Counter gear snapring
5. Bearing snapring
6. Transfer rear case assembly
7. Transmission and transfer case

Major components disassembly—late P'up, Trooper, Amigo and Rodeo

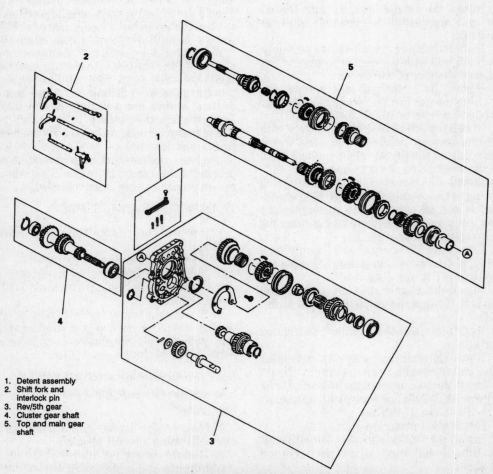

1. Detent assembly
2. Shift fork and interlock pin
3. Rev/5th gear
4. Cluster gear shaft
5. Top and main gear shaft

Transmission disassembly—late P'up, Trooper, Amigo and Rodeo

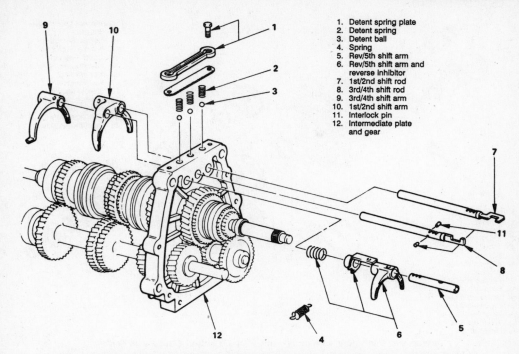

1. Detent spring plate
2. Detent spring
3. Detent ball
4. Spring
5. Rev/5th shift arm
6. Rev/5th shift arm and reverse inhibitor
7. 1st/2nd shift rod
8. 3rd/4th shift rod
9. 3rd/4th shift arm
10. 1st/2nd shift arm
11. Interlock pin
12. Intermediate plate and gear

Intermediate plate and shift arm assemblies—late P'up, Trooper, Amigo and Rodeo

3. Remove the 1st/2nd shift rod, 3rd/4th shift rod, 3rd/4th shift arm and 1st/2nd shift arm.

NOTE: *Place a round bar under the shift rods before removing spring pins.*

4. Remove the interlock pins from the 3rd/4th shift rod.

ASSEMBLY

1. Onto the intermediate plate and gear assemblies, install the 1st/2nd shift arm, 3rd/4th shift arm, 3rd/4th shift rod, interlock pins and 1st/2nd shift rod. Drive in the spring pins to hold in place.

2. Install the 5th/rev shift arm and inhibitor, 5th/rev shift rod and spring.

3. Install the detent balls, springs and plate. Torque the plate bolts to 11 ft. lbs. (15 Nm).

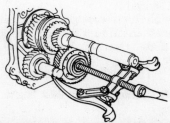

5th counter gear removal—late P'up, Trooper, Amigo and Rodeo

Reverse and 5th Gear

DISASSEMBLY

1. Remove the oil seal collar and pull the bearing off with retainer remover tool J–37222 or equivalent and a puller.

2. Remove the thrust plate, thrust washer and lock ball.

3. Remove the idler gear snapring, 5th counter gear snapring and pull off the 5th counter gear and bearing using a puller.

4. Remove the reverse idler shaft, reverse idler gear, thrust washer and idle shaft pin.

5. Remove the reverse counter gear, 5th blocker ring and needle bearings.

6. Engage the 3rd/4th synchronizer with the 3rd gear, engage the 1st/2nd synchronizer with the 1st gear and remove the clutch hub nut using a hub wrench J–37219.

7. Remove the 5th/rev synchronizer assembly by prying upwards with a pair of prybars.

8. Remove the reverse ring, reverse gear and needle bearing.

9. Using a Torx® bit wrench J–37225, remove the bearing plate screws and plate.

10. Remove the bearing snapring and intermediate plate.

ASSEMBLY

1. Mesh the counter gear with the mainshaft, install the holding fixture J–37224 or equivalent to the assembly and install the intermediate plate.

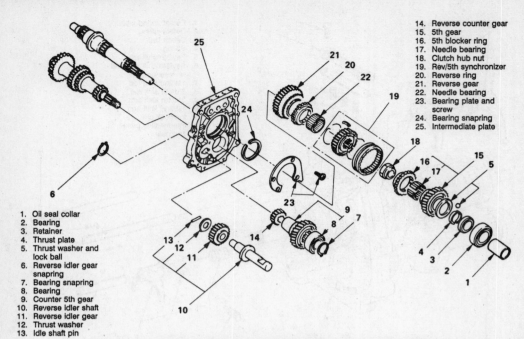

14. Reverse counter gear
15. 5th gear
16. 5th blocker ring
17. Needle bearing
18. Clutch hub nut
19. Rev/5th synchronizer
20. Reverse ring
21. Reverse gear
22. Needle bearing
23. Bearing plate and screw
24. Bearing snapring
25. Intermediate plate

1. Oil seal collar
2. Bearing
3. Retainer
4. Thrust plate
5. Thrust washer and lock ball
6. Reverse idler gear snapring
7. Bearing snapring
8. Bearing
9. Counter 5th gear
10. Reverse idler shaft
11. Reverse idler gear
12. Thrust washer
13. Idle shaft pin

Reverse and 5th gear assembly—late P'up, Trooper, Amigo and Rodeo

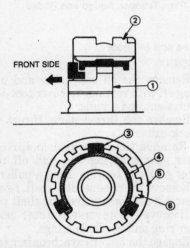

FRONT SIDE

Rev/5th synchronizer assembly—1. clutch hub, 2. small groove, 3. inserts, 4. springs, 5. clutch hub, 6. sleeve

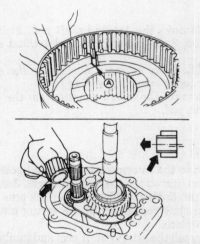

Clutch hub and reverse counter gear installation— late P'up, Trooper, Amigo and Rodeo

2. Apply thread locking compound to the bearing plate screws and torque to 11 ft. lbs. (15 Nm).

3. Install the 5th/rev synchronizer assembly, clutch hub nut, torque to 94 ft. lbs. (128 Nm) and stake the nut with a punch.

4. Install the needle bearings, 5th blocker ring and 5th gear.

5. Install the reverse counter gear with the projection facing the intermediate plate. Install the idler shaft pin, thrust washer, reverse idler gear, 5th counter gear and idler shaft, using a plastic hammer to drive in place.

6. Install the idler shaft bearing and selective snapring that meets the clearance of 0–0.0059 in. (0–0.15mm).

7. Install the reverse gear snapring.

8. Install the thrust washer and lock ball, thrust plate, retainer, bearing and oil seal collar.

Mainshaft, Counter and Top Gear Shafts
DISASSEMBLY

1. Remove the top shaft snapring, top gear shaft, needle bearings and press off the bearing.

1. Top gear shaft
   snapring
2. Top gear shaft
3. Ball bearing
4. Needle bearing
5. Top blocker ring
6. Mainshaft snapring
7. 3rd/4th synchronizer
8. 3rd blocker ring
9. 3rd gear
10. Needle bearing
11. Needle bearing collar
12. Mainshaft bearing
13. 1st gear thrust
    bearing
14. 1st gear
15. 1st blocker ring
16. Needle bearing
17. Clutch hub snapring
18. 1st/2nd synchronizer
19. 2nd blocker ring

20. 2nd gear
21. Needle bearings
22. Mainshaft
23. Bearing snapring
24. Center roller bearing
25. Counter gear

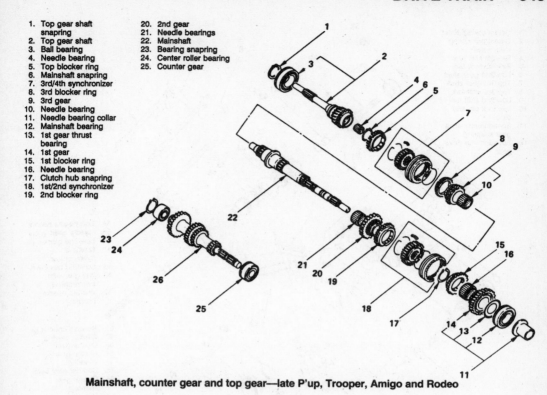

Mainshaft, counter gear and top gear—late P'up, Trooper, Amigo and Rodeo

2. Remove the top blocker ring, mainshaft snapring and 3rd/4th synchronizer assembly.

3. Remove the 3rd blocker ring, 3rd gear, needle bearings and press off the needle bearing collar.

4. Press off the mainshaft bearing, the thrust bearing and 1st gear.

5. Remove the 1st blocker ring, needle bearings and clutch hub snapring.

6. Remove the 1st/2nd synchronizer assembly, 2nd blocker ring, 2nd gear and needle bearings. A press may be needed.

7. From the counter gear, remove the bearing snapring and both bearings with a press.

ASSEMBLY

1. Onto the mainshaft, install the needle bearings and 2nd gear so the dog teeth are facing rearward.

2. Install the 2nd blocker ring and 1st/2nd

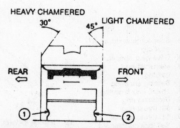

Low/2nd synchronizer assembly—4-speed

synchronizer assembly. Turn the shallow clutch hub face toward the side of the sleeve with the small groove on the outer circumference. Check to see if the sleeve slides smoothly.

3. Install the clutch hub selective snapring, needle bearings, 1st blocker ring, 1st gear and 1st gear thrust bearing. Thrust bearing face must face forward.

4. Press on the mainshaft bearing and bearing collar.

5. Install the 3rd gear needle bearings, 3rd gear, 3rd blocker ring and 3rd/4th synchronizer assembly. The 3rd gear dog teeth must face forward. Turn the synchronizer clutch hub face with the heavy boss toward the side of the sleeve with the small groove on the outer circumference. Make sure the sleeve slides smoothly.

6. Install the mainshaft selective snapring,

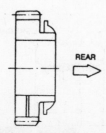

2nd gear positioning—4-speed

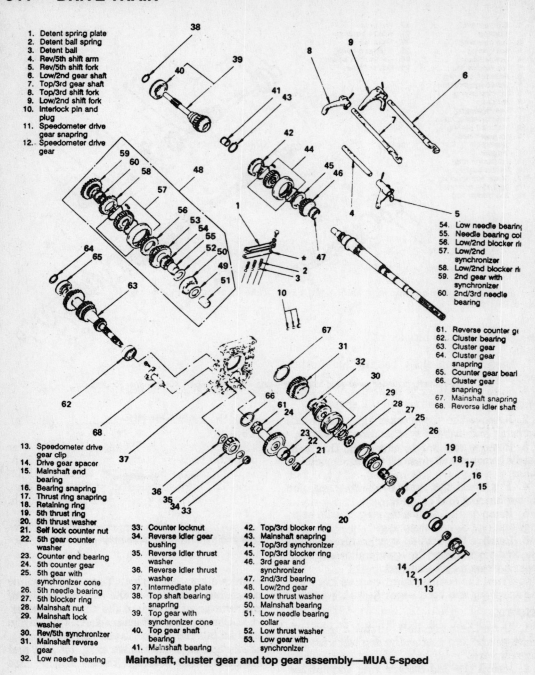

1. Detent spring plate
2. Detent ball spring
3. Detent ball
4. Rev/5th shift arm
5. Rev/5th shift fork
6. Low/2nd gear shaft
7. Top/3rd gear shaft
8. Top/3rd shift fork
9. Low/2nd shift fork
10. Interlock pin and plug
11. Speedometer drive gear snapring
12. Speedometer drive gear

54. Low needle bearing
55. Needle bearing co
56. Low/2nd blocker ri
57. Low/2nd synchronizer
58. Low/2nd blocker ri
59. 2nd gear with synchronizer
60. 2nd/3rd needle bearing

61. Reverse counter g
62. Cluster bearing
63. Cluster gear
64. Cluster gear snapring
65. Counter gear bear
66. Cluster gear snapring
67. Mainshaft snapring
68. Reverse idler shaft

13. Speedometer drive gear clip
14. Drive gear spacer
15. Mainshaft end bearing
16. Bearing snapring
17. Thrust ring snapring
18. Retaining ring
19. 5th thrust ring
20. 5th thrust washer
21. Self lock counter nut
22. 5th gear counter washer
23. Counter end bearing
24. 5th counter gear
25. 5th gear with synchronizer cone
26. 5th needle bearing
27. 5th blocker ring
28. Mainshaft nut
29. Mainshaft lock washer
30. Rev/5th synchronizer
31. Mainshaft reverse gear
32. Low needle bearing

33. Counter locknut
34. Reverse idler gear bushing
35. Reverse idler thrust washer
36. Reverse idler thrust washer
37. Intermediate plate
38. Top shaft bearing snapring
39. Top gear with synchronizer cone
40. Top gear shaft bearing
41. Mainshaft bearing

42. Top/3rd blocker ring
43. Mainshaft snapring
44. Top/3rd synchronizer
45. Top/3rd blocker ring
46. 3rd gear and synchronizer
47. 2nd/3rd bearing
48. Low/2nd gear
49. Low thrust washer
50. Mainshaft bearing
51. Low needle bearing collar
52. Low thrust washer
53. Low gear with synchronizer

Mainshaft, cluster gear and top gear assembly—MUA 5-speed

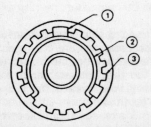

Synchronizer assembly, 1. key, 2. spring, 3. clutch 4-speed

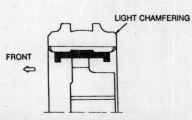

LIGHT CHAMFERING

FRONT

Top/3rd synchronizer assembly—4-speed

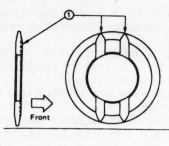

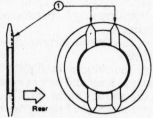

Low/rev thrust washer oil groove position—MUA 5-speed, top is low

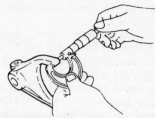

Shift arm thickness check—4-speed

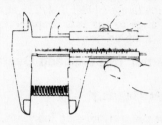

Detent spring check—4-speed

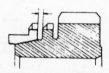

Blocker ring to gear clearance check—4-speed

needle bearings, top blocker ring, and top gear shaft.

7. Press on top shaft bearing and install snapring.

8. Onto the counter gear, press on the front and rear bearings and install the snapring.

INSPECTION

1. Using a micrometer, check the shift arm thickness where it rides on the synchronizer. 1st/2nd = 0.354–0.388 in. (9.0–9.8mm), 3rd/4th = 0.354–0.386 in. (9.0–9.9mm), transfer = 0.354–0.388 in. (9.0–9.8mm) and 5th/reverse = 0.354–0.386 in. (9.0–9.9mm).

2. Using a inside slide ruler, check the free length of the detent springs. All springs (except transfer) 1.03–1.06 in. (26.2–26.8mm) and transfer interlock = 0.603–0.626 in. (1.53–1.59).

3. Using a spring tension tester, check the detent spring tension. 1st/2nd, 3rd/4th and 5th/rev = 20.0–22.0 lbs. (8.9–9.9 kg), transfer = 15.0–17.0 lbs. (6.6–7.6 kg) and transfer interlock = 2.2 lbs. (1.0 kg).

4. Using a feeler gauge, check the clearance between the blocker ring and dog teeth. Standard clearance 0.032–0.059 in. (0.8–1.5mm).

5. Using a feeler gauge, check the clearance between the blocker rings and inserts. Standard clearance for 3rd/4th = 0.138–0.158 in. (3.51–4.00mm), 1st/2nd & transfer = 0.171–0.193 in. (4.34–5.00mm) and 5th = 0.141–0.161 in. (3.59–4.10mm).

6. Using a feeler gauge, check the clearance between the clutch hub and inserts. Standard clearance 0.0004–0.012 in. (0.01–0.3mm).

7. Using a dial indicator and holding fixture,

check the mainshaft run-out. Limit 0.0019 in. (0.05mm).

8. Using an inside T-gauge, check the gear inside diameter. 1st–3rd = 1.773–1.777 in. (45.0–45.1mm), 2nd gear = 2.047–2.051 in. (52.0–52.1mm), transfer/rev = 1.893–1.900 in. (48.0–48.1mm) and 5th = 1.246–1.260 in. (32.0–32.1mm).

9. Using a micrometer, check the clearance between the bushing and idler gear shaft. Standard clearance 0.0016–0.0059 in. (0.041–0.150mm).

10. Using a dial indicator, check the spline play. Clutch hub 0.0–0.0079 in. (0.0–0.20mm) and reverse gear 0.0–0.0120 in. (0.0–0.3mm).

11. Using a dial indicator, check the play in the ball bearings. Limit 0.068 in. (0.2mm).

12. Replace components that do not meet specifications.

ASSEMBLY

1. Apply liquid sealer to the transfer rear case fitting surfaces.

2. Shift the high/low synchronizer to the 4H side. Turn the select rod counterclockwise so that the select block projection may enter into the 4 × 2/4 × 4 shift block.

3. Install the gear shafts and intermediate plate into the main and transfer housing. The cut away portion the select rod head should

align with the rear case hole stopper in the transfer housing.

4. Install the transfer case-to-transmission bolts and torque to 28 ft. lbs. (37 Nm).

5. Install the front countershaft and top shaft bearing snaprings.

6. Apply liquid gasket to the front cover and install a new seal with a seal installer tool J–26540. Install the cover and torque the bolts to 14 ft. lbs. (19 Nm).

7. Using a flange holder J–27221, install the transfer flange to the rear transfer case and speedometer driven gear.

Borg-Warner T5R 5-Speed Overhaul Rodeo

CASE DISASSEMBLY

1. Drain the transmission lubricant.

2. Use a pin punch and hammer to remove the offset lever-to-shift rail roll pin.

3. Remove the extension housing adapter. Remove the housing and the offset lever as an assembly.

4. Remove the detent ball and spring from the offset lever. Remove the roll pin from the extension housing or adapter.

5. Remove the countershaft rear thrust bearing and race.

6. Remove the transmission cover and shift fork assembly. Two of the transmission cover bolts are alignment type dowel pins. Mark their location so that they may be reinstalled in their original locations.

7. Remove the reverse lever to reverse lever pivot bolt C-clip.

8. Remove the reverse lever pivot bolt. Remove the reverse lever and fork as an assembly.

9. Mark the position of the front bearing cap to case, then remove the bearing cap bolts and cap.

10. Remove the front bearing race and the

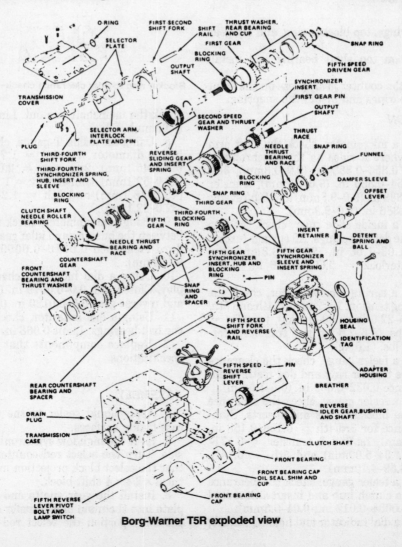

Borg-Warner T5R exploded view

shims from the bearing cap. Use a small pry bar and remove the front seal from the bearing cap.

11. Rotate the main drive gear shaft until the flat portion of the gear faces the countershaft, then remove the main drive gear shaft assembly.

12. Remove the thrust bearing and 15 roller bearings from the clutch shaft. Remove the output shaft bearing race. Tap the output shaft with a plastic hammer to loosen it if necessary.

13. Tilt the output shaft assembly upward and remove the assembly from the case.

14. Carefully pull off the countershaft rear bearing with the proper puller after marking the position for reinstallation.

15. Move the countershaft rearward and tilt it upward to remove it from the transmission case. Remove the countershaft bearing spacer.

16. Remove the reverse idler shaft roll pin, then remove the reverse idler shaft and gear.

17. Press off the countershaft front bearing. Use the appropriate pullers and remove the bearing from the main drive gear shaft.

18. Remove the extension housing or adapter oil seal and remove the back-up light switch from the case.

OUTPUT SHAFT DISASSEMBLY

1. Remove the thrust bearing washer from the front of the output shaft.

2. Scribe matchmarks on the hub and sleeve of the 3rd-4th synchronizer so that these parts may be reassembled properly.

3. Remove the 3rd-4th synchronizer blocking ring, sleeve and hub as an assembly.

4. Remove the insert springs and the inserts from the 3rd-4th synchronizer and separate the sleeve from the hub.

5. Remove the 3rd speed gear from the shaft.

6. Remove the 2nd speed gear to output shaft snapring, the tabbed thrust washer and the 2nd speed gear from the shaft.

7. Use an appropriate puller and remove the the output shaft bearing.

8. Remove the 1st gear thrust washer, the roll pin, the 1st speed gear and the blocking ring.

9. Scribe matchmarks on the 1st-2nd synchronizer sleeve and the output shaft.

10. Remove the insert spring and the inserts from the 1st-reverse sliding gear, then remove the gear from the output hub.

OUTPUT SHAFT ASSEMBLY

1. Coat the output shaft and the gear bores with transmission lubricant.

2. Align the matchmarks and install the 1st-2nd synchronizer sleeve on the output shaft hub.

3. Install the three inserts and two springs into the 1st-reverse synchronizer sleeve.

NOTE: *The tanged end of each spring should be positioned on the same insert but the open face of each spring should be opposite each other.*

4. Install the blocking ring and the 2nd speed gear onto the output shaft.

5. Install the tabbed thrust washer and 2nd gear snapring in the output shaft; be sure that the washer is properly seated in the notch.

6. Install the blocking ring and the 1st speed gear onto the output shaft, then install the 1st gear roll pin.

7. Press the rear bearing onto the shaft.

8. Install the remaining components onto the output shaft: The 1st gear thrust washer. The 3rd speed gear. The 3rd-4th synchronizer hub inserts and the sleeve (the hub offset must face forward). The thrust bearing washer on the rear of the countershaft.

COVER & FORKS DISASSEMBLY

1. Place the selector arm plates and the shift rail centered in the Neutral position.

2. Rotate the shift rail counterclockwise until the selector arm disengages from the selector arm plates; the selector arm roll pin should now be accessible.

3. Pull the shift rail rearward until the selector contacts the 1st-2nd shift fork.

4. Use a $3/16$ in. (5mm) pin punch and remove the selector arm roll pin and the shift rail.

5. Remove the shift forks, the selector arm, the roll pin and the interlock plate.

6. Remove the shift rail oil seal and O-ring.

7. Remove the nylon inserts and the selector arm plates from the shift forks.

NOTE: *Mark the position of the parts so that they may be properly installed.*

COVER & FORK ASSEMBLY

1. Attach the nylon inserts to the selector arm plates and through the shift forks.

2. If removed, coat the edges of the shift rail plug with sealer and install the plug.

3. Coat the shift rail and the rail bores with petroleum jelly, then slide the shift rail into the cover until the end of the rail is flush with the inside edge of the cover.

4. Position the 1st-2nd shift fork into the cover; with the offset of the shift fork facing the rear of the cover. Push the shift rail through the fork. The 1st-2nd fork is the larger of the two forks.

5. Position the selector arm and the C-shaped interlock plate into the cover, then push the shift rail through the arm. The widest part of the interlock plate must face away from the

cover and the selector arm roll pin must face downward, toward the rear of the cover.

6. Position the 3rd-4th shift fork into the cover with the fork offset facing the rear of the cover. The 3rd-4th shift selector arm plate must be positioned under the 1st-2nd shift fork selector arm plate.

7. Push the shift rail through the 3rd-4th shift fork and into the front cover rail bore.

8. Rotate the shift rail until the forward selector arm plate faces away from parallel to the cover.

9. Align the roll pin holes of the selector arm and the shift rail and install the roll pin. The roll pin must be installed flush with the surface of the selector arm to prevent selector arm plate to pin interference.

10. Install the O-ring into the groove of the shift rail oil seal, then install the oil seal carefully after lubricating it.

CASE ASSEMBLY

1. Apply a coat of Loctite® 601, or equivalent, to the outer cage of the front countershaft bearing, then press the bearing into the bore until it is flush with the case.

2. Apply petroleum jelly to the tabbed countershaft thrust washer and install the washer with the tab engaged in the corresponding case depression.

3. Tip the transmission case on end and install the countershaft into the front bearing bore.

4. Install the rear countershaft bearing spacer and coat the rear bearing with petroleum jelly. Install the rear countershaft bearing using the appropriate tools. The rear bearing is properly installed when 3mm is extended beyond the case surface.

5. Position the reverse idler into the case (the shift lever groove must face rearward) and install the reverse idler shaft into the case. Install the shaft retaining pin.

6. Install the output shaft assembly into the transmission case.

7. Install the main drive gear bearing onto the main drive shaft using the appropriate tools. Coat the roller bearings with petroleum jelly and install them in the main drive gear recess. Install the thrust bearing and race.

8. Install the 4th gear blocking ring onto the output shaft. Install the rear output shaft bearing race.

9. Install the main drive gear assembly into the case, engaging the 3rd-4th synchronizer blocking ring.

10. Install a new seal in the front bearing cap and in the rear extension or adapter.

11. Install the front bearing into the front bearing cap but do not (at this time) install the shims. Temporarily install the cap to the transmission without applying sealer.

12. Install the reverse lever, the pivot pin (coat the threads with non-hardening sealer) and the retaining C-clip. Be sure the reverse lever fork is engaged with the reverse idler gear.

13. Coat the countershaft rear bearing race and the thrust bearing with petroleum jelly, then install the parts into the extension housing or adapter.

14. Temporarily install the extension housing or adapter without sealer, tighten the retaining bolts slightly, but do not final torque them.

15. Turn the transmission case on end and mount a dial indicator in position to measure output shaft end play. To eliminate end play the bearings must be preloaded from 0.025-0.130mm. Check the endplay. Select a shim pack that measures 0.025-0.130mm thicker than the measured endplay.

16. Install the shims under the front bearing cap. Apply a ⅛ in. (3mm) bead of RTV sealer to the cap. Align the reference marks and install the cap on the front of the transmission. Torque the mounting bolts to 15 ft. lbs. Recheck the output shaft end play, none should exist. Adjust if necessary.

17. Remove the extension housing or adapter. Move the shift forks and synchronizer sleeves to their neutral position. Apply a ⅛ in. (3mm) bead of RTV sealer to the cover to case mounting surface. Align the forks with their sleeves and carefully lower the cover into position. Center the cover and install the alignment dowels. Install the mounting bolts and tighten to 9 ft. lbs.

NOTE: *The offset lever to shift rail roll pin must be position vertically; if not, repeat Step 17.*

18. Apply a ⅛ in. (3mm) bead of RTV sealer to the extension housing or adapter and install over the output shaft.

NOTE: *The shift rail must be positioned so that it just enters the shift cover opening.*

19. Install the detent spring into the offset lever and place the steel ball into the Neutral guide plate detent. Apply pressure to the detent spring and offset lever, then slide the offset lever on the shift rail and seat the extension housing or adapter plate against the transmission case. Install and tighten the mounting bolts to 25 ft. lbs. (34 Nm).

20. Install the roll pin into the offset lever and shift rail. Install the damper sleeve in the offset lever. Coat the back up lamp switch threads with sealer and install the switch, tighten to 15 ft. lbs. (20 Nm).

MANUAL TRANSAXLE

Identification

The FWD I-Mark, Impulse and Stylus are equipped with a MR8 5-speed manual transaxle. The identification tag is attached to one of the lower case retaining bolts or shift quadrant bolts.

Shifter and Cables

REMOVAL AND INSTALLATION

1. Disconnect the negative (–) battery cable.
2. Remove the transaxle snap pins from the cable retainers.
3. Remove the cable retaining clips from the cables.
4. Remove the cable nut, and front snap pin.
5. Remove the cable cover, grommet and select cable. Remove the shift cable.

To install:

1. Install the cable cover, grommet and select cable. Install the shift cable.
2. Install the cable nut, and front snap pin.
3. Install the cable retaining clips to the cables.

4. Install the transaxle snap pins to the cable retainers.
5. Connect the negative (–) battery cable.
6. **Cable Adjustment:** make sure the transaxle is in the NEUTRAL position.
7. Turn the adjusting nuts (2) until the change lever (1) is at right angle to the pivot case (3) as viewed from the side of the shifter.
8. After adjustment, tighten the adjusting nuts (2) securely.
9. Turn the adjusting nuts (4) until the change lever (1) is front or rear of the shift control. Tighten the adjusting nuts.

FWD Impulse and Stylus

1. Remove the intercooler, air duct and air cleaner.
2. Remove the snap pins from the cables at the transaxle.
3. Remove the front console panel and console.
4. Remove the shift cable nut, snap pin and adjusting nut.
5. Remove the cable cover and grommet.
6. Pull the cables forward and remove.

To install:

1. Push the cables forward and install.

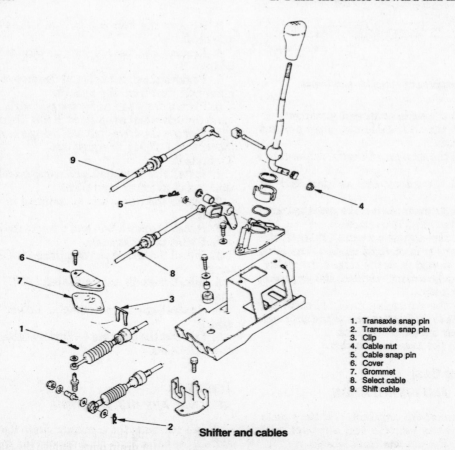

1. Transaxle snap pin
2. Transaxle snap pin
3. Clip
4. Cable nut
5. Cable snap pin
6. Cover
7. Grommet
8. Select cable
9. Shift cable

Shifter and cables

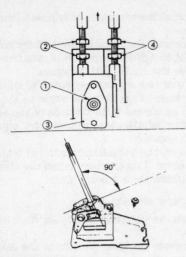

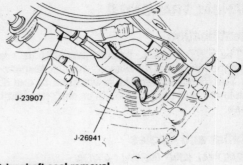

Driveshaft seal removal

Shifter cable adjustment—I-Mark

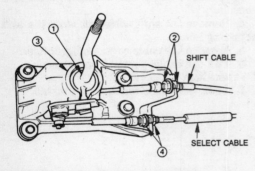

SHIFT CABLE

SELECT CABLE

Shift cable adjustment—Impulse and Stylus

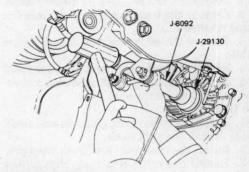

Driveshaft seal installation

2. Install the cable cover and grommet.

3. Install the shift cable nut, snap pin and adjusting nut.

4. Install the snap pins from the cables at the transaxle.

5. Install the intercooler, air duct and air cleaner.

6. **Cable Adjustment:** make sure the transaxle is in the NEUTRAL position.

7. Turn the adjusting nuts (2) until the change lever (1) is at right angle to the pivot case (3) as viewed from the side of the shifter.

8. After adjustment, tighten the adjusting nuts (2) securely.

9. Turn the adjusting nuts (4) until the change lever (1) is front or rear of the shift control. Tighten the adjusting nuts.

10. Install the console assembly.

Driveshaft Seal

REMOVAL AND INSTALLATION

1. Disconnect the negative (–) battery cable.

2. Raise the vehicle and support with jackstands. Remove the front wheels.

3. Remove the hub nut for the left (4WD) axle shaft.

4. Remove the tie rod end as outlined in Chapter 8.

5. Remove the pinch bolt and disconnect the lower ball joint from the knuckle.

6. Place a drain pan under the transaxle. Remove the driveshaft as outlined in this Chapter.

7. Remove the driveshaft seal using a seal remover tool J–26941 or equivalent.

To install:

1. Install the driveshaft seal using a seal install tool J–29130 or equivalent.

2. Install the driveshaft as outlined in this Chapter.

3. Install the pinch bolt and connect the lower ball joint to the knuckle.

4. Install the tie rod end as outlined in Chapter 8.

5. Install the hub nut for the left (4WD) axle shaft.

6. Install the front wheels. Lower the vehicle.

7. Connect the negative (–) battery cable and check for leaks.

Transaxle

REMOVAL AND INSTALLATION

Before removing the transaxle; drain the fluid from the lower drain plug, remove the engine

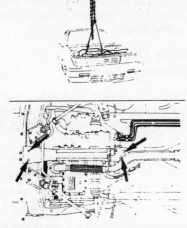

Removing lower crossmember—FWD I-Mark

hood and air duct and disconnect the wiring from the transaxle.

FWD I-Mark

1. Disconnect the negative (–) battery cable.
2. Raise the vehicle and support with jackstands.
3. Remove the front wheels.
4. Disconnect the tension rod from the lower control arm.
5. Disconnect the driveshaft as outlined in this Chapter.
6. Remove the bellhousing lower cover.
7. Support the engine and remove lower engine crossmember.

To install:

1. Support the engine and install the transaxle and lower crossmember.
2. Install the bellhousing lower cover.
3. Install the driveshaft as outlined in this Chapter.
4. Connect the tension rod to the lower control arm.
5. Install the front wheels.
6. Lower the vehicle.
7. Connect the negative (–) battery cable and check operation.

FWD Impulse and Stylus (2WD)

1. Disconnect the negative (–) battery cable.
2. Remove the battery and battery tray.
3. Remove the air duct and air cleaner.
4. Raise the vehicle and support with jackstands. Remove the front wheels.
5. Disconnect all electrical terminals from the transaxle.
6. Disconnect the clutch cable, shift, select and speedometer cables.

7. Disconnect the tie rod end and ball joints as outlined in Chapter 8.
8. Disconnect the driveshafts as outlined in this Chapter.
9. Disconnect the front exhaust pipe.
10. Remove the torque rod and bracket.
11. Remove the left rubber mount.
12. Support the engine with a holding fixture.
13. Remove the center support beam with rear mount.
14. Disconnect the engine strut and flywheel under cover. Place a transmission jack under the transaxle.
15. Remove the transaxle-to-engine bolts.
16. Lower the transaxle with the transmission jack.

To install:

1. Raise the transaxle with the transmission jack.
2. Install the transaxle-to-engine bolts.
3. Connect the engine strut and install the flywheel under cover. Remove the transmission jack.
4. Install the center support beam with rear mount.
5. Remove the engine holding fixture.
6. Install the left rubber mount.
7. Install the torque rod and bracket.
8. Connect the front exhaust pipe.
9. Connect the driveshafts as outlined in this Chapter.
10. Connect the tie rod end and ball joints as outlined in Section 8.
11. Connect the clutch cable, shift, select and speedometer cables.
12. Connect all electrical terminals to the transaxle.
13. Install the front wheels and lower the vehicle.
14. Install the air duct and air cleaner.
15. Install the battery and battery tray.
16. Connect the negative (–) battery cable and check operation.

All Wheel Drive Impulse

1. Disconnect the negative (–) battery cable.
2. Remove the battery and battery bracket.
3. Remove the intercooler, air duct and air cleaner.
4. Disconnect all electrical harnesses and cables from the transaxle.
5. Remove the transfer case as outlined in this Chapter.
6. Disconnect the torque rod and bracket to the lower control arm.
7. Remove the left mounting rubber.
8. Place a transmission jack under the transaxle and raise the engine with an engine holding fixture.
9. Remove the transaxle-to-engine bolts.

10. Lower the transaxle case from the vehicle.

To install:

1. Raise the transaxle case into the vehicle.

2. Install the transaxle-to-engine bolts.

3. Install the left mounting rubber and remove the transmission jack.

4. Connect the torque rod and bracket to the lower control arm.

5. Install the transfer case as outlined in this Chapter.

6. Connect all electrical harnesses and cables to the transaxle.

7. Install the intercooler, air duct and air cleaner.

8. Install the battery and battery bracket.

9. Connect the negative (–) battery cable and check operation.

Transaxle Overhaul

DISASSEMBLY

1. Remove the clutch release bearing assembly from the transaxle. Attach the transaxle assembly to a suitable transaxle holding fixture.

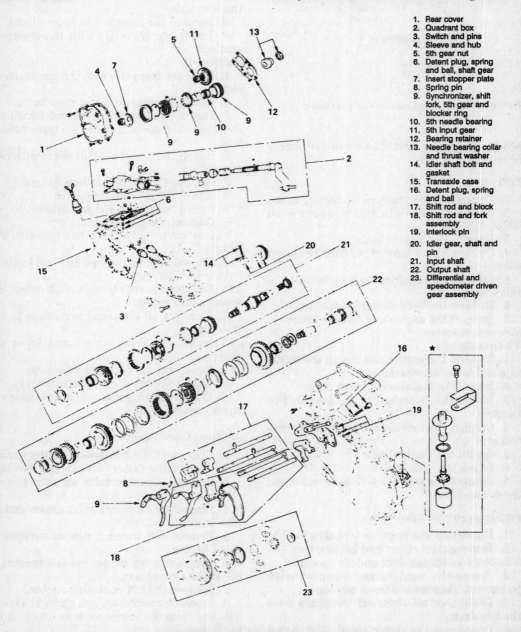

1. Rear cover
2. Quadrant box
3. Switch and pins
4. Sleeve and hub
5. 5th gear nut
6. Detent plug, spring and ball, shaft gear
7. Insert stopper plate
8. Spring pin
9. Synchronizer, shift fork, 5th gear and blocker ring
10. 5th needle bearing
11. 5th input gear
12. Bearing retainer
13. Needle bearing collar and thrust washer
14. Idler shaft bolt and gasket
15. Transaxle case
16. Detent plug, spring and ball
17. Shift rod and block
18. Shift rod and fork assembly
19. Interlock pin
20. Idler gear, shaft and pin
21. Input shaft
22. Output shaft
23. Differential and speedometer driven gear assembly

MR8 manual transaxle exploded view

2. Remove the rear cover assembly from the transaxle case.

3. Remove the control box assembly from the transaxle case.

4. Using a suitable tool, shift transaxle into gear. Remove the 5th speed shaft and discard the retaining nuts from the input and output shaft and discard the the retaining nuts. Shift transaxle back into neutral, aligning the detents of the shift rails.

5. Remove the detent spring retaining bolts for 1st/2nd, 3rd/4th and 5th speeds and remove the detent springs and detent balls. Remove the reverse detent spring retaining bolts, spring and detent ball. Remove switches for 1st/2nd and 3rd/4th gear switch hole, if so equipped with shift speed indicator light.

6. Place 5th speed synchronizer in neutral. Remove the roll pin at 5th gear shift fork and discard the roll pin. Remove 5th gear synchronizer hub, sleeve, roller bearing and gear with the shift fork as an assembly from the output shaft. Using a suitable gear puller, remove 5th speed gear from the input shaft.

7. Remove 7 bearing retainer screws with Torx® bit (No. 45) from the bearing retainer assembly.

8. Remove the bearing retainer and shims from the input and output shafts. Keep shims in order.

9. Remove the reverse idler retaining bolt used to retain the reverse idler shaft at the transaxle case.

10. Remove the collar and thrust washer from the output shaft using a suitable gear puller.

11. Remove the 14 bolts retaining the transaxle case and separate the transaxle from the clutch housing.

12. Lift the 5th gear shaft. With the detent aligned facing the same way, remove 5th and reverse shafts at the same time.

13. Remove the reverse idle gear and reverse idle shaft.

14. Using a punch and hammer, remove the roll pin from the 1st/2nd shift fork and discard the roll pin. Slide 1st/2nd shaft upward to clear housing and remove fork and shaft from case.

15. Remove the cotter pin and then remove the pin and reverse shift lever.

16. Remove the input and output shafts with 3rd/4th shift fork and shaft as an assembly.

17. Remove the differential case assembly.

18. Remove the reverse shaft bracket and take out 3 interlock pins.

19. Remove the rear bearing outer races (input and output) from the transaxle case.

20. Remove the outer races for the input shaft front bearing, output shaft front and differential side bearings. Use special tool J-26941 with J-33367 or equivalent for removing the input

and output races in the housing and the differential race in the case. Use special tool J-26941 or equivalent with a slide hammer to remove the differential race in the housing.

21. Remove the input shaft seal from the housing. Remove the clutch shaft only if replacement of bushing, bearing or shaft is required.

22. Remove the outer clutch shaft seal and outer clutch shaft bushing using special tools J-37245 with J-36190 or equivalent. Drive the bushings towards the outside of clutch housing.

23. Remove the clutch shaft and inner clutch shaft seal.

24. Remove the inner clutch shaft needle bearing using special tool J-37158 or equivalent. Position the puller legs under bearing and thread rod down to expand legs. Hold rod while tightening nut to remove the bearing.

Input Shaft

DISASSEMBLY

1. Remove the front bearing using special tool J-22912-01 or equivalent (inverted when installed on the shaft) with a suitable press.

2. Pull off the rear bearing, 4th gear, 3rd/4th synchronizer assembly and 3rd gear as a unit, using special tool J-22912-01 or equivalent (inverted when installed on the shaft) and a suitable press.

3. Remove the remaining parts from the input shaft.

INSPECTION

1. Clean parts with solvent and air dry.

2. Inspect shaft, spline wear for cracks.

3. Inspect gear teeth for scuffed, nicked, burred or broken teeth.

4. Inspect bearings for roughness of rotation, burred or pitted condition.

5. Inspect bearing races for scoring, wear or overheating.

6. Inspect synchronizers for damage or wear.

7. Measure the clearance between synchronizer blocker ring and inserts. Replace components if 0.146 in. (3.7mm) or less clearance exist.

8. Measure the clearance between blocker ring and gear. Replace components if not within 0.031 in. (0.8mm). This specification is the wear limit.

9. When reassembling synchronizer assemblies, each insert spring should support all 3 keys and each opening portion of the insert spring should face the opposite direction from the other.

ASSEMBLY

NOTE: *Before assembling apply oil to the thrust surfaces on all gears and washers.*

1. Install needle bearing, 3rd gear and the blocker ring on the input shaft.

2. Match the inserts of the 3rd/4th sleeve and hub assembly with the grooves of the blocker ring and press the sleeve and hub assembly and collar using special tool J-33374 or equivalent and a suitable press. Before installing, apply oil to the collar and hub of the collar. Check to ensure the insert springs do not interfere with the hub after installation.

3. Install the blocker ring, needle bearing, 4th gear and thrust washer on the input shaft. When installing the thrust washer install with the recessed area facing 4th gear.

4. Install the front and rear bearings using special tool J-33374 or equivalent and a suitable press. Before installing, apply oil to the bearing inside and race surfaces.

Output Shaft
DISASSEMBLY

1. Remove the front bearing using special tool J-22227-A and special tool J-33369 or equivalent and a suitable press.

2. Remove the rear bearing and 3rd/4th gear at the same time using special tool J-22912-01 (inverted when installed on the shaft) and a suitable press.

3. Remove the needle bearing, collar, 2nd gear, 1st/2nd gear synchronizer assembly, 1st gear and key as a unit using a suitable press.

4. Remove the thrust bearing and washer from the output shaft.

INSPECTION

1. Clean parts with solvent and air dry.

2. Inspect shaft, spline wear for cracks.

3. Inspect gear teeth for scuffed, nicked, burred or broken teeth.

4. Inspect bearings for roughness of rotation, burred or pitted condition.

5. Inspect bearing races for scoring, wear or overheating.

6. Inspect synchronizers assembly for damage or wear.

7. Measure the clearance between synchronizer blocker ring and inserts. Replace components if 0.154 in. (4mm) or less clearance exist.

8. Measure the clearance between blocker ring and gear. Replace components if not with 0.031 in. (0.8mm). This specification is the wear limit.

9. Measure the clearance between blocker rings and synchronizing cones for 1st and 2nd gears by positioning 1st gear then 1st/2nd synchronizer assembly then 2nd gear in the correct position. Replace the 1st/2nd gear synchronizer components if the measurement exceeds 0.059 in. (1.5mm).

10. When reassembling synchronizer assem-

blies, each insert spring should support all 3 keys and each opening portion of the insert spring should face the opposite direction from the other.

ASSEMBLY

NOTE: *Before assembling, apply oil to the thrust surfaces on all gear. Apply oil to all the bearing inside and race surfaces.*

1. Install the thrust washer, thrust bearing, needle bearing, 1st gear, inner, outer ring and blocker ring for 1st gear on the output shaft.

2. Match the inserts of the sleeve and hub assembly with the grooves of the blocker ring and press the sleeve and hub assembly together with the collar using special tool J-8853-01, pilot tool J-33369 or equivalent and a suitable press. Before installing the sleeve and hub assembly, oil should be applied to the hub and collar inside surface. After installation, apply oil to the collar outside surface. Check to ensure that the insert springs do not interfere with the hub after installation.

NOTE: *Install the 1st/2nd gear synchronizer in the correct position.*

3. Install the blocker ring, outer and inner ring for 2nd gear, needle bearing, 2nd gear and then the key. Make sure the key is positioned properly in the key groove.

4. Apply oil to the 3rd/4th gear inner surface, match the key with the key groove and fit the key together with the rear bearing. using special tool J-33374 or equivalent and a suitable press, press bearing on the shaft.

5. Press the front bearing on the shaft using special tool J-33368 or equivalent and a suitable press.

Differential
DISASSEMBLY

1. Remove the side bearing using a suitable gear puller.

2. Remove the 10 retaining bolts and remove the ring gear. Discard the ring gear bolts.

3. Using a small tool, pry the speedometer drive gear and or rotor from the differential case. Do not reuse the speedometer drive gear and or rotor.

4. Using a punch, drive out the lock pin and pull out the cross pin.

5. Remove the pinion gears, thrust washers, side gears and thrust washers.

INSPECTION

1. Clean with solvent and air dry.

2. Inspect the housing bearing race bore for wear, scratches or grooves.

3. Inspect the housing bushings for scores, burrs, roundness or evidence of overheating.

4. Inspect housing for cracks, threaded open-

ings for damaged threads, mounting faces for nicks, burrs or scratches.

5. Inspect gear teeth for scuffed, nicked, burred or broken teeth.

ASSEMBLY

NOTE: *Before assembling, apply oil to the bearing inner and outer race surfaces.*

1. Install the 2 side gears on the differential case together with the thrust washers. Next, position the 2 thrust washers with pinion gears opposite of each other and install them in their positions by turning the side gear.

2. Insert the cross pin and make sure the backlash is within the rated range 0.0012-0.0032 in. (0.03-0.08mm). If the backlash is outside the rated range, adjust it by installing different size thrust washers.

3. Install lock pin and cross pin.

4. Heat using a suitable tool (do not use hot water) a new speedometer drive gear or rotor to about 200°F (93°C) and then install it on the differential.

5. Heat using a suitable tool the rear gear to 122-212°F (50-100°C), then apply oil on the inside diameter of the ring gear then position the gear on the differential case. Apply a small amount of oil to the bottom side of the 10 new bolt heads only, then install bolts and tighten to 73-79 ft. lbs. in a diagonal sequence. Apply oil to the cross pin, differential gears, thrust portion, side gear shaft portion and side gear spline portion before installation.

6. Install the side bearing on the differential case using special tool J-22919 or equivalent and an arbor press.

TRANSAXLE ASSEMBLY

1. Install the new input shaft seal in housing using special tool J-26540 or equivalent.

2. Install the front outer bearing races for the input shaft, output shaft and differential into the clutch housing. Always apply oil to the bearing races before installation and use suitable tools.

3. Apply grease to the 3 interlock pins and install on the clutch housing.

4. Install the reverse shift bracket on the clutch housing. Use 3rd/4th shift shaft to align bracket to housing. Install retaining bolts and tighten to 13 ft. lbs. (17 Nm) make sure shaft operates smoothly after installation.

5. Install the differential assembly, then install the input, output shaft with the 3rd/4th shift fork and shaft together as an assembly into the clutch housing. Make sure the lock pin is in the 3rd/4th shifter shaft before installing. The 3rd/4th shift shaft is installed into the raised collar of reverse shift lever bracket.

6. Install the 1st/2nd gear shift fork onto the synchronizer sleeve and insert the shift shaft into the reverse shift lever bracket. Align hole in fork with the shaft and install a new double roll pin.

7. Install the reverse lever on shift bracket.

8. Install the reverse and 5th gear shifter shaft and at the same time, engage reverse shaft with reverse shift lever. Make sure lock pin is in the 5th gear shifter shaft before installing.

9. Install the reverse idle shaft with the gear into the clutch housing. Make sure reverse lever is engaged in collar of gear.

10. Measure and determine correct shim size using special tool J-33373. To determine correct shim size follow assembly procedure Steps 11-17.

11. Position the outer bearing races on the input, output and differential bearings. Position the shim selection gauges on the bearings races in the correct position.

NOTE: *The 3 gauges are marked as input, output and differential.*

12. Position 7 spacers provided with special tool J-33373 evenly around the perimeter of the clutch housing.

13. Install the bearing and shim retainer on transaxle case. Torque retaining screws to 13 ft. lbs. (17 Nm). After final torque on screws, stake screws to the retaining plate.

14. Carefully position the transaxle case over the gauges and on the spacer. Install the 7 bolts alternately until case is seated on spacers. Install the 7 bolts alternately until case is seated on spacers. Tighten bolts to 10 ft. lbs. (13 Nm).

15. Rotate each gauge to seat the bearings. Rotate the differential case through 3 revolutions in each direction.

16. With the 3 gauges compressed, measure the gap between the outer sleeve and base pad using available shim sizes in preload shim sizes chart. The input shaft shim should be 2 sizes smaller than the largest shim that will fit in the gap. The differential should use a shim 3 sizer larger than that which will smoothly fit in the gap. The output shaft should use the largest shim that can be placed into the gap and drawn through without binding.

17. When each of the 3 correct shims have been selected, remove the transaxle case, 7 spacers and 3 gauges.

18. Position the shim selected for the input, output and differential into the bearing race bores in the transaxle case.

19. Install the rear input and output shaft bearing races using suitable tools.

20. Install the rear differential case bearing race using special tools J-8611-01 with J-8092 or equivalent and a press. Apply oil to the bear-

ing race before installation. Press the bearing until seated in its bore.

21. Position the magnet in clutch housing. Clean the clutch housing and transaxle case mating surface, then apply a ⅛ in. (3mm) bead of Loctite No. 518 sealer or equivalent to the mating surfaces.

22. Install the transaxle case on the clutch housing. Install the reverse idle shaft bolt into the transaxle case. Tighten the retaining bolt to 28 ft. lbs. (38 Nm).

23. Install the 14 case bolts. Torque bolts to 28 ft. lbs. (38 Nm) in a diagonal sequence.

24. Install the drive axle seals using suitable tools.

25. Install the thrust washer and collar to the output shaft using special tool J-33374. Before installing, apply oil to the thrust surfaces and collar.

26. Install 5th gear to the input shaft. Install the needle bearing, 5th gear, blocker ring, hub/sleeve assembly with shift fork in its groove and back plate on the output shaft. Align shift fork on shift shaft and install a new double roll pin. Before installing apply oil to the output gear thrust surfaces.

27. Install the detent balls and detent springs for the reverse, 1st/2nd, 3rd/4th and 5th speeds. Install the retaining bolts and tighten to 18 ft. lbs. (25 Nm).

28. Install the 1st/2nd gear switch. Install the short pin and then the long pin into the 3rd/4th gear hole. Install 3rd/4th gear switch, if vehicle is equipped with a shift speed indicator light.

29. Apply Loctite No 262 sealer or equivalent to the threads of the input and output shafts. Install new retaining nuts and torque to 94 ft. lbs. (128 Nm). Stake nuts after reaching final torque.

30. Install a new gasket with the control box assembly on the transaxle case and torque the 4 bolts to 13 ft. lbs. (17 Nm). Stake the retaining nuts after final torque is applied and make sure transaxle shifts properly before installing the rear cover.

31. Install a new gasket with the rear cover. Install the retaining bolts and torque to 13 ft. lbs. (17 Nm).

32. If the clutch shaft, bushing, bearing and seals have been removed, installed new bearing into the clutch housing using special tools J-37159 with J-36190 or equivalent. Install new oil seal and clutch shaft. Install new outer bushing using special tool J-36037 or equivalent. Drive bushing inward until line on tool is flush with housing. Before installing, apply grease to both the inside and outside of bushing and bearing.

33. Install the clutch release bearing.

34. Measure the rotating torque on the input shaft. When measuring, the input shaft should be to the upper side and the differential assembly to the lower side. The rotating torque specification should be less than 7 inch lbs.

Halfshafts (Driveshafts)
REMOVAL AND INSTALLATION
Except All Wheel Drive Impulse

1. Disconnect the negative (–) battery cable.
2. Remove the ball joint-to-lower control arm, strut rod and stabilizer bar bolts or nuts.
3. Remove the driveshaft nut and washer. Dislodge the shaft from the spindle splines with a plastic hammer.
4. Support the driveshaft to the strut with a piece of wire to prevent the shaft from falling.
5. Place a drain pan under the driveshaft. Using a suitable prybar, remove the driveshaft from the transaxle. The inner joint is retained by a circlip inside the differential housing. Be careful not to damage the inner joint by pulling the shaft apart.

To install:

1. Install the driveshaft into the transaxle. Push the shaft in until the circlip engages the differential groove.
2. Insert the driveshaft into the splined hole in the spindle.
3. Install the driveshaft nut and washer. Torque the nut to 100 ft. lbs. (136 Nm).
4. Install the ball joint-to-lower control arm, strut rod and stabilizer bar bolts.
5. Refill the transaxle with the proper amount of fluid. Connect the negative (–) battery cable and check operation.

FWD Impulse and Stylus

1. Disconnect the negative (–) battery cable.
2. Raise the vehicle and support with jackstands.
3. Drain the oil from the transaxle and transfer case (4WD only).
4. Pry the hub nut open and loosen the nut. The brake may have to applied when loosening.
5. Using a tie rod removing tool J-21687–02 or equivalent, disconnect the tie rod from the knuckle.
6. Remove the lower ball joint bolts and swing out of the way.

Disconnecting driveshaft from transaxle

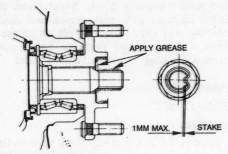

Driveshaft nut installation

7. Pull the hub and knuckle away from the driveshaft. Be careful not to allow the shaft to fully extend. Damage to the inner joint may result.

8. Use a prybar to dislodge the inner joint from the differential. The shaft is held in by a circlip at the end of the splined shaft.

To install:

1. Install the inner joint into the differential and engage the circlip.

2. Insert the outer joint into the splined hub. Be careful not to allow the shaft to fully extend. Damage to the inner joint may result.

3. Install the lower ball joint bolts and tighten.

4. Install the hub nut and tighten. The brake may have to applied when tighten.

5. Refill the transaxle and transfer case (4WD only) with the specified oil.

6. Lower the vehicle.

7. Connect the negative (–) battery cable.

CV-JOINT OVERHAUL

Double Offset Joint

DISASSEMBLY

1. Disconnect the negative (–) battery cable. Clean the assembly of all grease and dirt.

2. Remove the inner joint boot clamps. Slide the boot off of the joint.

3. From inside the inner joint, remove the circular clip from inside the offset joint. Pull the joint and shaft off of the inner joint.

4. Remove the ball retainer snapring and ball retainer. Pull the ball retainer and ball guide from the splined shaft.

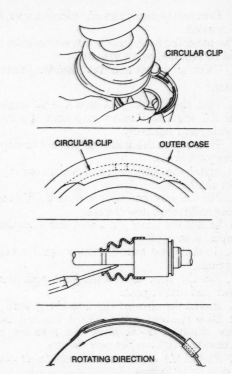

Assembly of Double Offset CV-joint

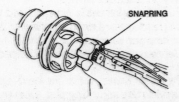

Remove the snapring and ball retainer

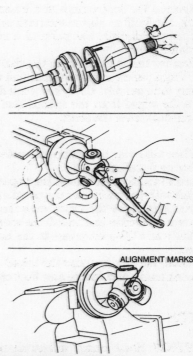

Disassembly of Tripot CV-joint

5. Remove the boots and vibration damper, if so equipped.

The outer (birfield) joint is not serviceable, it must be replaced as an assembly.

7. Clean all grease and dirt from the joints.

ASSEMBLY

1. With the birfield joint bent at a 40° angle, turn the shaft and make sure that it turns smoothly and normally.

2. Place tap on the splines to prevent damage to the joint boots.

3. Install the outer boot and clamps onto the outer shaft.

4. Fill the joint and boot with new CV-joint grease and install new clamps.

5. Install the inner joint boot and vibration damper, if so equipped.

6. Install the ball retainer, guide and snapring.

7. Fill the boot and off-set joint with new grease and install joint.

8. Install the circular clip into the groove.

9. Slide the boot onto the joint, insert a tool under the boot lip to allow the pressure to equalize and tighten the new clamps.

10. Install the shaft into the vehicle as outlined in this Chapter.

Tripod Joint

DISASSEMBLY

1. Remove the driveshaft from the vehicle as outlined in this Chapter.

2. Remove the boot clamps and inner joint housing. Mark off an alignment mark on both the housing and shaft. Use paint or a marker instead of a punch.

3. Remove the snapring from the shaft.

4. Using a punch, mark the shaft and tripod assembly for assembly. Using a wooden driver, remove the tripod from the splined shaft. Remove the boot from the shaft.

ASSEMBLY

1. Place tape over the splines to protect the boot during installation.

2. Install the boot and insert the tripod onto the shaft with the shorter spline positioned on the outer side. Drive the tripod onto the shaft with a wooden driver and install the snapring.

3. Apply new CV-joint grease to the housing and boot.

4. Install the housing onto the tripod at the alignment marks and install new boot clamps.

CLUTCH

CAUTION: *Some clutch driven discs contain asbestos, which has been determined to be a cancer causing agent. Never clean the clutch surfaces with compressed air! Avoid inhaling any dust from any clutch surface! When cleaning clutch surfaces, use a commercially available brake cleaning fluid.*

Adjustments

CLUTCH CABLE

I-Mark (RWD)

1. Loosen the lock and adjusting nuts on the clutch cable.

2. Pull the cable forward toward the front of the car to take up slack.

3. Turn the adjusting nut inward until the clutch pedal free travel is 5/8 in. (16mm).

4. Tighten the locknut and check the adjustment.

NOTE: *Correct pedal height from the floor is 6.2 in. (157.5mm), adjust the clutch switch to obtain, then lock the switch in position with the lock nut.*

I-Mark (FWD)

1. Loosen the clutch cable adjusting nut and pull the cable to the rear of the vehicle until the adjustment nut turns freely.

2. Turn the adjusting nut either clockwise or counterclockwise to adjust the cable length.

3. When the clutch pedal free play travel reaches 0.59 in. ± 0.20 in. (15mm ± 5mm) release the cable.

4. Check the adjustment and then tighten the lock nut.

FWD Impulse and Stylus

1. Pull the cable to the rear until the adjusting nut turns freely.

2. Turn the adjusting nut either clockwise or counterclockwise to adjust the cable length.

3. Repeat step 2 so that the play between the clutch release arm and clutch cable is at the (M) specification of 0.08 in. ± 0.04 in. (2mm ± 1mm).

4. Make sure the clutch pedal play is within the (L) specification of 0.39 in. ± 0.20 in. (10mm ± 5mm).

P'up, Amigo and Trooper

The late model trucks have a hydraulic clutch master cylinder that is self-adjusting and does not need periodic servicing.

1. Pull the outer cable forward and turn the adjusting nut inward until the rubber lip on the washer damper touches the firewall.

2. Depress and release the clutch pedal three times.

3. Pull the outer cable forward again and fully tighten the adjusting nut. Loosen the nut to provide a 5mm clearance.

Troubleshooting Basic Clutch Problems

Problem	Cause
Excessive clutch noise	Throwout bearing noises are more audible at the lower end of pedal travel. The usual causes are: • Riding the clutch • Too little pedal free-play • Lack of bearing lubrication A bad clutch shaft pilot bearing will make a high pitched squeal, when the clutch is disengaged and the transmission is in gear or within the first 2″ of pedal travel. The bearing must be replaced. Noise from the clutch linkage is a clicking or snapping that can be heard or felt as the pedal is moved completely up or down. This usually requires lubrication. Transmitted engine noises are amplified by the clutch housing and heard in the passenger compartment. They are usually the result of insufficient pedal free-play and can be changed by manipulating the clutch pedal.
Clutch slips (the car does not move as it should when the clutch is engaged)	This is usually most noticeable when pulling away from a standing start. A severe test is to start the engine, apply the brakes, shift into high gear and SLOWLY release the clutch pedal. A healthy clutch will stall the engine. If it slips it may be due to: • A worn pressure plate or clutch plate • Oil soaked clutch plate • Insufficient pedal free-play
Clutch drags or fails to release	The clutch disc and some transmission gears spin briefly after clutch disengagement. Under normal conditions in average temperatures, 3 seconds is maximum spin-time. Failure to release properly can be caused by: • Too light transmission lubricant or low lubricant level • Improperly adjusted clutch linkage
Low clutch life	Low clutch life is usually a result of poor driving habits or heavy duty use. Riding the clutch, pulling heavy loads, holding the car on a grade with the clutch instead of the brakes and rapid clutch engagement all contribute to low clutch life.

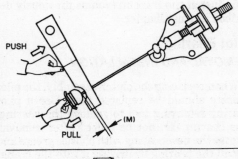

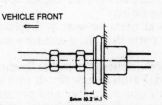

Clutch cable adjustment—late P'up, Trooper and Amigo equipped with cable

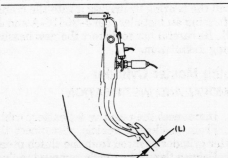

Clutch adjustment—FWD Impulse and Stylus

4. Release the outer cable and tighten the nut.

Driven Disc and Pressure Plate
REMOVAL AND INSTALLATION

1. Remove the transmission as previously described in this Chapter.
2. Mark the clutch assembly position on the flywheel with paint or a scribe.
3. Install clutch aligning tool J–24547 or equivalent and remove the pressure plate retaining bolts. Remove the clutch assembly.

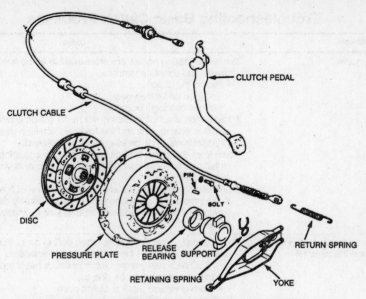

CLUTCH PEDAL

CLUTCH CABLE

DISC

PRESSURE PLATE

RELEASE BEARING SUPPORT

PIN

BOLT

RETAINING SPRING

YOKE

RETURN SPRING

Clutch assembly—cable type shown, hydraulic type similar

4. Remove the release bearing-to-yoke retaining springs, and then remove the release bearing with its support.

5. Remove the release yoke from the transmission ball stud.

6. Wash all metal parts of the clutch assembly, except the release bearing and friction plate in suitable cleaning solution.

CAUTION: *Soaking the release bearing in cleaning solution will ruin the bearing, soaking the clutch plate in cleaning solution will damage the facings.*

7. Inspect all parts for wear or deep scoring. Replace any parts that show excessive wear.

To install:

Due to clutch friction, the engine flywheel becomes scored. Putting a new clutch with an old flywheel can cause chatter and premature clutch plate wear. It is good insurance to remove the flywheel and have it resurfaced at a qualified machine shop. You have spent a lot of time removing the clutch assembly and you do not want to do it twice.

1. Lubricate the ball stud when installing the release yoke. Align the clutch with scribe marks and use an aligning tool to assure proper positioning of the clutch.

2. Apply grease and install the release yoke to the transmission ball stud.

3. Install the release bearing-to-yoke retaining springs and release bearing.

4. Install the clutch aligning tool J-24547 or equivalent and install the driven disc, pressure plate and retaining bolts to the marked position.

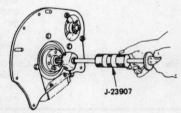

J-23907

Removing pilot bearing

5. Install the transmission as previously described in this Chapter.

Pilot Bearing

REMOVAL AND INSTALLATION

When replacing the clutch assembly, the pilot bearing should be replaced also. Use a pilot bearing removing tool to remove the bearing. The bearing can not be reused after removal. Grease the new bearing with chassis grease and install the bearing by driving it into the crankshaft using an installer tool J-26516–A and J-8092. Be careful not to distort the new bearing during installation.

Clutch Master Cylinder

REMOVAL AND INSTALLATION

1. Disconnect the negative (–) battery cable.

2. From inside the vehicle, disconnect the master cylinder pushrod from the clutch pedal.

3. Using a flarenut wrench, remove the fluid line from the master cylinder.

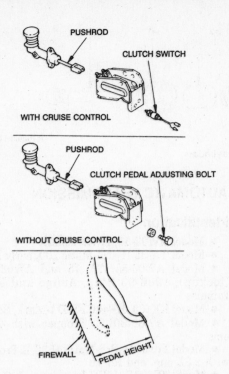

Clutch master cylinder and pedal height adjustment

4. Remove the cylinder retaining bolts from the firewall and remove the cylinder.

To install:

1. Install the cylinder and retaining bolts to the firewall.

2. Using a flarenut wrench, install the fluid line to the master cylinder.

3. From inside the vehicle, connect the master cylinder pushrod to the clutch pedal.

4. **To bleed the hydraulic system,** fill the reservoir with DOT 3 brake fluid to the top and install the cap. Open the slave cylinder bleeder

screw. With an assistance pumping the clutch pedal slowly, watch the bleeder until clean fluid comes out. Close the bleeder. Open the bleeder and have the assistant push the pedal to the floor and hold. Close the bleeder and release the pedal. NEVER ALLOW THE FLUID RESERVOIR TO RUN DRY. Repeat until all air bubbles are removed. Repeat the procedure at the damper valve, if so equipped.

5. Connect the negative (–) battery cable and check operation.

OVERHAUL

1. Remove the master cylinder from the vehicle as outlined in this Chapter.

2. Remove the yoke and nut from the pushrod.

3. Remove the snapring from the cylinder housing and remove pushrod and boot.

4. Using compressed air if needed, blow the piston from the housing.

5. Remove the reservoir clamp and reservoir.

6. Clean all parts in denatured alcohol and dry with compressed air.

To assemble

1. Install the reservoir and clamp.

2. Coat all rubber parts with rubber grease or clean brake fluid. Install the piston into the bore.

3. Install the pushrod, boot and snapring to the cylinder housing.

4. Install the yoke and nut to the pushrod.

5. Install the master cylinder to the vehicle as outlined in this Chapter.

Clutch Slave Cylinder

REMOVAL AND INSTALLATION

1. Disconnect the negative (–) battery cable.

2. Disconnect the slave cylinder pushrod from the clutch release fork.

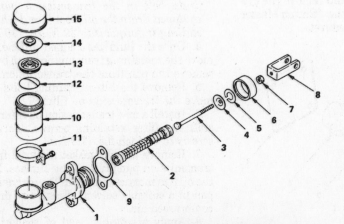

1. Cylinder body
2. Piston
3. Pushrod
4. Plate
5. Snapring
6. Boot
7. Nut
8. Yoke
9. Gasket
10. Reservoir
11. Clip
12. Float
13. Seal
14. Inner cap
15. Reservoir cap

Slave cylinder exploded view

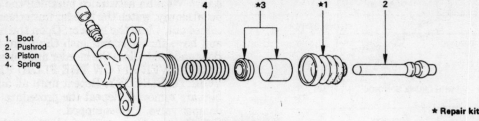

1. Boot
2. Pushrod
3. Piston
4. Spring

★ **Repair kit**

Clutch slave cylinder

3. Using a flarenut wrench, remove the fluid line from the slave cylinder.

4. Remove the cylinder retaining bolts from the clutch housing and remove the cylinder.

To install:

1. Install the cylinder and retaining bolts to the clutch housing.

2. Using a flarenut wrench, install the fluid line to the slave cylinder.

3. Connect the cylinder pushrod to the clutch release fork.

4. **To bleed the hydraulic system,** fill the reservoir with DOT 3 brake fluid to the top and install the cap. Open the slave cylinder bleeder screw. With an assistance pumping the clutch pedal slowly, watch the bleeder until clean fluid comes out. Close the bleeder. Open the bleeder and have the assistant push the pedal to the floor and hold. Close the bleeder and release the pedal. NEVER ALLOW THE FLUID RESERVOIR TO RUN DRY. Repeat until all air bubbles are removed. Repeat the procedure at the damper valve, if so equipped.

5. Connect the negative (–) battery cable and check operation.

Damper Cylinder

REMOVAL AND INSTALLATION

Disconnect the fluid line and remove the cylinder retaining bolts. Refer the "Clutch Master Cylinder" for bleeding procedures

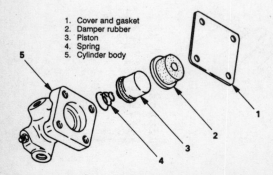

1. Cover and gasket
2. Damper rubber
3. Piston
4. Spring
5. Cylinder body

Clutch damper cylinder—if so equipped

AUTOMATIC TRANSMISSION

Identification

- Model AW03-55, RWD I-Mark
- Model Turbo Hydra-Matic 200, early P'up
- Model AW03-55, 70, 75 and AW03-72L (lockup), 1986-90 P'up, Amigo and RWD Impulse
- Model KF100, KF400 FWD I-Mark, Stylus
- Model AW30-80LE, Trooper with 4ZE1 eng.
- Model Turbo Hydra-Matic 4L30-E Trooper with 2.8L eng. and Rodeo
- Model JF403E, FWD Impulse

Fluid Pan

REMOVAL AND INSTALLATION

1. Disconnect the battery cables and raise the vehicle. Make sure it is supported safely.

2. Place a suitable transmission jack under the transmission. Remove the bolts and nuts retaining the transmission frame support rail. Slide the support rail back so as to let the transmission tailshaft rest upon the support rail.

3. Remove several of the transmission pan retaining bolts and loosen all of the others so as to let the fluid drain out into a suitable drain pan.

NOTE: *Some models may be equipped with a drain bolt in the transmission pan. If so equipped drain the oil from it and when reinstalling it, torque it to 29 ft. lbs. (40 Nm).*

4. Once the fluid has drained sufficiently, remove the remaining transmission pan bolts and remove the pan from the transmission.

5. Remove the filter retaining bolts and remove the transmission oil filter.

6. Install a new transmission oil filter and install the filter retaining screws. Torgue the screws to 60 inch lbs. (7.0 Nm).

7. Remove the old gasket material from the transmission pan and mating surface. Remove the oil pan magnet and clean the magnet and oil pan in a suitable solvent. Be sure to dry using compressed air.

8. Apply a suitable bead of sealant to the transmission gasket mating surface and install

Troubleshooting Basic Automatic Transmission Problems

Problem	Cause	Solution
Fluid leakage	• Defective pan gasket	• Replace gasket or tighten pan bolts
	• Loose filler tube	• Tighten tube nut
	• Loose extension housing to transmission case	• Tighten bolts
	• Converter housing area leakage	• Have transmission checked professionally
Fluid flows out the oil filler tube	• High fluid level	• Check and correct fluid level
	• Breather vent clogged	• Open breather vent
	• Clogged oil filter or screen	• Replace filter or clean screen (change fluid also)
	• Internal fluid leakage	• Have transmission checked professionally
Transmission overheats (this is usually accompanied by a strong burned odor to the fluid)	• Low fluid level	• Check and correct fluid level
	• Fluid cooler lines clogged	• Drain and refill transmission. If this doesn't cure the problem, have cooler lines cleared or replaced.
	• Heavy pulling or hauling with insufficient cooling	• Install a transmission oil cooler
	• Faulty oil pump, internal slippage	• Have transmission checked professionally
Buzzing or whining noise	• Low fluid level	• Check and correct fluid level
	• Defective torque converter, scored gears	• Have transmission checked professionally
No forward or reverse gears or slippage in one or more gears	• Low fluid level	• Check and correct fluid level
	• Defective vacuum or linkage controls, internal clutch or band failure	• Have unit checked professionally
Delayed or erratic shift	• Low fluid level	• Check and correct fluid level
	• Broken vacuum lines	• Repair or replace lines
	• Internal malfunction	• Have transmission checked professionally

the transmission oil pan. Install the transmission oil pan retaining bolts and torque them to 60–120 inch lbs. (7.0–14.0 Nm).

FILTER SERVICE

After removing the fluid pan, remove the filter retainers and allow the remaining fluid to drain. Install a new filter and retainers.

Adjustments
Throttle Cable
RWD I-Mark and Impulse

1. Check that the throttle valve is held closed completely.
2. Adjust the setting of the adjustment nut as necessary so that the clearance between the inner cable stopper and the end of the rubber boot on the outer cable is adjusted to 0.032–0.059 in. (0.8–1.5mm) the specification for the diesel models is 0–0.04 in. (0–1mm).
3. Open the throttle valve fully and check that the inner cable stroke is within the range of 1.30–1.36 in. (33–34mm).

Trucks with Gasoline Engines
1981–87

1. Loosen the throttle valve control cable adjusting nuts.
2. Check that the carburetor throttle adjusting screw is in contact with the stopper for normal idling.

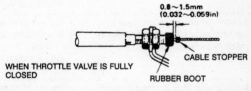

Throttle valve cable adjustment—gasoline engine

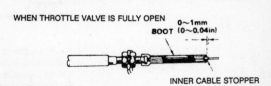

Throttle valve cable adjustment—diesel engine

Lockup Torque Converter Service Diagnosis

Problem	Cause	Solution

No lockup	• Faulty oil pump
	• Sticking governor valve
	• Valve body malfunction
	   (a) Stuck switch valve
	   (b) Stuck lockup valve
	   (c) Stuck fail-safe valve
	• Failed locking clutch
	• Leaking turbine hub seal
	• Faulty input shaft or seal ring
		• Replace oil pump
		• Repair or replace as necessary
		• Repair or replace valve body or its
		   internal components as neces-
		   sary
		
		• Replace torque converter
		• Replace torque converter
		• Repair or replace as necessary

Will not unlock	• Sticking governor valve
	• Valve body malfunction
	   (a) Stuck switch valve
	   (b) Stuck lockup valve
	   (c) Stuck fail-safe valve
		• Repair or replace as necessary
		• Repair or replace valve body or its
		   internal components as neces-
		   sary

Stays locked up at too low a speed in direct	• Sticking governor valve
	• Valve body malfunction
	   (a) Stuck switch valve
	   (b) Stuck lockup valve
	   (c) Stuck fail-safe valve
		• Repair or replace as necessary
		• Repair or replace valve body or its
		   internal components as neces-
		   sary

Locks up or drags in low or second	• Faulty oil pump
	• Valve body malfunction
	   (a) Stuck switch valve
	   (b) Stuck fail-safe valve
		• Replace oil pump
		• Repair or replace valve body or its
		   internal components as neces-
		   sary

Sluggish or stalls in reverse	• Faulty oil pump
	• Plugged cooler, cooler lines or
	   fittings
	• Valve body malfunction
	   (a) Stuck switch valve
	   (b) Faulty input shaft or seal
	      ring
		• Replace oil pump as necessary
		• Flush or replace cooler and flush
		   lines and fittings
		• Repair or replace valve body or its
		   internal components as neces-
		   sary

Loud chatter during lockup engagement (cold)	• Faulty torque converter • Failed locking clutch • Leaking turbine hub seal	• Replace torque converter • Replace torque converter • Replace torque converter

Vibration or shudder during lockup engagement	• Faulty oil pump
	
	• Valve body malfunction
	
	• Faulty torque converter
	• Engine needs tune-up
		• Repair or replace oil pump as nec-
		   essary
		• Repair or replace valve body or its
		   internal components as neces-
		   sary
		• Replace torque converter
		• Tune engine

Vibration after lockup engagement	• Faulty torque converter • Exhaust system strikes underbody • Engine needs tune-up • Throttle linkage misadjusted	• Replace torque converter • Align exhaust system • Tune engine • Adjust throttle linkage

Vibration when revved in neutral Overheating: oil blows out of dip stick tube or pump seal	• Torque converter out of balance
	• Plugged cooler, cooler lines or fit-
	   tings
	• Stuck switch valve
		• Replace torque converter
		• Flush or replace cooler and flush
		   lines and fittings
		• Repair switch valve in valve body
		   or replace valve body

Shudder after lockup engagement	• Faulty oil pump
	• Plugged cooler, cooler lines or
	   fittings
	• Valve body malfunction
	
	• Faulty torque converter
	• Fail locking clutch
	• Exhaust system strikes underbody
	• Engine needs tune-up
	• Throttle linkage misadjusted
		• Replace oil pump
		• Flush or replace cooler and flush
		   lines and fittings
		• Repair or replace valve body or its
		   internal components as neces-
		   sary
		• Replace torque converter
		• Replace torque converter
		• Align exhaust system
		• Tune engine
		• Adjust throttle linkage

Transmission Fluid Indications

The appearance and odor of the transmission fluid can give valuable clues to the overall condition of the transmission. Always note the appearance of the fluid when you check the fluid level or change the fluid. Rub a small amount of fluid between your fingers to feel for grit and smell the fluid on the dipstick.

If the fluid appears:	It indicates:
Clear and red colored	• Normal operation
Discolored (extremely dark red or brownish) or smells burned	• Band or clutch pack failure, usually caused by an overheated transmission. Hauling very heavy loads with insufficient power or failure to change the fluid, often result in overheating. Do not confuse this appearance with newer fluids that have a darker red color and a strong odor (though not a burned odor).
Foamy or aerated (light in color and full of bubbles)	• The level is too high (gear train is churning oil) • An internal air leak (air is mixing with the fluid). Have the transmission checked professionally.
Solid residue in the fluid	• Defective bands, clutch pack or bearings. Bits of band material or metal abrasives are clinging to the dipstick. Have the transmission checked professionally.
Varnish coating on the dipstick	• The transmission fluid is overheating

NOTE: *If the adjusting screw is not resting on the stopper, the fast idle mechanism is working and setting of the adjusting screw should be adjusted to obtain normal idling.*

3. To obtain normal idling, perform the following procedures:

a. Disconnect the battery ground cable.

b. Remove the air cleaner cover.

c. Fully depress the accelerator pedal to place the choke in the wide open position and release the pedal; do not depress the pedal again.

d. Check the the throttle adjusting screw is in contact with the stopper.

e. Install the air cleaner.

f. Connect the battery cable.

4. Remove the rubber boot from the outer

Location of the throttle adjusting screw—1987–88 gasoline engine

View of the throttle cable adjustment—1987–88 gasoline engine

cable and turn the adjusting nuts to adjust the outer cable setting to 0.032–0.059 in. (0.8–1.5mm) and tighten the adjusting nuts; the setting is the distance between the outer cable end and the inner cable stopper.

5. After adjusting, check that the inner cable stroke, from the closed position of the throttle valve to the wide open position is 1.30–1.36 in. (32.9–33.9mm).

6. Install the rubber boot onto the outer cable.

1988–90

1. Depress the accelerator pedal all the way and check that the throttle valve opens fully.

NOTE: *If the valve does not open fully, adjust the accelerator link.*

2. Fully depress the accelerator.

3. Loosen the adjustment nuts.

4. Adjust the cable housing so the distance between the end of the boot and stopper on the cable is the 0.03–0.06 in. (0.8–1.5mm).

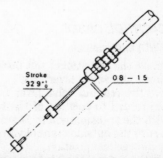

View of the throttle cable adjustment—1988–90 gasoline engine

5. Tighten the adjusting nuts.

6. Recheck the adjustment.

Trucks with Diesel Engine

1. Loosen the throttle valve control cable adjusting nuts.

2. Fully depress the accelerator pedal to place the injection pump lever in contact with the maximum speed adjusting screw and hold the lever in that position.

NOTE: *If the injection pump lever is not in contact with the adjusting screw, adjust the accelerator linkage.*

3. Turn the outer cable adjusting nuts to adjust the outer cable setting to 0.032–0.059 in. (0.8–1.5mm) and tighten the adjusting nuts; the setting is the distance between the upper face of the rubber boot, on the end of the outer cable, and the inner cable stopper.

4. After adjusting, check that the inner cable stroke, from the normal idling position the maximum speed position is 1.30–1.36 in. (32.9–33.9mm).

NOTE: *Normal idling position can not be obtained with the air conditioner operating and the engine coolant temperature higher than 59°F (15°C).*

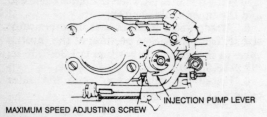

MAXIMUM SPEED ADJUSTING SCREW — INJECTION PUMP LEVER

View of the injection pump maximum speed adjusting screw—diesel engine

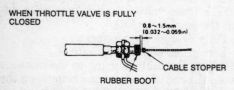

WHEN THROTTLE VALVE IS FULLY CLOSED

0.8~1.5mm (0.032~0.059in)

CABLE STOPPER

RUBBER BOOT

View of the throttle cable adjustment—diesel

SHIFT CONTROL CABLE

I-Mark (RWD) and Impulse

1. Remove the adjustment nut fastening the control lever and select lever link.

2. Move the manual valve lever forward to stop, then return to position of Neutral (third stop). With the transmission in Neutral, check to make sure the outside manual valve shift lever is in the vertical position.

3. Hold the manual shaft in that position and place the shift lever in the Neutral position.

4. To remove the play, tighten the adjusting nuts with the lower lever (control shaft lever) on the shift lever pushed rearward together with the shift control lever and tighten the adjust nut.

5. Check that the control lever moves smoothly and that position indicator works correctly.

Trooper, P'up and Amigo

1981–87

1. Loosen the control rod locknuts so the trunnion will slide on the control rod.

2. Turn the manual shaft on the transmission fully clockwise, viewed from the left side of the transmission, then, back it off to the 3rd stop and set it in the **N** position.

3. While holding the shaft in this position, move the shift lever to the **N** position.

4. Push the shift shift, with the shift control lower lever rearward to remove play and tighten the adjusting nuts.

5. Road test the vehicle and check for proper operation of the transmission in all ranges.

1988–90

1. Loosen the shift linkage adjusting nut.

2. Push the shift lever fully rearward.

3. Return the shift lever 2 notches to the **N** position.

4. While holding the selector lever lightly toward the **R** range side, tighten the shift linkage nut.

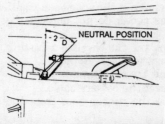

1 - 2 D NEUTRAL POSITION

Adjusting the automatic transmission shift linkage—1981–87

Neutral Safety Switch Adjustment

The neutral safety switch for the late model transmissions is mounted onto the transmission at the shift lever. The backup switch is incorporated into this assembly.

REMOVAL AND INSTALLATION

1. Disconnect the negative (–) battery cable.

2. Disconnect the electrical connectors and remove the shift lever from the transmission.

3. Remove the retaining bolts and switch.

This adjustment is necessary only if the engine will start with the shift selector in any range except **N** or **P**.

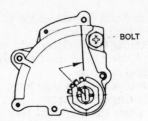

View of the neutral start switch

1. Loosen the neutral start switch bolt and set the shift selector into the **N** range.
2. Align the groove and the neutral basic line.
3. Hold it in position and torque the bolt to 9 ft. lbs. (12 Nm).

Transmission

REMOVAL AND INSTALLATION

RWD I-Mark and Impulse

1. Disconnect the battery cables and raise the vehicle. Make sure it is supported safely.
2. Remove the transmission dipstick. Drain the fluid into a suitable container and discard.
3. Remove the starter toward the front of the vehicle.
4. Disconnect the drive shaft from the central joint, then slide the propeller shaft rearward and remove it.
5. Disconnect the shift control rod from the shift lever.
6. Disconnect the speedometer cable.
7. Remove the exhaust pipe bracket.
8. Disconnect the oil cooler lines by loosening the joint nuts at the transmission.
NOTE: *Secure the cooler lines closer to the body to avoid damage during transmission removal.*
9. Remove the four bolts attaching the converter housing lower cover and remove the cover.
10. Remove the lower cover on the front part of the engine to permit turning of the engine and torque converter.
11. Remove the six bolts fastening the torque converter and drive plate by turning the crankshaft pulley.
12. Remove the bolt on the center part of the rear mounting from bracket.
13. Raise the engine and transmission using a suitable jack and support the rear end of the engine to hold it in position when the transmission is removed.
14. Remove the four bolts or nuts securing the rear mounting frame bracket, then remove the bracket.
15. Lower the transmission slightly then remove the bolts and nuts fixing the converter

housing, then remove the transmission toward the rear.
CAUTION: *When removing the transmission, exercise care so as not to let the torque converter slide out.*

To install:
1. Raise the transmission with a tranmission jack and install the bolts and nuts fixing the converter housing.
2. Install the four bolts or nuts securing the rear mounting frame bracket.
3. Raise the engine and transmission using a suitable jack and support the rear end of the engine to hold it in position when the transmission is installed.
4. Install the bolt on the center part of the rear mounting to bracket.
5. Install the six bolts fastening the torque converter and drive plate by turning the crankshaft pulley.
6. Install the cover and four bolts attaching the converter housing lower cover.
7. Connect the oil cooler lines by tightening the joint nuts at the transmission.
8. Install the exhaust pipe bracket.
9. Connect the speedometer cable.
10. Connect the shift control rod to the shift lever.
11. Connect the drive shaft to the central joint.
12. Install the starter toward the front of the vehicle.
13. Install the transmission dipstick and refill the fluid.
14. Connect the battery cables and raise the vehicle. Make sure it is supported safely.
15. Run the engine until it reaches normal temperature. Run the transmission through all gears and recheck fluid. Make sure the vehicle is supported safely and DO NOT overfill the transmission.

P'up, Amigo, Trooper and Rodeo

2-WHEEL DRIVE VEHICLES
1981–87

1. Disconnect the negative battery cable. Raise and safely support the vehicle.
2. Remove the undercover, if equipped.
3. Remove the transmission dipstick assembly. Drain the transmission fluid. Disconnect and plug the oil cooler lines from the transmission.
4. Remove the torque converter cover. Matchmark the torque converter-to-flywheel location and remove the torque converter-to-flywheel bolts; rotate the torque converter to expose the bolts.
5. Remove the exhaust pipe-to-exhaust manifold nuts and separate the pipe from the manifold.

6. Disconnect the shift lever control rod from the transmission shift lever.

7. Disconnect the back-up light switch and transmission wiring from the transmission.

8. Using an engine hoist, connect it to the engine hangers and support the engine.

9. Raise and safely support the vehicle.

10. Remove the starter motor. Disconnect the speedometer from the transmission.

11. Matchmark and remove the driveshaft. Remove the transmission-to-crossmember bolts.

12. Lift the engine/transmission slightly and remove the transmission frame bracket from the crossmember. Remove the rear mount from the crossmember. Remove the exhaust pipe bracket from the transmission.

13. Support the transmission.

14. Remove the bell housing-to-engine bolts and the transmission from the vehicle.

NOTE: *Be careful that the torque converter does not drop from the transmission.*

To install:

1. Raise the transmission on a jack and install the bell housing-to-engine bolts.

2. Support the transmission.

3. Lift the engine/transmission slightly and install the transmission frame bracket to the crossmember. Install the rear mount to the crossmember. Install the exhaust pipe bracket to the transmission.

4. Install the driveshaft. Install the transmission-to-crossmember bolts.

5. Install the starter motor. Connect the speedometer to the transmission.

6. Lower the vehicle.

7. Remove the engine support.

8. Connect the back-up light switch and transmission wiring to the transmission.

9. Connect the shift lever control rod to the transmission shift lever.

10. Install the exhaust pipe-to-exhaust manifold nuts and tighten.

11. Install the torque converter-to-flywheel bolts and flywheel cover.

12. Reconnect the cooler lines. Install the transmission dipstick assembly and refill the transmission.

13. Install the undercover, if equipped.

14. Connect the negative battery cable.

15. Run the engine until it reaches normal temperature. Run the transmission through all gears and recheck fluid. Make sure the vehicle is supported safely and DO NOT overfill the transmission.

2-WHEEL DRIVE VEHICLES
1988–90

1. Disconnect the negative battery cable.

2. Remove the undercover, if equipped.

3. Label and disconnect the necessary hoses and electrical connectors.

4. Remove the back-up light switch connector and the speedometer cable from the transmission.

5. Remove the gear shift lever by performing the following procedures:

a. Place the gear shift lever in **N**.

b. Remove the front console from the floor panel.

c. Pull the shift lever boot and grommet upward.

d. Remove the shift lever cover bolts and the shift lever.

6. Raise and safely support the vehicle. Remove the front wheels.

7. Drain the transmission fluid.

8. Remove the oil level gauge and the tube.

9. Disconnect the shift select control link rod from the select lever.

10. Disconnect the downshift cable from the transmission.

11. Disconnect and plug the fluid coolant lines from the transmission.

12. If equipped with a 1-piece driveshaft, remove the driveshaft flange-to-pinion nuts, lower the driveshaft and pull it from the transmission.

13. If equipped with a 2-piece driveshaft, perform the following procedures:

a. Remove the rear driveshaft flange-to-pinion nuts.

b. Remove the rear driveshaft flange-to-front driveshaft flange bolts and the rear driveshaft.

c. Remove the center bearing-to-chassis bolts, move the front driveshaft rearward and from the transmission.

14. Remove the starter-to-engine bolts and the starter.

15. Remove the exhaust pipe-to-exhaust manifold nuts, the exhaust pipe bracket-to-transmission bolts, the front exhaust pipe-to-2nd exhaust pipe bolts and the front exhaust pipe from the vehicle.

16. Attach an engine hanger to the rear of the exhaust manifold.

17. Using an engine hoist, connect it to the engine hangers and support the engine.

NOTE: *Removal of the transmission will require an assistant.*

18. Remove the torque converter-to-flex plate bolts through the starter hole.

19. Using a transmission jack, place it under the transmission; do not support it.

20. Remove the rear mount-to-transmission nuts.

21. Remove the rear mount-to-crossmember nuts/bolts and the mount.

22. Remove the transmission-to-engine bolts.

23. Move the transmission rearward into the crossmember and floor pan area; the transmission may rest on the crossmember.

24. Lower the front of the transmission toward the jack.

25. Firmly, grasp the transmission the rear cover while the assistant raises the jack toward the transmission.

26. Carefully, lower the transmission onto the jack and center it.

27. Lower the jack and move the transmission rearward.

To install:

NOTE: *Installation of the transmission will require an assistant.*

1. Raise the transmission into position.

2. Raise the rear of the transmission and move it into position on the crossmember.

3. Move the transmission forward and engage it with the engine.

4. Install the engine-to-transmission bolts.

5. Install the mount and the rear mount-to-crossmember nuts/bolts.

6. Install the rear mount-to-transmission nuts.

7. Install the torque converter-to-flex plate bolts through the starter hole.

8. Remove the engine hoist and the engine hanger from the rear of the exhaust manifold.

9. Install the front exhaust pipe, exhaust pipe-to-exhaust manifold nuts, the exhaust pipe bracket-to-transmission bolts, the front exhaust pipe-to-2nd exhaust pipe bolts.

10. Install the starter and the starter-to-engine bolts.

11. If equipped with a 2-piece driveshaft, perform the following procedures:

a. Install the front driveshaft into the transmission and the center bearing-to-chassis bolts.

b. Install the rear driveshaft and the rear driveshaft flange-to-front driveshaft flange bolts.

c. Install the rear driveshaft flange-to-pinion nuts.

12. If equipped with a 1-piece driveshaft, install the driveshaft into the transmission and the driveshaft flange-to-pinion nuts.

13. Connect the fluid coolant lines to the transmission.

14. Connect the downshift cable to the transmission.

15. Connect the shift select control link rod to the select lever.

16. Install the oil level gauge and the tube.

17. Install the front wheels and lower the vehicle.

18. Install the gear shift lever by performing the following procedures:

a. Install the shift lever and the shift lever cover bolts.

b. Push the grommet and shift lever boot downward.

c. Install the front console to the floor panel.

19. Install the back-up light switch connector and the speedometer cable to the transmission.

20. Connect the necessary hoses and electrical connectors.

21. Refill the transmission. Install the undercover, if equipped.

22. Connect the negative battery cable.

23. Run the engine until it reaches normal temperature. Run the transmission through all gears and recheck fluid. Make sure the vehicle is supported safely and DO NOT overfill the transmission.

24. Run the engine and check for leaks.

4-WHEEL DRIVE VEHICLES

1. Disconnect the negative battery cable.

2. Remove the undercover, if equipped.

3. Remove the air cleaner (4ZD1 engine) or air cleaner duct and hose (4ZE1 engine). Using a clean shop cloth, cover the air cleaner port to prevent dirt from entering the engine.

4. Label and disconnect the necessary hoses and electrical connectors.

5. Remove the back-up light switch connector and the speedometer cable from the transmission.

6. Remove the gear shift lever by performing the following procedures:

a. Place the gear shift lever in **N**.

b. Remove the front console from the floor panel.

c. Pull the shift lever boot and grommet upward.

d. Remove the shift lever cover bolts and the shift lever.

7. Remove the transfer shift lever by performing the following procedures:

a. Place the transfer shift lever in **H** (except 2.8L engine) or **2H** (2.8L engine).

b. Pull the shift lever boot and dust cover upward.

c. Remove the shift lever retaining bolts.

d. Pull the shift lever from the transfer case.

8. Raise and safely support the vehicle with jackstands at the front and rear of the vehicle. Remove the front wheels.

9. Drain the transmission and transfer case fluid.

10. Remove the oil level gauge and the tube.

11. Disconnect the shift select control link rod from the select lever.

12. Disconnect the downshift cable from the transmission.

13. Disconnect and plug the fluid coolant lines from the transmission.

14. If equipped with a 1-piece driveshaft, remove the driveshaft flange-to-pinion nuts, lower the driveshaft and pull it from the transmission.

15. If equipped with a 2-piece driveshaft, perform the following procedures:

   a. Remove the rear driveshaft flange-to-pinion nuts.

   b. Remove the rear driveshaft flange-to-front driveshaft flange bolts and the rear driveshaft.

   c. Remove the center bearing-to-chassis bolts, move the front driveshaft rearward and from the transmission.

16. Remove the front driveshaft's splinded yoke flange-to-transfer case bolts and separate the front driveshaft from the transfer case; do not allow the splined flange to fall away from the driveshaft.

17. Remove the starter-to-engine bolts and the starter.

18. Remove the exhaust pipe-to-exhaust manifold nuts, the exhaust pipe bracket-to-transmission bolts, the front exhaust pipe-to-2nd exhaust pipe bolts and the front exhaust pipe from the vehicle.

19. Attach an engine hanger to the rear of the exhaust manifold.

20. Using an engine hoist, connect it to the engine hangers and support the engine.

21. If equipped with a 2.8L engine, remove the catalytic converter and the parking brake cable bracket.

22. Using a transmission jack, place it under the transmission and support the assembly.

23. Remove the rear mount-to-transmission nuts.

24. Remove the rear mount-to-side mount member nuts/bolts and the mount.

25. Remove the transmission-to-engine bolts.

26. Move the transmission assembly rearward.

27. Carefully lower the transmission.

To install:

1. Raise the transmission into position.

2. Move the transmission forward and engage it with the engine.

3. Install the engine-to-transmission bolts.

4. Install the rear mount and the rear mount-to-side mount member nuts/bolts.

5. Install the rear mount-to-transmission nuts.

6. Remove the transmission jack.

7. If equipped with a 2.8L engine, install the catalytic converter and the parking brake cable bracket.

8. Remove the engine hoist and the engine hanger from the rear of the exhaust manifold.

9. Install the front exhaust pipe, exhaust pipe-to-exhaust manifold nuts, the exhaust pipe bracket-to-transmission bolts, the front exhaust pipe-to-2nd exhaust pipe bolts.

10. Install the starter and the starter-to-engine bolts.

11. Install the front driveshaft's splinded yoke flange-to-transfer case bolts.

12. If equipped with a 2-piece driveshaft, perform the following procedures:

   a. Install the front driveshaft into the transmission and the center bearing-to-chassis bolts.

   b. Install the rear driveshaft and the rear driveshaft flange-to-front driveshaft flange bolts.

   c. Install the rear driveshaft flange-to-pinion nuts.

13. If equipped with a 1-piece driveshaft, install the driveshaft into the transmission and the driveshaft flange-to-pinion nuts.

14. Connect the fluid coolant lines to the transmission.

15. Connect the downshift cable to the transmission.

16. Connect the shift select control link rod to the select lever.

17. Install the oil level gauge and the tube.

18. Install the front wheels and lower the vehicle.

19. Install the transfer shift lever by performing the following procedures:

   a. Position the shift lever into the transfer case.

   b. Install the shift lever retaining bolts.

   c. Push the dust cover and the shift lever boot downward.

20. Install the gear shift lever by performing the following procedures:

   a. Install the shift lever and the shift lever cover bolts.

   b. Push the grommet and shift lever boot downward.

   c. Install the front console to the floor panel.

21. Install the back-up light switch connector and the speedometer cable to the transmission.

22. Connect the necessary hoses and electrical connectors.

23. Install the air cleaner (4ZD1) or air cleaner duct and hose (4ZE1).

24. Refill the transmission and the transfer case. Install the undercover, if equipped.

25. Connect the negative battery cable.

26. Run the engine until it reaches normal temperature. Run the transmission through all gears and recheck fluid. Make sure the vehicle is supported safely and DO NOT overfill the transmission.

AUTOMATIC TRANSAXLE

Identification

- Model KF-100 I-Mark and KF-400 Stylus, 3-speed
- Model JF403E Impulse, 4-speed electronic

Fluid Pan

REMOVAL AND INSTALLATION

1. Disconnect the battery cables and raise the vehicle. Make sure it is supported safely.

2. Remove several of the transmission pan retaining bolts and loosen all of the others so as to let the fluid drain out into a suitable drain pan.

3. Once the fluid has drained sufficiently, remove the remaining transmission pan bolts and remove the pan from the transmission.

4. Remove the filter retaining bolts and remove the transmission oil filter.

5. Install a new transmission oil filter and install the filter retaining screws. Torgue the screws to 5 ft. lbs.

6. Remove the old gasket material from the transmission pan and mating surface. Remove the oil pan magnet and clean the magnet and oil pan in a suitable solvent. Be sure to dry using compressed air.

7. Apply a suitable bead of sealant to the transmission gasket mating surface and install the transmission oil pan. Install the transmission oil pan retaining bolts and torque them to 60–120 inch lbs. (7.0–14.0 Nm).

Adjustments

SHIFT LINKAGE ADJUSTMENT

Remove the front console cover to expose the shifter assembly. Refer to the back drive cable and shift lock operation adjustment illustration and adjust the cables to specifications.

1. Loosen the adjusting nuts.

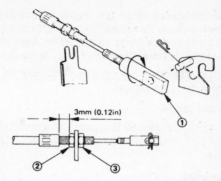

3mm (0.12in)

Back drive cable adjustment—FWD I-Mark and Stylus

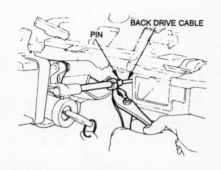

BACK DRIVE CABLE

PIN

Backup cable located at ignition switch

2. Place the transaxle and the shift lever in the Neutral position.

3. Turn the adjusting nuts until the shift lever is in the vertical position.

4. Tighten the adjusting nuts.

KICKDOWN SWITCH ADJUSTMENT

1. Connect a multi-purpose tester to the kickdown switch solenoid terminals.

2. Make sure there is continuity when depressing the throttle pedal fully.

Conditions			Restrict	
Key position	Lever position (X; Except "P")	B/pedal step	Solenoid	Explanation
ON or Engine ON	P	ON	Released	When engine "ON" or key "ON" and lever is in "P" position, can't shift from "P" position without stepping on brake pedal.
	P	OFF	LOCK	
	X	ON	Released	When engine "ON" or key "ON" and lever is out of "P" position, can shift regardless of brake pedal operation.
	X	OFF	Released	
ACC. OFF LOCK or Engine OFF	P	ON	Released	When engine "OFF" or key "ACC.", "OFF", "LOCK", can shift regardless of brake pedal operation.
	P	OFF	Released	
	X	ON	Released	
	X	OFF	Released	

Checking shift lock operation—Stylus

3. If continuity does not exist, adjust the kickdown switch. To adjust the switch, turn the switch so that continuity exists when depressing the throttle pedal more than ⅞ of its stroke.

NEUTRAL SAFETY SWITCH OR INHIBITOR SWITCH ADJUSTMENT

I-Mark and Stylus

The inhibitor switch is located on lower left side of the transmission no adjustment is possible.

FWD Impulse

1. Loosen the retaining bolts.
2. Set the gear selector in the NEUTRAL position.

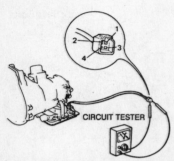

Shift position	Coupler terminal			
	1	2	3	4
P	o—o			
R			o—o	
N	o—o			

Neutral safety switch—FWD I-Mark and Stylus

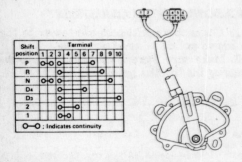

Shift position	Terminal									
	1	2	3	4	5	6	7	8	9	10
P	o-o	o				o				
R		o						o		
N	o-o	o								
D₄		o			o					
D₃		o							o	
2		o-o	o							
1		o-o								

o—o : Indicates continuity

Neutral safety switch—FWD Impulse

PIN (4MM DIAMETER)

Neutral safety switch adjustment—FWD Impulse

3. Insert a pin into the adjustment holes in both the switch and lever as nearly vertical as possible. Tighten the retaining bolts and check operation.

Backup Light Switch

The neutral and backup light switch are the same assembly.

Transaxle

REMOVAL AND INSTALLATION

I-Mark (FWD) and Stylus

1. Disconnect the negative battery cable.
2. Remove the air duct tube from the air cleaner.
3. At the transaxle, disconnect the shift cable, speedometer cable, vacuum diaphragm hose, engine wiring harness clamp and the ground cable.
4. At the left fender, disconnect the inhibitor switch and the kickdown solenoid wiring connectors.
5. Disconnect the oil cooler lines from the transaxle.
6. Remove the 3 upper transaxle-to-engine mounting bolts and raise and support the vehicle safely.
7. Remove both front wheels and the left front fender splash shield.
8. Disconnect the right control arm end at the knuckle. Remove the left tension rod with bracket. Disconnect both tie rod ends at the knuckle using tool J–21687–02 or equivalent.
9. Use a suitable tool and pull out the drive shafts. Be careful with the transaxle oil seals when pulling out the drive shafts. Remove the motor mount bolts.
10. Using a suitable engine lift, raise the engine. Remove the bolts of the center beam and then remove the 3 upper transaxle to engine mounting bolts.
11. Remove the flywheel dust cover and the converter-to-flywheel attaching bolts. Lower the engine and slant the engine from the engine support fixture.
12. Remove the transaxle rear mount through bolt.
13. Disconnect the starter wiring and the starter. Support the transaxle.
14. Remove the lower transaxle-to-engine mounting bolts and remove the transaxle.
To install:
1. Install the transaxle and lower transaxle-to-engine mounting bolts.
2. Connect the starter wiring and the starter. Support the transaxle.
3. Install the transaxle rear mount through bolt.
4. Install the converter-to-flywheel attach-

ing bolts and flywheel dust cover.5. Using a suitable engine lift, lower the engine. Install the bolts of the center beam and then install the 3 upper transaxle to engine mounting bolts.

6. Install the drive shafts. Be careful with the transaxle oil seals when install the drive shafts. Install the motor mount bolts.

7. Connect the right control arm end at the knuckle. Install the left tension rod with bracket. Connect both tie rod ends at the knuckle using tool J–21687–02 or equivalent.

8. Install both fender splash shields and front wheels.

9. Install the 3 upper transaxle-to-engine mounting bolts.

10. Connect the oil cooler lines to the transaxle.

11. At the left fender, connect the inhibitor switch and the kickdown solenoid wiring connectors.

12. At the transaxle, connect the shift cable, speedometer cable, vacuum diaphragm hose, engine wiring harness clamp and the ground cable.

13. Refill any lost transaxle fluid with the engine running. Install the air duct tube to the air cleaner.

14. Connect the negative battery cable.

a. Transaxle assembly to engine bolts — 56 ft. lbs.

b. Center beam bolts — 56 ft. lbs.

c. Torque converter-to-flywheel bolts — 30 ft. lbs.

d. Lower engine mounts — 61 ft. lbs.

e. Driveshaft/tie rod to knuckle — 42 ft. lbs.

f. Tension rod bracket bolts — 48 ft. lbs.

g. Right control arm end bolts — 80 ft. lbs.

h. Front wheel lugs aluminum — 87 ft. lbs. and steel are — 65 ft. lbs.

Impulse

1. Disconnect the negative (–) battery cable and place a drain pan under the transaxle.

2. Remove the battery and battery tray.

3. Remove the air cleaner and breather hose.

4. Remove the ignition coil and bracket.

5. Disconnect all wiring and control cables at the transaxle.

6. Raise the vehicle and support with jackstands. Remove the front tire assemblies.

7. Remove the undercover and disconnect the oil cooler lines.

8. Disconnect the ball joint and tie rod ends as outlined in Chapter 8.

9. Place a drain pan under the transaxle and remove the driveshafts as outlined in this Chapter.

10. Disconnect the front exhaust pipe and torque rod.

11. Remove or disconnect the left, center and rear rubber mount.

12. Disconnect the engine stiffener and remove the flywheel dust cover.

13. Remove the converter-to-flywheel and engine-to-transaxle bolt.

14. Using a suitable transaxle jack, remove the assembly from the vehicle.

To install:

1. Using a suitable transaxle jack, install the assembly into the vehicle.

2. Install the converter-to-flywheel and engine-to-transaxle bolt.

3. Connect the engine stiffener and install the flywheel dust cover.

4. Install the left, center and rear rubber mount.

5. Connect the front exhaust pipe and torque rod.

6. Install the driveshafts as outlined in this Chapter.

7. Connect the ball joint and tie rod ends as outlined in Section 8.

8. Install the undercover and connect the oil cooler lines.

9. Install the front tires and lower the vehicle.

10. Connect all wiring and control cables at the transaxle.

11. Install the ignition coil and bracket.

12. Install the air cleaner and breather hose.

13. Install the battery and battery tray.

14. Connect the negative (–) battery cable.

15. Start the engine and allow to reach operating temperature. Fill the transaxle to the proper level. NEVER overfill the transaxle.

Halfshafts (Driveshaft)

REMOVAL AND INSTALLATION

Except All Wheel Drive Impulse

1. Disconnect the negative (–) battery cable.

2. Remove the ball joint-to-lower control arm, strut rod and stabilizer bar bolts or nuts.

3. Remove the driveshaft nut and washer. Dislodge the shaft from the spindle splines with a plastic hammer.

4. Support the driveshaft to the strut with a piece of wire to prevent the shaft from falling.

5. Place a drain pan under the driveshaft. Using a suitable prybar, remove the driveshaft from the transaxle. The inner joint is retained by a circlip inside the differential housing. Be careful not to damage the inner joint by pulling the shaft apart.

To install:

1. Install the driveshaft into the transaxle. Push the shaft in until the circlip engages the differential groove.

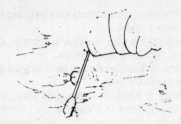

Disconnecting driveshaft from transaxle

2. Insert the driveshaft into the splined hole in the spindle.

3. Install the driveshaft nut and washer. Torque the nut to 100 ft. lbs. (136 Nm).

4. Install the ball joint-to-lower control arm, strut rod and stabilizer bar bolts.

5. Refill the transaxle with the proper amount of fluid. Connect the negative (–) battery cable and check operation.

FWD Impulse and Stylus

1. Disconnect the negative (–) battery cable.

2. Raise the vehicle and support with jackstands.

3. Drain the oil from the transaxle and transfer case (4WD only).

4. Pry the hub nut open and loosen the nut. The brake may have to applied when loosening.

5. Using a tie rod removing tool J–21687–02 or equivalent, disconnect the tie rod from the knuckle.

6. Remove the lower ball joint bolts and swing out of the way.

7. Pull the hub and knuckle away from the driveshaft. Be careful not to allow the shaft to fully extend. Damage to the inner joint may result.

8. Use a prybar to dislodge the inner joint

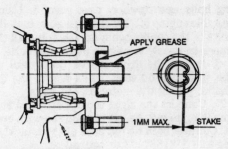

Driveshaft nut installation

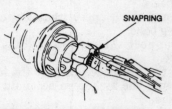

Remove the snapring and ball retainer

from the differential. The shaft is held in by a circlip at the end of the splined shaft.

To install:

1. Install the inner joint into the differential and engage the circlip.

2. Insert the outer joint into the splined hub. Be careful not to allow the shaft to fully extend. Damage to the inner joint may result.

3. Install the lower ball joint bolts and tighten.

4. Install the hub nut and tighten. The brake may have to applied when tighten.

5. Refill the transaxle and transfer case (4WD only) with the specified oil.

6. Lower the vehicle.

7. Connect the negative (–) battery cable.

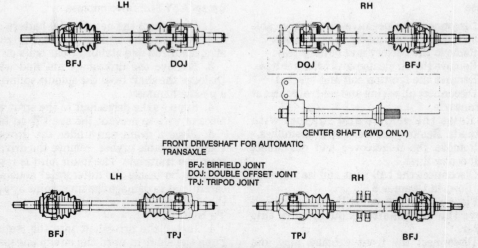

FWD driveshaft assemblies

CV-JOINT OVERHAUL

Double Offset Joint

DISASSEMBLY

1. Disconnect the negative (–) battery cable. Clean the assembly of all grease and dirt.

2. Remove the inner joint boot clamps. Slide the boot off of the joint.

3. From inside the inner joint, remove the circular clip from inside the offset joint. Pull the joint and shaft off of the inner joint.

4. Remove the ball retainer snapring and ball retainer. Pull the ball retainer and ball guide from the splined shaft.

5. Remove the boots and vibration damper, if so equipped.

The outer (birfield) joint is not serviceable, it must be replaced as an assembly.

7. Clean all grease and dirt from the joints.

ASSEMBLY

1. With the birfield joint bent at a 40° angle, turn the shaft and make sure that it turns smoothly and normally.

2. Place tap on the splines to prevent damage to the joint boots.

3. Install the outer boot and clamps onto the outer shaft.

4. Fill the joint and boot with new CV-joint grease and install new clamps.

5. Install the inner joint boot and vibration damper, if so equipped.

6. Install the ball retainer, guide and snapring.

7. Fill the boot and off-set joint with new grease and install joint.

8. Install the circular clip into the groove.

9. Slide the boot onto the joint, insert a tool under the boot lip to allow the pressure to equalize and tighten the new clamps.

10. Install the shaft into the vehicle as outlined in this Chapter.

Tripod Joint

DISASSEMBLY

1. Remove the driveshaft from the vehicle as outlined in this Chapter.

2. Remove the boot clamps and inner joint housing. Mark off an alignment mark on both the housing and shaft. Use paint or a marker instead of a punch.

3. Remove the snapring from the shaft.

4. Using a punch, mark the shaft and tripod assembly for assembly. Using a wooden driver, remove the tripod from the splined shaft. Remove the boot from the shaft.

ASSEMBLY

1. Place tape over the splines to protect the boot during installation.

2. Install the boot and insert the tripod onto the shaft with the shorter spline positioned on

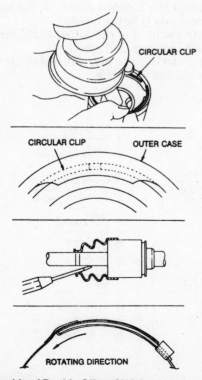

CIRCULAR CLIP

CIRCULAR CLIP   OUTER CASE

ROTATING DIRECTION

Assembly of Double Offset CV-joint

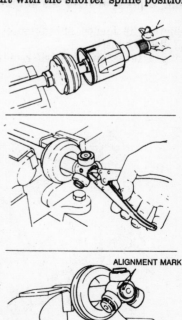

ALIGNMENT MARK

Disassembly of Tripot CV-joint

the outer side. Drive the tripod onto the shaft with a wooden driver and install the snapring.

3. Apply new CV-joint grease to the housing and boot.

4. Install the housing onto the tripod at the alignment marks and install new boot clamps.

TRANSFER CASE

1981-87 P'up and Trooper

REMOVAL AND INSTALLATION

The transfer case is part of the extension housing assembly. The transmission and transfer case has to be removed as an assembly. Refer to the "Transmission" removal and installation procedures in this Chapter.

OVERHAUL

DISASSEMBLY

1. Remove the countershaft lockplate, distance piece, and counter shaft assembly.

2. From the countershaft, remove the rubber O-ring, thrust washer, counter gear, two sets of needle bearings and thrust washer.

3. From the front end of the output shaft, remove the spacer, needle bearings and high/low sleeve.

4. From the rear end of the output shaft, remove the locknut.

5. Using a press, remove the output shaft bearing.

6. Remove the spacer, speedometer drive gear and distance piece.

7. Using a press and bearing remover J-

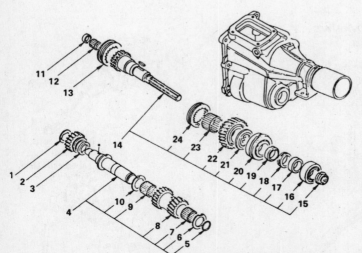

Removing output shaft snapring—1981-87 P'up and Trooper

22912-01 or equivalent, remove the middle bearing.

8. Remove the thrust washer, output gear, needle bearings and $4 \times 2/4 \times 4$ sleeve.

ASSEMBLY

1. Onto the output shaft, install the $4 \times 2/4 \times 4$ sleeve, needle bearings, output gear and thrust washer with the oil groove facing forward.

2. Install the middle bearing using a press.

3. Install the distance piece, speedometer drive gear, spacer and end bearing using a press.

4. Install the output shaft nut and torque to 116 ft. lbs. (160 Nm).

5. Install the output shaft assembly into the case.

6. Onto the counter shaft, install the thrust washer, needle bearings, counter gear, needle bearings, thrust washer and a new O-ring.

7. Install the countershaft into the case.

8. Install the high/low sleeve so the heavy chamfered side is facing forward.

9. Into the front of the output shaft, install the needle bearings and spacer.

10. Into the transfer case end, install the distance piece and lock plate.

1. Thrust washer
2. Reverse idler gear
3. Spacer
4. Transfer countershaft
5. O-ring
6. Thrust washer
7. Counter gear
8. Needle roller bearing
9. Needle roller bearing
10. Thrust washer
11. Spacer
12. Needle bearing
13. High/low sleeve
14. Output shaft
15. Nut
16. Ball bearing
17. Spacer
18. Speedometer drive gear
19. Distance piece
20. Ball bearing
21. Thrust washer
22. Output gear
23. Needle bearing
24. $4 \times 4/4 \times 2$ sleeve

Transfer case assembly—1981-87 P'up and Trooper

1988-91 P'up, Amigo, Trooper and Rodeo

REMOVAL AND INSTALLATION

The transfer case is part of the extension housing assembly. The transmission and transfer case has to be removed as an assembly. Refer to the "Transmission" removal and installation procedures in this Chapter.

OVERHAUL

DISASSEMBLY

1. Remove the rear case assembly.
2. Remove the shift arms, interlock pin and detent assemblies. Drive the spring pins out of the rod to remove the shift rod and arms.
3. Remove the mainshaft snapring and mainshaft end bearings using a bearings remover J–37217 and puller J–8433 or their equivalent.

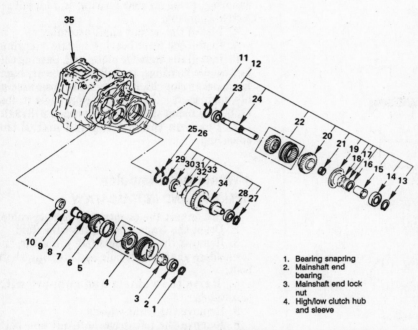

1. Bearing snapring
2. Mainshaft end bearing
3. Mainshaft end lock nut
4. High/low clutch hub and sleeve
5. High/low block ring (M/T only)
6. Transfer input gear
7. Needle bearing
8. Bearing collar
9. Ball
10. Plate
11. Bearing snapring
12. Front output gear
13. Bearing snapring
14. Bearing
15. Bearing collar
16. Sub gear snapring (M/T only)
17. Spacer (M/T only)
18. Belleville spring (M/T only)
19. Sub gear (M/T only)
20. Front output gear
21. Needle bearing
22. Clutch hub and sleeve
23. Bearing
24. Front output shaft
25. Bearing snapring
26. Counter gear
27. Snapring
28. Ball bearing
29. Snapring
30. Ball bearing
31. Spacer (M/T only)
32. Belleville spring (M/T only)
33. Sub gear (M/T only)
34. Counter gear
35. Transfer case

Transfer case assembly—1988–91 P'up, Amigo, Trooper and Rodeo

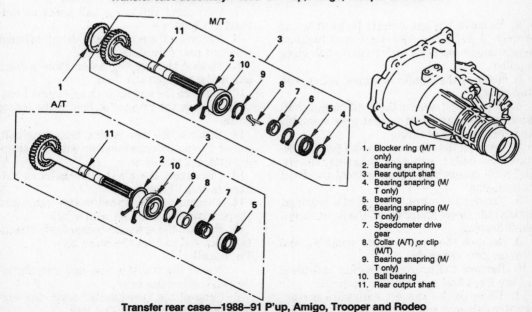

1. Blocker ring (M/T only)
2. Bearing snapring
3. Rear output shaft
4. Bearing snapring (M/T only)
5. Bearing
6. Bearing snapring (M/T only)
7. Speedometer drive gear
8. Collar (A/T) or clip (M/T)
9. Bearing snapring (M/T only)
10. Ball bearing
11. Rear output shaft

Transfer rear case—1988–91 P'up, Amigo, Trooper and Rodeo

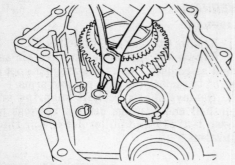

Bearing snapring removal

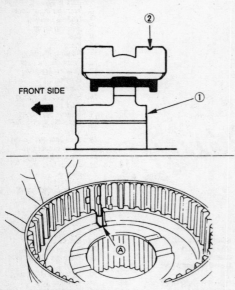

High/low clutch hub and sleeve

4. Remove the mainshaft locknut using wrench J–37219 or equivalent and high/low synchronizer assembly with transfer hub using a puller.

5. Remove the needle bearings, collar, ball and plate.

6. Expand and remove the front output shaft bearing snapring, front output gear assembly and rear bearing snapring.

7. Press off the rear output shaft bearing, remove the collar, sub-gear snapring, spacer, Belleville spring and sub-gear from the front output gear.

8. Remove the output gear needle bearings, clutch hub, sleeve and press off the front output shaft bearing.

9. Remove the counter gear snapring and counter gear assembly.

10. Remove the bearing snapring and press off the front and rear counter bearings.

11. Remove the spacer, belleville spring, counter sub-gear and counter gear.

ASSEMBLY

1. Cover the output shaft spline with adhesive tape to protect the oil seal. Apply liquid sealer to the transfer case sealing surfaces

2. Onto the counter gear, install the sub-gear, belleville spring, spacer and press on the front and rear bearings. Install the bearing-to-shaft snaprings.

3. Onto the front output shaft, install the front bearing, clutch and hub, needle bearings, sub-gear, belleville spring, spacer, sub-gear snapring, press on rear bearing and install selective snapring.

4. Install the output shaft assembly.

5. Install the front bearing-to-case snapring.

6. Install the transfer plate, ball, bearing collar, needle bearings, transfer input gear, high/low blocker ring, high/low synchronizer assembly, mainshaft locknut and torque to 94 ft. lbs. (130 Nm) using the installer wrench J–37219.

7. Press on the bearing and install the snapring.

4-Wheel Drive Impulse
REMOVAL AND INSTALLATION

1. Disconnect the negative (–) battery cable.
2. Drain the transaxle and transfer fluid.
3. Remove the steering shaft protector, intermediate shaft pinch bolt and steering shaft boot.
4. Raise the vehicle and support with jackstands.
5. Remove the front wheels.
6. Remove the left driveshaft nut and both tie rod ends as outlined in Chapter 8.
7. Disconnect the lower ball joints as outlined in Chapter 8.
8. Remove all undercovers, front exhaust pipe and rear driveshaft.
9. Remove the steering hoses. Place a drain pan under to catch the fluid.
10. Support the engine with an engine hoist.
11. Remove the torque rod bolt at the center beam.
12. Remove the rear rubber mounting bolt, center beam and crossmember with the steering unit and stabilizer.
13. Disconnect the FWD driveshafts as outlined in this Chapter.
14. Disconnect the speedometer cable and support the transfer case with a jack.
15. Remove the transfer-to-transaxle attaching bolts and remove the assembly.
To install:
1. Install the transfer case and transfer-to-transaxle attaching bolts.
2. Connect the speedometer cable and support the transfer case with a jack.

3. Connect the FWD driveshafts as outlined in this Chapter.

4. Install the rear rubber mounting bolt, center beam and crossmember with the steering unit and stabilizer.

5. Install the torque rod bolt at the center beam.

6. Install the steering hoses.

7. Install all undercovers, front exhaust pipe and rear driveshaft.

8. Connect the lower ball joints as outlined in Chapter 8.

9. Install the left driveshaft nut and both tie rod ends as outlined in Chapter 8.

10. Install the front wheels.

11. Lower the vehicle.

12. Install the steering shaft protector, intermediate shaft pinch bolt and steering shaft boot.

13. Refill the the transaxle and transfer fluid.

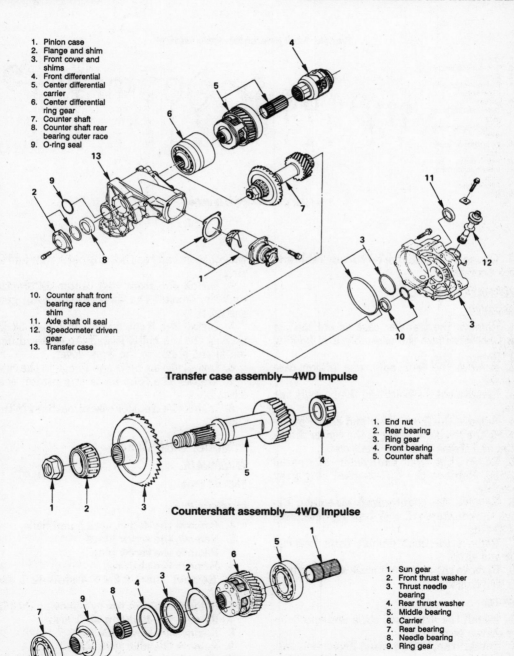

1. Pinion case
2. Flange and shim
3. Front cover and shims
4. Front differential
5. Center differential carrier
6. Center differential ring gear
7. Counter shaft
8. Counter shaft rear bearing outer race
9. O-ring seal
10. Counter shaft front bearing race and shim
11. Axle shaft oil seal
12. Speedometer driven gear
13. Transfer case

Transfer case assembly—4WD Impulse

1. End nut
2. Rear bearing
3. Ring gear
4. Front bearing
5. Counter shaft

Countershaft assembly—4WD Impulse

1. Sun gear
2. Front thrust washer
3. Thrust needle bearing
4. Rear thrust washer
5. Middle bearing
6. Carrier
7. Rear bearing
8. Needle bearing
9. Ring gear

Transfer center differential—4WD Impulse

1. Speedometer drive gear
2. Side bearing
3. Lock pin
4. Cross pin
5. Pinion gears and thrust washers
6. Side gears and thrust washers
7. Differential case

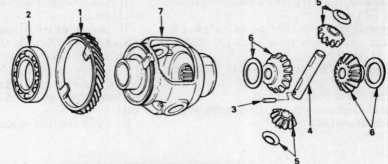

Transfer front differential—4WD Impulse

1. O-ring
2. End nut and washer
3. Flange
4. Distance piece and thrust washer
5. Oil seal
6. Outer bearing inner race
7. Outer bearing outer race
8. Inner bearing outer race
9. Pinion case
10. Inner bearing inner race
11. Pinion shaft
12. Shim

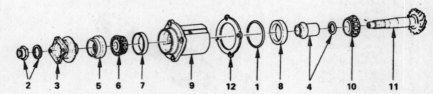

Transfer pinion—4WD Impulse

14. Connect the negative (–) battery cable and check operation.

OVERHAUL

DISASSEMBLY

1. Remove the transfer case as outlined in this Chapter. Place the assembly in a holding fixture.

2. Remove the four bolts and pinion case assembly.

3. Remove the six bolts and flange from the case.

4. Remove the front cover and shims by removing the ten bolts. Remove the center differential and shims from the front cover.

5. Remove the front and center differential carrier. Remove the differential ring gear assembly.

6. Remove the countershaft assembly. Remove the countershaft rear bearing outer race and O-ring.

7. Remove the countershaft front bearing, race and shim.

8. Remove the axle shaft seals and speedometer driven gear.

ASSEMBLY

1. Install the axle shaft seals and speedometer driven gear.

2. Install the countershaft front bearing, race and shim.

3. Install the countershaft assembly. Install the countershaft rear bearing outer race and O-ring.

4. Install the front and center differential carrier. Install the differential ring gear assembly.

5. Install the front cover and shims by installing the ten bolts. Install the center differential and shims to the front cover.

6. Install the six bolts and flange to the case.

7. Install the four bolts and pinion case assembly.

8. Install the transfer case as outlined in this Chapter.

Transfer Side Case

OVERHAUL

1981-87 P'up

DISASSEMBLY

1. Remove the detent spring and balls.
2. Remove the screw plugs.
3. Remove the screw plug.
4. Remove the shift rod.
5. Remove the $4 \times 2/4 \times 4$ shift arm and block.
6. Remove the shift rod by removing the pin.
7. Remove the high/low shift arm.
8. Remove the dowel pin.
9. Remove the idler gear shaft.
10. Remove the idler gear and needle bearings.

11. Remove the thrust washer.
12. Remove the thrust washer.
13. Remove the front output shaft cover.
14. Remove the Distance piece.
15. Remove the front output shaft.
16. Remove the front output gear.
17. Remove the front output shaft front bearing.
18. Remove the front output shaft rear bearing.

ASSEMBLY

1. Install the front output shaft rear bearing.
2. Install the front output shaft front bearing.

3. Install the front output gear.
4. Install the front output shaft.
5. Install the Distance piece.
6. Install the front output shaft cover.
7. Install the thrust washer.
8. Install the thrust washer.
9. Install the idler gear and needle bearings.
10. Install the idler gear shaft.
11. Install the dowel pin.
12. Install the high/low shift arm.
13. Install the shift rod by removing the pin.
14. Install the 4 × 2/4 × 4 shift arm and block.
15. Install the shift rod.
16. Install the screw plug.
17. Install the screw plugs.
18. Install the detent spring and balls.

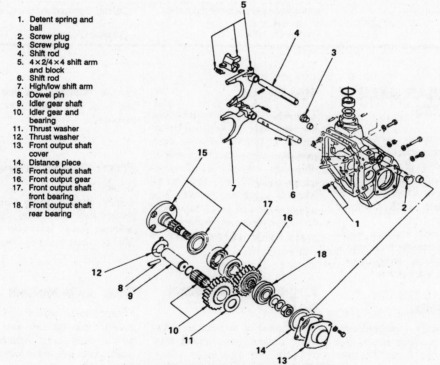

1. Detent spring and ball
2. Screw plug
3. Screw plug
4. Shift rod
5. 4 × 2/4 × 4 shift arm and block
6. Shift rod
7. High/low shift arm
8. Dowel pin
9. Idler gear shaft
10. Idler gear and bearing
11. Thrust washer
12. Thrust washer
13. Front output shaft cover
14. Distance piece
15. Front output shaft
16. Front output gear
17. Front output shaft front bearing
18. Front output shaft rear bearing

Transfer side case—1981–87 P'up and Trooper

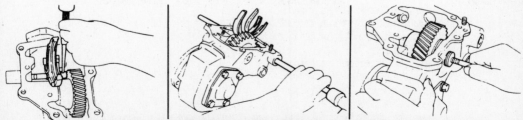

Shift rod and idler gear removal for transfer side case—1981–87 P'up and Trooper

Troubleshooting Basic Driveshaft and Rear Axle Problems

When abnormal vibrations or noises are detected in the driveshaft area, this chart can be used to help diagnose possible causes. Remember that other components such as wheels, tires, rear axle and suspension can also produce similar conditions.

BASIC DRIVESHAFT PROBLEMS

Problem	Cause	Solution
Shudder as car accelerates from stop or low speed	• Loose U-joint • Defective center bearing	• Replace U-joint • Replace center bearing
Loud clunk in driveshaft when shifting gears	• Worn U-joints	• Replace U-joints
Roughness or vibration at any speed	• Out-of-balance, bent or dented driveshaft • Worn U-joints • U-joint clamp bolts loose	• Balance or replace driveshaft • Replace U-joints • Tighten U-joint clamp bolts
Squeaking noise at low speeds	• Lack of U-joint lubrication	• Lubricate U-joint; if problem persists, replace U-joint
Knock or clicking noise	• U-joint or driveshaft hitting frame tunnel • Worn CV joint	• Correct overloaded condition • Replace CV joint

BASIC REAR AXLE PROBLEMS

First, determine when the noise is most noticeable.

Drive Noise: Produced under vehicle acceleration.

Coast Noise: Produced while the car coasts with a closed throttle.

Float Noise: Occurs while maintaining constant car speed (just enough to keep speed constant) on a level road.

Road Noise

Brick or rough surfaced concrete roads produce noises that seem to come from the rear axle. Road noise is usually identical in Drive or Coast and driving on a different type of road will tell whether the road is the problem.

Tire Noise

Tire noises are often mistaken for rear axle problems. Snow treads or unevenly worn tires produce vibrations seeming to originate elsewhere. **Temporarily** inflating the tires to 40 lbs will significantly alter tire noise, but will have no effect on rear axle noises (which normally cease below about 30 mph).

Engine/Transmission Noise

Determine at what speed the noise is most pronounced, then stop the car in a quiet place. With the transmission in Neutral, run the engine through speeds corresponding to road speeds where the noise was noticed. Noises produced with the car standing still are coming from the engine or transmission.

Front Wheel Bearings

While holding the car speed steady, lightly apply the footbrake; this will often decease bearing noise, as some of the load is taken from the bearing.

Rear Axle Noises

Eliminating other possible sources can narrow the cause to the rear axle, which normally produces noise from worn gears or bearings. Gear noises tend to peak in a narrow speed range, while bearing noises will usually vary in pitch with engine speeds.

NOISE DIAGNOSIS

The Noise Is	Most Probably Produced By
• Identical under Drive or Coast	• Road surface, tires or front wheel bearings
• Different depending on road surface	• Road surface or tires
• Lower as the car speed is lowered	• Tires
• Similar with car standing or moving	• Engine or transmission
• A vibration	• Unbalanced tires, rear wheel bearing, unbalanced driveshaft or worn U-joint
• A knock or click about every 2 tire revolutions	• Rear wheel bearing
• Most pronounced on turns	• Damaged differential gears
• A steady low-pitched whirring or scraping, starting at low speeds	• Damaged or worn pinion bearing
• A chattering vibration on turns	• Wrong differential lubricant or worn clutch plates (limited slip rear axle)
• Noticed only in Drive, Coast or Float conditions	• Worn ring gear and/or pinion gear

DRIVELINE

Front Driveshaft and CV-Joint

REMOVAL AND INSTALLATION

P'up, Amigo, Trooper and Rodeo

1. Raise and safely support the vehicle.
2. Disconnect the front driveshaft from the differential.
3. Remove the wheels and skid plate.
4. Loosen the torsion bar completely with the height control adjusting bolts.
5. Remove the strut bars.
6. Disconnect the stabilizer bars from the lower control arms.
7. Remove the caliper assemblies and wire them to the frame; do not disconnect the brake lines.
8. Remove the ball joints from the tie rods.
9. Disconnect the upper control arms from the frame; make sure to note the number and positions of the shims.
10. Remove the steering link ends from the lower control arms.
11. Disconnect the shock absorbers from the lower control arms.
12. Disconnect the lower control arms from the frame.
13. Remove the locking hub.
14. Remove the rotors and upper links.
15. Remove the pitman arm and idler arm along with the steering linkage assembly.
16. Support the differential housing and lower it clear of the vehicle. Take care to avoid damaging the Birfield joints.
17. Drain the differential case and remove the 4 bolts attaching the axle mounting bracket to the case.
18. Pull the shaft assemblies from the case on both sides.

To install:

1. Install the axle assembly and 4 bolts attaching the axle mounting bracket to the case.
2. Install the pitman arm and idler arm along with the steering linkage assembly.
3. Install the rotors and upper links.
4. Install the locking hub.
5. Connect the lower control arms to the frame.
6. Connect the shock absorbers to the lower control arms.
7. Install the steering link ends to the lower control arms.
8. Connect the upper control arms to the frame; make sure to note the number and positions of the shims.
9. Install the ball joints to the tie rods.
10. Install the caliper assemblies.
11. Connect the stabilizer bars to the lower control arms.
12. Install the strut bars.
13. Tighten the torsion bar completely with the height control adjusting bolts to their original position.
14. Install the wheels and skid plate.
15. Connect the front driveshaft to the differential.
16. Lower the vehicle and check operation. Refill the differential with fluid. Bleed the brake system if needed.

4-Wheel Drive Impulse

Refer to the "Halfshaft" procedures in this Chapter.

CV-JOINT OVERHAUL

Double Offset Joint

DISASSEMBLY

1. Disconnect the negative (–) battery cable. Clean the assembly of all grease and dirt.

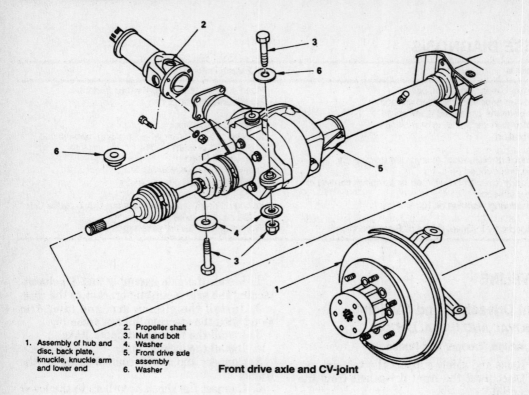

1. Assembly of hub and
   disc, back plate,
   knuckle, knuckle arm
   and lower end
2. Propeller shaft
3. Nut and bolt
4. Washer
5. Front drive axle
   assembly
6. Washer

Front drive axle and CV-joint

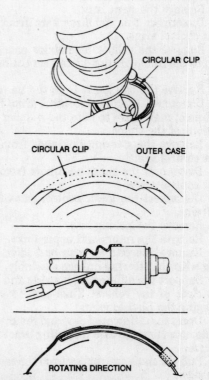

2. Remove the inner joint boot clamps. Slide the boot off of the joint.

3. From inside the inner joint, remove the circular clip from inside the offset joint. Pull the joint and shaft off of the inner joint.

4. Remove the ball retainer snapring and ball retainer. Pull the ball retainer and ball guide from the splined shaft.

5. Remove the boots and vibration damper, if so equipped.

The outer (birfield) joint is not serviceable, it must be replaced as an assembly.

7. Clean all grease and dirt from the joints.

ASSEMBLY

1. With the birfield joint bent at a 40° angle, turn the shaft and make sure that it turns smoothly and normally.

2. Place tap on the splines to prevent damage to the joint boots.

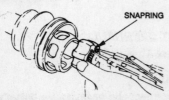

Remove the snapring and ball retainer

Assembly of Double Offset CV-joint

3. Install the outer boot and clamps onto the outer shaft.

4. Fill the joint and boot with new CV-joint grease and install new clamps.

5. Install the inner joint boot and vibration damper, if so equipped.

6. Install the ball retainer, guide and snapring.

7. Fill the boot and off-set joint with new grease and install joint.

8. Install the circular clip into the groove.

9. Slide the boot onto the joint, insert a tool under the boot lip to allow the pressure to equalize and tighten the new clamps.

10. Install the shaft into the vehicle as outlined in this Chapter.

Front Driveshaft and U-Joints

REMOVAL AND INSTALLATION

P'up, Amigo, Trooper and Rodeo

1. Raise and safely support the vehicle.

2. Matchmark the driveshaft flange-to-transfer case flange and the driveshaft-to-differential pinion flange.

3. Remove the front driveshaft's splinded yoke flange-to-transfer case bolts and separate the front driveshaft from the transfer case; do not allow the splined flange to fall away from the transmission.

4. Remove the driveshaft flange-to-differential pinion flange bolts and separate the driveshaft from the front differential.

To install:

5. Align the matchmarks and install the driveshaft.

6. Install the driveshaft flange-to-differential pinion flange bolts.

7. Install the front driveshaft's splinded

yoke flange-to-transfer case bolts and separate the front driveshaft to the transfer case.

8. Lower the vehicle.

U-JOINT OVERHAUL

1. Raise and support the vehicle safely. Remove the driveshaft.

2. If the front yoke is to be disassembled, matchmark the driveshaft and sliding splined yoke so that driveline balance is preserved upon reassembly. Remove the snaprings that retain the bearing caps.

3. Select 2 press components, with 1 small enough to pass through the yoke holes for the bearing caps and the other large enough to receive the bearing cap.

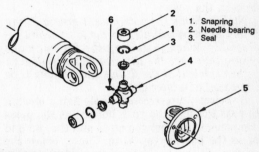

1. Snapring
2. Needle bearing
3. Seal

U-joint assembly

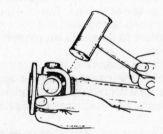

Dislodging bearing cap

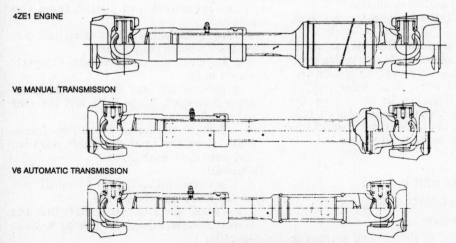

4ZE1 ENGINE

V6 MANUAL TRANSMISSION

V6 AUTOMATIC TRANSMISSION

Typical front driveshaft

4. Use a vise or a press and position the small and large press components on either side of the U-joint. Press in on the smaller press component so it presses the opposite bearing cap out of the yoke and into the larger press component. If the cap does not come all the way out, grasp it with a pair of pliers and work it out.

5. Reverse the position of the press components so that the smaller press component presses on the cross. Press the other bearing cap out of the yoke.

6. Repeat the procedure on the other bearings.

To install:

7. Grease the bearing caps and needles thoroughly if they are not pregreased. Start a new bearing cap into a side of the yoke. Position the cross in the yoke.

NOTE: *Some U-joints have a grease fitting that must be installed in the joint before assembly. When installing the fitting, make sure that once the driveshaft is installed in the vehicle that the fitting is accessible to be greased at a later date.*

8. Select 2 press components small enough to pass through the yoke holes. Put the press components against the cross and the cap and press the bearing cap ¼ in. (6mm) below the surface of the yoke. If there is a sudden increase in the force needed to press the cap into place, or if the cross starts to bind, the bearings are cocked. They must be removed and restarted in the yoke. Failure to do so will cause premature bearing failure.

9. Install a new snapring.

10. Start the new bearing into the opposite side. Place a press component on it and press in until the opposite bearing contacts the snapring.

11. Install a new snapring. It may be necessary to grind the facing surface of the snapring slightly to permit easier installation.

12. Install the other bearings in the same manner.

13. Check the joint for free movement. If binding exists, smack the yoke ears with a brass or plastic faced hammer to seat the bearing needles. If binding still exists, disassemble the joint and check to see if the needles are in place. Do not strike the bearings unless the shaft is supported firmly. Do not install the driveshaft until free movement exists at all joints.

Rear Driveshaft and U-Joint

REMOVAL AND INSTALLATION

RWD I-Mark and Impulse

1. Raise the rear of the car and support it safely on jack stands at the rear jack brackets.

2. Disconnect the parking brake return spring from the rod.

3. Mark the mating parts of the U-joint and the drive pinion extension shaft flange.

4. Remove the bolts and nuts connecting the U-joint and the extension shaft flange.

5. Work the propeller shaft slightly forward, lower the rear end of the shaft and slide the assembly rearward. Remove the thrust spring from the front of the shaft.

6. Install a plug (or wrap a small plastic bag) on the transmission extension housing to prevent the loss of oil.

CAUTION: *When replacing any fasteners or attaching bolts, be sure to use the proper grade bolt. Substitution of lesser quality hardware could cause failure and serious damage.*

To install:

7. Make sure that the transmission rear seal is not damaged. Align all marks and torque the bolts to 18 ft. lbs. (25 Nm).

8. Connect the parking brake return spring.

P'up, Amigo, Trooper and Amigo

2-WHEEL DRIVE DRIVESHAFT

1. Raise and support the vehicle safely.

2. Matchmark the driveshaft to the yokes.

3. Remove the driveshaft retaining bolts and remove the driveshaft.

4. To install, align the driveshaft to the matchmarked position and tighten the retaining bolts.

4-WHEEL DRIVE REAR DRIVESHAFT

1. Raise and safely support the vehicle.

2. Matchmark the driveshaft flange-to-differential pinion flange.

3. If equipped with a 1-piece driveshaft, remove the driveshaft flange-to-pinion nuts, lower the driveshaft and pull it from the transmission.

4. If equipped with a 2-piece driveshaft, perform the following procedures:

    a. Remove the rear driveshaft flange-to-pinion nuts.

    b. Remove the rear driveshaft flange-to-front driveshaft flange bolts and the rear driveshaft.

    c. Remove the center bearing-to-chassis bolts, move the front driveshaft rearward and from the transmission.

To install:

5. If equipped with a 2-piece driveshaft, perform the following procedures:

    a. Install the front driveshaft into the transmission and the center bearing-to-chassis bolts.

    b. Install the rear driveshaft and the rear

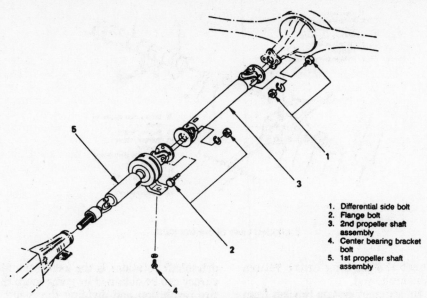

1. Differential side bolt
2. Flange bolt
3. 2nd propeller shaft assembly
4. Center bearing bracket bolt
5. 1st propeller shaft assembly

Exploded view of the rear driveshaft assembly—1981–87 similar

driveshaft flange-to-front driveshaft flange bolts.

c. Install the rear driveshaft flange-to-pinion nuts.

6. If equipped with a 1-piece driveshaft, install the driveshaft into the transmission and the driveshaft flange-to-pinion nuts.

Center Bearing
REMOVAL AND INSTALLATION

1. Remove the driveshaft assembly from the vehicle as outlined in this Chapter.
2. Remove the locknut and flange with a gear puller.
3. Remove retainer bolt and retainer.
4. Remove the supporting ring and cushion rubber.

5. Remove the bearing assembly using a gear puller.

To install:

6. Install the bearing assembly and repack with grease.
7. Install the cushion rubber and support ring.
8. Install the retainer, bolt, flange and locknut.
9. Torque the locknut to 90 ft. lbs. (122 Nm).

Central Joint
REMOVAL AND INSTALLATION
I-Mark (RWD) and Impulse

1. Raise and support the rear of the car safely under the axle tubes.

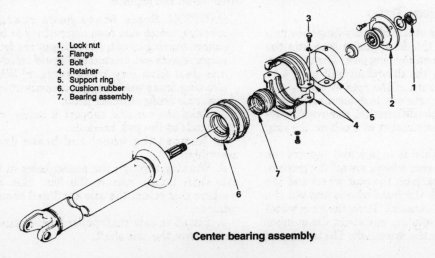

1. Lock nut
2. Flange
3. Bolt
4. Retainer
5. Support ring
6. Cushion rubber
7. Bearing assembly

Center bearing assembly

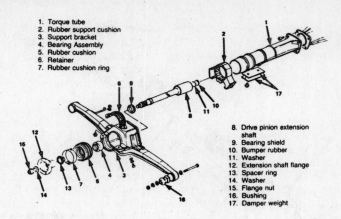

1. Torque tube
2. Rubber support cushion
3. Support bracket
4. Bearing Assembly
5. Rubber cushion
6. Retainer
7. Rubber cushion ring

8. Drive pinion extension shaft
9. Bearing shield
10. Bumper rubber
11. Washer
12. Extension shaft flange
13. Spacer ring
14. Washer
15. Flange nut
16. Bushing
17. Damper weight

Exploded view of central joint

2. Disconnect the parking brake return spring from the brake rod.

3. Unhook the exhaust system bracket from the central joint support bracket.

4. Mark the universal joint and flange, then disconnect the propeller shaft from the flange and support it out of the way.

5. Support the torque tube with a floor jack using minimum pressure.

6. Remove the central joint support bracket to underbody attaching bolts.

7. Allow the floor jack to lower the torque tube.

8. Disconnect the torque tube from the differential carrier by removing the attaching bolts.

9. Installation is the reverse of removal. Align all marks, torque all bolts to specifications.

REAR AXLE

Determining Axle Ratio

An axle ratio is obtained by dividing the number of teeth on the drive pinion gear into the number of teeth on the ring gear. For instance, on a 4.11 ratio, the driveshaft will turn 4.11 times for every turn of the rear wheel.

The most accurate way to determine the axle ratio is to drain the differential, remove the cover, and count the number of teeth on the ring and pinion.

An easier method is to jack and support the car so that both rear wheels are off the ground. Make a chalk mark on the rear wheel and the driveshaft. Block the front wheels and put the transmission in Neutral. Turn the rear wheel one complete revolution and count the number of turns made by the driveshaft. The number of

driveshaft rotations is the axle ratio. More accuracy can be obtained by going more than one tire revolution and dividing the result by the number of tire rotations.

The axle ratio is also identified by the axle serial number prefix on the axle; the axle ratios are listed in dealer's parts books according to prefix number. Some axles have a tag on the cover.

Differential Overhaul

A differential overhaul is a complex, highly technical, and time-consuming operation, which requires a great many tools, extensive knowledge of the unit and the way it works, and a high degree of mechanical experience and ability. It is highly advisable that the amateur mechanic not attempt any work on the differential unit.

Rear Axle Shaft, Bearing and Seal

REMOVAL AND INSTALLATION

RWD I-Mark and Impulse

CAUTION: *Some brake pads contain asbestos, which has been determined to be a cancer causing agent. Never clean the brake surfaces with compressed air! Avoid inhaling any dust from any brake surface! When cleaning brake surfaces, use a commercially available brake cleaning fluid.*

1. Raise the car and support it safely with jackstands at the jack brackets.

2. Remove the wheel and brake drum assembly.

3. Working through the access holes in the axle shaft flange, remove the four nuts and washers that retain the axle shaft and bearing retainer.

4. Install an axle shaft puller (slap-hammer) and remove the axle shaft.

5. To replace the bearing parts, first remove the retaining ring by cutting it off with a chisel. The bearing must be pressed off with a suitable bench press.

To install:

6. Press the new bearing on to the axle shaft with a suitable press.

7. Check the axle shaft endplay by using a depth gauge to measure the depth of the rear axle bearing seat in the axle housing with the backing plate in place.

8. Measure the width of the bearing outer race. The difference between the two measurements indicates the required thickness of the shims. If necessary to increase endplay, add shims. To decrease endplay, remove shims. Standard endplay is 0–0.008 in. (0.2mm) thickness. Shims are only available in 0.006 in. (0.15mm) thickness.

9. Coat all rear axle components with gear oil before installation. Torque the lock washers and nuts to 28 ft. lbs. (38 Nm).

FWD I-Mark

CAUTION: *Some brake pads contain asbestos, which has been determined to be a cancer causing agent. Never clean the brake surfaces with compressed air! Avoid inhaling any dust from any brake surface! When cleaning brake surfaces, use a commercially available brake cleaning fluid.*

1. Raise the vehicle and support with jackstands.

2. Remove the rear wheels.

3. Remove the hub cap, split pin and hub nut.

4. Remove the washer, pull the drum off of the axle and remove the outer bearing.

5. Remove the oil seal using a suitable puller.

6. Remove the inner bearing.

7. If replacing the bearings, remove the outer bearing race by driving out the race with a

brass drift. Remove the races from the hub notch.

To install:

8. Install the new races with a brass drift. Be careful not to damage the race, bearing damage will result.

9. Repack the bearings and hub with grease.

10. Install the inner bearing and oil seal.

11. Install the drum onto the axle and install the washer and hub nut.

12. Adjust the wheel bearings as follows: torque the nut to 22 ft. lbs. (30 Nm). Rotate the drum two times, loosen the nut completely and tighten the nut fully by hand.

13. Insert a new split pin and bend over.

14. Install the rear wheels and lower the vehicle.

FWD Impulse and Stylus

CAUTION: *Some brake pads contain asbestos, which has been determined to be a cancer causing agent. Never clean the brake surfaces with compressed air! Avoid inhaling any dust from any brake surface! When cleaning brake surfaces, use a commercially available brake cleaning fluid.*

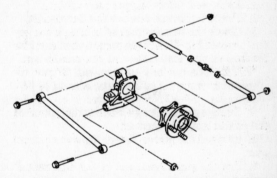

Rear bearing/hub assembly—FWD Impulse and Stylus

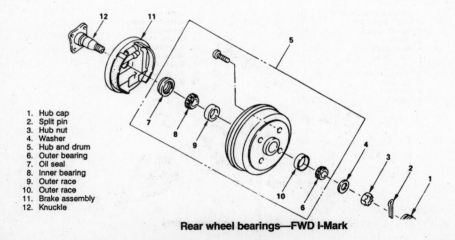

1. Hub cap
2. Split pin
3. Hub nut
4. Washer
5. Hub and drum
6. Outer bearing
7. Oil seal
8. Inner bearing
9. Outer race
10. Outer race
11. Brake assembly
12. Knuckle

Rear wheel bearings—FWD I-Mark

The hub and bearing are a complete assembly and can NOT be serviced separately.

1. Raise the vehicle and support with jackstands.

2. Remove the brake drum or rotor from the hub as outlined in Chapter 9.

3. Remove the four retaining bolts and hub/bearing assembly.

4. Install the hub/bearing assembly and torque the bolts to 49 ft. lbs. (66 Nm).

5. Install the brake drum or rotor, rear wheels and lower the vehicle.

P'up, Amigo, Trooper and Amigo

AXLE SHAFT

1. Raise and safely support the vehicle.

2. Remove the rear wheel assembly and brake drum.

3. Remove the 4 axle retainer bolts.

4. Using a slide hammer on the axle, pull the axle out of the housing.

5. To install, reverse the removal procedures.

6. Torque the axle retainer bolts to 51–58 ft. lbs. (68–81 Nm).

PINION SEAL

1. Raise and safely support the vehicle.

2. Matchmark and remove the driveshaft.

3. Check the turning torque of the pinion before proceeding. This is the torque that must be reached during installation of the pinion nut.

NOTE: *The amount of turning torque required to move the pinion gear should be 20–30 ft. lbs. (27–40 Nm) of torque.*

4. Using a pinion flange holding tool, remove the pinion nut and washer.

5. Remove the pinion flange from the pinion gear.

6. Pry the pinion seal out of the differential carrier.

7. Clean and inspect the sealing surface of the carrier.

To install:

8. Using a seal driver tool, drive the new seal into the carrier until the flange on the seal is flush with the carrier.

9. With the seal installed, the pinion bearing preload must be set.

10. Tighten the pinion nut while holding the flange, until the turning torque is the same as before removal of the nut.

11. Align the matchmarks and install the driveshaft.

12. Check the level of the differential lubricant when finished.

AXLE SHAFT SEAL

1. Raise and safely support the vehicle.

2. Remove the axle shaft from the housing.

3. Support the axle shaft and remove the bearing retainer locknut.

4. Remove the retainer, bearing and seal from the axle shaft.

5. Using a seal driver tool, remove the seal and install the new seal in the retainer.

To install:

6. Torque the bearing retainer nut to 188–195 ft. lbs. (250–275 Nm).

7. Check the level of the axle lubricant when finished.

Differential Carrier

REMOVAL AND INSTALLATION

Front Drive Axle

1. Raise and safely support the vehicle.

2. Drain the differential oil.

3. Matchmark and remove the front driveshaft.

4. Remove the axle shafts from the differential.

5. Remove the differential carrier mounting bolts and remove the carrier.

To install:

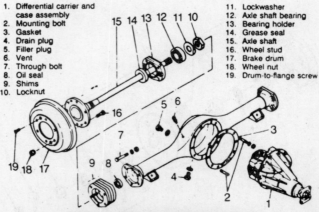

1. Differential carrier and case assembly
2. Mounting bolt
3. Gasket
4. Drain plug
5. Filler plug
6. Vent
7. Through bolt
8. Oil seal
9. Shims
10. Locknut
11. Lockwasher
12. Axle shaft bearing
13. Bearing holder
14. Grease seal
15. Axle shaft
16. Wheel stud
17. Brake drum
18. Wheel nut
19. Drum-to-flange screw

Exploded view of the rear axle assembly

6. Use a new gasket when installing. Install the housing and nuts.

7. Fill the differential to the correct level when finished.

Rear Drive Axle

1. Raise and safely support the vehicle.
2. Drain the differential oil.
3. Matchmark and remove the rear driveshaft.
4. Remove the axle shafts from the differential.
5. Remove the differential carrier mounting bolts and the carrier.

To install:

6. Use a new gasket when installing.
7. Fill the differential to the correct level when finished.

Pinion Seal

REMOVAL AND INSTALLATION

1. Raise and safely support the vehicle. If necessary, remove the skid plate.
2. Matchmark and remove the front driveshaft.
3. Check the turning torque of the pinion before proceeding. This is the torque that must be reached during installation of the pinion nut.

NOTE: *The amount of turning torque required to move the pinion gear should be 20–30 ft. lbs. (27–40 Nm) of torque.*

4. Using a pinion flange holding tool, remove the pinion nut and washer.

5. Remove the pinion flange from the pinion gear.

6. Pry the pinion seal out of the differential carrier.

7. Clean and inspect the sealing surface of the carrier.

To install:

8. Using a seal driver tool, drive the new seal into the carrier until the flange on the seal is flush with the carrier.

9. With the seal installed, the pinion bearing preload must be set.

10. Tighten the pinion nut while holding the flange, until the turning torque is the same as before removal of the nut.

11. Align the matchmarks and install the driveshaft.

12. Check the level of the differential lubricant when finished.

Axle Housing

REMOVAL AND INSTALLATION

RWD I-Mark and Impulse with G200Z Engine

1. Disconnect the negative (–) battery cable.
2. Raise the vehicle, support with jackstands and remove the rear wheels.
3. Remove the driveshaft as outlined in this Chapter.
4. Disconnect the exhaust pipe, stabilizer bar, shock absorbers and brake hose.
5. Disconnect the lateral rod.
6. Place a jack under the rear axle assembly.
7. Disconnect the insulator and springs.

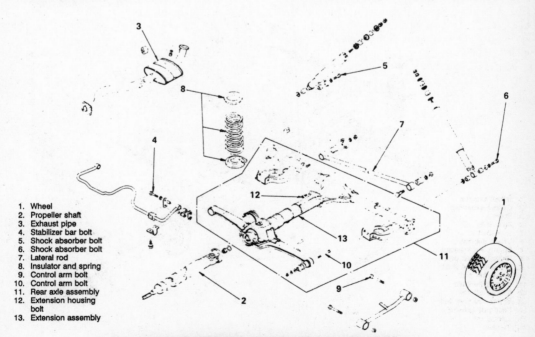

1. Wheel
2. Propeller shaft
3. Exhaust pipe
4. Stabilizer bar bolt
5. Shock absorber bolt
6. Shock absorber bolt
7. Lateral rod
8. Insulator and spring
9. Control arm bolt
10. Control arm bolt
11. Rear axle assembly
12. Extension housing bolt
13. Extension assembly

Rear axle assembly—RWD I-Mark and Impulse with G200Z eng.

8. Remove the control arm and bridge to body bolts.

9. Remove the rear axle assembly with the extension assembly.

To install:

1. Raise the rear axle assembly with the extension assembly into position and install the springs and insulators.

2. Install the control arm and bridge to body bolts.

3. Connect the lateral rod.

4. Connect the exhaust pipe, stabilizer bar, shock absorbers and brake hose.

5. Install the driveshaft as outlined in this Chapter.

6. Install the wheels and lower the vehicle.

7. Bleed the brake system as outlined in Chapter 9.

8. Connect the negative (–) battery cable and check operation.

RWD Impulse with 4ZC1-Turbo Engine

1. Disconnect the negative (–) battery cable.

2. Raise the vehicle, support with jackstands and remove the rear wheels.

3. Remove the caliper assemblies as outlined in Chapter 9.

4. Remove the plate to rear axle bolt.

5. Remove the lower link bolt, spring and insulator. Place a floor jack under the rear axle.

6. Disconnect the stabilizer, propeller shaft, upper link, brake hose, lateral link and shock absorbers.

To install:

7. Connect the stabilizer, propeller shaft, upper link, brake hose, lateral link and shock absorbers.

8. Install the lower link bolt, spring and insulator.

9. Install the plate to rear axle bolt.

10. Install the caliper assemblies as outlined in Chapter 9.

11. Install the rear wheels, lower the vehicle and bleed the brake system.

12. Connect the negative (–) battery cable.

P'up, Amigo, Trooper and Rodeo

1. Raise and safely support the vehicle. Remove the rear wheels.

2. Disconnect the shock absorbers from the spring plates.

3. Disconnect and plug the brake lines on the rear axle housing.

4. Disconnect the parking brake cables from the rear axle housing.

5. Support the rear axle housing and remove the housing to leaf spring U-bolts.

6. Remove the rear axle housing from the vehicle.

To install:

7. To install, reverse the removal procedures.

8. Torque the housing U-bolts to 36–43 ft. lbs. (47–60 Nm) and the shock absorber bolts to 27–30 ft. lbs. (30–41 Nm).

9. Bleed the brake system and check the level of the axle lubricant when finished.

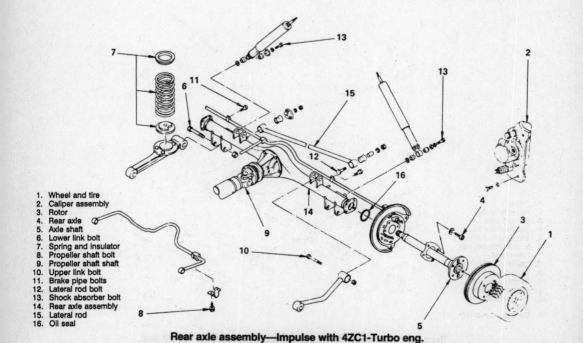

1. Wheel and tire
2. Caliper assembly
3. Rotor
4. Rear axle
5. Axle shaft
6. Lower link bolt
7. Spring and insulator
8. Propeller shaft bolt
9. Propeller shaft shaft
10. Upper link bolt
11. Brake pipe bolts
12. Lateral rod bolt
13. Shock absorber bolt
14. Rear axle assembly
15. Lateral rod
16. Oil seal

Rear axle assembly—Impulse with 4ZC1-Turbo eng.

FRONT DRIVE AXLE

Front Axle Shaft, Bearings and Seal

REMOVAL AND INSTALLATION

Axle Shaft

1. Raise and safely support the vehicle.
2. Disconnect the front driveshaft from the differential.
3. Remove the wheels and skid plate.
4. Loosen the torsion bar completely with the height control adjusting bolts.
5. Remove the strut bars.
6. Disconnect the stabilizer bars from the lower control arms.
7. Remove the caliper assemblies and wire them to the frame; do not disconnect the brake lines.
8. Remove the ball joints from the tie rods.
9. Disconnect the upper control arms from the frame; make sure to note the number and positions of the shims.
10. Remove the steering link ends from the lower control arms.
11. Disconnect the shock absorbers from the lower control arms.
12. Disconnect the lower control arms from the frame.
13. Remove the locking hub.
14. Remove the rotors and upper links.
15. Remove the pitman arm and idler arm along with the steering linkage assembly.
16. Support the differential housing and lower it clear of the vehicle. Take care to avoid damaging the Birfield joints.
17. Drain the differential case and remove the

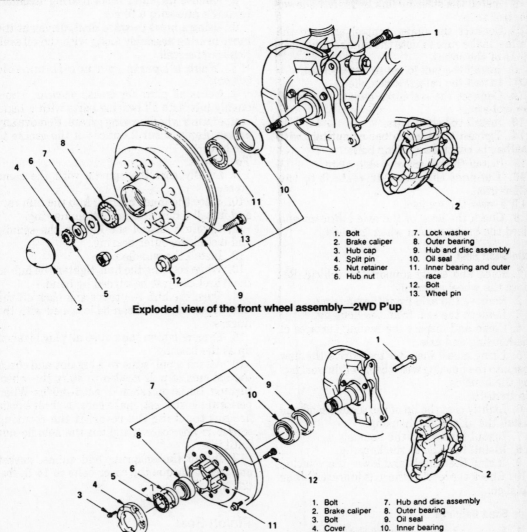

1.	Bolt	7.	Lock washer
2.	Brake caliper	8.	Outer bearing
3.	Hub cap	9.	Hub and disc assembly
4.	Split pin	10.	Oil seal
5.	Nut retainer	11.	Inner bearing and outer race
6.	Hub nut	12.	Bolt
		13.	Wheel pin

Exploded view of the front wheel assembly—2WD P'up

1.	Bolt	7.	Hub and disc assembly
2.	Brake caliper	8.	Outer bearing
3.	Bolt	9.	Oil seal
4.	Cover	10.	Inner bearing
5.	Lock washer	11.	Bolt
6.	Hub nut	12.	Wheel pin

Exploded view of the front wheel assembly—2WD Amigo

4 bolts attaching the axle mounting bracket to the case.

18. Pull the shaft assemblies from the case on both sides.

To install:

1. Install the shaft assemblies into the case on both sides.

2. Raise the differential housing and install the 4 bolts attaching the axle mounting bracket to the case.

3. Install the pitman arm and idler arm along with the steering linkage assembly.

4. Install the rotors and upper links.

5. Install the locking hub.

6. Connect the lower control arms to the frame.

7. Connect the shock absorbers to the lower control arms.

8. Install the steering link ends to the lower control arms.

9. Connect the upper control arms to the frame; make sure to note the number and positions of the shims.

10. Install the ball joints to the tie rods.

11. Install the caliper assemblies.

12. Connect the stabilizer bars to the lower control arms.

13. Install the strut bars.

14. Tighten the torsion bar completely with the height control adjusting bolts.

15. Install the wheels and skid plate.

16. Connect the front driveshaft to the differential.

17. Lower the vehicle.

18. Check the level of the axle lubricant and bleed the brake system when finished.

Axle Shaft Seal

1. Raise and safely support the vehicle. Remove the wheel assembly.

2. Remove the axle from the housing.

3. Remove the seal from the housing.

4. Clean and inspect the sealing surfaces of the housing and axle.

5. Using a seal installer tool, drive the new seal into the housing with the lip of the seal facing the housing.

To install:

6. Lightly coat the lip of the seal with oil and install the axle in the housing.

7. Install the seal to the housing.

8. Install the axle to the housing.

9. Install the wheels and lower the vehicle.

10. Check the level of the axle lubricant when finished.

Axle Shaft Bearings

1. Raise and safely support the vehicle.

2. Remove the axle shaft from the housing.

3. Support the axle shaft and remove the bearing retainer locknut and washer.

4. Remove the retainer, bearing and seal from the axle shaft.

To install:

5. Always replace the seal and lock washer when removing the axle shaft from the housing. Torque the bearing retainer nut to 188–195 ft. lbs. (250–320 Nm).

Wheel Bearings

1. Place the transfer case in **2H**. Raise and safely support the vehicle.

2. Remove the free wheeling hub cover assembly.

3. Remove the snapring and shims from the spindle.

4. Remove the free wheeling hub body and lock washer.

5. Remove the outer roller bearing assembly from the hub with a finger.

6. Using a brass or wood drift, drive out the inner bearing assembly along with the oil seal. Replace the seal.

7. Wash all parts in a non-flammable solvent.

8. Check all parts for cracks or wear. Thoroughly lubricate all bearing parts with a high-temperature wheel bearing grease. Remove any excess. Apply about 2 ounces of the grease to the hub.

To install:

9. Lightly coat the spindle with the same grease.

10. Place the inner bearing into the hub race and install a new seal and retaining ring.

11. Carefully install the hub on the spindle and install the outer bearing.

12. Install the spindle nut.

13. While rotating the hub, tighten the hub so the wheel can just be turned by hand.

14. Turn the hub 2–3 turns and back off the nut just enough so it can be loosened with the fingers.

15. Finger-tighten the nut so all play is taken up at the bearing.

16. Attach a pull scale to a lug nut and check the amount of pull needed to start the wheel turning. Initial pull should be 2.6–4.0 lbs. When performing this test, make sure the brake pads are not touching the rotor. If the rotating torque is not correct, tighten the spindle nut until it is.

17. Install the snapring and shims, gasket and cover. Torque the cover bolts to 14 ft. lbs. (20 Nm).

Pinion Seal

REMOVAL AND INSTALLATION

1. Raise and safely support the vehicle. If necessary, remove the skid plate.

2. Matchmark and remove the front driveshaft.

3. Check the turning torque of the pinion before proceeding. This is the torque that must be reached during installation of the pinion nut.

NOTE: *The amount of turning torque required to move the pinion gear should be 20–30 inch lbs. of torque.*

4. Using a pinion flange holding tool, remove the pinion nut and washer.

5. Remove the pinion flange from the pinion gear.

6. Pry the pinion seal out of the differential carrier.

7. Clean and inspect the sealing surface of the carrier.

To install:

8. Using a seal driver tool, drive the new seal into the carrier until the flange on the seal is flush with the carrier.

9. With the seal installed, the pinion bearing preload must be set.

10. Tighten the pinion nut while holding the flange, until the turning torque is the same as before removal of the nut.

11. Align the matchmarks and install the driveshaft.

12. Check the level of the differential lubricant when finished.

Manual Locking Hubs

REMOVAL AND INSTALLATION

1. Place the transfer case in the **2H** position. Raise and safely the vehicle.

2. Set the hubs in the **FREE** position.

3. Remove the hub cover bolts and the hub cover.

4. While pushing the follower toward the knob, turn the clutch assembly clockwise and then remove the clutch assembly from the knob.

5. Remove the snapring and the knob from the cover. Do not loose the detent ball.

6. Remove the ball and spring from the knob.

7. Remove the X-ring from the knob by pressing it off.

NOTE: *Do not use a sharp instrument to remove this ring because it may scratch the ring.*

8. Remove the compression spring, retaining spring and the follower from the clutch assembly.

9. Remove the retaining spring from the clutch assembly by turning it counterclockwise.

10. Remove the snapring and the inner assembly from the body.

11. Separate the ring, inner and spacer by removing the snapring.

To install:

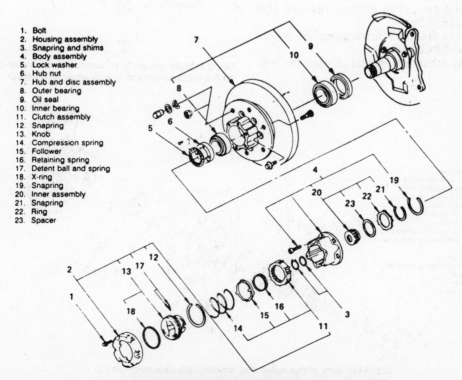

1. Bolt
2. Housing assembly
3. Snapring and shims
4. Body assembly
5. Lock washer
6. Hub nut
7. Hub and disc assembly
8. Outer bearing
9. Oil seal
10. Inner bearing
11. Clutch assembly
12. Snapring
13. Knob
14. Compression spring
15. Follower
16. Retaining spring
17. Detent ball and spring
18. X-ring
19. Snapring
20. Inner assembly
21. Snapring
22. Ring
23. Spacer

Exploded view of the manual locking hub assembly—4WD

12. Apply grease to the X-ring, the inner cover and the outside circumference of the knob.

13. Install the snapring and the inner assembly to the body.

14. Install the retaining spring to the clutch assembly by turning it clockwise.

15. Install the compression spring, retaining spring and the follower to the clutch assembly.

16. Install the X-ring to the knob by pressing it on.

17. Install the ball and spring to the knob.

18. Install the snapring and the knob to the cover.

19. Install the hub cover bolts and the hub cover.

20. Set the hubs in the **FREE** position.

21. Install the front wheels and lower the vehicle.

Automatic Locking Hubs

REMOVAL AND INSTALLATION

1. Move the transfer case shift lever into **2H** and move the vehicle forward and rearward about 3 ft.

2. Remove the hub cap-to-housing bolts and the cap.

3. Loosen the wheel nuts

4. Raise and safely support the vehicle. Remove the front wheel(s).

5. Remove the brake caliper-to-steering knuckle bolts and support the caliper on a wire; do not disconnect the brake hose.

6. Using snapring pliers, remove the snapring and shims.

7. Remove the drive clutch assembly, the inner cam and lockwasher.

8. Using a hub nut wrench, loosen the hub nut.

9. Pull the hub from the spindle.

10. If necessary, use a brass drift and a hammer to drive the wheel bearings from the hub.

11. If removing the disc from the hub, scribe matchmarks, remove the disc-to-hub bolts and separate the disc from the hub.

To install:

12. To install, reverse the removal procedures.

13. When installing the hub nut, perform the following procedures:

   a. Torque the hub nut to 22 ft. lbs. and loosen the nut.

   b. Using a spring gauge, connect it to the stud bolt at 90°.

   c. Retorque the hub nut until the spring gauge measures a bearing preload of 4.4–5.5 lbs. (new bearing and oil seal) or 2.6–4.0 lbs. (used bearing and new oil seal).

14. Adjust the snapring clearance by performing the following procedures:

   a. Install the special adjusting tool onto the hub until it comes in contact with the lock washer.

   b. Using a feeler gauge, measure the clearance **t** between the hub and the snapring groove on the axle shaft.

   c. If the clearance is larger than the

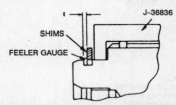

Using a feeler gauge to measure the shim clearance on the automatic locking hub assembly—4WD

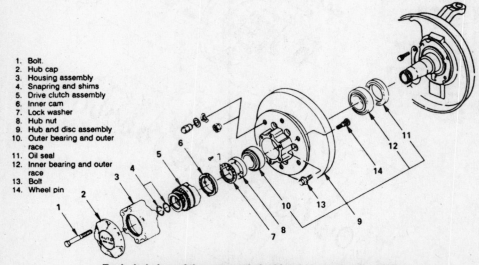

1. Bolt.
2. Hub cap
3. Housing assembly
4. Snapring and shims
5. Drive clutch assembly
6. Inner cam
7. Lock washer
8. Hub nut
9. Hub and disc assembly
10. Outer bearing and outer race
11. Oil seal
12. Inner bearing and outer race
13. Bolt
14. Wheel pin

Exploded view of the automatic locking hub assembly—4WD

snapring groove, install shims on the shaft so clearance **t** is 0–0.039 in. (0–0.1mm).

15. To complete the installation, reverse the removal procedures. Apply Loctite® to the hub cap bolts and torque the hub cap-to-hub assembly bolts to 43 ft. lbs. (60 Nm).

Differential Carrier

REMOVAL AND INSTALLATION

1. Raise and safely support the vehicle.
2. Drain the differential oil.
3. Matchmark and remove the front driveshaft.
4. Remove the axle shafts from the differential.
5. Remove the differential carrier mounting bolts and remove the carrier.

To install:

6. Install the carrier and use a new gasket when installing.
7. Install the axle shafts to the differential.
8. Install the front driveshaft.
9. Refill the differential oil.
10. Lower the vehicle.

Axle Housing

REMOVAL AND INSTALLATION

1. Raise and safely support the vehicle.
2. Matchmark and disconnect the front driveshaft from the differential.

3. Remove the wheels and skid plate.
4. Loosen the torsion bar completely with the height control adjusting bolts.
5. Remove the strut bars.
6. Disconnect the stabilizer bars from the lower control arms.
7. Remove the caliper assemblies and suspend them on a wire; do not disconnect the brake lines.
8. Remove the tie rod ends from the steering knuckles.
9. Disconnect the upper control arms from the frame; note the number and positions of the shims.
10. Remove the steering link ends from the lower control arms.
11. Disconnect the shock absorbers from the lower control arms.
12. Disconnect the lower control arms from the frame.
13. Remove the locking hub.
14. Remove the rotors and upper links.
15. Remove the pitman arm and idler arm along with the steering linkage assembly.
16. Support the differential housing and lower it clear of the vehicle. Take care to avoid damaging the Birfield joints.

To install:

1. Support the differential housing and raise into position. Take care to avoid damaging the Birfield joints.

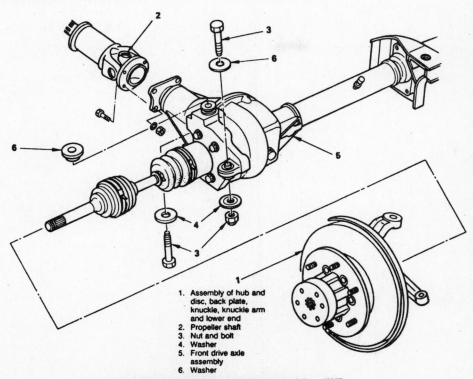

1. Assembly of hub and disc, back plate, knuckle, knuckle arm and lower end
2. Propeller shaft
3. Nut and bolt
4. Washer
5. Front drive axle assembly
6. Washer

Exploded view of the front axle assembly—4WD

2. Install the pitman arm and idler arm along with the steering linkage assembly.

3. Install the rotors and upper links.

4. Install the locking hub.

5. Connect the lower control arms to the frame.

6. Connect the shock absorbers to the lower control arms.

7. Install the steering link ends to the lower control arms.

8. Connect the upper control arms to the frame; note the number and positions of the shims.

9. Install the tie rod ends to the steering knuckles.

10. Install the caliper assemblies.

11. Connect the stabilizer bars to the lower control arms.

12. Install the strut bars.

13. Adjust the torsion bar completely with the height control adjusting bolts.

14. Install the wheels and skid plate.

15. Connect the front driveshaft to the differential.

16. Lower the vehicle.

Suspension and Steering

FRONT SUSPENSION

Coil Springs
REMOVAL AND INSTALLATION

RWD I-Mark and Impulse

1. Raise the car and safely support it with jackstands. Remove the wheel.

2. Remove the tie rod end cotter pin and castle nut. Discard the cotter pin.

3. Use a suspension fork to separate the tie rod end from the steering knuckle.

4. Remove the lower shock absorber bolt and push the shock up as far as possible.

5. Remove the stabilizer bar bolt and grommet assembly from the lower control arm.

Troubleshooting Basic Steering and Suspension Problems

Problem	Cause	Solution
Hard steering (steering wheel is hard to turn)	• Low or uneven tire pressure	• Inflate tires to correct pressure
	• Loose power steering pump drive belt	• Adjust belt
	• Low or incorrect power steering fluid	• Add fluid as necessary
	• Incorrect front end alignment	• Have front end alignment checked/adjusted
	• Defective power steering pump	• Check pump
	• Bent or poorly lubricated front end parts	• Lubricate and/or replace defective parts
Loose steering (too much play in the steering wheel)	• Loose wheel bearings	• Adjust wheel bearings
	• Loose or worn steering linkage	• Replace worn parts
	• Faulty shocks	• Replace shocks
	• Worn ball joints	• Replace ball joints
Car veers or wanders (car pulls to one side with hands off the steering wheel)	• Incorrect tire pressure	• Inflate tires to correct pressure
	• Improper front end alignment	• Have front end alignment checked/adjusted
	• Loose wheel bearings	• Adjust wheel bearings
	• Loose or bent front end components	• Replace worn components
	• Faulty shocks	• Replace shocks
Wheel oscillation or vibration transmitted through steering wheel	• Improper tire pressures	• Inflate tires to correct pressure
	• Tires out of balance	• Have tires balanced
	• Loose wheel bearings	• Adjust wheel bearings
	• Improper front end alignment	• Have front end alignment checked/adjusted
	• Worn or bent front end components	• Replace worn parts
Uneven tire wear	• Incorrect tire pressure	• Inflate tires to correct pressure
	• Front end out of alignment	• Have front end alignment checked/adjusted
	• Tires out of balance	• Have tires balanced

6. Remove the upper brake caliper bolt and slide the hose retaining clip back about ½ in. (13mm).

7. Place the lifting pad of a hydraulic floor jack under the outer extreme of the control arm and raise the lower control arm until it is level.

CAUTION: *Secure a safety chain through one coil near the top of the spring and attach it to the upper control arm to prevent the spring from coming out unexpectedly. The coil spring will come out with a lethal force, so don't take any chances.*

8. Loosen the lower ball joint lock nut until the top of the nut is flush with the top of the ball joint. Using tool J–26407 or equivalent, disconnect the lower ball joint from the steering knuckle.

9. Remove the hub assembly and steering knuckle from the lower ball joint and support with a wire or rope out of the way.

10. Pry the lower control arm down, using extreme caution so as not to injure yourself. Remove the spring.

To install:

CAUTION: *Properly seat the spring and use the safety chain. Use the hydraulic jack to compress the new spring until the control arm is stable.*

Torque the ball joint lock nut to 58 ft. lbs. Torque the lower shock absorber mounting nuts to 25 ft. lbs. (34 Nm).

1. Install the spring and pry the lower control arm up, using extreme caution so as not to injure yourself!

2. Install the hub assembly and steering knuckle to the lower ball joint.

3. Tighten the lower ball joint lock nut until the top of the nut is flush with the top of the ball joint.

4. Install the upper brake caliper bolt.

5. Install the stabilizer bar, bolts and grommet assembly to the lower control arm.

6. Install the lower shock absorber bolt.

7. Install the tie rod end to the steering knuckle.

8. Install the tie rod end cotter pin and castle nut.

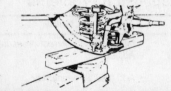

Using a hydraulic jack to control coil spring

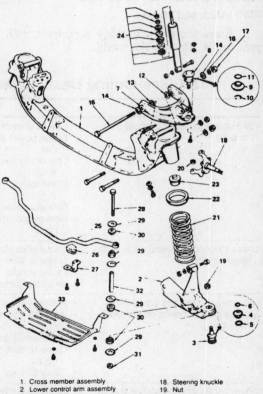

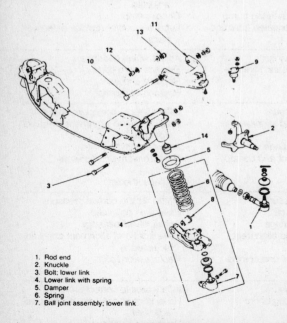

1. Rod end		
2. Knuckle		
3. Bolt; lower link		
4. Lower link with spring		
5. Damper		
6. Spring		
7. Ball joint assembly; lower link		

Front suspension system—RWD Impulse

1. Cross member assembly	18. Steering knuckle
2. Lower control arm assembly	19. Nut
3. Lower ball joint assembly	20. Nut
4. Boot	21. Front coil spring
5. Clamp ring	22. Damper rubber
6. Clamp ring	23. Bumper rubber
7. Upper control arm assembly	24. Shock absorber
8. Upper ball joint	25. Stabilizer bar
9. Boot	26. Rubber bushing
10. Clamp ring	27. Clamp
11. Clamp ring	28. Bolt
12. Washer	29. Retainer
13. Washer	30. Grommet
14. Washer	31. Nut
15. Through-bolt	32. Distance tube
16. Spring washer	33. Under cover
17. Nut	

Front suspension system—RWD I-Mark

9. Install the wheels and lower the vehicle.

FWD I-Mark
Impulse
Stylus

Refer to "MacPherson Strut" overhaul for specific coil spring removing procedures.

All Trucks
2-WHEEL DRIVE VEHICLES

1. Raise and safely support the vehicle.
2. Remove the adjusting bolt from the height control arm.

3. Mark the location and remove the height control arm from the torsion bar and the third crossmember.
4. Mark the location and withdraw the torsion bar from the lower control arm.
To install:
5. To install, apply a generous amount of grease to the serrated ends of the torsion bar.
6. Hold the rubber bumpers in contact with the lower control arm. Raise the vehicle up under the lower control arm to accomplish this.
7. Insert the front end of the torsion bar into the control arm.

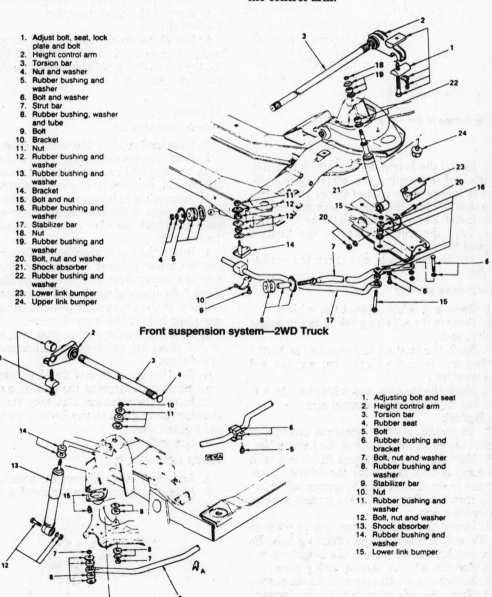

1. Adjust bolt, seat, lock plate and bolt
2. Height control arm
3. Torsion bar
4. Nut and washer
5. Rubber bushing and washer
6. Bolt and washer
7. Strut bar
8. Rubber bushing, washer and tube
9. Bolt
10. Bracket
11. Nut
12. Rubber bushing and washer
13. Rubber bushing and washer
14. Bracket
15. Bolt and nut
16. Rubber bushing and washer
17. Stabilizer bar
18. Nut
19. Rubber bushing and washer
20. Bolt, nut and washer
21. Shock absorber
22. Rubber bushing and washer
23. Lower link bumper
24. Upper link bumper

Front suspension system—2WD Truck

1. Adjusting bolt and seat
2. Height control arm
3. Torsion bar
4. Rubber seat
5. Bolt
6. Rubber bushing and bracket
7. Bolt, nut and washer
8. Rubber bushing and washer
9. Stabilizer bar
10. Nut
11. Rubber bushing and washer
12. Bolt, nut and washer
13. Shock absorber
14. Rubber bushing and washer
15. Lower link bumper

Front suspension system—4WD Truck

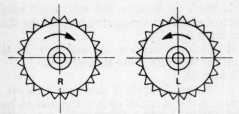

Each torsion bar is matched for Right and Left sides

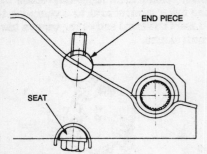

Apply grease to the end piece

8. Install the height control arm in position so it's end is reaching the adjusting bolt. Be sure to lubricate the part of the height control arm that fits into the chassis with grease.

9. Install a new cotter pin in the control arm.

10. Turn the adjusting bolt to the location marked before removal.

11. Lower the vehicle and check the vehicle height.

4-WHEEL DRIVE VEHICLES

1. Raise and safely support the vehicle.

2. Remove the adjusting bolt from the height control arm.

3. Mark the location and remove the height control arm from the torsion bar and the 3rd crossmember.

4. Mark the location and withdraw the torsion bar from the lower control arm.

To install:

5. To install, apply a generous amount of grease to the serrated ends of the torsion bar.

6. Hold the rubber bumpers in contact with the lower control arm. Raise the vehicle up under the lower control arm to accomplish this.

7. Insert the front end of the torsion bar into the control arm.

8. Install the height control arm in position so it's end is reaching the adjusting bolt. Be sure to lubricate the part of the height control arm that fits into the chassis with grease.

9. Install a new cotter pin in the control arm.

10. Turn the adjusting bolt to the location marked before removal.

11. Lower the vehicle and check the vehicle height.

Shock Absorbers

REMOVAL AND INSTALLATION

RWD I-Mark
RWD Impulse

1. Raise the car and support it safely. Remove the front wheel.

2. Disconnect the shock absorber from the upper control arm using two wrenches.

3. Remove the shock absorber nuts from the engine compartment. On the Impulse models, remove the lower shock absorber through bolt from the shock absorber bushing.

4. Remove the shock absorber.

To install:

5. Install the shock absorber and torque the control arm nut to 25 ft. lbs. (34 Nm). Tighten the top nut to the end of the threads on the rod. Use lock nuts.

All Trucks

2-WHEEL DRIVE VEHICLES

1. Raise and support the vehicle safely.

2. Hold the upper stem of the shock absorber from turning and remove the upper stem retaining nut, retainer and rubber grommet.

3. Remove the bolt retaining the lower shock absorber pivot to the lower control arm and remove the shock absorber from the vehicle.

To install:

4. Install the shock absorber by first installing the lower retainer and rubber grommet over the upper stem and then, installing the shock fully extended up through the upper control arm so the upper stem passes through the mounting hole in the frame bracket.

5. Install the upper rubber grommet, retainer and attaching nut over the shock absorber upper stem.

6. Hold the upper stem of the shock absorber from turning and tighten the retaining nut.

7. Install the retainers attaching the shock absorber lower pivot to the lower control arm and tighten them.

8. Lower the vehicle.

4-WHEEL DRIVE VEHICLES

1. Raise and safely support the vehicle.

2. Hold the upper stem of the shock absorber

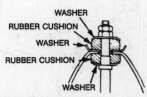

Shock absorber installation in engine compartment—RWD I-Mark and Impulse

from turning and remove the upper stem retaining nut, retainer and rubber grommet.

3. Remove the bolt retaining the lower shock absorber pivot to the lower control arm and remove the shock absorber from the vehicle.

To install:

4. Install the shock absorber by first installing the lower retainer and rubber grommet over the upper stem and then, installing the shock fully extended up through the upper control arm so the upper stem passes through the mounting hole in the frame bracket.

5. Install the upper rubber grommet, retainer and attaching nut over the shock absorber upper stem.

6. Hold the upper stem of the shock absorber from turning and tighten the retaining nut.

7. Install the retainers attaching the shock absorber lower pivot to the lower control arm and tighten them.

8. Lower the vehicle.

TESTING

Visually inspect the shock absorber. If there is evidence of leakage and the shock absorber is covered with oil, the shock is defective and should be replaced.

If there is no sign of excessive leakage (a small amount of weeping is normal) bounce the car at one corner by pressing down on the fender or bumper and releasing. When you have the car bouncing as much as you can, release the fender or bumper. The car should stop bouncing after the first rebound. If the bouncing continues past the center point of the bounce more than once, the shock absorbers are worn and should be replaced.

MacPherson Struts

REMOVAL AND INSTALLATION

FWD I-Mark

1. Loosen the front wheel lug nuts, raise and support the front of the vehicle safely and remove the wheel and tire assembly.

2. Remove the brake hose clip-to-strut bolt (if so equipped). Install a drive axle cover, to protect the axle boot.

3. Remove the bolts attaching the strut to the steering knuckle.

4. Remove the two strut tower nuts and remove the strut assembly from the vehicle.

To install:

5. Install the strut assembly and two strut tower nuts.

6. Install the bolts attaching the strut to the steering knuckle.

7. Install the brake hose clip-to-strut bolt (if so equipped).

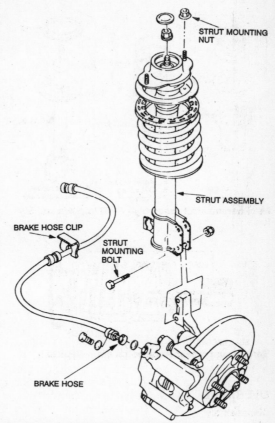

MacPherson strut assembly—FWD I-Mark

8. Install the front wheel.

9. Lower the vehicle.

10. The two strut tower nuts must be tightened before the lower strut bolts. The strut tower nuts should be torqued to 40 ft. lbs. (54 Nm) and the lower strut bolts should be torqued to 86 ft. lbs. (117 Nm).

FWD Impulse
Stylus

1. Disconnect the flexible brake hose from the strut.

2. Disconnect the speed sensor from the strut, if equipped with ABS.

3. Remove the knuckle-to-strut bolts.

4. Open the hood and remove the three upper mount nuts.

5. Remove the strut assembly.

To install:

1. Install the strut and three upper nuts. Torque the nuts to 58 ft. lbs. (78 Nm).

2. Install the knuckle-to-strut bolts with new lock nuts. Torque to 115 ft. lbs. (156 Nm).

3. Install the brake hose and bleed the system as outlined in Chapter 9.

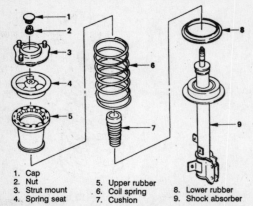

1. Cap
2. Nut
3. Strut mount
4. Spring seat
5. Upper rubber
6. Coil spring
7. Cushion
8. Lower rubber
9. Shock absorber

MacPherson strut assembly—FWD Impulse and Stylus

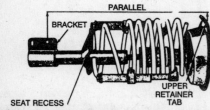

Spring compressor installed on strut—typical

OVERHAUL

Disassembly

CAUTION: *The MacPherson strut and spring are under extreme pressure! NEVER remove the center strut nut without first installing an approved MacPherson strut spring compressor! Severe personal injury may result if this procedure is not followed correctly!*

1. Remove the strut assembly from the vehicle and place in holding fixture.
2. Remove the cap from the upper mount to expose the center nut. DO NOT remove at this time.
3. Install an approved MacPherson strut spring compressor to the spring. DO NOT over compress the spring! Compress far enough to release the pressure from the spring seat.
4. After compressing the spring, remove the center nut, upper mount, spring seat, rubber and spring.
5. Remove the cushion and lower rubber from the strut.

Assembly

1. Check the strut for oil leaks, coil spring for cracks and distortion and upper mount bearing for abnormal noise and defective turning. Replace components if damage is found.
2. Install the cushion and lower rubber to the strut.

3. Install the spring, rubber, upper mount and center nut after compressing the spring.
4. Install the cap to the upper mount to expose the center nut. Remove the spring compressor after releasing the pressure.
5. Install the strut assembly to the vehicle.

Upper Ball Joint

INSPECTION

Grasp the top of the front wheel and pull it in and out several times to check for excessive movement of the ball joint; if no movement exist, the joint is in good shape.

REMOVAL AND INSTALLATION

RWD I-Mark and Impulse

1. Raise the car and support it safely. Remove the wheel.
2. Remove the upper brake caliper bolt and slide the hose retaining clip back about ½ in. (13mm).
3. Remove the lower shock absorber nut and bolt and push the shock absorber up.
4. Place a hydraulic jack under the outer extreme of the lower control arm and raise until level.
5. Loosen the upper ball joint nut until the top of the nut is flush with the top of the ball joint.
6. Using special tool J–26407 or equivalent, disconnect the upper ball joint from the steering knuckle.

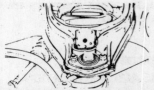

Installing the upper ball joint in the control arm—RWD I-Mark and Impulse

Removing the upper control arm from the crossmember—RWD I-Mark and Impulse

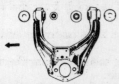

Installation of the upper control arm—RWD I-Mark and Impulse

7. Remove the two bolts connecting the upper ball joint to the upper control arm. Remove the ball joint.

To install:

8. Install the new ball joint in the control arm so that the cut-off portion is facing outward. Torque all attaching nuts and bolts.

NOTE: *The car should be aligned whenever any suspension components are replaced. The cut-off portion of the ball joint is to change the suspension camber 1 degree.*

All Trucks

1. Raise and safely support the vehicle. Remove the wheel and tire assembly.
2. Remove the tension from the torsion bar.
3. Remove the upper ball joint-to-steering knuckle nut.
4. Using a ball joint separator tool, separate the upper ball joint from the steering knuckle.
5. Remove the upper ball joint-to-upper control arm bolts and the ball joint.

To install:

6. Install the ball joint and torque the upper ball joint-to-upper control arm bolts to 21–25 ft. lbs. (29–35 Nm) and the upper ball joint-to-steering knuckle nut to 72–87 ft. lbs. (96–117 Nm) for 2WD or to 65–80 ft. lbs. (88–108 Nm) for 4WD.
7. Adjust the tension on the torsion bar and lower the vehicle.

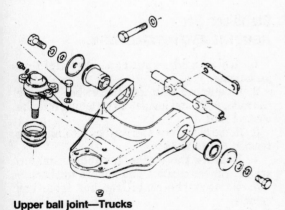

Upper ball joint—Trucks

Lower Ball Joint

INSPECTION

1. Raise and safely support the front of the vehicle.
2. Using a large pry bar, place it under the front wheel and try to pry the wheel upwards.
3. If excessive upward movement or clunking is noticed, the ball joint is damaged and requires replacement.

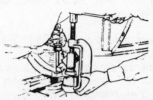

Removing the lower ball joint from the steering knuckle

Removing the lower ball joint from the lower control arm—RWD I-Mark

REMOVAL AND INSTALLATION

RWD I-Mark

1. Raise the car and support it safely. Remove the front wheel.
2. Remove the tie rod end cotter pin and castle nut. Discard the pin and separate the tie rod end with a suspension fork. Remove the tie rod from the steering knuckle.
3. Remove the stabilizer bar bolt and grommet assembly from the lower control arm.
4. Remove the upper brake caliper bolt and slide the brake hose retaining clip back about ½ in. (13mm).
5. Remove the shock absorber lower bolt and push the shock up.

CAUTION: *Secure a safety chain through the upper and lower control arms to prevent the possibility of the spring coming out and causing serious damage or injury. Allow enough room to get the ball joint out.*

6. Place a hydraulic jack under the outer extremity of the lower control arm and raise it until level.
7. Loosen the ball joint lock nut until the top of the nut is flush with the top of the ball joint.
8. Using special tool J–26407 or equivalent, disconnect the lower ball joint from the steering knuckle.
9. Remove the hub assembly and steering knuckle from the lower ball joint and support with a wire or rope.
10. Remove the lower ball joint from the control arm using tool J–9519–03 or equivalent.

To install:

1. Install the lower ball joint into the control arm using tool J–9519–03 or equivalent.
2. Install the hub assembly and steering knuckle to the lower and upper ball joint.
3. Tighten the ball joint lock nut until the slot in the nut is aligned to the hole in the stud.

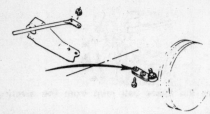

Lower ball joint—FWD I-Mark shown, Impulse and Stylus similar

Do NOT overtighten. About 25 ft. lbs. (34 Nm) is enough.

4. Install the shock absorber lower bolt.

5. Install the upper brake caliper bolt and the brake hose retaining clip.

6. Install the stabilizer bar bolt and grommet assembly to the lower control arm.

7. Install the tie rod end cotter pin and castle nut.

8. Install the front wheel and lower the vehicle.

FWD I-Mark, Impulse and Stylus

1. Loosen the wheel nuts.

2. Raise the vehicle and support it on jackstands.

3. Remove the wheel and tire assembly.

4. Remove the two nuts retaining the ball joint to the tension rod and control arm assembly.

5. Remove the pinch bolt retaining the ball joint to the steering knuckle.

6. Remove the ball joint.

To install:

7. Install the ball joint.

8. Install the pinch bolt retaining the ball joint to the steering knuckle.

9. Install the two nuts retaining the ball joint to the tension rod and control arm assembly.

10. Install the wheel and tire assembly.

11. Lower the vehicle.

12. Torque the steering knuckle arm nut to 51 ft. lbs. (68 Nm) and the tension rod nut to 80 ft. lbs. (108 Nm).

P'up, Amigo, Trooper and Rodeo

1. Raise and safely support the vehicle.

2. Remove the wheel and tire assembly.

3. Release the torsion bar tension.

4. Remove the cotter pin and castellated nut which retains the ball joint to the steering knuckle.

5. Remove the lower ball joint-to-lower control arm and strut rod.

6. Remove the ball joint.

To install:

7. Install the lower ball joint by mounting the joint to the lower control arm and torque

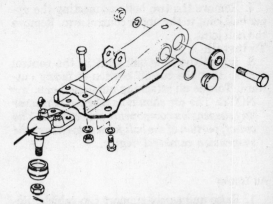

Lower ball joint—P'up and Amigo shown, Trooper and Rodeo similar

the bolts to 45–56 ft. lbs. (61–76 Nm) for 2WD or to 68–83 ft. lbs. (93–113 Nm) for 4WD.

8. Install the ball joint stud into the steering knuckle and install the castellated nut and torque it to 101–116 ft. lbs. (137–157 Nm) for 2WD or to 87–111 ft. lbs. (117–137 Nm) for 4WD and just enough additional torque to align the cotter pin hole with a castellation on the nut. Install a new cotter pin.

9. Lubricate the lower ball joint through the grease fitting.

10. Adjust the torsion bar tension.

11. Install the wheel assembly and lower the vehicle.

Stabilizer Bar

REMOVAL AND INSTALLATION

1. Raise and support the vehicle on jackstands.

2. If equipped with a stabilizer bar, remove the nuts, bolts and insulators retaining it to the control arm.

3. Remove the nut and washer retaining the tension rod to the body.

4. Remove the washers, rubber cushion spacer, rubber cushion and 2 more washers.

5. Remove the stabilizer bar from the vehicle.

To install:

6. Install the stabilizer bar to the vehicle.

7. Install the washers, rubber cushion spacer, rubber cushion and 2 more washers.

8. Install the nut and washer retaining the tension rod to the body.

9. Install the nuts, bolts and insulators retaining it to the control arm.

10. Install the front wheels and lower the vehicle.

11. Torque the stabilizer bar nut to 51 ft. lbs. (68 Nm).

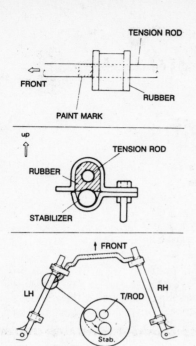

Stabilizer bar—FWD I-Mark

Strut Rod

REMOVAL AND INSTALLATION

FWD I-Mark

1. Raise the vehicle and support with jackstands. Remove the front wheel.
2. Remove the stabilizer bar, if so equipped.
3. Remove the strut rod-to-control arm bolts.

4. Remove the strut rod-to-body nut and washers.
5. Remove the rubber cushions and strut rod.

To install:

6. Install the rubber cushions and strut rod.
7. Install the strut rod-to-body nut and washers.
8. Install the strut rod-to-control arm bolts.
9. Install the stabilizer bar, if so equipped.
10. Install the wheels and lower the vehicle.

RWD Impulse

1. Raise the vehicle and support with jackstands.
2. Remove the strut bar cross bar.
3. Remove the locknut and nut from the end of the strut rod.
4. Remove the strut rod-to-lower control arm bolts and remove the rod.

To install:

5. Install the strut rod and fasteners.
6. Tighten the strut rod to the dimensions as shown in the illustration.
7. Torque the locknuts to 80 ft. lbs. (108 Nm).
8. Install the wheels and lower the vehicle.

P'up and Amigo (2WD)

1. Raise the vehicle and support with jackstands.
2. Remove the strut bar cross bar.
3. Remove the locknut and nut from the end of the strut rod.
4. Remove the strut rod-to-lower control arm bolts and remove the rod.

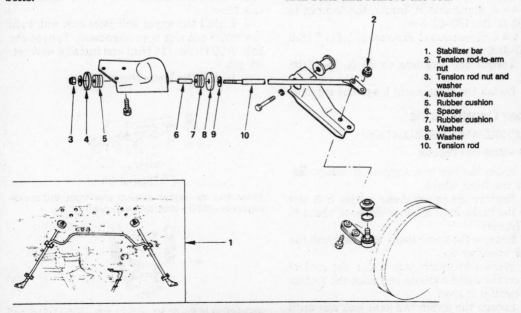

1. Stabilizer bar
2. Tension rod-to-arm nut
3. Tension rod nut and washer
4. Washer
5. Rubber cushion
6. Spacer
7. Rubber cushion
8. Washer
9. Washer
10. Tension rod

Strut rod and stabilizer bar—FWD I-Mark

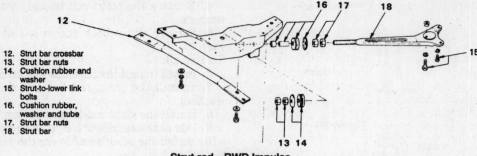

12. Strut bar crossbar
13. Strut bar nuts
14. Cushion rubber and washer
15. Strut-to-lower link bolts
16. Cushion rubber, washer and tube
17. Strut bar nuts
18. Strut bar

Strut rod—RWD Impulse

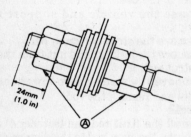

Strut rod positioning—RWD Impulse

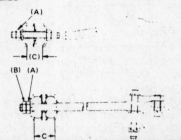

Strut rod positioning—P'up and Amigo (2WD on top)

To install:

5. Install the strut rod and fasteners.

6. Tighten the strut rod to the dimensions as shown in the illustration.

- 4 × 2, dimension A, torque nut to 58–72 ft. lbs. (78–98 Nm)
- 4 × 2, dimension C, distance of 1.2–1.3 inch (30.5–32.5mm)
- 4 × 4, dimension A, torque nut to 14 ft. lbs. (20 Nm)
- 4 × 4, dimension B, torque the locknut to 41–61 ft. lbs. (55–81 Nm)
- 4 × 4, dimension C, distance of 1.4–1.5 inch (36.0–38.0mm)

7. Torque the locknuts to 80 ft. lbs. (108 Nm).

8. Install the wheels and lower the vehicle.

Upper Control Arms

REMOVAL AND INSTALLATION

RWD I-Mark and Impulse

1. Raise the car and support it safely. Remove the front wheel.

2. Remove the upper brake caliper bolt and slide the brake hose retainer clip back about ½ in. (13mm).

3. Remove the lower shock bolt and push the shock absorber up.

4. Place a hydraulic jack under the control arm on the outer extreme and raise the control arm until it is level.

5. Loosen the upper ball joint lock nut until the top of the nut is flush with the top of the ball joint. Disconnect the upper ball joint from the steering knuckle using tool J–26407 or equivalent.

6. Disconnect and remove the through bolt connecting the upper control arm to the crossmember. Remove the upper control arm.

To install:

7. Install the upper control arm and install the through bolt connecting the upper control arm to the crossmember. Do NOT tighten at this time.

8. Install the upper ball joint lock nut until the cotter pin slot is in alignment. Torque the bolt to 20 ft. lbs. (25 Nm) and install a new cotter pin.

9. Install the lower shock bolt.

Removing the upper control arm from the crossmember—RWD I-Mark and Impulse

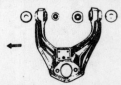

Installation of the upper control arm—RWD I-Mark and Impulse

10. Install the upper brake caliper bolt and slide the brake hose retainer clip into retainer.

11. Install the front wheel and lower the vehicle.

12. Installation is the reverse of removal. On installation, make sure the smaller washer is on the inner face of the front arm and larger washer is on the inner face of the rear arm.

13. With the vehicle resting on the suspension torque the upper control arm through bolt to 65 ft. lbs. (88 Nm).

NOTE: *Always check the camber when working around the upper control arm area.*

All Trucks

NOTE: *The upper control arm and ball joint are replaced as an assembly on some vehicles.*

1. Raise and safely support the vehicle on the lower control arms.

2. Remove the wheel and tire assembly.

3. Remove the cotter pin nut fastening the upper control arm and upper ball joint assembly and disconnect the upper control arm from the steering knuckle.

NOTE: *Do not allow the steering knuckle to hang by the flexible brake line. Wire the steering knuckle up to the frame temporarily.*

4. Remove the bolts from the upper pivot shaft and remove the upper control arm from the bracket. Be sure to note the position and number of shims used for adjusting the camber and caster angles when removing the upper control arm. The shims must be replaced in their original position.

5. To remove the pivot shaft and bushings from the upper control arm assembly, remove the bushing nuts from the pivot shaft by loosening them alternately, then remove the pivot shaft.

To install:

6. To install the upper control arm and ball joint assembly, first install the pivot shaft boots to the pivot shaft.

7. Fill the internal part of the bushings with grease and screw the bushings into the pivot shaft. Be sure to screw the right-side and the left-side bushings alternately into the pivot shafts carefully avoiding getting grease on the outer face of the bushings. Tighten the nuts to 250 ft. lbs.

NOTE: *Be sure that the control arm and bushings are centered properly and that the control arm rotates with resistance but not binding on the pivot shaft when tightened to the proper torque.*

To install:

8. Install the grease fittings and lubricate the parts with grease through the grease fittings.

9. Install the ball joint stud through the steering knuckle. Install the castellated nut and tighten it to 75 ft. lbs. and just enough additional torque to install the cotter pin. Use a new cotter pin.

10. Mount the upper control arm to the chassis frame and install the shims in their original positions between the pivot shaft and bracket. Tighten the pivot shaft attaching nuts to 55 ft. lbs.

NOTE: *Tighten the thinner shim pack's nut first for improved shaft-to-frame clamping force and torque retention.*

1. Nut and cotter pin
2. Nut and cotter pin
3. Nut and cotter pin
4. Steering link end
5. Knuckle
6. Upper end
7. Bolt and washer
8. Nut assembly
9. Upper link assembly
10. Nut and plate
11. Bushing
12. Fulcrum pin
13. Lower end
14. Bolt, nut and washer
15. Lower link assembly
16. Bushing

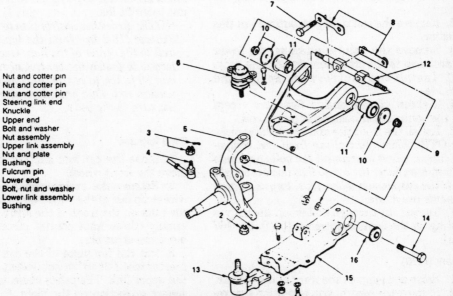

Steering knuckle and control arm—2WD truck

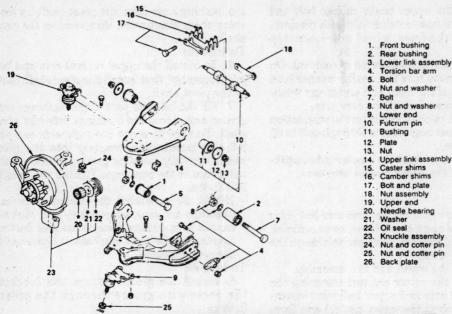

1. Front bushing
2. Rear bushing
3. Lower link assembly
4. Torsion bar arm
5. Bolt
6. Nut and washer
7. Bolt
8. Nut and washer
9. Lower end
10. Fulcrum pin
11. Bushing
12. Plate
13. Nut
14. Upper link assembly
15. Caster shims
16. Camber shims
17. Bolt and plate
18. Nut assembly
19. Upper end
20. Needle bearing
21. Washer
22. Oil seal
23. Knuckle assembly
24. Nut and cotter pin
25. Nut and cotter pin
26. Back plate

Exploded view of the steering knuckle and control arm assembly—4WD

11. Install the dust cover.

12. Install the wheel assembly and lower the vehicle.

Lower Control Arm

REMOVAL AND INSTALLATION

RWD I-Mark

1. Raise the vehicle and support with jackstands. Remove the front wheels. Lower the control arm onto floor jack or equivalent to release the spring tension before removing the spring.

2. Remove the coil spring as outlined in this Chapter.

3. Remove the bolts connecting the lower control arm to the crossmember and the body.

4. Install the control arm, spring and knuckle.

5. Tighten all suspension fasteners except for the control arm bushing through bolt.

6. Install the front tire and lower the vehicle.

NOTE: *When reinstalling front end components, it's best to snug all the bolts and nuts first, then lower the car so that there is weight on the suspension when final torque adjustments are made.*

7. Torque the through bolt when the body is resting on the front suspension (50 ft. lbs. [67 Nm]).

I-Mark (FWD)

1. Raise and support the front of the vehicle.

2. Remove the control arm to tension arm retaining nuts and bolts.

3. Remove the nut/bolt securing the control arm to the body.

4. Remove the control arm and check for cracking or distortion.

To install:

NOTE: *When reinstalling front end components, it's best to snug all the bolts and nuts first, then lower the car so that there is weight on the suspension when final torque adjustments are made.*

5. Install the control arm and torque the knuckle side nut to 80 ft. lbs. and the body side nut to 40 ft. lbs.

NOTE: *Raise the control arm to a distance of 386mm (15.2 in.) from the top of the wheel well to the center of the hub. Use 41 ft. lbs. of torque to fasten the control arm to the body and 80 ft. lbs. to secure the control arm to the tension rod. This procedure aligns the bushing arm to the body.*

RWD Impulse

1. Raise the car and support it safely. Remove the front wheel.

2. Remove the brake caliper assembly and wire it up out of the way. Mark the position of the nuts on the front of the strut bar for reassembly (these nuts control caster). Then remove the strut bar.

3. Put the top plate of the coil spring compressor tool J-36567 or equivalent on the top of the upper link. The safety chain is welded to a square projection on the plate. Run on end of the safety chain through the spring, about 3

coils from the top and secure the ends of the chain together. Be sure when setting this up, not to interfere with the brake pipe.

CAUTION: *During all the following Steps, do not work directly beside the coil spring. Although it is held by the upper and lower links and should not come loose, it is a good idea to stay out its direct line of removal.*

4. Place a floor jack under the lower control arm an apply slight upward pressure. Remove the knuckle and rotor assembly from the lower ball joint. Reinstall the old nuts on the ball joint studs to prevent damage to the threads.

5. Lower the floor jack slowly. The lower link will swing down to its lowest point. The spring ends will be held by the upper and lower seats. Remove the floor jack completely.

6. Set the lower plate of the special coil compressing tool into the coil spring. On the right hand side of the vehicle, put the plate into the 3rd space between the coils counting from the lower link. On the left hand side of the vehicle, put the plate into the 2nd space between the coils counting from the lower control arm. Install the threaded rods, bearing spacers and t-handles to the top of the lower plate.

NOTE: *Do not allow the spring to angle toward the front or rear of the vehicle.*

7. Press downward and inward on the lower control arm until the spring end is free of the lower seat. If necesary, loosen the lower link pivot bolt to allow more link travel. Remove the lower link bolt, then remove the coil spring together with the lower control arm.

8. After the spring has cleared the lower spring seat, turn the t-handle of the tool equal amounts to release the spring tension.

9. Remove the bushing through bolt and lower control arm.

To install:

a. When installing the upper control arm washers install the small washer on the inboard side of the rear end.

b. Leave the upper and lower control arm link bolts semi-tight as they are to be torqued to specifications after completion of installation with the wheels lowered to the floor.

c. When installing the upper ball joint to the control arm the cutaway portion of the ball joint should be turned outward.

10. Use the following torque guide:
- Upper link retaining bolt — 47 ft. lbs.
- Upper link ball joint retaining nut — 41 ft. lbs.
- Lower link retaining bolt — 68 ft. lbs.
- Lower link ball joint retaining nut — top bolt 76 ft. lbs.; lower bolt 47 ft. lbs.
- Upper ball joint retaining nut — 39 ft. lbs.
- Lower ball joint retaining nut — 58 ft. lbs.
- Stabilizer self lock nut — 19 ft. lbs.

- Stabilizer bracket bolt — 14 ft. lbs.
- Strut bar bolt — 72 ft. lbs.
- Strut bar front nut — 47 ft. lbs.
- Strut bar rear nut — 114 ft. lbs.
- Tie rod end nut — 61 ft. lbs.
- Brake caliper assembly bolt — 36 ft. lbs.

FWD Impulse and Stylus

1. Raise the vehicle and support with jackstands.

2. Disconnect the stabilizer bar from the lower control arm.

3. Remove the pinch bolt from the ball joint.

4. Remove the front and rear LCA bushing bolts and remove the control arm.

To install:

NOTE: *When reinstalling front end components, it's best to snug all the bolts and nuts first, then lower the car so that there is weight on the suspension when final torque adjustments are made.*

5. Install the control arm and bolts. Do NOT tighten the bolts at this time.

6. Install the pinch bolt at the ball joint and connect the stabilizer bar.

7. Install the front wheel and lower the vehicle.

8. Torque the rear LCA bushing bolt to 50 ft. lbs. (68 Nm) and the front bolt to 94 ft. lbs. (128 Nm).

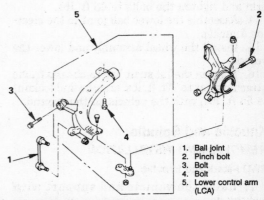

1. Ball joint
2. Pinch bolt
3. Bolt
4. Bolt
5. Lower control arm (LCA)

Lower control arm—FWD Impulse and Stylus

All Trucks

1. Raise and safely support the vehicle.

2. Remove the wheel and tire assembly.

3. Remove the strut bar by removing the frame side bracket and the double nuts, washer and the rubber bushing from the front side of the strut bar. Remove the strut bar-to-lower control arm bolts and remove the bar.

4. Disconnect the stabilizer bar from the lower control arm.

5. Remove the torsion bar.

6. Disconnect the shock absorber from the lower control arm.

7. Remove the lower ball joint from the lower control arm joint.

8. Remove the retaining nut and drive out the bolt holding the lower control arm to the chassis with a soft metal drift. Remove the lower control arm from the vehicle.

To install:

NOTE: *When reinstalling front end components, it's best to snug all the bolts and nuts first, then lower the car so that there is weight on the suspension when final torque adjustments are made.*

9. To install the lower control arm, install the lower ball joint to the lower control arm. Tighten the retaining nuts to 45 ft. lbs.

10. Mount the lower control arm to the frame. Drive the bolt into position carefully. Use care not to damage the serrated portions. Tighten the nut on the end of the pivot bolt to 135 ft. lbs.

11. Install the stabilizer bar to the lower control arm.

12. Place the washers and bushings on the strut rod and install it through the frame bracket. Install the second set of washers and bushings on the strut rod together with the lockwashers and nut. Leave the nut loose temporarily.

13. Install the strut rod to the lower control arm and tighten the bolts to 45 ft. lbs.

14. Assemble the lower ball joint to the steering knuckle.

15. Install the wheel assembly and lower the vehicle.

16. Tighten the 1st strut bar-to-chassis frame attaching nut to 175 ft. lbs. and the 2nd locknut to 55 ft. lbs. with the vehicle on the ground.

Knuckle and Spindle

REMOVAL AND INSTALLATION

RWD I-Mark and Impulse

1. Raise the vehicle and support with jackstands.

2. Remove the lower shock bolt and push the shock upward.

3. Remove the disc brake caliper and support it out of the way with wire.

4. Remove the tie rod end nut, cotter pin and assembly with the use of a tie rod removing tool J-21687-02 or equivalent. Refer to the tie rod procedures in this Chapter.

5. Remove the front hub and rotor assembly.

6. Remove the dust cover.

7. Place a hydraulic jack under the outer edge of the control arm and raise until level.

8. Loosen the upper and lower ball joint nuts until the top of the nut is flush with the top of the ball stud. Disconnect the ball joints from the steering knuckle using ball joint separator tool J-26407.

To install:

1. Install the steering knuckle and connect the upper and lower ball joints to the knuckle. Install the nuts and torque to 45 ft. lbs. (61 Nm). Align the cott pin hole and install a new cotter pin.

2. Install the dust cover.

3. Install the front hub and rotor assembly.

4. Install the tie rod end, nut and cotter pin. Torque the nut to 25 ft. lbs. (34 Nm) and install a new cotter pin.

5. Install the disc brake caliper.

6. Install the lower shock bolt.

7. Install the front wheel and lower the vehicle.

FWD I-Mark, Impulse and Stylus

1. Raise the vehicle and support with jackstands. Remove the front wheel.

2. Remove the brake caliper and support with a piece of wire.

3. Remove the rotor and hub nut.

4. Remove the tie rod end using a tie rod remover J-21687-02.

5. Remove the pinch bolt and disconnect the lower ball joint.

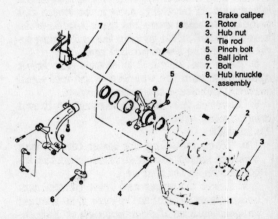

1. Brake caliper
2. Rotor
3. Hub nut
4. Tie rod
5. Pinch bolt
6. Ball joint
7. Bolt
8. Hub knuckle assembly

Steering knuckle—FWD I-Mark, Impulse and Stylus

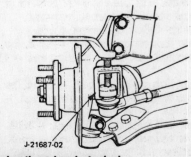

J-21687-02

Removing tie rod end—typical

6. Remove the strut-to-knuckle bolts and knuckle.

To install:

7. Install the knuckle and the strut-to-knuckle bolts.

8. Install the pinch bolt and connect the lower ball joint.

9. Install the tie rod end using a tie rod remover J–21687–02.

10. Install the rotor and hub nut.

11. Install the brake caliper.

12. Install the front wheel and lower the vehicle.

Trucks

2-WHEEL DRIVE

1. **Raise the vehicle and support with jackstands. Remove the front wheel.**

2. Place a hydraulic jack under the lower control arm and raise to release the spring pressure.

3. Remove the upper and lower ball joint cotter pins and loosen the nuts until they are flush with the top of the stud.

4. Using a tie rod end removing tool, disconnect the tie rod end from the knuckle.

5. Remove the brake caliper and hang by a wire as outlined in Chapter 9.

6. Remove the brake rotor and backing plate as outlined in this Chapter.

7. Disconnect the upper and lower ball joints as outlined in this Chapter.

8. Remove the knuckle/spindle assembly. Be careful not to damage the ball joint boots.

To install:

9. Install the knuckle/spindle assembly into the ball joint studs. Be careful not to damage the ball joint boots.

10. Connect the upper and lower ball joints as outlined in this Chapter. Torque the nuts to 10 ft. lbs. (14 Nm) and install new cotter pins.

11. Install the brake rotor and backing plate as outlined in this Chapter.

12. Install the brake caliper as outlined in Chapter 9.

13. Install the tie rod end and torque to 12 ft. lbs. (16 Nm). Install a new cotter pin.

15. Install the front wheels and lower the vehicle. Have the front end aligned by a qualified alignment technician.

4-WHEEL DRIVE

1. **Raise the vehicle and support with jackstands. Remove the front wheels.**

2. Remove the brake caliper, rotor and backing plate as outlined in Chapter 9.

3. Place a hydraulic jack under the lower control arm and raise to release the spring pressure.

4. Remove the upper and lower ball joint cotter pins and loosen the nuts until they are flush with the top of the stud.

5. Using a tie rod end removing tool, disconnect the tie rod end from the knuckle.

1. Nut and cotter pin
2. Nut and cotter pin
3. Nut and cotter pin
4. Steering link end
5. Knuckle
6. Upper end
7. Bolt and washer
8. Nut assembly
9. Upper link
10. Nut and plate
11. Bushing
12. Fulcrum pin
13. Lower end
14. Nut, washer and bolt
15. Lower link
16. Bushing

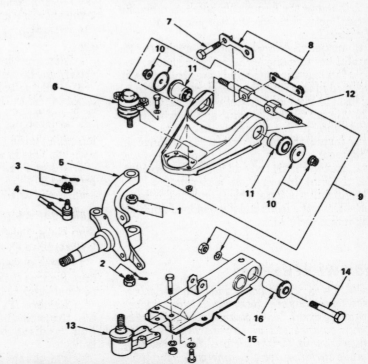

Knuckle and spindle assembly—2WD P'up and Amigo

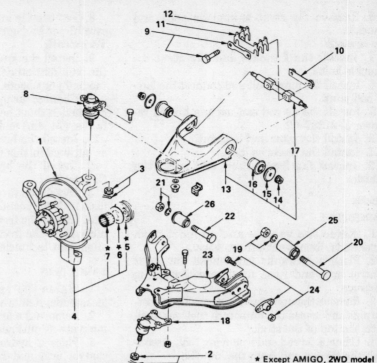

1. Back plate and hub
2. Nut and cotter pin
3. Nut and cotter pin
4. Knuckle
5. Oil seal
6. Washer
7. Needle bearing
8. Upper end
9. Bolt and plate
10. Nut assembly
11. Camber shims
12. Caster shims
13. Upper link
14. Nut
15. Plate
16. Bushing
17. Fulcrum pin
18. Lower end
19. Nut and washer
20. Bolt
21. Nut and washer
22. Bolt
23. Lower link
24. Torsion bar arm bracket
25. Rear side bushing
26. Front side bushing

★ Except AMIGO, 2WD model

Knuckle and spindle—4WD P'up, Amigo, Trooper and Amigo

6. Disconnect the upper and lower ball joints as outlined in this Chapter.

7. Remove the knuckle/spindle assembly. Be careful not to damage the ball joint boots.

To install:

8. Install the knuckle/spindle assembly. Be careful not to damage the ball joint boots.

9. Connect the upper and lower ball joints as outlined in this Chapter. Torque the nuts to 10 ft. lbs. (14 Nm) and install new cotter pins.

10. Install the brake rotor and backing plate as outlined in this Chapter.

11. Install the brake caliper as outlined in Chapter 9.

12. Install the tie rod end and torque to 12 ft. lbs. (16 Nm). Install a new cotter pin.

13. Install the front wheels and lower the vehicle. Have the front end aligned by a qualified alignment technician.

Front Wheel Bearings

CAUTION: *Some brake pads contain asbestos, which has been determined to be a cancer causing agent. Never clean the brake surfaces with compressed air! Avoid inhaling any dust from any brake surface! When cleaning brake surfaces, use a commercially available brake cleaning fluid.*

ADJUSTMENT

RWD I-Mark, Impulse
2-Wheel Drive P'up

1. Raise the car and support it at the lower arm.

2. Remove the hub dust cover and spindle cotter pin. Loosen the nut.

3. While spinning the wheel, snug the nut down to seat the bearings. Do not exert over 12 ft. lbs. of force on the nut.

4. Back the nut off ¼ turn or until it is just lose. Line up the cotter pin hole in the spindle with the hole in the nut.

5. Insert a new cotter pin. Endplay should be between 0.03-0.13mm. If play exceeds this tolerance, the wheel bearings should be replaced.

REMOVAL AND INSTALLATION

RWD I-Mark, Impulse
2-Wheel Drive P'up

1. Raise the car and support it at the lower arm. Remove the wheel. Remove the brake caliper and support it on a wire.

2. Remove the dust cap, cotter pin, castle nut, thrust washer and outside wheel bearing. Pull the disc/hub assembly from the steering knuckle.

3. Pry out the inner seal and remove the inner bearing. If necessary to remove the inner

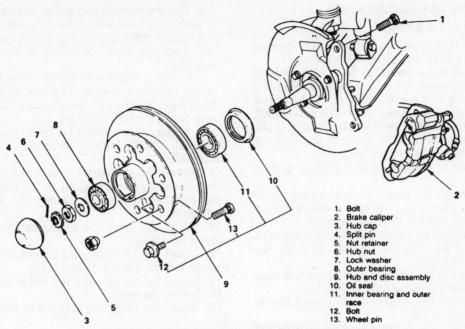

1. Bolt
2. Brake caliper
3. Hub cap
4. Split pin
5. Nut retainer
6. Hub nut
7. Lock washer
8. Outer bearing
9. Hub and disc assembly
10. Oil seal
11. Inner bearing and outer race
12. Bolt
13. Wheel pin

Exploded view of the front wheel assembly—RWD vehicles

bearing races, use a hammer and a brass drift to drive the bearing races from the hub.

4. Clean all parts in kerosene or equivalent, DO NOT use gasoline. After cleaning, check parts for excessive wear and replace damaged parts.

To install:

5. Smear grease inside of hub. Install the bearing races into hub, using a hammer and a brass drift. Drive the races in until they seat against the shoulder of the hub.

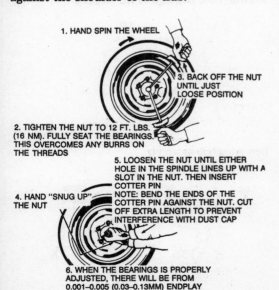

1. HAND SPIN THE WHEEL

3. BACK OFF THE NUT UNTIL JUST LOOSE POSITION

2. TIGHTEN THE NUT TO 12 FT. LBS. (16 NM). FULLY SEAT THE BEARINGS. THIS OVERCOMES ANY BURRS ON THE THREADS

5. LOOSEN THE NUT UNTIL EITHER HOLE IN THE SPINDLE LINES UP WITH A SLOT IN THE NUT. THEN INSERT COTTER PIN

4. HAND "SNUG UP" THE NUT

NOTE: BEND THE ENDS OF THE COTTER PIN AGAINST THE NUT. CUT OFF EXTRA LENGTH TO PREVENT INTERFERENCE WITH DUST CAP

6. WHEN THE BEARINGS IS PROPERLY ADJUSTED, THERE WILL BE FROM 0.001–0.005 (0.03–0.13MM) ENDPLAY

Wheel bearing adjustment—RWD vehicles

6. Pack the bearings with grease and install the inner bearing in the hub. Install a new grease seal, be careful not to damage the seal.

7. Install the disc/hub assembly onto the steering knuckle. Install the outer bearing, thrust washer and castle nut. Tighten the nut until the wheel does not turn freely.

8. Back off the nut until the wheel turns freely and install the cotter pin. Install the dust cap, caliper and wheel. Lower the car.

PACKING

Clean the wheel bearings thoroughly with solvent and check their condition before installation.

CAUTION: *Do not blow the bearing dry with compressed air as this would allow the bearing to turn without lubrication.*

Place a sizable amount of lubricant in the palm of one hand. Using your other hand, work the bearing into the lubricant so that the grease is pushed through the rollers and out the other side. Keep rotating the bearing while continuing to push the lubricant through it.

Front Hub and Wheel Bearing

CAUTION: *Some brake pads contain asbestos, which has been determined to be a cancer causing agent. Never clean the brake surfaces with compressed air! Avoid inhaling any dust from any brake surface! When cleaning brake surfaces, use a commercially available brake cleaning fluid.*

REMOVAL AND INSTALLATION

Front Wheel Drive Cars

DO NOT remove the hub from the steering knuckle unless it is absolutely necessary!

1. Raise and support the front of the vehicle safely and block the rear wheels. Loosen the wheel nuts. Remove the cotter pin, hub nut and thrust washer. Make sure the driveshaft splines are loose inside the hub. Damage to the driveshaft may result if the shaft is pulled out while remove the hub assembly.

2. Remove the caliper and support it on a wire.

3. Remove the rotor. With hub remover J-34866 and slide hammer J-2619-01 or eqivalents, remove the hub assembly.

4. Remove the tie rod nut. Using a ball joint removal tool, separate the tie rod from the steering knuckle.

5. Remove the two ball joint-to-control arm/tension rod retaining nuts and bolts.

6. Remove the strut-to-steering knuckle retaining nuts/bolts.

7. Remove the steering knuckle, bearing and oil seal. When removing the axle shaft from the steering knuckle, be careful not to drop it and support it with a wire.

NOTE: *A arbor press or equivalent is used to separate the hub and bearing from the steering knuckle.*

8. **To remove the bearing from the steering knuckle,** use the following procedure:

a. Using a suitable seal puller, remove the oil seals from both sides of the hub assembly.

b. Using suitable snapring pliers, remove the snaprings from both sides of the hub assembly.

c. Using a suitable arbor press and the proper bearing removal tools, press the inside inner race, bearing and outside inner bearing race out of the hub assembly.

d. Using a press, install the bearings, seals and hub into the knuckle assembly.

To install:

9. Install the steering knuckle assembly. When installing the driveshaft to the steering knuckle, be careful not to damage the driveshaft boots.

10. Install the strut-to-steering knuckle retaining nuts/bolts.

11. Install the two ball joint-to-control arm/tension rod retaining nuts and bolts.

12. Install the tie rod, nut and cotter pin.

13. Install the rotor.

14. Install the caliper as outlined in Chapter 9.

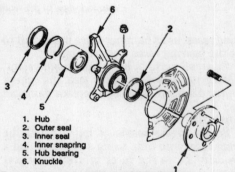

1. Hub
2. Outer seal
3. Inner seal
4. Inner snapring
5. Hub bearing
6. Knuckle

Front hub and bearings—FWD vehicles

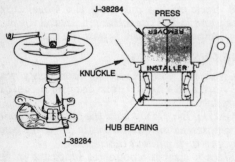

Installing wheel bearing and hub

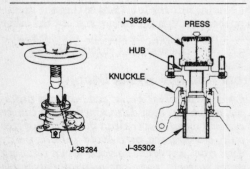

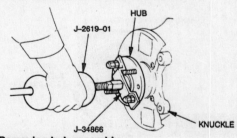

Removing hub assembly

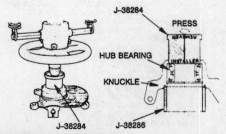

Removing wheel bearings

15. Install the front wheel and lower the vehicle.

  a. Tension rod to control arm bolts — 80 ft. lbs.

  b. Strut to steering knuckle — 87 ft. lbs.

  c. Tie rod castle nut — 29 ft. lbs.

  d. Wheel bearing nut — 137 ft. lbs.

4-Wheel Drive Trucks

1. Raise and safely support the vehicle. Remove the wheel assembly.

2. Remove the brake caliper and support it on a wire. Remove the rotor and dust shield.

3. Remove the axle shaft from the hub.

4. Remove the tie rod end-to-steering knuck-

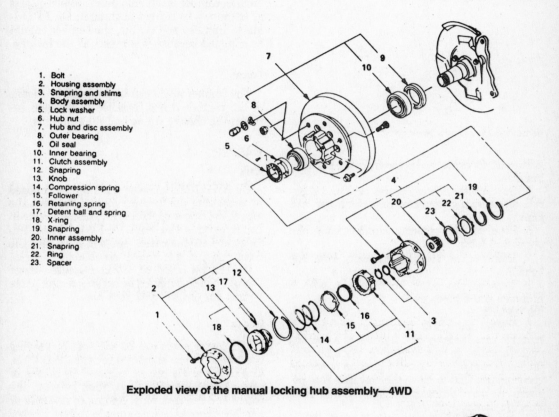

1. Bolt
2. Housing assembly
3. Snapring and shims
4. Body assembly
5. Lock washer
6. Hub nut
7. Hub and disc assembly
8. Outer bearing
9. Oil seal
10. Inner bearing
11. Clutch assembly
12. Snapring
13. Knob
14. Compression spring
15. Follower
16. Retaining spring
17. Detent ball and spring
18. X-ring
19. Snapring
20. Inner assembly
21. Snapring
22. Ring
23. Spacer

Exploded view of the manual locking hub assembly—4WD

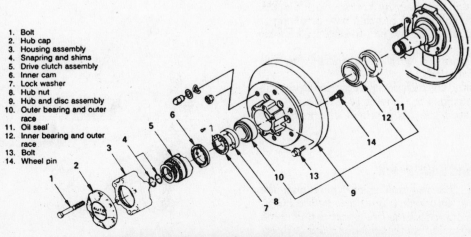

1. Bolt
2. Hub cap
3. Housing assembly
4. Snapring and shims
5. Drive clutch assembly
6. Inner cam
7. Lock washer
8. Hub nut
9. Hub and disc assembly
10. Outer bearing and outer race
11. Oil seal
12. Inner bearing and outer race
13. Bolt
14. Wheel pin

Exploded view of the automatic locking hub assembly—4WD

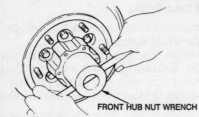

FRONT HUB NUT WRENCH

Removing the spindle nut

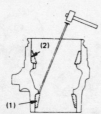

Removing the outer bearing races

le nut and separate the tie rod from the steering knuckle.

5. Support the lower control arm and separate the steering knuckle from the lower ball joint.

6. Separate the steering knuckle from the upper ball joint.

7. Remove the steering knuckle from the vehicle.

8. Remove the outer bearing race with a hammer and a brass drift.

To install:

9. Install the outer bearing races using a suitable race installer and a press. If a bearing race installer is not available. Grind about 0.25–0.50mm off of the outer portion of the old race and use that to drive the new race into position. Be careful not to damage the new race. Bearing damage will result.

10. Torque the ball joint nuts to 75 ft. lbs.

11. Install the steering knuckle to the vehicle.

12. Install the steering knuckle to the upper ball joint. Install the nut and new cotter pin.

13. Install the tie rod end-to-steering knuckle nut.

14. If equipped with 4WD, install the axle shaft to the hub.

15. Install the dust cover, rotor and brake caliper as outlined in Chapter 9.

16. Install the front wheel and lower the vehicle.

Front End Alignment

NOTE: *Steering problems are not always the result of improper alignment. Before aligning the car, check the tire pressure and check all suspension components for damage or excessive wear.*

CAMBER

Cars

On all I-Mark (RWD) and early model Impulse, camber angle can be increased approximately 1 degree by removing the upper ball joint, rotating it ½ turn and reinstalling it with the cut-off portion of the upper flange on the inboard side of the control arm. On late Impulse models, camber is not adjustable. Replace parts as necessary to correct alignment. On FWD I-Mark, Impulse and Stylus, the camber cannot be adjusted because it is preset at the factory.

Trucks

The camber angle can be adjusted by means of the camber shims installed in position between the chassis frame and fulcrum pins.

CASTER

Cars

On RWD I-Mark caster angle can be changed by realigning the washers located between the legs of the upper control arm. Washers come in two sizes 3mm and 9mm. On FWD I-Mark, Impulse and Stylus caster angle is built into the front end and is not itself adjustable.

NOTE: *On 1983–89 RWD Impulse, caster angle can be adjusted by varying length of the strut bar (adjust with lock nut).*

Trucks

The caster angle can be adjusted by varying the length of the strut rod for the 2WD P'up. The caster angle can be adjusted by means of caster shims installed in position between the frame and fulcrum pins. Adding to one side or another change the caster angle. Adjust camber after adjusting caster.

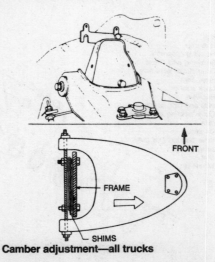

FRONT

FRAME

SHIMS

Camber adjustment—all trucks

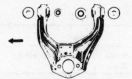

Caster adjustment—RWD I-Mark and Impulse

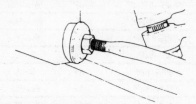

Caster adjustment—2WD P'up

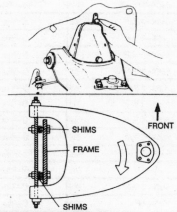

SHIMS
FRAME
FRONT
SHIMS

Caster adjustment—4WD trucks

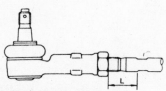

Toe-in adjustment—all vehicles

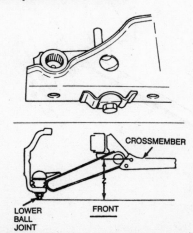

CROSSMEMBER

LOWER
BALL
JOINT

FRONT

Adjusting vehicle height—all trucks

TOE-IN ANGLE

All Vehicles

Toe in is controlled by adjusting the tie rod. To adjust the toe in setting loosen the nuts at the tie rod end. Rotate the rod as required to adjust the toe in. Retighten the cover and locknuts, check that the rubber bellows is not twisted on vehicles equipped with rack and pinion steering systems. For all specifications, see the Alignment Specs in this Chapter.

VEHICLE HEIGHT ADJUSTMENT

The vehicle height can be adjusted by turning the torsion bar adjusting bolts to achieve the desired vehicle height.

CAUTION: *Do NOT over or under tighten the torsion bar adjusters. The torsion bar may break due to over extension. A broken torsion bar may cause the vehicle to loose control causing personal injury.*

REAR SUSPENSION

Coil Springs

REMOVAL AND INSTALLATION

RWD I-Mark and Impulse

1. Raise the rear of the car on the axle housing and support it at the jack side brackets with jackstands.
2. Position a hydraulic jack under the differential housing, but use a light contact pressure.
3. Disconnect the shock absorber lower mounting bolts.
4. Slowly lower or separate the axle assembly from the car body to the point where the spring becomes loose enough to allow removal.

CAUTION: *Do not stress the brake hoses when lowering the axle.*

To install:

5. Position the spring correctly. Make sure that the insulator is in position on top of the spring.
6. Torque the shock absorber lower bolts to 29 ft. lbs. (40 Nm).

FWD I-Mark

1. Raise the rear of the car on the axle housing and support it at the jack side brackets with jackstands.
2. Position a hydraulic jack under the differential rear axle, but use a light contact pressure.
3. Disconnect the shock absorber lower mounting bolts and stabilizer bar.
4. Slowly lower or separate the axle assembly from the car body to the point where the spring becomes loose enough to allow removal.

Wheel Alignment

Year	Model	Caster Range (deg.)	Caster Preferred Setting (deg.)	Camber Range (deg.)	Camber Preferred Setting (deg.)	Toe-in (in.)	Wheel Turning Angle (deg.)
1981–85	RNDI-Mark	3¹¹/₁₆P–6³/₁₆P	5³/₁₆P	⅞N–⅝P	⅛P	⁵/₆₄–⁵/₃₂	7⅞
1985–86	INDI-Mark	1¾P–2¾P	2¼P	¹¹/₁₆N–1⁵/₁₆P	⁵/₁₆P	⁵/₆₄–⁵/₆₄	11¹³/₁₆
1987–89	I-Mark Non-Turbo	1¾P–2¾P	2¼P	¹¹/₁₆N–1⁵/₁₆P	⁵/₁₆P	⁵/₆₄–⁵/₆₄	11¹³/₁₆
1987–89	I-Mark Turbo	1¾P–2¾P	2¼P	½N–1½P	½P	⁵/₆₄–⁵/₆₄	12⅛
1983–87	Impulse	3½P–6P	4¾P	1N–½P	¼N	0–⅛	8
1988–89	Impulse	3¾P–5¼P	4½P	½N–½P	¼N	0–⅛	8
1990–91	Impulse	2P–4P	3P	1¼N–¼P	½N	¹/₃₂–³/₃₂	NA
1991	Stylus	2P–4P	3P	1¼N–¼P	½N	¹/₃₂–³/₃₂	NA
1981–87	P'Up (4 × 2)	0–1P	½P	0–1P	½P	0–⁵/₃₂	7½
1981–87	P'Up (4 × 4)	³/₁₆N–1¹³/₁₆P	⁵/₁₆P	¹/₁₆P–1¹/₁₆P	⁹/₁₆P	⁵/₆₄–⁵/₆₄	7⁷/₁₆
1988–89	P'Up (4 × 2) Short Bed	⅞P–2⅜P	1⅝P	½N–1½P	½P	0–⁵/₃₂	10
1988–89	P'Up (4 × 2) Long Bed	1P–2¾P	1⅞P	½N–1½P	½P	0–⁵/₃₂	10
1988–89	P'Up (4 × 4) Short Bed	1³/₁₆P–2¹¹/₁₆P	1¹⁵/₁₆P	½N–1½P	½P	0–⁵/₃₂	10
1988–89	P'Up (4 × 4) Long Bed	1⁷/₁₆P–2¹⁵/₁₆P	1¹⁵/₁₆P	½N–1½P	½P	0–⁵/₃₂	10
1990–91	P'Up (4 × 2) Short Bed	⅞P–2⅜P	1⅝P	½N–1½P	½P	0–³/₁₆	10
1990–91	P'Up (4 × 2) Long Bed	1P–2¾P	1⅞P	½N–1½P	½P	0–³/₁₆	10
1990–91	P'Up (4 × 4) Short Bed	1³/₁₆P–2¹¹/₁₆P	1¹⁵/₁₆P	½N–1½P	½P	0–³/₁₆	10
1990–91	P'Up (4 × 4) Long Bed	1⁷/₁₆P–2¹⁵/₁₆P	2³/₁₆P	½N–1½P	½P	0–³/₁₆	10
1985–86	Trooper	0–1P	½P	¹/₁₆P–1¹/₁₆P	⁹/₁₆P	⁵/₆₄–⁵/₆₄	7⁷/₁₆
1987–91	Trooper	2P–3P	2½P	0–1P	½P	0–⁵/₃₂	10
1989–91	Amigo	1¾P–3¼P	2½P	½N–1½P	½P	0–³/₁₆	10
1991	Rodeo	2P–3P	2½P	0–1P	½P	0–⁵/₃₂	10

1. Rubber bumper
2. Bushing
3. Leaf spring assembly
4. Spring pin, bolt and washer
5. Nut and washer
6. Rubber bushing
7. Rubber bushing
8. Shackle
9. Shackle plate
10. Nut and washer
11. Nut and washer
12. Lower clamp
13. U-bolt and nut
14. Shock absorber
15. Nut and washer
16. Nut and washer

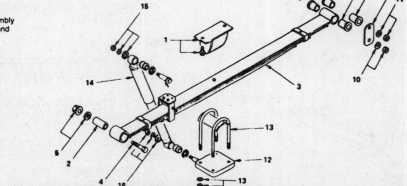

Exploded view of the rear suspension assembly—all trucks

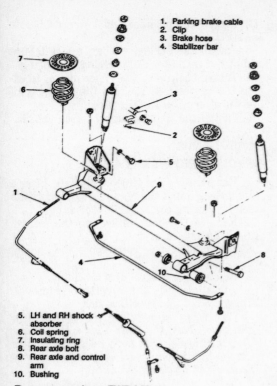

1. Parking brake cable
2. Clip
3. Brake hose
4. Stabilizer bar

5. LH and RH shock absorber
6. Coil spring
7. Insulating ring
8. Rear axle bolt
9. Rear axle and control arm
10. Bushing

Rear suspension—FWD I-Mark

CAUTION: *Do not stress the brake hoses when lowering the axle!*

To install:

5. Position the spring correctly. Make sure that the insulator is in position on top of the spring.

6. Torque the shock absorber lower bolts to 29 ft. lbs. (40 Nm).

Leaf Springs

REMOVAL AND INSTALLATION

1. Raise and safely support the vehicle so the leaf springs are hanging freely.

2. Remove the rear shock absorbers.

3. Remove the parking brake cable clips.

4. Remove the nuts from the U-bolts holding the springs to the axle housing.

5. Support the rear axle housing to remove the weight of the axle housing from the springs.

6. Remove the front and rear shackle pin nuts.

7. Drive out the rear shackle pin by using a hammer and drift. Lower the rear end of the leaf spring assembly to the floor.

8. Drive out the front shackle pin and remove the leaf spring assembly rearward.

9. Remove the shackle pin from the rear spring bracket and remove the shackle.

10. Check the leaf springs for cracks, wear and broken leaves. Replace any leaves found to be cracked, broken, fatigued or seriously worn.

11. Check the shackles for bending and the pins for wear.

12. Check the U-bolts for distortion or other damage.

To install:

13. Mount the shackle to the bracket.

14. Align the front end of the leaf spring assembly with the front bracket and install the shackle pin.

15. Align the rear end of the leaf spring assembly with the shackle and install the shackle pin.

16. Loosely install the shackle pin nuts and install the U-bolts. Tighten the U-bolt nuts to 40 ft. lbs. (54 Nm).

17. Install the shock absorbers.

18. Clip the parking brake cable to the bracket.

19. Remove the axle housing support and lower the vehicle so the weight is on the leaf springs.

20. Tighten the shackle pin nuts to 130 ft. lbs. (176 Nm).

Shock Absorbers

REMOVAL AND INSTALLATION

1. Raise and safely support the vehicle.

2. Remove the shock absorber-to-lower mount nut, washers and bushings.

3. Remove the shock absorber-to-chassis nut, washers and bushings.

4. Remove the shock absorber.

5. Install the shock and torque the retainers to 25 ft. lbs. (34 Nm).

MacPherson Strut

REMOVAL AND INSTALLATION

FWD Impulse and Stylus

1. Raise the vehicle and support with jackstands. Remove the rear wheels.

2. Disconnect and plug the rear brake hose. If equipped with ABS, disconnect the speed sensor.

3. Remove the stabilizer bar and bolt from the strut-to-knuckle.

4. From inside the vehicle, remove the upper strut tower cover and three mount retaining nuts. Remove the strut from the vehicle.

To install:

1. Install the strut and retaining bolts.

2. Connect the brake hose and bleed the system as outlined in Chapter 9.

3. Connect the ABS speed sensor, if so equipped.

4. Install the rear wheel and lower the vehicle.

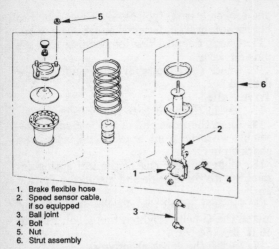

1. Brake flexible hose
2. Speed sensor cable, if so equipped
3. Ball joint
4. Bolt
5. Nut
6. Strut assembly

Rear MacPherson strut—FWD Impulse and Stylus

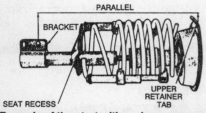

Example of the strut with spring compressor

OVERHAUL

Disassembly

CAUTION: *The MacPherson strut and spring are under extreme pressure! NEVER remove the center strut nut without first installing an approved MacPherson strut spring compressor! Severe personal injury may result if this procedure is not followed correctly!*

1. Remove the strut assembly from the vehicle and place in holding fixture.

2. Remove the cap from the upper mount to expose the center nut. DO NOT remove at this time.

3. Install an approved MacPherson strut spring compressor to the spring. DO NOT over compress the spring! Compress far enough to release the pressure from the spring seat.

4. After compressing the spring, remove the center nut, upper mount, spring seat, rubber and spring.

5. Remove the cushion and lower rubber from the strut.

Assembly

1. Check the strut for oil leaks, coil spring for cracks and distortion and upper mount bearing for abnormal noise and defective turning. Replace components if damage is found.

2. Install the cushion and lower rubber to the strut.

3. Install the spring, rubber, upper mount and center nut after compressing the spring.

4. Install the cap to the upper mount to expose the center nut. Remove the spring compressor after releasing the pressure.

5. Install the strut assembly to the vehicle.

Control Arms

REMOVAL AND INSTALLATION

1. Raise the car and support it safely. Place a suitable jack under the rear axle to support the assembly during control arm removal.

2. Remove the bolt connecting the control arm to the axle case.

3. Remove the bolt connecting the control arm to the body.

4. Remove the control arm assembly.

5. Installation is the reverse of removal. Torque the bolts to specifications.

NOTE: *When reinstalling the control arm assembly, leave the bolts semi-tight. Lower the car before torquing any nuts. The vehicle weight should be on all suspension components when torquing the nuts.*

Sway Bar

REMOVAL AND INSTALLATION

1. Raise the vehicle and support with jackstands.

2. Disconnect the outer sway bar attaching points.

3. Remove the sway bar-to-body retaining clamps and sway bar assembly.

4. Install the sway bar and retaining bolts.

Rear Wheel Bearings

ADJUSTMENT

FWD I-Mark

1. Raise the car and support it with jackstands.

2. Remove the hub dust cover and spindle cotter pin. Loosen the nut.

3. While spinning the wheel, snug the nut down to seat the bearings. Do not exert over 12 ft. lbs. of force on the nut.

4. Back the nut off ¼ turn or until it is just lose. Line up the cotter pin hole in the spindle with the hole in the nut.

5. Insert a new cotter pin. Endplay should be between 0.03-0.13mm. If play exceeds this tolerance, the wheel bearings should be replaced.

REMOVAL AND INSTALLATION

CAUTION: *Some brake pads contain asbestos, which has been determined to be a cancer*

1. Ball joint
2. Bracket
3. Sway bar

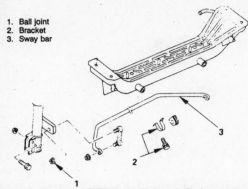

Rear sway bar—FWD Impulse and Stylus, others similar

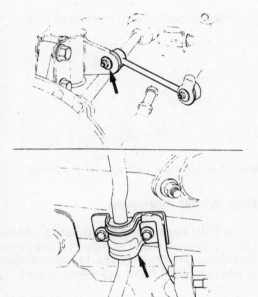

Sway bar attaching points

Removing bearing outer race with a brass drift

causing agent. Never clean the brake surfaces with compressed air! Avoid inhaling any dust from any brake surface! When cleaning brake surfaces, use a commercially available brake cleaning fluid.

1. Raise the car and support it with jackstands. Remove the wheel.

2. Remove the dust cap, cotter pin, castle nut, thrust washer and outside wheel bearing. Pull the drum assembly from the spindle.

3. Pry out the inner seal and remove the inner bearing. If necessary to remove the inner bearing races, use a hammer and a brass drift to drive the bearing races from the hub.

4. Clean all parts in kerosene or equivalent, DO NOT use gasoline. After cleaning, dry the parts with compressed air and check parts for excessive wear and replace damaged parts. Do NOT allow the bearings to spin while blowing dry.

To install:

5. Smear grease inside of hub. Install the bearing races into hub, using a hammer and a brass drift. Drive the races in until they seat against the shoulder of the hub.

6. Pack the bearings with grease and install the inner bearing in the hub. Install a new grease seal, be careful not to damage the seal.

7. Install the drum assembly onto the spin-

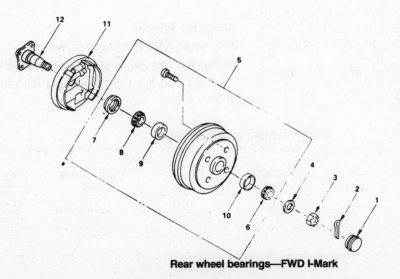

1. Hub cap
2. Split pin
3. Hub nut
4. Washer
5. Hub and drum assembly
6. Outer bearing
7. Oil seal
8. Inner bearing
9. Inner bearing outer race
10. Outer bearing outer race
11. Brake assembly
12. knuckle

Rear wheel bearings—FWD I-Mark

dle. Install the outer bearing, thrust washer and castle nut. Tighten the nut until the wheel does not turn freely.

8. Back off the nut until the wheel turns freely and install the cotter pin. Install the dust cap and lower the vehicle.

PACKING

Clean the wheel bearings thoroughly with solvent and check their condition before installation.

CAUTION: *Do not blow the bearing dry with compressed air as this would allow the bearing to turn without lubrication.*

Apply a sizable amount of lubricant to the palm of one hand. Using your other hand, work the bearing into the lubricant so that the grease is pushed through the rollers and out the other side. Keep rotating the bearing while continuing to push the lubricant through it.

FWD Impulse and Stylus

The rear hub and bearing assembly is a complete unit. It is not serviceable and has to be replaced as a complete unit.

CAUTION: *Some brake pads contain asbestos, which has been determined to be a cancer causing agent. Never clean the brake surfaces with compressed air! Avoid inhaling any dust from any brake surface! When cleaning brake surfaces, use a commercially available brake cleaning fluid.*

1. Raise the vehicle and support with jackstands.

2. Remove the rear wheel, caliper and rotor as outlined in Chapter 9.

3. Remove the hub nut and washer, 4WD only.

4. Remove the hub retaining bolts and hub assembly.

To install:

5. Install the hub and retaining bolts. Torque the bolts to 49 ft. lbs. (69 Nm).

6. Install the hub nut and washer, 4WD only. Torque to 137 ft. lbs. (186 Nm).

7. Install the rear wheel, caliper and rotor as outlined in Section 9.

8. Lower the vehicle.

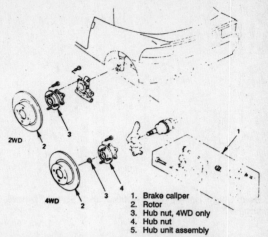

1. Brake caliper
2. Rotor
3. Hub nut, 4WD only
4. Hub nut
5. Hub unit assembly

Rear hub and bearing—FWD Impulse and Stylus

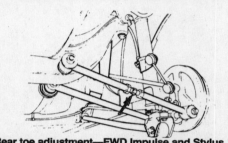

Rear toe adjustment—FWD Impulse and Stylus

Rear Wheel Alignment

The FWD Impulse and Stylus has an adjustable rear support arm. The support arm adjusts the rear toe. No other adjustments are available unless specialized frame equipment is used.

STEERING

Steering Wheel

REMOVAL AND INSTALLATION

Without SIR (Supplemental Inflatable Restraint)

1. Raise the hood and disconnect the battery ground cable.

Rear Wheel Alignment

| Year | Model | Caster | | Chamber | | Toe-in (In.) |
		Range (deg)	Preferred Setting (deg)	Range (deg)	Preferred Setting (deg)	
1985–86	FWD I-Mark	①	①	0 ①	0 ①	5/64 out ①
1987–89	FWD I-Mark	①	①	1⅛N–⅞P ①	⅛N ①	5/32–0 ①
1990–91	FWD Stylus Impulse	①	①	1¼N–¼P ①	½N ①	1/16–1/4

① Not adjustable

Troubleshooting the Steering Column

Problem	Cause	Solution
Will not lock	• Lockbolt spring broken or defective	• Replace lock bolt spring
High effort (required to turn ignition key and lock cylinder)	• Lock cylinder defective	• Replace lock cylinder
	• Ignition switch defective	• Replace ignition switch
	• Rack preload spring broken or deformed	• Replace preload spring
	• Burr on lock sector, lock rack, housing, support or remote rod coupling	• Remove burr
	• Bent sector shaft	• Replace shaft
	• Defective lock rack	• Replace lock rack
	• Remote rod bent, deformed	• Replace rod
	• Ignition switch mounting bracket bent	• Straighten or replace
	• Distorted coupling slot in lock rack (tilt column)	• Replace lock rack
Will stick in "start"	• Remote rod deformed	• Straighten or replace
	• Ignition switch mounting bracket bent	• Straighten or replace
Key cannot be removed in "off-lock"	• Ignition switch is not adjusted correctly	• Adjust switch
	• Defective lock cylinder	• Replace lock cylinder
Lock cylinder can be removed without depressing retainer	• Lock cylinder with defective retainer	• Replace lock cylinder
	• Burr over retainer slot in housing cover or on cylinder retainer	• Remove burr
High effort on lock cylinder between "off" and "off-lock"	• Distorted lock rack	• Replace lock rack
	• Burr on tang of shift gate (automatic column)	• Remove burr
	• Gearshift linkage not adjusted	• Adjust linkage
Noise in column	• One click when in "off-lock" position and the steering wheel is moved (all except automatic column)	• Normal—lock bolt is seating
	• Coupling bolts not tightened	• Tighten pinch bolts
	• Lack of grease on bearings or bearing surfaces	• Lubricate with chassis grease
	• Upper shaft bearing worn or broken	• Replace bearing assembly
	• Lower shaft bearing worn or broken	• Replace bearing. Check shaft and replace if scored.
	• Column not correctly aligned	• Align column
	• Coupling pulled apart	• Replace coupling
	• Broken coupling lower joint	• Repair or replace joint and align column
	• Steering shaft snap ring not seated	• Replace ring. Check for proper seating in groove.
	• Shroud loose on shift bowl. Housing loose on jacket—will be noticed with ignition in "off-lock" and when torque is applied to steering wheel.	• Position shroud over lugs on shift bowl. Tighten mounting screws.
High steering shaft effort	• Column misaligned	• Align column
	• Defective upper or lower bearing	• Replace as required
	• Tight steering shaft universal joint	• Repair or replace
	• Flash on I.D. of shift tube at plastic joint (tilt column only)	• Replace shift tube
	• Upper or lower bearing seized	• Replace bearings
Lash in mounted column assembly	• Column mounting bracket bolts loose	• Tighten bolts
	• Broken weld nuts on column jacket	• Replace column jacket
	• Column capsule bracket sheared	• Replace bracket assembly

Troubleshooting the Steering Column (cont.)

Problem	Cause	Solution
Lash in mounted column assembly (cont.)	• Column bracket to column jacket mounting bolts loose	• Tighten to specified torque
	• Loose lock shoes in housing (tilt column only)	• Replace shoes
	• Loose pivot pins (tilt column only)	• Replace pivot pins and support
	• Loose lock shoe pin (tilt column only)	• Replace pin and housing
	• Loose support screws (tilt column only)	• Tighten screws
Housing loose (tilt column only)	• Excessive clearance between holes in support or housing and pivot pin diameters	• Replace pivot pins and support
	• Housing support-screws loose	• Tighten screws
Steering wheel loose—every other tilt position (tilt column only)	• Loose fit between lock shoe and lock shoe pivot pin	• Replace lock shoes and pivot pin
Steering column not locking in any tilt position (tilt column only)	• Lock shoe seized on pivot pin	• Replace lock shoes and pin
	• Lock shoe grooves have burrs or are filled with foreign material	• Clean or replace lock shoes
	• Lock shoe springs weak or broken	• Replace springs
Noise when tilting column (tilt column only)	• Upper tilt bumpers worn	• Replace tilt bumper
	• Tilt spring rubbing in housing	• Lubricate with chassis grease
One click when in "off-lock" position and the steering wheel is moved	• Seating of lock bolt	• None. Click is normal characteristic sound produced by lock bolt as it seats.
High shift effort (automatic and tilt column only)	• Column not correctly aligned	• Align column
	• Lower bearing not aligned correctly	• Assemble correctly
	• Lack of grease on seal or lower bearing areas	• Lubricate with chassis grease
Improper transmission shifting— automatic and tilt column only	• Sheared shift tube joint	• Replace shift tube
	• Improper transmission gearshift linkage adjustment	• Adjust linkage
	• Loose lower shift lever	• Replace shift tube

Troubleshooting the Ignition Switch

Problem	Cause	Solution
Ignition switch electrically inoperative	• Loose or defective switch connector	• Tighten or replace connector
	• Feed wire open (fusible link)	• Repair or replace
	• Defective ignition switch	• Replace ignition switch
Engine will not crank	• Ignition switch not adjusted properly	• Adjust switch
Ignition switch wil not actuate mechanically	• Defective ignition switch	• Replace switch
	• Defective lock sector	• Replace lock sector
	• Defective remote rod	• Replace remote rod
Ignition switch cannot be adjusted correctly	• Remote rod deformed	• Repair, straighten or replace

Troubleshooting the Turn Signal Switch

Problem	Cause	Solution
Turn signal will not cancel	• Loose switch mounting screws • Switch or anchor bosses broken • Broken, missing or out of position detent, or cancelling spring	• Tighten screws • Replace switch • Reposition springs or replace switch as required
Turn signal difficult to operate	• Turn signal lever loose • Switch yoke broken or distorted • Loose or misplaced springs • Foreign parts and/or materials in switch • Switch mounted loosely	• Tighten mounting screws • Replace switch • Reposition springs or replace switch • Remove foreign parts and/or material • Tighten mounting screws
Turn signal will not indicate lane change	• Broken lane change pressure pad or spring hanger • Broken, missing or misplaced lane change spring • Jammed wires	• Replace switch • Replace or reposition as required • Loosen mounting screws, reposition wires and retighten screws
Turn signal will not stay in turn position	• Foreign material or loose parts impeding movement of switch yoke • Defective switch	• Remove material and/or parts • Replace switch
Hazard switch cannot be pulled out	• Foreign material between hazard support cancelling leg and yoke	• Remove foreign material. No foreign material impeding function of hazard switch—replace turn signal switch.
No turn signal lights	• Inoperative turn signal flasher • Defective or blown fuse • Loose chassis to column harness connector • Disconnect column to chassis connector. Connect new switch to chassis and operate switch by hand. If vehicle lights now operate normally, signal switch is inoperative • If vehicle lights do not operate, check chassis wiring for opens, grounds, etc.	• Replace turn signal flasher • Replace fuse • Connect securely • Replace signal switch • Repair chassis wiring as required
Instrument panel turn indicator lights on but not flashing	• Burned out or damaged front or rear turn signal bulb • If vehicle lights do not operate, check light sockets for high resistance connections, the chassis wiring for opens, grounds, etc. • Inoperative flasher • Loose chassis to column harness connection • Inoperative turn signal switch • To determine if turn signal switch is defective, substitute new switch into circuit and operate switch by hand. If the vehicle's lights operate normally, signal switch is inoperative.	• Replace bulb • Repair chassis wiring as required • Replace flasher • Connect securely • Replace turn signal switch • Replace turn signal switch
Stop light not on when turn indicated	• Loose column to chassis connection • Disconnect column to chassis connector. Connect new switch into system without removing old.	• Connect securely • Replace signal switch

Troubleshooting the Turn Signal Switch (cont.)

Problem	Cause	Solution
Stop light not on when turn indicated (cont.)	Operate switch by hand. If brake lights work with switch in the turn position, signal switch is defective.	
	• If brake lights do not work, check connector to stop light sockets for grounds, opens, etc.	• Repair connector to stop light circuits using service manual as guide
Turn indicator panel lights not flashing	• Burned out bulbs • High resistance to ground at bulb socket • Opens, ground in wiring harness from front turn signal bulb socket to indicator lights	• Replace bulbs • Replace socket • Locate and repair as required
Turn signal lights flash very slowly	• High resistance ground at light sockets • Incorrect capacity turn signal flasher or bulb • If flashing rate is still extremely slow, check chassis wiring harness from the connector to light sockets for high resistance • Loose chassis to column harness connection • Disconnect column to chassis connector. Connect new switch into system without removing old. Operate switch by hand. If flashing occurs at normal rate, the signal switch is defective.	• Repair high resistance grounds at light sockets • Replace turn signal flasher or bulb • Locate and repair as required • Connect securely • Replace turn signal switch
Hazard signal lights will not flash— turn signal functions normally	• Blow fuse • Inoperative hazard warning flasher • Loose chassis-to-column harness connection • Disconnect column to chassis connector. Connect new switch into system without removing old. Depress the hazard warning lights. If they now work normally, turn signal switch is defective. • If lights do not flash, check wiring harness "K" lead for open between hazard flasher and connector. If open, fuse block is defective	• Replace fuse • Replace hazard warning flasher in fuse panel • Conect securely • Replace turn signal switch • Repair or replace brown wire or connector as required

2. On models with the 2-spoke wheel, remove the two screws retaining the horn shroud and disconnect the horn contact.

3. On models with the 3-spoke wheel, remove the medallion cover from the center of the wheel by prying lightly around the edge with a small screwdriver.

4. On models with paded horn shrouds, use a suitable prybar to unsnap the shroud from the retaining clip.

5. Remove the steering wheel nut and washer. Mark the steering wheel and shaft to assure proper positioning later.

6. Using a steering wheel puller, remove the steering wheel.

7. Align the marks you made earlier and install the wheel, washer and nut.

7. Torque the steering wheel nut to 26 ft. lbs. (35 Nm). Install the horn shroud or center medallion.

With SIR (Supplemental Inflatable Restraint)

CAUTION: *Remove and tape the negative (−) battery cable before servicing the SIR system. Failure to do so can result in accidental deployment and personal injury.*

Troubleshooting the Manual Steering Gear

Problem	Cause	Solution
Hard or erratic steering	• Incorrect tire pressure	• Inflate tires to recommended pressures
	• Insufficient or incorrect lubrication	• Lubricate as required (refer to Maintenance Section)
	• Suspension, or steering linkage parts damaged or misaligned	• Repair or replace parts as necessary
	• Improper front wheel alignment	• Adjust incorrect wheel alignment angles
	• Incorrect steering gear adjustment	• Adjust steering gear
	• Sagging springs	• Replace springs
Play or looseness in steering	• Steering wheel loose	• Inspect shaft spines and repair as necessary. Tighten attaching nut and stake in place.
	• Steering linkage or attaching parts loose or worn	• Tighten, adjust, or replace faulty components
	• Pitman arm loose	• Inspect shaft splines and repair as necessary. Tighten attaching nut and stake in place
	• Steering gear attaching bolts loose	• Tighten bolts
	• Loose or worn wheel bearings	• Adjust or replace bearings
	• Steering gear adjustment incorrect or parts badly worn	• Adjust gear or replace defective parts
Wheel shimmy or tramp	• Improper tire pressure	• Inflate tires to recommended pressures
	• Wheels, tires, or brake rotors out-of-balance or out-of-round	• Inspect and replace or balance parts
	• Inoperative, worn, or loose shock absorbers or mounting parts	• Repair or replace shocks or mountings
	• Loose or worn steering or suspension parts	• Tighten or replace as necessary
	• Loose or worn wheel bearings	• Adjust or replace bearings
	• Incorrect steering gear adjustments	• Adjust steering gear
	• Incorrect front wheel alignment	• Correct front wheel alignment
Tire wear	• Improper tire pressure	• Inflate tires to recommended pressures
	• Failure to rotate tires	• Rotate tires
	• Brakes grabbing	• Adjust or repair brakes
	• Incorrect front wheel alignment	• Align incorrect angles
	• Broken or damaged steering and suspension parts	• Repair or replace defective parts
	• Wheel runout	• Replace faulty wheel
	• Excessive speed on turns	• Make driver aware of conditions
Vehicle leads to one side	• Improper tire pressures	• Inflate tires to recommended pressures
	• Front tires with uneven tread depth, wear pattern, or different cord design (i.e., one bias ply and one belted or radial tire on front wheels)	• Install tires of same cord construction and reasonably even tread depth, design, and wear pattern
	• Incorrect front wheel alignment	• Align incorrect angles
	• Brakes dragging	• Adjust or repair brakes
	• Pulling due to uneven tire construction	• Replace faulty tire

Always wear gloves and safety glasses when handling a deployed SIR module and wash your hands with mild soap and water afterwards.

The SIR module should always be carried with the urethane cover away from your body and should always be laid on a flat surface with the urethane side up. This is necessary because a free space is provided to allow the air cushion to expand in the unlikely event of accidental deployment. If so, personal injury may result.

Troubleshooting the Power Steering Gear

Problem	Cause	Solution
Hissing noise in steering gear	• There is some noise in all power steering systems. One of the most common is a hissing sound most evident at standstill parking. There is no relationship between this noise and performance of the steering. Hiss may be expected when steering wheel is at end of travel or when slowly turning at standstill.	• Slight hiss is normal and in no way affects steering. Do not replace valve unless hiss is extremely objectionable. A replacement valve will also exhibit slight noise and is not always a cure. Investigate clearance around flexible coupling rivets. Be sure steering shaft and gear are aligned so flexible coupling rotates in a flat plane and is not distorted as shaft rotates. Any metal-to-metal contacts through flexible coupling will transmit valve hiss into passenger compartment through the steering column.
Rattle or chuckle noise in steering gear	• Gear loose on frame	• Check gear-to-frame mounting screws. Tighten screws to 88 N·m (65 foot pounds) torque.
	• Steering linkage looseness	• Check linkage pivot points for wear. Replace if necessary.
	• Pressure hose touching other parts of car	• Adjust hose position. Do not bend tubing by hand.
	• Loose pitman shaft over center adjustment **NOTE:** A slight rattle may occur on turns because of increased clearance off the "high point." This is normal and clearance must not be reduced below specified limits to eliminate this slight rattle.	• Adjust to specifications
	• Loose pitman arm	• Tighten pitman arm nut to specifications
Squawk noise in steering gear when turning or recovering from a turn	• Damper O-ring on valve spool cut	• Replace damper O-ring
Poor return of steering wheel to center	• Tires not properly inflated • Lack of lubrication in linkage and ball joints	• Inflate to specified pressure • Lube linkage and ball joints
	• Lower coupling flange rubbing against steering gear adjuster plug	• Loosen pinch bolt and assemble properly
	• Steering gear to column misalignment	• Align steering column
	• Improper front wheel alignment • Steering linkage binding • Ball joints binding • Steering wheel rubbing against housing	• Check and adjust as necessary • Replace pivots • Replace ball joints • Align housing
	• Tight or frozen steering shaft bearings	• Replace bearings
	• Sticking or plugged valve spool	• Remove and clean or replace valve
	• Steering gear adjustments over specifications	• Check adjustment with gear out of car. Adjust as required.
	• Kink in return hose	• Replace hose
Car leads to one side or the other (keep in mind road condition and wind. Test car in both directions on flat road)	• Front end misaligned • Unbalanced steering gear valve **NOTE:** If this is cause, steering effort will be very light in direction of lead and normal or heavier in opposite direction	• Adjust to specifications • Replace valve

Troubleshooting the Power Steering Gear (cont.)

Problem	Cause	Solution
Momentary increase in effort when turning wheel fast to right or left	• Low oil level • Pump belt slipping • High internal leakage	• Add power steering fluid as required • Tighten or replace belt • Check pump pressure. (See pressure test)
Steering wheel surges or jerks when turning with engine running especially during parking	• Low oil level • Loose pump belt • Steering linkage hitting engine oil pan at full turn • Insufficient pump pressure • Pump flow control valve sticking	• Fill as required • Adjust tension to specification • Correct clearance • Check pump pressure. (See pressure test). Replace relief valve if defective. • Inspect for varnish or damage, replace if necessary
Excessive wheel kickback or loose steering	• Air in system • Steering gear loose on frame • Steering linkage joints worn enough to be loose • Worn poppet valve • Loose thrust bearing preload adjustment • Excessive overcenter lash	• Add oil to pump reservoir and bleed by operating steering. Check hose connectors for proper torque and adjust as required. • Tighten attaching screws to specified torque • Replace loose pivots • Replace poppet valve • Adjust to specification with gear out of vehicle • Adjust to specification with gear out of car
Hard steering or lack of assist	• Loose pump belt • Low oil level **NOTE:** Low oil level will also result in excessive pump noise • Steering gear to column misalignment • Lower coupling flange rubbing against steering gear adjuster plug • Tires not properly inflated	• Adjust belt tension to specification • Fill to proper level. If excessively low, check all lines and joints for evidence of external leakage. Tighten loose connectors. • Align steering column • Loosen pinch bolt and assemble properly • Inflate to recommended pressure
Foamy milky power steering fluid, low fluid level and possible low pressure	• Air in the fluid, and loss of fluid due to internal pump leakage causing overflow	• Check for leak and correct. Bleed system. Extremely cold temperatures will cause system aeriation should the oil level be low. If oil level is correct and pump still foams, remove pump from vehicle and separate reservoir from housing. Check welsh plug and housing for cracks. If plug is loose or housing is cracked, replace housing.
Low pressure due to steering pump	• Flow control valve stuck or inoperative • Pressure plate not flat against cam ring	• Remove burrs or dirt or replace. Flush system. • Correct
Low pressure due to steering gear	• Pressure loss in cylinder due to worn piston ring or badly worn housing bore • Leakage at valve rings, valve body-to-worm seal	• Remove gear from car for disassembly and inspection of ring and housing bore • Remove gear from car for disassembly and replace seals

Troubleshooting the Power Steering Pump

Problem	Cause	Solution
Chirp noise in steering pump	• Loose belt	• Adjust belt tension to specification
Belt squeal (particularly noticeable at full wheel travel and stand still parking)	• Loose belt	• Adjust belt tension to specification
Growl noise in steering pump	• Excessive back pressure in hoses or steering gear caused by restriction	• Locate restriction and correct. Replace part if necessary.
Growl noise in steering pump (particularly noticeable at stand still parking)	• Scored pressure plates, thrust plate or rotor • Extreme wear of cam ring	• Replace parts and flush system • Replace parts
Groan noise in steering pump	• Low oil level • Air in the oil. Poor pressure hose connection.	• Fill reservoir to proper level • Tighten connector to specified torque. Bleed system by operating steering from right to left—full turn.
Rattle noise in steering pump	• Vanes not installed properly • Vanes sticking in rotor slots	• Install properly • Free up by removing burrs, varnish, or dirt
Swish noise in steering pump	• Defective flow control valve	• Replace part
Whine noise in steering pump	• Pump shaft bearing scored	• Replace housing and shaft. Flush system.
Hard steering or lack of assist	• Loose pump belt • Low oil level in reservoir **NOTE:** Low oil level will also result in excessive pump noise • Steering gear to column misalignment • Lower coupling flange rubbing against steering gear adjuster plug • Tires not properly inflated	• Adjust belt tension to specification • Fill to proper level. If excessively low, check all lines and joints for evidence of external leakage. Tighten loose connectors. • Align steering column • Loosen pinch bolt and assemble properly • Inflate to recommended pressure
Foaming milky power steering fluid, low fluid level and possible low pressure	• Air in the fluid, and loss of fluid due to internal pump leakage causing overflow	• Check for leaks and correct. Bleed system. Extremely cold temperatures will cause system aeriation should the oil level be low. If oil level is correct and pump still foams, remove pump from vehicle and separate reservoir from body. Check welsh plug and body for cracks. If plug is loose or body is cracked, replace body.
Low pump pressure	• Flow control valve stuck or inoperative • Pressure plate not flat against cam ring	• Remove burrs or dirt or replace. Flush system. • Correct
Momentary increase in effort when turning wheel fast to right or left	• Low oil level in pump • Pump belt slipping • High internal leakage	• Add power steering fluid as required • Tighten or replace belt • Check pump pressure. (See pressure test)
Steering wheel surges or jerks when turning with engine running especially during parking	• Low oil level • Loose pump belt • Steering linkage hitting engine oil pan at full turn • Insufficient pump pressure	• Fill as required • Adjust tension to specification • Correct clearance • Check pump pressure. (See pressure test). Replace flow control valve if defective.

Troubleshooting the Power Steering Pump (cont.)

Problem	Cause	Solution
Steering wheel surges or jerks when turning with engine running especially during parking (cont.)	• Sticking flow control valve	• Inspect for varnish or damage, replace if necessary
Excessive wheel kickback or loose steering	• Air in system	• Add oil to pump reservoir and bleed by operating steering. Check hose connectors for proper torque and adjust as required.
Low pump pressure	• Extreme wear of cam ring • Scored pressure plate, thrust plate, or rotor • Vanes not installed properly • Vanes sticking in rotor slots • Cracked or broken thrust or pressure plate	• Replace parts. Flush system. • Replace parts. Flush system. • Install properly • Freeup by removing burrs, varnish, or dirt • Replace part

1. **Very Important.** Disconnect the negative (−) battery cable.

2. Remove the SIR module retaining screws and disconnect the module/horn wiring.

3. Remove the steering wheel fixing nut and washer.

4. Using a steering wheel puller J–1859–03 or equivalent, remove the steering wheel.

To install:

1. Install the steering wheel and nut.

2. Torque the nut to 25 ft. lbs. (34 Nm).

3. Connect the wheel wiring and install the SIR module.

4. Connect the negative battery cable.

Turn Signal Switch (Combination Switch)

REMOVAL AND INSTALLATION

Cars

1. Remove the steering wheel as previously described.

2. Remove the steering column covers and disconnect the electrical connectors to the switches.

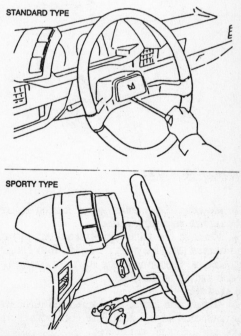

STANDARD TYPE

SPORTY TYPE

Steering pad removal

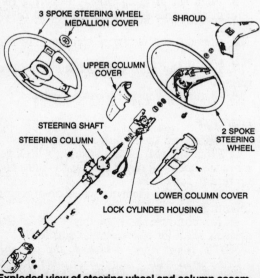

3 SPOKE STEERING WHEEL MEDALLION COVER

SHROUD

UPPER COLUMN COVER

STEERING SHAFT

STEERING COLUMN

2 SPOKE STEERING WHEEL

LOWER COLUMN COVER

LOCK CYLINDER HOUSING

Exploded view of steering wheel and column assembly—RWD I-Mark, others similar

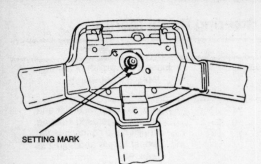

SETTING MARK

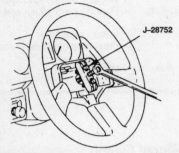

J-28752

Steering wheel removal

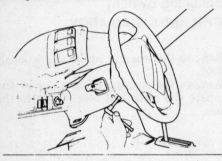

Removing SIR module

3. Remove the washer/wiper switch by removing the retaining screws.

4. Remove the turn signal/headlight switch and hazard switch by removing the four retaining screws. Disconnect the harness connector as the switch is removed.

To install:

5. Install the switch and make all electrical connections. Make sure the connectors are tight and properly connected.

NOTE: *The light, wiper/washer, turn signal*

switches etc. on the Impulse, are contained in a control panel which is removed as an assembly.

Trucks

P'UP

1. Disconnect the negative battery cable.

2. From the rear of the steering wheel, remove the horn pad screw and lift the horn pad upward to remove it.

3. Disconnect the electrical connector from the horn pad.

4. Remove the steering wheel-to-steering column nut.

5. Matchmark the steering wheel to the steering shaft for reinstallation purposes.

NOTE: *Never apply a blow to the steering wheel shaft with a hammer or other impact tool, to remove the steering wheel, for the steering shaft may become damaged.*

6. Using a steering wheel puller, press the steering wheel from the steering column.

NOTE: *Use steering wheel puller J-29752 (LS model) or J-24292-B (except LS model).*

7. Remove the contact ring.

8. Remove the steering column covers.

9. Disconnect the electrical connector from the combination switch.

10. Remove the combination switch-to-steering column screws and the switch.

To install:

11. Install the combination switch to the steering column and secure it with screws.

12. Connect the combination switch electrical connector.

13. Install the steering column covers.

14. Install the contact ring.

15. Align the steering wheel-to-steering column matchmarks and torque the nut to 18–25 ft. lbs.

16. Connect the electrical connector to the horn pad.

17. Install the horn pad and the horn pad screw.

18. Connect the negative battery cable.

EXCEPT P'UP

1. Disconnect the negative battery cable.

2. From the rear of the steering wheel, remove the horn pad screw and lift the horn pad upward to remove it.

3. Remove the steering wheel-to-steering column nut.

4. Matchmark the steering wheel to the steering shaft for reinstallation purposes.

NOTE: *Never apply a blow to the steering wheel shaft with a hammer or other impact tool, to remove the steering wheel, for the steering shaft may become damaged.*

5. Using a steering wheel puller, press the steering wheel from the steering column.

6. Remove the contact ring.

7. Remove the steering column covers.

8. Disconnect the electrical connector from the combination switch.

9. Remove the combination switch-to-steering column screws and the switch.

To install:

10. Install the combination switch to the steering column and secure it with screws.

11. Connect the combination switch electrical connector.

12. Install the steering column covers.

13. Install the contact ring.

14. Align the steering wheel-to-steering column matchmarks and torque the nut to 22–29 ft. lbs.

15. Install the horn pad and the horn pad screw.

16. Connect the negative battery cable.

Ignition Lock/Switch

REMOVAL AND INSTALLATION

All Cars

1. Disconnect the negative battery cable. Using the steering wheel removal procedure, (as previously outlined), remove the steering wheel.

2. Remove the screws retaining the upper and lower steering column covers.

3. Disconnect all the electrical connectors.

4. On the RWD I-Mark models, remove the combination windshield wiper and washer switch by removing the two retaining screws. Then remove the combination turn signal, headlight dimmer and hazard warning switch by removing the two retaining screws.

5. Remove the ignition lock cylinder housing by removing the snapring and washer, along with the lock cylinder housing retaining bolts on the column flange. On Impulse models, remove the ignition lock cylinder in position except for the **LOCK** position.

6. Remove the lock cylinder housing from the steering column shaft.

To install:

1. Install the lock cylinder housing to the steering column shaft.

2. Install the ignition lock cylinder housing.

3. On the RWD I-Mark models, install the combination windshield wiper and washer switch by installing the two retaining screws.

4. Connect all the electrical connectors.

5. Install the screws retaining the upper and lower steering column covers.

6. Install the steering wheel as previously outlined. Connect the battery cable and check operation.

Trucks

SWITCH

The ignition switch is located on the lower right side of the dash.

1. Disconnect the negative battery cable.

2. Disconnect and label the ignition switch wiring under the dashboard.

4. Remove the ignition switch locknut and the switch from the dash.

To install:

5. Install the ignition switch to the dash and secure with the locknut.

6. Connect the electrical connector to the ignition switch.

7. Connect the negative battery cable.

LOCK

1. Remove the combination switch.

2. Remove the ignition lock-to-steering column clamp bolts and the ignition lock.

To install:

3. Install the ignition lock to the steering column and secure with bolts.

4. Install the combination switch.

P'up and Amigo

1. Disconnect the negative battery cable.

2. From the rear of the steering wheel, remove the horn pad screw and lift the horn pad upward to remove it.

3. Remove the steering wheel-to-steering column nut.

4. Matchmark the steering wheel to the steering shaft for reinstallation purposes.

NOTE: *Never apply a blow to the steering wheel shaft with a hammer or other impact tool, to remove the steering wheel, for the steering shaft may become damaged.*

5. Using a steering wheel puller, press the steering wheel from the steering column.

6. Remove the contact ring.

7. Remove the steering column covers.

8. Disconnect the electrical connector from the combination switch.

9. Remove the combination switch-to-steering column screws and the switch.

10. Remove the ignition lock/switch-to-steering column snapring and bushing.

11. Disconnect the electrical connector from the ignition lock/switch assembly.

12. Remove the ignition lock/switch-to-steering column bolts and the lock/switch assembly.

To install:

13. Install the ignition lock/switch-to-steering column bolts, the bushing and the snapring.

14. Install the combination switch to the steering column and secure it with screws.

15. Connect the combination switch electrical connector.

16. Install the steering column covers.

17. Install the contact ring.

18. Align the steering wheel-to-steering column matchmarks and torque the nut to 22–29 ft. lbs.

19. Install the horn pad and the horn pad screw.

20. Connect the negative battery cable.

Steering Column

REMOVAL AND INSTALLATION

CAUTION: *Remove and tape the negative (−) battery cable before servicing the SIR system. Failure to do so can result in accidental deployment and personal injury!*

Always wear gloves and sdafety glasses when handling a deployed SIR module and wash your hands with mild soap and water afterwards.

The SIR module should always be carried with the urethane cover away from your body and should always be laid on a flat surface with the urethane side up. This is necessary because a free space is provided to allow the air cushion to expand in the unlikely event of accidental deployment. If so, personal injury may result.

1. Disconnect the negative (−) battery cable.

2. Remove the steering wheel and cover as outlined in this Chapter.

3. Disconnect all electrical connectors.

4. Remove combination switch assembly.

5. Remove the flexible joint key bolt at the bottom of the shaft.

6. Remove column-to-dash board flange bolts.

7. Remove the column and shaft assembly from the vehicle.

To install:

8. Install the column and shaft assembly to the vehicle.

9. Install column-to-dash board flange bolts.

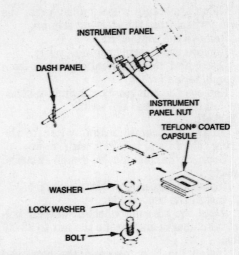

Steering column retainers

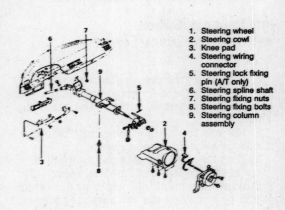

1. Steering wheel
2. Steering cowl
3. Knee pad
4. Steering wiring connector
5. Steering lock fixing pin (A/T only)
6. Steering spline shaft
7. Steering fixing nuts
8. Steering fixing bolts
9. Steering column assembly

Steering column assembly—FWD Impulse and Stylus

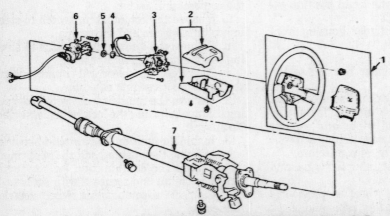

1. Steering wheel
2. Steering cowl
3. Combination switch
4. Snapring
5. Bushing
6. Steering lock and bearing
7. Steering column assembly

Steering column—Rodeo shown, others similar

10. Install the flexible joint key bolt at the bottom of the shaft.

11. Install combination switch assembly.

12. Connect all electrical connectors.

13. Install the steering wheel and cover as outlined in this Chapter.

14. Connect the negative (−) battery cable.

Steering Linkage

REMOVAL AND INSTALLATION

Outer Tie Rod Ends

ALL MODELS

1. Raise the vehicle and remove the front wheel.

2. Remove the cotter pin and castle nut from the tie rod end. Using a tie rod removal tool, separate the tie rod from the steering knuckle.

3. Mark the thread portion of the steering link with tape or paint. Loosen the locknut and remove the tie rod end from the steering link.

4. Install the tie rod to the marked position on the threaded steering link. Torque the lock nut to 25 ft. lbs. (34 Nm).

5. Install the tie rod and nut into the knuckle. Torque the nut to 29 ft. lbs. (39 Nm) and align the cotter pin hole. Install a new cotter pin.

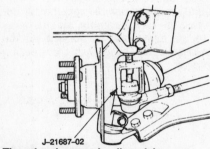

J−21687−02
Tie rod end removal—all models

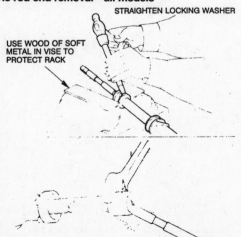

STRAIGHTEN LOCKING WASHER

USE WOOD OF SOFT METAL IN VISE TO PROTECT RACK

Removing inner tie rod end—rack and pinion steering

6. Install the front wheel and lower the vehicle. Have the front end aligned by a qualified alignment technician.

Inner Tie Rod End (Rack and Pinion)

1. Remove the rack and pinion assembly as outlined in this Chapter.

2. Remove the outer tie rod end and steering boot.

3. Place the assembly in a soft vise with the rack gear being held in position.

4. Straighten the locking washer with a hammer and chisel.

5. Use a wrench to remove the inner tie rod and steering link.

To install:

6. Use a wrench to install the inner tie rod, new lock washer and steering link. Torque to 65 ft. lbs. (88 Nm).

7. Stake the new locking washer with a hammer and chisel.

8. Install the steering boot and outer tie rod end.

9. Install the rack and pinion assembly as outlined in this Chapter.

Intermediate Rod and Tie Rods (Trucks)

1. Raise and safely support the vehicle.

2. Remove cotter pin from the ball studs connecting tie rods-to-intermediate rod and the steering damper. Remove the castellated nuts. Using a ball joint separator tool, separate the parts.

3. Remove the nut and lockwasher on ball stud connecting the intermediate rod to idler arm. Using a ball joint separator tool, separate the intermediate rod from the idler arm.

4. Remove the intermediate rod with tie rods.

5. If the tie rod is replaced, disconnect the intermediate rod from tie rod.

To install:

6. Make sure the threads on the ball studs and nuts are clean and smooth.

7. Install the intermediate rod-to-idler arm and torque the nut to 50 ft. lbs.

8. Raise the end of the rod and install it on the pitman arm. Torque the nut to 44 ft. lbs. Tighten the nut just enough to insert cotter pin and install new cotter pin.

9. Install intermediate rod to steering damper end. Torque nut to 87 ft. lbs., then, advance nut just enough to insert cotter pin and install new cotter pin.

10. Install the tie rods to adapter, torque nut to 44 ft. lbs., then, advance nut just enough to insert cotter pin and install new cotter pin and lubricate tie rod ball studs.

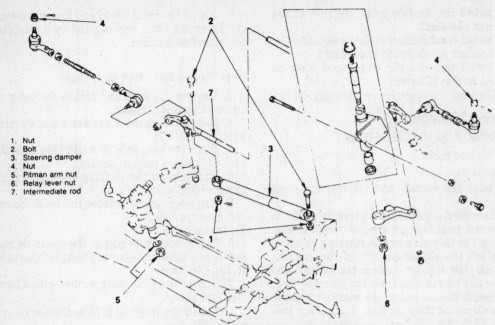

1. Nut
2. Bolt
3. Steering damper
4. Nut
5. Pitman arm nut
6. Relay lever nut
7. Intermediate rod

Steering linkage assembly—trucks and 4WD

Manual Steering Gear
REMOVAL AND INSTALLATION

RWD I-Mark and Impulse

1. Raise the car and safely support it with jackstands. Remove the lower engine shrouds.

2. Remove the steering shaft coupling bolt.

3. Remove both tie rod ends cotter pin and castle nut. Discard the pins and use tool J–21687–02 or equivalent to disconnect the tie rod ends from the steering knuckles.

4. Disconnect the rack retaining bolts from the crossmember. Expand the steering shaft coupling and remove the assembly.

5. Installation is the reverse of removal. Before installing the rack assembly, set the steering gear to the high point by positioning the front wheels straight ahead with the steering wheel centered.

LOCK NUT
SCREW PLUG
FLEXIBLE COUPLING
ADJUSTING SCREW
THRUST SPRING
BEARING SHELL
LOCK NUT
OIL SEAL
PINION SHAFT
STEERING GEAR HOUSING
RUBBER BUSHING
TIE-ROD
RETAINER RING
RUBBER BELLOWS
RETAINER RING
RETAINER RING
RUBBER BELLOWS
RETAINER RING
LOCK NUT
TIE-ROD END
RACK

Manual rack and pinion assembly

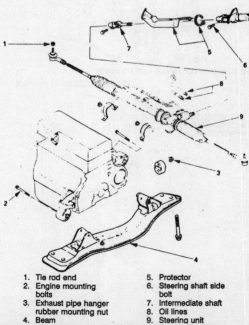

1. Tie rod end
2. Engine mounting bolts
3. Exhaust pipe hanger rubber mounting nut
4. Beam
5. Protector
6. Steering shaft side bolt
7. Intermediate shaft
8. Oil lines
9. Steering unit

Steering assembly removal—power shown, manual similar

6. Torque the crossmember retaining bolts to 14 ft. lbs. (20 Nm). Torque the steering shaft coupling bolt to 19 ft. lbs. (25 Nm).

FWD I-Mark

1. Disconnect the negative battery cable and remove the engine hood.

2. Loosen the front wheel lugs and raise and support the front of the vehicle safely. Remove both front tires.

3. Remove the tie rod ends from the steering knuckles.

4. Using a suitable engine hoist, slightly raise the engine. Support the lower part of the engine with a suitable engine jack or jack stand.

5. Remove the engine mounting bolts.

6. Remove the front exhaust pipe hange mounting rubber nut. Detach the mounting rubber from the beam. Remove the intermediate shaft mounting bolt (steering shaft side bolt).

7. Remove the bracket nut(s) holding the manual steering unit.

8. Remove the steering unit and when removing the right and left steering unit boots through the body be careful not to damage the boots.

To install:

9. Install the through bolts and steering unit. Be careful not to damage the boots.

10. Install the bracket nut(s) holding the manual steering unit.

11. Install the front exhaust pipe hange mounting rubber nut. Attach the mounting rubber to the beam. Install the intermediate shaft mounting bolt (steering shaft side bolt).

12. Lower the engine and install the engine mounting bolts.

13. Install the tie rod ends to the steering knuckles.

14. Install the front wheels and lower the vehicle.

15. Connect the negative battery cable and install the engine hood.
   a. Steering unit bracket nut—30 ft. lbs.
   b. Steering shaft side bolt—19 ft. lbs.
   c. Support beam bolts—56 ft. lbs.
   d. Engine mounting bolts—61 ft. lbs.
   e. Tie rod end nut—29 ft. lbs.

Trucks

1. Disconnect the negative battery cable. Raise and safely support the vehicle. Remove the skid plate, if equipped.

2. Remove pitman arm nut and washer. Matchmark the pitman arm-to-pitman shaft.

3. Using a puller tool, press the pitman arm from the pitman shaft.

4. Remove the steering gear-to-steering shaft clamp bolt.

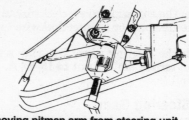
Removing pitman arm from steering unit

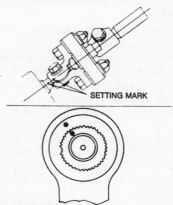
Steering unit setting marks

5. Remove the steering gear-to-frame bolts and the steering gear from vehicle.

To install:

6. Place the steering gear in position and install and tighten the mounting bolts.

7. Install the steering gear-to-steering shaft clamp bolt and torque to 29–40 ft. lbs. (40–49 Nm).

8. Torque the steering column mounting bolts to 13 ft. lbs.

9. Install the pitman arm-to-pitman shaft and torque the nut to 145–174 ft. lbs. (196–236 Nm).

10. Install the skid plate, if equipped.

11. Lower the vehicle.

ADJUSTMENTS

Cars

1. Tighten the adjusting plug to 3.6 ft. lbs. (5.3 Nm).

2. Loosen the adjusting nut and repeat steps 1 and 2.

3. Back down the adjusting plug by a maximum of 25°.

4. Hold the adjusting plug with a lock nut.

5. Apply liquid gasket to the lock nut and torque to 49 ft. lbs. (67 Nm).

Trucks

1. Position the front wheel in the straight ahead position.

2. Loosen the locknut on the adjusting screw of the steering unit.

3. Turn the adjusting screw clockwise to decrease the free-play or counterclockwise to increase it.

4. With the steering wheel free-play set at 10–30mm, torque the locknut to 15–22 ft. lbs. (20–29 Nm).

Power Steering Gear

REMOVAL AND INSTALLATION

RWD Impulse

1. Disconnect the negative battery cable and remove the engine hood.

2. Loosen the front wheel lugs and raise and support the front of the vehicle safely. Remove both front tires. On the Impulse models, remove the hub and rotor assembly.

3. Remove the tie rod ends from the steering knuckles.

4. Using a suitable engine hoist, slightly raise the engine. Support the lower part of the engine with a suitable engine jack or jack stand. On the Impulse models it may not be necessary to raise the engine.

5. Remove the engine mounting bolts.

6. Remove the exhaust pipe hanger rubber mounting and separate the mounting rubber and the beam.

7. Remove the intermediate shaft mounting bolt and remove the intermediate shaft.

8. Remove the power steering unit oil line and place the lines in a suitable container. Turn the steering wheel fully to the left and right to force the oil out of the cylinder.

9. Remove the bracket nut(s) holding the power steering unit in the vehicle. Remove the unit from the vehicle and be careful not to damage the boots.

To install:

10. Install the steering unit and bracket nut(s) holding the power steering unit in the vehicle. Be careful not to damage the boots.

11. Install the power steering unit oil lines.

12. Install the intermediate shaft and mounting bolt.

13. Install the exhaust pipe hanger rubber mounting.

14. Lower the engine and install the engine mounting bolts.

15. Install the tie rod ends to the steering knuckles.

16. Install the front wheels and lower the vehicle.

17. Connect the negative battery cable and install the engine hood. Have the front end aligned.

18. Use the same torque specifications as the manual steering unit. The feed oil line is torqued to 25 ft. lbs. and the return line is torqued to 33 ft. lbs.

ADJUSTMENTS

Adjustment of the steering gear assembly is accomplished by turning the adjusting screw in or out.

Cars

1. Set the steering to the high point by positioning the front wheels straight ahead with the steering wheel centered.

2. Thread the adjusting screw into the steering gear housing and torque the adjusting screw to 11 ft. lbs.

3. Back off the adjusting screw slightly, then torque the locknut to 58 ft. lbs.

Trucks

1. Raise and safely support the vehicle. Remove the skip plate, if equipped.

2. Remove pitman arm nut and washer. Matchmark the pitman arm-to-pitman shaft.

3. Using a puller tool, press the the pitman arm from the pitman shaft.

4. Disconnect and plug the power steering lines at the steering gear.

5. Remove the steering gear-to-steering shaft clamp bolt.

6. Remove the steering gear-to-frame bolts and the steering gear from vehicle.

To install:

1. Disc brake front
2. Hub and rotor; front brake
3. Rod end assembly; outer
4. Shaft, steering, 2nd
5. Pipe assembly, return
6. Pipe assembly, feed
7. Bolt, bracket to crossmember
8. Washer, spring, bracket to crossmember
9. Bracket, steering unit to crossmember

Power steering unit removal and installation—RWD Impulse

7. Place the steering gear in position and install and tighten the mounting bolts.

8. Install steering gear-to-steering shaft bolts and torque to 29–40 ft. lbs. (40–49 Nm).

9. Torque steering column mounting bolts to 13 ft. lbs.

10. Install the pitman arm to the pitman shaft. Install washer and torque nut to 145–174 ft. lbs. (196–236 Nm).

11. Install the skid plate, if equipped.

12. Lower the vehicle. Refill and bleed the power steering system.

ADJUSTMENT

1. Position the front wheel in the straight ahead position.

2. Loosen the locknut on the adjusting screw of the steering unit.

3. Turn the adjusting screw clockwise to decrease the free-play or counterclockwise to increase it.

4. With the steering wheel free-play set at 10mm, torque the locknut to 26–35 ft. lbs. (37–47 Nm).

Power Steering Pump

REMOVAL AND INSTALLATION

Cars

1. Disconnect the negative battery cable. Remove all necessary drive belts.

2. Disconnect the high pressure lines from the power steering pump and let them and the pump drain out into a suitable drain pan. On the Impulse G200Z engine it is necessary to remove the under the engine dust cover in order to reach the high pressure lines and to remove the drive belt.

3. In the I-Mark models, remove the power steering pump adjusting plate, brackets and retaining bolts. Then remove the power steering pump from the vehicle.

4. On the G200Z Impulse, remove the power steering pump pulley, brackets and retaining bolts and remove the pump from the vehicle.

5. On the 4ZCI-T Impulse, remove the V-belt, pump pulley, idler pulley, brackets and retaining bolts. Then remove the pump from the vehicle.

6. Installation is the reverse order of the removal procedure. Tighten the drive belts to specifications, refill the power steering reservoir, bleed the system and start the car and check for leaks.

BLEEDING

1. Turn the wheels to the extreme left.

2. With the engine stopped, add power steering fluid to the **MIN** mark on the fluid indicator.

3. Start the engine and run it for 15 seconds at fast idle.

4. Stop the engine, recheck the fluid level and refill to the **MIN** mark.

5. Start the engine and turn the wheels from side to side (3 times).

6. Stop the engine check the fluid level.

NOTE: *If air bubbles are still present in the fluid, the procedure must be repeated.*

Trucks

1. Disconnect the negative battery cable.

2. Disconnect and plug the inlet and outlet fluid lines from the power steering pump.

3. Remove the drive belt from the pump.

4. Remove the pump-to-bracket bolts and the pump from the brackets.

5. To install, reverse the removal procedures.

6. Connect the negative battery cable. Refill and bleed the power steering system.

BELT ADJUSTMENT

1. Loosen the power steering pump adjusting bolts.

2. Using finger pressure, between the idler pulley and the power steering pump pulley, check the belt deflection; it should be 10mm.

3. With the power steering pump adjusted to the correct belt deflection, tighten the pump bolts.

SYSTEM BLEEDING

1. Fill the power steering reservoir to the proper level when cold.

2. Start and operate the engine until it reaches normal operating temperatures.

3. Turn the engine **OFF** and check the fluid level. If necessary, fill the reservoir to the proper level.

4. Run the engine and turn the steering wheel from lock-to-lock, in both directions, 3–4 times; do not hold the steering wheel at the lock position for more than 5 seconds or temperature rise will result.

5. Return the steering wheel to center, turn the engine **OFF** and allow the fluid to sit for 5 minutes before adding any more.

6. If necesary, repeat the bleeding procedure until the air bubbles are removed from the system.

7. Fill the system to the proper level when finished.

Brakes

BRAKE SYSTEM

Adjustments

DRUM BRAKES

1. Raise and support vehicle safely.
2. Mark relationship of wheel to axle flange. Remove wheel nuts, wheel assembly and brake drum.
3. Using a drum brake gauge (J–21177), or equivalent, measure the inside diameter of brake drum.
4. Adjust brake shoes to dimension obtained in Step 3. Use a brake adjusting tool (available at local parts stores) to turn the auto adjuster lever until correct diameter is reached. It may be necessary to relieve pressure on the adjuster latch by using a piece of wire to hold it open when decreasing diameter.
5. Install brake drum and wheel assembly. Lower vehicle.
NOTE: *Pump brake pedal to seat brake shoes before moving vehicle.*

BRAKE PEDAL

1. Measure brake pedal height (L_2) after engine is started and engine speed increased sev-

eral times. Ensure pedal is fully returned by the pedal return spring.
2. Measure distance from floor panel to top of pedal (see illustration).
3. Measure free play (L_2) after engine is stopped and brake pedal pumped several times.
4. If measurements are not in specification, adjust brake pedal as follows:
   a. Disconnect stop light switch connector.
   b. Loosen stop light switch lock nut and back switch away from brake pedal.
   c. Loosen lock nut on push rod and adjust brake pedal to the specified height.
   d. Tighten lock nut to 15 ft. lbs.
   e. Adjust stop light switch (A) to specification, tighten nut and install connector.

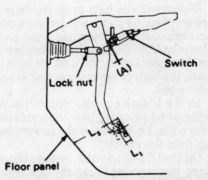

Brake pedal adjustment (except RWD Impulse). (L_1) pedal free play (L_2) pedal height (A) brake light switch housing to pedal clearance

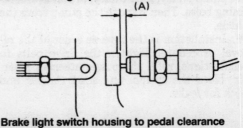

Brake light switch housing to pedal clearance

Brake pedal adjustment on the RWD Impulse

Troubleshooting the Brake System

Problem	Cause	Solution
Low brake pedal (excessive pedal travel required for braking action.)	• Excessive clearance between rear linings and drums caused by inoperative automatic adjusters	• Make 10 to 15 alternate forward and reverse brake stops to adjust brakes. If brake pedal does not come up, repair or replace adjuster parts as necessary.
	• Worn rear brakelining	• Inspect and replace lining if worn beyond minimum thickness specification
	• Bent, distorted brakeshoes, front or rear	• Replace brakeshoes in axle sets
	• Air in hydraulic system	• Remove air from system. Refer to Brake Bleeding.
Low brake pedal (pedal may go to floor with steady pressure applied.)	• Fluid leak in hydraulic system	• Fill master cylinder to fill line; have helper apply brakes and check calipers, wheel cylinders, differential valve tubes, hoses and fittings for leaks. Repair or replace as necessary.
	• Air in hydraulic system	• Remove air from system. Refer to Brake Bleeding.
	• Incorrect or non-recommended brake fluid (fluid evaporates at below normal temp).	• Flush hydraulic system with clean brake fluid. Refill with correct-type fluid.
	• Master cylinder piston seals worn, or master cylinder bore is scored, worn or corroded	• Repair or replace master cylinder
Low brake pedal (pedal goes to floor on first application—o.k. on subsequent applications.)	• Disc brake pads sticking on abutment surfaces of anchor plate. Caused by a build-up of dirt, rust, or corrosion on abutment surfaces	• Clean abutment surfaces
Fading brake pedal (pedal height decreases with steady pressure applied.)	• Fluid leak in hydraulic system	• Fill master cylinder reservoirs to fill mark, have helper apply brakes, check calipers, wheel cylinders, differential valve, tubes, hoses, and fittings for fluid leaks. Repair or replace parts as necessary.
	• Master cylinder piston seals worn, or master cylinder bore is scored, worn or corroded	• Repair or replace master cylinder
Decreasing brake pedal travel (pedal travel required for braking action decreases and may be accompanied by a hard pedal.)	• Caliper or wheel cylinder pistons sticking or seized	• Repair or replace the calipers, or wheel cylinders
	• Master cylinder compensator ports blocked (preventing fluid return to reservoirs) or pistons sticking or seized in master cylinder bore	• Repair or replace the master cylinder
	• Power brake unit binding internally	• Test unit according to the following procedure: (a) Shift transmission into neutral and start engine (b) Increase engine speed to 1500 rpm, close throttle and fully depress brake pedal (c) Slow release brake pedal and stop engine (d) Have helper remove vacuum check valve and hose from power unit. Observe for backward movement of brake pedal. (e) If the pedal moves backward, the power unit has an internal bind—replace power unit

Troubleshooting the Brake System (cont.)

Problem	Cause	Solution
Spongy brake pedal (pedal has abnormally soft, springy, spongy feel when depressed.)	• Air in hydraulic system • Brakeshoes bent or distorted • Brakelining not yet seated with drums and rotors • Rear drum brakes not properly adjusted	• Remove air from system. Refer to Brake Bleeding. • Replace brakeshoes • Burnish brakes • Adjust brakes
Hard brake pedal (excessive pedal pressure required to stop vehicle. May be accompanied by brake fade.)	• Loose or leaking power brake unit vacuum hose • Incorrect or poor quality brakelining • Bent, broken, distorted brakeshoes • Calipers binding or dragging on mounting pins. Rear brakeshoes dragging on support plate. • Caliper, wheel cylinder, or master cylinder pistons sticking or seized • Power brake unit vacuum check valve malfunction • Power brake unit has internal bind • Master cylinder compensator ports (at bottom of reservoirs) blocked by dirt, scale, rust, or have small burrs (blocked ports prevent fluid return to reservoirs). • Brake hoses, tubes, fittings clogged or restricted • Brake fluid contaminated with improper fluids (motor oil, transmission fluid, causing rubber components to swell and stick in bores • Low engine vacuum	• Tighten connections or replace leaking hose • Replace with lining in axle sets • Replace brakeshoes • Replace mounting pins and bushings. Clean rust or burrs from rear brake support plate ledges and lubricate ledges with molydisulfide grease. **NOTE:** If ledges are deeply grooved or scored, do not attempt to sand or grind them smooth—replace support plate. • Repair or replace parts as necessary • Test valve according to the following procedure: (a) Start engine, increase engine speed to 1500 rpm, close throttle and immediately stop engine (b) Wait at least 90 seconds then depress brake pedal (c) If brakes are not vacuum assisted for 2 or more applications, check valve is faulty • Test unit according to the following procedure: (a) With engine stopped, apply brakes several times to exhaust all vacuum in system (b) Shift transmission into neutral, depress brake pedal and start engine (c) If pedal height decreases with foot pressure and less pressure is required to hold pedal in applied position, power unit vacuum system is operating normally. Test power unit. If power unit exhibits a bind condition, replace the power unit. • Repair or replace master cylinder **CAUTION:** Do not attempt to clean blocked ports with wire, pencils, or similar implements. Use compressed air only. • Use compressed air to check or unclog parts. Replace any damaged parts. • Replace all rubber components, combination valve and hoses. Flush entire brake system with DOT 3 brake fluid or equivalent. • Adjust or repair engine

Troubleshooting the Brake System (cont.)

Problem	Cause	Solution
Grabbing brakes (severe reaction to brake pedal pressure.)	• Brakelining(s) contaminated by grease or brake fluid	• Determine and correct cause of contamination and replace brakeshoes in axle sets
	• Parking brake cables incorrectly adjusted or seized	• Adjust cables. Replace seized cables.
	• Incorrect brakelining or lining loose on brakeshoes	• Replace brakeshoes in axle sets
	• Caliper anchor plate bolts loose	• Tighten bolts
	• Rear brakeshoes binding on support plate ledges	• Clean and lubricate ledges. Replace support plate(s) if ledges are deeply grooved. Do not attempt to smooth ledges by grinding.
	• Incorrect or missing power brake reaction disc	• Install correct disc
	• Rear brake support plates loose	• Tighten mounting bolts
Dragging brakes (slow or incomplete release of brakes)	• Brake pedal binding at pivot	• Loosen and lubricate
	• Power brake unit has internal bind	• Inspect for internal bind. Replace unit if internal bind exists.
	• Parking brake cables incorrrectly adjusted or seized	• Adjust cables. Replace seized cables.
	• Rear brakeshoe return springs weak or broken	• Replace return springs. Replace brakeshoe if necessary in axle sets.
	• Automatic adjusters malfunctioning	• Repair or replace adjuster parts as required
	• Caliper, wheel cylinder or master cylinder pistons sticking or seized	• Repair or replace parts as necessary
	• Master cylinder compensating ports blocked (fluid does not return to reservoirs).	• Use compressed air to clear ports. Do not use wire, pencils, or similar objects to open blocked ports.
Vehicle moves to one side when brakes are applied	• Incorrect front tire pressure	• Inflate to recommended cold (reduced load) inflation pressure
	• Worn or damaged wheel bearings	• Replace worn or damaged bearings
	• Brakelining on one side contaminated	• Determine and correct cause of contamination and replace brakelining in axle sets
	• Brakeshoes on one side bent, distorted, or lining loose on shoe	• Replace brakeshoes in axle sets
	• Support plate bent or loose on one side	• Tighten or replace support plate
	• Brakelining not yet seated with drums or rotors	• Burnish brakelining
	• Caliper anchor plate loose on one side	• Tighten anchor plate bolts
	• Caliper piston sticking or seized	• Repair or replace caliper
	• Brakelinings water soaked	• Drive vehicle with brakes lightly applied to dry linings
	• Loose suspension component attaching or mounting bolts	• Tighten suspension bolts. Replace worn suspension components.
	• Brake combination valve failure	• Replace combination valve
Chatter or shudder when brakes are applied (pedal pulsation and roughness may also occur.)	• Brakeshoes distorted, bent, contaminated, or worn	• Replace brakeshoes in axle sets
	• Caliper anchor plate or support plate loose	• Tighten mounting bolts
	• Excessive thickness variation of rotor(s)	• Refinish or replace rotors in axle sets
Noisy brakes (squealing, clicking, scraping sound when brakes are applied.)	• Bent, broken, distorted brakeshoes	• Replace brakeshoes in axle sets
	• Excessive rust on outer edge of rotor braking surface	• Remove rust

Troubleshooting the Brake System (cont.)

Problem	Cause	Solution
Noisy brakes (squealing, clicking, scraping sound when brakes are applied.) (cont.)	• Brakelining worn out—shoes contacting drum of rotor	• Replace brakeshoes and lining in axle sets. Refinish or replace drums or rotors.
	• Broken or loose holdown or return springs	• Replace parts as necessary
	• Rough or dry drum brake support plate ledges	• Lubricate support plate ledges
	• Cracked, grooved, or scored rotor(s) or drum(s)	• Replace rotor(s) or drum(s). Replace brakeshoes and lining in axle sets if necessary.
	• Incorrect brakelining and/or shoes (front or rear).	• Install specified shoe and lining assemblies
Pulsating brake pedal	• Out of round drums or excessive lateral runout in disc brake rotor(s)	• Refinish or replace drums, re-index rotors or replace

Stoplight Switch

REMOVAL AND INSTALLATION

1. Disconnect the negative battery cable.
2. Locate the stoplight switch on the brake pedal support.
3. Disconnect the electrical connector from the stoplight switch.
4. Remove the locknut and the stoplight switch.

To install:

5. Install switch on brake pedal support and adjust to specification.
6. Torque the locknut to 14 ft. lbs.
7. Install the connector and the negative battery cable.
8. Check the operation of the switch.

Master Cylinder

REMOVAL AND INSTALLATION

1. Disconnect reservoir fluid level indicator connector at the master cylinder.
2. Remove all brake lines from master cylinder using a *flare nut* wrench.

NOTE: *Brake fluid is highly corrosive to paint. Take care not to spill brake fluid on any painted surface of vehicle.*

3. Remove the master cylinder by pulling straight out.
4. Installation is the reverse of removal. Tighten master cylinder to power booster bolts to 7–12 ft. lbs. torque. Tighten brake line fittings to 6–11 ft. lbs. torque.
5. Bleed master cylinder and brakes.

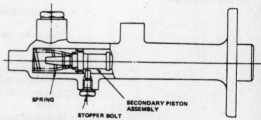

Installing secondary piston stop bolt

BRAKE PEDAL ADJUSTMENTS

Model	Free Play (in.)	Pedal Height (in.)	Switch Housing To Brake Pedal (in.)
RWD I-Mark	0	6.75	0
FWD I-Mark	0	6.07	0
RWD Impulse	0.24–0.39	5.52	0.0039 ①
4WD-FWD Impulse	0	6.22	0.02–0.04
Stylus	0	6.22	0.02–0.04
Trooper	0.28–0.43	7.80–8.20	0.02–0.04
Pick-up/Amigo	0.23–0.39	6.85–7.24	0.02–0.04
Rodeo	0.23–0.39	6.85–7.24	0.02–0.04

① Plus ½ Turn

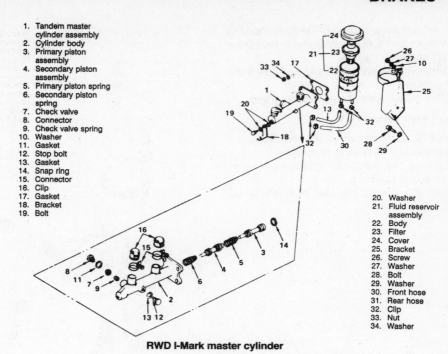

1. Tandem master cylinder assembly
2. Cylinder body
3. Primary piston assembly
4. Secondary piston assembly
5. Primary piston spring
6. Secondary piston spring
7. Check valve
8. Connector
9. Check valve spring
10. Washer
11. Gasket
12. Stop bolt
13. Gasket
14. Snap ring
15. Connector
16. Clip
17. Gasket
18. Bracket
19. Bolt

20. Washer
21. Fluid reservoir assembly
22. Body
23. Filter
24. Cover
25. Bracket
26. Screw
27. Washer
28. Bolt
29. Washer
30. Front hose
31. Rear hose
32. Clip
33. Nut
34. Washer

RWD I-Mark master cylinder

OVERHAUL

RWD I-Mark

1. Pour brake fluid out of the reservoir.

2. Disconnect the front and rear rubber hoses from the master cylinder and separate the fluid reservoir.

3. Place the master cylinder in a soft jawed vice and remove the pipe connector, check valve, spring and retainer.

4. Push IN on the primary piston with an appropriate tool and remove the secondary piston stop bolt and gasket. Maintain pressure and remove snapring.

NOTE: *DO NOT remove the spring from the piston.*

5. Remove the primary and secondary piston assembly from the master cylinder.

6. Clean all parts with DOT-3 brake fluid and dry with compressed air.

7. Measure master cylinder bore diameter. Specification for bore diameter is 22.22mm (0.875in.). Replace master cylinder if not within specification.

8. Measure primary and secondary piston outside diameter. Subtract the piston outside diameter from the master cylinder bore diameter to obtain the clearance. Specifications call for 0.025–0.127mm (0.001–0.005in.) with a maximum service limit of 0.15mm (0.006in.). If the clearance is larger, replace the master cylinder.

9. Check the master cylinder inner wall for wear, rust or damage. Check the pistons for wear or damage. Replace pistons if any wear is evident.

10. Inspect check valve for poor contact. Replace as necessary.

11. Check return port for obstructions and clean with wire. Blow away foreign matter with compressed air.

12. Inspect brake fluid reservoir and rubber hoses for cracking or damage. Inspect gaskets and snaprings for fatigue or damage. Replace as necessary.

To assemble:

13. Inspect parts carefully for foreign matter and lubricate with clean brake fluid. Lubricate the cylinder bore with clean rubber grease.

14. Clamp the cylinder into a soft jawed vice. Install the spring, check valve and gasket. Install the pipe connector hand tight. Torque pipe connector to 47 ft. lbs.

15. Install the primary and secondary piston assemblies. Push the piston in with an appropriate tool and install the snapring.

NOTE: *Be careful not to scratch the piston cups when installing the piston assemblies.*

16. Maintain pressure on the piston an install the stopper bolt and gasket hand tight. Torque stopper bolt to 14 ft. lbs.

17. Install the front and rear rubber hoses on the master cylinder. Install the fluid reservoir.

18. Apply rubber grease to the entrance of the cylinder housing.

19. Press the piston all the way into the cylin-

der and release several times. Check for smooth piston return and brake fluid being forced from the front and rear outlets.

20. Fill the reservoir with fluid and bleed the master cylinder.

21. After installation, bleed brake system.

All Except RWD I-Mark

1. Pour brake fluid out of the reservoir.
2. Remove the dust seal, if equipped.
3. Remove the reservoir attaching screw, reservoir and grommets.
4. Place the master cylinder in a soft jawed

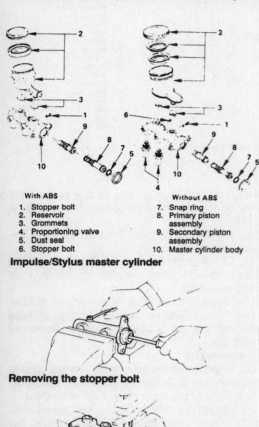

With ABS

1. Stopper bolt
2. Reservoir
3. Grommets
4. Proportioning valve
5. Dust seal
6. Stopper bolt

7. Snap ring
8. Primary piston assembly
9. Secondary piston assembly
10. Master cylinder body

Without ABS

Impulse/Stylus master cylinder

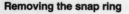

Removing the stopper bolt

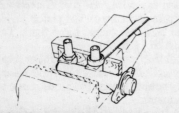

Removing the snap ring

Removing the proportioning valves

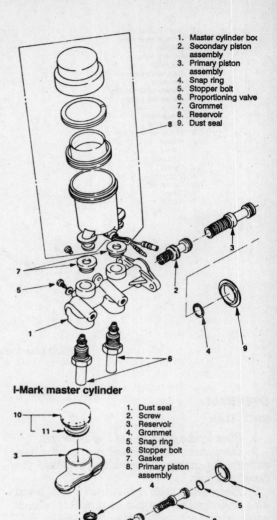

1. Master cylinder boc
2. Secondary piston assembly
3. Primary piston assembly
4. Snap ring
5. Stopper bolt
6. Proportioning valve
7. Grommet
8. Reservoir
9. Dust seal

I-Mark master cylinder

1. Dust seal
2. Screw
3. Reservoir
4. Grommet
5. Snap ring
6. Stopper bolt
7. Gasket
8. Primary piston assembly
9. Secondary piston assembly
10. Reservoir cover
11. Seal
12. Master cylinder assembly

Truck master cylinder

vise and remove the proportioning valve assemblies, if equipped.

5. Push IN on the primary piston with an appropriate tool and remove the secondary piston stop bolt and gasket. Maintain pressure and remove snapring.

NOTE: *DO NOT remove the spring from the piston.*

6. Remove the primary and secondary piston assembly from the master cylinder.

7. Clean all parts with DOT-3 brake fluid and dry with compressed air.

8. Measure master cylinder bore diameter. Specification for bore diameter for all vehicles **except P'up/Amigo is 22.22mm (0.875in.).**

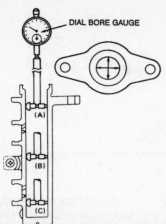

Measuring the master cylinder bore with a dial bore gauge. Measure the bore at 3 positions (A) top, (B) middle, (C) bottom

Specification for P'up/Amigo with 2.3L engine is 23.85mm (0.938in.); 2.6L enigne is 25.5mm (1.000in.). Replace master cylinder if not within specification.

9. Measure primary and secondary piston outside diameter. Subtract the piston outside diameter from the master cylinder bore diameter to obtain the clearance. Specifications call for 0.025–0.127mm (0.001–0.005in.) with a maximum service limit of 0.15mm (0.006in.). If the clearance is larger, replace the master cylinder.

10. Check the master cylinder inner wall for wear, rust or damage. Check the pistons for wear or damage. Replace pistons if any wear is evident.

11. Check return port for obstructions and clean with wire. Blow away foreign matter with compressed air.

12. Inspect brake fluid reservoir and grommets (rubber hoses) for cracking or damage. Inspect gaskets and snaprings for fatigue or damage. Replace as necessary.

To assemble:

13. Inspect parts carefully for foreign matter and lubricate with clean brake fluid. Lubricate the cylinder bore with clean rubber grease.

14. Install the primary and secondary piston assemblies. Push the piston in with an appropriate tool and install the snapring.

NOTE: *Be careful not to scratch the piston cups when installing the piston assemblies.*

15. Maintain pressure on the piston an install the stopper bolt and gasket hand tight. Torque stopper bolt to 5–7 ft. lbs. (RWD I-Mark 14 ft. lbs.).

16. Install the proportioning valve, if equipped. Torque to 29 ft. lbs.

17. Install the grommets, fluid reservoir and attaching screw.

18. Install the dust seal (if equipped) with the notch at the bottom.

19. Press the piston all the way into the cylinder and release several times. Check for smooth piston return and brake fluid being forced from the front and rear outlets.

20. Fill the reservoir with fluid and bleed the master cylinder.

21. Torque master cylinder nuts and brake line fittings to 12 ft. lbs. After installation, bleed the brake system.

Power Brake Booster

REMOVAL AND INSTALLATION

1. Disconnect the negative battery cable. Firmly, set the parking brake and block the wheels.

2. Disconnect the vacuum hose to the vacuum booster.

3. Disconnect and plug the brake fluid lines at the master cylinder. Place rags under the master cylinder to catch any leaking fluid.

NOTE: *Be careful not to spill any brake fluid on any painted surface. Permanent damage to the paint will result.*

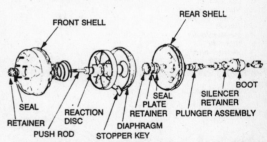

Exploded view of the RWD I-Mark power brake booster

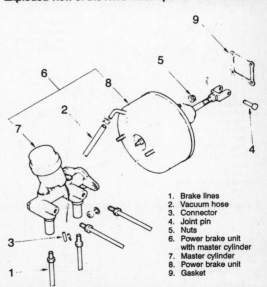

1. Brake lines
2. Vacuum hose
3. Connector
4. Joint pin
5. Nuts
6. Power brake unit with master cylinder
7. Master cylinder
8. Power brake unit
9. Gasket

Removing the power brake booster on the FWD I-Mark

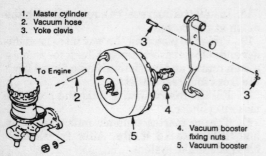

1. Master cylinder
2. Vacuum hose
3. Yoke clevis

To Engine

4. Vacuum booster fixing nuts
5. Vacuum booster

Removing the power brake booster on the FWD Impulse

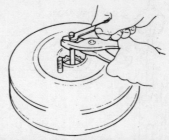

Adjusting power brake booster push rod

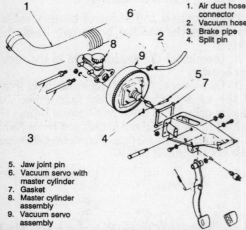

1. Air duct hose connector
2. Vacuum hose
3. Brake pipe
4. Split pin

5. Jaw joint pin
6. Vacuum servo with master cylinder
7. Gasket
8. Master cylinder assembly
9. Vacuum servo assembly

Removing the power brake booster on the RWD Impulse

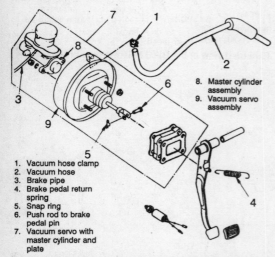

8. Master cylinder assembly
9. Vacuum servo assembly

1. Vacuum hose clamp
2. Vacuum hose
3. Brake pipe
4. Brake pedal return spring
5. Snap ring
6. Push rod to brake pedal pin
7. Vacuum servo with master cylinder and plate

Removing the power brake booster on the Isuzu truck

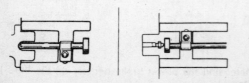

Measuring power brake booster push rod projection

4. Inside the vehicle, remove the snapring from the clevis pin and separate the clevis pin from the brake pedal.

5. Remove the vacuum booster mounting nuts at the firewall and lift out the power unit and master cylinder/reservoir as an assembly.

To install:

6. Before installing power brake booster, check the distance from the flange face of the booster to the end of the push rod. Projection should be 18.0–18.2mm (0.709–0.717in.) for Isuzu trucks and RWD Impulse; 18.6mm (0.733in.) for RWD I-Mark.

7. The procedure for measuring projection for front wheel drive vehicles involves the use of a push rod gauge (tool J–34873).

   a. Set the push rod gauge on the master cylinder and lower the pin until its tip slightly touches the piston.

   b. Turn the gauge upside down and set it on the power brake booster.

   c. Adjust the push rod length until the push rod lightly touches the pin head.

8. Installation is the reverse of removal. Torque vacuum booster nuts to 14 ft. lbs.; master cylinder and brake line fittings to 12 ft. lbs.

9. Bleed the master cylinder and brake system.

Proportioning Valve

REMOVAL AND INSTALLATION

Proportioning valves on Isuzu vehicles are mounted in two locations: (1) On the master cylinder, inline with the rear brake lines. (2) On the frame rail below the master cylinder.

1. Disconnect the negative battery cable.

2. Disconnect and plug the brake lines at the master cylinder (proportioning valve).

3. Remove the proportioning valve(s).

4. Installation is the reverse of the removal procedure. Torque the proportioning valves attached to the master cylinder to 30 ft. lbs. Torque brake lines to 12 ft. lbs.

5. Bleed the brake system.

Brake Hoses

REMOVAL AND INSTALLATION

1. Raise and support vehicle safely. Remove wheel.

2. Clean dirt and foreign matter from both hoe end fittings.

3. Disconnect brake pipe from hose fitting using a backup wrench on fitting. Be careful not to bend frame bracket or brake pipe. It may be necessary to soak connections with penetrating oil. Place an appropriate container under the work area to catch any spilled brake fluid.

NOTE: *Be careful not to spill any brake fluid on any painted surface. Permanent damage to the paint will result.*

4. Remove the 'U' clip from the female fitting at the bracket. Remove hose from the bracket.

5. Remove hose from caliper.

To install:

6. Connect brake hose at each end. Install 'U' clip and torque brake hose to 12 ft. lbs.

7. Install wheel. Inspect to see that hose does not rub against wheel or suspension. If hose makes contact, loosen fittings and correct.

8. Bleed the brake system.

Brake System Bleeding

1. Set the parking brake and start the engine.

NOTE: *The vacuum booster will be damaged if the bleeding operation is performed with the engine off.*

2. Remove the master cylinder reservoir cap and fill the reservoir with brake fluid. Keep the reservoir at least half full during the bleeding operation.

3. If the master cylinder is replaced or overhauled, first bleed the air from the master cylinder and then from each caliper or wheel cylinder. Bleed the master cylinder as follows:

a. Disconnect the left front wheel brake line from the master cylinder.

b. Have an assistant depress the brake pedal slowly once and hold it depressed.

c. Seal the delivery port of the master cylinder where the line was disconnected with a

finger, then release the brake pedal slowly.

d. Release the finger from the delivery port when the brake pedal returns completely.

e. Repeat Steps C–E until the brake fluid comes out of the delivery port during Step C.

f. Reconnect the brake line to the master cylinder.

g. Have an assistant depress the brake pedal slowly once and hold it depressed.

h. Loosen the front wheel brake line at the master cylinder.

i. Retighten the brake line, then release the brake pedal slowly.

j. Repeat Steps G–I until no air comes out from the port when the brake line is loosened.

k. Bleed the air from the right front wheel brake line connection by repeating Steps A–J.

4. Bleed the air from each wheel in the following order: Left front caliper, Right rear caliper or wheel cylinder, Right front caliper, Left rear caliper or wheel cylinder. Bleed the air as follows:

a. Place the proper size box wrench over the bleeder screw.

b. Cover the bleeder screw with a transparent tube and submerge the free end of the tube in a transparent container containing brake fluid.

c. Have an assistant pump the brake pedal 3 times, then hold it depressed.

d. Remove the air along with the brake fluid by loosening the bleeder screw.

e. Retighten the bleeder screw, then release the brake pedal slowly.

f. Repeat Steps C–E until the air is completely removed. It may be necessary to repeat the bleeding procedure 10 or more times for front wheels and 15 or more times for rear wheels.

g. Go to the next wheel in sequence after each wheel is bled.

5. Depress the brake pedal to check if sponginess is felt after the air has been removed from all wheel cylinders and calipers. If the pedal feels spongy, the entire bleeding procedure must be repeated.

6. After the bleeding operation is completed on each individual wheel, check the level of brake fluid in the reservoir and replenish up to the **MAX** level, if necessary.

7. Install the master cylinder reservoir cap and stop the engine.

DISC BRAKES

Disc Brake Pads

Most disc brake pads are equipped with wear indicators. If a squealing noise occurs from the

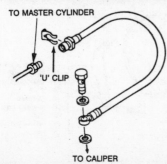

TO MASTER CYLINDER

'U' CLIP

TO CALIPER

Brake hose installation

brakes while driving, check the pad wear indicator plate. If there is evidence of the indicator plate contacting the rotor disc, the brake pad should be replaced.

CAUTION: *Brake shoes contain asbestos, which has been determined to be a cancer causing agent. Never clean the brake surfaces with compressed air! Avoid inhaling any dust from any brake surface! When cleaning brake surfaces, use a commercially available brake cleaning fluid.*

REMOVAL AND INSTALLATION

1. Remove half of the volume of brake fluid from the master cylinder.
2. Raise and safely support the vehicle.
3. Remove the wheel and tire assemblies.
4. Remove the brake caliper without disconnecting the brake line. Support the caliper with a length of wire. Do not let the caliper hang from the brake hose.

NOTE: *On some rear disc brake systems it is*

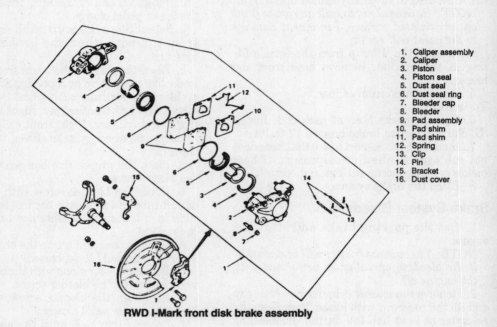

1. Caliper assembly
2. Caliper
3. Piston
4. Piston seal
5. Dust seal
6. Dust seal ring
7. Bleeder cap
8. Bleeder
9. Pad assembly
10. Pad shim
11. Pad shim
12. Spring
13. Clip
14. Pin
15. Bracket
16. Dust cover

RWD I-Mark front disk brake assembly

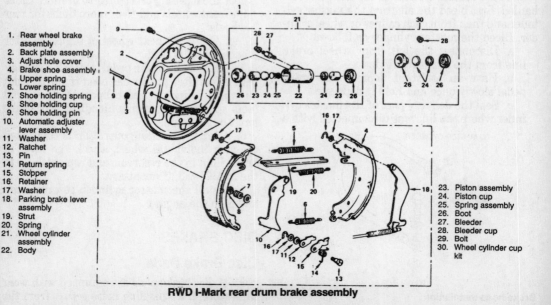

1. Rear wheel brake assembly
2. Back plate assembly
3. Adjust hole cover
4. Brake shoe assembly
5. Upper spring
6. Lower spring
7. Shoe holding spring
8. Shoe holding cup
9. Shoe holding pin
10. Automatic adjuster lever assembly
11. Washer
12. Ratchet
13. Pin
14. Return spring
15. Stopper
16. Retainer
17. Washer
18. Parking brake lever assembly
19. Strut
20. Spring
21. Wheel cylinder assembly
22. Body

23. Piston assembly
24. Piston cup
25. Spring assembly
26. Boot
27. Bleeder
28. Bleeder cup
29. Bolt
30. Wheel cylinder cup kit

RWD I-Mark rear drum brake assembly

not necessary to remove the caliper when installing new brake pads. Remove the lower slide bolt and rotate the caliper upward to remove the pads.

5. Remove the brake pads and shims. Inspect the brake rotor and machine or replace as necessary. Check the minimum thickness (specification is cast into the rotor) before machining.

To install:

6. Use a suitable tool to push the caliper piston into it's bore. On FWD Impulse and truck rear calipers, push the piston in by rotating it clockwise until it stops, then set the piston, aligning the uneven section on the piston surface with the caliper center.

7. Apply a thin coat of grease to the rear face of the brake pad and install the shim. Install the brake pads. On FWD Impulse rear calipers, the brake pad is provided with a pinion. The automatic adjuster becomes inoperative when the

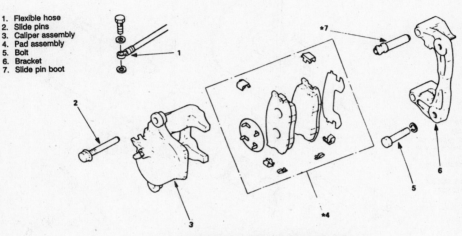

1. Flexible hose
2. Slide pins
3. Caliper assembly
4. Pad assembly
5. Bolt
6. Bracket
7. Slide pin boot

FWD I-Mark front disk brake assembly

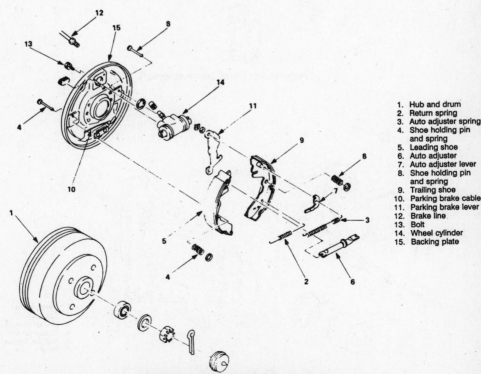

1. Hub and drum
2. Return spring
3. Auto adjuster spring
4. Shoe holding pin and spring
5. Leading shoe
6. Auto adjuster
7. Auto adjuster lever
8. Shoe holding pin and spring
9. Trailing shoe
10. Parking brake cable
11. Parking brake lever
12. Brake line
13. Bolt
14. Wheel cylinder
15. Backing plate

FWD I-Mark rear drum brake assembly

pinion is not placed correctly into the indentation of the piston.

8. Install the calipers. Install the wheel and tire assemblies and lower the vehicle.

9. Apply the brakes several times to seat the pads. Check the fluid in the master cylinder and add as necessary.

Brake Caliper
REMOVAL AND INSTALLATION
Front

CAUTION: *Brake shoes contain asbestos, which has been determined to be a cancer causing agent. Never clean the brake surfaces*

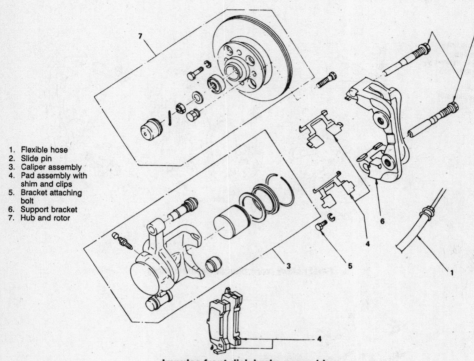

1. Flexible hose
2. Slide pin
3. Caliper assembly
4. Pad assembly with shim and clips
5. Bracket attaching bolt
6. Support bracket
7. Hub and rotor

Impulse front disk brake assembly

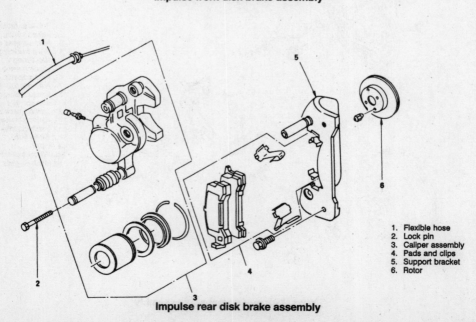

1. Flexible hose
2. Lock pin
3. Caliper assembly
4. Pads and clips
5. Support bracket
6. Rotor

Impulse rear disk brake assembly

with compressed air! Avoid inhaling any dust from any brake surface! When cleaning brake surfaces, use a commercially available brake cleaning fluid.

1. Raise and safely support the vehicle.

2. Remove the front wheel and tire assemblies.

3. Disconnect and plug the brake hose at the caliper. Use a container to catch the fluid.

4. Remove the caliper slide pin(s) and remove the caliper (some models may have a support bracket which also needs to be removed).

5. Installation is the reverse of the removal procedure. Tighten the slide pin(s) to 36 ft. lbs. except on RWD Impulse and Isuzu trucks where they are tightened to 27 ft. lbs.

6. Bleed the brake system.

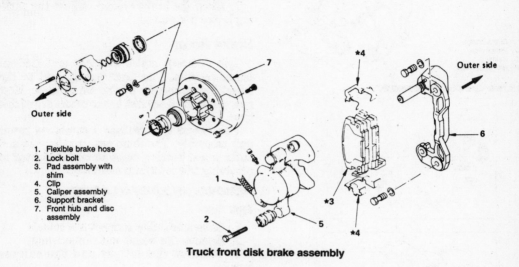

1. Flexible brake hose
2. Lock bolt
3. Pad assembly with shim
4. Clip
5. Caliper assembly
6. Support bracket
7. Front hub and disc assembly

Truck front disk brake assembly

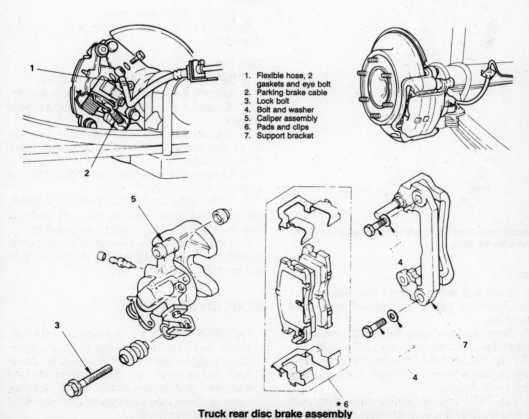

1. Flexible hose, 2 gaskets and eye bolt
2. Parking brake cable
3. Lock bolt
4. Bolt and washer
5. Caliper assembly
6. Pads and clips
7. Support bracket

Truck rear disc brake assembly

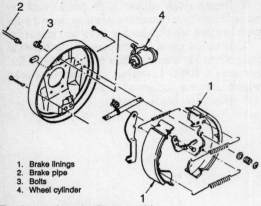

1. Brake linings
2. Brake pipe
3. Bolts
4. Wheel cylinder

Truck rear drum brake assembly

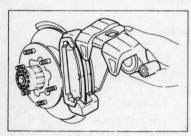

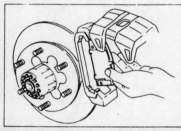

Remove the lower bolt, rotate the caliper upward and remove brake pads

Rear

1. Raise and safely support the vehicle.
2. Remove the rear wheel and tire assemblies.
3. Disconnect and plug the brake hose at the caliper. Use a container to catch the fluid.

NOTE: *On 1990–91 Impulse, the bolt retaining the brake hose on the right hand side has left hand thread.*

4. On FWD Impulse and trucks, disconnect the rear parking brake cable from the front ca-

ble, remove the brake cable from the cable support bracket and disconnect the brake cable from the brake lever.

5. Remove the lower slide pin and remove the caliper assembly.
6. Installation is the reverse of the removal procedure. Tighten the slide pin to 36 ft. lbs. on Stylus, 32 ft. lbs. on FWD Impulse and 14.5 ft. lbs. on RWD Impulse and trucks.
7. Bleed the brake system. Adjust the parking brake if removed.

Brake Rotor

Two different styles of rotor are used on Isuzu vehicles. The first type is held to the wheel hub assembly by the wheel nuts. Most rear and some front disc brake rotors are of this type.

The second type utilizes a combined rotor/hub assembly. The dust cap, spindle nut and outer wheel bearing must be removed prior to removing the rotor/hub assembly.

REMOVAL AND INSTALLATION

Type One

1. Raise and safely support the vehicle.
2. Remove the wheel and tire assembly.
3. Remove the caliper and the caliper bracket.
4. Remove the brake rotor.
5. Installation is the reverse of the removal procedure.

Type Two

1. Raise and safely support the vehicle.
2. Remove the front wheel and tire assembly.
3. Remove the caliper and the caliper bracket.
4. Remove the dust cap and cotter pin. Remove the castle nut, washer and the outer wheel bearing.
5. Remove the rotor/hub assembly with the inner wheel bearing.
6. If the rotor is machined while removed, the wheel bearings must be removed and the hub thoroughly cleaned before installation.
7. Installation is the reverse of the removal procedure. Properly adjust the wheel bearings and install a new cotter pin.

REAR DRUM BRAKES

CAUTION: *Brake shoes contain asbestos, which has been determined to be a cancer causing agent. Never clean the brake surfaces with compressed air! Avoid inhaling any dust from any brake surface! When cleaning brake surfaces, use a commercially available brake cleaning fluid.*

Brake Drums

REMOVAL AND INSTALLATION

1. Raise and safely support the vehicle.
2. Remove the rear wheel and tire assembly.
3. Remove the dust cap and cotter pin. Remove the castle nut, washer and outer wheel bearing.
4. Remove the brake drum/hub assembly with the inner wheel bearing.
5. Installation is the reverse of the removal procedure. Properly adjust the wheel bearings and install a new cotter pin.

Brake Shoes

REMOVAL AND INSTALLATION

1. Raise and safely support the vehicle.
2. Remove the rear wheel and tire assemblies.
3. Remove the brake drums.
4. Remove the brake return springs.
5. Remove the leading shoe holding pin and spring and the leading shoe.
6. Remove the self adjuster and the adjuster lever.
7. Remove the trailing shoe holding pin and spring.
8. Disconnect the parking brake cable from the trailing shoe and remove the trailing shoe. Remove the parking brake lever from the trailing shoe.
9. Installation is the reverse of the removal procedure. Apply a thin coat of suitable high temperature grease to the shoe contact pads on the brake backing plate prior to installation.
10. Check the brake drum for scoring or other wear and machine or replace as necessary. Check the maximum brake drum diameter specification when machining. If the drum is machined, the wheel bearings must be removed and the hub thoroughly cleaned before reinstalling.
11. Adjust the brake shoes.

Wheel Cylinder

REMOVAL AND INSTALLATION

1. Raise and safely support the vehicle.
2. Remove the rear wheel and tire assembly.
3. Remove the brake drum and the brake shoes.
4. Disconnect and plug the brake line at the wheel cylinder.
5. Remove the wheel cylinder attaching bolts and the wheel cylinder.
6. Installation is the reverse of the removal procedure. Bleed the brake system.

PARKING BRAKE

Parking Brake Cable

ADJUSTMENT

FWD Impulse vehicles are equipped with parking brake shoes which are located inside the disc brake rotor. These shoes are adjusted by turning the adjuster until shoe contact can be felt, then backing off 6 notches.

1. Release the parking brake lever.
2. Adjust the brake shoes on I-Mark and 1987–89 Impulse.
3. On I-Mark, adjust the parking brake by turning the turnbuckle until the parking brake lever stroke is 7–9 notches when pulled with a force of approximately 66 lbs.
4. On FWD Impulse, turn the nuts at the equalizer until the parking brake lever stroke is 11–13 notches when pulled with a force of approximately 66 lbs.

NOTE: *The parking brake shoes on 1987–89 Impulse must be broken down periodically or after replacement of the shoes or rotor in order to ensure effective operation. Drive the vehicle at about 30 mph on a safe, dry and level surface. Pull the brake lever up with a force of approximately 20 lbs. with the brake release button depressed. Drive the vehicle approximately ¼ mile with the parking brake partly applied. Repeat this operation 2–3 times.*

5. On 1990–91 FWD Impulse, adjust the cable by turning the adjust nuts until the parking brake lever stroke is 7–8 notches when pulled with a force of approximately 66 lbs.

REMOVAL AND INSTALLATION

I-Mark

1. Raise and safely support the vehicle.
2. Remove the rear wheel and tire assemblies.
3. Remove the brake drums.
4. Disconnect the rear cables from the parking brake levers and the brake backing plates.
5. Disconnect the front parking brake cable from the parking brake lever. Disconnect the front cable from the rear cables and remove the tension spring from the rear axle.
6. Remove the cable-to-body mounting bolts and remove the cables.
7. Installation is the reverse of the removal procedure. Adjust the parking brake.

1987–89 Impulse

1. Raise and safely support the vehicle.
2. Remove the rear wheel and tire assemblies.
3. Remove the rear disc brake calipers and the rotors. Disconnect the rear cable from the

parking brake levers and the brake backing plate.

4. Remove the return spring and the rear nut at the equalizer.

5. Remove the clips and the cable mounting bolts and remove the rear cable.

6. Remove the rear console assembly and the parking brake lever cover.

7. Remove the parking brake cable bolt from the parking brake lever.

NOTE: *The parking brake cable bolt has left hand thread.*

8. Remove the front cable mounting bolts and remove the front cable.

9. Installation is the reverse of the removal procedure. Adjust the parking brake.

1990–91 Impulse

1. Raise and safely support the vehicle.

2. Remove the rear wheel and tire assemblies.

3. Loosen the adjusting nuts at the left side rear cable.

4. Remove the right side rear cable from the bracket and disconnect it from the front cable.

5. Disconnect the rear cables from the parking brake levers at the disc brake assemblies.

6. Remove the cable mounting bolts and remove the rear cables.

7. Remove the console box.

8. Disconnect the front parking brake cable from the parking brake lever, remove the mounting nuts and remove the front cable.

9. Installation is the reverse of the removal procedure. Adjust the parking brake.

ANTI-LOCK BRAKE SYSTEM — IMPULSE

Hydraulic Unit

REMOVAL AND INSTALLATION

1. Disconnect negative battery cable.

2. Raise and support vehicle safely.

3. Remove under cover to gain access to hydraulic unit.

4. Remove tire if needed and remove inner fender liner.

5. Disconnect harness connectors from hydraulic unit.

6. Remove radiator reservoir tank.

7. Remove brake lines using a *flare nut* wrench. Cap or tape brake line ends to prevent entry of foreign matter.

8. Disconnect hydraulic motor ground cable.

9. Remove bracket attaching bolt, hydraulic unit attaching nut, bracket and hydraulic unit.

10. Installation is the reverse of removal. Torque hydraulic unit attaching nut, bracket

attaching bolt and ground cable bolt to 17 ft. lbs. Torque brake line to 9 ft. lbs.

11. Bleed the brake system.

NOTE: *Replace all components included in repair kits used to service this system. Lubricate rubber parts with clean, fresh brake fluid to ease assembly. Do not use lubricated shop air to clean parts, as damage to rubber components may result. Always bleed the braking system after repairing or replacing hydraulic components.*

Electric Brake Control Unit (EBCM)

REMOVAL AND INSTALLATION

The EBCM is located under the passenger side seat on the Impulse.

1. Disconnect the negative battery cable.

2. It may be necessary to move the passenger seat out of the way to gain access to the EBCM. If so, remove the seat attaching bolts and move the seat.

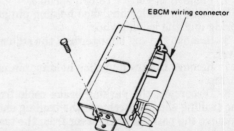

Electronic brake control module (EBCM) removal and installation

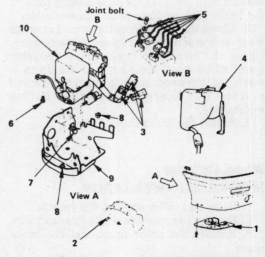

1. Under cover
2. Inner liner
3. Harness connector
4. Radiator reservoir tank
5. Brake pipes
6. Ground cable
7. Bracket fixing bolt
8. Hydraulic unit fixing nuts
9. Bracket
10. Hydraulic unit

ABS hydraulic unit removal and installation

3. Remove the EBCM attaching bolts.

4. Remove the EBCM wiring harness connector. Remove the EBCM.

5. Installation is the reverse of removal. Tighten EBCM attaching bolts to 62 inch lbs.

G-Sensor

REMOVAL AND INSTALLATION

1. Disconnect negative battery cable.

2. Remove center console as per illustration.

3. Remove G-Sensor wiring harness connector.

4. Remove G-Sensor attaching bolt. Remove G-Sensor.

5. Place G-Sensor on a known level surface and check continuity between terminals (see illustration). If no continuity, replace the G-Sensor.

6. Incline the G-Sensor at a 30° angle and re-test for continuity. If continuity, replace the G-Sensor.

NOTE: *Ensure that G-Sensor is installed in the correct direction.*

7. Installation is the reverse of removal. Torque attaching bolts to 53 inch lbs.

Speed Sensor

REMOVAL AND INSTALLATION

1. Disconnect negative battery cable.

2. Raise and support vehicle safely.

3. Remove wheel assembly. Remove inner fender liner.

4. Disconnect speed sensor wire connector.

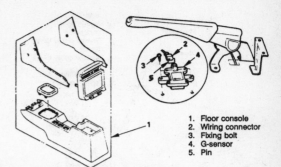

1. Floor console
2. Wiring connector
3. Fixing bolt
4. G-sensor
5. Pin

G-sensor location on the 1981 Impulse

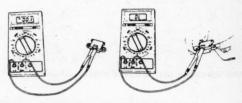

Checking continuity on the G-sensor

5. Remove sensor cable attaching bolts and screws.

6. Remove sensor attaching bolts. Remove sensor.

7. Inspect the speed sensor for damage.

   a. Check speed sensor pole piece for dirt and remove.

   b. Check the pole piece for damage and replace if necessary.

   c. Check for continuity while flexing the sensor cable. Replace sensor cable if short or open is found.

   d. Check the sensor rotor for damage in-

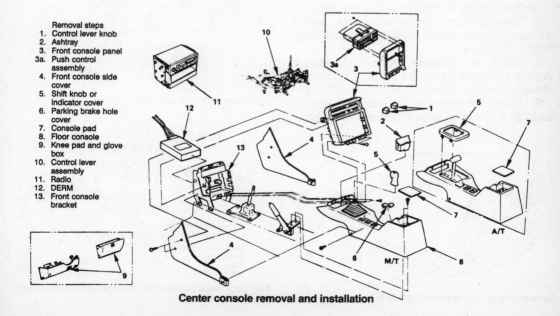

Removal steps
1. Control lever knob
2. Ashtray
3. Front console panel
3a. Push control assembly
4. Front console side cover
5. Shift knob or indicator cover
6. Parking brake hole cover
7. Console pad
8. Floor console
9. Knee pad and glove box
10. Control lever assembly
11. Radio
12. DERM
13. Front console bracket

Center console removal and installation

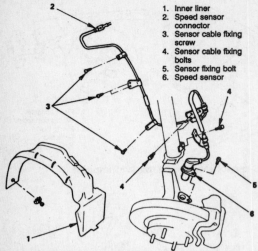

1. Inner liner
2. Speed sensor connector
3. Sensor cable fixing screw
4. Sensor cable fixing bolts
5. Sensor fixing bolt
6. Speed sensor

Front speed sensor removal and installation

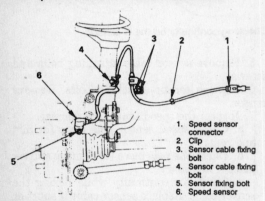

1. Speed sensor connector
2. Clip
3. Sensor cable fixing bolt
4. Sensor cable fixing bolt
5. Sensor fixing bolt
6. Speed sensor

Rear speed sensor removal and installation

cluding tooth chipping. Replace the drive shaft assembly if sensor rotor is damaged.

8. Install the speed sensor taking care not to damage the pole piece. Tighten the attaching bolt to 62 inch lbs.

9. Check the clearance between the speed sensor pole piece and the rotor. Clearance should be 0.20–0.80mm (0.0079 to 0.0315in.).

10. Install the sensor cable fixing bolt (tighten to 13 ft. lbs.) and screw (tighten to 9 ft. lbs.).

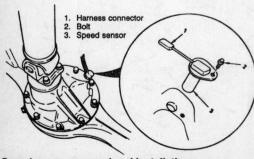

1. Harness connector
2. Bolt
3. Speed sensor

Speed sensor removal and installation

11. Ensure the white line marked on the cable is not twisted. If so, loosen connections and straighten cable.

12. Reconnect sensor wire connector, install inner liner, install wheel, lower vehicle and reconnect negative battery cable.

REAR WHEEL ANTI-LOCK (RWAL) BRAKE SYSTEM — P'UP/RODEO

RWAL Electronic Control Module (ECM)
REMOVAL AND INSTALLATION

1. Disconnect negative battery cable.
2. Remove passenger seat assembly.
3. Remove ECM wire harness connector.
4. Remove ECM harness bracket. Remove ECM.
5. Installation is reverse of removal. Torque attaching bolt to 29 ft. lbs.

Anti-Lock (Isolation/Dump) Valve
REMOVAL AND INSTALLATION

1. Disconnect negative battery cable.
2. Disconnect valve harness connector.

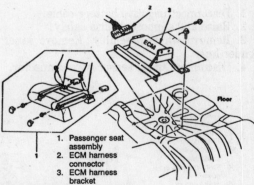

1. Passenger seat assembly
2. ECM harness connector
3. ECM harness bracket

ECM removal and installation

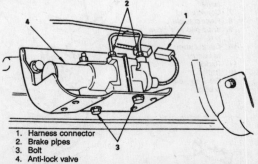

1. Harness connector
2. Brake pipes
3. Bolt
4. Anti-lock valve

Anti-Lock (isolation/dump) valve removal and installation

3. Disconnect brake pipes using a *flare nut* wrench.

4. Remove attaching bolt then remove anti-lock valve from frame rail.

5. Installation is the reverse of removal. Torque attaching bolt to 18 ft. lbs. and brake pipe to 12 ft. lbs.

Speed Sensor

REMOVAL AND INSTALLATION

1. Disconnect negative battery cable.

2. Remove speed sensor wiring harness connector.

3. Remove attaching bolt and speed sensor.

4. Installation is the reverse of removal. Torque attaching bolt to 18 ft. lbs.

Body

10

EXTERIOR

Doors

REMOVAL AND INSTALLATION

RWD I-Mark

NOTE: *To prevent door glass from breaking, lower glass prior to removal or alignment of door.*

1. If door is equipped with power accessories or front door speakers, the inside door panel must be removed to disconnect the wiring harness. See illustrations for locations of inside door panel fasteners.

2. Fully open and balance door on a floor jack (an assistant may be needed). Use a bundled rag or a block of wood to protect the painted surface of the door edge.

3. Remove the door checker rivet with a hammer and a chisel (punch).

4. Remove the door hinge plugs that cover the door hinge pins.

5. Using a hinge pin removal tool (J-21688-01), remove the upper and lower hinge pins.

6. Slowly pull the door away from the hinges.

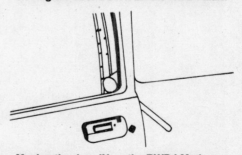

Moving the door DOWN on the RWD I-Mark

Removing the door hinge pins on the RWD I-Mark

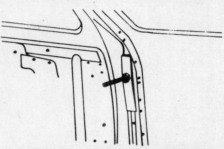

Moving the door IN on the RWD I-Mark

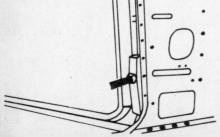

Moving the door UP on the RWD I-Mark

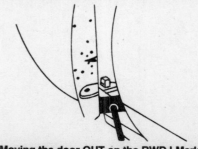

Moving the door OUT on the RWD I-Mark

To install:

7. Clean surfaces of hinges with sandpaper to remove any burrs. Lubricate the hinges and the inside of the door pin hole with grease.

8. Balance door on floor jack and align two halves of hinge.

9. Using a hammer and punch, install hinge pins in the same direction of removal. First the upper, then the lower. Replace hinge plugs. Remove floor jack.

10. Install new rivet on door checker and secure with caulking.

11. Close door slowly to check alignment. DO NOT slam door closed.

12. Adjust the door using the following procedure:

a. Move the door UP by putting a piece of metal over the lower hinge and closing the door.

b. Move the door DOWN by putting a piece of metal over the upper hinge and closing the door.

c. Move the door IN by putting a rubber hammer between the door and pillar, just under the window frame, and push the lower part of the door in.

d. Move the door OUT by putting a rubber hammer between the lower part of the door and pillar and pushing the center of the door in.

e. Move the door FORWARD by disconnecting the door checker and opening the door wide enough to bend the hinges.

f. Move the door REARWARD by putting a piece of metal over the upper and lower hinges and closing the door.

g. Poor sealing in the upper part of the door is corrected by hitting the outer door panel with a rubber hammer or hitting the weatherstrip flange with a hammer.

h. Poor sealing in the lower part of the door is corrected be hitting the weatherstrip flange with a hammer.

13. Reconnect door accessory wiring harness.

14. Install all previously disconnected inner door panel components.

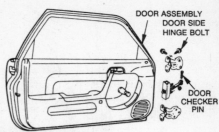

FWD Impulse door hinges

All Except RWD I-Mark

NOTE: *To prevent door glass from breaking, lower glass prior to removal or alignment of door.*

1. If door is equipped with power accessories or front door speakers, the inside door panel must be removed to disconnect the wiring harness. See illustrations for locations of inside door panel fasteners.

2. Fully open and balance door on a floor jack (an assistant may be needed). Use a bundled rag or a block of wood to protect the painted surface of the door edge.

3. Remove the door checker pin with a hammer. Place a block of wood under the checker to prevent bending it while removing the pin.

4. Remove the door-side hinge mounting bolts

5. Slowly pull the door away from the hinges.

To Install:

6. Clean and lubricate the hinges, hinge bolt holes and door checker assembly with grease.

7. Balance door on floor jack and align the door with the hinges.

8. Install door-side hinge bolts and tighten with moderate torque. DO NOT tighten down all the way.

9. Remove floor jack and close door slowly to check alignment. DO NOT slam door closed. In most cases door adjustment will be necessary.

10. Open door, loosen hinge bolts and adjust door so that all clearances are even. Hold clearance as far as possible.

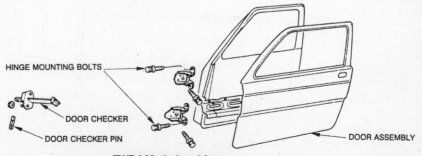

FWD I-Mark door hinges

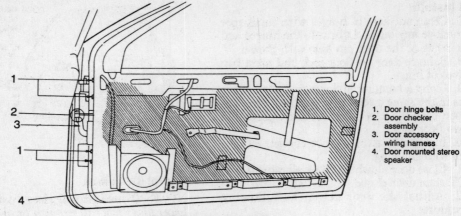

1. Door hinge bolts
2. Door checker assembly
3. Door accessory wiring harness
4. Door mounted stereo speaker

RWD Impulse door hinges

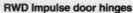

UPPER HINGE

LOWER HINGE

P'up/Amigo door hinges

Door striker

Door checker

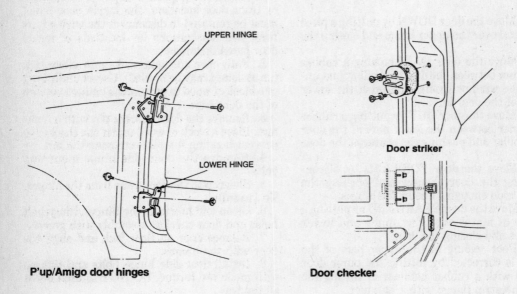

1. Door accessory wiring harness
2. Door checker assembly
3. Door hinge bolts
4. Door

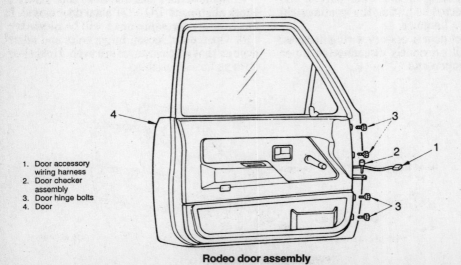

Rodeo door assembly

NOTE: *It may be necessary to loosen door-side and/or body-side hinge bolts to correctly adjust door. Body shims may be necessary to adjust door or striker with body.*

11. After alignment is satisfactory, tighten door-side hinge bolts to 18-25 ft. lbs.

12. Adjust door striker by loosening mounting screws and tapping with a plastic hammer. The striker should be parallel with the dovetail on the door latch mechanism. One or two shims are needed to control correct engagement of striker with door latch. Torque striker screws to 10 ft. lbs.

Hood

REMOVAL AND INSTALLATION

1. Scribe a mark showing the location of the hinges on the hood.

2. Disconnect under hood light connector (if equipped).

3. On RWD Impulse disconnect headlight actuator terminal connector.

4. On FWD I-Mark remove washer nozzle tubes.

5. Disconnect hood strut (if equipped) by removing bolts, or lower prop rod.

CAUTION: *An assistant is needed to hold the hood in position during removal. Serious injury can result if hood should close during removal.*

RWD I-Mark hood hinge

6. Remove hood mounting bolts and lift hood from vehicle.

To install:

7. Position hood on hinges and line up scribe line.

8. Install and tighten mounting bolts with moderate torque. DO NOT tighten down all the way.

9. Close hood slowly to check alignment. DO NOT slam hood closed. In most cases hood adjustment will be necessary.

10. Open hood, loosen hinge bolts and adjust hood so that all clearances are even and panel is flush with body. Hold clearance as far as possible.

NOTE: *Body shims may be necessary to adjust hood.*

11. After alignment is satisfactory, tighten hood hinge bolts to 18-25 ft. lbs.

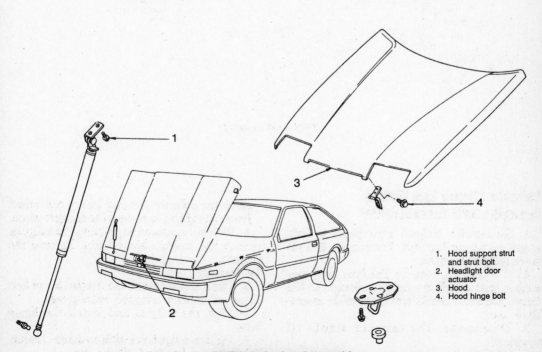

1. Hood support strut and strut bolt
2. Headlight door actuator
3. Hood
4. Hood hinge bolt

RWD Impulse hood assembly

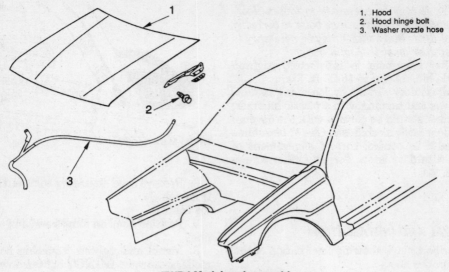

1. Hood
2. Hood hinge bolt
3. Washer nozzle hose

FWD I-Mark hood assembly

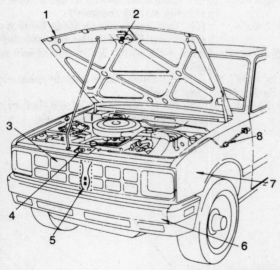

1. Hood
2. Striker assembly
3. Grille
4. Hood lock assembly
5. Support deflector
   panel
6. Front bumper
   assembly
7. Front fender
8. Hood lock control
   cable

P'up hood assembly

Tailgate (Trunk Lid, Hatch)
REMOVAL AND INSTALLATION

1. Disassemble tailgate inner panel to gain access to wiring harness. Disconnect and remove tailgate harness.

2. If equipped, remove the bolt, nut and washer that attach the tailgate checker to the frame. On some trucks a tailgate cable assembly is used.

3. Disconnect the tailgate struts (if equipped).

CAUTION: *An assistant is necessary to re-move the tailgate. Serious injury can result from attempting to remove the tailgate alone.*

4. With an assistant supporting the tailgate, remove the tailgate hinge bolts. Remove the tailgate.

To Install:

5. Clean and lubricate the hinges, hinge bolt holes and checker assembly with grease.

6. Align the tailgate and install the hinge bolts.

7. Tighten hinge bolts with moderate torque. DO NOT tighten down all the way.

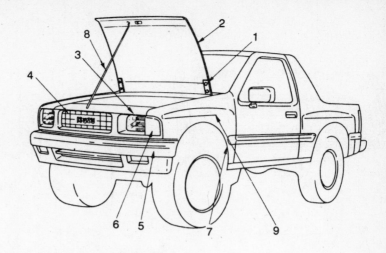

1. Hood hinge and hinge bolt
2. Hood
3. Head light
4. Grille
5. Front bumper assembly
6. Turn signal lamp
7. Inner fender well
8. Hood prop rod
9. Front fender

Amigo hood assembly

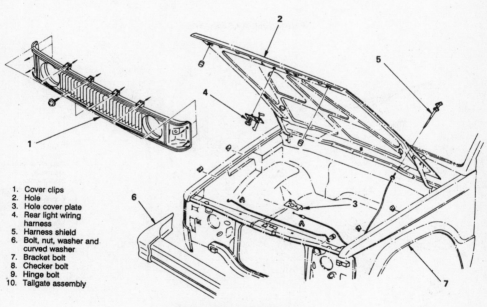

1. Cover clips
2. Hole
3. Hole cover plate
4. Rear light wiring harness
5. Harness shield
6. Bolt, nut, washer and curved washer
7. Bracket bolt
8. Checker bolt
9. Hinge bolt
10. Tailgate assembly

Trooper hood assembly

8. Close tailgate slowly to check alignment. DO NOT slam tailgate closed. In most cases tailgate adjustment will be necessary.

9. Open tailgate, loosen hinge bolts and adjust so that all clearances are even and panel is flush with body. Hold clearance as far as possible.

NOTE: *It may be necessary to loosen tailgate and/or body-side hinge bolts to correctly adjust tailgate. Body shims may be necessary to* *adjust tailgate or striker with body.*

10. After alignment is satisfactory, tighten hinge bolts to 18-25 ft. lbs.

11. Adjust striker by loosening mounting screws and tapping with a plastic hammer. The striker should be parallel with the dovetail on the latch mechanism. One or two shims are needed to control correct engagement of striker with the latch. Torque striker screws to 10 ft. lbs.

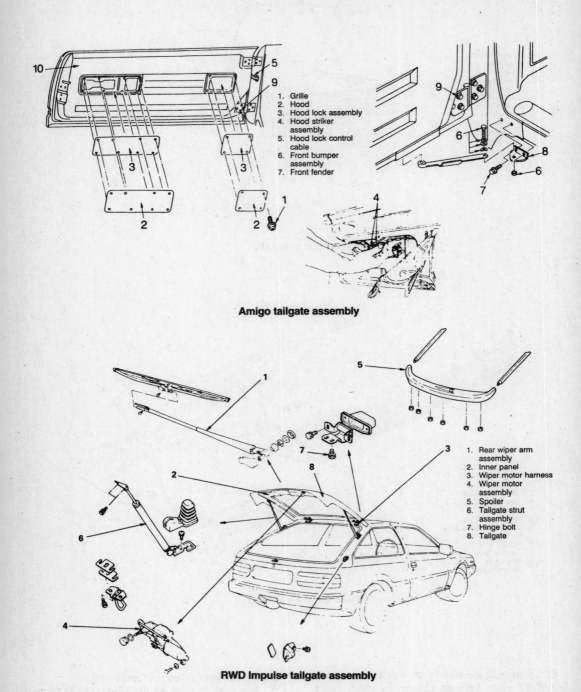

1. Grille
2. Hood
3. Hood lock assembly
4. Hood striker assembly
5. Hood lock control cable
6. Front bumper assembly
7. Front fender

Amigo tailgate assembly

1. Rear wiper arm assembly
2. Inner panel
3. Wiper motor harness
4. Wiper motor assembly
5. Spoiler
6. Tailgate strut assembly
7. Hinge bolt
8. Tailgate

RWD Impulse tailgate assembly

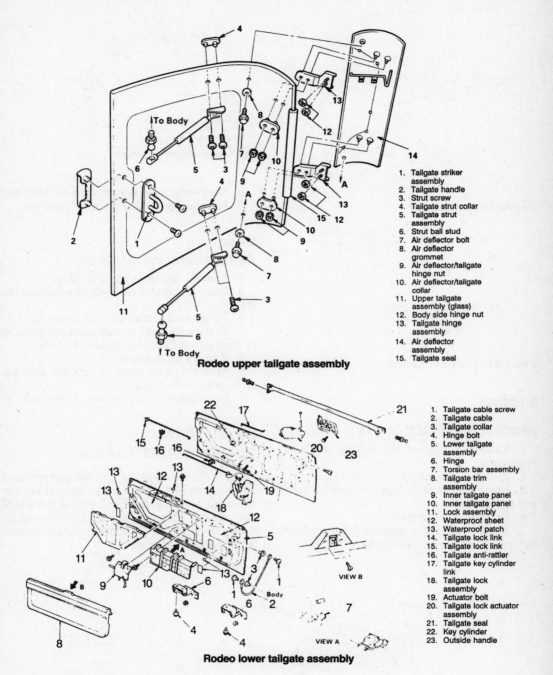

Rodeo upper tailgate assembly

1. Tailgate striker assembly
2. Tailgate handle
3. Strut screw
4. Tailgate strut collar
5. Tailgate strut assembly
6. Strut ball stud
7. Air deflector bolt
8. Air deflector grommet
9. Air deflector/tailgate hinge nut
10. Air deflector/tailgate collar
11. Upper tailgate assembly (glass)
12. Body side hinge nut
13. Tailgate hinge assembly
14. Air deflector assembly
15. Tailgate seal

Rodeo lower tailgate assembly

1. Tailgate cable screw
2. Tailgate cable
3. Tailgate collar
4. Hinge bolt
5. Lower tailgate assembly
6. Hinge
7. Torsion bar assembly
8. Tailgate trim assembly
9. Inner tailgate panel
10. Inner tailgate panel
11. Lock assembly
12. Waterproof sheet
13. Waterproof patch
14. Tailgate lock link
15. Tailgate lock link
16. Tailgate anti-rattler
17. Tailgate key cylinder link
18. Tailgate lock assembly
19. Actuator bolt
20. Tailgate lock actuator assembly
21. Tailgate seal
22. Key cylinder
23. Outside handle

VIEW B

VIEW A

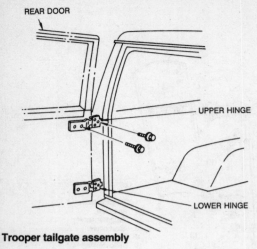

REAR DOOR

UPPER HINGE

LOWER HINGE

Trooper tailgate assembly

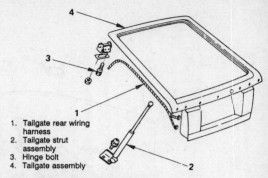

1. Tailgate rear wiring harness
2. Tailgate strut assembly
3. Hinge bolt
4. Tailgate assembly

FWD I-Mark tailgate assembly

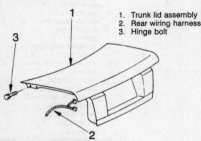

1. Trunk lid assembly
2. Rear wiring harness
3. Hinge bolt

FWD I-Mark trunk lid assembly

Bumpers

REMOVAL AND INSTALLATION

1. Raise and support the vehicle safely (if necessary).
2. Remove mud guards (if equipped).
3. Disconnect parking light and marker light wiring harness.
4. Remove side bumpers.
5. Remove all bolts necessary to separate bumper (cover) from backing bars.

6. Remove bumper (cover) from backing bar.
7. Installation is the reverse of removal.

Grille

REMOVAL AND INSTALLATION

1. Remove the front grille emblem.
2. Raise the setting tip of all clips holding the grille.
3. Remove all screws holding the grille.
4. Disconnect front wiring harness if parking or turn signal lights are located in grille.
5. Remove grille assembly.
6. Attaching clips must be installed into the grille prior to installation.
7. Installation is the reverse of removal.

Outside Mirrors

REMOVAL AND INSTALLATION

There are two types of outside mirrors used on Isuzu vehicles. The first type (type 1) has the mounting screws accessible from the outside of the vehicle. This design may be removed/installed by prying off the screw cover and removing the attaching screws.

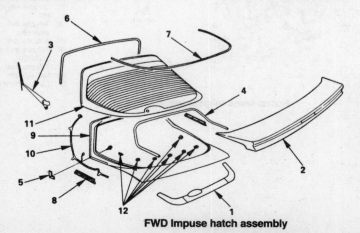

1. Hatch trim panel
2. Hatch spoiler
3. Rear wiper motor assembly
4. Hatch finisher
5. Molding joint
6. Upper molding
7. Lower molding
8. Molding holder
9. Rear hatch
10. Rear wiring harness
11. Hatch glass
12. Clip

FWD Impuse hatch assembly

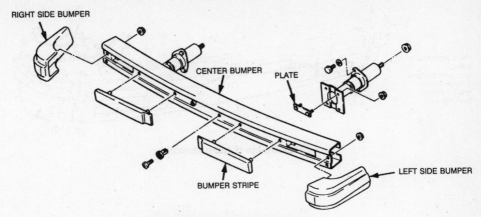

RIGHT SIDE BUMPER

CENTER BUMPER

PLATE

LEFT SIDE BUMPER

BUMPER STRIPE

RWD I-Mark bumper assembly

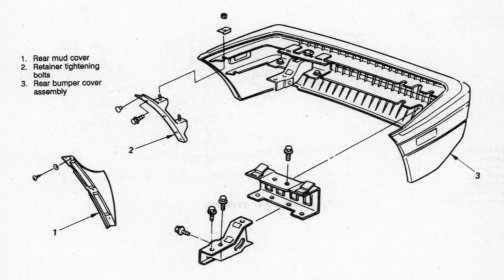

1. Rear mud cover
2. Retainer tightening bolts
3. Rear bumper cover assembly

FWD I-Mark rear bumper assembly

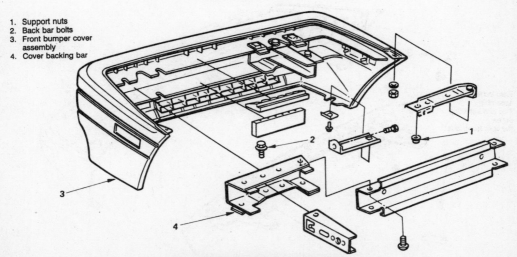

1. Support nuts
2. Back bar bolts
3. Front bumper cover assembly
4. Cover backing bar

FWD I-Mark front bumper assembly

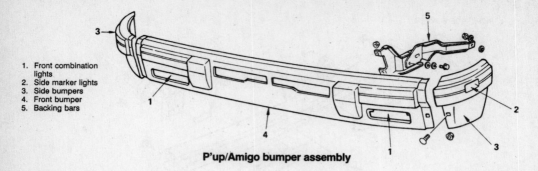

1. Front combination lights
2. Side marker lights
3. Side bumpers
4. Front bumper
5. Backing bars

P'up/Amigo bumper assembly

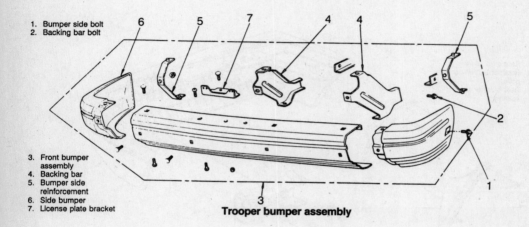

1. Bumper side bolt
2. Backing bar bolt

3. Front bumper assembly
4. Backing bar
5. Bumper side reinforcement
6. Side bumper
7. License plate bracket

Trooper bumper assembly

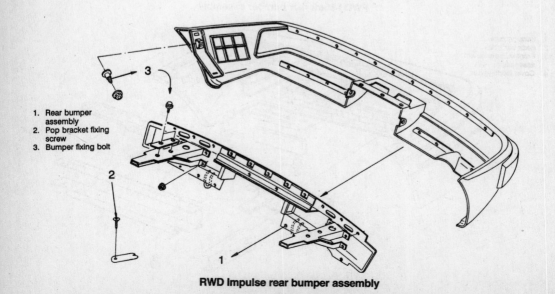

1. Rear bumper assembly
2. Pop bracket fixing screw
3. Bumper fixing bolt

RWD Impulse rear bumper assembly

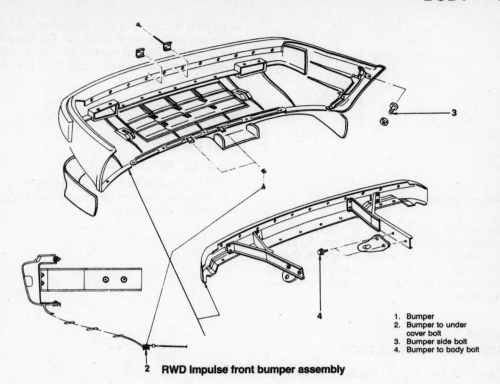

1. Bumper
2. Bumper to under cover bolt
3. Bumper side bolt
4. Bumper to body bolt

RWD Impulse front bumper assembly

RWD I-Mark grille assembly

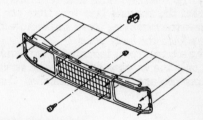

Trooper grille assembly

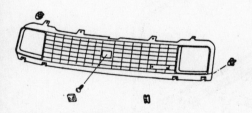

FWD I-Mark grille assembly

Clips ends must be raised prior to grille removal

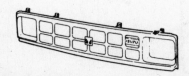

P'up grille assembly

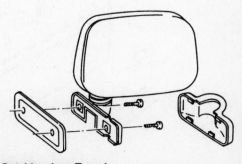

Outside mirror Type 1

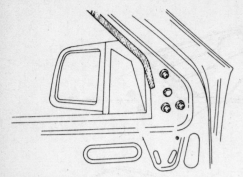

Outside mirror Type 2

The second type (type 2) of outside mirror has mounting screws accessible from the inside of the vehicle only. This design requires the removal of the inner door panel and trim. After this is removed the three mounting screws can be removed.

Antenna

REMOVAL AND INSTALLATION

There are two types of antennae used on Isuzu vehicles. The first type is mounted on the body. To remove/install this type, simply disconnect the antenna lead wire from the radio, remove the mounting screw and remove the antenna from the body panel.

The second type is mounted in the windshield and only the antenna cable may be serviced.

Once the new antenna is installed, the radio

must be trimmed. The trim adjustment is located on the back panel of the radio. Set the radio to a weak AM station around 1400 on the dial. Use a trim adjusting tool to fine tune the radio for the best reception.

INTERIOR

Door Panels

REMOVAL AND INSTALLATION

1. Remove arm rest attaching screws.
2. Remove window crank handle with appropriate clip removal tool.

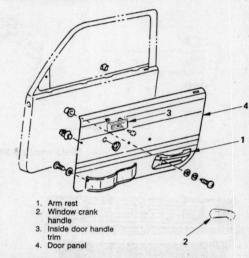

1. Arm rest
2. Window crank handle
3. Inside door handle trim
4. Door panel

I-Mark door panel

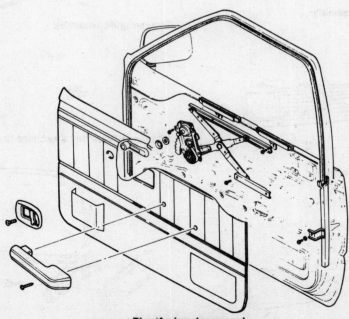

P'up/Amigo door panel

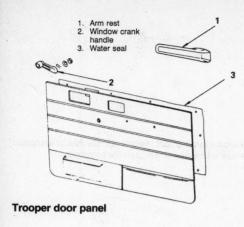

1. Arm rest
2. Window crank handle
3. Water seal

Trooper door panel

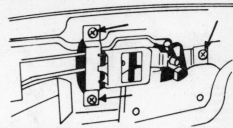

RWD I-Mark inside door handle

1. Key cylinder
2. Key cylinder attaching clip
3. Inside handle connecting rod
4. Door lock assembly
5. Door lock assembly mounting screw
6. Outside handle

FWD I-Mark door lock assembly

Impulse attaching screw/clip location

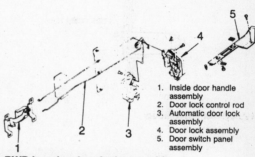

1. Inside door handle assembly
2. Door lock control rod
3. Automatic door lock assembly
4. Door lock assembly
5. Door switch panel assembly

RWD Impulse door lock assembly

3. Remove inside door handle cover attaching screw and trim plate.

4. Remove all external screws securing the door panel. Insert an appropriate pry tool between the door panel and door frame to remove the hidden clips securing the panel.

5. Holding door panel vertical lift straight up to release upper clip.

6. If equipped with power windows or door locks, the door panel must be removed first to gain access to the wiring harness. DO NOT remove door panel completely, but just enough to disconnect wiring harness.

7. Prior to installation, ensure that all clips remaining in door frame are removed and installed in door panel.

8. Installation is reverse of removal.

Door Locks

REMOVAL AND INSTALLATION

1. Remove door panel as described above. Remove water seal carefully it must be reused.

2. Disconnect the inside handle rod clips. Disconnect and remove all lock control rods, noting their position for installation.

3. Remove the door lock assembly mounting screws from the outside of the door and remove the door lock assembly.

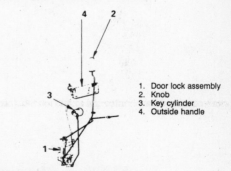

1. Door lock assembly
2. Knob
3. Key cylinder
4. Outside handle

P'up/Amigo door lock assembly

4. Remove the key cylinder by prying the retaining clip with an appropriate tool.

5. Remove the outside door handle by loosening the two outside handle mounting bolts from inside the door.

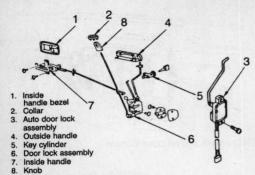

1. Inside handle bezel
2. Collar
3. Auto door lock assembly
4. Outside handle
5. Key cylinder
6. Door lock assembly
7. Inside handle
8. Knob

Trooper door lock assembly

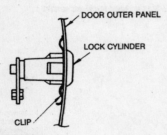

LOCKING ROD

OUTSIDE HANDLE   OPENING ROD

DOOR LOCK ASSEMBLY

RWD I-Mark door lock assembly

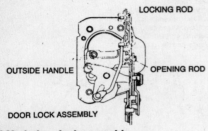

DOOR OUTER PANEL

LOCK CYLINDER

CLIP

Key cylinder installation

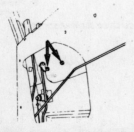

Tighten outside door handle nuts to 48 inch lbs. torque

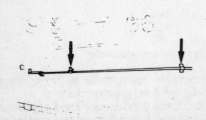

Inside handle control rod retaining clip location

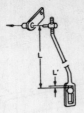

Adjust lock control rod length (L) so that clearance (L') is zero when lock rod is in lock position

CLIP

Adjust inside handle control rod so that inside handle is parallel with door panel

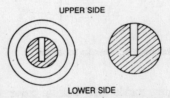

UPPER SIDE

LOWER SIDE

Install key cylinder in the correct position

6. Remove the inside door handle by loosening the retaining screws. Some inside handles may be attached with rivets. In this case drill the rivets out with the appropriate size drill bit.

7. If equipped with power door locks, disconnect the power door lock wiring harness, remove the attaching screws, then remove the assembly.

8. Lubricate all components prior to installation.

9. Install components in reverse order of removal.

10. On vehicles equipped with an adjustable lock rod, set play to zero when door lock rod is in lock position.

11. Torque door lock assembly and outside door handle mounting screws to 48inch lbs. torque.

Door Glass and Regulator
REMOVAL AND INSTALLATION

NOTE: *Power window motors on Isuzu vehicles are an intergal part of the window regulator assembly. The regulators are not*

CHILTON'S
AUTO BODY
REPAIR TIPS

Tools and Materials • Step-by-Step Illustrated Procedures
How To Repair Dents, Scratches and Rust Holes
Spray Painting and Refinishing Tips

With a little practice, basic body repair procedures can be mastered by any do-it-yourself mechanic. The step-by-step repairs shown here can be applied to almost any type of auto body repair.

TOOLS & MATERIALS

You may already have basic tools, such as hammers and electric drills. Other tools unique to body repair — body hammers, grinding attachments, sanding blocks, dent puller, half-round plastic file and plastic spreaders — are relatively inexpensive and can be obtained wherever auto parts or auto body repair parts are sold. Portable air compressors and paint spray guns can be purchased or rented.

Auto Body Repair Kits

The best and most often used products are available to the do-it-yourselfer in kit form, from major manufacturers of auto body repair products. The same manufacturers also merchandise the individual products for use by pros.

Kits are available to make a wide variety of repairs, including holes, dents and scratches and fiberglass, and offer the advantage of buying the materials you'll need for the job. There is little waste or chance of materials going bad from not being used. Many kits may also contain basic body-working tools such as body files, sanding blocks and spreaders. Check the contents of the kit before buying your tools.

BODY REPAIR TIPS

Safety

Many of the products associated with auto body repair and refinishing contain toxic chemicals. Read all labels before opening containers and store them in a safe place and manner.

• Wear eye protection (safety goggles) when using power tools or when performing any operation that involves the removal of any type of material.

• Wear lung protection (disposable mask or respirator) when grinding, sanding or painting.

Sanding

1 Sand off paint before using a dent puller. When using a non-adhesive sanding disc, cover the back of the disc with an overlapping layer or two of masking tape and trim the edges. The disc will last considerably longer.

2 Use the circular motion of the sanding disc to grind *into* the edge of the repair. Grinding or sanding away from the jagged edge will only tear the sandpaper.

3 Use the palm of your hand flat on the panel to detect high and low spots. Do not use your fingertips. Slide your hand slowly back and forth.

WORKING WITH BODY FILLER

Mixing The Filler

Cleanliness and proper mixing and application are extremely important. Use a clean piece of plastic or glass or a disposable artist's palette to mix body filler.

1 Allow plenty of time and follow directions. No useful purpose will be served by adding more hardener to make it cure (set-up) faster. Less hardener means more curing time, but the mixture dries harder; more hardener means less curing time but a softer mixture.

2 Both the hardener and the filler should be thoroughly kneaded or stirred before mixing. Hardener should be a solid paste and dispense like thin toothpaste. Body filler should be smooth, and free of lumps or thick spots.

Getting the proper amount of hardener in the filler is the trickiest part of preparing the filler. Use the same amount of hardener in cold or warm weather. For contour filler (thick coats), a bead of hardener twice the diameter of the filler is about right. There's about a 15% margin on either side, but, if in doubt use less hardener.

3 Mix the body filler and hardener by wiping across the mixing surface, picking the mixture up and wiping it again. Colder weather requires longer mixing times. Do not mix in a circular motion; this will trap air bubbles which will become holes in the cured filler.

Applying The Filler

1 For best results, filler should not be applied over ¼″ thick.

Apply the filler in several coats. Build it up to above the level of the repair surface so that it can be sanded or grated down.

The first coat of filler must be pressed on with a firm wiping motion.

Apply the filler in one direction only. Working the filler back and forth will either pull it off the metal or trap air bubbles.

REPAIRING DENTS

Before you start, take a few minutes to study the damaged area. Try to visualize the shape of the panel before it was damaged. If the damage is on the left fender, look at the right fender and use it as a guide. If there is access to the panel from behind, you can reshape it with a body hammer. If not, you'll have to use a dent puller. Go slowly and work the metal a little at a time. Get the panel as straight as possible before applying filler.

1 This dent is typical of one that can be pulled out or hammered out from behind. Remove the headlight cover, headlight assembly and turn signal housing.

2 Drill a series of holes ½ the size of the end of the dent puller along the stress line. Make some trial pulls and assess the results. If necessary, drill more holes and try again. Do not hurry.

3 If possible, use a body hammer and block to shape the metal back to its original contours. Get the metal back as close to its original shape as possible. Don't depend on body filler to fill dents.

4 Using an 80-grit grinding disc on an electric drill, grind the paint from the surrounding area down to bare metal. Use a new grinding pad to prevent heat buildup that will warp metal.

5 The area should look like this when you're finished grinding. Knock the drill holes in and tape over small openings to keep plastic filler out.

6 Mix the body filler (see Body Repair Tips). Spread the body filler evenly over the entire area (see Body Repair Tips). Be sure to cover the area completely.

7 Let the body filler dry until the surface can just be scratched with your fingernail. Knock the high spots from the body filler with a body file ("Cheese-grater"). Check frequently with the palm of your hand for high and low spots.

8 Check to be sure that trim pieces that will be installed later will fit exactly. Sand the area with 40-grit paper.

9 If you wind up with low spots, you may have to apply another layer of filler.

10 Knock the high spots off with 40-grit paper. When you are satisfied with the contours of the repair, apply a thin coat of filler to cover pin holes and scratches.

11 Block sand the area with 40-grit paper to a smooth finish. Pay particular attention to body lines and ridges that must be well-defined.

12 Sand the area with 400 paper and then finish with a scuff pad. The finished repair is ready for priming and painting (see Painting Tips).

Materials and photos courtesy of Ritt Jones Auto Body, Prospect Park, PA.

REPAIRING RUST HOLES

There are many ways to repair rust holes. The fiberglass cloth kit shown here is one of the most cost efficient for the owner because it provides a strong repair that resists cracking and moisture and is relatively easy to use. It can be used on large and small holes (with or without backing) and can be applied over contoured areas. Remember, however, that short of replacing an entire panel, no repair is a guarantee that the rust will not return.

1 Remove any trim that will be in the way. Clean away all loose debris. Cut away all the rusted metal. But be sure to leave enough metal to retain the contour or body shape.

2 Grind away all traces of rust with a 24-grit grinding disc. Be sure to grind back 3-4 inches from the edge of the hole down to bare metal and be sure all traces of paint, primer and rust are removed.

3 Block sand the area with 80 or 100 grit sandpaper to get a clear, shiny surface and feathered paint edge. Tap the edges of the hole inward with a ball peen hammer.

4 If you are going to use release film, cut a piece about 2-3″ larger than the area you have sanded. Place the film over the repair and mark the sanded area on the film. Avoid any unnecessary wrinkling of the film.

5 Cut 2 pieces of fiberglass matte to match the shape of the repair. One piece should be about 1″ smaller than the sanded area and the second piece should be 1″ smaller than the first. Mix enough filler and hardener to saturate the fiberglass material (see Body Repair Tips).

6 Lay the release sheet on a flat surface and spread an even layer of filler, large enough to cover the repair. Lay the smaller piece of fiberglass cloth in the center of the sheet and spread another layer of filler over the fiberglass cloth. Repeat the operation for the larger piece of cloth.

7 Place the repair material over the repair area, with the release film facing outward. Use a spreader and work from the center outward to smooth the material, following the body contours. Be sure to remove all air bubbles.

8 Wait until the repair has dried tack-free and peel off the release sheet. The ideal working temperature is 60°-90° F. Cooler or warmer temperatures or high humidity may require additional curing time. Wait longer, if in doubt.

9 Sand and feather-edge the entire area. The initial sanding can be done with a sanding disc on an electric drill if care is used. Finish the sanding with a block sander. Low spots can be filled with body filler; this may require several applications.

10 When the filler can just be scratched with a fingernail, knock the high spots down with a body file and smooth the entire area with 80-grit. Feather the filled areas into the surrounding areas.

11 When the area is sanded smooth, mix some topcoat and hardener and apply it directly with a spreader. This will give a smooth finish and prevent the glass matte from showing through the paint.

12 Block sand the topcoat smooth with finishing sandpaper (200 grit), and 400 grit. The repair is ready for masking, priming and painting (see Painting Tips).

Materials and photos courtesy Marson Corporation, Chelsea, Massachusetts

PAINTING TIPS

Preparation

1 SANDING — Use a 400 or 600 grit wet or dry sandpaper. Wet-sand the area with a 1/4 sheet of sandpaper soaked in clean water. Keep the paper wet while sanding. Sand the area until the repaired area tapers into the original finish.

2 CLEANING — Wash the area to be painted thoroughly with water and a clean rag. Rinse it thoroughly and wipe the surface dry until you're sure it's completely free of dirt, dust, fingerprints, wax, detergent or other foreign matter.

3 MASKING — Protect any areas you don't want to overspray by covering them with masking tape and newspaper. Be careful not get fingerprints on the area to be painted.

4 PRIMING — All exposed metal should be primed before painting. Primer protects the metal and provides an excellent surface for paint adhesion. When the primer is dry, wet-sand the area again with 600 grit wet-sandpaper. Clean the area again after sanding.

Painting Techniques

P aint applied from either a spray gun or a spray can (for small areas) will provide good results. Experiment on an old piece of metal to get the right combination before you begin painting.

SPRAYING VISCOSITY (SPRAY GUN ONLY) — Paint should be thinned to spraying viscosity according to the directions on the can. Use only the recommended thinner or reducer and the same amount of reduction regardless of temperature.

AIR PRESSURE (SPRAY GUN ONLY) — This is extremely important. Be sure you are using the proper recommended pressure.

TEMPERATURE — The surface to be painted should be approximately the same temperature as the surrounding air. Applying warm paint to a cold surface, or vice versa, will completely upset the paint characteristics.

THICKNESS — Spray with smooth strokes. In general, the thicker the coat of paint, the longer the drying time. Apply several thin coats about 30 seconds apart. The paint should remain wet long enough to flow out and no longer; heavier coats will only produce sags or wrinkles. Spray a light (fog) coat, followed by heavier color coats.

DISTANCE — The ideal spraying distance is 8″-12″ from the gun or can to the surface. Shorter distances will produce ripples, while greater distances will result in orange peel, dry film and poor color match and loss of material due to overspray.

OVERLAPPING — The gun or can should be kept at right angles to the surface at all times. Work to a wet edge at an even speed, using a 50% overlap and direct the center of the spray at the lower or nearest edge of the previous stroke.

RUBBING OUT (BLENDING) FRESH PAINT — Let the paint dry thoroughly. Runs or imperfections can be sanded out, primed and repainted.

Don't be in too big a hurry to remove the masking. This only produces paint ridges. When the finish has dried for at least a week, apply a small amount of fine grade rubbing compound with a clean, wet cloth. Use lots of water and blend the new paint with the surrounding area.

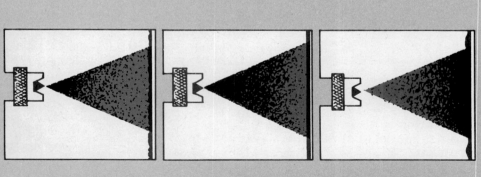

WRONG	CORRECT	WRONG
Thin coat. Stroke too fast, not enough overlap, gun too far away.	*Medium coat. Proper distance, good stroke, proper overlap.*	*Heavy coat. Stroke too slow, too much overlap, gun too close.*

interchangable. The service removal/installation procedure is similar to that manual windows with a two exceptions. The power window wiring harness must be disconnected prior to servicing the assembly and the inside handle is replaced by the power window switch assembly.

RWD I-Mark

FRONT GLASS

1. Remove inside door panel and waterproof seal.
2. Remove screws holding lower channel to sash.
3. Raise glass to UP position and support.
4. Remove window regulator attaching bolts then remove regulator through opening in door frame.
5. Lower glass to the DOWN position and remove upper glass run strip.
6. Tilt the front of the glass down and remove the rear portion first.
7. Measure position of sash on glass and remove by prying with an appropriate tool.
8. When reinstalling sash, lubricate sash channel and install glass with a rubber hammer.
9. Installation is the reverse of removal.

REAR GLASS

1. Remove inside door panel and waterproof seal.
2. Remove the attaching screw on the upper and lower portion of the guide rail. Remove the guide rail.
3. Move the door glass forward and remove together with the weatherstrip.
4. Remove the door glass from the window

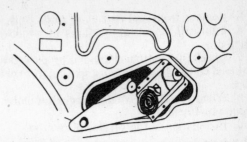

Removing window regulator on the RWD I-Mark

regulator guide rail, then from door frame by pulling straight up.
5. Install channel and glass and apply soapy water to door window glass weatherstrip. Set glass in door frame.
6. Install door glass and then attach to window regulator guide rail.
7. Set the lip of the weatherstrip to the door frame. Apply adhesive Diabond or equivalent to the joining face of the door glass and weatherstrip.
8. Install inside door panel, applying sealant 880-C or equivalent to the trim pad clips and arm rest base.

FWD I-Mark

FRONT GLASS

1. Remove inside door panel, weather proof sheet, waist seal and weather strip.
2. Temporarily install the inside door handle and lower window to the inside panel holes.
3. Remove window attaching screws and glass.
4. Remove window regulator mounting bolts and nuts. Remove window regulator.

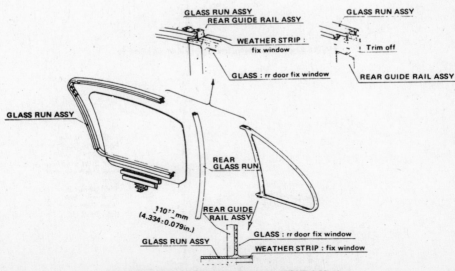

Installing channel and glass on the RWD I-Mark

5. Remove front and rear glass guide rails.

6. Lubricate operating surfaces of window regulator.

7. Check that bottom channel is properly positioned on the glass. Measure spacing from old glass.

8. When installing window regulator bolts, torque to 48inch lbs.

9. Installation is the reverse of removal.

REAR GLASS

1. Remove inside door panel, weather proof sheet and door trim.

2. Remove front guide rail, inner and outer waist seal. Then remove rear guide rail.

3. Remove door window quarter glass. Then remove door glass.

4. Remove window regulator assembly.

5. Lubricate operating surfaces of window regulator.

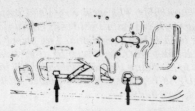

Door glass attaching screws on the FWD I-Mark

6. When installing window regulator bolts, torque to 48inch lbs.

7. Installation is the reverse of removal.

RWD Impulse

1. Remove the inside door panel and waterproof sheet.

2. Remove the inside trim cover.

3. Position glass to gain access to stopper bolts and remove.

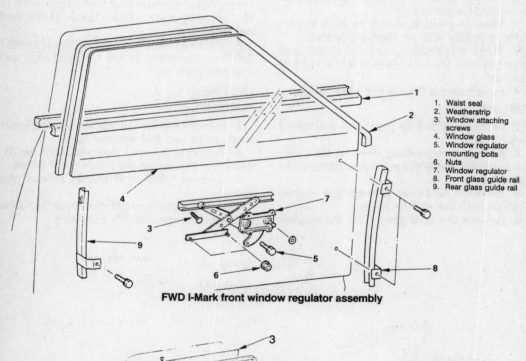

1. Waist seal
2. Weatherstrip
3. Window attaching screws
4. Window glass
5. Window regulator mounting bolts
6. Nuts
7. Window regulator
8. Front glass guide rail
9. Rear glass guide rail

FWD I-Mark front window regulator assembly

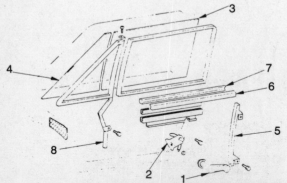

1. Regulator handle
2. Window regulator assembly
3. Door glass assembly
4. Door window quarter glass
5. Front guide rail
6. Inner waist seal
7. Outer waist seal
8. Rear guide rail

FWD I-Mark rear window regulator assembly

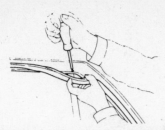

Removing the rear guide rail on the FWD I-Mark

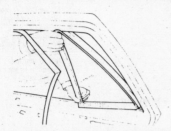

Removing the rear quarter glass on the FWD I-Mark

4. Remove guide rail, weatherstrip and waist seal. Remove door glass.

5. Remove window regulator assembly.

6. Installation is the reverse of removal. See illustration for special instructions.

FWD Impulse

1. Remove inside door panel and weather proof sheet.

2. Remove guide rail.

3. Remove the glass fixing bolts from the regulator. Remove the door glass.

4. Remove the window regulator.

5. Installation is the reverse of removal. Torque window regulator bolts to 71 inch lbs.

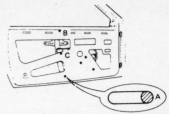

Tighten screws with portion (A) moved forward. Pull front of glass up and rear down. Check clearance between garnish molding and glass (2–5mm). Roll up window and position where proper seal is made. Tighten screw at (B)

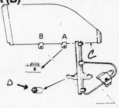

Install glass assembly into door frame placing it into the guide rail. Raise portion (C) and tighten screw (A). Push portion (D) to the lower-rear and tighten screw (B)

P'up/Amigo

1. Remove the inside door panel and weatherproof sheet.

2. Remove the inner and outer waist seals by prying with an appropriate tool.

3. Remove the two screws attaching the bottom channel and regulator. remove the glass by tilting as necessary.

4. Remove the regulator attaching screws and remove the regulator through the access hole in the door frame.

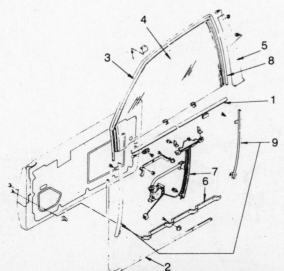

1. Outer door waist seal
2. Drip weatherstrip
3. Door inboard weatherstrip
4. Door glass assembly
5. Door garnish
6. Door trim reinforcement
7. Window regulator assembly
8. Glass guide weatherstrip
9. Guide rail assembly

RWD Impulse window regulator assembly

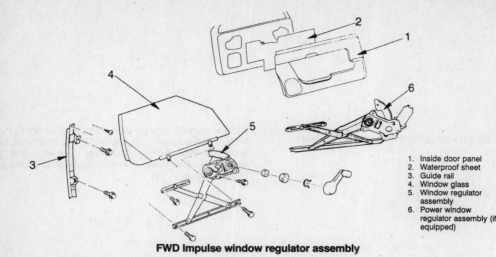

1. Inside door panel
2. Waterproof sheet
3. Guide rail
4. Window glass
5. Window regulator assembly
6. Power window regulator assembly (if equipped)

FWD Impulse window regulator assembly

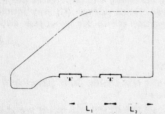

FWD Impulse channel positioning. (L₁) 270mm (L₂) 290.5mm

5. Installation is the reverse of removal.

6. Install window glass and insure that bottom channel is properly positioned. See illustration.

7. Install waist seal with the cut away portion turned inward.

Trooper/Rodeo

1. Remove inside door panel and weatherproof sheet. If equipped with power windows, disconnect wiring harness.

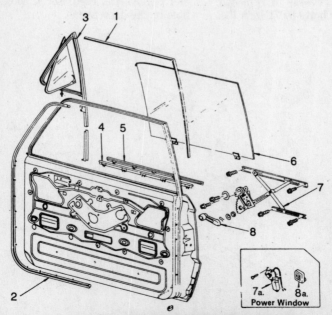

1. Glass run
2. Weatherstrip
3. Cross vent assembly
4. Inner waist seal
5. Outer waist seal
6. Window glass
7. Window regulator
7a. Power window regulator
8. Regulator handle
8a. Power window switch

Trooper front window regulator assembly

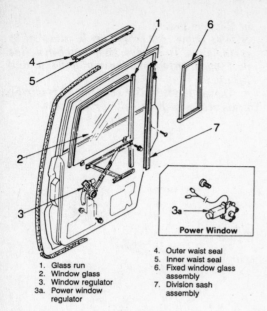

2. Remove the inner and outer waist seals by prying with an appropriate tool.

3. Remove cross vent screws. Then remove cross vent by pulling upward.

4. Remove channel attaching screws and remove door glass.

5. Remove the window regulator attaching screws and remove regulator through access hole in door frame.

6. Installation is the reverse of removal.

NOTE: *The procedure for removal/installation is the same for front and rear doors.*

Power Window

1. Glass run
2. Window glass
3. Window regulator
3a. Power window regulator
4. Outer waist seal
5. Inner waist seal
6. Fixed window glass assembly
7. Division sash assembly

Trooper rear window regulator assembly

Inside Rear View Mirror

The rear view mirror on most Isuzu vehicles is attached to the center of the windsheild brace in the interior. It is removed by simply unscrewing the attaching screw(s). On some models, the attaching screw(s) may be covered with plastic trim.

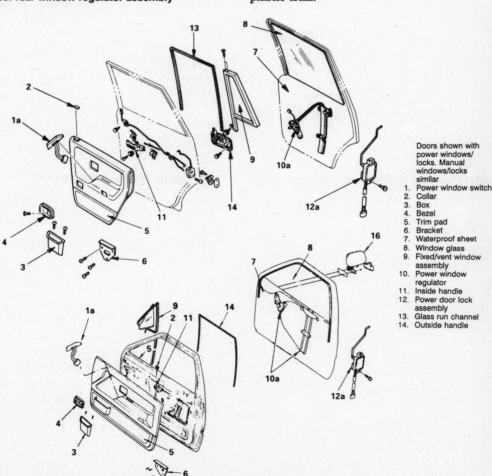

Doors shown with power windows/locks. Manual windows/locks similar
1. Power window switch
2. Collar
3. Box
4. Bezel
5. Trim pad
6. Bracket
7. Waterproof sheet
8. Window glass
9. Fixed/vent window assembly
10. Power window regulator
11. Inside handle
12. Power door lock assembly
13. Glass run channel
14. Outside handle

Rodeo front/rear window regulator assembly

Seats

REMOVAL AND INSTALLATION

1. Remove door sill plate if necessary.
2. Remove the seat adjuster bracket cover. Loosen and remove the seat adjuster attaching bolts.

3. Remove seat.
NOTE: *Some rear seats may be attached by spring clips. To remove, push seat bench (the part you sit on) toward the rear of the car and lift up.*
4. Installation is the reverse of removal. Torque seat attaching bolts to 29 ft. lbs.

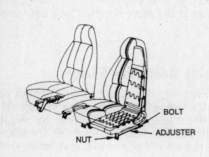

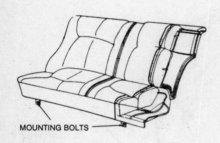

RWD I-Mark front and rear seat assembly

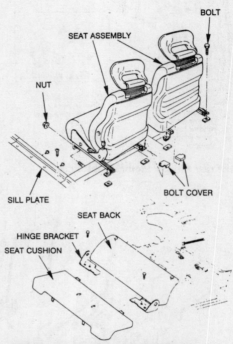

FWD Impulse front/rear seat assembly

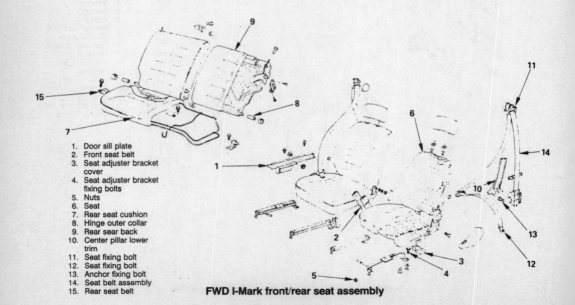

1. Door sill plate
2. Front seat belt
3. Seat adjuster bracket cover
4. Seat adjuster bracket fixing bolts
5. Nuts
6. Seat
7. Rear seat cushion
8. Hinge outer collar
9. Rear sear back
10. Center pillar lower trim
11. Seat fixing bolt
12. Seat fixing bolt
13. Anchor fixing bolt
14. Seat belt assembly
15. Rear seat belt

FWD I-Mark front/rear seat assembly

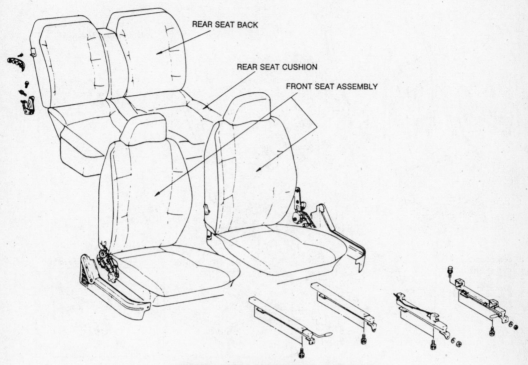

REAR SEAT BACK

REAR SEAT CUSHION

FRONT SEAT ASSEMBLY

RWD Impulse front/rear seat assembly

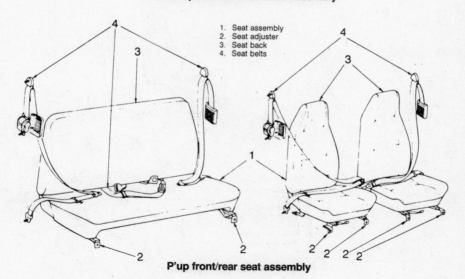

1. Seat assembly
2. Seat adjuster
3. Seat back
4. Seat belts

P'up front/rear seat assembly

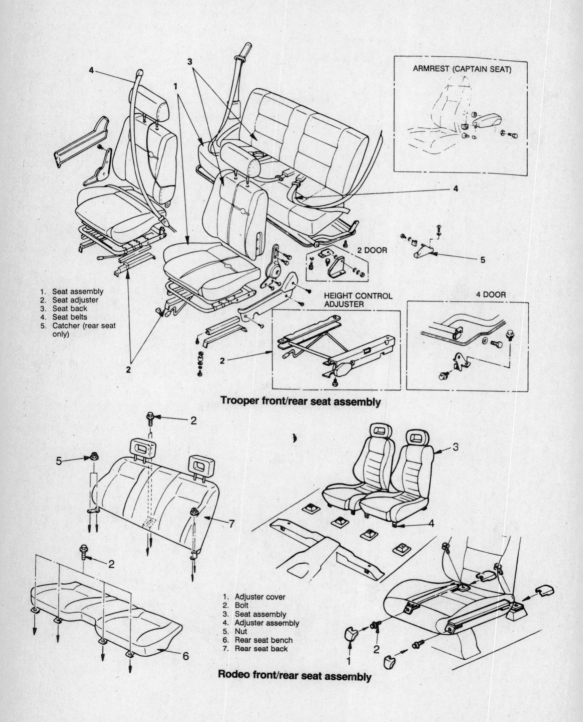

ARMREST (CAPTAIN SEAT)

1. Seat assembly
2. Seat adjuster
3. Seat back
4. Seat belts
5. Catcher (rear seat only)

2 DOOR

HEIGHT CONTROL ADJUSTER

4 DOOR

Trooper front/rear seat assembly

1. Adjuster cover
2. Bolt
3. Seat assembly
4. Adjuster assembly
5. Nut
6. Rear seat bench
7. Rear seat back

Rodeo front/rear seat assembly

How to Remove Stains from Fabric Interior

For best results, spots and stains should be removed as soon as possible. Never use gasoline, lacquer thinner, acetone, nail polish remover or bleach. Use a 3' x 3" piece of cheesecloth. Squeeze most of the liquid from the fabric and wipe the stained fabric from the outside of the stain toward the center with a lifting motion. Turn the cheesecloth as soon as one side becomes soiled. When using water to remove a stain, be sure to wash the entire section after the spot has been removed to avoid water stains. Encrusted spots can be broken up with a dull knife and vacuumed before removing the stain.

Type of Stain	How to Remove It
Surface spots	Brush the spots out with a small hand brush or use a commercial preparation such as K2R to lift the stain.
Mildew	Clean around the mildew with warm suds. Rinse in cold water and soak the mildew area in a solution of 1 part table salt and 2 parts water. Wash with upholstery cleaner.
Water stains	Water stains in fabric materials can be removed with a solution made from 1 cup of table salt dissolved in 1 quart of water. Vigorously scrub the solution into the stain and rinse with clear water. Water stains in nylon or other synthetic fabrics should be removed with a commercial type spot remover.
Chewing gum, tar, crayons, shoe polish (greasy stains)	Do not use a cleaner that will soften gum or tar. Harden the deposit with an ice cube and scrape away as much as possible with a dull knife. Moisten the remainder with cleaning fluid and scrub clean.
Ice cream, candy	Most candy has a sugar base and can be removed with a cloth wrung out in warm water. Oily candy, after cleaning with warm water, should be cleaned with upholstery cleaner. Rinse with warm water and clean the remainder with cleaning fluid.
Wine, alcohol, egg, milk, soft drink (non-greasy stains)	Do not use soap. Scrub the stain with a cloth wrung out in warm water. Remove the remainder with cleaning fluid.
Grease, oil, lipstick, butter and related stains	Use a spot remover to avoid leaving a ring. Work from the outisde of the stain to the center and dry with a clean cloth when the spot is gone.
Headliners (cloth)	Mix a solution of warm water and foam upholstery cleaner to give thick suds. Use only foam—liquid may streak or spot. Clean the entire headliner in one operation using a circular motion with a natural sponge.
Headliner (vinyl)	Use a vinyl cleaner with a sponge and wipe clean with a dry cloth.
Seats and door panels	Mix 1 pint upholstery cleaner in 1 gallon of water. Do not soak the fabric around the buttons.
Leather or vinyl fabric	Use a multi-purpose cleaner full strength and a stiff brush. Let stand 2 minutes and scrub thoroughly. Wipe with a clean, soft rag.
Nylon or synthetic fabrics	For normal stains, use the same procedures you would for washing cloth upholstery. If the fabric is extremely dirty, use a multi-purpose cleaner full strength with a stiff scrub brush. Scrub thoroughly in all directions and wipe with a cotton towel or soft rag.

Mechanic's Data

11

General Conversion Table

Multiply By	To Convert	To	
		LENGTH	
2.54	Inches	Centimeters	.3937
25.4	Inches	Millimeters	.03937
30.48	Feet	Centimeters	.0328
.304	Feet	Meters	3.28
.914	Yards	Meters	1.094
1.609	Miles	Kilometers	.621
		VOLUME	
.473	Pints	Liters	2.11
.946	Quarts	Liters	1.06
3.785	Gallons	Liters	.264
.016	Cubic inches	Liters	61.02
16.39	Cubic inches	Cubic cms.	.061
28.3	Cubic feet	Liters	.0353
		MASS (Weight)	
28.35	Ounces	Grams	.035
.4536	Pounds	Kilograms	2.20
—	To obtain	From	Multiply by

Multiply By	To Convert	To	
		AREA	
.645	Square inches	Square cms.	.155
.836	Square yds.	Square meters	1.196
		FORCE	
4.448	Pounds	Newtons	.225
.138	Ft./lbs.	Kilogram/meters	7.23
1.36	Ft./lbs.	Newton-meters	.737
.112	In./lbs.	Newton-meters	8.844
		PRESSURE	
.068	Psi	Atmospheres	14.7
6.89	Psi	Kilopascals	.145
		OTHER	
1.104	Horsepower (DIN)	Horsepower (SAE)	.9861
.746	Horsepower (SAE)	Kilowatts (KW)	1.34
1.60	Mph	Km/h	.625
.425	Mpg	Km/1	2.35
—	To obtain	From	Multiply by

Tap Drill Sizes

National Coarse or U.S.S.

Screw & Tap Size	Threads Per Inch	Use Drill Number
No. 5	40	39
No. 6	32	36
No. 8	32	29
No. 10	24	25
No. 12	24	17
1/4	20	8
5/16	18	F
3/8	16	5/16
7/16	14	U
1/2	13	27/64
9/16	12	31/64
5/8	11	17/32
3/4	10	21/32
7/8	9	49/64

National Coarse or U.S.S.

Screw & Tap Size	Threads Per Inch	Use Drill Number
1	8	7/8
1 1/8	7	63/64
1 1/4	7	1 7/64
1 1/2	6	1 11/32

National Fine or S.A.E.

Screw & Tap Size	Threads Per Inch	Use Drill Number
No. 5	44	37
No. 6	40	33
No. 8	36	29
No. 10	32	21

National Fine or S.A.E.

Screw & Tap Size	Threads Per Inch	Use Drill Number
No. 12	28	15
1/4	28	3
6/16	24	1
3/8	24	Q
7/16	20	W
1/2	20	29/64
9/16	18	33/64
5/8	18	37/64
3/4	16	11/16
7/8	14	13/16
1 1/8	12	1 3/64
1 1/4	12	1 11/64
1 1/2	12	1 27/64

Drill Sizes In Decimal Equivalents

Inch	Decimal	Wire	mm	Inch	Decimal	Wire	mm	Inch	Decimal	Wire & Letter	mm	Inch	Decimal	Letter	mm	Inch	Decimal	mm
1/64	.0156		.39		.0730	49			.1614		4.1		.2717		6.9		.4331	11.0
	.0157		.4		.0748		1.9		.1654		4.2		.2720	I		7/16	.4375	11.11
	.0160	78			.0760	48			.1660	19			.2756		7.0		.4528	11.5
	.0165		.42		.0768		1.95		.1673		4.25		.2770	J		29/64	.4531	11.51
	.0173		.44	5/64	.0781		1.98		.1693		4.3		.2795		7.1	15/32	.4688	11.90
	.0177		.45		.0785	47			.1695	18		9/32	.2812		7.14		.4724	12.0
	.0180	77			.0787		2.0	11/64	.1719		4.36		.2835		7.2	31/64	.4844	12.30
	.0181		.46		.0807		2.05		.1730	17			.2854		7.25		.4921	12.5
	.0189		.48		.0810	46			.1732		4.4		.2874		7.3	1/2	.5000	12.70
	.0197		.5		.0820	45			.1770	16							.5118	13.0
	.0200	76			.0827		2.1		.1772		4.5		.2900	L		33/64	.5156	13.09
	.0210	75			.0846		2.15		.1800	15			.2913		7.4	17/32	.5312	13.49
	.0217		.55		.0860	44			.1811		4.6		.2950	M			.5315	13.5
	.0225	74			.0866		2.2		.1820	14			.2953		7.5	35/64	.5469	13.89
	.0236		.6		.0886		2.25		.1850	13		19/64	.2969		7.54		.5512	14.0
	.0240	73			.0890	43			.1850		4.7		.2992		7.6	9/16	.5625	14.28
	.0250	72			.0906		2.3		.1870		4.75		.3020	N			.5709	14.5
	.0256		.65		.0925		2.35	3/16	.1875		4.76		.3031		7.7	37/64	.5781	14.68
	.0260	71			.0935	42			.1890		4.8		.3051		7.75		.5906	15.0
	.0276		.7	3/32	.0938		2.38		.1890	12			.3071		7.8	19/32	.5938	15.08
	.0280	70			.0945		2.4		.1910	11			.3110		7.9	39/64	.6094	15.47
	.0292	69			.0960	41			.1929		4.9		.3125		7.93		.6102	15.5
	.0295		.75		.0965		2.45		.1935	10		5/16	.3150		8.0	5/8	.6250	15.87
	.0310	68			.0980	40			.1960	9			.3160	O			.6299	16.0
1/32	.0312		.79		.0981		2.5		.1969		5.0		.3189		8.1	41/64	.6406	16.27
	.0315		.8		.0995	39			.1990	8			.3228		8.2		.6496	16.5
	.0320	67			.1015	38			.2008		5.1		.3230	P		21/32	.6562	16.66
	.0330	66			.1024		2.6		.2010	7			.3248		8.25		.6693	17.0
	.0335		.85		.1040	37		13/64	.2031		5.16		.3268		8.3	43/64	.6719	17.06
	.0350	65			.1063		2.7		.2040	6		21/64	.3281		8.33	11/16	.6875	17.46
	.0354		.9		.1065	36			.2047		5.2		.3307		8.4		.6890	17.5
	.0360	64			.1083		2.75		.2055	5			.3320	Q		45/64	.7031	17.85
	.0370	63		7/64	.1094		2.77		.2067		5.25		.3346		8.5		.7087	18.0
	.0374		.95		.1100	35			.2087		5.3		.3386		8.6	23/32	.7188	18.25
	.0380	62			.1102		2.8		.2090	4			.3390	R			.7283	18.5
	.0390	61			.1110	34			.2126		5.4	11/32	.3438		8.73	47/64	.7344	18.65
	.0394		1.0		.1130	33			.2130	3			.3445		8.75		.7480	19.0
	.0400	60			.1142		2.9		.2165		5.5		.3465		8.8	3/4	.7500	19.05
	.0410	59			.1160	32		7/32	.2188		5.55		.3480	S		49/64	.7656	19.44
	.0413		1.05		.1181		3.0		.2205		5.6						.7677	19.5
	.0420	58			.1200	31			.2210	2			.3504		8.9	25/32	.7812	19.84
	.0430	57			.1220		3.1		.2244		5.7		.3543		9.0		.7874	20.0
	.0433		1.1	1/8	.1250		3.17		.2264		5.75		.3580	T		51/64	.7969	20.24
	.0453		1.15		.1260		3.2		.2280	1			.3583		9.1		.8071	20.5
3/64	.0465	56			.1280		3.25		.2283		5.8	23/64	.3594		9.12	13/16	.8125	20.63
	.0469		1.19		.1285	30			.2323		5.9		.3622		9.2		.8268	21.0
	.0472		1.2		.1299		3.3		.2340	A			.3642		9.25	53/64	.8281	21.03
	.0492		1.25		.1339		3.4	15/64	.2344		5.95		.3661		9.3	27/32	.8438	21.43
	.0512		1.3		.1360	29			.2362		6.0		.3680	U			.8465	21.5
	.0520	55			.1378		3.5		.2380	B			.3701		9.4	55/64	.8594	21.82
	.0531		1.35		.1405	28			.2402		6.1		.3740		9.5		.8661	22.0
	.0550	54		9/64	.1406		3.57		.2420	C		3/8	.3750		9.52	7/8	.8750	22.22
	.0551		1.4		.1417		3.6		.2441		6.2		.3770	V			.8858	22.5
	.0571		1.45		.1440	27			.2460	D			.3780		9.6	57/64	.8906	22.62
	.0591		1.5		.1457		3.7		.2461		6.25		.3819		9.7		.9055	23.0
	.0595	53			.1470	26			.2480		6.3		.3839		9.75	29/32	.9062	23.01
	.0610		1.55		.1476		3.75	1/4	.2500	E	6.35		.3858		9.8	59/64	.9219	23.41
1/16	.0625		1.59		.1495	25			.2520		6.		.3860	W			.9252	23.5
	.0630		1.6		.1496		3.8		.2559		6.5		.3898		9.9	15/16	.9375	23.81
	.0635	52			.1520	24			.2570	F		25/64	.3906		9.92		.9449	24.0
	.0650		1.65		.1535		3.9		.2598		6.6		.3937		10.0	61/64	.9531	24.2
	.0669		1.7		.1540	23			.2610	G			.3970	X			.9646	24.5
	.0670	51		5/32	.1562		3.96		.2638		6.7		.4040	Y		31/32	.9688	24.6
	.0689		1.75		.1570	22		17/64	.2656		6.74	13/32	.4062		10.31		.9843	25.0
	.0700	50			.1575		4.0		.2657		6.75		.4130	Z		63/64	.9844	25.0
	.0709		1.8		.1590	21			.2660	H			.4134		10.5	1	1.0000	25.4
	.0728		1.85		.1610	20			.2677		6.8	27/64	.4219		10.71			

GLOSSARY OF TERMS

AIR/FUEL RATIO: The ratio of air to gasoline by weight in the fuel mixture drawn into the engine.

AIR INJECTION: One method of reducing harmful exhaust emissions by injecting air into each of the exhaust ports of an engine. The fresh air entering the hot exhaust manifold causes any remaining fuel to be burned before it can exit the tailpipe.

ALTERNATOR: A device used for converting mechanical energy into electrical energy.

AMMETER: An instrument, calibrated in amperes, used to measure the flow of an electrical current in a circuit. Ammeters are always connected in series with the circuit being tested.

AMPERE: The rate of flow of electrical current present when one volt of electrical pressure is applied against one ohm of electrical resistance.

ANALOG COMPUTER: Any microprocessor that uses similar (analogous) electrical signals to make its calculations.

ARMATURE: A laminated, soft iron core wrapped by a wire that converts electrical energy to mechanical energy as in a motor or relay. When rotated in a magnetic field, it changes mechanical energy into electrical energy as in a generator.

ATMOSPHERIC PRESSURE: The pressure on the Earth's surface caused by the weight of the air in the atmosphere. At sea level, this pressure is 14.7 psi at 32°F (101 kPa at 0°C).

ATOMIZATION: The breaking down of a liquid into a fine mist that can be suspended in air.

AXIAL PLAY: Movement parallel to a shaft or bearing bore.

BACKFIRE: The sudden combustion of gases in the intake or exhaust system that results in a loud explosion.

BACKLASH: The clearance or play between two parts, such as meshed gears.

BACKPRESSURE: Restrictions in the exhaust system that slow the exit of exhaust gases from the combustion chamber.

BAKELITE: A heat resistant, plastic insulator material commonly used in printed circuit boards and transistorized components.

BALL BEARING: A bearing made up of hardened inner and outer races between which hardened steel ball roll.

BALLAST RESISTOR: A resistor in the primary ignition circuit that lowers voltage after the engine is started to reduce wear on ignition components.

BEARING: A friction reducing, supportive device usually located between a stationary part and a moving part.

BIMETAL TEMPERATURE SENSOR: Any sensor or switch made of two dissimilar types of metal that bend when heated or cooled due to the different expansion rates of the alloys. These types of sensors usually function as an on/off switch.

BLOWBY: Combustion gases, composed of water vapor and unburned fuel, that leak past the piston rings into the crankcase during normal engine operation. These gases are removed by the PCV system to prevent the buildup of harmful acids in the crankcase.

BRAKE PAD: A brake shoe and lining assembly used with disc brakes.

BRAKE SHOE: The backing for the brake lining. The term is, however, usually applied to the assembly of the brake backing and lining.

BUSHING: A liner, usually removable, for a bearing; an anti-friction liner used in place of a bearing.

BYPASS: System used to bypass ballast resistor during engine cranking to increase voltage supplied to the coil.

CALIPER: A hydraulically activated device in a disc brake system, which is mounted straddling the brake rotor (disc). The caliper contains at least one piston and two brake pads. Hydraulic pressure on the piston(s) forces the pads against the rotor.

CAMSHAFT: A shaft in the engine on which are the lobes (cams) which operate the valves. The camshaft is driven by the crankshaft, via a belt, chain or gears, at one half the crankshaft speed.

CAPACITOR: A device which stores an electrical charge.

CARBON MONOXIDE (CO): a colorless, odorless gas given off as a normal byproduct of combustion. It is poisonous and extremely dangerous in confined areas, building up slowly to toxic levels without warning if adequate ventilation is not available.

CARBURETOR: A device, usually mounted on the intake manifold of an engine, which mixes the air and fuel in the proper proportion to allow even combustion.

CATALYTIC CONVERTER: A device installed in the exhaust system, like a muffler, that converts harmful byproducts of combustion into carbon dioxide and water vapor by means of a heat-producing chemical reaction.

CENTRIFUGAL ADVANCE: A mechanical method of advancing the spark timing by using flyweights in the distributor that react to centrifugal force generated by the distributor shaft rotation.

CHECK VALVE: Any one-way valve installed to permit the flow of air, fuel or vacuum in one direction only.

CHOKE: A device, usually a moveable valve, placed in the intake path of a carburetor to restrict the flow of air.

CIRCUIT: Any unbroken path through which an electrical current can flow. Also used to describe fuel flow in some instances.

CIRCUIT BREAKER: A switch which protects an electrical circuit from overload by opening the circuit when the current flow exceeds a predetermined level. Some circuit breakers must be reset manually, while other reset automatically

COIL (IGNITION): A transformer in the ignition circuit which steps of the voltage provided to the spark plugs.

COMBINATION MANIFOLD: An assembly which includes both the intake and exhaust manifolds in one casting.

COMBINATION VALVE: A device used in some fuel systems that routes fuel vapors to a charcoal storage canister instead of venting

them into the atmosphere. The valve relieves fuel tank pressure and allows fresh air into the tank as fuel level drops to prevent a vapor lock situation.

COMPRESSION RATIO: The comparison of the total volume of the cylinder and combustion chamber with the piston at BDC and the piston at TDC.

CONDENSER: 1. An electrical device which acts to store an electrical charge, preventing voltage surges.
2. A radiator-like device in the air conditioning system in which refrigerant gas condenses into a liquid, giving off heat.

CONDUCTOR: Any material through which an electrical current can be transmitted easily.

CONTINUITY: Continuous or complete circuit. Can be checked with an ohmmeter.

COUNTERSHAFT: An intermediate shaft which is rotated by a mainshaft and transmits, in turn, that rotation to a working part.

CRANKCASE: The lower part of an engine in which the crankshaft and related parts operate.

CRANKSHAFT: The main driving shaft of an engine which receives reciprocating motion from the pistons and converts it to rotary motion.

CYLINDER: In an engine, the round hole in the engine block in which the piston(s) ride.

CYLINDER BLOCK: The main structural member of an engine in which is found the cylinders, crankshaft and other principal parts.

CYLINDER HEAD: The detachable portion of the engine, fastened, usually, to the top of the cylinder block, containing all or most of the combustion chambers. On overhead valve engines, it contains the valves and their operating parts. On overhead cam engines, it contains the camshaft as well.

DEAD CENTER: The extreme top or bottom of the piston stroke.

DETONATION: An unwanted explosion of the air fuel mixture in the combustion chamber caused by excess heat and compression, advanced timing, or an overly lean mixture. Also referred to as "ping".

DIAPHRAGM: A thin, flexible wall separating two cavities, such as in a vacuum advance unit.

DIESELING: A condition in which hot spots in the combustion chamber cause the engine to run on after the key is turned off.

DIFFERENTIAL: A geared assembly which allows the transmission of motion between drive axles, giving one axle the ability to turn faster than the other.

DIODE: An electrical device that will allow current to flow in one direction only.

DISC BRAKE: A hydraulic braking assembly consisting of a brake disc, or rotor, mounted on an axle, and a caliper assembly containing, usually two brake pads which are activated by hydraulic pressure. The pads are forced against the sides of the disc, creating friction which slows the vehicle.

DISTRIBUTOR: A mechanically driven device on an engine which is responsible for electrically firing the spark plug at a predetermined point of the piston stroke.

DOWEL PIN: A pin, inserted in mating holes in two different parts allowing those parts to maintain a fixed relationship.

DRUM BRAKE: A braking system which consists of two brake shoes and one or two wheel cylinders, mounted on a fixed backing plate, and a brake drum, mounted on an axle, which revolves around the assembly. Hydraulic action applied to the wheel cylinders forces the shoes outward against the drum, creating friction and slowing the vehicle.

DWELL: The rate, measured in degrees of shaft rotation, at which an electrical circuit cycles on and off.

ELECTRONIC CONTROL UNIT (ECU): Ignition module, module, amplifier or igniter. See Module for definition.

ELECTRONIC IGNITION: A system in which the timing and firing of the spark plugs is controlled by an electronic control unit, usually called a module. These systems have not points or condenser.

ENDPLAY: The measured amount of axial movement in a shaft.

ENGINE: A device that converts heat into mechanical energy.

EXHAUST MANIFOLD: A set of cast passages or pipes which conduct exhaust gases from the engine.

FEELER GAUGE: A blade, usually metal, of precisely predetermined thickness, used to measure the clearance between two parts. These blades usually are available in sets of assorted thicknesses.

F-Head: An engine configuration in which the intake valves are in the cylinder head, while the camshaft and exhaust valves are located in the cylinder block. The camshaft operates the intake valves via lifters and pushrods, while it operates the exhaust valves directly.

FIRING ORDER: The order in which combustion occurs in the cylinders of an engine. Also the order in which spark is distributed to the plugs by the distributor.

FLATHEAD: An engine configuration in which the camshaft and all the valves are located in the cylinder block.

FLOODING: The presence of too much fuel in the intake manifold and combustion chamber which prevents the air/fuel mixture from firing, thereby causing a no-start situation.

FLYWHEEL: A disc shaped part bolted to the rear end of the crankshaft. Around the outer perimeter is affixed the ring gear. The starter drive engages the ring gear, turning the flywheel, which rotates the crankshaft, imparting the initial starting motion to the engine.

FOOT POUND (ft.lb. or sometimes, ft. lbs.): The amount of energy or work needed to raise an item weighing one pound, a distance of one foot.

FUSE: A protective device in a circuit which prevents circuit overload by breaking the circuit when a specific amperage is present. The device is constructed around a strip or wire of a lower amperage rating than the circuit it is designed to protect. When an amperage higher than that stamped on the fuse is present in the circuit, the strip or wire melts, opening the circuit.

GEAR RATIO: The ratio between the number of teeth on meshing gears.

GENERATOR: A device which converts mechanical energy into electrical energy.

HEAT RANGE: The measure of a spark plug's ability to dissipate heat from its firing end. The higher the heat range, the hotter the plug fires.

HUB: The center part of a wheel or gear.

HYDROCARBON (HC): Any chemical compound made up of hydrogen and carbon. A major pollutant formed by the engine as a byproduct of combustion.

HYDROMETER: An instrument used to measure the specific gravity of a solution.

INCH POUND (in.lb. or sometimes, in. lbs.): One twelfth of a foot pound.

INDUCTION: A means of transferring electrical energy in the form of a magnetic field. Principle used in the ignition coil to increase voltage.

INJECTION PUMP: A device, usually mechanically operated, which meters and delivers fuel under pressure to the fuel injector.

INJECTOR: A device which receives metered fuel under relatively low pressure and is activated to inject the fuel into the engine under relatively high pressure at a predetermined time.

INPUT SHAFT: The shaft to which torque is applied, usually carrying the driving gear or gears.

INTAKE MANIFOLD: A casting of passages or pipes used to conduct air or a fuel/air mixture to the cylinders.

JOURNAL: The bearing surface within which a shaft operates.

KEY: A small block usually fitted in a notch between a shaft and a hub to prevent slippage of the two parts.

MANIFOLD: A casting of passages or set of pipes which connect the cylinders to an inlet or outlet source.

MANIFOLD VACUUM: Low pressure in an engine intake manifold formed just below the throttle plates. Manifold vacuum is highest at idle and drops under acceleration.

MASTER CYLINDER: The primary fluid pressurizing device in a hydraulic system. In automotive use, it is found in brake and hydraulic clutch systems and is pedal activated, either directly or, in a power brake system, through the power booster.

MODULE: Electronic control unit, amplifier or igniter of solid state or integrated design which controls the current flow in the ignition primary circuit based on input from the pickup coil. When the module opens the primary circuit, the high secondary voltage is induced in the coil.

NEEDLE BEARING: A bearing which consists of a number (usually a large number) of long, thin rollers.

OHM: (Ω) The unit used to measure the resistance of conductor to electrical flow. One ohm is the amount of resistance that limits current flow to one ampere in a circuit with one volt of pressure.

OHMMETER: An instrument used for measuring the resistance, in ohms, in an electrical circuit.

OUTPUT SHAFT: The shaft which transmits torque from a device, such as a transmission.

OVERDRIVE: A gear assembly which produces more shaft revolutions than that transmitted to it.

OVERHEAD CAMSHAFT (OHC): An engine configuration in which the camshaft is mounted on top of the cylinder head and operates the valve either directly or by means of rocker arms.

OVERHEAD VALVE (OHV): An engine configuration in which all of the valves are located in the cylinder head and the camshaft is located in the cylinder block. The camshaft operates the valves via lifters and pushrods.

OXIDES OF NITROGEN (NOx): Chemical compounds of nitrogen produced as a byproduct of combustion. They combine with hydrocarbons to produce smog.

OXYGEN SENSOR: Used with the feedback system to sense the presence of oxygen in the exhaust gas and signal the computer which can reference the voltage signal to an air/fuel ratio.

PINION: The smaller of two meshing gears.

PISTON RING: An open ended ring which fits into a groove on the outer diameter of the piston. Its chief function is to form a seal between the piston and cylinder wall. Most automotive pistons have three rings: two for compression sealing; one for oil sealing.

PRELOAD: A predetermined load placed on a bearing during assembly or by adjustment.

PRIMARY CIRCUIT: Is the low voltage side of the ignition system which consists of the ignition switch, ballast resistor or resistance wire, bypass, coil, electronic control unit and pick-up coil as well as the connecting wires and harnesses.

PRESS FIT: The mating of two parts under pressure, due to the inner diameter of one being smaller than the outer diameter of the other, or vice versa; an interference fit.

RACE: The surface on the inner or outer ring of a bearing on which the balls, needles or rollers move.

REGULATOR: A device which maintains the amperage and/or voltage levels of a circuit at predetermined values.

RELAY: A switch which automatically opens and/or closes a circuit.

RESISTANCE: The opposition to the flow of current through a circuit or electrical device, and is measured in ohms. Resistance is equal to the voltage divided by the amperage.

RESISTOR: A device, usually made of wire, which offers a preset amount of resistance in an electrical circuit.

RING GEAR: The name given to a ring-shaped gear attached to a differential case, or affixed to a flywheel or as part a planetary gear set.

ROLLER BEARING: A bearing made up of hardened inner and outer races between which hardened steel rollers move.

ROTOR: 1. The disc-shaped part of a disc brake assembly, upon which the brake pads bear; also called, brake disc.
2. The device mounted atop the distributor shaft, which passes current to the distributor cap tower contacts.

SECONDARY CIRCUIT: The high voltage side of the ignition system, usually above 20,000 volts. The secondary includes the ignition coil, coil wire, distributor cap and rotor, spark plug wires and spark plugs.

SENDING UNIT: A mechanical, electrical, hydraulic or electromagnetic device which transmits information to a gauge.

SENSOR: Any device designed to measure engine operating conditions or ambient pressures and temperatures. Usually electronic in nature and designed to send a voltage signal to an on-board computer, some sensors may operate as a simple on/off switch or they may provide a variable voltage signal (like a potentiometer) as conditions or measured parameters change.

SHIM: Spacers of precise, predetermined thickness used between parts to establish a proper working relationship.

SLAVE CYLINDER: In automotive use, a device in the hydraulic clutch system which is activated by hydraulic force, disengaging the clutch.

SOLENOID: A coil used to produce a magnetic field, the effect of which is produce work.

SPARK PLUG: A device screwed into the combustion chamber of a spark ignition engine. The basic construction is a conductive core inside of a ceramic insulator, mounted in an outer conductive base. An electrical charge from the spark plug wire travels along the conductive core and jumps a preset air gap to a grounding point or points at the end of the conductive base. The resultant spark ignites the fuel/air mixture in the combustion chamber.

SPLINES: Ridges machined or cast onto the outer diameter of a shaft or inner diameter of a bore to enable parts to mate without rotation.

TACHOMETER: A device used to measure the rotary speed of an engine, shaft, gear, etc., usually in rotations per minute.

THERMOSTAT: A valve, located in the cooling system of an engine, which is closed when cold and opens gradually in response to engine heating, controlling the temperature of the coolant and rate of coolant flow.

TOP DEAD CENTER (TDC): The point at which the piston reaches the top of its travel on the compression stroke.

TORQUE: The twisting force applied to an object.

TORQUE CONVERTER: A turbine used to transmit power from a driving member to a driven member via hydraulic action, providing changes in drive ratio and torque. In automotive use, it links the driveplate at the rear of the engine to the automatic transmission.

TRANSDUCER: A device used to change a force into an electrical signal.

TRANSISTOR: A semi-conductor component which can be actuated by a small voltage to perform an electrical switching function.

TUNE-UP: A regular maintenance function, usually associated with the replacement and adjustment of parts and components in the electrical and fuel systems of a vehicle for the purpose of attaining optimum performance.

TURBOCHARGER: An exhaust driven pump which compresses intake air and forces it into the combustion chambers at higher than atmospheric pressures. The increased air pressure allows more fuel to be burned and results in increased horsepower being produced.

VACUUM ADVANCE: A device which advances the ignition timing in response to increased engine vacuum.

VACUUM GAUGE: An instrument used to measure the presence of vacuum in a chamber.

VALVE: A device which control the pressure, direction of flow or rate of flow of a liquid or gas.

VALVE CLEARANCE: The measured gap between the end of the valve stem and the rocker arm, cam lobe or follower that activates the valve.

VISCOSITY: The rating of a liquid's internal resistance to flow.

VOLTMETER: An instrument used for measuring electrical force in units called volts. Voltmeters are always connected parallel with the circuit being tested.

WHEEL CYLINDER: Found in the automotive drum brake assembly, it is a device, actuated by hydraulic pressure, which, through internal pistons, pushes the brake shoes outward against the drums.

ABBREVIATIONS AND SYMBOLS

A: Ampere

AC: Alternating current

A/C: Air conditioning

A-h: Ampere hour

AT: Automatic transmission

ATDC: After top dead center

μA: Microampere

bbl: Barrel

BDC: Bottom dead center

bhp: Brake horsepower

BTDC: Before top dead center

BTU: British thermal unit

C: Celsius (Centigrade)

CCA: Cold cranking amps

cd: Candela

cm^2: Square centimeter

cm^3, cc: Cubic centimeter

CO: Carbon monoxide

CO_2: Carbon dioxide

cu.in., in^3: Cubic inch

CV: Constant velocity

Cyl.: Cylinder

DC: Direct current

ECM: Electronic control module

EFE: Early fuel evaporation

EFI: Electronic fuel injection

EGR: Exhaust gas recirculation

Exh.: Exhaust

F: Fahrenheit

F: Farad

pF: Picofarad

μF: Microfarad

FI: Fuel injection

ft.lb., ft. lb., ft. lbs.: foot pound(s)

gal: Gallon

g: Gram

HC: Hydrocarbon

HEI: High energy ignition

HO: High output

hp: Horsepower

Hyd.: Hydraulic

Hz: Hertz

ID: Inside diameter

in.lb.; in. lb.; in. lbs: inch pound(s)

Int.: Intake

K: Kelvin

kg: Kilogram

kHz: Kilohertz

km: Kilometer

km/h: Kilometers per hour

kΩ: Kilohm

kPa: Kilopascal

kV: Kilovolt

kW: Kilowatt

l: Liter

l/s: Liters per second

m: Meter

mA: Milliampere

mg: Milligram

mHz: Megahertz

mm: Millimeter

mm^2: Square millimeter

m^3: Cubic meter

MΩ: Megohm

m/s: Meters per second

MT: Manual transmission

mV: Millivolt

μm: Micrometer

N: Newton

N-m: Newton meter

NOx: Nitrous oxide

OD: Outside diameter

OHC: Over head camshaft

OHV: Over head valve

Ω: Ohm

PCV: Positive crankcase ventilation

psi: Pounds per square inch

pts: Pints

qts: Quarts

rpm: Rotations per minute

rps: Rotations per second

R-12: A refrigerant gas (Freon)

SAE: Society of Automotive Engineers

SO$_2$: Sulfur dioxide

T: Ton

t: Megagram

TBI: Throttle Body Injection

TPS: Throttle Position Sensor

V: 1. Volt; 2. Venturi

μV: Microvolt

W: Watt

∝: Infinity

<: Less than

>: Greater than

Index

CHILTON'S REPAIR MANUAL MODEL INDEX
Car and truck model names are listed in alphabetical and numerical order

Part No.	Model	Repair Manual Title
6980	Accord	Honda 1973-88
7747	Aerostar	Ford Aerostar 1986-90
7165	Alliance	Renault 1975-85
7199	AMX	AMC 1975-86
7163	Aries	Chrysler Front Wheel Drive 1981-88
7041	Arrow	Champ/Arrow/Sapporo 1978-83
7032	Arrow Pick-Ups	D-50/Arrow Pick-Up 1979-81
6637	Aspen	Aspen/Volare 1976-80
6935	Astre	GM Subcompact 1971-80
7750	Astro	Chevrolet Astro/GMC Safari 1985-90
6934	A100, 200, 300	Dodge/Plymouth Vans 1967-88
5807	Barracuda	Barracuda/Challenger 1965-72
6844	Bavaria	BMW 1970-88
5796	Beetle	Volkswagen 1949-71
6837	Beetle	Volkswagen 1970-81
7135	Bel Air	Chevrolet 1968-88
5821	Belvedere	Roadrunner/Satellite/Belvedere/GTX 1968-73
7849	Beretta	Chevrolet Corsica and Beretta 1988
7317	Berlinetta	Camaro 1982-88
7135	Biscayne	Chevrolet 1968-88
6931	Blazer	Blazer/Jimmy 1969-82
7383	Blazer	Chevy S-10 Blazer/GMC S-15 Jimmy 1982-87
7027	Bobcat	Pinto/Bobcat 1971-80
7308	Bonneville	Buick/Olds/Pontiac 1975-87
6982	BRAT	Subaru 1970-88
7042	Brava	Fiat 1969-81
7140	Bronco	Ford Bronco 1966-86
7829	Bronco	Ford Pick-Ups and Bronco 1987-88
7408	Bronco II	Ford Ranger/Bronco II 1983-88
7135	Brookwood	Chevrolet 1968-88
6326	Brougham 1975-75	Valiant/Duster 1968-76
6934	B100, 150, 200, 250, 300, 350	Dodge/Plymouth Vans 1967-88
7197	B210	Datsun 1200/210/Nissan Sentra 1973-88
7659	B1600, 1800, 2000, 2200, 2600	Mazda Trucks 1971-89
6840	Caballero	Chevrolet Mid-Size 1964-88
7657	Calais	Calais, Grand Am, Skylark, Somerset 1985-86
6735	Camaro	Camaro 1967-81
7317	Camaro	Camaro 1982-88
7740	Camry	Toyota Camry 1983-88
6695	Capri, Capri II	Capri 1970-77
6963	Capri	Mustang/Capri/Merkur 1979-88
7135	Caprice	Chevrolet 1968-88
7482	Caravan	Dodge Caravan/Plymouth Voyager 1984-89
7163	Caravelle	Chrysler Front Wheel Drive 1981-88
7036	Carina	Toyota Corolla/Carina/Tercel/Starlet 1970-87
7308	Catalina	Buick/Olds/Pontiac 1975-90
7059	Cavalier	Cavalier, Skyhawk, Cimarron, 2000 1982-88
7309	Celebrity	Celebrity, Century, Ciera, 6000 1982-88
7043	Celica	Toyota Celica/Supra 1971-87
8058	Celica	Toyota Celica/Supra 1986-90
7309	Century FWD	Celebrity, Century, Ciera, 6000 1982-88
7307	Century RWD	Century/Regal 1975-87
5807	Challenger 1965-72	Barracuda/Challenger 1965-72
7037	Challenger 1977-83	Colt/Challenger/Vista/Conquest 1971-88
7041	Champ	Champ/Arrow/Sapporo 1978-83
6486	Charger	Dodge Charger 1967-70
6845	Charger 2.2	Omni/Horizon/Rampage 1978-88
6739	Cherokee 1974-83	Jeep Wagoneer, Commando, Cherokee, Truck 1957-86
7939	Cherokee 1984-89	Jeep Wagoneer, Comanche, Cherokee 1984-89
6840	Chevelle	Chevrolet Mid-Size 1964-88
6836	Chevette	Chevette/T-1000 1976-88
6841	Chevy II	Chevy II/Nova 1962-79
7309	Ciera	Celebrity, Century, Ciera, 6000 1982-88
7059	Cimarron	Cavalier, Skyhawk, Cimarron, 2000 1982-88
7049	Citation	GM X-Body 1980-85
6980	Civic	Honda 1973-88
6817	CJ-2A, 3A, 3B, 5, 6, 7	Jeep 1945-87
8034	CJ-5, 6, 7	Jeep 1971-90
6842	Colony Park	Ford/Mercury/Lincoln 1968-88
7037	Colt	Colt/Challenger/Vista/Conquest 1971-88
6634	Comet	Maverick/Comet 1971-77
7939	Comanche	Jeep Wagoneer, Comanche, Cherokee 1984-89
6739	Commando	Jeep Wagoneer, Commando, Cherokee, Truck 1957-86
6842	Commuter	Ford/Mercury/Lincoln 1968-88
7199	Concord	AMC 1975-86
7037	Conquest	Colt/Challenger/Vista/Conquest 1971-88
6696	Continental 1982-85	Ford/Mercury/Lincoln Mid-Size 1971-85
7814	Continental 1982-87	Thunderbird, Cougar, Continental 1980-87
7830	Continental 1988-89	Taurus/Sable/Continental 1986-89
7583	Cordia	Mitsubishi 1983-89
5795	Corolla 1968-70	Toyota 1966-70
7036	Corolla	Toyota Corolla/Carina/Tercel/Starlet 1970-87
5795	Corona	Toyota 1966-70
7004	Corona	Toyota Corona/Crown/Cressida/Mk.II/Van 1970-87
6962	Corrado	VW Front Wheel Drive 1974-90
7849	Corsica	Chevrolet Corsica and Beretta 1988
6576	Corvette	Corvette 1953-62
6843	Corvette	Corvette 1963-86
6542	Cougar	Mustang/Cougar 1965-73
6696	Cougar	Ford/Mercury/Lincoln Mid-Size 1971-85
7814	Cougar	Thunderbird, Cougar, Continental 1980-87
6842	Country Sedan	Ford/Mercury/Lincoln 1968-88
6842	Country Squire	Ford/Mercury/Lincoln 1968-88
6983	Courier	Ford Courier 1972-82
7004	Cressida	Toyota Corona/Crown/Cressida/Mk.II/Van 1970-87
5795	Crown	Toyota 1966-70
7004	Crown	Toyota Corona/Crown/Cressida/Mk.II/Van 1970-87
6842	Crown Victoria	Ford/Mercury/Lincoln 1968-88
6980	CRX	Honda 1973-88
6842	Custom	Ford/Mercury/Lincoln 1968-88
6326	Custom	Valiant/Duster 1968-76
6842	Custom 500	Ford/Mercury/Lincoln 1968-88
7950	Cutlass FWD	Lumina/Grand Prix/Cutlass/Regal 1988-90
6933	Cutlass RWD	Cutlass 1970-87
7309	Cutlass Ciera	Celebrity, Century, Ciera, 6000 1982-88
6936	C-10, 20, 30	Chevrolet/GMC Pick-Ups & Suburban 1970-87

Chilton's Repair Manuals are available at your local retailer or by mailing a check or money order for **$15.95** per book plus **$3.50** for 1st book and **$.50** for each additional book to cover postage and handling to:

Chilton Book Company
Dept. DM
Radnor, PA 19089

NOTE: When ordering be sure to include your name & address, book part No. & title.

CHILTON'S REPAIR MANUAL MODEL INDEX
Car and truck model names are listed in alphabetical and numerical order

Part No.	Model	Repair Manual Title
8055	C-15, 25, 35	Chevrolet/GMC Pick-Ups & Suburban 1988-90
6324	Dart	Dart/Demon 1968-76
6962	Dasher	VW Front Wheel Drive 1974-90
5790	Datsun Pickups	Datsun 1961-72
6816	Datsun Pickups	Datsun Pick-Ups and Pathfinder 1970-89
7163	Daytona	Chrysler Front Wheel Drive 1981-88
6486	Daytona Charger	Dodge Charger 1967-70
6324	Demon	Dart/Demon 1968-76
7462	deVille	Cadillac 1967-89
7587	deVille	GM C-Body 1985
6817	DJ-3B	Jeep 1945-87
7040	DL	Volvo 1970-88
6326	Duster	Valiant/Duster 1968-76
7032	D-50	D-50/Arrow Pick-Ups 1979-81
7459	D100, 150, 200, 250, 300, 350	Dodge/Plymouth Trucks 1967-88
7199	Eagle	AMC 1975-86
7163	E-Class	Chrysler Front Wheel Drive 1981-88
6840	El Camino	Chevrolet Mid-Size 1964-88
7462	Eldorado	Cadillac 1967-89
7308	Electra	Buick/Olds/Pontiac 1975-90
7587	Electra	GM C-Body 1985
6696	Elite	Ford/Mercury/Lincoln Mid-Size 1971-85
7165	Encore	Renault 1975-85
7055	Escort	Ford/Mercury Front Wheel Drive 1981-87
7059	Eurosport	Cavalier, Skyhawk, Cimarron, 2000 1982-88
7760	Excel	Hyundai 1986-90
7163	Executive Sedan	Chrysler Front Wheel Drive 1981-88
7055	EXP	Ford/Mercury Front Wheel Drive 1981-87
6849	E-100, 150, 200, 250, 300, 350	Ford Vans 1961-88
6320	Fairlane	Fairlane/Torino 1962-75
6965	Fairmont	Fairmont/Zephyr 1978-83
5796	Fastback	Volkswagen 1949-71
6837	Fastback	Volkswagen 1970-81
6739	FC-150, 170	Jeep Wagoneer, Commando, Cherokee, Truck 1957-86
6982	FF-1	Subaru 1970-88
7571	Fiero	Pontiac Fiero 1984-88
6846	Fiesta	Fiesta 1978-80
5996	Firebird	Firebird 1967-81
7345	Firebird	Firebird 1982-90
7059	Firenza	Cavalier, Skyhawk, Cimarron, 2000 1982-88
7462	Fleetwood	Cadillac 1967-89
7587	Fleetwood	GM C-Body 1985
7829	F-Super Duty	Ford Pick-Ups and Bronco 1987-88
7165	Fuego	Renault 1975-85
6552	Fury	Plymouth 1968-76
7196	F-10	Datsun/Nissan F-10, 310, Stanza, Pulsar 1976-88
6933	F-85	Cutlass 1970-87
6913	F-100, 150, 200, 250, 300, 350	Ford Pick-Ups 1965-86
7829	F-150, 250, 350	Ford Pick-Ups and Bronco 1987-88
7583	Galant	Mitsubishi 1983-89
6842	Galaxie	Ford/Mercury/Lincoln 1968-88
7040	GL	Volvo 1970-88
6739	Gladiator	Jeep Wagoneer, Commando, Cherokee, Truck 1962-86
6981	GLC	Mazda 1978-89
7040	GLE	Volvo 1970-88
7040	GLT	Volvo 1970-88

Part No.	Model	Repair Manual Title
7593	Golf	VW Front Wheel Drive 1974-90
7165	Gordini	Renault 1975-85
6937	Granada	Granada/Monarch 1975-82
6552	Gran Coupe	Plymouth 1968-76
6552	Gran Fury	Plymouth 1968-76
6842	Gran Marquis	Ford/Mercury/Lincoln 1968-88
6552	Gran Sedan	Plymouth 1968-76
6696	Gran Torino	Ford/Mercury/Lincoln Mid-Size 1971-85
7346	Grand Am	Pontiac Mid-Size 1974-83
7657	Grand Am	Calais, Grand Am, Skylark, Somerset 1985-86
7346	Grand LeMans	Pontiac Mid-Size 1974-83
7346	Grand Prix	Pontiac Mid-Size 1974-83
7950	Grand Prix FWD	Lumina/Grand Prix/Cutlass/Regal 1988-90
7308	Grand Safari	Buick/Olds/Pontiac 1975-87
7308	Grand Ville	Buick/Olds/Pontiac 1975-87
6739	Grand Wagoneer	Jeep Wagoneer, Commando, Cherokee, Truck 1957-86
7199	Gremlin	AMC 1975-86
6575	GT	Opel 1971-75
7593	GTI	VW Front Wheel Drive 1974-90
5905	GTO	Tempest/GTO/LeMans 1968-73
7346	GTO 1974	Pontiac Mid-Size 1974-83
5821	GTX	Roadrunner/Satellite/Belvedere/GTX 1968-73
5910	GT6	Triumph 1969-73
6542	G.T.350, 500	Mustang/Cougar 1965-73
6930	G-10, 20, 30	Chevy/GMC Vans 1967-86
6930	G-1500, 2500, 3500	Chevy/GMC Vans 1967-86
8040	G-10, 20, 30	Chevy/GMC Vans 1987-90
8040	G-1500, 2500, 3500	Chevy/GMC Vans 1987-90
5795	Hi-Lux	Toyota 1966-70
6845	Horizon	Omni/Horizon/Rampage 1978-88
7199	Hornet	AMC 1975-86
7135	Impala	Chevrolet 1968-88
7317	IROC-Z	Camaro 1982-88
6739	Jeepster	Jeep Wagoneer, Commando, Cherokee, Truck 1957-86
7593	Jetta	VW Front Wheel Drive 1974-90
6931	Jimmy	Blazer/Jimmy 1969-82
7383	Jimmy	Chevy S-10 Blazer/GMC S-15 Jimmy 1982-87
6739	J-10, 20	Jeep Wagoneer, Commando, Cherokee, Truck 1957-86
6739	J-100, 200, 300	Jeep Wagoneer, Commando, Cherokee, Truck 1957-86
6575	Kadett	Opel 1971-75
7199	Kammback	AMC 1975-86
5796	Karmann Ghia	Volkswagen 1949-71
6837	Karmann Ghia	Volkswagen 1970-81
7135	Kingswood	Chevrolet 1968-88
6931	K-5	Blazer/Jimmy 1969-82
6936	K-10, 20, 30	Chevy/GMC Pick-Ups & Suburban 1970-87
6936	K-1500, 2500, 3500	Chevy/GMC Pick-Ups & Suburban 1970-87
8055	K-10, 20, 30	Chevy/GMC Pick-Ups & Suburban 1988-90
8055	K-1500, 2500, 3500	Chevy/GMC Pick-Ups & Suburban 1988-90
6840	Laguna	Chevrolet Mid-Size 1964-88
7041	Lancer	Champ/Arrow/Sapporo 1977-83
5795	Land Cruiser	Toyota 1966-70
7035	Land Cruiser	Toyota Trucks 1970-88
7163	Laser	Chrysler Front Wheel Drive 1981-88
7163	LeBaron	Chrysler Front Wheel Drive 1981-88
7165	LeCar	Renault 1975-85

Chilton's Repair Manuals are available at your local retailer or by mailing a check or money order for **$15.95** per book plus **$3.50** for 1st book and **$.50** for each additional book to cover postage and handling to:

Chilton Book Company
Dept. DM
Radnor, PA 19089

NOTE: When ordering be sure to include your name & address, book part No. & title.

CHILTON'S REPAIR MANUAL MODEL INDEX
Car and truck model names are listed in alphabetical and numerical order

Part No.	Model	Repair Manual Title
6817	4 × 4-63	Jeep 1981-87
6817	4-73	Jeep 1981-87
6817	4 × 4-73	Jeep 1981-87
6817	4-75	Jeep 1981-87
7035	4Runner	Toyota Trucks 1970-88
6982	4wd Wagon	Subaru 1970-88
6982	4wd Coupe	Subaru 1970-88
6933	4-4-2 1970-80	Cutlass 1970-87
6817	6-63	Jeep 1981-87
6809	6.9	Mercedes-Benz 1974-84
7308	88	Buick/Olds/Pontiac 1975-90
7308	98	Buick/Olds/Pontiac 1975-90
7587	98 Regency	GM C-Body 1985
5902	100LS, 100GL	Audi 1970-73
6529	122, 122S	Volvo 1956-69
7042	124	Fiat 1969-81
7042	128	Fiat 1969-81
7042	131	Fiat 1969-81
6529	142	Volvo 1956-69
7040	142	Volvo 1970-88
6529	144	Volvo 1956-69
7040	144	Volvo 1970-88
6529	145	Volvo 1956-69
7040	145	Volvo 1970-88
6529	164	Volvo 1956-69
7040	164	Volvo 1970-88
6065	190C	Mercedes-Benz 1959-70
6809	190D	Mercedes-Benz 1974-84
6065	190DC	Mercedes-Benz 1959-70
6809	190E	Mercedes-Benz 1974-84
6065	200, 200D	Mercedes-Benz 1959-70
7170	200SX	Nissan 200SX, 240SX, 510, 610, 710, 810, Maxima 1973-88
7197	210	Datsun 1200, 210, Nissan Sentra 1971-88
6065	220B, 220D, 220Sb, 220SEb	Mercedes-Benz 1959-70
5907	220/8 1968-73	Mercedes-Benz 1968-73
6809	230 1974-78	Mercedes-Benz 1974-84
6065	230S, 230SL	Mercedes-Benz 1959-70
5907	230/8	Mercedes-Benz 1968-73
6809	240D	Mercedes-Benz 1974-84
7170	240SX	Nissan 200SX, 240SX, 510, 610, 710, 810, Maxima 1973-88
6932	240Z	Datsun Z & ZX 1970-87
7040	242, 244, 245	Volvo 1970-88
5907	250C	Mercedes-Benz 1968-73
6065	250S, 250SE, 250SL	Mercedes-Benz 1959-70
5907	250/8	Mercedes-Benz 1968-73
6932	260Z	Datsun Z & ZX 1970-87
7040	262, 264, 265	Volvo 1970-88
5907	280	Mercedes-Benz 1968-73
6809	280	Mercedes-Benz 1974-84
5907	280C	Mercedes-Benz 1968-73
6809	280C, 280CE, 280E	Mercedes-Benz 1974-84
6065	280S, 280SE	Mercedes-Benz 1959-70
5907	280SE, 280S/8, 280SE/8	Mercedes-Benz 1968-73
6809	280SEL, 280SEL/8, 280SL	Mercedes-Benz 1974-84
6932	280Z, 280ZX	Datsun Z & ZX 1970-87
6065	300CD, 300D, 300SD, 300SE	Mercedes-Benz 1959-70
5907	300SEL 3.5, 300SEL 4.5	Mercedes-Benz 1968-73
5907	300SEL 6.3, 300SEL/8	Mercedes-Benz 1968-73
6809	300TD	Mercedes-Benz 1974-84
6932	300ZX	Datsun Z & ZX 1970-87
5982	304	Peugeot 1970-74
5790	310	Datsun 1961-72
7196	310	Datsun/Nissan F-10, 310, Stanza, Pulsar 1977-88
5790	311	Datsun 1961-72
6844	318i, 320i	BMW 1970-88
6981	323	Mazda 1978-89
6844	325E, 325ES, 325i, 325iS, 325iX	BMW 1970-88
6809	380SEC, 380SEL, 380SL, 380SLC	Mercedes-Benz 1974-84
5907	350SL	Mercedes-Benz 1968-73
7163	400	Chrysler Front Wheel Drive 1981-88
5790	410	Datsun 1961-72
5790	411	Datsun 1961-72
7081	411, 412	Volkswagen 1970-81
6809	450SE, 450SEL, 450 SEL 6.9	Mercedes-Benz 1974-84
6809	450SL, 450SLC	Mercedes-Benz 1974-84
5907	450SLC	Mercedes-Benz 1968-73
6809	500SEC, 500SEL	Mercedes-Benz 1974-84
5982	504	Peugeot 1970-74
5790	510	Datsun 1961-72
7170	510	Nissan 200SX, 240SX, 510, 610, 710, 810, Maxima 1973-88
6816	520	Datsun/Nissan Pick-Ups and Pathfinder 1970-89
6844	524TD	BMW 1970-88
6844	525i	BMW 1970-88
6844	528e	BMW 1970-88
6844	528i	BMW 1970-88
6344	530i	BMW 1970-88
6844	533i	BMW 1970-88
6844	535i, 535iS	BMW 1970-88
6980	600	Honda 1973-88
7163	600	Chrysler Front Wheel Drive 1981-88
7170	610	Nissan 200SX, 240SX, 510, 610, 710, 810, Maxima 1973-88
6816	620	Datsun/Nissan Pick-Ups and Pathfinder 1970-89
6981	626	Mazda 1978-89
6844	630 CSi	BMW 1970-88
6844	633 CSi	BMW 1970-88
6844	635CSi	BMW 1970-88
7170	710	Nissan 200SX, 240SX, 510, 610, 710, 810, Maxima 1973-88
6816	720	Datsun/Nissan Pick-Ups and Pathfinder 1970-89
6844	733i	BMW 1970-88
6844	735i	BMW 1970-88
7040	760, 760GLE	Volvo 1970-88
7040	780	Volvo 1970-88
6981	808	Mazda 1978-89
7170	810	Nissan 200SX, 240SX, 510, 610, 710, 810, Maxima 1973-88
7042	850	Fiat 1969-81
7572	900, 900 Turbo	SAAB 900 1976-85
7048	924	Porsche 924/928 1976-81
7048	928	Porsche 924/928 1976-81
6981	929	Mazda 1978-89
6836	1000	Chevette/1000 1976-88
6780	1100	MG 1961-81
5790	1200	Datsun 1961-72
7197	1200	Datsun 1200, 210, Nissan Sentra 1973-88
6982	1400GL, 1400DL, 1400GF	Subaru 1970-88
5790	1500	Datsun 1961-72

Chilton's Repair Manuals are available at your local retailer or by mailing a check or money order for **$15.95** per book plus **$3.50** for 1st book and **$.50** for each additional book to cover postage and handling to:

Chilton Book Company
Dept. DM
Radnor, PA 19089

NOTE: When ordering be sure to include your name & address, book part No. & title.

CHILTON'S REPAIR MANUAL MODEL INDEX

Car and truck model names are listed in alphabetical and numerical order

Chilton's Repair Manuals are available at your local retailer or by mailing a check or money order for **$15.95** per book plus **$3.50** for 1st book and **$.50** for each additional book to cover postage and handling to:

**Chilton Book Company
Dept. DM
Radnor, PA 19089**

NOTE: When ordering be sure to include your name & address, book part No. & title.

CHILTON'S REPAIR MANUAL MODEL INDEX
Car and truck model names are listed in alphabetical and numerical order

Part No.	Model	Repair Manual Title
7675	Skylark	Calais, Grand Am, Skylark, Somerset 1985-86
7657	Somerset	Calais, Grand Am, Skylark, Somerset 1985-86
7042	Spider 2000	Fiat 1969-81
7199	Spirit	AMC 1975-86
6552	Sport Fury	Plymouth 1968-76
7165	Sport Wagon	Renault 1975-85
5796	Squareback	Volkswagen 1949-71
6837	Squareback	Volkswagen 1970-81
7196	Stanza	Datsun/Nissan F-10, 310, Stanza, Pulsar 1976-88
6935	Starfire	GM Subcompact 1971-80
7583	Starion	Mitsubishi 1983-89
7036	Starlet	Toyota Corolla/Carina/Tercel/Starlet 1970-87
7059	STE	Cavalier, Skyhawk, Cimarron, 2000 1982-88
5795	Stout	Toyota 1966-70
7042	Strada	Fiat 1969-81
6552	Suburban	Plymouth 1968-76
6936	Suburban	Chevy/GMC Pick-Ups & Suburban 1970-87
8055	Suburban	Chevy/GMC Pick-Ups & Suburban 1988-90
6935	Sunbird	GM Subcompact 1971-80
7059	Sunbird	Cavalier, Skyhawk, Cimarron, 2000, 1982-88
7163	Sundance	Chrysler Front Wheel Drive 1981-88
7043	Supra	Toyota Celica/Supra 1971-87
8058	Supra	Toyota Celica/Supra 1986-90
6837	Super Beetle	Volkswagen 1970-81
7199	SX-4	AMC 1975-86
7383	S-10 Blazer	Chevy S-10 Blazer/GMC S-15 Jimmy 1982-87
7310	S-10 Pick-Up	Chevy S-10/GMC S-15 Pick-Ups 1982-87
7383	S-15 Jimmy	Chevy S-10 Blazer/GMC S-15 Jimmy 1982-87
7310	S-15 Pick-Up	Chevy S-10/GMC S-15 Pick-Ups 1982-87
7830	Taurus	Taurus/Sable/Continental 1986-89
6845	TC-3	Omni/Horizon/Rampage 1978-88
5905	Tempest	Tempest/GTO/LeMans 1968-73
7055	Tempo	Ford/Mercury Front Wheel Drive 1981-87
7036	Tercel	Toyota Corolla/Carina/Tercel/Starlet 1970-87
7081	Thing	Volkswagen 1970-81
6696	Thunderbird	Ford/Mercury/Lincoln Mid-Size 1971-85
7814	Thunderbird	Thunderbird, Cougar, Continental 1980-87
7055	Topaz	Ford/Mercury Front Wheel Drive 1981-87
6320	Torino	Fairlane/Torino 1962-75
6696	Torino	Ford/Mercury/Lincoln Mid-Size 1971-85
7163	Town & Country	Chrysler Front Wheel Drive 1981-88
6842	Town Car	Ford/Mercury/Lincoln 1968-88
7135	Townsman	Chevrolet 1968-88
5795	Toyota Pickups	Toyota 1966-70
7035	Toyota Pickups	Toyota Trucks 1970-88
7004	Toyota Van	Toyota Corona/Crown/Cressida/Mk.II/Van 1970-87
7459	Trail Duster	Dodge/Plymouth Trucks 1967-88
7046	Trans Am	Firebird 1967-81
7345	Trans Am	Firebird 1982-90
7583	Tredia	Mitsubishi 1983-89
7040	Turbo	Volvo 1970-88
5796	Type 1 Sedan 1949-71	Volkswagen 1949-71
6837	Type 1 Sedan 1970-80	Volkswagen 1970-81
5796	Type 1 Karmann Ghia 1960-71	Volkswagen 1949-71
6837	Type 1 Karmann Ghia 1970-74	Volkswagen 1970-81
5796	Type 1 Convertible 1964-71	Volkswagen 1949-71
6837	Type 1 Convertible 1970-80	Volkswagen 1970-81
5796	Type 1 Super Beetle 1971	Volkswagen 1949-71
6837	Type 1 Super Beetle 1971-75	Volkswagen 1970-81
5796	Type 2 Bus 1953-71	Volkswagen 1949-71
6837	Type 2 Bus 1970-80	Volkswagen 1970-81
5796	Type 2 Kombi 1954-71	Volkswagen 1949-71
6837	Type 2 Kombi 1970-73	Volkswagen 1970-81
6837	Type 2 Vanagon 1981	Volkswagen 1970-81
5796	Type 3 Fastback & Squareback 1961-71	Volkswagen 1949-71
7081	Type 3 Fastback & Squareback 1970-73	Volkswagen 1970-70
5796	Type 4 411 1971	Volkswagen 1949-71
6837	Type 4 411 1971-72	Volkswagen 1970-81
5796	Type 4 412 1971	Volkswagen 1949-71
6845	Turismo	Omni/Horizon/Rampage 1978-88
5905	T-37	Tempest/GTO/LeMans 1968-73
6836	T-1000	Chevette/T-1000 1976-88
6935	Vega	GM Subcompact 1971-80
7346	Ventura	Pontiac Mid-Size 1974-83
6696	Versailles	Ford/Mercury/Lincoln Mid-Size 1971-85
6552	VIP	Plymouth 1968-76
7037	Vista	Colt/Challenger/Vista/Conquest 1971-88
6933	Vista Cruiser	Cutlass 1970-87
6637	Volare	Aspen/Volare 1976-80
7482	Voyager	Dodge Caravan/Plymouth Voyager 1984-88
6326	V-100	Valiant/Duster 1968-76
6739	Wagoneer 1962-83	Jeep Wagoneer, Commando, Cherokee, Truck 1957-86
7939	Wagoneer 1984-89	Jeep Wagoneer, Comanche, Cherokee 1984-89
8034	Wrangler	Jeep 1971-90
7459	W100, 150, 200, 250, 300, 350	Dodge/Plymouth Trucks 1967-88
7459	WM300	Dodge/Plymouth Trucks 1967-88
6842	XL	Ford/Mercury/Lincoln 1968-88
6963	XR4Ti	Mustang/Capri/Merkur 1979-88
6696	XR-7	Ford/Mercury/Lincoln Mid-Size 1971-85
6982	XT Coupe	Subaru 1970-88
7042	X1/9	Fiat 1969-81
6965	Zephyr	Fairmont/Zephyr 1978-83
7059	Z-24	Cavalier, Skyhawk, Cimarron, 2000 1982-88
6735	Z-28	Camaro 1967-81
7318	Z-28	Camaro 1982-88
6845	024	Omni/Horizon/Rampage 1978-88
6844	3.0S, 3.0Si, 3.0CS	BMW 1970-88
6817	4-63	Jeep 1981-87

Chilton's Repair Manuals are available at your local retailer or by mailing a check or money order for **$15.95** per book plus **$3.50** for 1st book and **$.50** for each additional book to cover postage and handling to:

**Chilton Book Company
Dept. DM
Radnor, PA 19089**

NOTE: When ordering be sure to include your name & address, book part No. & title.

CHILTON'S REPAIR MANUAL MODEL INDEX
Car and truck model names are listed in alphabetical and numerical order

Part No.	Model	Repair Manual Title	Part No.	Model	Repair Manual Title
6844	1500	DMW 1970-88	6844	2000	BMW 1970-88
6936	1500	Chevy/GMC Pick-Ups & Suburban 1970-87	6844	2002, 2002Ti, 2002Tii	BMW 1970-88
8055	1500	Chevy/GMC Pick-Ups & Suburban 1988-90	6936	2500	Chevy/GMC Pick-Ups & Suburban 1970-87
6844	1600	BMW 1970-88	8055	2500	Chevy/GMC Pick-Ups & Suburban 1988-90
5790	1600	Datsun 1961-72			
6982	1600DL, 1600GL, 1600GLF	Subaru 1970-88	6844	2500	BMW 1970-88
6844	1600-2	BMW 1970-88	6844	2800	BMW 1970-88
6844	1800	BMW 1970-88	6936	3500	Chevy/GMC Pick-Ups & Suburban 1970-87
6982	1800DL, 1800GL, 1800GLF	Subaru 1970-88	8055	3500	Chevy/GMC Pick-Ups & Suburban 1988-90
6529	1800, 1800S	Volvo 1956-69	7028	4000	Audi 4000/5000 1978-81
7040	1800E, 1800ES	Volvo 1970-88	7028	5000	Audi 4000/5000 1978-81
5790	2000	Datsun 1961-72	7309	6000	Celebrity, Century, Ciera, 6000 1982-88
7059	2000	Cavalier, Skyhawk, Cimarron, 2000 1982-88			